THE FRENCH REVOLUTION
AND NAPOLEONIC ERA

THE FRENCH REVOLUTION AND NAPOLEONIC ERA

Second Edition

Owen Connelly

Harcourt Brace Jovanovich College Publishers
Fort Worth   Philadelphia   San Diego
New York   Orlando   Austin   San Antonio
Toronto   Montreal   London   Sydney   Tokyo

Publisher	Ted Buchholz
Acquisitions Editor	David Tatom
Developmental Editor	Martin Lewis
Project Editor	Vicki Young
Production Manager	Tad Gaither
Art & Design Supervisor	John Ritland
Text Designer	Greg Draper
Cover Designer	Nancy Turner

EG05259

944.04 CON

3 wk Main

Library of Congress Cataloging-in-Publication Data
Connelly, Owen, 1929–
    French Revolution/Napoleonic Era / Owen Connelly
    Includes bibliographical references and index.
    1. France—History—Revolution, 1789–1799. 2. France—History—Consulate
    and Empire, 1799–1815. I. Title.
    DC148.C73 1991
    944.04—dc20 90-41975

ISBN: 0-03-053329-5

Address editorial correspondence to: 301 Commerce Street, Suite 3700, Fort Worth, TX
76102. *Address orders to:* 6277 Sea Harbor Drive, Orlando, FL 32887 1-800-782-4479,
or 1-800-433-0001 (in Florida)

Printed in the United States of America

    4 090 9 8 7 6 5 4

Harcourt Brace Jovanovich, Inc.
The Dryden Press
Saunders College Publishing

THE AUTHOR

OWEN CONNELLY is the author of *Napoleon's Satellite Kingdoms* (1965 and 1969), *The Gentle Bonaparte: A Biography of Joseph, Napoleon's Elder Brother* (1968), *The Epoch of Napoleon* (1972 and 1978), *Blundering to Glory: Napoleon's Military Campaigns* (1987 and 1990), and other books. He is Professor of Modern European History at the University of South Carolina, a Member of the Institute for Advanced Study, Princeton, New Jersey (1989 and 1990), a director of the Consortium on Revolutionary Europe, and past-president of the Society for French Historical Studies (1988).

ACKNOWLEDGMENTS

This is a work of synthesis, based on the studies of hundreds of specialists in the field. Their works are listed in the Bibliography at the end of the book. Few are cited elsewhere, unless quoted directly, since it seemed inadvisable to overload the book with academic paraphernalia. I am nonetheless indebted to all these authors. They are not to be blamed, of course, for my interpretations and opinions. I assume full responsibility also for translations from primary sources.

For their help with the first edition I remain grateful to Harold T. Parker of Duke University and Keith Eubank of Queens College of the City University of New York. Harold Parker read draft after draft of the manuscript, patiently suggesting revisions based on his extraordinary knowledge of the Revolutionary Era. Keith Eubank was instrumental (with Clifford Snyder of Holt, Rinehart and Winston) in getting me the contract for the book, constantly encouraged me, and did a most helpful critique of the final draft. I wish to express my appreciation also to Gerlof D. Homan of Illinois State University and J. Harvey Smith of Northern Illinois University, who read the manuscript and gave constructive advice. Other scholars reassured me in various ways. Harold Parker and Keith Eubank, however, truly helped to shape this text. I humbly thank them.

Though it is not usual, I would like also to enter a word of appreciation for the editors who saw me through a "time of troubles." Some have moved on to higher things, but, at any rate, my thanks go to Clifford Snyder, Seibert Adams, William Brisick, Raymond Ashton, Denise Rathbun, Joan Greene, and, especially, Pamela Forcey, managing editor for the final production stages. Also, I acknowledge the kind permission of the Macmillan Publishing Company to use four maps dealing with the Peninsular War, three from my *The Gentle Bonaparte* (1968) and one from my *Napoleon's Satellite Kingdoms* (1965).

For the Second Edition, I would like to thank my editors—David Tatom, who was my advocate at Holt, Rinehart and Winston, Martin Lewis, and Vicki Young who saw the manuscript through production. I must also express my sincere appreciation to the readers selected by the company, who submitted very useful critiques of the original edition, *viz.*, Peter Paret of the Institute for Advanced Study, Gunther Rothenberg of Purdue University, Eric Arnold of the University of Denver, Gordon Bond of Auburn, and Matthew Ramsey of Vanderbilt; my special thanks go to Gunther and Matthew for their attention to detail and the information and references they supplied.

I especially acknowledge my great debt to the Institute for Advanced Study at Princeton, New Jersey, and its director, Dr. Marvin L. Goldberger, for allowing me to work on the textbook (among other projects) while a resident member in the fall of 1989, and to the University of South Carolina, especially Provost Arthur Smith, for the sabbatical that enabled me to accept membership in the Institute.

Among the Institute's distinguished scholars, I owe most to Peter Paret for his careful advice, notably on Germany in the Napoleonic period. However, Professors Glen Bowersock, Giles Constable, and John Elliott (now Regius Professor at Oxford) were invariably supportive. My friend and fellow member, Leandro Polverini, of the University of Perugia, advised me on Italian questions and helped me trace the origins of the Phrygian Bonnet.

Lastly, I must, literally, render homage to my longtime friend R. R. Palmer, still first among America's scholars of the French Revolution and a font of rare wisdom and wry humor. I am grateful for the privilege of his frequent company and good counsel.

Owen Connelly

CONTENTS

"La Grande Nation" • Causes of the Revolution: Summary • Population Explosion • The Power Struggle • Military Power: France and Britain • Commercial Rivalry • Industrial Revolution • The "Business Revolution" • The Enlightenment • The Populationists • Enlightenment and Revolution • The American Revolution and the French • Atlantic Revolutions and Enlightened Monarchy • French "Absolutism" • Society and Privilege • First Estate: The Clergy • The Nobility • The Third Estate • Population Growth and Society • Society, Government, Political Culture, and Revolution

Louis XVI and Marie Antoinette • The Economic Background • The Fiscal Crisis • Louis XVI Attempts Reform • The Nobles' Revolt • Doubling the Third • The Elections • The Cahiers • The Estates General • The Revolution Begins

Paris Eternal and in 1789 • Paris Erupts • The Bastille • Municipal Revolutions • The Great Fear • The Night of 4 August • Declaration of Rights and the Veto • The March of the Women • Press/Clubs/Salons • The Problem of Equality • The National Assembly and the Economy • The Assignats • Civil Constitution of the Clergy • Administration and Judiciary • The Flight to Varennes • The Rise of Republicanism • The Drift to the Left (an Aside) • Constitution of 1791

TABLE OF MAPS

THE FRENCH REVOLUTION
AND NAPOLEONIC ERA

INTRODUCTION
The Era and Its Legacies

The French Revolutionary-Napoleonic Era was a magnificently complex overture to modern times in that the themes of ideas, forms, systems, and movements were sounded which would be played out in future generations and in part have yet to be fully orchestrated. For this reason it has been studied in more detail than any period in human history. It was also, of course, an epoch of incomparable drama.

Surging mobs shouting the "Marseillaise." The roll of drums; the crash of the guillotine; heads dropping bloody into baskets. Characters worthy of fiction: Lafayette, the "Hero of Two Worlds"; Robespierre, the "Incorruptible"; Marat, the "Friend of the People," murdered in his bath by the beautiful Charlotte Corday; Danton on the scaffold: "Show my head to the people; it is a sight to see!" Bonaparte, the Corsican, the "Little Corporal," the emperor on horseback in his faded green coat, trailed by the sinister Mameluke Roustan, surrounded by the guard, the legion of heroes; prancing steeds, a blaze of colors and flashing steel. "Through this village I saw him ride, followed by kings. . . . " The snows of Russia. Waterloo; Wellington; the red-haired Marshal Ney with his broken sword leading the final charge of the guard.

For almost two centuries, the spectacle of the period, exploited by major creative talents in every generation, has captivated the public. Today, it seems more popular than ever, perhaps because its heroes loom larger to people who feel they have none and whose daily lives are ordered by the computers of public and private bureaucracies.

Ironically, the first modern bureaucracy was spawned by the Revolution (specifically the government of Terror), and Napoleon later created the proto-type of the contemporary bureaucratic state—or, put less kindly, the first modern police state. These are among the reasons scholars of all nationalities maintain a consuming interest in the Revolution and the Napoleonic adventure. There are many more.

The era saw experiments in almost every contemporary system of government. Every political and socioeconomic concept important since 1815 was voiced—at least in nascent form. Government involvement in society and economy was vastly increased, and the secularization of society fairly begun. The principles of the Revolution became fixed as ideals in the Western mind—if in various interpretations. Modern nationalism and mass warfare with popular involvement originated. There were significant changes in French society, and to some degree European society, presaging more. Napoleon Bonaparte deliberately "revolutionized" a large part of Europe and came closer to forming a European state than any ruler since Roman times.

These developments will be briefly interpreted here, but readers should feel free to draw their own conclusions from the evidence presented in this text or other works, to which the bibliography (p. 352) is a guide. The *causes* of the Revolution will not be discussed, since they are treated fully in Chapter 1. Its deepest roots, however, were in awesome, silent, changes (to a degree international)—population increase, expanding commerce, nascent industrialization, urbanization, and the rise of new elites of wealth and intellect. These trends demanded a redefinition of the role of governments, of the relation of individuals to government, and of the "right" behavior of citizens.

The Revolution proper (1789–1799) saw an incredible succession of governments—absolute monarchy, constitutional monarchy (in various forms), representative republic, authoritarian republic, bourgeois republic—and under Napoleon (1799–1815) popularly sanctioned dictatorship and empire (under three constitutions). In the ten years before Bonaparte finished "the romance of the revolution" (his own words), the leaders ran the gamut from liberal monarchists to Socialists, of whom there were two on the Committee of Public Safety of the Terror. Their outlooks ranged from Lafayette's Americanized royalism to Robespierre's determination that the people should be "forced to be free," (in the words of J. J. Rousseau's *Social Contract*, the Terrorists' "bible").

In the wings there were militant Communists, such as Gracchus Babeuf, who agitated for the abolition of private property as the first step toward human equality. "Let the people . . . break their chains. . . . " His theories were tinged with anarchism as well: "Perish, if need be, all the arts, if real equality be left us. . . . " And there were feminists too, among them the striking Mary Wollstonecraft, a sexually liberated Englishwoman who was in France during the bloodiest years of the Revolution (1792–1795). In *The Rights of Woman* she damned the revolutionaries for excluding women from the "Mankind" of their glorious declarations and called men's chivalry "systematically degrading." She and Babeuf represented extremes of opinion in the ongoing dispute over the meaning of equality and the best means to achieve it. Precedents for their ideas can be found in the literature of the eighteenth-century Enlightenment, or earlier tracts.

Nevertheless, these people were not theorists, but activists, as were most other protagonists in the great revolutionary debates. Babeuf lost his life; Wollstonecraft hid in the countryside during the Terror.[1]

Of the bywords of the early Revolution, "Liberty, Equality, and Fraternity," the last was innocuous, and the first two contradictory. The issue of the balance between liberty and equality was basic to all the conflicts of ten years of revolution. Equality, at first merely equality before the law, had to be imposed by force by the central government. Soon the broader implications of equality were broached—social, economic—in terms of service of the state to citizens and of citizens to the state. The advocates of greater equality became the proponents of greater central power. Successive governments were toppled by "new democrats" with ever-expanding plans to improve the lot of the common man by exerting more state authority.

The trend reached its apex in the Terror when the guillotine stood as a guarantee of obedience to the law. The bureaucracy of the Committee of Public Safety imposed mass military conscription (the first in history); mobilized economic resources for war; controlled prices and wages; purged local governments; spawned a plethora of schemes (mostly stillborn) for the public welfare, including free, public education; attempted to destroy the Catholic Church (and all others); and initiated a new "rational" state religion.

The weakness of the Directory, formed in reaction to the Terror, enabled Napoleon Bonaparte to seize power and to install an even more authoritarian regime—if more restrained in punishing its opponents. Liberty was the loser. Bureaucracy grew apace to regiment the people for the sake of power and, by Napoleon's standards, to promote equality of opportunity and to provide better education and public services.

Nevertheless, "Liberty, Equality, and Fraternity," and the principles of constitutionalism, government by the popular will, and the natural rights of man became permanent legacies of the Revolution. They were affirmed by every revolutionary government and were trumpeted to Europe by Napoleon for another fifteen years. These ideals owed much to traditional British concepts and to the American example, but it took the French Revolution and Napoleon to impress them on Europe and the world. Today, no major nation is without a written constitution (except Great Britain, the "Mother of Parliaments"). That of the USSR has a bill of rights, which (if historically honored in the breach) is longer than that of the United States.

Modern nationalism, defined as loyalty to the abstract concept of the nation (*La Patrie*) originated in 1789, but more positively with the abolition of the monarchy and the disestablishment of the Church. (Traditional nationalism involved loyalty to the king and Church.) With the onset of war (1792) it was

---

[1] Olympe de Gouges, an actress of the Comédie-Française, who published a "Declaration of the Rights of Woman and the Citizeness," was not so lucky. She died at the Guillotine in 1793.

connected in the public mind with the defense of "The Revolution" against forces of the Old Regime. Increasingly systematic government propaganda demanded that every citizen serve the cause (and hate the enemy). The *levée en masse* (mass draft) of 1793 produced the largest armies Europe had ever seen, and conscription was continued under the Directory, Consulate, and Empire. Napoleon instituted monarchical forms but utilized the new nationalism to the maximum. "The Imperial Guard always marched to the 'Marseillaise,'" he said at St. Helena. His propaganda, which dramatized his triumphs and celebrated the victories and heroes of the Grande Armée, raised national pride to such heights that his name is still synonymous with French glory.

Overall, a pattern was set for national wars, with total popular involvement—as opposed to the wars of the Old Regime, which were fought by professionals with minimal attention to public attitudes. Ultimately the French would be emulated by all nations. However, during that era, France's enemies followed her example only tentatively and for short periods. The old monarchs were too fearful of the masses to appeal to popular passion or even to institute the draft. Spanish nationalism, which was a real force in bringing Napoleon down, was of the ancient mold—the nationalism of crown and Church. The Kings of England and Prussia and the Emperors of Austria and Russia continued to depend largely on professional armies. In the final struggle against Napoleon, however, they did benefit from anti-French sentiment, heightened by Napoleon's conscription and taxes in conquered areas. In 1813–1815, German and Italian nationalism existed largely in the minds of intellectuals, though nationalism would become a vital force in the nineteenth century.

The Revolution destroyed "feudalism" in France—more properly a society of legal privilege, dominated by a hereditary aristocracy. It may be cogently argued that the Revolution produced a society dominated by an aristocracy of wealth. Without doubt, in some of its phases and at many levels, the Revolution was a struggle between the rich and the poor, out of which the very poor emerged as miserable as ever. However, it was not exactly a victory of the *bourgeoisie* (middle class), if the term is defined to mean industrial-commercial capitalists. If anything, it was a victory for property holders, and the largest holdings, in 1815 as in 1789, were in *land*. Although the number of capitalists in large-scale enterprise increased, the bourgeoisie expanded generally on traditional lines—in numbers of officeholders (bureaucrats), lawyers, professional men, investors, and government-connected businessmen and bankers. Gains in landholding transcended class lines. The nobles retained large amounts, the city bourgeoisie gained more, the "rural bourgeoisie" of prosperous peasants expanded, and more peasant farmers acquired enough land to support their families. The most depressed people remained the landless peasants and the unskilled workers of the cities.

The Revolution eliminated *caste* (dependent on birth) as a legal factor in social status. However, the *classes* (defined by wealth and occupation) had transcended the castes of the Old Regime, and each "class" was extremely heterogeneous. (This will be explained fully in Chapter 1.) Further, the "revolutionary bourgeoisie," which supposedly overthrew the aristocracy early in the Revolution, had among its top leaders more liberal nobles (such as Lafayette) than businessmen. The ruling "bourgeoisie," at all stages, even under the Terror, had nobles in its ranks.

No group had sufficient class consciousness to formulate, much less implement, a long-term program to promote its interests. The bourgeois leaders of 1789, 1791–1792, of the Convention (1792–1795), and the Directory (1795–1799) were consistent in their determination to protect the institution of private property. In this, however, they were supported by the peasants, strongly attached to the family smallhold, the nobles who remained in France, and even the proletariat of the cities. To the Paris *sans-culottes*, the ideal citizen was the artisan-manufacturer who worked with his hands, even if an employer.

Nevertheless, in general, the middle class (very loosely defined) did triumph. Its ranks were vastly expanded and moved upward in society to meet the needs of the new bureaucracy and the expanding capitalist economy. Since free public education never became a reality, people of means and their children could most easily qualify for office or managerial positions. It was significant for the future, however, that the principle of equality was upheld.

The Revolution did not destroy the Catholic Church, but it did confiscate the Church's business property and did eliminate the Church as an official arm of the government. The principle of freedom of religion was firmly established, and state supervision of the churches became routine. Society was secularized in that it became possible for people to live normally without any church affiliation. Civil marriage and divorce were legalized; births, marriages (civil and religious), and deaths had to be registered with the state. Thus one could marry, produce legal heirs, and bequeath property without benefit of clergy. The Church's monopoly on education was broken as well, though it retained a vital role.

In civil rights, Protestants and belatedly Jews and blacks in France were granted full equality before the law and in officeholding. Slavery was not abolished in the colonies until 1794, however, for fear of destroying the economy of the French West Indies, disrupting trade, and reducing government revenues. Napoleon restored slavery in the colonies in 1802, which contributed to the loss of Haiti. This was in contradiction to his policies in Europe—and even in Egypt—but was done for economic reasons.

Napoleon Bonaparte was brought to power by moderate politicians to insure against a return of the Terror (not imminently, but, they thought, eventually). They are often pictured as a high bourgeoisie bent on protecting their economic interests, and Napoleon, as Consul and Emperor, is credited with advancing their cause. It is true that to strengthen the economy and his government he rewarded enterprisers and expanded the ranks of bourgeois civil servants. However, he also made maximum use of nobles of the Old Regime— including exiles who were invited back, along with Jacobins and others—in the administration, judiciary, and military. At the same time, Napoleon catered to commercial and industrial entrepreneurs and bankers and made it profitable for them to serve him. (Gabriel

Julien Ouvrard in France and Mayer Anselm Rothschild in Frankfurt are out-standing examples.) Bonaparte also favored tax collectors who could pay in advance. These men, however, were salaried and removable, like the rest of his officials. More important, in the Revolutionary-Napoleonic bureaucracy, unlike that of the Old Regime, no man *owned* his office or could pass it to an heir. Careers were indeed "open to talent." Undoubtedly, Napoleon did expand and strengthen the bourgeoisie and did so on the basis of merit (of which he, admittedly, was the judge). He did not create, whole, some strange new class of capitalist "predators."

The Corsican may have halted the path of the Revolution toward greater democracy or may have saved it from total destruction. The issue is academic. He seems to have been right for this time. He governed more absolutely than the Bourbons, but under constitutions approved by universal manhood suffrage. For the sake of national unity, he reintegrated the old nobility into society, but without its privileges. He restored the Catholic Church for its social value, but did not reestablish it. He preserved the secular state. The new monarchy (Empire) he founded had an aristocracy of service.

Though Napoleon built on the work of the Revolution, his legacy to France was enormous. "I am so much identified . . . with . . . our institutions . . . that no one would know how to separate me from them. . . . " he said at St. Helena. That is true today. The Code Napoléon is still the basic law. In essence, his adminis-trative, judicial, and police systems persist. National education is administered along the lines he laid down; the baccalaureate exam he introduced is still the key to higher education and high position. There is much more. One could even say that Charles de Gaulle founded the present Fifth Republic through a Napoleonic appeal to the people, in plebiscite, over the heads of the politicians.[2]

Napoleon produced a stronger French nation than had ever existed before by his superb organizational skill and leadership, which included an actor's flair for the dramatic and an almost hypnotic ability to control people. With ample resources, cadres of veterans of the wars of the Revolution, conscripts and volunteers, and the advantage of vital French patriotism, he built an army, which, until 1812, was invincible. Augmented increasingly by contingents from his satellites and allies, this army gave him domination of Europe.

If he was a conservative in France, Bonaparte was positively a revolutionary in Europe. In the kingdoms and lesser states he founded, he promulgated constitutions; instituted the Code Napoléon (in seven languages); guaranteed equal rights (to the point that he was considered pro-Jewish in eastern Europe); abolished feudalism (and serfdom where it existed); reformed administrative and judicial systems; disestablished churches; founded schools; pensioned eminent scientists, writers, and artists; renovated cities; and built roads, bridges, and other

---

[2] That is not to say that Napoleon's reforms were original with him. See p. 215f. on the civil reforms, especially 220 on the law. See also p. 228f on the absence of military innovations. Bonaparte's forte was *action* (implementation in France; improvision in battle).

public works. He also instituted conscription and raised taxes—from his viewpoint a small price for the preservation of the empire—for citizenship in Europe.

Napoleon's ultimate Grand Design was to create a European state—a "federation of free peoples," he said at St. Helena. Probably he wanted a centralized, bureaucratic state. In either case, he believed that the unification of Europe would enable the peoples to reach their greatest potential. It would also eliminate the balance-of-power system by which Britain, and latterly Russia, had benefited by pitting the European states against each other. His Continental System, which banned British goods from Europe, was intended both to wreck the British economy and to make Europe more self-sufficient.

By 1812, Napoleon was "Emperor of Europe," enough to mobilize the whole Continent against Russia. The Grande Armée that crossed the Niemen was only one-third French. The Empire was not so strong as this seems to indicate because of the cost in blood and money of the war in Spain (in progress since 1808); the concealed hostility of some of France's allies, notably Prussia and Austria; and the restiveness of Europeans, burdened by war taxes and conscription. Nevertheless, Bonaparte seemed sure to win. But, of course, he did not. If he had, his empire might have survived, and the history of Europe and the world might have been much different. In our century, for example, neither world war could have begun as it did if there had been a European state.

After the Russian disaster, the "Crowned Jacobin," as the European princes so aptly called Napoleon, was vulnerable. Backed by Britain, the monarchs of the Old Regime brought him down. But they could not undo all his reforms or erase his memory. He had set the stage for further European revolutions in the nineteenth century. Moreover, he had shaken the whole world. For example, he had handed Louisiana to the United States and had drawn the United States into the War of 1812 against Britain, in effect, on the side of France.

Today, Napoleon is remembered best as a great military commander and has become a legendary hero with worldwide appeal. Without him, however, the Revolution would surely not have had the effect it did on Europe and the world. He made French bureaucratic systems the model for European states, and later, for their colonies and the rest of the world. His penchant for legislating solutions to all problems and for creating organizations to implement them gradually affected every major government as population increased and societies became more complex. The Code Napoléon, at first viewed outside France as radical, was later referred to for its comprehensiveness (as was the old Roman law, which "covered all cases," real or anticipated) and has affected law codes throughout the world. It is also well adapted to the bureaucratic state because it attempts to protect "rational authority" and to promote law and order. The more serious scholars of the Napoleonic Era are now giving more attention to his role as civil executive in France and Europe than to his military achievements. In both, however, his leadership is worthy of study.

In the Revolution proper, persons of every political persuasion have their heroes, including authoritarian democrats (who believe in government *for*, but not *by*, the people) and proponents of representative democracy. European statesmen are identified politically (most notably in France) by the revolutionary figures they praise or damn. Americans tend to view the Revolution whole, generally as "a good thing," but few congressmen would quote Robespierre in public. Revolutionaries, theoretical and actual, from Karl Marx and Lenin to Frantz Fanon and Ho Chi Minh, have studied it. The latter two, one black, one Oriental, both French-educated, illustrate the truth of Herbert Luethy's observation: "France lives in the hearts of those who rebel against her." Liberalism and nationalism, the most immediate by-products of the Revolution, are still vital forces—in many manifestations and mutations. In 1989 nationalism suddenly became an explosive force in eastern Europe and parts of the USSR. It is present among all the emerging nations of Africa, Asia, and the Middle East, whatever the political proclivities of their leaders.

Few raise the old question of whether the French Revolution was a "watershed" in history, though many want to extend the revolutionary period—some to one hundred years, 1750–1850—but the central focus is still on the French Revolution. For better or worse, it is still alive today. All the issues raised have not been resolved, even the most basic—the proper balance between liberty and equality.

In eastern Europe, nationalities seem to be gaining freedom, and to prefer Western-style, representative governments. But how much liberty (especially economic liberty) will the peoples tolerate at the cost of losing "equality" in the form of certain Socialist "benefits." The peoples' lives have been drab but "insured." Can Western-style democracies solve the problem? We hope so. In developing countries, governments find it difficult to grant liberty and representation while trying to educate populations and build viable economies to support them. Even in the United States, there are perpetual questions about the proper balance between public and private interest in the economy, and in the definition of rights and parameters of freedoms granted by the Constitution.

Nonetheless, *Liberté, Egalité et Fraternité* seem to be enjoying triumphs. Yet in every nation, no matter what its politico-economic system, the bureaucratic machinery which originated in the Revolutionary Era is being perfected. Increasingly, it controls people's lives and even thoughts. It has the potential, thus, for effecting great human betterment—or for making slaves of us all.

The Revolution was an affair of many phases, and a thing of many faces and contradictions. This became baldly evident in 1989, the Revolution's bicentennial year. France's president, François Mitterand, had hoped for a full year of festivities, beginning with the Bastille Day parade on 14 July. In the years preceding 1989, however, the French had proved so divided over the Revolution that he settled for a celebration of *La Réconciliation*, which translates literally: "reconciliation, the effecting of harmony among all factions." There were many. Hardly any of the French were prepared to simply commemorate the Great Revolution. A multitude of factions was ready to rejoice over one phase or another; some saw no good in the Revolution at all. The Left plumped for the Terror; the extreme Right pictured the Revolution as an evil and destructive.

For the first time in the twentieth century, questions over the interpretation of the Revolution (most recently, Marxist class-struggle or not) or over causes (intellectual, political, economic, social, cultural, or combinations of these) gave way to the blunt question: Was the Revolution *good* or *bad*? Was it necessary or unnecessary for progress? Could not its gains (some said, "if any") have been achieved without ten years of turmoil and bloodshed, the crashing guillotine, massacres in the countryside, civil and foreign war, all ending not with a great republic (as in America) or a hereditary "legitimate" constitutional monarchy, but in the Consulate and Empire of General Bonaparte (or, said some, fifteen years of Napoleonic dictatorship)?

"Revolution: Good or Bad???" That question had not been asked in a hundred years except by persons considered eccentrics by the vast majority of scholars. (The public, nevertheless, bawled at the cruel fate of gentle people in Dickens' *Tale of Two Cities,* latterly offered in movie and TV versions.) The issue was argued with passion during the Revolution itself, of course, and, with decreasing fervor, until the late nineteenth century.[3] In 1989, the bicentennial year, the more prominent historians of the Revolution again addressed the question.[4]

Students might find "The Revolution: Good or Bad?" a challenging issue to debate.

---

[3] These arguments may be found in the works of Edmund Burke, *Reflections on the Revolution in France* (1790); Joseph Barnave, in *Introduction à la Révolution française* (written before 1793, when he was executed, published 1843); the Abbé Barruel's *Mémoires pour servir à l'histoire du jacobinisme* (1797); and Jean-Joseph Mounier in *On the Influence Attributed to Philosophers* (1801). Somewhat later, Alexis de Tocqueville in his much cited *L'Ancien régime et la Révolution* (1856) postulated that France, in fact, had changed more by evolution, despite the revolution. However, condemning the Revolution outright was already out of style. Three great multi-volume French histories—by Louis-Adolphe Thiers, Louis Blanc, and Jules Michelet—praised the Revolution; only Hippolyte Taine, in truth a royalist, damned the Revolution—and Napoleon too.

[4] Simon Schama's magnificently written *Citizens* and William Doyle's Oxford *French Revolution* were conservative in tone, even to the point of lauding the Old Regime. So was J. F. Bosher's *French Revolution* (1988) and Emmet Kennedy's *Cultural History of the French Revolution* (1989). The divided French contented themselves with contentious monographs and articles; a few bland, comprehensive histories like Michel Vovelle's *Révolution française: Images et récit,* 5 vols. (1986), and Godechot's *Chronologie commentée* (1988); and reprints of old syntheses, including that of Soboul (see Bibliography).

Of course, one should have been alerted by Donald Sutherland's *France 1789–1815* (1986), and the *Dictionnaire critique de la Révolution française,* edited by François Furet and Mona Ozouf (1987), and translated into English in 1989. Conor Cruise O'Brien titled his review in the *New York Review of Books* (13 Feb. 1990) "The Decline and Fall of the French Revolution." Another bellwether of the new conservatism was the popularity in France of books that roundly damned the Revolution: Reynauld Secher, in *La génocide franco-français: la Vendée-vengé* (1986), accused Robespierre's government of Terror of genocide—the systematic slaughter of God-fearing peasants in the Vendée; René Sédillot in *Le Coût de la Révolution française* (1987) ["The Cost of the French Revolution"] said, with impassioned verbosity, that the cost was too high by far.

All, implicitly or explicitly, questioned whether or not the Revolution was a "good" or a "bad" thing. For one with his eye on historiographical developments, however, a "funny thing happened on the way to the Bicentennial."

Generally, in the 1980s (see Bibliography), the emphasis among scholars shifted from social history, per se, to cultural-social, cultural, or intellectual history, and that of *mentalités*. The French *Mentalités* school attributes developments to mind-sets of certain groups, which in turn are fostered by ideas, tradition, rhetoric, art, symbols, myth, festivals, celebrations, and even trinkets (minor cultural artifacts of the time). These involve the history of the theater, press, art, architecture, religion, ethnicity (mostly in France), medicine, science, demography, and much else. A solid example is Michel Vovelle's *Mentalité révolutionnaire: Sociétés et mentalités sous la Révolution française* (1985). All this is new, and yet not. In some ways it is a continuation of the work of the *Annales* School, identified with Lucien Febvre, Marc Bloch, and (into the 1980s) Fernand Braudel, as well as Emmanuel Le Roy Ladurie, who has changed direction, but is still at work. So is Geneviève Bollème, whose *La bibliothèque bleue* (1971) and *Contes bleus* (1983) have improved our understanding of the impact of the Enlightenment on ordinary people.

A defector from the *Annales* School and an early leader in cultural-intellectual history was François Furet. He emphasized the impact of ideas in *Penser la révolution française* (1978), translated as *Interpreting the French Revolution* (1981), by Elborg Forster. At least equally important were the works of the quixotic Richard Cobb, *Reactions to the French Revolution* (1972), *The Police and the People* (1976), and *Death in Paris* (1978), with their sympathetic, yet realistic treatment of the views of people at the lowest levels of society—bums, prostitutes, thieves, and others. Mona Ozouf's *Fête révolutionnaire* (1976; English 1988) has had enormous influence. Many of the current leaders in the "new history" are Americans (or teach in the U.S., like Furet and Ozouf), Canadians, or British. The Bibliography will show multiple works by Keith Baker, Robert Darnton, Jack Censer, Lynn Hunt, Colin Lucas, Jeremy Popkin, and many others.

If course, much women's history is being produced, some of it following the new trends, much of it simply devoted to giving women—leaders and rank-and-file alike—a fairer place in the chronicle of the Era.

On recent trends, one can consult: Jacques Godechot, *Les Révolutions, 1770–1799, Nouvelle Clio*, No. 36, 4th ed. (1986) and his "Bulletins historiques: La périod révolutionnaire et impériale," in *Revue Historique*, 533 and 536 (1980), 561 (janvier–mars 1987) and 587 (juillet—sept. 1988); François Furet, *L'Atelier de l'histoire (1982) and Marx et la Révolution française* (1985); Albert Soboul, *Comprehendre la Révolution: Problèmes politiques de la Révolution française (1981); Journal of Modern History*, Vol. 56, No. 4 (Dec. 1984), a Special Issue on Political Practice in the French Revolution; Gunther Horst (ed.), *Die Franzosische Revolution: Berichte und Deutungen deutscher Schriftsteller und Historiker* (1985); Frank Kafker and James Laux, *The French Revolution: Conflicting Interpretations*, 4th ed. (1989); Donald M. G. Sutherland, "Introduction," *French Historical Studies*, Vol. 16, No. 2 (Fall 1989); *Special Issue: The French Revolution*; edited by D.G.M. Sutherland: Chap. 5 (pp. 881–1021) of F. Furet and Mona Ozouf, *Critical Dictionary of the French Revolution* (translated 1989); Jack Censer, "Commencing the Third Century of Debate," *American Historical Review*; Vol. 94, No. 5 (Dec. 1989); and *Journal of Modern History*, Vol. 60, "Supplement" (Sept. 1988), on the End of the Old Regime. Throughout the 1980s, American periodicals carried an unusual number of articles on the Old Regime, French Revolution, and Napoleonic Era. They were more sparse in the French journals, notably the *Revue d'Histoire Moderne et Contemporaine*, which treated 1989 as a normal year.

On the older controversies see: Alfred Cobban, "The Myth of the French Revolution," in *Aspects of the French Revolution* (1970); Gerald J. Cavanaugh, "The Present State of French Revolutionary Historiography," *French Historical Studies* (1972); R. R. Palmer, "Popular Democracy in the French Revolution," *French Historical Studies* (1960); George V. Taylor, "Noncapitalist Wealth and the Causes of the French Revolution," *American Historical Review* (1967); Elizabeth Eisenstein, "Who Intervened in 1788?" *American Historical Review* (1965); Elizabeth Behrens, "Nobles, Privileges, and Taxes in France at the End of the Ancien Regime," *Economic History Review* (1963); G. J. Cavanaugh, "Nobles, Privileges and Taxes in France: A Revision Reviewed," *French Historical Studies* (1974); François Furet, "Le Catechisme révolutionnaire," *Annales, E.S.C.* (1971); Daniel Guerin, "D'une nouvelle interpretation de la Révolution française," *Annales E.S.C.* (1965); Albert Soboul, "La Révolution française dans l'histoire du monde contemporain," *Information Historique* (1969); Claude Mauzaric, "Sur une nouvelle conception de la Révolution," *Annales historique de la Revolution Francaise* (1967); Stanley Mellon, "Nineteenth Century Perceptions of Revolution," *Proceedings of the Consortium on Revolutionary Europe* (1975); Philip Dawson, "The Bourgeois de Robe in 1789," *French Historical Studies* (1965);

Jeffry Kaplow, *New Perspectives on the French Revolution* (1967); Frank A. Kafker and James M. Laux (eds.), *The French Revolution: Conflicting Interpretations* (1968 and 1989); Ralph W. Greenlaw (ed.), *The Social Origins of the French Revolution* (1975) and *The Economic Origins of the French Revolution* (1958); Alfred Cobban, *Historians and Causes of the French Revolution* (1958) and *Social Interpretation of the French Revolution* (1964); A. Gérard, *Révolution française: Mythes et interpretations* (1970); Jacques Godechot, *Un jury pour la Révolution: Les historiens de la Révolution française* (1975); Claude Mazauric, *Sur la Révolution française* (1970); George Rudé, *Interpretations of the French Revolution* (1961); John Hall Stewart, *The French Revolution: Some Trends in Historical Writing, 1945–1965* (1967). Many of the above also discuss the "Atlantic Revolution" thesis advanced by R. R. Palmer and Jacques Godechot. The best references are Jacques Godechot, "Révolution française ou occidentale?," in *Les Révolutions*, 3rd ed. (1970) and Peter Amann, *The Eighteenth Century Revolution: French or Western?* (1963). In a more general vein, that is, on the historiography of the Revolution over two centuries, see Cobban, Godechot and Gérard, cited above, and Richard Cobb, *The French Revolution in Historical Thought* (1967); Stanley Mellon, *Political Uses of History: A Study of the Historians of the French Revolution* (1969); Hedva Ben-Israel, *English Historians and the French Revolution* (1968). These works have discussions of, for example: the conservative-liberal war of the nineteenth century, with opposing "generals" F. Adolphe Thiers and Hippolyte Taine; Jules Michelet's "hymn to the people"; and the shorter literary spectacular of Thomas Carlyle, the *French Revolution* of the Utopian Socialist Louis Blanc, and the more "scientific" *Histoire Socialiste* of Jean Jaurès.

In our century, two of the greatest scholars capped their work with miscellanies emphasizing their major theories: François Alphonse Aulard, the liberal eminence of the early Third Republic, in *Etudes et leçons sur la Révolution française*, 9 vols., Paris, 1893–1924, and George Lefebvre, in *Etudes sur la Révolution française* (1954).

Napoleonic historiography of the old style is represented by Pieter Geyl, *Napoleon: For and Against* (1949); Albert Guérard, *Reflections on the Napoleonic Legend* (1924); David H. Pinckney (ed.), *Napoleon: Historical Enigma* (1969); Jean Tulard (ed.), *L'Anti-Napoleon: La legende noire de l'empereur* (1965) and *Le mythe de Napoleon* (1971); Jean Lucas-Dubreton, *Le culte de Napoleon, 1814–1848* (1960); and H.A.L. Fisher's erudite *Bonapartism* (1908). Along similar lines, Jacques Godechot's *L'Epoque Napoléonienne* (1967), cited above, has a fine "Pour ou Contre" chapter. This approach to Napoleonic historiography, however, seems to be passé.

A new direction of studies was signalled by the subject matter of colloquia held in 1969 (the bicentenary of Napoleon's birth). For example: *La France à l'Epoque Napoléonienne*, a special issue of *Revue d'Histoire Moderne et Contemporaine*, Tome XVII (juillet–septembre, 1970); and *Colloque de Bruxelles: Occupants—Occupes 1792–1815* (1969). Other colloquia were held in Germany, Elba, Corsica, and Lyons. All had multinational participation and papers on almost everything but military subjects.

Napoleon-as-Hero (or Villain) was finally being abandoned in favor of the history of the Napoleonic Era. Institutional, legal, social, economic, and political, cultural, and other studies were being written, focusing on limited areas of France or the Empire, and utilizing the methods and tools of statistical and prosopographic history. A striking example was "L'Italie jacobine et napoléonienne," a special number of the *Annales Historiques de la Révolution Française*, 230 (octobre–dec. 1977).

The trend has continued toward studying the Napoleonic Era, rather than the Man, in France, Europe, and the world. Scholars in Napoleonic history now have more in common with those in French Revolutionary studies. See, for example, Henry Laurens, *Les origines intellectuelles de l'expédition d'Egypte: L'orientalisme islamisant en France, 1698–1798* (1987).

For France, there is Louis Bergeron, *L'Episode Napoléonien: Aspects intérieurs* (1972), translated as *France under Napoléon* by R. R. Palmer (1981), with improved graphs and maps; Jean Paul Bertaud, *La France de Napoleon, 1799–1815* (1987); and some American contributions: June K. Burton, *Napoleon and Clio: Historical Writing, Teaching and Thinking during the First Empire* (1979) and Edward A. Whitcomb, *Napoleon's Diplomatic Service* (1979). There is also local history: E. Erlanning, *La resistance bretonne à Napoléon, 1799–1815* (1986); Thierry Lentz and Denis Imhoff, *La Moselle et Napoleon: Etude d'un departement sous le Consulat et l'Empire* (1988), and much more. And much economic history is now available, some in "sweepthroughs": William Reddy, *The Rise of Market Culture: The Textile Trade and French Society, 1750–1900* (1984) and Denis Woronoff, *L'industrie siderurgique en France pendant la Révolution et l'Empire* (1984).

Outside France, the Italians led the way, with works such as Edoardo Bressan's *Poverta e assistenza in Lombardia nell'eta napoleonica* (1985); Pasquale Villani's *Italia napoleonica* (1978); Paolo Morachiello and G. Teyssot's *Nascita delle citta di Stato: ingegneri e architetti sotto il Consolato e l'Impero* (1983); and the works of the prolific Carlo Zaghi, including *Potere, chiesa, e società: studi e ricerche sull'Italia giocobina e napoleonica* (1984) and *L'Italia di Napoleone* (1986). (See Bibliography.)

The Germans, with help from England, France, and North America, also have come on strong. See Helmut Berding, *Privat Kapital, Staatfinanzen und Reformpolitik im Deutschlander Napoleonischen Zeit* (1981); Geoffrey Ellis, *Napoleon's Continental Blockade: The Case of Alsace* (1981); Michel Hau, *L'Industrialisation d'Alsace (1803–1939)* (1987); Marcus Junkelmann, *Napoleon und Bayern: von den Anfangen des Königreiches* (1985); Herbert Kisch, *From Domestic Manufacture to Industrial Revolution: The Case of the Rhineland Textile Districts* (1989).

Spanish contributions feature familiar names: Miguel Artola, *La Hacienda del siglo XIX: Progresistas y Moderatos* (1986) and Juan Mercader Riba, *José Bonaparte Rey de España (1808–1813): estructura del estado español bonapartista* (1983). The same is true for Poland, where Monika Senkowska-Gluck and W. Sobocinski dominate Napoleonic studies. And at last there are works on long-neglected areas, for example: Frank J. Bundy, *The Administration of the Illyrian Provinces of the French Empire, 1809–1813* (1987); Demokos Kosary, *Napoléon et l'Hongrie* (1979); and Pierre Pluchon, *Histoire des Antilles et de la Guyane* (1982). We also have a new diplomatic history of Portugal: Antonio Pedro Manique, *Portugal e as potencias europeias, 1807–1847* (1988).

Jean Tulard's *Le Grand Empire, 1804–1815* (1982) deals with its announced subject quite fully. Of general interest also are François Collaveri, *La franc-maçonnerie des Bonaparte* (1982) and Margaret M. O'Dwyer, *The Papacy in the Age of Napoleon and the Restoration: Pius VII, 1800–1823* (1985). Also, Owen Connelly's *Napoleon's Satellite Kingdoms* will be reprinted in 1990.

Peter Paret, king of military theory, top expert on Prussia, the military and other reforms, and Clausewitz, is still at work. His *Clausewitz and the State* had a new edition in 1985, and he edited (with Gordon Craig and Felix Gilbert) *Makers of Modern Strategy* (1986). Other titles dot the Bibliography.

Inevitably, as it were, much military history was written in the 1980s. However, it is better than ever, and some of it, like the works of Geoffrey Best, Alan Forrest, Sam Scott, and Isser Woloch is social-cultural as well as military. Please see the Bibliography for books by David Chandler, Gunther Rothenberg, John Elting, Steven Ross, Isser Wolloch, Samuel Scott, Gordon Bond, Geoffrey Parker, Christopher Duffy, John Keegan, and Alan Forrest, as well as Geoffrey Best, Thomas Mack Barker, Charles E. White, T.C.W. Blanning, John Lynn, Peter Wenzler, Azar Gat, and Owen Connelly. R. R. Palmer has done a real service for military historians of the period by translating Jean-Paul Bertaud, *La Révolution Armée: Les soldats-citoyens et la Révolution française* (1979) [*The Army of the French Revolution: From Citizen Soldiers to Instrument of Power*, Princeton, 1988]. It is *the* place to begin in studying war both under the Revolution and Napoleon.

There are many new references and bibliographies on the Napoleonic Era. For example: Donald D. Horward, *Napoleonic Military History: A Bibliography* (1986); Ronald J. Caldwell, *The Era of the French Revolution: A Bibliography of the History of Western Civilization, 1789–1799* (1985); Jean Tulard (ed.), *Dictionnaire Napoléon* (1987); Owen Connelly (ed.), with P. W. Becker, H. T. Parker, June Burton, and Janice Berbin, *Historical Dictionary of Napoleonic France* (1985); and David G. Chandler, *Dictionary of the Napoleonic Wars* (1979). More titles in all categories are to be found in the Bibliography.

There is a deep lying struggle in the whole of society;
a boundless grinding collision of the New with the Old.
The French Revolution . . . was not the parent
of this mighty movement, but its offspring.
— *Thomas Carlyle*

THE EIGHTEENTH CENTURY

"LA GRANDE NATION"

It is easy to form the impression that in the decades before 1789 France swarmed with prophets of revolution. King Louis XV intoned his famous *"Après moi, le déluge."* Voltaire predicted a revolution and regretted that he would probably not live to see it. The Count de Chamfort, a renowned dilettante, forecast a holocaust and said he would "die of it." (He did.) However, the king spoke in a fit of pique, Voltaire equated revolution with enlightenment, and Chamfort was so unconcerned with his safety that he lived in the teeming Palais-Royal quarter of Paris.

In fact, even in the spring of 1789 most contemporaries would have judged France a near-impossible locus for revolution. The nation was considered very strong by her own officials and foreign observers alike, as well as by her brilliant, hyperactive, and contentious intellectuals, however critical they were. She had the largest population in Europe—26,000,000, perhaps 27,000,000—greater than Russia's, three times that of England, and twice that of Spain, and it was rising. To most people, numbers connoted strength; only the most astute observers saw the dangers involved. France had emerged victorious from the War of the American Revolution, and, ignoring her losses earlier in the century, optimists crowed that she had won the "Second Hundred Years War." The income of the French government was several times that of the British, which seemed to signal greater strength.[1] Though British predominance in industrial development was

---

[1] 640,000,000 livres to £10,000,000 (about 250,000,000 livres). The livre was worth a little less than a shilling, or about $.20 in U.S. currency.

recognized, the Physiocrats, who dominated French economic thought, emphasized that a nation's basic wealth was in the products of the land.

Faith in the monarchy was strong. Louis XVI was not hated. Arthur Young, the famous English traveler, recorded (1787) with astonishment that the king had no fear of the masses. Even beggars in rags roamed about Versailles unchecked, some venturing into the royal chateau itself. The monarch was still seen as the "father of the people," above all classes and political factions.

France had seen bread riots almost every year from 1763 onward.[2] These were largely confined to the countryside, since the crown was seeing to the supply of the cities. Political implications, however, were nil. The peasants invariably seized granaries, warehouses, and village bakeries, then appealed to the king and/or local authorities to reduce prices to a "just" level. Often they claimed to be fighting for the king, who, at one time or another, had imposed price controls almost everywhere. Violence was done to property but seldom was anyone hurt, except by accident.[3]

Such repeated incidents might have been taken as evidence that all was not well, but they were not. After all, England, not destined for a revolution, had bread riots, too, though fewer (1766, 1772, 1773, and 1783). And nothing in all Europe compared to the Pugachev rebellion in Russia (1773). The giant Cossack's bands ravaged the Ukraine for two years before Pugachev was finally captured and executed.

Paris, soon to be the center of the Revolution, seemed to present no problems. Its inhabitants were staunchly loyal to the king. Paradoxically, they had often rioted to protest against unpopular royal edicts (or in support of courts that refused to register them)—but it was the king's ministers whom they blamed for new tax levies and similar impositions. Louis XVI, like Louis XV before him, went among Parisians without fear.

The French capital, moreover, was considered the best-managed and best-policed city in Europe. Joseph II of Austria had remarked on the cleanliness of the streets and buildings and on the attention of officials to public hygiene and charity.[4] Compared to London or Vienna, the rate of violent crime was very low. And the Paris police did not even carry firearms. The French had scoffed at Londoners after the breakdown of order during the Gordon Riots of 1780. Nothing like that could happen in Paris!

Arthur Young, who had cataloged France's ills, still saw no signs of imminent revolution in the fall of 1788. The government, he wrote in his journal, must use its "clearest and most decided talents"; otherwise it could not "last half a century longer." Entries for the spring of 1789 show that he was caught unaware by the cataclysm.

---

[2] 1769, 1779, and 1780 were the only years of total quiet.

[3] This applies only to the rioters; police and troops took quite a number of lives.

[4] By today's (western) standards, they were filthy, of course. (See p. 75.)

The Revolution was a great surprise; so much seems beyond dispute. How, then, did it happen? What were the causes?

CAUSES OF THE REVOLUTION: SUMMARY

The Revolution was possible because of a political culture that had evolved in the eighteenth century. (See p. 53.) It began, however, as a result of a fiscal crisis in the French government, rooted in general economic stress. It was made possible by a theoretically absolute king who was too weak to exert his powers and who allowed hereditary, noble officeholders to disable his government. Once in motion, the Revolution was carried forward by people inspired by the ideals of the Enlightenment and the American Revolution, but motivated by a determination to solve specifically *French* problems. These included an anachronistic absolute monarchy; a government dominated by holders of venal, often hereditary, office; an untoward power of the Church in political and economic affairs; a society-of-legal-privilege (often called "feudal"); and the tensions, lack of social mobility and opportunity, and economic disabilities that resulted. The Revolution could not have occurred, however, or moved into successively more radical phases, without the action of angry masses—particularly in Paris—who were motivated by some idealism, much hope, and, at critical junctures, terrible hunger.

The French Revolution was unique and stemmed from French circumstances. However, France was to some degree shaped by eighteenth-century developments that were international, though of most impact in the Atlantic world. These included enormous population growth and power-political and commercial rivalries (and resulting world wars). In addition, there were technological advancement, commercial expansion, nascent industrial revolution, and innovation in business methods and banking, which demanded new kinds of leadership that the old landed aristocracy was neither qualified nor inclined to offer and which mandated radical changes in society.

We shall discuss the broader developments first, then move to the ills of the French government, society, and economy.

POPULATION EXPLOSION

Sudden, vast population expansion in the eighteenth century cannot be singled out as the sole cause of any of the many changes in Western society, much less revolutions. Nevertheless, there is no event that is unrelated to this phenomenon. An indication of the scale of increase is given in the following table. As we can see, the demographic growth in some parts of Europe was 100 percent. The table does not cover Asia, but the rough figures show that between 1750 and 1800 the population there jumped from 497,000,000 to 602,000,000—a 25 percent increase. This compares to the growth in Europe, from 140,000,000 to 187,000,000 in the same fifty years.

DEMOGRAPHIC GROWTH: EIGHTEENTH CENTURY

Country or Area	1701 (or as indicated)	1800 (or as indicated)	Percent Increase
France	18,000,000 (1715)	26,000,000 (1789)	44
England and Wales	5,800,000	9,150,000 (1801)	58
Ireland	2,500,000	5,200,000	108
Scotland	1,000,000	1,600,000	60
Spain	6,000,000	10,400,000 (1787)	73
Italy (all states)	13,000,000	17,000,000	31
Germany (all states)	10,000,000	20,000,000	100
Austrian Empire	9,000,000	18,000,000	100
Russia	12,500,000 (1724)	26,000,000 (1796) (part of population annexed)	108
Thirteen Colonies (U.S.)	270,000	2,500,000 (est. 1776)	825
Central and South America	11,000,000 (1750)	19,000,000	72

Adapted from Reinhard, *Population mondiale*, 3d ed. (1968).

There was what Dévèze called *"une demographie trop gallopante"* ("a galloping population growth") throughout the world. And there is no accepted explanation for it. The best guess is that it was rooted in climatic change, which affected human health and behavior and promoted food production. Also, we know that the plagues of the seventeenth century and earlier did not recur in the eighteenth century, perhaps because rats seem to have lost their ability to carry bubonic bacteria.

For Europe, there is a combination of possible causes. The mortality rate dropped, and, though the birth rate remained relatively stable, there were more women of childbearing age and thus more births. The decreased death rate, in turn, is usually attributed to advances in medicine and hygiene and to better nourishment. The greatest medical advance was the introduction of smallpox inoculation, which was, however, spottily applied. The growth of cities undoubtedly worsened the state of public hygiene. Nourishment improved when food production increased and Europeans began to grow new American crops such as corn (maize), potatoes, tomatoes, and squash and to import sugar, chocolate, and so on. But if American foods contributed to population growth in Europe, how can equal growth in Asia be explained? Moreover, Europeans used corn and potatoes mostly to feed stock; therefore their introduction may have served only to put more meat into the diets of the rich, while removing land from the production of grain and worsening the diets of the poor. Fortunately, we do not have to explain exactly why a population explosion occurred in the eighteenth century. We know that there was one and that its impact was international and created both problems and opportunities.[5]

THE EUROPEAN RESPONSE   Britain, which took an early lead in industrialization, was able to utilize additional people in her factories and "exported" thousands to her colonies (though fewer after 1776). She weathered the century in relative domestic peace. In central and eastern Europe the problem was met by "internal colonization"—moving people onto previously unused land—or into adjacent territories acquired by conquest. Generally, the existing social system was simply extended. The nobility, however, especially in Prussia, Poland, and Russia, gained power at the expense of the peasant population, which was driven into more formalized serfdom. Prussia had a modicum of industrialization, which helped absorb excess population, and manufacturing grew in the other German states as well, most markedly in the Rhineland. Scandinavia had modest increases in industry and greatly expanded trade. In Belgium (the Austrian Netherlands), industrialization paralleled that of Britain. In Holland (the United Provinces of the Netherlands), commerce and the processing of colonial goods kept employment fairly high, though Dutch commerce declined in the face of British competition.

In Italy, there was extensive industrialization in the north and accelerated commerce in the old maritime cities such as Venice, Genoa, and Leghorn (Livorno). In the Papal States and Naples, there were no effective responses to burgeoning population. The crisis intensified as the century progressed, and in Naples, widespread banditry began. Thus in 1789 both seemed more ripe for revolution than France, because the people were surely more downtrodden.

France, however, had a population with increasing expectations, since, until 1778, she had enjoyed unusual prosperity, apparently aided by population growth. In fact she lagged behind Britain in industrialization and had lost important colonies during the century. Thus unemployment in the cities had gradually increased as had the "squeeze on the land" in the countryside, producing more landless peasants, unemployment, banditry, and movement toward the cities. After 1778 the adverse effects of relative overpopulation (a rise of 44 percent

[5] As of 1990, we still have no positive explanation of population growth. However, see the Bibliography for the works of Matthew Ramsey and Thomas McKeown (medical history), P. E. Razzell (smallpox vaccination), and James C. Riley (hygiene).

between 1715 and 1789) contributed heavily to her general malaise. These will be discussed in detail in connection with French social problems (pp. 52–53).

THE POWER STRUGGLE

When Louis XIV died at the age of seventy-seven in 1715, Paris celebrated, and the people threw stones and shouted insults as his funeral cortege passed. He had presided over France in her golden age, expanded her frontiers, and installed his grandson on the throne of Spain. To do so, however, he had kept the nation at war for a total of twenty-seven years and had taxed his subjects unmercifully.

Nonetheless, only thirty-six years later, Voltaire, in his *Siècle de Louis XIV*, wrote that the king "did more for his people than twenty of his predecessors put together." He stressed French intellectual and artistic achievements in the seventeenth century, which, he said, had made Louis' age more brilliant than that of Periclean Athens, Augustan Rome, or the Renaissance. But just as Tacitus' *Germania* had been a lament for the lost virtues of Rome, Voltaire's history was a cry of anguish for the lost glory of France. Moreover, the sardonic king of the *philosophes* well knew that the glory had been based on power. He pointedly deplored the decline of the French navy since 1715 and praised the discipline of the Sun King's armies. Radical-in-exile and citizen of the world, he was still Frenchman enough to be dumbfounded at the decline of France's prestige.

The decline was relative. France was still the first power in Europe, but she became accustomed to being preponderant in the *world*, and was clearly losing ground to Britain overseas. The trend began with the last war of Louis XIV, that of the Spanish Succession (1701–1714), after which Britain gained Newfoundland, Nova Scotia, and the Hudson's Bay area from France, and Gibraltar and the *asiento*, a monopoly on slavetrading with the Spanish colonies, from Spain. Louis XIV's foreign policy had given Europe first priority. He favored the army and neglected the navy.

The Sun King's successors continued his Europe-centered *politique*. As a result, in five costly wars, Louis XV (1715–1774) gained only the Duchy of Lorraine (and otherwise added only Corsica to France by purchase from Genoa). Overseas, at the end of the Seven Years' War (1763), he ceded Canada, North America east of the Mississippi, and Senegal, in Africa, to Britain and gave over Louisiana to his ally, Spain. In India, France was left with trading stations at Pondichery and Chandernagor.

Louis XVI was given an unprecedented opportunity for revenge against Britain by the revolt of the American colonies (1775). He delayed committing French forces until 1778, however, and then managed the war badly, considering that he had the Spanish and Dutch as allies, and, for once, no enemies in Europe. In the end (1783), he contented himself with seeing the new American nation born and with receiving back Senegal. The effort had cost France 2,000,000,000 livres. Five years later (1788) it was the debt, by then 4,000,000,000 livres (and a political crisis), that forced Louis to call the Estates General of 1789, which began the Revolution.[6]

MILITARY POWER: FRANCE AND BRITAIN

France's concentration on European problems was partly a matter of necessity. Unlike her rival, Britain, protected by the sea, she had potential enemies on three frontiers and (considering the slow communications of the time) long coastlines on the Atlantic and Mediterranean that had to be guarded. In the eighteenth century, French kings maintained a peacetime standing army of 150,000, of whom about 50,000 were foreign mercenaries. Britain's was one-third that size, and most of it was stationed in India or other colonies. (She depended in emergencies on militia.)

Britain steadily built up her navy. In 1715 she had 120 ships-of-the-line (fifty guns or more) versus thirty-nine for France. In 1783, Britain had 174 ships-of-the-line and 294 other warships; France had about seventy line vessels and perhaps 150 others. Britain's fleet was scattered around the world, but with attention to guarding the channel. France kept squadrons in the West Indies (where she still had colonies) but concentrated her strength in Atlantic and Mediterranean ports. Curiously, the French, thanks to the work of the Academies des Sciences and de Marine, led in naval technology. France had both faster and more maneuverable ships and bigger ones with more guns. The French also had better navigation instruments. But the British excelled in seamanship—and borrowed French technology freely.

The French developed a more professional corps of army officers and better land weapons. Louis XV founded the École Militaire in Paris in 1751. (The British Royal Military College at Sandhurst dates from 1802.) Louis XVI perfected a system of twelve "feeder schools" (including Brienne, where Napoleon got his initial training) from which the top students went to the École Militaire to finish their training. In addition, there were postgraduate schools for officers of artillery and engineers. Jean-Baptiste de Gribeauval was commissioned by Louis XV to design a new field cannon, which he continued to improve as Inspector of Artillery under Louis XVI. His light, smooth-bore, 12-, 8-, 6-, and 4-pound guns remained the best in Europe until 1825.

The Old Regime laid the groundwork for French strength on the Continent. This was a basic reason that French Revolutionary armies could be challenged only by coalitions of powers. The Imperial French armies of Napoleon were defeated, ultimately, only by the combined forces of all of Europe. Even at that, victory owed much to British supremacy on the high seas.

---

[6] Livre (or franc) = 1 English shilling = $.20 in U.S. currency in 1789. Some recent studies argue that the French debt increased only 1,000,000,000+ as a result of the American Revolution. Even if true, the amount was still very significant.

During the eighteenth century, Britain had become not only the dominant naval power in the world, but the top colonial and commercial power as well. During the French Revolutionary-Napoleonic period, she continued to control the seas, and, with revenues from international trade (and industry, sparked by commerce), was able to support allies on the Continent.

COMMERCIAL RIVALRY

Commerce was the lifeblood of the great nations, and its pattern followed that of the extension of their power. The fate of the British and French East India companies illustrates this. During the eighteenth century the British company, backed by its own and crown troops, gained control of India and its trade to the virtual exclusion of the French, extended its operations into Burma, Malaya, and China, and cut into Dutch and Portuguese trade in the Indies. The British East India Company's capital worth accrued by 1000 percent during the century, and fabulous profits were paid to investors. The French East India Company was founded in 1664 by Louis XIV, with the crown supplying 60 percent of the capital (9,000,000 of 15,000,000 livres). It required continuous government subsidies, and in 1769 was abolished—as was the West India Company, also a failure. A combined company was revived in 1785, but it, too, failed and was dissolved during the Revolution.

The British company was a crown-chartered free enterprise; the French, a government operation. This proves little in itself, however. The French company was created to venture where private capital would not. Private French investment (and most crown money too) was in European and Middle Eastern trade, where there were sure profits and where French forces were disposed to protect both overland and maritime commerce. The heaviest profits even from colonial goods—French and other—made by the merchants of French ports were in transshipment to other European countries or the Ottoman Empire.

Exploiting the nearby markets, France increased the value of her exports from 120,000,000 livres in 1716 to over 500,000,000 in 1789. The growth rate of British commerce was only slightly higher. The British merchant marine grew from 260,000 tons in 1702 to 1,300,000 tons in 1800 and was almost three times the size of France's. In fact, however, it had to grow if Britain were to compete with France. Britain could only trade by sea; the French had a heavy overland trade with adjoining European states, as well as sea trade with Italy and Spain, in addition to the Ottoman Empire and Egypt.

On the other hand, British commercial enterprisers were preparing a greater future than they imagined by breaking freely with mercantilist theory, while the French stuck doggedly to it. Mercantilism dictated that a nation establish a favorable balance of trade (export goods of greater value than it imported) and amass bullion (precious metal), exporting as little as possible, since a "heavy" treasury was equated with power.

The British cheerfully sustained an unfavorable balance with the Far East. As late as 1790 the worth of exports to India was £700,000; imports from India £3,000,000. The difference—£2,300,000—had been sent in cash (bullion) to India. Spices, indigo, saffron, textiles, tea, saltpeter, and other items were re-exported largely to Europe. The most profitable of all was Indian (and Chinese) cotton cloth. The colorful printed fabrics, in exotic designs, became the rage among ladies-of-fashion and some (calico, for example) were cheap enough for the common people. European textiles—French, Spanish, German, Italian—could not compete in lure or price. Various princes banned these fabrics, but since aristocratic ladies wanted them, they got them—the French via Switzerland or Holland. By 1789 the British grossed £1,000,000 a year from Europe on cotton cloth alone. (By 1792 the figure was £2,000,000 and in 1809 an incredible £19,000,000.)

In this and other ways, the British in the 1780s were cutting into traditional French markets. After 1786, because of an unwise commercial treaty negotiated by the government of Louis XVI, they sold in volume in France, driving many textile manufacturers and others into bankruptcy and adding to France's already acute economic problems. British advances in mechanizing her industry were a factor in her success.

INDUSTRIAL REVOLUTION

The Industrial Revolution in Britain began in textiles, and not by accident. It was inspired by the ready market for Oriental cottons in Europe. Sources of raw cotton were found in Egypt, India, China, the East and West Indies, North America, and elsewhere. British entrepreneurs were quick to see that if they could manufacture cloth, greater profit could be made than in the re-export trade. The Parliament cooperated by protecting industry from Indian competition, and gradually, as machines were invented to speed production, the cost dropped toward the level of Oriental handmade fabrics. Thus British cloth began to share the European and world market.

Commerce, of course, furnished the capital for industrial development and also fostered the development of stock exchanges for investment, banking, and techniques and specialities of large-scale business. Manpower was at hand in the burgeoning cities. To feed the urban masses, British agriculture had undergone a slow evolution from manorial and smallholder production to large-scale capi-talistic farming. An "agricultural revolution" facilitated the process by introduc-ing machinery, fertilizing techniques, and improved stockbreeding. More food was produced by fewer people. (This too was made possible by commercial profits; scientific farming required heavy capital investments.)

The concentration on textile manufacturing is illustrated by the dreary catalog of inventions, from John Kay's flying shuttle (1733) to Edmund Cartwright's power loom (1785). Really rapid advances began with the invention by James Watt of the reciprocating steam engine to drive the machines (1769). Improvements by Watt and Matthew Boulton were made possible by independent developments in metallurgy. Processes for making better steel had been discovered by Benjamin Huntsman and Henry Cort. In 1774, John Wilkinson designed a mill to bore cannon and also used it to cut precision cylinders for the Watt engine, thus enabling mass production of engines. Hundreds were put into use in the 1780s.

France did not have a single steam engine until 1785. In 1789 she had 900 spinning machines operating, compared to 20,000 in Britain. She lagged in metallurgy as well; her first large furnace—an English model—was put into service just before the Revolution. In terms of mechanization, France was behind the Austrian Netherlands (Belgium) and some areas of the German Rhineland. There were beginnings. France had some 100 factories producing printed cloth, and at Aubenas there were 120 machines for spooling silk thread (from cocoons) under one roof. Industry, generally, was of the traditional small-shop variety. Mostly hand-driven machinery was used in the few large enterprises, such as the Anzin coal mining complex (4000 employees), the Van Robais textile works at Abbéville (3000), and the Royal mirror plant at Caen (1000).

The French saw no necessity to ape the English until the 1760s. They were doing well with traditional manufactures. The mercantilist regulations of Louis XIV and his great minister, Colbert, established quality standards for manufacturers and helped to make French luxury goods the exemplars of excellence and taste throughout Europe. The laws had been little modified. French clothing, jewelry, crystal, mirrors, tapestries, furniture, and perfumes, not to mention wines—everything accruing to French fashion—were still the vogue in the eighteenth century, and even today France's stock-in-trade. They bore the hallmarks of master craftsmen, designers, winemakers, and the like. The French, however, were catering to the aristocracy of Europe, while the British had caught the wave of the future and were beginning to cater to the masses with machine-produced goods.

France was the slave of habit, tradition, and past success. She had a surplus of talent. René de Réaumur wrote a treatise on steelmaking in 1822 that presaged the work of Huntsman, in England, thirty years later. Pierre Trésaguet pioneered in paved roads, but John McAdam, in Britain, actually built them, adding a blacktop of pulverized coal. Jacques de Vaucanson built a metal drill and lathe, which the British put into production. The Montgolfier brothers made the first balloon ascent. Claude Chappe invented a workable wigwag telegraph and experimented with an electrical model. Superior technologists were available in France, but the nation took little economic advantage from their work.

As the population of the cities expanded at the end of the century, the lack of industry to provide employment generated increasing problems. No single group was more important in setting the course of the Revolution than the workers of Paris, and even Marxist writers, such as Albert Soboul, agree that the masses would not have moved but for hunger and unemployment.

THE "BUSINESS REVOLUTION"

Britain also moved ahead of France in banking and business methods. Private banks by the score sprang up beginning in the 1600s. (London alone had over sixty in 1789.) In 1695 the Banks of England and Scotland were founded and began to issue notes backed by the credit of the government.[7] This created reliable paper money, less subject to inflation than the multitude of private issues already in circulation and also immune from collapse. Paper was easier to handle than coin, but the real reason for its appearance was that large-scale business demanded an expanded money supply.

The London Stock Exchange was founded in 1698, and shortly after, one in Edinburgh. The British perfected the joint-stock company. Meanwhile the needs of commerce and industry produced specialists and specialized firms for investment banking, insurance, and brokerage. Lawyers narrowed their practices to serve particular branches of business.

During the minority of Louis XV, his regent, the Duke d'Orléans, attempted to give France the benefit of British experience. Defying Catholic doctrine, which decried banking as usury, he allowed the Scottish financier John Law to establish a Royal Bank (1718), which issued paper money, and gave Law's Company of the West a monopoly to exploit Louisiana. Overspeculation ruined the company, however, and the bank went down with it (1720). France returned to her time-honored practice of depending for credit on foreigners, largely Swiss and Dutch, allied with a few French financiers, mostly Protestants. France had no bank until 1776, when the Caisse d'Escompte was created to handle the royal accounts (the term *banque* was deliberately avoided, even then).

The psychological scars of Law's abortive schemes, manifest in a deep suspicion of stock enterprises and paper money, retarded French economic growth in the eighteenth century. The full impact was not felt, however, until after 1778.

THE BRITISH "EXAMPLE" As world preponderance shifted from France to Britain in the eighteenth century, French intellectuals manifested an untoward interest in British institutions. Directly or indirectly, they questioned whether or not parliamentary government, traditional rights, greater religious tolerance, and a less rigid social system were contributing to Britain's strength.

In the seventeenth century, while France had moved toward greater royal absolutism, the English parliament (and that of Great Britain after 1707) had achieved a decisive role in government. It was far from democratic but did seem to reflect the popular will, though dominated by the landed aristocracy and gentry and by the upper crust of the middle class. Whatever their differences otherwise,

---

[7] The model was the Exchange Bank of Amsterdam, whose notes continued to command more respect than those of the British until the 1790s.

its members cooperated in fostering economic growth, particularly in promoting commerce and in providing a navy to protect it.

This attitude seemed suddenly evident in the eighteenth century but had really developed over the centuries with increasing commercial success and the growth of the enterprising middle class. The "triumph" of parliament was dramatized in the Civil War (1642–1647) and by the expulsion of James II in favor of William and Mary (1688). However, these were only benchmarks in an evolutionary process. The East India Company was chartered by Elizabeth I in 1600, long before the Civil War. The first Navigation Acts, favorable to private shipping, were the work of Cromwell. Throughout the century, whatever the government, the planting of colonies was consigned to private companies, groups, and individuals. Agricultural enterprise was encouraged by "enclosure" laws, which enabled lords to seize or acquire the commons (village property under medieval custom) and to undertake large-scale farming.

Society, at all stages, allowed great mobility. One factor was the Englishman's ingrained belief that he had *rights*, law-in-custom "since Good King Alfred's" time, which gave him courage to demand, and often get, equal treatment under the law. In addition, the English law of primogeniture gave titles only to the eldest sons of nobles (not all of them, as in France). Thus younger sons—the majority of "gentlemen" —were *commoners* and often without fortune. Many entered (or married into) the middle class. Similarly, with minimal fuss, successful middle class businessmen married noble ladies. No stigma was placed on being "in trade" in Britain.

Such was not the case in France, as will be discussed below (p. 45). Nobles engaged in business and invested, but their status required that they be lords-of-the-land first and at least pretend not to take demeaning business too seriously. Social mobility was also more limited. For these reasons, together with the specter of rising British power, commercial success, industrial growth, and accompanying primacy in technology, the British example was a decided factor in the intellectual movement called the "Enlightenment," whose center was France. Among others, the Baron de Montesquieu, in *The Spirit of the Laws* (1748), and Jean-Jacques Rousseau, in *The Social Contract* (1762), analyzed the English government at length (though neither recommended a similar system for France). Voltaire, in his *Letters on the English* (1733), praised British individual freedom and religious tolerance so highly that his book was banned and he had to flee Paris.[8]

The fascination of such men with things British surely helped to erode the faith of Frenchmen in their own institutions. And if the eighteenth-century Enlightenment helped cause the Revolution, it was by challenging everything traditional. Its aims, however, were much more grandiose.

---

[8] French titles of the books are *De l'esprit des loix*, *Le Contrat Social*, and *Lettres Anglaises*, though the last was first printed in English.

THE ENLIGHTENMENT

The architects of the Enlightenment, called *philosophes* (philosophers, broadly defined) sought to lead mankind out of the darkness of ignorance and into a new era of "light." They were motivated by the belief that man, through the application of reason and science, would soon be able to control his own destiny. At the same time, they saw themselves as perpetuating the "natural" leadership of France in matters of the mind. Had not seventeenth-century France produced such as Racine, Corneille, Molière, Descartes, Pascal, Cyrano de Bergerac, and La Fontaine? Was not French the language of diplomacy and of the aristocracy of Europe (and even England)?

The works of the *lumières* were directed to an international audience, nevertheless. They were the "party of humanity." In that spirit, the French publicized the work of foreign thinkers as well as their own, and none got higher praise than British notables of the seventeenth century.

Sir Isaac Newton, wrote the astronomer Jean d'Alembert, "created physics" by his relevations in the *Principia Mathematica* (1687) and established the major natural laws of the universe. John Locke, he said, "created metaphysics," through his *Essay Concerning Human Understanding* (1690). Man's mind, Locke had said, was *Tabula rasa* (a blank tablet) at birth. All information entered the mind through the senses; thinking was a juggling of received data. Thus, by extension, men's minds could be shaped and "right thinking" citizens created. Education and environment were therefore the keys to an ideal society. No two concepts were more important in the Enlightenment than those of natural law (applied to everything from biology to politics and even religion) and environmentalism.

A belief in immutable natural laws flew in the face of Christian doctrine, both Catholic and Protestant, under which God was involved in daily human affairs (otherwise why pray?). Environmentalism dictated that one consider man as "naturally good" (perfectible), which also contradicted Christian dogma that man was a fallen creature, in need of salvation. If not, what was the reason for churches? Thus many *philosophes* turned to deism, which made God only the first mover and creator of natural laws, and some became atheists. Most people simply ignored the contradictions—as many of us still do today—accepting the "best of both worlds."

On whatever lofty plain the philosophes began their treatises, however, they inevitably related to French problems.

MONTESQUIEU/VOLTAIRE/ROUSSEAU The most influential figure of the early Enlightenment was the Baron de Montesquieu (1689–1755), a lawyer and hereditary judge (noble-of-the-robe) of Bordeaux, made famous by his *Spirit of the Laws*.[9] This work explained the evolution of varying systems of government

---

[9] *De l'esprit des loix* (1748).

and laws in nations and regions, worldwide, with heavy emphasis on the role of climate and geography. France, he said, had developed a monarchy suitable to her needs but denied that it had ever been "absolute." The king's will had been limited by his noble counsellors. In the eighteenth century they were represented by the royal judges, notably those of the *parlements* (high courts),[10] who were the custodians of the unwritten constitution of France and guardians of the people against royal tyranny. A generation after Montesquieu's death, the *parlementaires*, citing his arguments, led the fight against the reforms of Louis XVI and helped force the calling of the Estates General of 1789.

The most vituperative crusader of the Enlightenment was Voltaire (François Arouet), whose life spanned the century (1694–1778). A fragile figure with glittering eyes that beamed sarcasm, Voltaire had a sharp tongue that got him an early introduction to the Bastille, and he spent most of his life in exile. (Though in an interlude peculiarly French, he was elected to the Académie Française (1746) and ennobled by Louis XV.) His literary output was astounding—poems, plays, tracts, essays, novels, histories, and over 19,000 letters, which fill 103 printed volumes. Voltaire was a master of merciless polemic, yet he produced works of fiction and history significant in themselves. His novel *Candide* (1759) is in print in a dozen languages today, perhaps because its hero is the victim of timeless human idiocies and prejudice. His *Age of Louis XIV* (1751) pioneered in social-cultural, economic, and intellectual history, and the *Essay on the Manners and Customs of Nations* (1757) in world history.[11]

Voltaire was a professional angry man, at his best on the attack. His crusade against the Church, which he accused of perpetuating superstition and ignorance, headlined by the repeated *"Ecrasez l'Infâme!"* shook the confidence of educated men in the heirarchy, if not religion. His constant indictments of the Jesuit Order for corruption were a factor in its dissolution in France (1766) and worldwide by the Pope (1773).[12] He fought for three years to win the exoneration of Jean Calas, a Protestant executed for murder on doubtful evidence by a Catholic *parlement* in Toulouse. It benefited only Calas' family—and Voltaire's crusade against intolerance. He also assailed inefficient government, aristocratic judiciary, noble privilege, and much else. He was pronouncedly *for* liberty, especially freedom of expression, but was not a democrat. Voltaire had no quarrel with absolute monarchy if it was "enlightened," thus he happily accepted the hospitality of Frederick the Great. In his old age, he extolled Louis XVI, who chose *philosophes* for ministers.

Jean-Jacques Rousseau (1712–1778) is today the most celebrated political theorist of the Enlightenment. In his own time, this erratic, reclusive, and usually

---

[10] The *parlements* are described below, p. 39. American students know Montesquieu better for having described a government of "independent" executive, legislative, and judicial branches. However, he did not recommend it for France.

[11] *Siècle de Louis XIV* and *Essai sur les moeurs et de l'esprit des nations*.

[12] It was reconstituted in 1815.

destitute Swiss-born writer was famed for his novels, *Julie, ou la Nouvelle Héloise* (1761) and *Émile* (1762). His major political works became famous after his death. *The Origins of the Inequalities of Man* (1755), which made private property the root of all evil, became a favorite of Socialists. *The Social Contract* (1762) was the "Bible" of the Terrorists during the Revolution.[13]

In *The Social Contract*, Rousseau proposed government by the "general will." But he defined the "general will" as what was *best* for the people—not what the majority, or even all of them, wanted. He condemned representative government (delegates spoke for themselves, not the people) and political parties (factions with their own aims, controlled by a few) and judged democracy suitable only for very small towns. How the "general will" was to be determined he left unclear. However, once a "social contract" was sealed between the people and "sovereign" (which could be one or many persons), the government had power to promote the general welfare and those who opposed its policies were to be "forced to be free." It is easy to see therefore why the *Social Contract* was so frequently cited by the Terrorists of 1793–1794 and has appealed to authoritarians of various stripes ever since.

Montesquieu, Voltaire, and Rousseau, the great eminences of the Enlightenment, had one thing in common: a belief in government by *"intelligent authority."* Montesquieu favored a monarchy limited by an aristocratic judiciary. Voltaire opted for enlightened monarchy—strong princes advised by such as himself. Rousseau proposed government which would see to the general welfare, whether or not the people approved. None of the *philosophes* were proponents of parliamentary government, much less democrats. This explains much in the French Revolution, taken together with the French tradition of authoritarian government. For example, why the French could never settle on a constitution and amend it peacefully or accept the results of elections as final. Each group in power felt it should maintain itself by any means—for the national good. Therefore the government was repeatedly changed by *coup d'état*, rather than by constitutional means.

THE ENCYCLOPEDIA The greatest common effort of the *philosophes* was *L'Encyclopédie*,[14] in twenty-eight quarto volumes, seventeen of text and eleven of illustrations, published 1751–1764. It was edited by Jean d'Alembert, mathematician and astronomer, and Denis Diderot, biologist (a forerunner of Darwin), chemist, novelist, playwright, essayist, and pornographer. Diderot actually did most of the work alone, however, getting help with the censors from friends in high places like Madame de Pompadour, mistress of Louis XV.

---

[13] *Discours sur l'origine et les fondements de l'inégalitié parmi les hommes* and *Le Contrat Social.*

[14] The title translates, in full: *The Encyclopedia, or Analytical Dictionary of the Sciences, Arts, and Professions, by The Society of Men of Letters.*

Among the some 200 contributors were Montesquieu (posthumously), Voltaire, Rousseau, and (to be identified below) Morellet, Quesnay, and Turgot. Advice came from Buffon, Condillac, Mably, Raynal, and dozens of others. The stated purpose of the *Encyclopedia* was to summarize human knowledge, so that posterity might be "happier and more virtuous." Rather than force "enlightened" opinion on readers (and invite censorship), Diderot balanced it with conservative views and overwhelmed both with factual and scientific articles. Human progress was the keynote. Natural explanations were postulated for everything. New political ideas were presented in pro-and-con dialogues, as in one between Rousseau and Diderot, writing anonymously. An article entitled "Bible" suggested a need for critical scholarship, but the Bible itself received orthodox treatment by individual books. Astrology and magic were given sober articles along with the empirical sciences. Religious toleration was praised in the article on England, but there was no article on the subject.

Diderot flatly stated that success depended on coverage of scientific advances, not *"philosophie."* The overwhelming emphasis, however, was on *technology*, not pure science. A huge volume of articles and the preponderance of illustrations were devoted to the machines and methods of industry and agriculture, the instruments and techniques of medicine, and the like. All were pictured in incredible detail in fine line engravings—true works of art. There was step-by-step coverage of the making of wire, cannon, battleships, plows, and movable stages for the theater; and the reader could learn how to fence, train a horse, or perform a brain operation.

Such technology, as Diderot saw it, was the best evidence of progress he could freely print. Nevertheless, for close readers, the *Encyclopedia* had a plethora of philosophic concepts: Lockian sensationalism, deism, laissez-faire economics, natural rights, liberty, tolerance, anticlericalism, utilitarianism, and even a mild version of the social contract.

The influence of the *Encyclopedia* is impossible to gauge. The original edition, however, was of 4000 sets, and some 16,000 in subsequent printings (legal and illegal); of these at least 15,000 were in French libraries in 1789. Whether or not he chose to read it, almost every literate Frenchman had access to a copy.

THE PHYSIOCRATS   Among the least censored of the *philosophes* were the economists—the *physiocrats*. Their founder was François Quesnay (1694–1774), court physician to Louis XV. His more famous followers were Jacques Turgot, Intendant of Limoges and later Comptroller General of Louis XVI, Pierre Samuel Dupont (whose sons became Americans), and the Marquis de Mirabeau (1715–1789), father of the great revolutionary.

The basic doctrines of the school were outlined by Quesnay and Turgot in the *Encyclopedia* and later expounded upon in Dupont's *Physiocratie* (1767), Mirabeau's *Economiques* (1769), and other works. The physiocrats believed that those who worked the land—farmers, miners, lurnbermen, and the like—produced all the new wealth and should be taxed least or not at all. *Land* was the basic national resource, yielding the "net product." They proposed a single tax, to be paid by proprietors on the "net product." Processors, manufacturers, and distributors were not to be taxed but would be limited to a price that reflected only the value they added to the product. They urged the crown to stop favoring manufacturers and to "feed the roots" of the economic system by minimizing the burdens of those nearest the soil.

More broadly, the physiocrats were laissez-faire economists—believers in free enterprise. They proposed the elimination of all barriers to internal trade and the abolition of controls on production and pressed the crown to work for international free trade (by stages). Otherwise, the government could contribute to economic growth best by building roads, bridges, harbors, and by facilitating trade and thereby production. Their general ideas "took." The majority in every revolutionary assembly believed in laissez-faire—even in the Convention, which spawned the Terror.[15]

Mirabeau and Dupont encouraged Adam Smith, the Scotsman, whose *Wealth of Nations* (1776) became a free-enterprise classic. His theory differed from theirs essentially only in that he considered *labor* rather than land the principal national resource—or element in production.

THE POPULATIONISTS

The *philosophes* were almost totally blind to France's population problem. Worse, they tended to feel (if they considered it at all) that the *nombre des habitants* should be increased for the sake of prosperity. Montesquieu set the tone. There had been 20,000,000 Gauls in Roman times, he wrote; the population of France had been declining ever since. "If this continues . . . the land will be nothing more than a desert." France had suffered severe losses in the seventeenth century—by the great plague of 1636 and at the end of the century, by crop failures, disease, and the wars of Louis XIV (mostly because of epidemics spread by the armies, not battle casualties). Thus depopulation was easy to accept as a permanent trend. Even the physiocrats, who should have been most knowledgeable on peasant problems, confined themselves to hatching schemes to repopulate the countryside. (Reduced taxes—free trade—higher prices—higher peasant income: Voilà! More people.)

The demographers of the day, called *populationistes*, also produced plans to increase population. Turmeau de la Morandière, in 1763, proposed reducing the number of celibate clergy and encouraging immigration and large families.

---

[15] It was "in" among the intelligentsia; the people did not understand it and often were hostile. Governments, notably that of Terror, tightly controlled the economy. See p. 147*ff*.

Messance, in his *Recherches sur la population* (1766), demonstrated that the French population was growing, but not, he thought, fast enough. He favored increasing food production and (disagreeing with the physiocrats) *lower* grain prices. The Chevalier de Cerfvol, in 1768, saw the solution in legalizing divorce and the marriage of the clergy, making cash grants to families for each new child, and the like. The Chevalier des Pommelles, in 1789, estimated the population of France fairly accurately—at 25,062,882 (based on the work of Messance, the Abbé Jean-Joseph Expilly, Moheau, and others). Again, however, he suggested "populationist" reforms.

Moheau would belatedly come to agree with the Reverend Thomas Malthus, in England, that uncontrolled growth could lead only to disaster. In the pre-revolutionary era, however, he crusaded against control. Contraception seemed a great evil to him:

> Rich women for whom pleasure is of the greatest interest and a unique occupation are not the only ones who regard the propagation of the species a duperie of olden times; already the disastrous secrets known to no animal but man have penetrated to the countryside: nature is tampered with even in the villages. . . .

He was right. Otherwise France might have had 40,000,000 people in 1789 rather than 26,000,000—and even greater economic problems. (The growth rate had been only half that of England's.) He did not note the tragic fact that among the desperately poor, infanticide was also common. Late marriage, the use of contraceptives, and *coitus interruptus* (advised even by some priests), however, were the major population-limiting measures.

Doubtless, the *philosophes* made France aware of many evils, but overpopulation was not one of them. On the contrary, their proposals, if implemented, would have exacerbated the problem which was one of the root causes of France's socioeconomic malaise in the 1780s.

MATERIALISTS, SCIENTISTS, SOCIALISTS   The *philosophes* were always a mixed bag. In the generation of Montesquieu, for example, was the atheist, La Mettrie, whose *Natural History of the Soul* (1745)[16] asserted that man's soul died with him and attributed insanity to chemical changes in the brain. To the generation of Diderot belonged the Count de Buffon, a pioneer naturalist; Étienne Condillac, who expanded on Locke's sensationalist psychology; and Joseph-Louis Lagrange, one of the fathers of modern mathematics. Also in this group was the most respectable tax farmer, Claude Adrienne Helvetius, materialist par excellence. His *Mind* (1758) and *Man* (1772)[17] held that man acts

[16] *Histoire naturelle de l'âme.*
[17] *De l'esprit* and *De l'homme.*

according to natural laws, that therefore what is natural is right (moral), that education is the key to perfecting society, and that science and legislation are the true religion.[18]

At midcentury, Socialists gained prominence, notably Gabriel Bonnet de Mably (brother of Condillac) and the pseudonymous Morelly (whose identity is still unknown). Mably's *History of France* (1765) and more positively *The Idea of History* (1788)[19] insisted that gradual communization of property should be accomplished as fast as the public could be educated to accept it. Otherwise, he deemed revolution probable. Morelly was more utopian; his *Code of Nature* (1755) envisioned the peaceful establishment of a Socialist state ruled by a senate of elder workers.

In the last generation was the Baron Henri Dietrich d'Holbach, the most famous atheist-materialist of them all. The more practical aspects of his *System of Nature* (1770) undoubtedly inspired Jeremy Bentham, whose name has become synonymous with utilitarianism. Holbach also patronized the "last of the *philosophes*," the Marquis de Condorcet, constitutionalist and educational planner in the early Revolution. Condorcet died in prison during the Terror (1794), but not before finishing *The Progress of the Human Mind*,[20] expressing undiminished optimism for the future of mankind.

ENLIGHTENMENT AND REVOLUTION

The *philosophes* had no common agreed-upon political program but presented theoretical bases upon which almost any sort of government could be founded. They expounded concepts that were sometimes irrational, romantic, or utopian. They lauded empirical science, where conclusions are drawn from verifiable data, but often stretched the evidence to unwarranted conclusions. Nevertheless, the *philosophes* educated the French people (or at least literate French people) to think in terms of rational and/or scientific solutions to their problems. They promulgated ideas of progress, intellectual freedom, liberty, and attacked the ills of the Old Regime. The last generation of *philosophes*, particularly the physiocrats, offered concrete schemes of reform.

It is certain that the *philosophes* did not reach the common people, who were mostly illiterate in any case.[21] The "Blue Books" and almanacs which circulated

---

[18] The spirit of the Enlightenment was utilitarian and irreligious, if not amoral. Surely the *philosophes* established a rationale for libertinism. If what is in accordance with natural law is moral and what is natural can be determined by the individual, then self-interest—even self-indulgence—might be reasonable. This sort of argument would only have been acceptable, however, to such as the Marquis de Sade, a contemporary of the last generation of *philosophes*, though hardly one of them.

[19] *Sur l'histoire de France* and *Sur l'Idée de l'histoire.*

[20] *Equisse d'une tableau historique des progrès de l'esprit humain.*

[21] Perhaps 15 percent of the entire population was able to read and write with reasonable facility. The truly literate, mostly among the nobility, clergy, and bourgeoisie, amounted to no more than 5 percent. For figures more flattering to the French, see D. Roche, *People of Paris* (1988).

among the peasants and workers contained few "enlightened" thoughts. Even educated provincials, to judge by their libraries, read principally traditional works and fiction, though owning the *Encyclopedia* became prestigious. The Enlightenment, in short, was confined mostly to Paris, and based in the salons of the great ladies, which were frequented by intellectuals, artists, aristocrats, rich bourgeois, and crown officials and bishops who often revelled in discussing books they had helped ban.

Without doubt, however, the ideas later expressed in the shibboleths of the Revolution percolated down to the literate people of the provinces, and to a degree lower. They were grist for discussion in the academies, the philosophic societies, and the lodges of the Freemasons (Masonic Order). The more radical of the works, like Rousseau's *Social Contract*, were read by a distinct minority, but among them were the greatest zealots and most forceful men of the Revolution, such as Maximilien Robespierre, a country lawyer from Arras.

The Freemasons were the best organized of the proponents of Enlightenment. Their intellectual elitism and secret semireligious ceremonies drew into their ranks liberal aristocrats and bourgeois, as well as the *philosophes* themselves. They were deists (or we might say today, nonsectarian); atheists were banned; the Almighty was revered as the creator of the universe, natural laws, and human intelligence. Membership transcended national boundaries and formal religious affiliation. Among French Masons were the Duke d'Orléans, the king's cousin; Lafayette, a marquis of ancient lineage; and many other nobles, together with the leading *philosophes*. Frederick the Great headed the Berlin lodge. Most of the British intelligentsia belonged, and in America, Washington, Jefferson, Adams, Madison, and others. The Order was anathema to the Catholic Church (though many French bishops attended meetings). It was considered the font of all radicalism and evil. After the Revolution began, the first thesis offered for its cause was that of a Masonic plot.[22] There was none, but the Masons, among others, popularized the concepts of the Enlightenment.

The Enlightenment did not cause the Revolution, but it created an atmosphere in which revolution was possible. (See p. 53)

THE AMERICAN REVOLUTION AND THE FRENCH

In 1778, Benjamin Franklin, American minister in Paris, took his grandson to meet Voltaire. The old *philosophe* blessed the boy in English: "God and

---

[22] The thesis was voiced in 1789 and fully developed by the Abbé Barreul, an émigré from France, in his *Mémoirs pour servir à l'histoire du Jacóbinism*, 5 vols. (Hamburg, 1798). This and other conservative theses were revived in the 1980s. See the Introduction, footnotes 3 and 4, p. 9. After generations of trying to find the causes of the Revolution chiefly in economic or socio-economic factors, it is suddenly again popular to blame it on *words*.

Liberty." Between 1775 and 1783, America and her ideals were the vogue in France, and Franklin, whose image was on everything from jewel cases to chamberpots, was a folk hero. He exemplified the virtues of the "noble primitive" (an act the sophisticate and world traveler carefully perfected). That American principles might infect the French people seemed to occur to no one. "How goes it with our darling republicans?" gushed Queen Marie Antoinette to Lafayette, home briefly on leave.

The "darling republicans" were barely surviving, but in France their ideas were marching unopposed. The mere *fact* of the revolution was important, and more so after it succeeded. Ideals had been transformed into action. The dreams of the *philosophes* seemed fulfilled, and Americans were happy to give credit to their influence.[23] American arguments for liberty, rights, and against "unconstitutional" and irrational taxes were widely circulated. The crown itself financed the publication of a collection of American state constitutions that was of special importance because *written* constitutions were alien to French tradition. (In 1789, however, the Third Estate would demand one.) Such as Diderot and Jacques Turgot decided that the United States was a model for the future.

Further, more than 9000 Frenchmen fought in the American Revolution, and many returned imbued with American ideas. Some thirty of the early leaders of the French Revolution were veterans of the struggle. These included the Marquis de Lafayette, the Count de Rochambeau, Alexandre de Lameth, Mathieu Dumas, the Count de Ségur (father of the famous chronicler of the Russian campaign), and the Viscount de Noailles.

France had entered the war of the American Revolution to strike at the British. Rochambeau's army, of course, went on orders. Lafayette was typical of the volunteers, mostly nobles. He admitted in his memoirs that he had gone to America for adventure, glory, and to fight the British. He returned, nevertheless, full of American ideas, though still a monarchist. The influence of the highly placed, such as Lafayette, Lameth, and Noailles is easily traced. More difficult is to evaluate the influence of the French soldiers who had served in the American colonies. Many do turn up as ardent republicans after 1792, however. An easy example is Jean Baptiste Jourdan, an enlisted man in America who became a general and national hero during the Revolution.[24]

The effect of America's success on the French mind was quite evident to contemporaries. Arthur Young wrote, "The American Revolution has laid the foundation of another in France, if government does not take care of itself." In this he was dead right.

---

[23] Though in fact the Americans were more influenced by John Locke's *Treatises on Government* (1690), William Blackstone's *Commentaries on the Laws of England* (1765–1769), and the English Bill of Rights.

[24] Napoleon made him a marshal but never trusted him fully because he felt that at heart he was always a republican. Jourdan had opposed the *coup* which brought Bonaparte to power.

ATLANTIC REVOLUTIONS AND ENLIGHTENED MONARCHY

Other revolutions also preceded the French Revolution and have been linked with it and the American Revolution in a pattern of "Atlantic" or "Democratic" revolutions.[25] There were also "revolutions from above," which are usually treated under "Enlightened Monarchy." None affected France profoundly but should be mentioned in passing, since all were assaults on the Old Regime in Europe, and, in a very broad sense, forecast the pattern of the early Revolution in France. There is a certain similarity among them—in all cases the authority of aristocratic "constituted bodies" (Estates, Diets, Parliaments) was challenged, either by democratic elements from below, the crown from above, or both. Americans, nominally, fought against George III, but actually fought against rule by the British Parliament.

During the American Revolution, Britain was wracked by the Gordon Riots (1780) and troubles in Ireland. The riots, in London, began as an anti-Catholic demonstration (Britain was at war with France, the major Catholic power) but ended as a week-long battle between the poor and rich. They were put down by royal troops and the London Military Association, composed of property owners (much like the French National Guard, formed after the storming of the Bastille in 1789). These disturbances served quiet parliamentary reformers (the nearest thing Britain had to revolutionaries), who feared further anarchy. Parliament and the crown were more dangerously challenged by the Irish Volunteers, organized to repel a French invasion that did not come. They forced the British government to approve an independent Irish Parliament (1782) representing both Protestants and Catholics, which would have made Ireland almost as independent as the United States. It was abolished, however, after peace in 1783.

Meanwhile, there were middle-class revolts against the Patrician rulers of Geneva in 1768 and 1782 and Freibourg in 1781, but they were quelled with the aid of French troops. In the Dutch Republic (United Provinces) the aristocratic regents rose against the Stadholder, the Prince of Orange (1781). Their revolution was taken over, however, by middle-class patriots. (Roughly the same thing happened in France in 1789–1790.) The regents then allied with the Stadholder, who in 1787 called in Prussian troops and ended it all. From these disturbances the French netted an influx of hundreds of revolutionary émigrés, including Etienne Clavière, Peter Ochs, and Étienne Dumont from Switzerland, and Johan Valckenaer and Herman Daendels from the Netherlands. They later participated in the formation of "sister republics" of France in their countries.

The *philosophes* all but ignored these revolutionaries, however, and gave their highest praise to "Enlightened Despots." The Despots expanded their power at the expense of their clergy and nobles (some times by giving them more authority

---

[25] The originators of this thesis were R. R. Palmer and Jacques Godechot. See the Bibliography.

over their peasants). They created more efficient, centralized governments; improved their armed forces; and promoted trade, industry, and agriculture, and at the same time (for practical reasons), granted degrees of religious toleration; befriended intellectuals (especially scientists); improved education; and the like. The toughest and most pragmatic were the most successful. These included Frederick II (the Great) of Prussia, Catherine II (the Great) of Russia, and Charles III of Spain. Gustavus III of Sweden, for twenty years, excelled them all. In 1772, backed by the army, he dissolved his aristocratic Riksdag (parliament), imprisoned the leaders, and systematically demolished noble privilege in the public interest. In 1792, however, the "royal democrat" was assassinated by high-born conspirators, and the Riksdag regained its power. Joseph II of Austria, the Holy Roman Emperor, perhaps the most genuinely enlightened of all, provoked defiance by the Hungarian Estates and open rebellion in Belgium (the Austrian Netherlands) led by the Estates. On his death (1790), his successor, Leopold II, was forced to compromise with the Estates, not only in Belgium and Hungary, but in Austria, Bohemia, and Lombardy as well, nullifying most of the reforms.

Louis XVI of France was as public-spirited, and positively more humanitarian, than Frederick the Great of Prussia. If he had been as strong, ruthless, wily, and energetic as "Old Fritz," he might be extolled today as an "Enlightened Monarch." But he was not, and his reforms were blocked by the aristocrats and clergy, with the *parlements* (high courts) in the vanguard; he was forced to call the Estates General, and the Revolution ensued.

FRENCH "ABSOLUTISM"

The building of modern France into a unified state, as opposed to a loose confederation with states ruled by dukes, counts, barons (and a king in Navarre), had been the story of the gradual destruction of the power of the nobles to govern and to judge. Since the fifteenth century, the kings, by all possible means, including warfare, had transferred authority in the duchies and counties to royal officials. The executive power was first given to royal provincial governors, chosen from the high nobility. Then, in the seventeenth century, the governors were reduced to ceremonial functions and their substantive powers given to *intendants* (new nobles or bourgeois).

Meanwhile, a system of royal courts evolved, of which the most important were the *parlements*. Their judges, almost to a man, were nobles with hereditary titles and offices. Noble-dominated provincial estates (legislatures) were dissolved one after another. By 1789 there were estates in only twelve of the thirty-six provinces (and one in Corisca). The provinces with estates (*pays d'états*) had some control over royal taxation. The others (*pays d'élections*, from the tax district, the *élection*) had none, unless the local *parlement* undertook to protest. (See Maps 1.1 and 1.2.)

Map 1.1

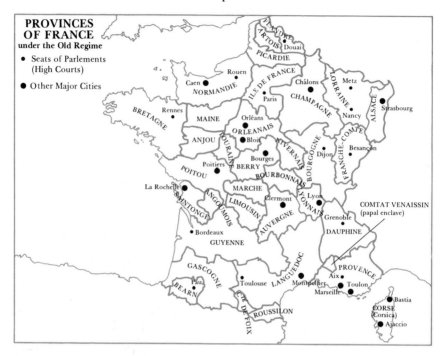

PROVINCES
OF FRANCE
under the Old Regime
● Seats of Parlements
  (High Courts)
● Other Major Cities

An administrative "absolute" monarchy was created. The king made law by edict and appointed the officials who administered it. The French equivalent of the British Parliament, the Estates General (*États Généraux*), which had earlier tempered royal authority, had sunk into atrophy. In 1469 it had voted the power to tax to the awesome Louis XI, "The Spider," and had since met only when kings were very weak or were minors. The Estates General met in 1614 to challenge the government of the boy-king, Louis XIII, to no avail. It did not meet again until 1789—175 years later—the year of the Revolution.

The nobles came to realize that they could only exert political power through control of the king. During the minority of Louis XIV, high nobles-of-the-sword (those of ancient title) and nobles-of-the-robe (principally judges), temporarily cooperating, revolted against the regency of the Queen Mother, Anne of Austria, and Cardinal Mazarin. A civil war, called the Fronde, raged sporadically between 1649 and 1653, during which the king and his government had to flee Paris twice.[26]

---

[26] The various sorts of nobles will be discussed below, p. 46. It should be understood that the nobles never sought to depose, much less *kill* the king. They were aware that if they tampered with *hereditary* monarchy, their *hereditary* privileges would have a shaky legal basis.

Map 1.2

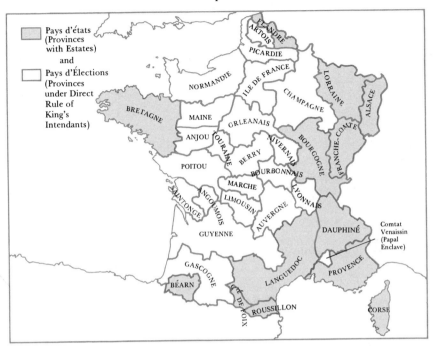

But the crown emerged victorious and the stage was set for the perfection of royal absolutism under Louis XIV.[27]

Under the system elaborated by Louis XIV, the king made law with the aid of councils, composed of his ministers and judges, clergymen, and experts as the occasion demanded. They *advised*; however, the king *decided*. The privy council (*Conseil d'état et privé*) was the supreme interpreter of the laws; the council of state (*d'état ou d'en haut*) conferred on war, peace, and great matters of state (defined by the king) and sometimes sat as a "supreme court"; the council of dispatches (*des depêches*) framed the laws. There were also councils of finance, war (army), marine (navy, merchant marine, ports), commerce, and others, composed as the king directed. Decisions in council were implemented by ministers (technically "secretaries of state") of finance, war, marine, foreign affairs, and religious affairs, and a chancellor, who was the top legal officer of the state. By far the most important was the minister of finance or Comptroller General.

---

[27] "Absolutism" is used here because it is customary. Due to poor communications, the persistence of traditions, and the prevalence of legalized privilege (see p. 43), the king's power over individuals, or even local governments, did not vaguely approach that of twentieth-century governments. He merely established a more efficient centralized government than had ever been seen before.

The channels of power ran from the king and his ministers to the people through four administrative structures: (1) the provincial governments, (2) the intendancies or *généralités* (thirty-four in 1789), (3) to a degree, the Church, and (4) the courts. The royal governors presided over state functions and also nominally commanded the king's troops, though many of them lived at Versailles (just outside Paris), the locus of the royal court and government, as pensioned sycophants. The real governors were the *intendants*, who ruled areas centered on major cities with sweeping powers, including authority over the revenue collection. Administratively, the *généralités* had replaced the provinces, some of which (e.g., Normandy) were divided and others (e.g., Maine, Touraine, and Anjou) were combined.

The Church was hardly servile, but the king had considerable control since he appointed (directly, or indirectly if he chose) all archbishops, bishops, abbots, and other high clergy.[28] Moreover, the prelates tended to gravitate to Versailles where the monarch could influence them directly (and vice versa). The judicial system included, at the top, the king's council of state, constituted at his command from among judges, ministers, princes-of-the-blood, and others. There were additional great "sovereign courts" for special purposes.[29] The majority of important cases and appeals, however, were handled by the thirteen *parlements*, of which the Parlement of Paris was the most important (though not a supreme court) because of its location and wide jurisdiction and because it received the king's edicts first.[30]

Louis XIV gave France the basic structure of a modern, bureaucratic state. There was one flaw in his system, however. Its maintenance and improvement depended almost solely on the Sun King's *hereditary* successors. He had created a government in which the king made all the major decisions. This required a man of enormous energy and dedication, which Louis XIV was (contrary to legend, which makes him a royal peacock, playing at Versailles). Neither Louis XV nor Louis XVI had the strength or will to "make the machine go." The government fell into disrepair in the eighteenth century. It remained for revolutionaries and Napoleon Bonaparte to carry forward the process of bureaucratization, adding elements of the welfare state.

INTENDANTS AND PARLEMENTAIRES The intendants of Louis XV and Louis XVI, on the average, were men of exceptional talent. Most were chosen by the council of state from among the most promising *maîtres de requêtes* (masters

---

[28] Under the provisions of the Concordat of Bologna, (1516) between Francis I and the Pope. In return the Pope was entitled to the *annates*, the first year's revenues of a new prelate.

[29] The *Chambre des Comptes* (royal finances and domains); the *Cour des Aides* (indirect taxes); the *Cour des Monnaies* (counterfeiting, etc.).

[30] The *parlements* were at Paris, Toulouse, Grenoble, Bordeaux, Dijon, Rouen, Aix-en-Provence, Rennes, Pau, Metz, Besançon, Douai, and Nancy. There were about 1000 judges (nobles-of-the-robe) in all these courts. (See Map 1.1.)

of requests; young men who did the legwork of the council). Jacques Turgot (the physiocrat), Intendant of Limoges, was, in all matters dependent on local authority, an "enlightened monarch." The Bertier de Sauvigny (father and son), Intendants of Paris, cooperating with the king's lieutenant of police (who ruled the city proper), improved roads and waterways, regularized the bread supply, reformed the police, erected new hospitals, and so on. Jean Baptiste de Montyon, Intendant of La Rochelle, improved institutions of charity, encouraged learning, and created a prize for literature still given yearly by the *Académie Française*. The intendants could do nothing to attack national problems, however, without the backing of the crown.

The king and his intendants were constantly at war with the *parlements*, manned by hereditary noble judges. The intendants were also nobles but were removable officials, whereas the *parlementaires* belonged to a "constituted" body with traditional rights and functions (the thirteen high courts claimed to act as one). Primarily, they claimed the "right to remonstrance" or to challenge the king's edicts as "unconstitutional" or as not according to tradition. In this they were supported by ancient texts, pseudo-history, and Montesquieu's writings. The law they administered was complex; deriving in the south from the Roman law and in the north from medieval feudal law (see Map 1.3). But the king's new edicts were national, and the royal objective—if fumblingly pursued—was to establish a common law. The *parlements* thus assumed the role of opposing innovation in favor of tradition, which meant protecting privileges written into law over the ages, including their own noble privileges.

In the eighteenth century the *parlementaires*, by their frequent challenges to the king's authority, had become the leaders of the nobility, a position grudgingly accorded since many of them were of relatively new title (first, second, or third generation nobles). Most of the presidents and subpresidents (chief and ranking justices) were of old families, such as the d'Ormesson, Lamoignon, and Molé, but the majority had fought their way up from the middle class. Some were liberals and sympathized with Lafayette, in the early Revolution. Most, however, considered their titles "earned" (they or their fathers or grandfathers had become sufficiently prosperous bourgeois to buy them) and guarded their noble privileges zealously, often more than their peers did.[31]

No one questioned the king's right to make law, but unless his edicts were registered by the *parlements*, they did not exist for the courts and were not enforced. Perforce when a *parlement* refused to register (Paris usually set the example), there was confrontation between the king and courts. This occurred in a ceremony called the *lit de justice* where the king, enthroned in full splendor, commanded the judges to register the law, and they did. Usually a compromise had been struck beforehand between the king's ministers and the *parlementaires*.

[31] See most recent studies, Bibliography: The Eighteenth-Century Background: France, Social and Institutional.

Map 1.3

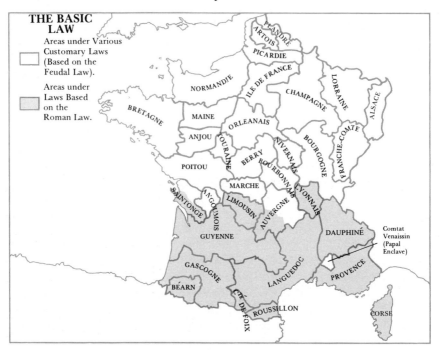

If not, the justices sometimes still balked (generally after returning to chambers). In such cases the king preserved his dignity by exiling a few judges to the country until an agreement could be reached. If there was a prolonged deadlock, the *parlements*, in theory, could demand that the king call the Estates General (in its traditional form an aristocratic body). More logically, in terms of maintaining royal power, the king could dissolve the courts and appoint new judges. After all, the king granted titles and controlled the army and police.

Louis XV (1715–1774), toward the end of his reign, found the courage to "roar" and to act. In 1766, in a *séance de flagellation* (whipping session), he excoriated the *Parlements* of Rennes and Paris for trying the royal governor of Brittany, the Duke d'Aiguillon, against his orders (and seemingly in retaliation for having to register new taxes). "Sovereignty resides in my person alone!" he thundered. Voltaire was overjoyed. "It has been a long time," he wrote, "since I have read anything so wise, so noble, so well-written." Other *philosophes* sounded "uncertain trumpets," however, and the *parlements*, nationwide, reacted angrily. In 1771, urged on by his chancellor, René Nicolas de Maupeou, the king abolished the Parlement of Paris, created a new one with new judges and a smaller jurisdiction and punished the more recalcitrant provincial *parlements* by creating five new courts which cut into their territories.[32] There were protests, but the king's will prevailed.

The basis was established for a forceful, enlightened monarchy, perhaps the only means, short of revolution, by which France's complex society-of-legal-privilege could be reformed (discussed further in more detail below, p. 43). In 1774, however, the weak-willed Louis XVI acceded to the throne and immediately restored the old *parlements* to power. This was his first step toward the guillotine.

Louis XVI was influenced by *philosophes* less hard-minded than Voltaire. But essentially he was a man-of-peace and easily frightened. He had been much impressed by the popularity of the *parlements*, expressed in some places by destructive riots. He wanted to please his people, who, in fact, saw the high courts as their protectors (not so much against the king as against his "evil" ministers). This attitude stemmed largely from the fact that the *parlements* almost invariably objected to new taxes. It escaped the public that tax laws were usually registered after they had been amended to exempt nobles and the clergy (dominated by noble bishops) from their provisions or to provide "loopholes" by which they could evade taxation.

TAXES, DUES, AND COLLECTION   Taxation was grossly unjust both in its impact and collection. The peasantry (farmers) bore the greatest burden; the artisans and the lower middle class were next heavily taxed; the upper middle class was often insulated by secondary royal office; the very rich, notably the financiers who lent to the crown, were untouched. The nobility and clergy were exempt from taxation or found means of avoiding it (though there were exceptions).

The principal direct royal taxes in 1789 were the *taille* (on income or property value, depending on the area), the three *vingtièmes* (one-twentieth, on income) and the *capitation* on the heads of households; the larger the family, the lower the tax. The royal *corvée*, in former times several days' work on the roads, had in most places become a tax. Collection was the responsibility of the minister of finances (Comptroller General), but his supervisory authority was limited since the administration was managed by sixty-eight Receivers General who *bought* their offices and netted a percentage of revenues. Under them were some 400 receivers and several thousand lesser officers whose income depended in part on the amount they collected—a great temptation to terrorize the taxpayers, which they did.

Indirect taxes—excise, sales taxes, tariffs, and others—were collected (with a few exceptions) by the Farmers General (Fermiers Généraux). The organization was run by sixty-odd directors, who bought their offices by contributing to a surity fund and contracted with the crown (normally every six years) to deliver a set annual revenue. They, in turn, subcontracted for the collection of various taxes

---

[32] The new courts were at Blois, Châlons, Clermont-Ferrand, Lyons, and Poitiers.

in particular areas with "farmers" whose hired "receivers" were notorious for their brutality. Those who collected the *gabelle* (salt tax) were the most feared. Almost everywhere, families were *required* to buy a specified amount of "legal" salt yearly from licensed producers and merchants.[33]

The profits of the Farmers General were incredible. In 1788, for example, they paid the king 208,000,000 livres and grossed 200,000,000 for themselves. The system was an obvious evil, but all attempts to abolish it failed because too many people had a vested interest in the system, including members of the royal court. The crown monopolies on tobacco, liqueurs, playing cards, and other items were similarly managed.

No tax was uniform. As to tariffs, the "Five Great Farms," comprising the twelve provinces nearest Paris, had almost no provincial tariffs among them. They, however, levied heavy duties on goods from "reputedly foreign provinces" (*provinces reputées étrangères*)—most of the rest of France, which had remained semi-independent of the crown for longer, and the "foreign provinces" such as Lorraine, acquired in the eighteenth century (see Map 1.4). The "foreign" provinces, in turn, had tariffs against each other and the Five Great Farms. In addition, cities and towns had import and export tariffs, and there were tolls on roads, waterways, bridges, and duties for passage through local areas. All were immensely profitable to officials and/or tax farmers and impediments to commerce. Often the most successful businessmen were the fastest with bribes.

In addition to royal taxes, the people were saddled with provincial and local taxes, and the peasants with seigneurial ("feudal") dues. These varied from province to province and within provinces. The most common was the *cens*, in most areas commuted to a fixed amount of money, and because of inflation not burdensome, but in some places up to 5 percent of the crop. The *champart, terrage,* or seigneurial *dîme*—by definition, 10 percent of the crop—taken in the fields, was a heavy imposition, though often less than 10 percent and in some areas replaced in part by flat money rents. The *lods et ventes*, paid when land was sold (in some places when inherited), amounted to 10 percent of the value.

Some landowning peasants were exempt, as we shall note later, but in general the rule was "No land without a Lord." Thus peasants paid dues on land they owned outright (as well as that rented or sharecropped) to the descendants of their medieval lords, or to those who had bought their rights along with the land. Among the most ridiculous dues were the *banalités*, levied since the medieval period for the use of the lord's mill, bakery, and winepress, which in the eighteenth century generally no longer existed. These had been commuted to money and were not heavy, but added to the peasants' sense of servility. There

[33] Brittany, Béarn, the coastal regions of Poitou, Picardy, and Aunis, and a few other scattered areas were exempt from the *gabelle*. The core of the "Five Great Farms" was most heavily taxed. The price of salt (tax included) in Paris, Mons, or Orléans was thirty to sixty times that paid in Brittany. In provinces outside the "Farms" it varied from one-tenth to one-half that inside the zone, but was seldom uniform, even within provinces.

Map 1.4

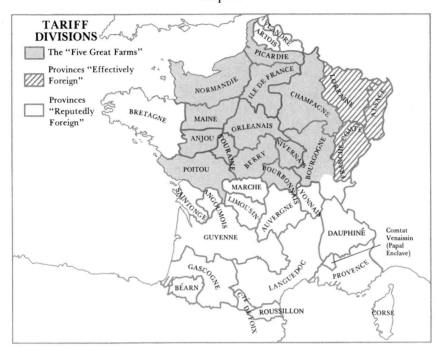

were dozens of minor dues of similar nature. Many that had lapsed were revived in the eighteenth century, which saw a "feudal reaction," led by new nobles and bourgeois landowners who wanted to maximize their profits. Their lawyers were set to work on the *terriers* (feudal records) for any dues customary (and thus legal) or agreed upon in the past.

The Church also took a share of the peasants' earnings. Its *dîme* (tithe) was a tax enforced by the crown. Nominally 10 percent of the crop, it was as low as 3 percent in some areas, and nowhere more than 8. If the proceeds had been used locally, there would have been few objections, but little of it was.

The inequities of the revenue system and feudal dues were part-and-parcel of the social system of the Old Regime.

SOCIETY AND PRIVILEGE

The ills of society under the prerevolutionary Old Regime are automatically associated with legal privilege, especially the rights and prerogatives of the nobility and high clergy. Privilege and feudal rights are often equated, and the society called "feudal." Actually most of the privileges did not derive from "Feudal

Times"—the medieval period—when the king had (loosely) ruled France through noble and knightly vassals whose estates were tilled by serfs. Instead, they had been generated during the 400-year period of transition from a subsistence to a capitalistic economy (though still basically agricultural) and represented, often, awkward compromises between the two. At the same time, the royal bureaucracy and judiciary had taken over most of the authority once exercised by the nobility.

The privileges of the nobility and clergy were quite real. However, the crown had also granted privileges to others—provinces, municipalities, guilds, manufacturing and trading companies, and individuals. French society was in fact a complex of more-or-less privileged groups.

In the bourgeoisie (middle class), for example, among the richest were directors of the Farmers General, which had the vested right to collect the king's indirect taxes. The silk manufacturers of Lyons were the masters of a guild called the "Grande Fabrique," which was protected and regulated by the crown. They had conflicts with their journeymen and apprentices, but all stood together against the abolition of the guild, and in the prerevolutionary years were demanding more royal protection and quality controls to preserve the city's monopoly on certain silk fabrics. City and town councils had the right to tax, impose tariffs at the gates, and regulate business. Peasant villages controlled the use of the *vaine pâture* (commons, left over from manorial days) where all had the right to graze stock and to gather wood, mushrooms, acorns, and so on. Often they controlled local water rights as well. The lowest *journalier* or *brassier* (landless peasant) had the privilege of using the commons.

The feudal rights of noble and clerical landlords were irrational in a capitalistic society, but so were those of guilds and of peasants to commons. All had value, whether precisely calculable or not, and thus represented property rights. Moreover, neither the nobles, nor any other privileged group, considered its rights evil. On the contrary, the majority saw their rights as legal, proper, traditional, and altogether necessary. This is why reform under the Old Regime was so difficult.

In order to illustrate further the ills of society during the Old Regime, it is important to discuss the numbers, status, condition, privileges, and burdens of the three traditional estates (*états*) of the realm—the clergy, the nobles, and "The Third" (everybody else).

FIRST ESTATE: THE CLERGY

The French Catholic clergy numbered about 150,000, or one-half of 1 percent of the population.[34] It was controlled by a hierarchy of some 10,000;

---

[34] The vast majority of the French people were Catholics. Protestant clergy had little or no influence under the Old Regime. The small minority of Protestants were not even recognized as French "subjects" until 1787, and did not get full civil rights until after the Revolution began in 1789. The Jews had to wait until 1791. See p. 90.

archbishops, bishops, abbots and prioresses of the monasteries and convents, vicars-general (adjunct bishops), several cardinals and others.

The Church was immensely rich. It owned about 15 percent of the land in France from which it drew income and (like the nobility) collected feudal dues. In good years the tithe alone netted the Church 130,000,000 livres, and its total income was about 300,000,000—equal to half that of the royal government. The Church also owned much commercial property, from tenements and houses in Paris to industries and shipping firms. Despite all this, the clergy was not taxed.[35] Instead, the Church Assembly (hierarchy) voted a gift to the king (the *don gratuit*) every few years, for an average of less than 5,000,000 livres a year. (Taxation would have yielded perhaps 50,000,000.) The Church felt no necessity for justifying its independence, which was traditional. However, it did manage and partly financed virtually all institutions of charity, hospitals, orphanages, schools, and even the universities. It also supported its own clergy, including retired priests, monks, and nuns. The crown, however, had been impelled to subsidize education and charity ever more heavily to meet growing needs.

The regular clergy (orders of monks, friars, and nuns) had a bad reputation, though most of them still performed useful functions—teaching, administering charity, nursing, and the like. But population shifts and changing times had left some monasteries idle, and the monks had become notorious for violating their vows of chastity and poverty. A few convents were actually retirement places or retreats for noble ladies who took no vows and were lavishly provided for, and where the younger "nuns" misbehaved grossly. Such places had been the subject of philosophic tracts and bawdy novels.

In 1789 the hierarchy (bishops, abbots, etc.) was composed totally of nobles. Though not necessarily irreligious or corrupt, most were career-oriented and viewed the Church as their cousins might, say, the army. The hierarchy controlled the church's wealth; talented bishops could move in the halls of power and could acquire political office. (Cardinal First Ministers had been common in France.) A typical aspiring bishop of 1789 was Talleyrand de Périgord, of ancient family, who was made an abbot before he was thirty, a bishop at thirty-five. He was the top legalist of the Church and probably would have made a name under the Old Regime if it had survived. As it turned out, Talleyrand shed his robes to become a revolutionary and diplomat.

The upper clergy lived in noble style, as they thought befitted their status. They had palaces and townhouses, carriages drawn by fine horses, stables of horses and kennels of dogs for hunting. Considering the times, this would not have brought great criticism except that the ranking clergy habitually lived at Versailles, or in Paris, and others in the larger cities where they were seldom seen by the people. Their clerical duties were performed by vicars or the deans of their

---

[35] Except for "foreign clergy" of the "new" provinces of Alsace, Lorraine, and Flanders, who paid small amounts.

cathedrals, while overseers managed the church lands. Moreover, multiple officeholding was common. The Cardinal de La Rochefoucauld (d. 1757) had been, at the same time, an archbishop, an abbot, and bishop of three dioceses— and had drawn income from all offices. His was an extreme case, of course.

The hierarchy was not corrupt, venal, or ineffective in the majority, however, or the Church would have collapsed. That it was all-noble was not altogether bad in a society such as that of the Old Regime. A noble bishop could move easily in high society, perhaps even be received by the king, and might, if he exerted himself, gain more benefits for his people than one of lower social status. Moreover, not all bishops were careerists, and many who began as such became sincerely religious. It became evident in 1789 that there were a number of liberal bishops, including Talleyrand and Champion de Cicé—enough so that when the Estates General met the hierarchy was split.

The curés (priests), in daily contact with the people, were dedicated, though often not well educated. They shared the hardships of their parishioners and received little of the church's income. In 1789 they tended to side with the Third Estate. This did not mean, however, that they opposed Louis XVI. Few questioned that the king ruled by divine right. They had taught this and obedience to the monarch from the pulpit and school platform. Whatever else they were in the beginning, the curés were monarchists.

THE NOBILITY

Nobles in France numbered about 350,000 or about 1.5 percent of the population. They belonged to one of four categories: (1) nobles-of-the-sword (*noblesse de l'épée*), who were of ancient title, presumed to have been won as medieval knights; (2) nobles-of-the-robe (*noblesse de la robe*), whose titles derived from royal judicial or administrative service; (3) nobles-of-the-bell (*noblesse de cloche*), honored for municipal service, and (4) *anoblis*, who had simply bought titles, often with no duties attached, such as "secretary to the king" (of whom there were some 900). The aristocrats owned 20 percent of the land in France and drew feudal dues from most of the rest. Traditionally, they disdained business, but some were investors and some even manufacturers. The Duke d'Aiguillon, sometime governor of Brittany, owned ironworks, the Ségur and Noailles families had sugar refineries in Santo Domingo. Most nobles considered income only from lands "respectable," however.

The nobles-of-the-sword, at heart, considered themselves the only true nobles—descendants of the ancient rulers of France—and in earlier centuries had disdained all others as glorified clerks. In the eighteenth century the nobility had become more unified, and generally accepted the leadership of the nobility-of-the-robe, as we have noted. Increasingly, wealth, as well as the origins of titles, had become important in determining status. Among nobles-of-the-sword, for example, a duke who was of ancient title and wealthy was more likely to be a

"Duke and Peer," be received by the king and live in Paris or Versailles. A man of equally distinguished lineage who had lost his wealth had little influence unless he earned it. He was of the group derisively called *hoberaux* (sparrow hawks). For young "hawks" (who traditionally disdained business) the best opportunities were often in the army, where their titles guaranteed their admission to the king's schools for officers or direct commissions. Poor country nobles (though not necessarily all destitute) were the mainstay of the officer corps, though high rank more often went to peers. (Young Napoleon Bonaparte got a scholarship from Louis XVI as an impecunious noble.) Age of title counted in all noble groups. A noble-of-the-robe was ranked according to the number of generations his family had held a title—but he could gain more status by taking a wife of a sword family.[36]

Nobles had a *de facto* monopoly on office in the royal administration and the judiciary. Their exclusive right to officers' commissions in the army had been affirmed by Royal Edict in 1781, though it was frequently honored in the breach in the engineers and artillery, for which not enough nobles qualified. To gain office, however, an aspirant bourgeois had only to acquire nobility, which was fairly easy—that is, if he were wealthy. Among the 426 lay judges of the *parlements* appointed during the last fifteen years of the Old Regime, 266 were "new" nobles and only 160 of old title.[37] Appointment to the Parlement of Paris and a few others carried nobility with it immediately. In others, title was acquired in the second or third generation. One could also buy a title and then secure appointment. (Necker's survey of 1781 listed 4000 venal offices which gave nobility immediately or eventually.) Similar arrangements applied to intendants. Some 66 percent of those who served Louis XVI were of first, second, or third generation nobility.[38] There was social mobility in eighteenth-century France, but it may be argued that this was not constructive, since, at the upper level, enterprising men were moved into a nobility that exalted landholding and disdained "moneygrubbing."

The aristocratic monopoly in office was nonetheless real. With rare exceptions, nobles were also exempt from or managed to evade most taxes. They got special treatment in courts of law. If guilty of a crime, a noble could not be whipped or maimed, as was legal for commoners. If guilty of a capital offense, such as murder, he could not be hanged, but was "privileged" to be beheaded. In civil suits, nobles were given the benefit of the doubt. They enjoyed the right of the *chasse* (hunting), which meant they could ride roughshod over the peasants' crops at will. For target practice, they had the right to keep pigeons, which roosted in hutches, but fed on the crops—a major nuisance. In remote areas, nobles still

[36] For those unfamiliar with noble rank: A prince (in France, at least) was of or closely related to the royal house. Other titles in descending order were duke (*duc*), marquis, count (*comte*), viscount (*vicomte*), and baron. A knight (*chevalier*) was technically not an hereditary noble, but those "of the sword" in fact, were, in France.

[37] According to Jean Égret. (See Bibliography: Prerevolution/Onset of Revolution.)

[38] Vivian Gruder. (See Bibliography: The Eighteenth-Century France: Social, Cultural, Institutional.)

judged "their people" in everyday criminal and civil cases, and there was no appeal unless allowed by them.

Like the church hierarchy, the nobility had its liberal element. And in the years 1787–1789 it was extremely vocal. This group included the Duke d'Orléans, cousin of the king; the Dukes de La Rochefoucauld and d'Aiguillon, both peers; the counts Charles and Alexandre Lameth, the Viscount de Barras; the Comte de Mirabeau; and, of course, the Marquis de Lafayette. In the years before the Revolution, they were tolerated as harmless by their fellow nobles and occasionally praised for opposing royal authority. As the Revolution gained heat, however, they were seen as traitors to their *caste*. The role of the nobility in "destroying itself" is, in fact, remarkable.

THE THIRD ESTATE

Everyone in France who was not a noble or clergyman belonged to the Third Estate—approximately 98 percent of the population. For discussion the Third Estate may be broken into three categories: (1) the bourgeoisie or middle class (perhaps 500,000), (2) the city workers (about 2,500,000) and (3) the peasants (farmers) numbering at least 22,500,000 or almost 87 percent of the people.

Each category will be discussed separately; however, we should remember that the people we describe did not view themselves as belonging to a "class" or social group based on wealth and occupation. Each group was extremely heterogeneous, and the "classes" cannot be defined in such a way that they do not overlap. For example, there were rich peasant landowners who could be considered high bourgeois, or even gentry, and among skilled workers there were those who could qualify, by income, as bourgeois. Even the terms which we use for convenience are anachronistic. There was no Marxist-style proletariat in eighteenth-century France. The term bourgeoisie was not then the equivalent of middle class. In most areas, a bourgeois was a member of the oligarchy of a *bourg* (town or city); one could be middle class by economic standards and yet not be bourgeois in status. Bearing such qualifications in mind, however, we should get a clear general picture of the "classes" in the Third Estate.

THE BOURGEOISIE   The bourgeoisie comprised extremely rich men with aspirations to nobility, as well as shopkeepers, artisans who employed helpers, country lawyers, minor bureaucrats, and others. The richest of the bourgeoisie were not, as an American might assume, industrialists and merchants, or technically, bankers. They were the "financiers" who lent money to the crown (among others). Under Louis XVI, two of the most prominent of these were Jacques Necker, a Swiss Protestant, long resident in Paris (who is discussed later), and Jean-Joseph Laborde, whose wife was of the old noble family of Noailles. Next richest were the collectors of the king's indirect taxes, headed by the directors of the Farmers General. (See above, p. 41.) Rivaling the farmers in wealth were the receivers of the direct royal taxes.

Next in affluence were the more successful lawyers, headed by the *avocats* of the Paris bar, of whom the upper crust aspired to judgeships in the *parlements*. On the same or a slightly lower level were some great merchants, particularly those in overseas shipping, a few private industrialists, and many managers of royal industries. Most of the richer manufacturers were servants of the crown, for example, the managers of the royal gun factories at Creusot, Nantes, and elsewhere, the royal mirror works at Caen, the tapestry plant of the Gobelins in Paris, and other enterprises. Since the time of Henry IV (1589–1610), who founded the silk industry at Lyons, the kings had steadily enlarged the scope of government manufacturing.[39]

French society discouraged successful businessmen from remaining in trade. The dream of the enterprising bourgeois was not to change society but to join the aristocracy. Once he had enough wealth, the businessman invariably sought to buy office and title—if not for himself for his son—and to acquire land so as to "live nobly." Thus funds that might have gone to expand commerce and industry were devoted instead to expanding and perpetuating the anachronistic society-of-legal-privilege.

Only a few private industrialists were richer than the "king's men." For example, Frederic Dietrich of Strasbourg owned metal works in Alsace with over 600 employees. (He ultimately became a baron.) Dollfuss of Mulhouse employed some 300 in his textile mills. Various entrepreneurs owned the coal mining Company of Anzin which employed 4000 miners and teamsters and was the largest single enterprise in France. Many men, of course, belonged simultaneously to several of the categories. A financier could also be an investor in the Farmers General and/or in industry and commerce and also be a landlord, and so on. The banker Jacques Necker qualified on all these counts.

As with the nobility, many members of the bourgeoisie were touched by the doctrines of the Enlightenment. The upper crust often suffered social slights from the nobility, with whom they consorted frequently, and sometimes even from the kind-hearted king. Necker, for example, whom Louis XVI made finance minister, was not a noble (and moreover was a Swiss and Protestant). He was styled Director General of Finances rather than (as was usual) Comptroller General. Nevertheless, neither Necker nor any other prominent bourgeois favored changing the basic social system. They were too near achieving nobility. Some wanted the power of the king limited but more were interested in removing impediments to economic growth than in reforming the royal administration. Though the high bourgeoisie took a part in the early Revolution, it was those of middle rank who steered it into ever more radical phases.

---

[39] Louis XIV bought the Gobelins, a going private enterprise. It still belongs to the French government. De Gaulle as president of France provided it with a new plant in Paris.

THE WORKERS   The workers were concentrated in the cities, none of which was very big by present day standards. Paris was the largest with a population between 500,000 and 650,000, second only to London in the Western world. Otherwise, only Marseilles and Lyons had as many as 100,000, and Nantes, Lille, and Toulouse 50,000.[40] Industry had grown in the eighteenth century, despite all handicaps. As mentioned above (p. 22), however, France's strength was still in luxury goods, as it had been for centuries. Chief exports were wines, liqueurs, cognac, silk cloth and silk clothing, perfumes, furniture, mirrors, jewelry, and the like. Industry was closely tied to agriculture. When one failed, so did the other. This was the case in 1789. The wine industry was dependent on grape production, cognac on apples and other fruit, silk on plentiful leaves of mulberry trees (on which silkworms fed), perfumes on flower blossoms, and so on. When these crops were poor, food crops tended to be also. Workers tended to be laid off at the same time when there were food shortages and prices rose. Similarly, when the workers were prone to riot, the poorer peasants of the countryside were also, which hampered government efforts to feed the cities.

Most industries were very small "family" affairs, run by master-workers (craftsmen, artisans, winemakers, brewers, and the like). A factory with fifty workers was considered large. Most masters were really of the bourgeoisie, the more successful definitely so, though many, including some of the richer ones, identified with the workers.

The best off among the genuine workers were the journeymen, whom the guilds kept down by severely limiting the number of new masters. Some became wealthy by establishing themselves outside their guild's jurisdiction. In Lyons, for example, a few managed to manufacture silk cloth outside the city by employing peasants, furnishing them with instruction, crude machines, and materials in their homes. Most, however, remained journeymen for life. They maintained steady employment and drew top wages through semi-legal "unions" called *compagnonnages* (brotherhoods) and to some degree led other workers. They could and did strike, if occasionally. In 1776, Paris bookbinders struck for a fourteen-hour day and won. In 1785 building workers blocked a reduction in their wages. In 1786 silk production in Lyons was halted for weeks, and there was bloodshed before the masters and merchants met the journeymen's demands. Before the Revolution, however, journeymen were the least violence-prone of all workers.

The most volatile element in the cities comprised unskilled workers, many recently arrived from the country. They were totally unprotected and subject to the laws of supply and demand. When they could get work, their wages were at subsistence level. In 1789 the average wage was about 135 sous a week (less than seven francs), in a year when the price of a four-pound loaf of bread (enough for a small family for one day) went from twelve sous to twenty (one franc) between

---

[40] In the range between 30,000 and 50,000 were Amiens, Angers, Orléans, Besançon, Caen, Nimes, Montpélier, and Deziers.

March and July. In times of high unemployment, hundreds of these unskilled workers literally died in the streets from hunger and exposure. In hard years, one of the tasks of the Paris police was to clear the gutters of corpses in the mornings. This element was as voiceless as it was volatile, and, when desperate, easily led and barbarous.

The leadership of the Paris masses in the Revolution fell to the now famous *sans-culottes*,[41] who were mostly skilled artisans and journeymen. A few were masters, and some lawyers, priests, and shopkeepers also stand out. Santerre, a wealthy Paris brewer, was perhaps the most famous of the masters who led the workers. When he rallied mobs of his section, he provided the people with beer to bolster their courage. The *sans-culottes* moved the great crowds of Paris, which played such a large role in charting the course of the Revolution.

The beliefs of the *sans-culottes* were curiously mixed. They firmly believed in the sanctity of private property, but only if the owner worked—preferably got his hands dirty. Those who lived on incomes from investments were anathema to them; however, men with inherited wealth were accepted if they *worked* and were not *too* rich. Their ideal man was the small, independent entrepreneur. They were against big business—large-scale capitalistic ventures—and thus backward looking. They favored the measures of the crown to feed the city and to provide welfare institutions. During the Revolution the *sans-culottes* came to favor even greater government intervention to guarantee jobs and control wages and prices. Their attitudes applied, generally, to all workers, who comprised a "preindustrial" proletariat.

THE PEASANTS The more than 22,000,000 peasant farmers varied widely in wealth and status. A few were rich enough to rival noblemen in living style. At the other end of the scale were the *brassiers*, the landless day laborers. Between the extremes were landowners (great and small), renters, and sharecroppers.[42] Most peasants were combinations of landowner and renter and/or sharecropper. About 75 percent of the peasants owned some land but in most cases not enough to support their families, so that they also had to rent or sharecrop. Overall, the peasants owned 54 percent of the land in France. In general, they were more prosperous than peasants anywhere on the Continent, but they had their complaints, especially about the heavy taxes and feudal dues already described. (See p. 41.) They did not appreciate the nobles' wasting their crops with hunting parties and hordes of ravenous pigeons, but until the Revolution gave them a voice, the French peasants took these abuses much as they did the weather.

---

[41] Literally "without knee breeches," which the upper classes wore. Workers wore long trousers, or, more precisely, trousers were part of the proud workers' "uniform." Sketches and paintings of the period reveal that many of them wore shabby culottes—probably cast-offs of the "aristos." After all, most of them were very poor, and wore whatever they could come by.

[42] Substantial landholders, confusingly, were called *laboureurs*. The richest, the *francsalleux*, paid no feudal dues. Renters were called *fermiers* (farmers); sharecropper translates *métayer*. *Brassiers* were also called *journaliers* (day workers).

Generally, the peasantry was stolid, solid, religious, loyal to the king, and anything but revolutionary. The one dangerous element was the landless *brassiers*, who were the first to suffer in hard times. As the economic depression which preceded the Revolution deepened, many became professional bandits and were at hand in 1789 to swell the ranks of rioters when bread shortages, fear of an "aristocratic plot," and fever of revolutionary expectations moved many more prosperous peasants to violence. Almost accidentally, the peasant did play a role in launching the Revolution.

The peasants were only occasionally involved in the Revolution after 1789, however. "Feudalism" was abolished (and most of the peasants stopped paying dues), prosperity began to return, and they fell back into their usual routines and the traditional business (aided somewhat by the Revolution) of expanding smallholds. They furnished the bulk of the revolutionary armies, of course, and those of Napoleon. But those most passionately involved on the domestic scene were *counter-revolutionaries*, as we shall see.

The burdens of the peasantry therefore should not be given great weight in the causal pattern of the Revolution, and surely not of its more radical later phases. It was largely an urban affair, to which the peasants, for the most part, passively consented. This is emphasized here because our extended treatment of "feudal" society might lead one to believe that the peasants *had to be* an enraged element. Perhaps they should have been, but they were not.

POPULATION GROWTH AND SOCIETY

Demographic growth, already touched on (p. 16–18, above) helps to explain much about French society in 1789, especially the condition of the peasants and workers. Population had increased 44 percent since 1715—from 18,000,000 to 26,000,000 (or more). It was a young population, with 36 percent under twenty, 40 percent between twenty and forty, and only 24 percent over forty. In the countryside, land tenure and farming methods had changed little. There was not enough land to go around. Where large-scale "scientific" farming had been introduced, labor requirements were reduced and more peasants were driven off the land.

The result was an increase in the number of landless *brassiers* in France, many of whom migrated to the cities, especially Paris, where the population more than doubled between 1715 and 1789 (when it stood at 600,000).[43] Industry, however, was underdeveloped, for reasons already discussed. There was an ever-increasing oversupply of labor. In Paris some 10 percent of the people were always unemployed. Half of this 60,000 were professional beggars and thieves. In times of

---

[43] This seems small by today's standards, but considering the primitive state of transportation, Paris was more difficult to feed and supply in 1789 than, say, New York is today.

crisis, unemployment went as high as 50 percent. The crown did its best to feed Paris, if for no other reason than to keep the populace quiet. Under extreme conditions, however, the administrative machinery was inadequate to the task.

Burgeoning population was also a factor in pushing up prices and depressing wages during the eighteenth century. For most of this period, wages lagged behind prices, to the advantage of enterprising employers. Thus the number of rich peasants had increased (and the number owning land); in the cities many more persons had achieved middle-class status. But at the lowest level of society, some 10 to 15 percent of the population was perpetually unemployed, and many on the verge of starvation. Severe economic shocks, such as those that came after 1778, had catastrophic consequences for the people, as will be described in Chapter 2.

SOCIETY, GOVERNMENT, POLITICAL CULTURE, AND REVOLUTION

The Old Regime in France was rife with injustices—for the most part institutionalized and legal. Nevertheless, to most Frenchmen, monarchial-aristocratic-clerical government seemed natural and even right. And until 1778 there was general prosperity. Most people had everyday complaints, usually connected with their pocketbooks. Educated men had ideas about reform, though generally of the government, especially the financial administration, and not of society, per se. Their plans for action, however (if any), were as vague and diverse as those of the *philosophes*. Those in the best position to propose and effect reforms were either paralyzed by the Byzantine complexity of the nation's institutions and laws[44] or disinclined to act because they had too much to lose. There was discontent in every sector of society, but most men, of whatever class, were inclined to work within the "eternal" system.

After 1778, however, "La Grande Nation" found herself in the throes of a prolonged—if sporadic—economic depression, and the irrationality of the structures of the Old Regime was brought brutally into focus. Reform became mandatory—at least of the royal administration, on which, given French history, everything depended. If that failed, the way was open to an attack on the Old Regime, root and branch.

The crisis had to be met by Louis XVI, and he was unequal to the challenge. Moreover, in addition to the evident problems, the king had a new disadvantage. Political languages and a political culture had been created in the eighteenth century. Alongside diehard absolute monarchists were liberals (constitutional monarchists, later moderate republicans) and radicals, all unconsciously condi-

---

[44] Eighteenth-century France was absolute heaven for lawyers—until economic conditions began to deteriorate after 1778—and for some even then.

tioned by the *philosophes* to vie for power. They were inspired largely by Rousseau, who had offered a rationale for transferring power from the king to the amorphous "people." A political atmosphere prevailed that fostered a mentality of action, that, in turn, netted rhetoric from the politicians and real action—ultimately violence—from the masses. Rhetoric and action continually drew life from drama, art, the press, rituals, festivals, symbols, slogans, the mystique of real and contrived heroes, and a plethora of other motivators.

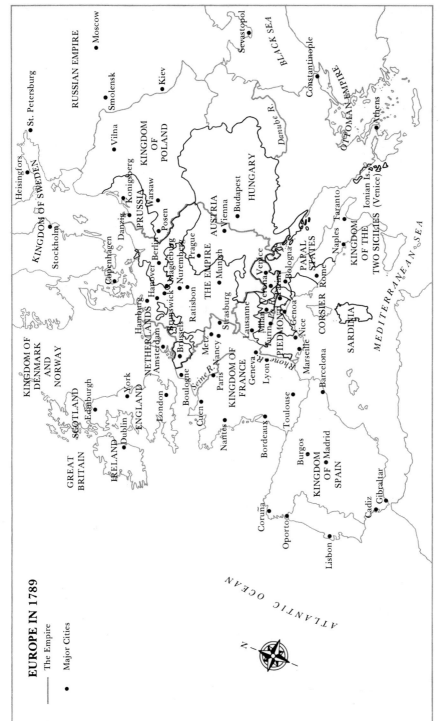

EUROPE IN 1789

The Empire

● Major Cities

Map 2.1

"Why, it's an uprising."
"No, Sire, it is a revolution."
—*Exchange between Louis XVI and the*
Duke de Liancourt, 14 July 1789

THE GREAT SURPRISE
The Onset of the Revolution

LOUIS XVI AND MARIE ANTOINETTE

Since Louis XVI was the king whom the French people sent to the guillotine, we are likely to picture him as old, ugly, and a tyrant. In fact, he was none of these. When he ascended the throne in 1774 he was not quite twenty; he was thirty-five in 1789 and thirty-eight when he was executed. Although fat, he was not unattractive. There was not a despotic bone in his body, which may have been his undoing.

Louis was good natured, with ordinary, regular habits, and a churchgoer who took religion very seriously. He was faithful to his wife (of which the reverse cannot be said). The welfare of his people concerned him deeply—insofar as he understood it. For example, in 1787, two years before the Revolution, he personally led a drive in Paris to raise funds for a new hospital for the indigent. It is unfortunately just as typical of him that he lacked the will to force the church authorities to abandon the Hôtel Dieu (the central charity hospital), an ancient eyesore near Notre Dame, which was notorious for its overcrowded conditions and high patient death rate.

The king was not unintelligent, nor was his judgment bad; he simply was bored by the business of government. His snores were a regular feature of extended cabinet meetings. He much preferred to be at his hobbies—making clocks, watches, and mechanical gadgets (at which he was quite skilled) or out hunting (for which he kept a huge stable of horses and several hundred hounds). When the weather was good, he was always out shooting. On 5 October 1789, the day of the march of the women to Versailles, perhaps the most momentous of the Revolution, Louis wrote one line in his diary: "Hunting at the gate Chatillon, killed 81 [birds]. Interrupted by events."

Whatever hunting might have done for his physique was offset by his eating. A typical breakfast, recorded in 1787 by a courtier, consisted of four veal cutlets, one whole baked chicken, six eggs, a slice of ham, and one and one-half bottles of champagne. Then, says the chronicler, he "left for hunting and returned for dinner [at noon] with an incredible appetite."

This was the man in the "genius seat" of Louis XIV. He had inherited a government which demanded an executive of abnormal energy and interest in affairs, but Louis XVI was not the man for the job. Assuming that he had inherited a fortune, he would have done marvelously as a small-town burgher. He would have been an exemplary family man, a pillar of the Church, a supporter of charities, a member of all the "right" organizations, and so on. Unfortunately, Louis XVI was not a small-town burgher, but the king of France.

To cement the Franco-Austrian alliance, Louis had been married three months before his sixteenth birthday to Marie Antoinette von Habsburg (fourteen and a half), daughter of the Empress Maria Theresa. A beautiful, blonde, vivacious spitfire, she was not enamored of her tongue-tied, shy husband, especially since it was seven years before he could consummate the marriage. Ultimately she produced two sons and two daughters for the king, but may have taken lovers. She was a woman of little education but of considerable intelligence and unbending will. She disliked the ceremonies at Versailles and at times refused to attend them. With a small circle of friends, she often went away for long sojourns at the king's other palaces.

Marie Antoinette's favorite occupations were playing cards at high stakes, listening to music or playing an instrument, performing in amateur theatricals, and spending money. She was continually in debt from her purchases and losses at gambling. Though the sums she spent could hardly have damaged the royal finances, the public thought otherwise. "Madame Deficit" she was called. In 1785 the queen's reputation had been further damaged by the "Affair of the Diamond Necklace." To all appearances the worldly Cardinal Rohan had hoped to buy her favors with the bauble. Actually the cardinal had been swindled, and the queen was innocent. That this was proved in a public trial held by special order of the king did not help matters. The public would believe no good of the queen.

Marie Antoinette never grew up. She continued to behave all of her life like a spoiled teenage princess. To satisfy one of her whims, Louis had built at Versailles a mill and peasant's hut where she and her ladies could play at being happy milkmaids. Not until the dark days of the Revolution, when the reality of captivity and the imminence of death bore in upon her, did she show signs of having matured. It was then, too late, that she gained some respect for her husband who, whatever his faults, was not a coward. And she herself mounted the scaffold with dignity and courage.

Even the anti-Austrian party at court, however, had to admit that when Marie Antoinette chose, she could be the most impressive of queens. Foreign visitors were invariably stunned by her beauty and grace. The staid Edmund Burke, writing in 1790, remembered her from the early days of her reign.

I saw her just above the horizon, decorating and cheering the elevated sphere she had just begun to move in, glittering like a morning star, full of life and splendor, and joy.

Those who loved the Old Regime—or like Burke tried to see some good in it—gave her pity, even affection, despite her faults. Who does not love a pretty child, even if spoiled?

The queen interfered in government often, though she knew little of state affairs. The king was never able to oppose her for long. Her party at court had disastrous influence after 1789, but her destructive powers were evident long before. In 1776, for example, she helped bring down Louis' reforming minister, Turgot. Marie Antoinette had scant understanding of his financial schemes, but he had "wronged" one of her favorites, the Count de Guines. She demanded not only that Louis oust Turgot, but that he send him to the Bastille forthwith. The minister was already under fire from the nobles, whom he wanted to tax, and for other reasons (see p. 60, below), but the queen played a part in his dismissal.

With Marie Antoinette by his side, Louis XVI faced the most serious economic crisis of the century—perhaps of French history.[1]

THE ECONOMIC BACKGROUND

During the eighteenth century, overall, the French economy expanded and improved, signalled by steadily rising prices. In 1778, however, a depression set in that, with jarring ups and downs, lasted until 1787, with businesses failing and prices falling. In 1787, prices began to climb, which is usually a sign of recovery. In this case, however, higher prices merely reflected shortages of food and other commodities. In 1789, when the Revolution began, both prices and unemployment were at an all-time high.

Some additional detail will better illustrate the state of the French economy. By 1778, prices had risen about 45 percent over the average for the period 1726–1741.[2] Wages went up also, but only by about 17 percent. Thus real wages (measured by buying power) went down. Employment was high, however, so that workers were relatively content. Peasant farmers benefited from high prices. Then came the depression of 1778–1787. The causes seem to have been overproduction on the farms, overexpansion in some industries, and the closing of overseas markets (the War of the American Revolution played a part). The latter was disastrous for manufacturing, and a tariff treaty with Britain (1786) made

---

[1] The newer biographies of Marie-Antoinette give the queen a much better image. See, for example, those of Olivier Bernier (1985) and Joan Haslip (1988). Also see Sarah Maza, "The Diamond Necklace Affair Revisited: The Case of the Missing Queen," *National Humanities Center Newsletter*, Vol. 10, No. 2 (Winter 1988–89).

[2] This is the "base" period taken by Ernest Labrousse.

matters worse, especially for French textiles, which could not compete with the English. Prices fell. By 1787, grain was down 40 percent, wine 50 percent. Wages of city workers also decreased, but not proportionately, thus their buying power was greater. However, unemployment was high. The industrial cities, notably Paris, were hard hit. Jobs were scarce for their inhabitants, and there was a continuous influx of people from the countryside seeking work. As for the peasants, the small farmers were hurt because their rents had been agreed upon when prices were high and were fixed by long-term leases. The prices of farm products were low and went lower with every harvest. (Thus inflationary rents had to be paid in deflated coin.) Leases, of course, came up for renewal, but population expansion had produced many bidders for any lease, therefore rents remained high. During the period of sharply rising prices (1787–1789, moderating somewhat in 1790) the lot of peasants and workers was even worse. Farm products drew good prices, but crops were poor, and farmers' incomes remained low. City workers faced a scarcity of jobs and skyrocketing prices at the same time. In short, there was simultaneous depression and inflation, an almost unprecedented situation.

The harvests of 1788 and 1789 were extremely bad. Prices soared—in 1789 wheat increased to 66 percent (over the 1726–1741 average), rye 71 percent, wood 91 percent. (These figures are averages.) The peak prices of July 1789 were up 150 percent for wheat and 165 percent for rye (the staple bread of the workers). At the same time, wages had risen only 5 percent since 1770. Unemployment in 1789 reached almost 50 percent in Paris.

In sum, the economic situation in the prerevolutionary years exacerbated the tempers of little men throughout France. During 1788 and 1789 there were bread riots in both the cities and the countryside. The city workers were the most desperate. Despite government action, which gave great quantities of cheap (or free) bread to Paris, the populace was extremely restive. Among the angry men, however, were also entrepreneurs—businessmen, manufacturers, and even farmers—who had been ruined by depression and inflation. Ex-employers, suddenly plunged into the proletariat, were among the most sullen, frustrated, and enraged people to be found.

THE FISCAL CRISIS

When the people were least willing and able to pay, the government was in dire need of funds. Under the circumstances, increasing taxes seemed unwise, though receipts were at an all-time low. The Budget of 1788 gave the crown's income as 640,500,000 livres (in round figures), but 140,000,000 of that was borrowed. Worse still, the figure for debt service was 318,000,000 livres—almost half the budget—and most of it was *interest* on loans, not amounts repaid. The total debt had gone over 4,000,000,000 livres, and financiers were reluctant to lend more. With the state's expenditures exceeding its income by 100,000,000 to

150,000,000 livres a year, how could the lenders ever expect to recover their capital? In an attempt to restore confidence, the king had already initiated programs to increase his revenues, notably by taxing the nobility and clergy—the best able to pay but also the most able to resist.[3]

LOUIS XVI ATTEMPTS REFORM

Louis XVI since his coronation (1774) had been aware of France's problems, particularly financial, and had solicited the aid of *philosophes* in solving them. His first ministry included Jacques Turgot as Comptroller General and Malesherbes. The former we know as the progressive Intendant of Limoges and a physiocrat; the latter as chief censor of Louis XV had facilitated the publication of Diderot's *Encyclopédie*. The intelligentsia applauded. To dissociate himself from the "despotism" of the previous regime, however, Louis also restored the *parlements* to their full power, thereby insuring the failure of any effective financial reforms.

Comptroller General Turgot began ambitiously. Over the royal signature, he reduced the authority of the tax farmers, which saved the government 6,000,000 livres a year. He abolished the guilds and freed the domestic grain trade from all controls and internal tariffs (measures intended to promote production). Finally, he abolished the royal *corvée* in favor of a tax on all three estates.

At this, the Parlement of Paris balked. The nobles-of-the-robe were especially disinclined to approve a new tax on themselves. They appealed to the unwritten constitution of France. Malesherbes, an ex-judge himself, angrily offered them their own traditional alternative. "Assemble the Estates General . . . [Otherwise] . . . the king . . . should himself judge, and judge in favor of the people. . . . "

The king did himself judge in solemn *lit de justice*. The *parlementaires* were ordered to register the decrees. An enormous uproar was created, however, by the Parlement of Paris, posing as the protector of the public against new taxation. And meanwhile, accidents of weather worked to discredit Turgot. The harvests of 1774–1775 had been unusually bad, and there were serious shortages of grain in some areas (including the Paris basin), which were blamed on the new free trade policy. There ensued in the summer of 1775 the famous "Flour War" (*guerre des farines*). Peasants and townsmen rioted. Wholesale installations and bakeries were seized; mobs demanded that prices be controlled. A huge crowd assembled at Versailles and petitioned the king to set prices at a "fair and just" level. Much to the chagrin of Turgot, Louis XVI ordered the governor of Versailles to do so.

---

[3] 4,000,000,000 livres (francs) in 1788 was the equivalent of about $800,000,000. In today's money the debt would still be less than $30,000,000,000, which seems very small in comparison to the U.S. debt (1989) of about $4,000,000,000,000—even if we consider that the population of France then was only one-tenth that of the United States today. We must remember, however, that deficit financing was abnormal in that era. Governments were expected to have reasonably balanced budgets, except perhaps in wartime.

The public was encouraged by the *parlementaires* and court nobles to believe that free trade had allowed profiteers to hoard grain and to drive up prices. Turgot, under fire from all quarters, resigned (1776). Shortly thereafter, the grain controls, the *corvée*, and the guilds were all restored. The king had lost his first bout against the nobility. Almost alone, Voltaire saw clearly what had happened: "A fatal day. . . . "

Jacques Necker replaced Turgot. This Protestant financier had come to Paris from Geneva in 1747 as an accountant and by 1765 had become a millionaire. Necker had the managerial talents and shrewdness the crown needed, a reputation for incorruptibility, and, importantly, he had connections with the banks of Switzerland, Holland, and Britain. In addition, he was well accepted socially; the dinners of his vivacious wife attracted the powerful and famous to their magnificent house in the Marais district. Necker had endeared himself to reactionaries by attacking the physiocrats in print. The Académie had awarded him a prize for a tribute to Colbert (prince of mercantilism). Necker was initially inclined merely to keep his masters happy, but his businessman's mentality gradually drove him to push for reforms.

To help finance the war of the American Revolution, he secured a second *vingtième* in 1776, with only mild protest from the *parlements*. Thereafter, he borrowed to cover deficits and concentrated on increasing the efficiency of tax collection and on introducing a salaried officiate to collect direct taxes at the district level. Necker also eliminated serfdom on the royal domains (as uneconomic). Perhaps inspired by a Swiss faith in federalism, he proposed that provincial estates be restored. Only one was established—in Le Berry. Both intendants and *parlements* were opposed to new estates, which they feared would infringe on the prerogatives.

In 1781, alarmed by the growth of the debt during the American Revolution, Necker asked the king for expanded powers. Simultaneously, he took the unprecedented step of publishing the crown budget, with commentary. This *Compte Rendu au Roi* criticized the tax system, but showed a small surplus, which Necker calculated by omitting war expenses (which he considered as nonrecurrent). This impressed the financial community. The royal court was outraged, however, since he revealed its expenses, including 28,000,000 livres in *pensions* (unearned lifetime salaries). Led by Marie Antoinette, the courtiers demanded Necker's dismissal and were backed by the *parlementaires* and the intendants. The king turned his back on Necker, who resigned. He was replaced by Joly de Fleury (1781–1783), a nonentity whose only accomplishment was putting through the third *vingtième*.

The next comptroller, Charles Alexandre de Calonne, borrowed heavily, and for a time gave the government the appearance of affluence. Each year, however, he had to pay higher rates of interest, until, in 1786, his credit was exhausted, and he had to consider fiscal reforms. Before his program could be put into royal decrees, however, the *parlements* heard that he planned to tax the nobility and Church, and the Parlement of Paris gave advance notice that it would oppose any new taxes.

Calonne persuaded the king to neutralize the *parlements* by calling a body of superior authority—not the Estates General, but an "Assembly of Notables" drawn from all estates and provinces. Louis summoned 144 persons—seven princes-of-the-blood, fourteen archbishops and bishops, thirty-six high nobles, thirty-seven *parlementaires*, four intendants, eight councillors of state, twelve representatives of provincial estates, and twenty-six of the cities.

The assembly met in February 1787, just as France entered its worst economic crisis of the century. Calonne proposed (1) the repeal of all three *vingtièmes* and their replacement by a *subvention territoriale* (land tax) to be paid by all orders; (2) the abolition of the royal *corvée*, and the reform of the *taille, gabelle*, and other taxes; (3) the abolition of internal tariffs; and (4) the establishment of a state bank.

Louis had expected that this hand-picked group of educated men-of-affairs would approve all or most of these measures, even if it meant the sacrifice of some of their privileges. Such was not the case. Among the princes, the Duke d'Orléans, a liberal but no friend of the king, led the opposition to Calonne. Archbishop Loménie de Brienne, a proponent of physiocracy had, nevertheless, solidified the clergy in defense of ancient church privileges. Among the high nobles, "The American," the Marquis de Lafayette, wavered and parleyed, but ended by questioning the authority of the assembly. Legally, he said, only a "true national assembly" could discuss taxation. Did he mean the Estates General? "Precisely," he replied.

The opposition outside the assembly was more violent than within. Calonne found himself *persona non grata* with the court nobility, the *parlementaires* and noble society generally. Fearing for his life, he fled Paris. When the king formally dismissed him in April 1787, he was already in London, where he remained until 1802—the "first émigré of the Revolution."

The king was now definitely on the defensive. He must be credited with *wanting* to reform his government, but he had failed to support, in turn, Turgot, Necker, and Calonne. Obviously, Calonne knew that Louis would not protect him, or he would not have fled, and the king *could* have. Though his power was not in fact absolute, at this juncture it was still enormous. Given the will power, he could have swept the court clean, exiled the *parlementaires*, and used the army, if necessary. Few noble officers, no matter what their feelings, would have risked their careers, fortunes, and lives by disobeying the king. Louis XVI demonstrated this fact, if haphazardly, during the next year.

THE NOBLES' REVOLT

After a month of temporizing, the king surprised the court by giving the post of Comptroller General to Loménie de Brienne, one of the chief spoilers in the Assembly of Notables. The archbishop, however, surprised the assembly by proposing that the Calonne program (with slight modifications) be adopted. He was now the king's advocate, not that of the Church (and in his heart, had been for reform all along).

Opposition was better organized than a month before. The demand for the Estates General, obliquely voiced earlier by Lafayette, was now bluntly presented. The most vocal proponents were among those who would later be called the "Patriot Party"—the Duke de La Rochefoucauld, Alexandre Lameth, the Duke d'Aiguillon (son of the famous governor of Brittany), Lafayette, of course, and some of the younger members of the Parlement of Paris, such as Adrien Duport and Hérault de Séchelles. Duport, more radical than the others, insisted that France must have a written constitution. All reforms were voted down, and Brienne dismissed the assembly.

Among the nobles and clergy—liberal and conservative alike—the universal demand became the calling of the Estates General. This is understandable only if it is realized that the traditional "parliament" had always been controlled by the nobility and church hierarchy (their noble cousins). This was so because there were three houses—one for each estate—each of which voted separately as a house and cast a single vote to decide issues. Thus the First and Second Estates could always outvote the Third, two to one.

In July 1787, Brienne asked the Parlement of Paris to register Calonne's *subvention territoriale*, taxing all three estates. The court refused and called for the Estates General. The edict was registered in August 1787 by *lit de justice*, but the demand for the Estates General was repeated to the king's face. Moreover, the next day the decree was declared null and void by the Parlement. The king exiled the *parlementaires* from Paris but quickly approved a compromise that allowed them to return. Brienne killed the *subvention territoriale* in return for the renewal of two *vingtièmes*, which, of course, the nobles and clergy did not pay. In November 1787 the Parlement refused to legalize loans for the next five years. It was called into *lit de justice* in its highest form, the Court of Peers (*Cour des Pairs*), which included princes and peers as well as judges. The Duke d'Orléans, the king's cousin, made bold to tell Louis that his edict was illegal. The king lost his temper. "It is legal because it is my will," he snarled, and the edict was registered. The next day Orléans and two leading judges were exiled from Paris.

Louis ordered plans drawn to suppress the Parlement of Paris and to reorganize others (in the manner of Maupeou under Louis XV).[4] Meanwhile, Brienne sought to reduce the power of provincial *parlements* by resurrecting provincial estates. Time was running against him, however. His most notable success was in Dauphiné and there the estates served to multiply the king's problems.[5]

---

[4] See p. 40. above.

[5] Brienne effected other liberal reforms, including granting Protestants the right to worship privately and the status of royal subjects. (See p. 90.) This had little to do with the central issue, however, unless one takes the far-fetched position that he was trying to better France's image among Protestant bankers in the Netherlands and Switzerland.

Court reform was delayed, which gave time for the nobility, the *parlementaires* in the vanguard, to organize its campaign for convening the Estates General. Nevertheless, but for severe economic conditions, the king might have prevailed. The causes were at base natural, but Brienne freed the grain trade and thus got the blame. In the fall of 1787 there were localized food shortages and the government could not import supplies fast enough to meet the need. In the spring of 1788, rains and hail ruined the crops and widespread hunger ensued. There were urban and rural bread riots—more severe in the countryside where the peasants were levied upon to feed the cities. Under such conditions, rumors of royal plans for taxes made it easy for the *parlements* to gain public support by publicizing their record of opposition to taxation. Few analyzed the judges' motives. They were against new taxes; the people were always against new taxes; hence, the judges protected the people. The *parlements* continually demanded the Estates General.

In May 1788 the king adjourned the Parlement of Paris pending reform of the courts. The provincial *parlements* protested, more so when they found that their powers were to be reduced. Some parlementaires were ordered into exile. In Rennes, days of rioting were inspired by the Parlement of Brittany and the noble-controlled Estates. There were disturbances in Toulouse, Dijon, Pau, and other cities. Grenoble defended its parlement in a "Day of Tiles," with the populace hurling shingles at the king's troops from rooftops. Disorders spread to the countryside.

The king's troops marched and countermarched to troublespots throughout France, restoring order. Busy in the spring, they were driven to exhaustion during the summer. Even in elite units, discipline began to deteriorate; others became undependable, and a few downright mutinous.

In June 1788 the Assembly of the Clergy met, voted the king an insultingly small *don gratuit*, and called for the Estates General. Some intendants and many peers recommended the same. The resurrected Estates of Dauphiné met at Vizille—an unusual assembly because Brienne had allowed double representation of the Third Estate and *vote-by-head*. This group was dominated by municipal deputies, and it, too, demanded the Estates General.

In August 1788 the king announced that he would call the Estates General in May 1789. At month's end he replaced Loménie de Brienne with Necker. In September he "suspended" court reforms and restored the *parlements*. The king had surrendered to his nobility and the only chance of retaining his traditional authority now lay in assembling an Estates General favorable to him.

The nobility and church hierarchy had forced the king's hand and set the stage for the Revolution. This is a great irony. No one, of course, anticipated the cataclysm to come. Only a liberal minority wanted more than to reassert the ancient role of the Estates. The conservative aristocracy expected to control the body, demonstrate its power, and chasten the king; it had no inkling that its privileges would be affected—beyond perhaps "freely granted" minor tax concessions. That seemed assured when the Parlement of Paris, in September 1788, ruled that the Estates General must be formed as in 1614, with clergy, nobles, and commoners sitting separately and voting on issues as estates.

DOUBLING THE THIRD

The reactionary decision of the Paris *parlement* on the composition of the Estates outraged the public and broke the coalition between conservative and liberal nobles and clergy. The liberals insisted that the Third Estate deserved as many delegates as the other two combined, which implied vote-by-head, or it would be meaningless. "Doubling the Third" quickly became *the* subject of discussion in academies, Masonic lodges, and *sociétés de pensée*. The "Patriot Party" organized a campaign in favor of the measure, for which the "Committee of Thirty" set the tone. The Thirty were organized by a young *parlementaire*, Adrien Duport and included the Marquis de Lafayette, the Marquis de Condorcet, the Count de Mirabeau, the Duke de Rochefoucauld, the Lameth brothers, Talleyrand, the Abbé Sieyès—mostly nobles and high clergy. (Even Sieyès was a vicar-general, or substitute bishop). The few identifiable members of the middle class were very rich Parisians. The Thirty wrote, financed, or inspired pamphlets by the thousands, of which Sieyès' *What is the Third Estate?* became most famous. Responding to this barrage of hostility, the Parlement of Paris reversed its decision (December 1788) that voting would be by estate, but to little avail. Its popularity was permanently lost.

Meanwhile, the king, in November 1788, recalled the Assembly of Notables to advise him on the composition and selection of the Estates General. Among other issues, the notables considered "doubling the Third" and voted against it. The king, however, on the advice of Necker, authorized doubling anyway. But he said nothing about voting. The public was left to assume what it liked, and, quite naturally, the Third Estate anticipated that there would be vote-by-head, which would mean that with a few votes from the other orders, the Third would dominate the Estates. In fact, the king had approved doubling the Third to frighten the privileged orders. He had no intention of allowing the commoners to control the assembly.

It seems curious today that the Patriots did not demand *more* than one-half the delegates for the Third. Sieyès had asked "What is the Third Estate?" and answered "Everything." Why then did the Thirty not fight for a single-chamber assembly with 98 percent of the deputies from the Third? The answer is that they felt "doubling" was enough to win popular support without totally alienating the conservative aristocrats (the *majority*, after all) with whose support the king might cancel the meeting of the Estates altogether. Moreover, a larger Third might reflect peasant opinion, which was conservative. Neither the Thirty nor the leaders of the Third at large were democrats. They wanted a delegation with a strong voice, but small enough to be dominated by "enlightened," educated men, who, with the cooperation of fellow spirits in the First and Second Estates, could effect reforms. Beyond that, their program remained to be formulated.

THE ELECTIONS

Barentin, the king's Keeper of the Seals, conducted research on previous Estates General, and produced information on protocol and procedure. As to elections, however, no rules were discernible—in fact there had been none, except among the elite of the three orders. The king was left to decide how the deputies would be selected, and he chose an astonishingly democratic procedure (for that time).

The vote was given to virtually all male adults[6]: commoners age twenty-five or over and on the tax rolls; nobles age twenty-five or over holding hereditary titles; clergy without regard to age. Minors and women holding fiefs (feudal lands) could vote by proxy.

In most of France, ballots were cast in some 250 constituencies, comprising existing judicial districts (*bailliages* or *sénéchaussées*) or groups of districts. In each constituency, each estate sent delegates to a "general assembly" in the chief city. Nobles chose their delegates directly, as did the clergy (except for monks, friars, and others in orders, who voted through representatives). Commoners voted in village and town "primary assemblies" for representatives to intermediate assemblies, which then picked delegates (sometimes in two stages) to the general assembly.

At the general assembly of the constituency, the estates, voting separately, chose deputies to the Estates General—normally four, that is, one noble, one cleric, and two representatives of the Third. However, the assemblies that met in the larger cities were allowed more. Bordeaux, Bourges, Lyons, Nîmes, Tours, and Toulouse each elected sixteen. Paris, designated a separate constituency, was allotted forty deputies for the city proper and twenty-four for the suburbs. The city's masses, though, were disenfranchised by high property qualifications.[7] This reflected the crown's fear of Paris, but the election in general reflected Louis' extraordinary faith in the people.

Louis XVI truly wanted to hear the popular voice. His liberal arrangements were not altogether based on that fact, however. He believed that rural France was monarchist (in that he was right) and would return deputies favorable to his tax proposals. He counted on the control of the First Estate by the priests and of the Second Estate by provincial nobles, traditionally the most loyal to the crown. The king calculated rightly on the composition of the First and Second Estates,

---

[6] Actors, bankrupts, felons, servants, and a few others were excluded.

[7] For a commoner to vote in Paris he had to pay a tax of not less than six *livres*—or be a university graduate, an official, a master workman, or hold a "position of trust" (*commission ou emploi*).

but not on the Third. Neither did he dream that his trusted curés would help the Third destroy the three-house organization.

The elections returned 578 deputies from the Third and seventy alternates who subsequently took seats. The label of "bourgeois" usually supplied to these 648 men[8] is not inaccurate. There were only seventy-six businessmen, eight manufacturers, and one banker. By contrast, there were 278 royal officeholders, many of whom were *procureurs, avocats*, and the like—that is, lawyers—and 166 additional lawyers who listed no office, but may have had one. As we have seen, however, the French bourgeoisie consisted heavily of officeholders or office seekers. Among the remaining 119 were five nobles, four clergymen, four non-noble army officers, and eighty-one landed proprietors—"rural bourgeoisie"—plus a scattering of doctors, scientists, writers, and others. The Third had selected a majority of vocal officials and lawyers, but no workers or peasants. The First and Second Estates each returned about 300 members. The clergy had a vast majority of curés and only forty-six bishops, including known liberals such as Talleyrand and Champion de Cicé. Among the nobles were ninety identifiable liberals, including Lafayette and Adrien Duport.

THE CAHIERS

To provide the government with a guide as to how it might satisfy public demands as well as solve its own problems, Louis XVI commanded the preparation of *cahiers de doléances* (bills of grievances and requests). *Cahiers* were to be prepared by electors of each estate at every level. Based on these, the district assemblies were supposed to produce "general" *cahiers* for each estate. Many parish, town, and intermediate assemblies sent no *cahiers* forward. In all, however, some 60,000 were written. Most constituencies sent general *cahiers* to Versailles, and some sent extra ones from lower assemblies. Paris sent one from each estate and another from the City Council. Some provincial estates also sent *cahiers*. In the end, some 600 *cahiers* reached the king, who had them carefully analyzed.

Actually, we now know that they were a poor gauge of the public temper. These *cahiers* were not syntheses of those of lower assemblies, but generally represented the thinking of the most literate and politically aware men in the constituencies.[9] In a representative sample from Paris and areas with heavy urban population 100 percent of the general *cahiers* asked that a constitution be "fixed," or "determined" (not that one be *written*, however); 90 to 100 percent mentioned individual rights; and 100 percent called for regular meetings of the Estates General and no taxation without its consent. Among the "particular" *cahiers*,

---

[8] This is the number identified by Alfred Cobban, *Aspects of the French Revolution* (New York, 1968), p. 110.

[9] All figures are based on an analysis of 741 *cahiers* of the Third by George V. Taylor.

(those written at the grassroots level), only those of the Parisian sections showed support for such "radical" reforms.

Of the *cahiers* from rural parishes only 10 percent mentioned individual rights, and 33 percent called for regular meetings of the Estates General. The peasant *cahiers*, moreover, demonstrated an astonishing apathy regarding the feudal system. Only 4 percent asked for the abolition of seigneurial property, usually with indemnity, 21 percent asked for the abolition of the *banalités*, and 8 percent mentioned other dues. Hunting rights and pigeon hutches drew the most fury, but only 46 percent demanded abolition.

On some matters, however, there was general agreement. Most notably, equality of taxation, demanded by 100 percent of the general *cahiers*, got the support of 89 percent of the Paris sections and 77 percent of the peasant assemblies. None of the *cahiers*, general or particular, even hinted at abolition of the monarchy or nobility. Only the most glaring abuses of the Church (for example, plurality of office) received emphasis in the general *cahiers*. There was a heavy peasant demand for fixed salaries for curés.

This simply means that the representatives of the Third who went to Versailles were much more radical than the French populace in general.

THE ESTATES GENERAL

The deputies to the Estates General assembled at Versailles on 2 May 1789, a Saturday. The king received them in the famous Hall of Mirrors, greeting each personally—a process which consumed nine hours.

On Monday, 4 May, the splendid death march of the Old Regime occurred. It was a spectacle the like of which would not be seen again in France. The Estates General assembled at Notre Dame to hear the *Veni Creator*, where the king and queen entered to the sound of trumpets, fifes, and drums, and were enthroned, each amid a glittering entourage of lords and ladies, before the choir screen, hung with cloth of gold. After the service, the deputies marched in procession to the Church of Saint Louis, escorted by Swiss and French guard cavalry, along a route lined with troops in colorful uniforms. The clergy led—two by two—in their magnificent vestments, followed by the gilded carriages of the royal party, escorted by Gardes-du-Corps. Then came the nobles, in black velvet and ermine, with plumed caps and ceremonial swords, and finally the Third, in drab black. Bands played. A quarter of a million people lined the route and watched from windows of buildings draped with tapestries.

At the Church of Saint Louis, built by Louis XIV and dedicated to his saintly predecessor, mass was celebrated, there was a sermon and a singing of the *Te Deum*, a ritual reserved for the celebration of great events. The king endured it all well, except the sermon, which lasted two hours; Louis went to sleep. He wakened with the *Te Deum*, however, and as the ceremony ended, all seemed to have begun well.

On 5 May 1789, the first regular session of the Estates General was held in the Salle des Menus Plaisirs, a huge old structure with a hall that could seat all the members and with rooms where the estates could meet separately.[10] The king spoke first, assuming a fatherly posture and warning the deputies against impulsive behavior and stirring up public opinion. He then left clarification of his views to Barentin, Keeper of the Seals, but the minister only mouthed more platitudes about responsible action.

Necker, impatiently awaited, came next, but his message was disappointing— if interminable. His voice gave out, and the speech was finished by a reader. He analyzed the royal budget, line by line, and admitted a deficit of 6,000,000 livres. The Estates expected legislative proposals to follow, but none came. Instead, Necker described his complex financial operations and seemed to ask only to continue "under the patronage of the people." Toward the end, he praised the judgment of the king and expressed the hope that the Estates would soon arrive at a consensus which the monarch could support. By implication, if the body did not reach a reasonable unanimity of opinion quickly, the king would have to act on his own. However interpreted, the statement was much more reactionary than had been expected from Necker. He seemed to be saying "Give me your support, recommend something, and go away."

In short, neither the king nor Necker provided the leadership expected by the Estates. They offered no program on which the deputies could act. This was a shocking disappointment, especially to the Third. During the excitement of elections and debates over the *cahiers*, the commoners had worked themselves into a state of euphoric optimism over the "new day" that was dawning in France. They had come to Versailles eager to cooperate with the crown in giving the nation new life, only to be met with stiff ceremony, double-talk, and indifference. Louis XVI had missed a great opportunity. After the opening session, the deputies increasingly turned away from him and looked for leadership within their own ranks.

THE THIRD ORGANIZES To the outrage of the Third, it became apparent that the three estates were expected to meet and vote separately. The First and Second proceeded to organize officially, but not the Third. The members refused to present their credentials merely as deputies of the Third, but, instead, insisted on being certified to the entire Estates General—the "National Assembly." Meanwhile, they met unofficially, and on 6 May passed a resolution refusing to recognize the three-estate organization. The nobles responded by voting 141 to 47 for separate houses. The clergy also affirmed tradition, but by the narrow margin of 133 to 114. The Estates General was deadlocked and could conduct no business; it remained this way for six weeks.

---

[10] This building was torn down in the fall of 1789 and is the only one at Versailles made famous by the Revolution which may no longer be visited. In Paris there are a number which no longer exist, as will be noted later.

By conceding to the Third on credentials (a technical matter) the king might have tamed the Estates. But he did nothing, and the radicals were able to build support for a single-house assembly which would decide everything. More important, they convinced the Third and many members of the other estates that France should have a *written* constitution, something few had conceived of before the Estates convened.

Among the leaders of the Third, the most spectacular orator was the Count de Mirabeau, who had abandoned his title. Huge, ugly, and fat, with a pockmarked face and a wild mane of hair, he had a reputation to match. In his youth he had been imprisoned (at his father's request) for dueling and debauchery and was still a womanizer. He was a brilliant writer, however, and as a speaker was thunderous, persuasive, and awesome. "When I shake my terrible head, no one dares interrupt me." Quieter, but a better politician, was the Abbé Sieyès, a handsome, poised strategist destined to figure in every phase of the Revolution. Finally, there was Jean-Sylvain Bailly, a noted astronomer and sometime royal official. Aristocratic in bearing, respected, and articulate, he was at this time the perfect figurehead for the Third. All three represented the opinions expressed in the radical *cahiers* of Paris.

Meeting undisturbed, the Third steadily gained confidence. It took heart from the First Estate, where the curés increasingly defied the conservative bishops, to whom they had initially deferred. When on 10 June the Third invited the other estates to meet with it to validate credentials, the nobles were unmoved, but the clergy debated angrily. The bishops were able to keep the order separate by parliamentary maneuvers (declaring no quorum, and the like). By this time some 100 "unionist" curés and some liberal bishops, led by the Abbé Grégoire, were holding nightly caucuses. On 13 June, three *curés* joined the Third, on 14 June, six more, including Grégoire, and on 16 June, ten more.

On 17 June, sure of its power, the Third Estate declared itself the National Assembly of France and invited the other estates to join it— not merely to validate credentials, but to assist the "representatives of the Major Part of the Nation" (Mirabeau) in legislating for the people. On 19 June the clergy, despite a walkout by die-hard bishops, voted 153 to 137 to join the National Assembly. The assembly meanwhile proclaimed to the people that they should continue to pay taxes, "however illegal," but should stop paying if their representatives were interfered with. This was meant to reinforce the assembly's hand against the king and was also an open invitation for many to evade all levies and to defy authority in general. This contributed to the disorder in the country during the next few months.

The king did not react immediately. The dauphin (heir to the throne) had died on 4 June at age seven and Louis was in mourning.

TENNIS COURT OATH   On 20 June the deputies of the Third arrived at the Salle des Menus Plaisirs to find the doors locked and a proclamation posted that the hall was closed for preparations for a royal session on 22 June. It was drizzling rain, therefore they made for shelter in an indoor tennis court nearby. Thus the defiant proclamation which they framed has gone down in history as the "Tennis Court Oath." It was read from an improvised platform by Bailly, the president of the "National Assembly." It declared that the National Assembly had been called to "establish the constitution of the Kingdom . . . and maintain the true principles of monarchy. . . . " (That this was questionable did not matter at all.) It pledged the deputies to continue to convene "whenever circumstances require" until "the constitution of the Kingdom is established." Damp and bedraggled, but exultant, the deputies swore orally and then pressed forward to sign the oath. Only one wrote "opposed" before his signature (and was almost lynched).[11]

A positive step toward revolution had been taken. Most of the delegates had come to Versailles bearing *cahiers* that said nothing about producing a written constitution. Now they were committed to do so, even if the task took months, or years. While it was done, as their previous proclamations had made clear, they expected the National Assembly to act as an interim legislature. If their will prevailed, Louis XVI would become a *de facto* constitutional monarch immediately.

ROYAL SESSION At the king's court, a battle raged between Necker's party and that of the queen. Necker proposed that the king announce partial abolition of noble tax privileges and allow voting by head on taxes and on some constitutional matters. The queen's party won the day, however, and the proposals the king decided on were restricted. Necker decided to absent himself from the royal session.

On 23 June the royal session assembled.[12] The king pronounced that the Estates consisted of three orders. Nevertheless, he authorized them to meet together and to vote by head on matters *not affecting the privileges* of the clergy and nobles. Any decision so made could be vetoed, however, by a two-thirds vote of *one order*. Without these provisos, the king's offer would have been fairly generous. He agreed to: (1) no taxation without the consent of the Estates (he would not use the word "Assembly") except in an emergency, and that vote on taxes would be by head; (2) equality of taxation; (3) modification of hunting rights; (4) liberty of the press; (s) abolition of *lettres de cachet*;[13] (6) abolition of serfdom; (7) creation of new provincial assemblies.

The king was standing pat, in effect, except on taxation, the problems of which had forced him to call the Estates. On hunting rights, he was unspecific.

---

[11] In 1788, Malesherbes had proposed to the king that he issue a constitution to avoid the possible embarrassment of having the Estates General force one on him. Necker had made a similar proposal in May 1789, suggesting a constitution on the British model providing for a chamber of peers and a chamber of deputies. Louis XVI turned a deaf ear. Ironically, the document much resembled that proclaimed by Louis XVIII in 1814 after the fall of Napoleon.

[12] Delayed a day for the removal of spectator seating.

[13] Arrest orders requiring only the king's signature.

The *lettres de cachet* had virtually gone out of use anyway; they had in recent years been issued largely at the request of families to incarcerate misbehaving or deranged members in prisons or asylums. The king had abolished serfdom on the royal lands in 1779, and most nobles had followed his example (though there were perhaps 1,000,000, mostly on church lands in the Franche Comté and Nivernais).[14] He had authorized Necker and Brienne, in turn, to create provincial estates in 1778 and 1787.

Nevertheless, Louis XVI felt he had made enormous concessions. He asked the deputies to limit their zeal and to remember that "never has a king done so much for any nation [as I have]." The Third, however, was too deeply committed to greater things. Moreover, the day before, 120 of the clergy had joined the Third (National Assembly).

The king and the majority of the nobles and clergy left the hall. The Third estate sat as if stunned, but the leaders quickly took control. "Remember your duty to 25,000,000 Frenchmen," thundered Mirabeau. The young Master of Ceremonies, the Marquis de Dreux-Brézé, pounded his staff and said mildly "Gentlemen, you have heard the king's order [to adjourn]." "We shall not move . . . except at the point of the bayonet," Mirabeau shot back. Bailly then informed the Master of Ceremonies that the National Assembly had decided beforehand to sit. "Is that the reply that I am to give to His Majesty?" asked the Marquis. "It is," replied Bailly. "No one can dictate to the assembled nation."

THE REVOLUTION BEGINS

The Revolution had begun. The king, however, displayed only irritation. "*Foutre*! Let them sit," he snapped at clamoring courtiers. Though his will had clearly been defied, he made no move to recover control of the Estates. Again, his indecisiveness helped the Third. On 24 June a majority of the clergy went over to the National Assembly. The next day, forty-seven nobles followed, led by the Duke d'Orléans. On 27 June, Louis ordered "my loyal clergy and nobility" to join the National Assembly.

The king had apparently capitulated—actually not. Marie Antoinette had said it: "*Il faut des troupes*." Troops were on the way.

---

[14] Contemporary estimates ranged from 140,000 to 1,500,000. Marcel Marion says 140,000; Henri Sée, 1,000,000; Soboul 1,000,000; Godechot, *Institutions*, p. 50, says 1,500,000.

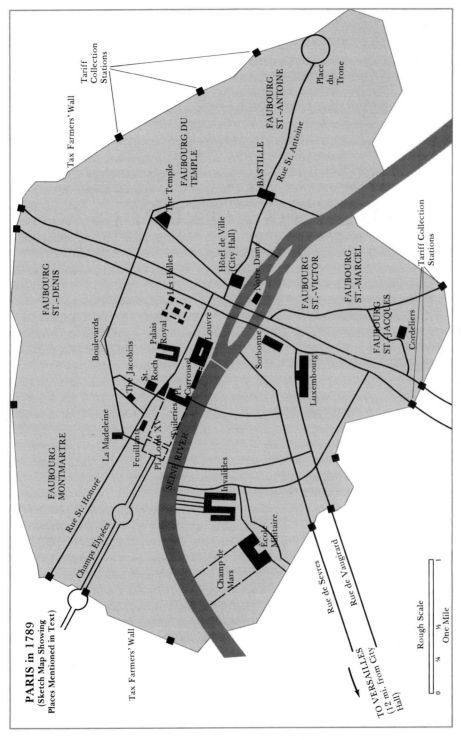

PARIS in 1789
(Sketch Map Showing Places Mentioned in Text)

FAUBOURG MONTMARTRE

FAUBOURG ST.-DENIS

Tax Farmers' Wall

Rue St. Honoré

La Madeleine

Boulevards

The Jacobins

St. Roch

Palais Royal

Les Halles

The Temple

FAUBOURG DU TEMPLE

Tariff Collection Stations

Feuillants

Pl. Louis XV

Tuileries

Pl. Carrousel

Louvre

SEINE RIVER

Hôtel de Ville (City Hall)

BASTILLE

FAUBOURG ST.-ANTOINE

Rue St. Antoine

Place du Trone

Champs Elysées

Invalides

École Militaire

Champ de Mars

Sorbonne

Notre Dame

FAUBOURG ST.-VICTOR

Luxembourg

FAUBOURG ST.-MARCEL

FAUBOURG ST.-JACQUES

Cordeliers

Tariff Collection Stations

Rue de Sevres

Rue de Vaugirard

Tax Farmers' Wall

TO VERSAILLES (12 mi. from City Hall)

Rough Scale

0   ¼   ½   1
One Mile

Map 3.1

I well know that M. de La Fayette wants to save us,
but who will save us from M. de La Fayette?
—*Marie Antoinette*

THE YEARS OF LAFAYETTE
(1789–1791)

Between 22 June and 1 July 1789, Louis XVI ordered some 20,000 troops, mostly Swiss and German mercenaries, from provincial garrisons to Paris. By 13 July, with units already present, he expected to have 30,000 men at his disposal. Command was given to a Swiss general, the Baron Besenval, who was instructed to maintain order in Paris, where as yet no great disorder existed. Nevertheless, the capital was the only source of possible interference with the king's will and had to be sealed off. More important, for any action against the National Assembly to be effective, Paris had to be kept quiet. If it appeared that the king had lost control of the capital, the rest of France might fall into anarchy. Paris had overwhelming importance in the minds of Frenchmen.

PARIS ETERNAL AND IN 1789

Possession of Paris was historically imperative for French rulers. The red-bearded Henry IV, "most French of French kings," had converted from Protestant to Catholic to secure the capital. Louis XIV was not truly king until Paris had been retaken from the *frondeurs*. To the French, he who held Paris, held France. This helps to explain much in the Revolution—why, for example, government after government—popular or not—generally got obedience in the provinces. It was a sort of reflex action.[1]

---

[1] Even in our century, this attitude toward Paris persists. In 1961, President Charles de Gaulle, threatened by a revolt of his generals in Algeria, fortified Paris. Since the main rebel divisions were paratroops, he was certain they would strike (if at all) at the capital.

74

Louis XIV had realized the power and fascination of Paris, but also that its crowds were dangerous. This was one reason he had built Versailles and moved his government there. During the eighteenth century, however, Paris had been friendly to the kings. Louis XVI did not fear the people—otherwise the course of the Revolution might have been different.

In the eyes of the French, Paris had been for centuries the hub of the world. True, the court was at Versailles, but it was only twelve miles from the Paris City Hall. Princes, peers, ministers, and cardinals of the church lived in Versailles or Paris. The capital was the center of politics and high society, which were tightly meshed under the Old Regime. Important to both (and to intellectual life) were the salons of the great ladies—most noble, some merely rich—held in mansions clustered in the suburbs of Paris nearest Versailles.

Paris was the home of the Académie Française, the Académies of Belles Lettres, Sciences, Painting and Sculpture, and Architecture, of the University of Paris and the École Militaire. It was the center of publishing, of *philosophie*, as well as of finance, commerce, and manufacturing. It was also the center of suffering. Its working class included the largest concentration of miserable people in France.

Visitors admired the great landmarks of Paris, most of which remain today. The spires of Notre Dame towered over the Île de la Cité. To the north was the Palace of the Louvre, and alongside, the Tuileries (destroyed in 1871) with its magnificent gardens. South of the Seine were the Hôtel des Invalides and the École Militaire with its parade ground, the Champ de Mars. Palaces of great noble houses such as that of Rohan-Soubise (now the National Archives), dotted the inner city. To the southeast, toward Versailles, the faubourgs were crowded with lavish townhouses.

Yet, Thompson quotes a British visitor who was not charmed by Paris. "It is the most ill-contrived, ill-built, dirty stinking town that can be possibly imagined. . . . As for the inhabitants, they are ten times more nasty than the inhabitants of Edinburgh." This man had seen the real Paris—the jammed central district, fanning to the north and east around Les Halles, the central market of Paris, from which in the warmer months the stench of the decaying blood and garbage reached even to the Louvre.

The Old City, within a circle about one mile in radius around the Île de la Cité, had perhaps 350,000 inhabitants (of 600,000 total), most of them on the north bank of the Seine. Workers lived there in tenements up to eight stories high, which shaded the narrow, cobblestone streets, perpetually wet as a sanitation measure and with gutters flowing with refuse and sewage. Conditions were little better in the working-class districts outside of the Old City, of which the largest was the Faubourg St.-Antoine, to the east. Whole families were jammed into single rooms with no sanitary facilities.

The crowded quarters literally forced people onto the streets when they were not working. On Sundays and holidays, in good weather, crowds filled the wide quais along the Seine and the streets, such as the Rue St.-Honoré, which led to the open areas near the palaces. Parisians, then as now, loved the Seine, where they swam, boated, and fished, unbothered by the fact that all the sewage of Paris flowed into it.

The thousands of workers were engaged in the food industry, glassmaking, tanning, paper making, the production of liqueurs, beer, and ale, and in fabricating shoes, clothing, and jewelry. Hundreds were servants. In addition, there was a floating population in normal times of around 50,000 people—professional beggars, police spies, thieves, prostitutes, and the like. In the summer of 1789, economic conditions added some 200,000 unemployed.

LAW AND ORDER   Although the Provost of Merchants nominally headed the Paris government, the real governor of Paris was the king's Lieutenant of Police, whose authority extended to everything relating to public order. The last lieutenant of Louis XV, Sartine, had provided the city with lighting—oil lamps on poles shaped like shepherds' crooks.[2] Le Noir, who served Louis XVI, had regularized the food supply by licensing grain merchants and bakers and by forcing the latter to bake a set amount of bread daily, all of which had to be sold or given away the same day.[3] For a decade before 1787, when grain supplies began to fail, the price of a four-pound loaf (family size) was kept at about nine sous (nine cents, U.S.), a price that a worker could afford. The Lieutenants of Police also controlled the city courts, which were the most efficient in France.

The police had been so effective that in 1789 a force of 1500 was considered adequate, though less than one-half were on duty at a given time. They did not carry firearms; some were not armed at all. Criminals returned the favor. The police could be reinforced by the Maréchaussée (mounted police) who patrolled the highways, but only a handful were assigned to Paris proper.

Also stationed in the capital was the Regiment called the Gardes Françaises (French Guards, 3600 men), a supposedly elite unit. The king had pampered these troops, however, and they were poorly disciplined and in the decade before 1789 had become identified with the city populace. Most of the men lived like civilians, reporting infrequently for training. Some had small businesses. Others, notably noncommissioned officers, profiteered in the Paris underground.

Versailles had one Swiss regiment, a few companies of Gardes-du-Corps, and the Royal Guard, composed of noble volunteers (membership was an honor). From Versailles, infantry could reach Paris in four or five hours, cavalry in about three.[4] Therefore, only the 1500 police and the 3600 men of the French Guards were available to handle an emergency.

The French Guards, however, proved themselves useless to the crown before the end of June 1789. News of the Tennis Court Oath (20 June) and succeeding

---

[2] The lamps were lowered on ropes to be lit, making the poles ready-made gallows. Hence the fearsome chant "To the lantern!" of the Revolution.

[3] Therefore, except in times of extreme shortage, the price went down as the day progressed.

[4] Infantry marched at about 2-1/2 miles per hour (the same as today). Cavalry horses had to be walked to Paris, or they would be ineffective on arrival.

events sparked minor disturbances. There were attacks on bakeries and wine-shops. Louis XVI ordered the French Guards to reinforce the police, but they let the people have their way at almost every encounter. On 28 June two whole companies laid down their arms and were wined and dined by the people at the Palais-Royal.

The Palais-Royal was the popular nerve center of Paris. Once a royal residence, it belonged in 1789 to the Duke d'Orléans, who had converted it into a complex of shops, cafés, restaurants, apartments, gambling houses, and the like. In its central square and in the cafés of the surrounding arcade, popular orators held forth. Here there was free speech, since the Palais was still royal property and the police could not interfere without Orléans' permission. News and rumors from Versailles flew quickly to the Palais Royal, and from there to the masses, who were extremely sensitive to any threat to the National Assembly. Somehow they expected the assembly to alleviate their miseries, a hope which probably had postponed widespread violence. Unemployment was at 50 percent; bread was at twenty sous per four-pound loaf (equal to a day's wages for the average worker), and the price was rising.

PARIS ERUPTS

Tension rose as troops from the provinces began arriving in Paris. In the first week in July, four Swiss regiments and the Royal German Cavalry were biv-ouacked on the Champ de Mars. More units, predominately foreign, appeared in the suburbs and nearby villages. Rumors flew. The troops were part of the aristocratic plot to starve Paris; the troops had been called to destroy the National Assembly; the nobles were about to kidnap the king and carry him to a frontier fortress, away from his people. (To most, the king was still "father of the people." His ministers were blamed for unpopular acts.)

If the mercenaries excited the people, however, they made the king more confident. On 11 July he dismissed the popular finance minister, Jacques Necker, and ordered him to leave France immediately. Necker departed, as did some timid members of the National Assembly.

News of Necker's dismissal reached Paris the next day and spread quickly. It was Sunday, and the streets were full of people. "To arms! To arms!" shouted Camille Desmoulins and other orators at the Palais-Royal. Defend Paris! Defend the National Assembly! Put on the green cockade (the color of Necker's livery). By midday the streets were full of marchers, carrying busts of Necker and the Duke d'Orléans (another "friend of the people"). Looting began, with gunshops the prime targets, but the police could not restore order.[5]

---

[5] There was a strict, long-standing law in Paris that prohibited owning or carrying arms of any sort, especially ones easily concealed on the person, including knives and daggers as well as pistols.

Late in the afternoon, General Besenval sent the Royal German Cavalry (300 horse) to disperse a mob in the Tuileries gardens. The people, however, were joined by a number of well-armed French Guards. The troopers hesitated, were surrounded and pommeled by the people, and finally withdrew. Disorder continued throughout the night of 12–13 July. Besenval ordered 9000 Swiss infantry to cross the Seine and to assist the Royal German Cavalry. In the darkness, however, the operation became very confused and by morning all the king's troops had withdrawn to the Champ de Mars.[6]

Meanwhile, on 12 July (the same Sunday) a few electors[7] had met at the Hôtel de Ville (City Hall) but could do little but vote to call all the electors (some 400) together. On 13 July the electors decreed formation of a militia, to be identified by a cockade of red and blue, the colors of Paris. The City Hall was besieged by volunteers, demanding arms. Jacques de Flesselles, the Provost of Merchants, gave out some 300 muskets stored there but could get no more. He was loudly accused of treachery by the crowd.

Flesselles had released arms reluctantly because he did not know who was getting them. The electors' intent was to arm trustworthy property holders who could take control of Paris, restore order, and destroy the king's rationale for keeping troops in the city. Such a legally constituted force would also give them bargaining power with the crown.

Building a militia required time, however. For the moment, therefore, many who were normally "rabid" proponents of law and order were backing the mobs. Necker's dismissal had alarmed the financial community, which feared government bankruptcy and the loss of investments. Bankers such as Laborde de Méréville, Boscary, and Dufresnoy were distributing money to the crowds. So was Delessert, who later claimed he had also turned his house into an arms factory. Until a strong militia could be organized these men were ready to risk property to prevent the triumph of the king's forces.

On 13 July, mobs destroyed most of the customs posts of Paris. They also attacked prisons (but none with dangerous inmates), freeing everyone and searching for arms. Thousands appeared before the Invalides, demanding muskets and shot, but royal troops were encamped nearby, and the governor was able to turn them away. Meanwhile, at the Monastery of St.-Lazare and other places, crowds seized hundreds of kegs and bottles of wine.

On 13 July, Paris was not only in fury, but roaring drunk. The same was true on the fateful Fourteenth.

---

[6] Besenval's orders were so incredible that some contemporaries accused him of treason. Instead of sending his regiments across the Seine by the bridges, he carried out a river crossing, as if on a field campaign, using available boats and ferries. This consumed a lot of time and resulted in the troops arriving piecemeal and disorganized.

[7] Those who had elected the deputies of Paris to the Estates General.

THE BASTILLE

At midmorning on 14 July, 80,000 people assailed the Invalides and appropriated 30,000 muskets. Royal troops stood by with loaded cannon but were never ordered to fire. The crowd moved to the City Hall, demanding powder and shot. Meanwhile, a huge mob was moving toward the Bastille, a massive fortress which stood (by accident) between central Paris and the workers' district of St.-Antoine.

The Bastille had been built in the 1300s to guard the city's eastern approaches, but since about 1660 had been a prison. The famous "man in the iron mask" (among others) had been incarcerated there by Louis XIV, who ordered the identity of prisoners kept secret, making the place more ominous. In the eighteenth century, however, it had housed fewer and fewer prisoners. Louis XVI considered the Bastille essentially useless and had long-standing plans to demolish it. The few arms there on 14 July were in the hands of the garrison. There were seven prisoners—five forgers and two insane persons held at the request of their families. But the Parisians were convinced that the Bastille held vast arms supplies and numerous prisoners. The crowd, nevertheless, approached fearfully, and with good reason.

The Bastille was a huge rectangle of solid rock around an inner court. Its eight towers, 90 feet high, were connected by walls which were 9 feet thick, or more. There were twelve rampart guns on the towers, and eighteen larger cannon at the middle and ground levels. The fortress had no windows, only barred slits and gun ports. The only way in was over two moats, both with drawbridges. The moats were empty, but nevertheless deep, formidable obstacles, though the first could be flanked over rooftops. Therefore the Bastille, given a small determined garrison, was virtually impregnable to attack even by a sizable military force, much less a mob.

The governor (commander) of the Bastille, Count de Launey, however, was an excitable and indecisive man.[8] His garrison consisted of eighty-two "invalids"—soldiers unfit for regular duty—recently augmented by thirty Swiss mercenaries. This force was probably sufficient, nevertheless, to defend the Bastille. But the decision to fight had to be de Launey's. He had no positive orders from the king or Besenval.

By 10 A.M., thousands of people swarmed the streets near the Bastille, but showed little inclination to attack.[9] De Launey ordered the drawbridges raised and waited. At 10:30, a delegation was admitted from City Hall and dined with the governor. De Launey was persuaded that he could quiet the crowds by withdrawing his cannon from firing position, which he did. The electors departed happy at the governor's nonbelligerent attitude, but could not get the word to the milling, noisy crowd outside. A delegation from the local district was let

[8] The name is spelled Launay in many records and subsequent histories.

[9] Lists made later of the "conquerers of the Bastille" show that only 954, at most, participated in the final "assault." The first list had only 662 names.

in next and demanded that the Bastille be turned over to the citizens' militia. De Launey refused, but promised that he would not fire unless fired upon. When this group left, some of the people began sniping at the fortress. A few daredevils went across the rooftops and cut the chains to the first drawbridge. The crowd surged across and to the second moat. Beyond its raised drawbridge was the gate of the Bastille. Two delegations arrived in town from the City Hall, but the crowd was so close that de Launey could not let them in.

The people kept sniping; the garrison began to return fire with small arms. Lieutenant Deflue, commanding the thirty Swiss, had holes cut in the fortress gate so that he could fire cannon through it if the mob got the drawbridge down. At about the same time, the people suddenly found leaders. One Hulin, a former soldier, arrived with 100 French Guards and two cannon and also Lieutenant Elie, of the Queen's Infantry Regiment, a veteran of forty-one, recently promoted from the ranks. Elie and Hulin brought the two cannon up before the fortress gate and prepared to try to blow it down.

Inside, the Count de Launey was beside himself. His veterans were urging him to surrender. Lieutenant Deflue was demanding that he fight. At about 5:00 P.M. he wrote a note, which Deflue passed to a man standing on a plank extended over the moat, who then passed it to Lieutenant Elie. In it the governor asked to be allowed to capitulate "with honor" (march out free with his men). He got no reply, but apparently assumed that his terms had been accepted. About 5:30, de Launey ordered the drawbridge dropped and the crowd poured into the Bastille. No one was killed in the final "assault." There was no massacre of the defenders either. The governor and garrison were arrested and escorted toward the City Hall. Enroute, the mob killed three officers and three veterans, and at the steps of the Hôtel de Ville, hacked de Launey to death, put his head on a pike and paraded it about. That was all.[10]

It was a strange victory. The Bastille fell, but it had not been taken. As Michelet put it, "It surrendered. It suffered from a bad conscience." Less romantically phrased, it fell because its commander had not used his weapons. If he had given the order to open fire with the Bastille's cannon, the people surely would have had no chance. To the Parisians, however, it mattered only that a great symbol of tyranny had fallen. They celebrated wildly, and in their enthusiasm began leveling the fortress, stone by stone.[11]

Victory of the people or not, the taking of the Bastille had concrete and immediate results. The king restored Necker to office. On 16 July, Louis himself "joined the victors" in Paris. He was received on the steps at the Hôtel de Ville

---

[10] Earlier in the day, however, random fire had killed eighty-two people and one soldier. The mob also killed Provost Flesselles as he left the City Hall, presumably in the belief that he had denied the people arms earlier in the day.

[11] The voluntary effort faltered, but commercial companies finished the job and made a good thing of selling the locks, chains, keys, and even stone. Americans should remember that the Bastille no longer exists. It is a standing joke among Parisians that they always ask to see it. Some taxi drivers regularly oblige them.

by Bailly, recently made mayor by the electors of Paris. To thunderous applause, the king donned the blue and red cockade of the Paris militia.[12] He had already ordered his troops back to their distant garrisons, removing any threat to the National Assembly.

In addition, Louis XVI legalized the Paris militia, which became the National Guard. Throughout France, cities and towns formed similar units of citizen-soldiers and "federated" to cooperate with each other. (Thus National Guardsmen were also referred to as *fédérés*.) Within a few months the National Guard had become a national army responsive more to the National Assembly than to the king. In Paris the commander was the Marquis de Lafayette, "the Hero of two Worlds." This dapper, vain soldier of thirty-two was well aware that this office gave him greater political prominence and power.[13]

MUNICIPAL REVOLUTIONS

There were revolutions in cities and towns throughout France in July and August. Some were triggered by bread shortages, others by fear of an "aristocratic plot" against the Revolution, and still others directly by events in Paris. All, however, resulted in the assertion of local authority against the king's officials. Most of the royal intendants "abdicated" and fled, and most of the parlements were dissolved. The tax collection system was left in shambles. In Strasbourg the city council was ejected by force and a revolutionary one installed; in Toulouse the old council maintained itself by assuming a revolutionary posture. In Lyons there were two upheavals: the first removed the old council and the second, in effect, replaced it.

In all cities a broader segment of the bourgeoisie gained a voice in government and that of the aristocratic element was reduced or nullified. There were some concessions to the proletariat, most pronounced in Rennes (Brittany) and Caen (Normandy) where severe laws were imposed to insure bread supplies and to keep prices down. All cities created National Guards. In Toulouse and Aix, they were nothing more than reorganized traditional militia. In most places, however, for example, Strasbourg in the north and Marseilles in the south, they were forces of the militant antiaristocratic, anticlerical bourgeoisie and upper-artisan classes. Some guardsmen got into politics early, as in Angers, where the guard ousted the council that had formed it and installed a more revolutionary one.

---

[12] In a short time, white, the color of the Bourbon dynasty was added to form red, white and blue of the "New Regime"—in time the tricolor of the Revolution.

[13] In commenting on this fact later, however, he vowed that he had wanted command only so as to use the guard as a mediating force between ultraroyalists and destructive radicals.

The municipal revolutions served to consolidate the power of the cities behind the Revolution. In the west, especially, they served to heighten the tension that already existed between town and country. (The peasants perennially felt they were exploited by the city folk.) These were the areas where counterrevolution would take hold later—Brittany, southern Normandy, Anjou, and Poitou (which included the later department of the Vendée). The city movements were applauded by the National Assembly, but the destruction of the royal centralized machinery of government demanded that the new legislative power replace it, and quickly.

THE GREAT FEAR

Apparently in support of Paris, violence also swept the countryside in July 1789. From Alsace, the Franche Comté, Dauphiné, Lorraine, Picardy, and Provence, it moved steadily westward. Here and there peasants marched on châteaux of lords, demanding the abolition of feudal dues. Often they burned feudal records and sometimes the châteaux as well. In other areas they attacked grain warehouses and bakeries, fixing prices or simply taking supplies. Some grain convoys were looted. Carriages of aristocrats were held up on the highways and robbed, with an occasional killing.

Contrary to appearances, however, the movement had little to do with events in Paris. It had begun months before as a series of traditional bread riots.

By decrees of January and April 1789, the king had authorized bonuses on imported grain to relieve the food shortage. Speculators responded by buying up French grain, smuggling it out of the country, and re-importing it at the bonus price. Meanwhile, royal procurers began to buy heavily in northern France to supply Paris. Thus in rich grain-producing areas, local supplies were depleted and prices rose. Processions of peasants, often led by women, "visited" proprietors, requisitioning grain. Mobs formed in provincial cities, demanding grain at a "just price." The mayors called frantically for the king's troops, who wore themselves out marching and countermarching, usually to little avail.

Meanwhile, elections were held for the Estates General and the *cahiers* were prepared. Though the peasants themselves only mildly protested against feudal abuses, they heard of protests from other quarters. (See above, p. 67f.) They came to expect immediate abolition of dues, at least. By July, the whole of eastern and northern France was in uproar. Respectable peasants refused to pay their dues, and some even joined the march on châteaux. Their example inspired crowds of landless workers (and professional bandits). Overall, however, *hunger* remained the root motivation. News from Versailles, however, which put the king's power in doubt, surely promoted lawlessness.

Old hatreds also came to the fore. In Alsace the property of Jews was attacked. One bandit chief masqueraded as the Count d'Artois (brother of the king) and issued "royal" proclamations canceling peasant debts and confiscating Jewish property. It took the king's troops two months to destroy this band.

Ecclesiastical as well as lay lords were assailed. In July the bishop of Mâcon, in Burgundy, was surrounded in his country palace by hordes of peasants. He asked them for a *cahier* stating their grievances. Astonishingly, they agreed, withdrew, and returned two days later to present the document. They demanded that the bishop distribute funds for charity, including royal funds. "Some five years ago, our King gave a considerable sum for all France, . . . but none of the poor have received a cent [sol]." They asked further that feudal records be burned. And as to feudal dues, they were blunt. "Monseigneur, . . . we have paid you all that we are going to." The bishop met the demands, and his properties were left undamaged.

As the violence spread across France, its force diminished. In most villages talk of action gave way to mass hysteria. The word spread that bandits were coming to destroy homes and to seize food. Supposedly, they were in the pay of the nobles who were determined to preserve their prerogatives by starving the peasants (a version of the "aristocratic plot" theme, recurrent in hard times for centuries). In town after town the inhabitants shut themselves inside their houses and merely waited. By the end of August 1789, it was over. The king's troops and mounted police, aided by the bourgeois militia of larger towns and cities, had reestablished order.

The final accounting was such that "The Great Fear" has become the standard designation of the peasant movement. Grain merchants suffered more losses than aristocrats. Most peasants had spent most of the period quailing inside their huts. The incidence of destruction of châteaux and other property was relatively small.

During the summer of 1789, however, hardly anyone at Versailles doubted that the peasants had joined Paris in the Revolution.

THE NIGHT OF 4 AUGUST

To the liberal members of the National Assembly, organized in the Breton Club,[14] the time was ripe to strike at feudalism. For maximum impact on the aristocracy, they appointed as their spokesman the Duke d'Aiguillon, one of the richest landholders in France who on 4 August was to propose abolition of rights and dues. The duke was upstaged, but the proposal was made by another high noble, the young Viscount de Noailles, a veteran of the American Revolution.

---

[14] The Breton Club, organized by delegates from Brittany, had many noble and clerical members, including Lafayette and Sieyès. It later became the Jacobin Club (see p. 89, below), and as such gradually became more radical and was abandoned by most of the early leaders.

The effect was astounding. In an all-night session, the aristocrats seemed to be vying with each other to sacrifice their rights. Debate centered on *how* dues and rights should be abolished. Hardly a voice was raised against the proposition. At dawn the assembly passed a resolution renouncing feudal rights, "pure and simple," and adjourned in a mood of exaltation. It appeared that all forms of inequality had been struck dead in a single night.

On 11 August, however, when the detailed law was passed, abolition was not so "pure and simple." Serfdom was abolished, and all dues derived therefrom, without indemnity, along with the tithe of the Church. In fact, this meant that lay lords would lose only minor revenues, for example, from the *banalités*; otherwise they were deprived only of nonincome producing rights—judicial, hunting, pigeon-keeping, and the like. The Church was to collect the tithe until the assembly provided otherwise for its support. Peasants had to pay for release from all other dues (on lay or ecclesiastical lands). A clarifying law of March 1790 specified that the *cens, champart, lods et ventes*, and others of real worth had to be bought off in installments over a thirty-year period. The dues were valued at twenty times the annual payment if in money, twenty-five if in kind.

The peasants, however, ignored the "fine print." Most stopped paying dues in August 1789 and never paid them again. (In 1793, the law was finally brought in line with practice.) Similarly, they generally ignored the tithe. The National Assembly had struck a heavier blow than it realized against property rights grounded in privilege, and thus against the society of the Old Regime. Its "statement of principle" would require vast legislative elaboration, not the least of it to "regulate" the Church.

For the moment therefore, the first order of business was the production of a written constitution for France.

DECLARATION OF RIGHTS AND THE VETO

On 26 August 1789 the assembly passed the "Declaration of the Rights of Man and the Citizen," the preface to the new constitution. "Men are born and remain free and equal in rights. . . . " it stated. Liberty, property, security, and resistance to oppression were the "natural and inalienable rights." The law was defined as the expression of the "general will," formulated by the representatives of the people. All men were declared equal before the law. Freedom from arrest without due process was guaranteed, as was freedom of speech and freedom of the press (but not of assembly or petition, perhaps in reaction to recent violence in Paris). There was to be no taxation without public consent. The king's ministers were made responsible to the nation. Property was declared sacred and inviolable. Religious freedom was guaranteed, with qualifications: "No one is to be disturbed for his opinions, even religious, provided their manifestation does not disturb the public order. . . . " Voting qualifications (already a subject of violent disagreement) were not mentioned. Such was the assembly's statement of first principles. To the king it was wildly egalitarian. He allowed it to be printed but declined to sign it.[15]

In September 1789 the chief issues became the king's veto and the form of the future national legislature. On these the "Patriot Party" split. The minority, styled *monarchiens*, were Anglophiles, led by Jean Joseph Mounier, who favored an absolute veto and a bicameral legislature (hereditary lords; elected commons). The majority Patriots, called *constitutionnels*, led by Lafayette, Bailly, and Sieyès, wanted the king to have *no* veto and favored a one-house legislature. Ultimately a unicameral legislature was voted and the parties compromised on a three-year suspensive veto.[16]

With an absolute veto, Louis could still negatively exercise his traditional power. If he approved the suspensive veto, however, the king believed he would be abdicating his divine right and divine duty to God. This he would not do. Therefore, in September, he began calling troops, this time to Versailles.

PARIS REACTS On 1 October 1789 the Regiment of Flanders reached Versailles. The king and queen gave a banquet for the officers at which the ladies of the court appeared wearing white gowns and lilies (the color and fleur-de-lis of Bourbon dynasty). As the affair ended, the king and queen made their appearance, the queen carrying the young Dauphin (crown prince) in her arms.[17] As if on signal, the officers took off their red, white, and blue cockades, trampled them on the floor, and donned white or black cockades. (Black was the color of the Habsburg dynasty of Marie Antoinette.) It was an unmistakable gesture of loyalty to the monarchy.

The news reached Paris the same night and spread like wildfire. Journalists and orators dramatized the story, as did agents of the Breton Club and the Duke d'Orléans, who declared the National Assembly in dire jeopardy. All the rumors current in July were revived, including the aristocratic plot to starve the people. During the next three days, Mirabeau and others visited Paris, while popular leaders went to Versailles, notably Jacques Danton (who will be discussed later) and Jean-Paul Marat, editor of *L'Ami du Peuple* (Friend of the People). All of them helped heat up the public temper. Seemingly none, however, could have predicted the bizarre events soon to occur.

---

[15] The king, as national executive, was sent all constitutional acts to sign (along with regular legislation). The constitution was not written all at once, but a section at a time. All the pieces, as amended, were finally brought together in 1791.

[16] Three years is an average. Actually the king could suspend a law for the term of two legislatures. Elections at two-year intervals was voted later. Thus a law could be suspended for as long as six years, depending on when the first and third legislatures voted on it.

[17] This was the second son of the king and queen—the first had died in June.

THE MARCH OF THE WOMEN

On 5 October, women made their usual morning trek to Les Halles and other markets, but found little to buy. (Many grain barges had failed to reach the Seine. Unseasonably cold weather had caused ice blockage on canals to the north.) As if by plan, the women gravitated toward the City Hall, where by midmorning 3000 were milling about before the steps, shouting for bread. The cries of babes in arms and children hanging to skirts added to the general din.

The municipal councillors, who had the bad luck to be there, stayed out of sight.[18] They had no food to offer, and talk seemed useless. What were they to do? Call the National Guard and disperse the crowd with bayonets? Fire on women and children?

To their astonishment, a "savior" appeared with a plan—one Stanislas Maillard, a dashing officer of the "Conquerors of the Bastille." He asked leave to persuade the women to march to Versailles and petition the king for bread. He would lead them, he said, but they would never get there. It was drizzling rain and cold. Women would never march four leagues (12 miles) in the rain and mud. Never! The councillors happily agreed.

Maillard harangued the crowd, and the march began. The women swept through the streets of Paris, gathering strength as they went, smashing shop windows, taking arms and supplies, confiscating carriages and even caissons of the National Guard. One Amazon emerged from Paris astride a horse-drawn cannon. Outside the city, the women broke into three lines and marched doggedly toward Versailles, confiscating peasants' food, horses and wagons, and dogcarts as they went. The mob grew to 6000, including a number of men, some appropriately dressed as women. The most spectacular female leader was the beautiful Théroigne de Méricourt, who appeared dressed in red on a prancing black horse.

Word soon reached City Hall that the plan had gone awry. The city fathers called out the National Guard and ordered the Marquis de Lafayette to lead the troops to Versailles. Lafayette refused, but his officers threatened to hang him from the nearest lamppost if he did not. (They suspected that he wanted an incident at Versailles, so that he could "save the day" and gain more political power.) In the late afternoon, the National Guard marched.

At Versailles, meanwhile, the women in midafternoon besieged the National Assembly. A delegation was admitted and cordially received. (Mirabeau was seen with a girl on each knee.) Maillard spoke, demanding bread for Paris, revenge on the Regiment of Flanders, an end to the aristocratic plot to starve the people, and an audience for the women with the king. The assembly voted for the audience.

At about 6 P.M., fifteen women and fifteen deputies presented themselves at the château and were taken to the sitting room of the king's upstairs apartments.

---

[18] The city government had been reorganized after 14 July. There were sixty councillors. The whole "commune" or municipal government was made up of 300 men elected by the voting districts. Bailly was still mayor.

When Louis entered the women fell on their knees, hardly able to believe they were in the presence of the "father of the people." He gently raised them. All talking at once, they told him of starving children, no bread at any price, and husbands without work. Begging his help, they began to cry; the king cried with them. When all were finally calm, he promised Paris would get food—immediately.

Louis at once ordered the release of available grain supplies to the capital. His decrees were sent to the National Assembly and copies were handed to Maillard to take to Paris. This overshadowed a greater victory for the assembly. The king also sent word that he had accepted the Bill of Rights and "Constitution," meaning the veto bill. Meanwhile, the authorities of Versailles had found shelter and food and wine for the crowd.

All was quiet at 10 P.M. when Lafayette arrived, an hour ahead of the National Guard. He was immediately granted an audience by the king. "Behold Cromwell!" shouted an officer of the guards as he went up to the royal apartments. Such was the ultraroyalist view of "The Hero of Two Worlds."

Lafayette persuaded Louis XVI that to please the crowd, his National Guardsmen should replace the royal troops outside the palace. (Gardes-du-Corps would remain within.) The change was made quietly around midnight. Versailles slept, but not Lafayette, according to Mathieu Dumas, though he was not seen for some hours. "Far from taking his rest, [he] . . . was having his hair dressed by his valet de chambre." This the Marquis' enemies never believed.

Early in the morning of 6 October, some men got by National Guardsmen and broke into the palace. They killed two Gardes-du-Corps at the door of the queen's apartment before National Guardsmen entered and drove them out. The crowd meanwhile collected around the palace, its leaders displaying the head of the queen's guard on a pike. Lafayette hurried in to see the king and queen. The people began shouting for the royal family to return to Paris with them. Lafayette urged the king to go, arguing that it was the only way to allay the fears of Paris.

Louis reluctantly agreed, and Lafayette led the king, queen, and dauphin onto a balcony in view of the crowd. To loud cheers, Lafayette shouted that the king would accompany his people to Paris. In midafternoon, the royal party departed, their caravan escorted by National Guards and regular troops and surrounded by happy Parisians. Sixty members of the National Assembly also went, and within a few days all the deputies had moved to Paris. The king took up residence in the Tuileries. The National Assembly was ensconced in a riding school (Manège) nearby.[19]

The march of the women surely ranks as the most dramatic *journée* of the Revolution. But it also marked a great turning point.

The king's decision to move to Paris, especially since the National Assembly also relocated there, was disastrous. The king only gradually became aware of it, but he was a prisoner of Paris. So was the National Assembly and the legislatures

---

[19] The arena, surrounded by plush galleries, was easily converted into a meeting hall.

which would succeed it. For the time being, all was quiet and the Parisians were friendly. But the people were in a position to intimidate the crown and the assembly, or worse. Mirabeau, who saw the danger, wrote to the Count de la Marque:

> Paris has great power and there are good reasons why she may boil over. Her populace, once agitated, is irresistible: winter is coming; food is scarce; bankruptcy may come; what will Paris be in three months? Certainly a poor-house—perhaps a chamber of horrors. Ought the chief of the nation to risk his very existence in such a place?

Actually the king was in no immediate danger, and would not be for almost two years, but he had signed his death warrant by coming to Paris. The *monarchiens* sensed this. In 1790, Mounier and others emigrated; for them the Revolution had gone too far.

For the Marquis de Lafayette, matters had worked out perfectly. Apparently he had the king's confidence. He had command of the National Guard and great influence (though not dominant) among the *constitutionnels*, the chief "party" in the National Assembly. Until mid-1791, he would be the most powerful political figure in France. Meanwhile, popular opinion, which would ultimately ruin him, found unprecedented expression in the press, clubs, and salons of Paris.

PRESS/CLUBS/SALONS

The freedom of the press, granted in the Declaration of Rights, already existed in Paris, where the king's censors had long since abdicated. The press was expanding unbelievably. In 1788, Paris had only thirty-five newspapers, most of them weeklies. In 1789, she had 169, of which about one half were dailies. There were hundreds more that failed after a few issues. The boom continued until 1791. Though most of the people could not read—perhaps 20 percent in Paris and 15 percent nationwide—the journals had an enormous influence.

The most spectacular by far—the most libelous and foul of language—was *L'Ami du Peuple* (Friend of the People), founded September 1789. Its editor, Jean-Paul Marat, was small and apparently a physical wreck, but a man of enormous drive and talent. A physician turned drifter and longtime exile in England, he found his element in the Revolution. His instinct for the popular will[20] and huge following assured his adoption by successive leftist factions until he was assassinated in 1793, but Marat was never truly a member of any party. The *Moniteur* of Charles Joseph Pancoucke was also prorevolution, but more

---

[20] Marat sensed the limits of Lafayette's liberalism as early as October 1790, when the "Hero of Two Worlds" supported the vicious suppression of a revolt by the garrison of Nancy, and attacked him as a "false friend" of the people. This was a year before Lafayette became a political "out."

respectable. Founded in 1789, it became an official paper in 1792 and served successive governments until the 1860s. Pancoucke also owned the royalist *Mercure*, edited by Mallet du Pan.[21] Other editors-publishers were Barère, Brissot (later leader of the Girondin faction), and the popular orator, Camille Desmoulins.

The focus of all papers was on the National Assembly and the Commune (municipal government) of Paris. They also had to cover the clubs, the most prominent of which was the Jacobins, so called because it met in a former Dominican—"Jacobin"—monastery. Founded at Versailles as the Breton Club, it was reconstituted formally in Paris as the "Society of Friends of the Constitution." In 1789–1790 it was the club of the National or Patriot party of Lafayette, Barnave, Bailly, Mirabeau, Sieyès, and other liberal monarchists.[22] On the back benches at the Jacobins was the man who would lead the club (or generally be thought to lead it) in its more notorious form—Maximilien Robespierre, an architect of the Terror. The upper-crust leadership already had its separate organization—the very exclusive *Société de '89*, founded by the Abbé Sieyès.

The "poor man's Jacobin Club" was the "Society of the Friends of Man and the Citizen"—the Cordeliers—called after the nickname of the Franciscans, in whose monastery they met. Among its members were the more active leaders of the *sans-culottes* of Paris, such as the brewer, Santerre; the journalists Hébert, Marat, and Desmoulins; and the popular lawyer, Jacques Danton, all prominent later during the more radical phases of the Revolution.

The conservative constitutionalists were represented by the *Club Monarchique*. Called *monarchiens*, and led by Mounier, Malouet, Lally-Tollendal, and Clermont-Tonnerre, they had fought for a British-style constitution at Versailles. The ultraroyalists (absolutists) were headquartered in the Salon Française on the Rue Royale. Called the "Blacks," they were very secretive; no known records remain of their activities. Both clubs were decimated by emigration in 1790 and had virtually ceased to exist after mid-1791.

There were many less influential clubs. One of the most radical was the Amis de la Vérité (Friends of Truth), of the Socialist Abbé Fauchet. It sponsored a newspaper called *La Bouche de Fer* (The Cannon). Its broadsides, however, did not rival those of Marat's *Friend of the People*.

In none of the clubs were the meetings social functions. They were devoted to hearings, political speeches, and debates. Women were excluded from all of them.

It was in the salons that women wielded influence, which was considerable. There, some of the frivolities of the old society were combined with serious discussion, and politicians and statesmen mingled with representatives of the literary, artistic, and scientific worlds. The leading hostesses during 1789–1791

---

[21] Pancoucke was not without political beliefs, but was decidedly more interested in money than ideals. He owned papers for every major faction.

[22] By 1791 the club became too radical for them, and they formed a new one, the *Feuillants*.

were Mme. de Tesse and the Princess de Henin. Madame Necker still held soirées, but when her husband left the finance ministry in 1790, she retired with him to Switzerland.

By that time, her daughter, Germaine Necker, Madame de Staël, was already stealing the scene. She had made an arranged marriage with the Swedish ambassador, the Baron de Staël-Holstein, in 1786, when she was nineteen. Her father gave her a fortune to go with her title and her aging husband soon absented himself from her frenetic world. Vivacious and intelligent, she made a reputation as a hostess, seductress, and writer. At twenty-one, she published a book on Rousseau (1788), the first of her many political and literary works. From the first, she was not very popular with the ladies. Wrote Mme. de Tesse, "Beautiful, ugly? I don't know. . . . I don't believe I've ever seen anything but her eyes and her mouth." From 1790 until she was exiled by Napoleon in 1804 (except for a year, when she fled the Terror), her salon was frequented by the famous and powerful. Even in exile, she was never without influence.

The press came under censorship again in 1791. The minor clubs lost importance gradually. The Cordeliers and Jacobins committed suicide by supporting the Terror. The salons, however, though the hostesses changed according to the fortunes of politics, retained a place in affairs throughout the period of the Revolution and Napoleon.

THE PROBLEM OF EQUALITY

The clubs and salons especially influenced the assembly on the matter of minority rights, which the deputies considered "minor" in the face of financial and other problems (discussed below). Equality was granted to "all men" in the Declaration of Rights. Nevertheless, the position of 700,000 Protestants, some 30,000 Jews, and perhaps 3000 blacks (mostly of mixed blood) remained unclear. The assembly squelched debate and referred motions to committees. What the committees proposed and the assembly voted reflected opinion formed in the salons and clubs, especially in the Jacobins.

Protestants had been granted "civil rights" in 1787,[23] and fifteen, all enthusiastic patriots, had been elected to the Estates General. In December 1789 the assembly easily affirmed Protestants' rights to vote and hold office. At the same time, they denied citizenship to Jews, despite the advocacy of the Abbé Grégoire, Talleyrand, Mirabeau, Robespierre, and others. Talleyrand, however, made a special plea for the Sephardim, who were well integrated into society in eastern and southern France,[24] and in January 1790 they were granted equality. That left

---

[23] In 1787 Protestants were recognized as French subjects and allowed to marry legally, produce legitimate children, and practice trades and professions. They were still barred from most offices.

[24] The Sephardim were descendants of refugees from the Spanish Inquisition, who had entered France c. 1500.

the Ashkenazim of Alsace and Lorraine, "German" Jews who lived in tight "corporate" communities sanctioned by the Old Regime. Grégoire, from Lorraine, became their advocate, and in September 1791 the assembly finally gave them citizenship—provided that they left their communities and liquidated loans to non-Jews. It remained for Napoleon to improve their condition further.

The cause of the blacks, meanwhile, was taken up by the Société des Amis des Noirs (Friends of the Blacks), a club whose members included Lafayette, Mirabeau, Sieyès, Brissot (famous in later assemblies) and the ever-crusading Abbé Grégoire. It was opposed tooth-and-nail by the Club Massiac, representing the planters of the Indies. The Amis were able to get slavery abolished in France in September 1791. The planters, however, frightened the assembly with predictions that abolition in the Indies would mean chaos and the ruin of colonial commerce. The assembly (also in September 1791) perpetuated slavery in the colonies and even repealed earlier legislation allowing free "persons of color" to vote in the colonies. The result was civil war in Santo Domingo. Slavery was finally abolished under the Terror (1794).[25]

THE NATIONAL ASSEMBLY AND THE ECONOMY

. Meanwhile, the assembly concerned itself with matters "closer to home." The revolutionary glories of the "Summer of '89" worked no magic on the government's financial problems. The crown's bankruptcy merely became the nation's, and it became more acute because of unsettled conditions. The Declaration of Rights provided for "equality" of taxation, but a statement of principle could produce no revenues without implementing laws.

The National Assembly began by abolishing the old royal taxes and establishing new ones on land, property, and revenues from industry and commerce. It favored abandoning the royal monopolies but could not afford the loss of income entailed. It returned only tobacco production and sale to free enterprise and retained monopolies on saltpeter, gunpowder, and many others. Paradoxically, the assembly continued to operate the Company of the Indies at a loss (until 1791) but abolished city monopolies, which had produced revenues.[26] Losses were partially offset by reviving the royal indirect taxes under different names, even the hated one on salt (the *gabelle*). The budget did not balance, however, and Necker could not borrow nearly enough to cover the deficit.[27] (Necker resigned in despair in September 1790.)

[25] See p. 147 below and Chapter 11, p. 304 on Napoleon's restoration of slavery.

[26] Obviously, the crown did not grant, or perpetuate, monopolies without compensation. That held by Marseilles on trade with the Near East had netted profits for both the city and crown for generations.

[27] Which Necker estimated would be at least 294,000,000 francs for 1790 (as opposed to 126,000,000 for 1788).

The most obvious means of relief was to appropriate and sell the property of the Church, which was made inviolable by the Declaration of Rights. But there was a loophole: "unless a legally established public necessity obviously requires it. . . . " Bishop Talleyrand (recently the Church's chief legalist) argued further that the Church had been allowed to *hold* property in order to provide welfare and other public services, which it had neglected. Thus the government had a duty to take and utilize the holdings.[28]

In October 1789 Talleyrand himself proposed the confiscation of the property. There should be no objection, he said, if the government assumed the Church's debts (a billion francs), took over the administration of education and charity, and put the clergy on salaries. There was, of course, violent objection from the conservative bishops, who cried out against the destruction of the independence of the Church and the reduction of the clergy to salaried lackeys. Nevertheless, in November 1789 the assembly voted to place Church properties "at the disposal of the Nation."

It was not the intention of the assembly to seize churches, or cathedrals, used regularly for services. Bona fide schools were supposed to be put under loose public supervision. What the new government wanted was the income-producing property of the Church—lands, industries, commercial buildings, tenements and houses, and the like, together with bonds, stocks, and other investment paper.[29] Monastic orders were treated more roughly. In February 1790, all were declared abolished and their property forfeit.[30] The holdings of the Church were designated the Biens Nationaux—the National Properties.

THE ASSIGNATS

A workable scheme for liquidating the National Properties was decreed in December 1789. Treasury bonds, called *assignats*, were issued, good only for the purchase of properties.[31] These were paid to the government's creditors, who were expected to return them for properties. Then the assignats would be burned. To discourage their use as money, the first issue was of bills of 1000, 300, and 200 francs, totaling a modest 400,000,000 francs.

Financiers, however, began to exchange assignats immediately, at a discount, for hard money. The value began to drop. In April 1790, the assembly, hoping

---

[28] The "basic" properties of the Church dated from medieval times, when all property (in theory) had been "held" in return for services—ultimately to the crown—both lay and ecclesiastical property. There had been no ownership, per se.

[29] The law, however, was so stated that everything could conceivably be forfeit, and at more radical stages of the Revolution, cathedrals and churches did in fact come up for sale.

[30] Retirement funds were provided for nuns or they could become lay teachers, nurses, and so on, and in some cases stay where they were. Monks could become secular (ordinary) clergy or retire on pensions.

[31] Until "spent" they drew interest at 5 percent.

to stop this trend, decreed that the paper was exchangeable at full value for metallic currency.

The market price of the assignats continued to fall all the same. There were various reasons. Sales were infrequent and property was often overpriced. The government, in desperate need of hard cash, sold many of the better properties for specie (metal money). The assignats used in purchases often were not burned, but returned to the market. In addition, the official volume of assignats was steadily expanded. In September 1790 the limit was raised to 1,200,000,000 francs; in 1792, to 1,800,000,000. In 1791, meanwhile, fifty and five franc notes were issued, and assignats went into everyday use as paper money. Merchants quickly developed two price scales, one for hard money and a higher one for paper (though they, of course, would never admit it).

The assignats did not pay the national debt or allow the government to meet all of its current expenses. They were not even a successful paper currency. By August 1792 assignats were worth 58 percent of face value; by the end of 1794, 24 percent, and by the end of 1796, almost nothing.

The assignats were a political success since they served to commit those who acquired property with them to the new government. (If the Revolution failed, they stood to lose.) The assignats did not serve to broaden the base of land ownership, however, as the liberals had hoped. Some peasants did acquire new land, but generally only those who already owned considerable amounts. Speculators were the greatest beneficiaries. Nevertheless, the overall measure freed a very large amount of property from *mortmain* and put it on the market.[32] This was a boon, in the long run, to the national economy.

The financial problems of the government, therefore, were not solved. In fact, they worsened. Meanwhile, inflation plagued the economy.

LAISSEZ-FAIRE As long as the assignats were held at a reasonable value, they served to expand the currency and to facilitate expansion of the economy. Expansion was also promoted by the abolition of internal tariffs, the guilds, some of the royal monopolies, and the privileges of cities. Along with the abolition of feudal rights, lands were freed by law for enclosure. However, no specific law for the division of the commons was promulgated and in most places the commons remained intact. During the Terror, the Convention (1793) acted on the matter. Its law was unenforceable, though, because of the resistance of the majority of the peasants who were poor and not inclined to give up their share of the commons.

---

[32] Mortmain means "dead hand"—of the Church, which held whatever it acquired "forever."

CIVIL CONSTITUTION OF THE CLERGY

After confiscating clerical property, the assembly assumed the right to regulate the Church, ultimately by the Civil Constitution of the Clergy (July 1790). It thereby took for the nation a prerogative which had been that of the king by law and Gallican tradition.[33] The most urgent reason was that the assembly had assumed heavy church financial obligations, including paying the clergy, and had to enact laws to meet them. (Dodging the issue by separating church and state was too radical even to occur to most deputies at this point.) Beyond that, the assembly wanted to give the Church a more efficient and economical organization (the state of finances made that mandatory); to root out all vestiges of privilege; to bring the Church in line with political institutions by introducing election of clergy; and to insure that the Church would perform its proper social function (producing citizens loyal to the Revolution) by requiring an oath of clergy to the government. (Even Rousseau had deemed religion a social asset.)

The Civil Constitution of the Clergy authorized eighty-three dioceses, one for each department (administrative reorganization is discussed below, p. 98). Thereby the number of bishops was reduced from 139 to 83. Those whose dioceses were eliminated had to resign. (Generally this meant bishops whose seats were not in major cities.) The dioceses were grouped in ten metropolitan districts (archbishopics), but the metropolitan (archbishop) was merely the principal bishop.

Bishops were to be elected by the departmental electors; parish priests by "active" (taxpaying) citizens of the districts (*arrondissements*). New bishops were to be invested by their metropolitans and were forbidden to ask the pope for confirmation. They were merely to inform him by letter since he was the "Visible Head of the Universal Church." Salaries specified for curés (priests) ranged from 1200 francs per year in rural parishes to 6000 in Paris. For most bishops the salary was 12,000 francs, though the bishop of Paris was allowed 50,000 francs, and those of the larger cities 20,000 francs. Incomes of the higher clergy thus were drastically reduced; those of the curés were increased. (Many country priests had been receiving less than 500 francs per year.)

The Civil Constitution required that bishops and curés take an oath to perform their duties faithfully and to be loyal to the king, the law, and the Constitution.[34]

---

[33] By the Pragmatic Sanction of Bourges (1438) the French Bishops had declared their decisions superior to any papal pronouncements, a virtual declaration of independence from Rome. Francis I, in 1516, had restored relations and granted the Pope the *annates* (first year's income of bishops), but in return for the right to appoint bishops and abbots. Since that time the French church had always been more responsive to the king than to Rome and very much a national church, though paying formal respect to the pontiff.

[34] Where parishes remained unchanged the curés did not have to be reelected. Neither did bishops in unaltered dioceses, for example, Paris. But all, elected or not, had to take the oath. The original Constitution, however, set no deadline.

The debate over the Civil Constitution began in the fall of 1789, and the Constitution was not passed until July 1790. Initially most of the curés in the assembly were for reorganizing the Church and the majority of bishops against. When the assembly refused to declare Catholicism the state religion, however, the curés began to side with the bishops and in the end the clerical deputies were all but united in opposition. Liberals such as Talleyrand, the Abbé Grégoire, and the Jansenist Camus supported the legislation, but laymen had to carry the vote. Nor was that the end of it.

The churchmen carried their "campaign" to the country. They argued doggedly against the election of clergy. To run for office would be demeaning to them and the Church. Nonbelievers including Protestants and Jews would be able to vote (though nowhere but in Alsace were there significant numbers). The Constitution, they objected, denied the spiritual authority of the pope. Christ had consecrated his disciples—the first "bishops"—by the "laying on of hands." The pope was his vicar. French bishops (though for centuries nominated by the king) had always received the blessing of Rome. Most effective, especially in country parishes, was the argument that the Constitution was the *work of the devil*—inspired by the *atheistic philosophes*—*sinful*.

For the clergy, nationwide, the oath presented the greatest problem. To a majority, it demanded a choice between duty to God and duty to country. If this issue had not been raised, the Civil Constitution might have been accepted by most of them. The lay deputies, however, insisted on the provision. In the matter of loyalty, they depended on the Gallican tradition of independence to dictate a choice (as they saw it) of Paris over Rome. On practical grounds, they expected some curés to be influenced by the promise of more decent incomes. Further, most curés had sympathized with the Revolution and the National Assembly from the beginning anyway. The laymen's arguments seemed logical to them, but they were dead wrong.

The clergy split. A majority of the curés came out against the Constitution as did almost all the bishops. On the publication of the law, more questions arose to trouble priests and their flocks. The pope had not approved the Civil Constitution. Were sacraments administered by French clergy efficacious? (Were persons married *truly* married, etc.) French bishops in council ruled they were not. The pope made no comment, but his silence was generally interpreted as agreement.

In November 1790, four months after the Constitution was promulgated, hardly any clergy had taken the oath. The National Assembly responded to this clerical revolution by decreeing that all clergy must take the oath within a week.[35] If they refused, their offices were forfeit.

This forced the rebels to identify themselves. The bolder ones did so openly, and a few, mostly in Paris, had to flee for their lives. The less courageous went

[35] If absent from their posts but in France, within a month, if out of the country, within two months. Law of 27 November 1790.

into hiding or ministered to the "faithful" secretly. In remote areas, some refractory priests retained their churches, however, since public opinion was heavily in their favor.

Less than half the priests took the oath. Of the bishops only seven out of 139 took it. Of these, six refused to consecrate new clergy—all but Talleyrand, bishop of Autun. Elevated to metropolitan, he consecrated the first new bishops (February 1791), who in turn invested more, including Grégoire and Claude Fauchet, the socialist founder of the "Friends of Truth."[36]

The schism in the French church remained, however. Most of the old bishops emigrated or went into retirement. Most of the priests, however, both those who refused the oath and those who took it, continued to administer the sacraments. France came to have, in effect, two churches—one loyal to the government, the other to Rome, with each considering itself quite as Catholic as the other. The government's clergy were called jurors or juring or Patriot clergy; the rebels were referred to as nonjuring, refractory or counterrevolutionary.

The king, during 1790, had gone through a terrible crisis of conscience. In July he had delayed approving the Civil Constitution, hoping for advice from Pope Pius VI. When no word came, he finally signed the bill and was appalled to receive a letter the next day from the pope, urging him not to sign. In November he signed the decree on the oath only after threats from the National Assembly and rumblings of violence in Paris. Deeply religious, Louis was certain he had sinned and was much troubled. The king was a victim, on the one hand, of the assembly, and on the other, of the pope, who was playing a waiting game.

PIUS VI Conveniently, for the historian, the pontificate of Pius VI spans the revolutionary period, 1775–1799. Born Giovanni Angelo Braschi, he was a handsome, cultivated Italian aristocrat, a man of the world, and a patron of literature, science, and the arts. He was conservative in church matters, however, and earlier had battled obstinately against the church reforms of Joseph II of Austria. By nature, however, he was a man of peace. His pet project was the clearing of the Pontine marshes,[37] and he was fond of digging for artifacts at Pompeii.

The pope was slow to condemn the Revolution, because he did not want to jeopardize the position of "Our Son and Most Catholic Majesty," Louis XVI. He was encouraged to "watch and wait" by the French ambassador, Cardinal Bernis—an aged former confidant of Madame de Pompadour—who was convinced that the radical National Assembly would soon alienate the people, who would return the king to power.

During this period, it should be remembered that the power of the papacy was at a low ebb. Catholic monarchs had forced Pius to dissolve the Jesuit order,

---

[36] On 2 January 1791 the National Assembly asked its clerical members to take the oath. Two bishops did so (Talleyrand and Gobel). Only one-third of the curés took the oath.

[37] A program later taken up by Napoleon, but not completed until the 1930s—by Mussolini.

his most militant support. The Holy Roman Emperor, Joseph II, had been positively anticlerical, and Pius distrusted his successor, Leopold II. In Spain, where medieval Catholicism had its last outpost and the Inquisition was active, Charles IV had begun his reign, as had Louis XVI of France, by appointing liberal ministers and encouraging "philosophic" ideas. The Revolution was promoting conservatism among Catholic monarchs, but slowly. (The same was true of Protestant monarchs such as the kings of Prussia and England.)

The August decrees of 1789 lost the pope 360,000 francs a year. In the same month the National Assembly abrogated the Concordat of Bologna of 1516, which cut off papal *annates* of 400,000 francs a year. Papal lands in France—the Comtat Venaissin and city of Avignon—were menaced.[38] Nevertheless, the pope raised no public objection to the laws of August 1789 or to the confiscation of church property in November. Throughout 1790, though increasingly alarmed, the pontiff resisted taking a public position on the Revolution. He consoled himself that Louis XVI was still on his throne and that the French church was intact, if impoverished.

As the schism caused by the oath became apparent, however, Pius had to break his silence. On 10 March 1791 he condemned the Civil Constitution of the Clergy. In April 1791 he issued the Bull *Charitas*, which suspended all clergy "whether secular or regular, who have taken the civil oath"—unless they recanted within forty days. The Bull named "Charles, Bishop of Autun" (Talleyrand) and other rebel prelates who were specifically made subject to excommunication if they did not retract their oaths. In May the pope withdrew his Nuncio from Paris. In subsequent Bulls he condemned the Revolution, root and branch, and began urging European princes—Protestant and Catholic —to come to the aid of Louis XVI.

The National Assembly retaliated by progressive moves against refractory clergy. In May 1791 it decreed that elected clergy who refused the oath would lose their rights as citizens. In June the assembly denied pensions to clergy who had refused the oath or refused it in the future. In November 1791 refractory priests were classified as traitors, exiled from their parishes, and made subject to imprisonment if they practiced. Meanwhile, the Comtat Venaissin was annexed to France.

Government propaganda made refractory priests co-villains with "the aristocrats." In the cities, they were often the targets of mobs. The peasants of the countryside, however, and France at large, remained disturbed by the schism. The country was plagued by religious strife until the time of Napoleon.

The problem might have been solved by the assembly except that its leaders, the Patriots, were torn between retaining the established Church, obviously

---

[38] The popes had resided at Avignon during the "Babylonian Captivity" (1309–1377), and the Comtat and city were still ruled by the pope—a foreign enclave on the Rhone, completely surrounded by French territory.

desired by most Frenchmen, and separating church and state. The Patriots preferred disestablishment, but tried to take a middle position, which pleased no one. They had included religious toleration in the Declaration of Rights, and granted full citizenship to Protestants (December 1789) and Jews except in Alsace (January 1790).[39] These measures offended the Catholic hierarchy as much as the Civil Constitution.

At the same time, the assembly was trapped between a recalcitrant king and a violence-prone, increasingly demanding Paris population. The religious legislation bred disorder in the countryside (conservative peasants versus more liberal townsmen). The assembly simultaneously had to deal with an authoritarian king, to write a constitution and to try to satisfy the conflicting demands of the French people. To this were added increasing international pressures. Nevertheless, sweeping domestic reforms were effected.

ADMINISTRATION AND JUDICIARY

Administrative and judicial reform had been contemplated for decades by the monarchy. Little had been done, however, because of fierce provincial loyalties and opposition of privileged estates, *parlements*, and municipalities. In the existing administrative system the authority of royal intendants and royal governors overlapped in the provinces. City governments were various in the extreme. Intermediate administrative units differed in size, organization, and population. The judicial system was a hodgepodge of royal, municipal, and provincial courts, where lines of appeal were never clear, and justice at the lowest level (until 4 August 1789) was often administered by seigneurs.

The assembly restructured both systems, the administration during the winter of 1789–1790 and the judiciary during 1790–1791. This would have warmed the heart of the king except for one thing: control was decentralized. In response to the wishes of leaders produced by the "municipal revolutions" of 1789, and to the influence of the American example, the assembly gave great authority to elected local officials. They were to be chosen indirectly—by electors named by the voters—except in the municipalities (and even there, in the larger cities). But the vote was given to virtually all male citizens twenty-one years or older who paid a nominal tax. Electors had to meet a higher property qualification, but they had to be citizens of the locality they served.[40]

France was divided into eighty-three departments. (See Map 3.2.) The old provinces, generalities, and local governments were abolished. The departments were subdivided into districts (*arrondissements*), cantons, and communes (municipalities). The municipal councils were elective, the president of the council serving as mayor. Electors who were chosen in the cantons then designated the

[39] See above, p.90.
[40] A full explanation is given in the description of the Constitution of 1791, p. 105.

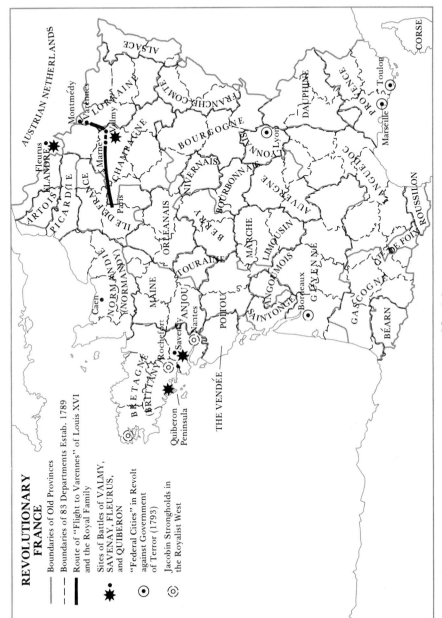

REVOLUTIONARY FRANCE

— Boundaries of Old Provinces

--- Boundaries of 83 Departments Estab. 1789

••• Route of "Flight to Varennes" of Louis XVI and the Royal Family

★ Sites of Battles of VALMY, SAVENAY, FLEURUS, and QUIBERON

⊙ "Federal Cities" in Revolt against Government of Terror (1793)

◎ Jacobin Strongholds in the Royalist West

AUSTRIAN NETHERLANDS

ALSACE

Montmédy

Varennes

LORRAINE

Valmy

FRANCHE-COMTÉ

Fleurus

FLANDRE

ARTOIS

PICARDIE

Marne

CHAMPAGNE

BOURGOGNE

DAUPHINÉ

PROVENCE

ÎLE DE FRANCE

Paris

NIVERNAIS

LYONNAIS

Lyon

Toulon

Marseille

CORSE

ORLÉANAIS

BERRY

BOURBONNAIS

AUVERGNE

LANGUEDOC

ROUSSILLON

CTÉ DE FOIX

Caen

NORMANDIE (NORMANDY)

MAINE

TOURAINE

MARCHE

LIMOUSIN

ANGOUMOIS

GUYENNE

Bordeaux

GASCOGNE

BÉARN

POITOU

SAINTONGE

ANJOU

Nantes

Savenay

Rochefort

BRETAGNE (BRITTANY)

Quiberon Peninsula

THE VENDÉE

Map 3.2

99

administrative councils of the districts. All the district electors assembled to elect departmental officials and representatives to the National Legislative Assembly. Each department had a council of thirty-six members headed by a *procureur-général-syndic*; each district had a *procureur-syndic* and smaller council. District and departmental administrations were renewed by one-half every two years. After the first two years, those to retire were to be chosen by lot; thereafter the term was four years. The king could suspend local officials, but they could appeal to the Legislative Assembly. Laws could be made by departmental, district, and municipal assemblies. The enforcement of national law was left completely in the hands of local officials.

A uniform judicial system was created to replace the old one, which was abolished entirely. Even before it was in place, seigneurial justice was eliminated (4 August 1789) and the *parlements* replaced by temporary courts (September 1790).

All judges were elected for six-year terms. Every canton had one or more justices of the peace, chosen directly by the voters.[41] There were courts-of-first-instance in each district for civil cases, with judges and a public prosecutor picked by district electors. Appeal from a district court was made to another district court. Final appeal was to the Court of Cassation in Paris (chosen by departmental electors) which, however, did not try cases, but ruled only on the legality of proceedings and ordered retrial where necessary in district courts.

For criminal cases, there was an elected criminal tribunal in each department (selected by all the district electors). The line of appeal was from the justice of the peace to the departmental criminal court to the Court of Cassation. All men were equal before the law; penalties were the same for all classes. There were two elected juries for criminal cases, one to determine if a crime had been committed (a grand jury); another to judge guilt. (There were no juries for civil cases.)

The king was not pleased. The National Assembly had cut the reins to his administrative and judicial "horses."

THE FLIGHT TO VARENNES

The king became more and more miserable. His accustomed routine was disrupted. He could not hunt except on weekends and then only at St. Cloud, in the outskirts of Paris. He could not even walk in peace in the gardens of the Tuileries without the "supervision" of hundreds of Parisians. Louis was a very shy man who loved privacy. At the Tuileries, he felt he had none. Even inside the palace the priggish Lafayette and his entourage were always there, spouting philosophic "nonsense." Louis had accepted Lafayette because he was both of the old nobility and popular, but the monarch did not like him.

---

[41] Communes had the equivalent of justices-of-the peace for simple police cases. They were reelected yearly.

In addition, the National Assembly steadily whittled away at the royal prerogative. The king could no longer make laws and had been put on a salary—"the civil list." His ministers were accountable to the assembly. He could not even remove a country mayor. What was left? Moreover, to Louis, religious questions related to everything that had been done.

In surrendering his prerogatives to the assembly, was he abandoning his duty to God? He was, after all, a divine-right monarch, chosen by God to rule. (This doubtless had been a convenient fable to Louis XIV, but was *believed* by Louis XVI.) Surely he had sinned in approving the Civil Constitution of the Clergy and the oath. Had not the pope condemned both? Louis' confessor, a nonjuring priest, affirmed the king's worst fears.

Moreover, there was the ever-present physical danger. What if the mood of the populace turned ugly? What if food supplies failed and the great beast of the people turned on him?

Mirabeau had been among the first to warn of this danger. He seems to have decided after the "October Days" that the Revolution had "gone too far." In the fall of 1789 he secretly entered the king's service.[42] From the first, he laid plans for the king's escape from Paris. The first involved his going to Rouen and summoning the assembly to follow. Rouen was rich, royalist, ecclesiastical, and center of the grain trade for Paris, which might give the king the upper hand. If necessary, moreover, he could easily reach Le Havre and sail abroad. Louis rejected the scheme, however. The German frontier seemed much safer to him. There were Austrian troops in Belgium that might give aid if Marie Antoinette appealed to her brother, Leopold II, the Holy Roman Emperor.

Louis also vetoed various new plans including flight to Compiègne and creation of a new provincial army which would lock Lafayette and his National Guard into Paris.

At the same time, Mirabeau (he said) tried to drive the National Assembly into ever more radical acts, particularly on religious questions, hoping the country would be antagonized. At any rate Mirabeau made violent anticlerical speeches in the assembly that served to counteract rumors that he was serving the king (the secret was out). He may have been loyal only to himself. No one will ever know. When he died suddenly, however, on 2 April 1791, pamphlets were circulating denouncing the former champion of liberty.

With Mirabeau's death, plotting the escape was taken over by Marie Antoinette and her sometime lover, the handsome Count Axel von Fersen, of the Royal Swedish Regiment. The king still wavered over making *any* attempt, but he was persuaded by events. First, organized agitation in the Paris sections forced him to remove all the royal ministers and to replace them with nominees of Lafayette and the Lameth brothers. Second, at Easter 1791, a mob prevented the king from

---

[42] In return for the payment of his considerable debts and the salary of 6000 francs a month. (Remember that persons who made over about 12,000 a year were considered upper middle class.)

going even to St. Cloud for the holiday. The royal carriage was stopped and forced to turn back to the Tuileries.

It was then finally decided that the royal party would make for Montmédy, in Lorraine (in France but near the Luxembourg border and also near Metz and other fortresses manned by loyal troops). Fersen was the key man in Paris. At the frontier, arrangements were made by the Marquis de Bouillé, commandant of Metz. In Paris, Quinton Craufurd, a Scottish financeer, and his mistress, a Mrs. Sullivan, assisted Fersen. Craufurd had money sent ahead in case the royal party had to flee into the Austrian Netherlands. Also involved were Mercy d'Argenteau, former Austrian ambassador to France, then stationed at Brussels, and Count Fernan Nuñez, the Spanish ambassador. The queen sent ahead 1,000,000 francs in cash and valuables; the king 2,000,000 (the quarterly installment on his "civil list"). Another 3,000,000 in borrowed money was available abroad. Fersen offered 600,000 of his own money if needed. All were acutely aware that even royal refugees are not wildly welcomed anywhere if they arrive penniless.

Once the king reached Montmédy, he intended to declare the National Assembly dissolved and the property of the Church restored. Thereby he hoped to destroy with one blow the central political institution and the credit of the revolutionary government. If, however, the tactic failed, he planned to march on Paris with an Austrian-French army. Leopold II had promised him Austrian troops, but only if he reached Montmédy and could mobilize a sizable French force. The king did not intend to leave France therefore, except as a last resort. (Refer to Map 3.2.)

On 20 June, all was in readiness. At 10 P.M. a berline (a heavy, roomy coach) drawn by four horses, pulled up at the south end of the Tuileries. On the box was the Count de Fersen, dressed as a coachman. He waited near the entrance to a secret corridor, well known to him, which led to the queen's apartment. At intervals until 11:30 he picked up members of the royal family, driving around between stops to be sure all was quiet—first the crown prince and his sister (both dressed as girls) and their governess (posing as a German baroness, the head of the party); next the king's sister; then Louis XVI (dressed as a valet); and finally the queen, dressed as the children's governess. Fersen drove the coach out of Paris, and then galloped ahead to prepare the way.

It had been carefully coordinated with the military that as the king's carriage passed through major cities and towns, troops would be nearby or cavalry passing through. If he kept on schedule he would be guarded all the way. Louis, however, did not. The next day, 21 June, was beautiful and sunny and the trip began to seem like an excursion. The king ordered extra stops and delayed at posting stations (where the horses were changed) to have his favorite foods cooked. Worse, he could not resist dropping hints as to who he *really* was. His troops lost him and at Ste.-Ménéhould (in Champagne) he was recognized by the posting master, an old soldier, J. B. Drouet.

After the king departed, at about 7 P.M., Drouet and a companion rode cross-country to Varennes, a small village which straddled a tributary of the

Meuse River just inside Lorraine. With the help of villagers, they blocked the bridge across the river with a cart and furniture. At 11:00 P.M. the royal party reached a hill overlooking Varennes, where they awaited cavalry which was now expected to openly escort the coach. A detachment was close by, commanded by the son of the Marquis de Bouillé. He had been in Varennes for hours, however, and had finally ordered his men to bivouac on the far side of the river. He and the other officers were at a hotel beyond the bridge.

About midnight, the king's party went on into Varennes. The carriage was stopped and the king, exhausted, immediately admitted who he was. The royal party was escorted to the local inn, wined and dined, and treated with greatest respect. Meanwhile, the tocsin was rung, and peasants swarmed in from the countryside—before daylight some 10,000 choked the village streets.

Young Captain Bouillé, roused by the uproar, sent an officer to the king, who asked His Majesty to give the order and the cavalry would cut a way out. This they might easily have done. It was dark, the citizens were not organized, and in any case would have been no match for a hundred well-armed horsemen. The king, however, refused to take any risk. He insisted instead on waiting for the arrival of the Marquis de Bouillé with a larger force.

This decision sealed his fate. At 6 A.M. on 22 June, long before Bouillé appeared, representatives of the National Assembly arrived, escorted by National Guardsmen. The royal party was put on the road for the capital. On 25 June, all members were back in the Tuileries.

The "flight to Varennes" exploded the myth of the king as father of the people. He had been captured in the company only of his family, coachmen and footmen. There was no sign of kidnappers. No official denials could long suppress the truth. It would be over a year before Parisians were willing to turn on the king, but the monarchy was doomed.

THE RISE OF REPUBLICANISM

In the king's absence the National Assembly had been in an uproar. If he escaped, who would supplant him as executive? The Duke d'Orléans could be made regent—but for whom? The dauphin had fled also; the king's brothers were already in exile. Paris might accept a republic, but the rest of the country— "never." Moreover, the great powers, already disturbed over the Revolution, would surely support Louis XVI. When the king was brought back, the simplest solution was to adopt the fiction that he had been abducted. Louis, in turn, swore to accept the Constitution, finished just before he fled.

The public, however, was not deceived. There was a sudden proliferation of republican literature and a flurry of republican action, something new in the Revolution. Up to this time, even in the most radical circles, there had been no question of a government without a king, no matter what its form. Now, republican pamphlets were circulated, including one by Tom Paine, of American Revolutionary fame, and antimonarchical placards appeared on walls and trees.

On 16 July 1791 the Cordeliers posted a petition on the speaker's platform on the Champ de Mars demanding the trial of the king and the establishment of a "new executive government." People by the hundreds rushed to sign it. On 17 July two men (presumed to be royal spies) were discovered under the platform and seized by the mob and hanged. The crowd swelled to enormous proportions and some sort of march was feared.

Lafayette moved in with detachments of the National Guard to restore order. His troops were pommeled and there was a fight. The troops fired, killing some twenty people and wounding more. The Paris newspapers played up the incident as the "Massacre of the Champ de Mars." The popularity of Lafayette plummeted.

The "Hero of Two Worlds," along with most of the early leaders of the Revolution, withdrew from the Jacobin Club at this point. They were no longer radical enough for the organization, which rapidly became republican. The constitutional monarchists formed their own club—the Feuillants. In the Jacobins the new leaders were the Abbé Grégoire, Jerôme Pétion, (who in August defeated Lafayette for the post of mayor of Paris) along with the more moderate Jacques Brissot and Jean Roland. The star of Maximilien Robespierre was rising, however.[43] Jacobin clubs all over France gradually followed the lead of the mother club in Paris and became republican.

THE DRIFT TO THE LEFT (AN ASIDE)

The upsurge of republicanism—or at least its ultimate coming—should not have been unexpected. "When you get mixed up with directing a revolution," Mirabeau had said in the fall of 1789, "the problem is not to make it go, but to hold it back." The horse of revolution, which he had earlier given a sharp slap on the buttocks, was galloping leftward, and he had lost the reins. Such was the experience of succeeding leadership groups in the revolutionary assemblies.

Calonne fled France in 1787 because of the "revolutionary" defiance of the king by the Assembly of Notables. Thereafter the aristocrats and high clergy remained a revolutionary block, until the king gave them what they wanted—the Estates General. A liberal minority—"traitors to their class"—assumed leadership of the Revolution.

In the National Assembly, these "traitors," joined by members of the Third, formed the "Patriot Party," which assumed leadership. Between July 1789 and

---

[43] At this time the lawyers mentioned were still using the aristocratic name style (though untitled). It was *de* Robespierre, Pétion *de* Villeneuve, Brissot *de* Warville, and Roland *de* la Platière. This shortly became unfashionable.

July 1791, however, the ranks gradually thinned as various members reached the limits of their liberalism. After the night of 4 August (abolition of feudal dues), the Viscount Noailles and the Duke d'Aiguillon were not very active. (They emigrated in 1792.) After October 1789 the *monarchiens* left the assembly over the defeat of their proposed British-style constitution. (Mounier emigrated in 1790; Malouet in 1792.) Mirabeau defected to the crown. Lafayette became a proponent of law-and-order, approved harsh suppressions of army mutinies in 1790, lost popularity, and came to favor conservative amendments to the draft constitution. Archbishop Talleyrand, after presiding over the Fête de la Fédération of 1790 (14 July), left the clergy and sought diplomatic assignments overseas. (Lafayette and Talleyrand emigrated in 1792.) Sieyès showed grave concern over the clerical legislation of 1790 (but voted for it) and devoted his best efforts to limiting the suffrage in the new constitution. Bailly developed the same law-and-order syndrome as Lafayette and was displaced as mayor of Paris. (He was executed in 1793.) In the spring of 1791 the leading Patriots (*constitutionnels*) in the assembly—Barnave, Adrien DuPort, and Alexandre Lameth—had come to favor limited suffrage and a watered-down bill of rights and had sponsored the Le Chapelier Law, which forbade labor organizations. After the "Flight to Varennes" (June 1791), the remaining Patriots almost unanimously plumped for amending the Constitution to limit power to the wealthy. The upcoming leadership was in the Jacobins, as noted above.

In the summer of 1791, Barnave summed up the attitude of the remaining "Men of '89":

> This revolutionary movement has destroyed all that it set out to destroy . . . it is necessary to halt. . . . One more step toward liberty will destroy the monarchy; one more step toward equality will abolish private property.

He placed his faith in the Constitution of 1791, to be promulgated in September. It would prove unworkable, however. By August 1792 most of his prominent colleagues had fled the country. He was guillotined in 1793.

CONSTITUTION OF 1791

The Constitution on which the National Assembly had labored since 1789 was finished in June 1791. The king had left behind a denunciation of it, and his subsequent change of heart could hardly be taken as sincere. Moreover, suspicion of him was heightened by the appearance of letters written prematurely by the pope and Holy Roman Emperor congratulating him on his escape and by a foolish letter from the Marquis de Bouillé threatening Paris and the assembly if any harm were done to the royal family. The assembly set about amending the Constitution to provide checks against any future rash action by the monarch.

These amendments provided that if the king placed himself at the head of an army and led it "against the nation" or approved any such undertaking, he would be considered to have abdicated. If he left the country, and, upon request of the legislative body, did not return within two months, he would have abdicated. If the king abandoned the throne under either of these provisions or by his own declaration, he was to be classed as a citizen and could be accused and tried as such for acts "subsequent to his abdication." The amendment also made specific that the king must take an oath to uphold the Constitution.

In the completed Constitution, the vote was given to "active citizens," defined as any male, twenty-five or older, who paid a tax equal to the three days wages of a common laborer. It excluded from suffrage debtors, servants, felons, those indicted for crimes, and the insane (and women, as seemed normal at the time). The status of blacks was ignored.[44] Actors, however, had been declared citizens.[45]

Perhaps 4,300,000 men (of a maximum electorate of 7,000,000) could vote. These participated only in "primary assemblies," however, where electors were chosen, who then selected deputies and other officials. Electors had to be *landowners* and to pay a tax of between 15 and 25 livres (francs), depending on the area. Any active citizen (any of the 4,300,000 voters) could be a deputy; he had to be chosen by fairly well-to-do electors, for which office almost 3,000,000 men qualified, but of whom only 50,000 were elected—nationwide.[46] This set a pattern for indirect election of assemblies that would be followed by most later governments.

The Constitution provided for a clear separation of powers among executive, legislative, and judicial authorities. The king was now described as the "King of the French" rather than of France. He was allowed a three-year suspensive veto, but not over constitutional or fiscal legislation. He could declare war and make peace with the consent of the (new) Legislative Assembly and was further empowered to appoint ministers, ambassadors, and military officers. The ministers, however, were responsible to the Legislative Assembly. The assembly was to be elected and to meet every two years, and the king was prohibited from dissolving it. It was to consist of 745 deputies from the eighty-three departments plus an unspecified number from the colonies. An elective judiciary was established, as previously described.

---

[44] See above, pp. 90–91. Protestants and all Jews had citizenship—and the vote—by the time the Constitution went into effect. The status of blacks was complicated by the existence of slavery in the colonies.

[45] Actors and actresses had been outcasts under the Old Regime, made more so by the Church, however, than the government. Priests were forbidden to perform marriage ceremonies for them or inter their bodies in holy ground.

[46] This is according to the final version of the Constitution, which, however, was amended (in August 1791) *after* the elections for the new Legislative Assembly were held. In the elections of 1791, electors had to pay a tax of only 10 francs, but deputies had to pay at least one *marc d'argent* (silver marc) or about 50 francs.

That the National Assembly had been chastened by its experiences both with the king and the people was rejected in the finished version of the Constitution. The Declaration of Rights,[47] though forceful, was more prosaic and hedged with qualifications than the Declaration of 1789, and some of its provisions were contradicted by the Constitution proper. It reiterated guarantees of liberty and equality of rights. However, not everyone had the right to vote. The Declaration of Rights stated that all citizens were admissible to office "without distinction other than as to virtues and talents," but property qualifications for electors all but insured that officeholders would be chosen from among the rich. It again specified equality of taxation and before the law, without qualification. But as to liberty, there were numerous reservations. Any man could speak, write, print, or publish, freely, "without having his writings subject to any censorship or inspections *before their publication*." Citizens were guaranteed the right to assemble, but "peaceably and without arms and in accordance with police regulation." *All* rights were guaranteed, but the legislature could make laws forbidding anything that "*might* be injurious to society" (emphasis added).

There were new features, however. With an eye to the Paris multitudes, "public relief" (welfare) was made a right, and the government made itself responsible for furnishing jobs to able-bodied men who could find none. Most radical—for the long term—was the promise to establish free public schools for "all men." Therein (had it been applied) lay the key to equality of opportunity.

Such was the Constitution of 1791. On 14 September the king swore to accept, maintain, and enforce it before the assembly. Afterward, Louis was carried on the shoulders of a jubilant crowd through the gardens of the Tuileries to the palace. The queen was cheered at the Opera. The goal of the early leaders had been reached. Public reaction seemed to certify that the Revolution was over. Surely Lafayette and the members of the Club des Feuillants thought so, too. The assembly had terminated the Declaration of Rights as if this were an accepted fact:

> National festivals shall be instituted to preserve the memory of the French Revolution to maintain fraternity among the citizens, and to bind them to the Constitution, the *Patrie*, and the laws.

Actually the Revolution had barely begun. Paris was alive with republican agitation. It was a bellwether of events to come that in 1791 Lafayette was defeated when he ran for mayor of Paris by the more radical Pétion. He resigned his post in the National Guard and went into temporary retirement.

The years of Lafayette were over. Constitutional monarchy was established in France, but the forces which would destroy it were already at work.

---

[47] In the final document divided between the Preamble and Title I: Fundamental Provisions Guaranteed by the Constitution.

The Revolution is like Saturn, it devours all its children.
—*Vergniaud*

DEATH OF THE MONARCHY
(1791–1793)

LEGISLATIVE ASSEMBLY

Deputies to the new Legislative Assembly were named between 29 August and 5 September 1791 by electors chosen by the voters in June, before the flight of the king. Nevertheless, the assembly was generally representative of the politically active in France, though perhaps not of the "active citizens," of whom no more than one-third voted. As in 1789, the majority of the legislators were lawyers. Most of them also had been officials either of the Old or New Regime, predominantly at the municipal, district, or departmental level.

By mid-1791, most ultraroyalists had emigrated, as had many conservative constitutionalists and as had some alarmed bankers and businessmen. The Count d'Artois, the king's younger brother, had left just after the Bastille fell. His more moderate brother, the Count de Provence (later Louis XVIII) had fled in June 1791. The departure of the émigrés—most of them for Germany, Switzerland, or England—tended to make suspects of aristocrats who remained in France. Initially, nevertheless, the majority in the Legislative Assembly was monarchist, and 100 percent swore to uphold the Constitution and therefore the constitutional monarchy.

The National Assembly had passed a "self-denying ordinance" that prohibited reelection of its members. Thus the Legislative Assembly was composed altogether of inexperienced parliamentarians. Moreover, the impression is inescapable that this was the "second team."[1] There were fewer idealists and statesmen and more politicians (in the most gross sense of the word) who scratched and

---

[1] Simon Schama disagrees, based on the powerful oratory and persuasiveness of the deputies, especially of the "crusaders" for patriotic war, the Brissotins. *Citizens*, 581*ff*.

clawed for position. To hear all who demanded the floor, the assembly was forced into a marathon seven-day-a-week schedule, with sessions running into the night. The delegates quickly divided into warring factions which carried their antipathies outside of the meeting hall.

The militant constitutional monarchists (Feuillants) had 250 of the 745 delegates, including Mathieu Dumas, the Marquis de Jaucourt, and Jacques Beugnot. Lafayette was still an important leader, though not in the assembly. The unconfessed republicans, numbering about 150, were directed from the Jacobin Club and the Cordeliers and were influenced by Robespierre's newspaper, *Le Défenseur de la Constitution (Defender of the Constitution)*. This most vocal group, in turn, broke into moderate and radical factions. The moderate republicans had their support in the provinces, whereas the radicals catered to the whims of Paris. During the relatively peaceful winter of 1791–1792 the moderates were best able to appeal to the huge uncommitted "center," since Paris was as yet unorganized, and gained ascendency in the assembly.

This group was called the Brissotins, after its leader, Jacques Pierre Brissot, or later, the Girondins, since many of them were from the department of the Gironde. Brissot de Warville, as he "nobly" styled himself, the son of a wealthy restauranteur of Chartres, was a successful lawyer. At thirty-eight, he was urbane, traveled, and experienced in politics. He had helped edit revolutionary papers in England, Switzerland, and America, studied with Marat, and participated in the revolution of 1780–1787 in Belgium. With the Abbé Grégoire, he had founded the Société des Amis des Noirs (Friends of the Blacks), which promoted the cause of "persons of color" in France and favored the abolition of slavery in the colonies.

As an orator, Brissot was upstaged by Pierre Vergniaud, who had presence and a golden tongue but had to be fed ideas. The "work horse" of the group was Jean Roland, whose wife, however, was perhaps more of a leader than he. The Girondins mapped strategy in the salon of Madame Roland (Manon Phlipon), the daughter of a Paris engraver, whose aristocratic air belied her origins. Blonde, graceful, and elegant, she seemed younger than thirty-seven (and was twenty years younger than Roland). Her charm and the amenities of her drawing room initially drew the Girondins there, but ultimately her intelligence, knowledge, and zeal for the revolutionary cause gave her enormous influence. She had a firm grasp of legislative problems, as well.

DOMESTIC AND FOREIGN PROBLEMS

France had a multitude of domestic difficulties. The financial ills of the government had still not been cured. The economy had recovered somewhat, but the possibility loomed that there would be food shortages again in 1792. The refractory clergy was causing trouble. In Paris itself, some priests made bold to lead bands against the National Guard under cover of darkness. Nationwide, refractory clergy held the loyalty of half the people, and in remote areas the peasants rejected patriot priests altogether. The religious schism bred defiance of the government in other matters; tax collection was difficult. In the south of France and in the Vendée, on the west coast, there were clashes between counterrevolutionary peasants (reinforced by small-town workers) and National Guards. These disturbances were no real danger in 1791–1792, but in the Vendée the groundwork was laid for a serious revolt in 1793.

Foreign affairs soon became the major concern of the Assembly. During the summer of 1791, Leopold II, Holy Roman Emperor, had begun organizing an alliance to restore absolute monarchy in France. His plans were destroyed, however, when Louis XVI accepted the Constitution. The emperor settled for a defensive alliance with Prussia. In the "Declaration of Pillnitz" (27 August 1791), Leopold and Frederick William II of Prussia mildly stated that the restoration of the monarchy in France was in the common interest of all the European powers. They proposed no action, however, except by concert of all the nations, which, at the time, was impossible. Even Frederick William did not want war. Catherine of Russia was more interested in Poland, and George III of England was decidedly cool to giving aid to Louis XVI, "sponsor" of the American Revolution. Nevertheless, the Declaration of Pillnitz alarmed the French assembly and was presented by the Paris press as a threat to France.

Almost simultaneously, Pope Pius VI began making frequent and vituperous condemnations of the Revolution. (The old National Assembly, as a parting gesture, had finally annexed Avignon to France.)

Most disturbing were the émigrés collected in the small states of the Rhineland. These included the king's brothers, the Count de Provence and the Count d'Artois. On 31 October 1791 the assembly ordered the Count de Provence to return within two months or lose his rights to the regency. The future Louis XVIII's reply displayed bravado and humor which he lost in the ensuing years. Describing the deputies as "madmen fit only for asylums," he ordered them to return to their senses within two months, on penalty of losing their titles as reasonable men. The assembly countered with a decree ordering all émigrés, including the princes, to return to France by 1 January 1792 or be legally classified as traitors, subject to punishment by death. The king vetoed this decree, but the *Moniteur* published it anyway. Louis tried to placate the legislature by sending a letter to his brothers ordering them to return because, he said, the Revolution was over, but they of course paid no attention. The assembly then forced the king (December 1791) to order the Elector of Trier to expel the émigrés or be treated as an enemy. Under pressure from the Holy Roman Emperor, Leopold II, the Elector-Archbishop complied. The emperor, however, notified the assembly that he considered the case of the émigrés closed.

The assembly was not satisfied. The Diet of the Holy Roman Empire (the German States) meanwhile had declared its sympathy for the émigrés. Individual German princes and nobles did the same. (Some had economic reasons—they had lost income from feudal dues on properties in Alsace and Lorraine.) It was known that there were émigrés in the Palatinate, the archbishopric of Cologne and in Hesse, Baden, Switzerland, and elsewhere. In the free city of Worms, the prince of Condé had collected an army of some 2000 men. This small force was hardly a danger to France, but its numbers were multiplied in the imaginations of the legislators, the press, and the public, and the name of Condé struck fear into many hearts. For centuries the family had produced outstanding generals. The present prince was a hero of the Seven Years War. His great-great grandfather, called the "Great Condé," with the equally famous Turenne, had brought glory to France in the Thirty Years' War.

In January 1792 the assembly forced Louis XVI to sign an "ultimatum" to the Holy Roman Emperor, demanding that Leopold renounce all anti-French treaties or face dire consequences. The emperor's reply was an impolite and defiant *no*. He blamed international tensions on the "dangerous conspiracies of the Jacobin party," which he proclaimed the enemy of the French people, their "most Christian King," and all of Europe. He would not be intimidated, he said, and declared that "the cause of the Emperor [himself] is that of all the powers." Leopold died in March 1792, but was succeeded by his son (and nephew of Marie Antoinette), Francis II, a known enemy of the Revolution.[2]

The Girondins found little difficulty in convincing the assembly that France was surrounded by enemies. Brissot, Vergniaud, and others demanded war—that France strike the first blow. The king, whose ministry consisted of Feuillants, was brought under heavy pressure. He had discredited himself by vetoing the legislation recalling émigrés (also a punitive bill against nonjuring priests). He was rumored to be in correspondence with foreign princes, "conspiring against the nation." He was, in fact, writing to other monarchs, but his language was extremely circumspect, and he was not so foolish as to suggest armed intervention in his behalf. There were agents to do that orally, and it was unnecessary. The European courts knew that he had sought Austrian aid in 1791 and were perfectly aware that his hostile pronouncements were made under duress. (The queen was not so discreet; her letters were indeed treasonable.)

In March 1792, to repair his reputation, Louis appointed a Girondin ministry headed by General Dumouriez and including Roland as minister of the interior. A soldier of the Old Regime, Dumouriez had secured rapid promotion since 1789 by associating himself successively with Mirabeau, Lafayette, and finally the Girondin faction. He now undertook to persuade the king to do the popular thing, to declare war. It was Dumouriez' belief that the war could be won. Many of the Girondins, however, hoped that the French would suffer initial defeats, which would discredit the king, whom they could then overthrow in favor of a republic.

---

[2] The Emperor's bellicose attitude was dictated by his foreign minister, Count Wenzel Anton von Kaunitz, who thought that the Declaration of Pillnitz had weakened the Brissotins in the Assembly and believed "talking tough" to the French (whom he considered incapable of fighting a war) would help Louis XVI to keep the peace. In fact, the Brissotin line remained that peoples would revolt against the Old Regime and support French armies wherever they appeared. See Steven Ross, *France against Europe*, 39; T.C.W. Blanning, *Origin of the French Revolutionary Wars*, 21ff.

Lafayette, who had returned to military service on the German front in December 1791, signaled the Feuillants in Paris to support the war. He was convinced that France could win and that the constitutional monarchy would be strengthened.[3]

Most surprisingly (at first brush), the queen and her party suddenly began to press for war. "The imbeciles!" she said of the Girondins. "They don't seem to know that they are playing into our hands." She had decided that, win or lose, the monarchy would be saved. If France were victorious, Louis' position would certainly be stronger. If France lost, then her nephew, Francis II, would restore the king to his absolute powers.

By April the only prominent voices against war were those of Robespierre and Marat, who feared that France was unprepared and that foreign armies would quickly overrun the country and destroy the Revolution.

With his ministers, Lafayette, the Legislative Assembly, the clubs, and even the queen pressing for war, Louis XVI was not one to stand against it. On 21 April 1792, with the unanimous consent of the assembly, he issued a declaration of war against Austria—Austria alone. Thereby he hoped to avoid conflict with Prussia or other German states. Prussia, however, honored her alliance with Austria.

Before the king's declaration, the assembly published a proclamation on war policy framed by the Girondins. The French nation, it said, renounced all desire for conquest but fought simply against the princes who harbored French traitors. France would never make war against peoples, only against princes. French soldiers would behave in occupied foreign territory just as they would behave at home. France would protect all foreigners who chose to fight under her banners and to dedicate themselves to liberty.

The document understated the true stance of the Girondins, however. They had become a party of international revolution. Doubtless the legislators' pronouncements were in part rhetorical. Nevertheless, they led France into a crusade which would involve an entire generation of Frenchmen and which would not really end until the defeat of Napoleon at Waterloo.

THE WAR

Dumouriez' plan was to win a quick victory by striking into the Austrian Netherlands, which was lightly garrisoned and as recently as 1790 had been in rebellion against the empire. He had served in the Prussian army and did not believe that the Prussians and Austrians could cooperate. Moreover, he knew that the Austrian court was in some confusion because of the change of emperors. It had also been distracted by the recent assassination of the king of Sweden. Dumouriez was encouraged primarily, however, by the fact that Russian troops were staging for an invasion of Poland. Prussia and Austria, which had partici-

---

[3] Schama may well be right that "patriotic war was . . . the logical consequence of everything the revolution represented." *Citizens*, p. 591.

pated in the first partition of Poland in 1772, seemed certain to demand a second share, and if denied it, would go to war with Russia. Quick French victories, it was hoped, would induce Francis II to come to terms. To make peace he had only to clear the émigrés from Germany.

Commanding the invasion of the Austrian Netherlands (Belgium) was the Count de Rochambeau of American Revolutionary fame, now a marshal of France. His army comprised two columns, one under General Dillon, an Irish soldier of fortune, and the other under the Duke de Biron. Forces on the German frontier, including the army of Lafayette, at Metz, were not to figure in the offensive campaign.

The French marched confidently into Belgium only to meet disaster. They were not only defeated, but routed. Dillon was murdered by his own troops. Biron completely lost control of his army, which fled across the frontier. In June 1792, Paris seethed with anger and fear of foreign invasion. The Austrians joked that the new motto of the French army was "Conquer or Run."

What was wrong with the French army? There was no shortage of manpower and most of the men, as Lafayette wrote Washington, were Patriots. One defect lay in the acute shortage of qualified officers. Those of the Old Regime had been nobles almost to a man and thousands had emigrated.[4] Their replacements, drawn from the middle class and the ranks of noncommissioned officers, were at considerable disadvantage. The bourgeois officers lacked the habit of command that came naturally to aristocrats. They had been reared to persuade and negotiate, not to give orders. Ex-sergeants tended either to overplay their roles as officers and to "crack the whip" too much or to overidentify with the troops. In any case, they were initially ineffective.

Moreover, the men were infused with ideas of equality and democracy appropriate for civilian life, but destructive of discipline. In one extreme case, Biron himself ordered a bayonet charge, only to be faced by his grenadiers who demanded a vote on the issue. The general was defeated, as was his army. Also making for the lack of discipline was the soldiers' distrust of the government in Paris. Still unaccustomed to a parliamentary system and a free press, they read or heard of newspaper attacks on ministers and deputies and of reports on debates in the assembly and the clubs. To many, it all seemed to reflect utter confusion in high places. Finally, the ranking generals, all still aristocrats at this point, were not all trusted by the men.[5] Three years before, officers such as Rochambeau and

[4] By August 1792, fully two-thirds had left the country.

[5] Enlisted men of the Royal Army and volunteers of '91 and '92 (or "whites" and "blues"; white was the Bourbon color) were generally of the same low social status. Thus, the "whites" reacted *much the same* as the "blues" to the Revolution. Initial hostility rapidly gave way to comaradarie. By 1792, volunteers were integrated into the line army; some divisions had Demi-Brigades of one "white" battalion and two "blue," some the reverse; some mixed the troops in battalions, others remained solidly regular. Overall, the army comprised about one-third volunteers of one year's service or less, and scant training. Despite the common *esprit* in the ranks, it was not a potent combat force. See Bertaud, *Army of the French Revolution*.

Lafayette would have been cheered anywhere as liberal friends of the people—but no more. Rochambeau sensed that he could no longer lead, and wisely retired.

The army was saved by factors which Dumouriez had thought would assure victory. As he had predicted, the Prussians and Austrians did not cooperate well. By concerted effort they might have taken Paris in May or June, but they did not. The major distracting factor was the issue of Poland. The Russian troops of Catherine the Great occupied eastern Poland in April 1792, and Prussia and Austria held their more effective regiments in the east, pending a new partition of Poland. Until this second truncation of Poland was completed in January of 1793, the war with France was a secondary matter. This did nothing, however, to allay the fears of Parisians. In fact, it gave them leisure to direct their energies to attacking those they held responsible for defeat—the government and the crown.

PARIS IN FERMENT

In May the Legislative Assembly, under Girondin leadership, passed decrees which abolished the constitutional guard of the king (1200 infantry, 600 cavalry), ordered nonjuring priests deported from France and called 20,000 provincial National Guardsmen (fédérés) to Paris. Louis XVI approved the first, as a gesture of confidence in Paris (he still had 900 Swiss guards) but vetoed the other two. This alarmed the Girondin ministers, who feared anticlerical Paris might rise against the king and were no longer certain that they would not fall with him. It was to protect themselves that they had invited the fédérés to Paris, where the National Guard was rapidly being taken over by the radical sections (wards) of the city.[6] The leaders of the sections held regular meetings and took their cues from the clubs of the Jacobins and Cordeliers. The mayor of Paris, Pétion, nominally a Girondin, was much in terror of the sections. The commander of the National Guard, Mandat, was a monarchist, but it was not known whether the troops would respond to his orders.

On 13 June 1792, Roland sent the king a letter predicting violence if he did not sanction the decrees on nonjuring priests and the fédérés:

> The Revolution is completed in men's minds; it will be finished at the price of blood and will be cemented with blood unless wisdom anticipates misfortunes which it is still possible to avoid.

Louis found the language threatening. He angrily dismissed the Girondin ministry and appointed a new one of Feuillants. The sectionnaires began arming for a march on the Tuileries. Pétion, the mayor of Paris, disappeared rather than

---

[6] The National Assembly had replaced the sixty electoral districts of Paris with forty-eight sections. This had temporarily disorganized the legions of the *sans-culottes*, but by 1792 they were stronger than ever.

oppose them, and they were encouraged by *sans-culottes* in high places, including Panis, head of the police, and Manuel, the public prosecutor. As usual, hunger as well as politics played a part. The crops had been mediocre and farmers preferred to hoard grain rather than sell it for assignats.

On 20 June, mobs surged from the Faubourgs St.-Antoine and St.-Marcel, and other quarters toward the Tuileries. They invaded the hall of the National Assembly, carrying the "heart of an aristocrat" (actually a calf's heart), dripping with blood, on a pike. In the Tuileries, the king was backed to the wall and forced to don the red liberty cap.[7] Louis remained calm, however, and was not harmed, nor was the royal family. At nightfall, the crowds withdrew.

Lafayette now complicated the situation. On 16 June he had written an emotional letter to the Legislative Assembly, predicting its demise if the Jacobin Club were not dissolved. On 28 June he appeared in Paris, demanding punishment of the instigators of the march on the Tuileries. The Legislative Assembly threatened him with trial for deserting his command and dispatched him back to Metz, an act which, as it turned out, saved his life. Paris growled disapproval.

The Girondins, frightened by the spectacle of 20 June, privately beseeched the king to return them to the ministry, and thereby save himself. Louis hotly refused and moreover decreed the suspension of Pétion as mayor and Manuel as prosecutor. The Girondins, with an eye on the angry sections, got a reversal of the suspensions by the assembly. The newly conservative Girondins, however, had lost influence in Paris to the Jacobins and Cordeliers. Robespierre, Hébert, Danton, and others began preparing for further action. Santerre was the principal organizer in the sections. Handsome, rich, famous for his horsemanship, Santerre was still a self-made man and identified with the *sans-culottes* who accepted him as one of them.

Meanwhile, in early July, the fédérés (National Guardsmen) began arriving in Paris in defiance of the king's veto. The contingent from Marseilles entered singing a *chant de guerre* which was soon famous as the "Marseillaise."[8] The arrival of the National Guardsmen brought cheer to the hearts of the Girondins, who felt that they now had protectors. They were disillusioned. The provincials, wined and dined in the sections, were easily won to the Jacobin cause.

"10 AUGUST"

Paris churned with unrest. The grain shortage remained acute and was aggravated by the diversion of large stocks to the army from the northern

---

[7] The "Phrygian Bonnet" was one of many revolutionary symbols drawn from the ancient Roman Republic. It had been brought to Rome by slaves from Phrygia (in modern-day Turkey), and had come to represent freedom and resistance to tyranny. There is an authentic Roman coin bearing on the obverse the head of Brutus, and on the reverse the Bonnet, suspended over a dagger. See C.H.V. Sutherland, *Roman Coins* (London, 1974), pp. 102, 326.

[8] In 1795, it was decreed the French National Anthem by the Convention, and though banned under the Bourbon restoration, still is. It had been composed in April 1792 by Rouget de Lisle for the Army of the Rhine, but had not caught on in Alsace.

provinces, which supplied Paris. In the summer of 1792, however, the people were moved less by hunger than distrust of the government, compounded by military defeats. Lafayette's visit had increased popular suspicion both of the commanders at the front and of the king's ministry. The Girondins, still bidding for support, attacked the Feuillant ministers, who resigned (10 July), but the king did not replace them with Girondins. Meanwhile, Dumouriez departed to command an army in Belgium. To add to the tension, news arrived that a Prussian army under the Duke of Brunswick had crossed the border and was marching on Paris. In the sections, and in the Jacobins and Cordeliers, there was intensified agitation to remove the king and to give power to a patriotic republican executive. The Girondins, still in control of the Legislative Assembly, hoped to stop short of that. On 11 July 1792 they induced the assembly to declare the "Nation in danger" and called 100,000 National Guardsmen to the colors.

On 14 July the king participated in the Bastille Day celebration (Fête de la Fédération). All went well. The parades and speeches took place on schedule. Afterward, however, there were disturbances in various quarters of Paris, with cries of "Vive Pétion" and "Hang Lafayette." On 15 July, in the Jacobins, Billaud-Varenne, Danton's secretary, called for the exile of the king, the election of a new commune, the arrest of Lafayette and "all public enemies," the dismissal of other generals, and the exemption of the poor from taxation.

A petition to this effect was circulated, and by the end of July, twenty-eight of the forty-eight sections had approved it. This was a small majority, however; not enough to support an uprising. Moreover, no one knew how the Paris National Guard would react, though most of the guardsmen seemed to be for the Jacobins.

On 1 August, however, antimonarchal opinion was suddenly crystallized by the arrival of a "Manifesto" of the Duke of Brunswick,[9] commander of the invading army. His troops, he said, would not harm civilians or loot the country, but meant to insure the safety of the French royal family.

> If the least violence, the least outrage, be done to their majesties . . . [my troops] will take . . . unforgettable vengeance by delivering the city of Paris to military punishment and total destruction. . . .

To the Parisians, this was proof positive that the royal family was in treasonous correspondence with the enemy.

By 3 August, forty-seven of the forty-eight sections had petitioned for the king's dismissal. On 4 August the Quinze-Vingts section of the Faubourg St.-Antoine—true *sans-culottes*—warned the Legislative Assembly to remove the king by 9 August or to face the wrath of Paris. Other sections sent similar messages.

---

[9] Though the duke signed the document, it had been framed by French émigrés who accompanied him. Dispatched on 25 July, it was published in Paris on 1 August.

Vergniaud and other Girondin leaders threatened Paris in return and demanded loyalty to the king. On 8 August, to the outrage of the people, the assembly absolved Lafayette of all wrongdoing. The sections, meanwhile, chose three representatives each to form a new commune and completed plans to storm the Tuileries on 10 August.

The new Commune invaded the City Hall during the night of 9–10 August. For some hours, it competed with the old Commune, which was in session. By morning, however, the rebels were in charge. They proceeded to replace all officials who were not in sympathy with them, retaining such as Pétion, Manuel, and Danton. They summoned the commander of the Paris National Guard, Mandat, a royalist, and put him under arrest. He was killed outside before he could be escorted to prison. Santerre, the knight of the *sans-culottes*, took command of the guard and withdrew it from the area of the Tuileries. The king was left under the protection of 900 Swiss guards and some 300 volunteers of the Order of Chevaliers de St. Louis.

Before the morning fog had lifted, the crowds were on the march. Howling the "Marseillaise," pikes high, they surged through the streets from the east and the north and surrounded the Tuileries. The king and royal family, guarded by the Chevaliers, withdrew to the Legislative Assembly. The Swiss, left without orders, retreated from the gardens, abandoning their cannon without firing a shot, and withdrew up the steps of the palace. As the crowd pressed in, the Swiss began firing. The crowd charged, or appeared to. Actually, those in front had heroism thrust upon them; thousands behind were pushing them forward.

At this moment, orders arrived from the king to defend the palace, but it was too late. If the elite Swiss mercenaries had been ordered earlier to use their cannon, they probably could have won the day. But left only with muzzle-loading muskets at close range, they had no chance. Most were able to get off only one shot, then had to resort to the bayonet. The masses overwhelmed them; only three hundred escaped to tell the story. By noon the people held the Tuileries and surrounded the Manège, where sat the now intimidated Legislative Assembly.

The Commune, supported by Paris, dictated to the assembly, which suspended the king from office and imprisoned him, with his family, in the Temple. It also decreed that a convention be called to write a new constitution (and when formed, to replace the Legislative Assembly, which would dissolve itself). The convention would be elected by universal manhood suffrage (through electors, but ones for which no property qualification was set), the first national assembly so chosen in the history of the world.

The events of 10 August sent a new wave of émigrés across the borders. One was the "Hero of Two Worlds," the Marquis de Lafayette, who was conspiring within the army to intervene in Paris when the capital erupted. Thus when further efforts failed, he left for England. He was captured enroute, however, by the Austrians, who imprisoned him at Olmütz (where he remained until released at the behest of Napoleon in 1797). Others who fled included the Lameth brothers, Duport, the Count de Noailles, the Duke d'Aiguillon, and the *monarchien*, Pierre

Malouet—all at some time heroes of the Revolution in earlier years. Barnave and Bailly, who remained in France, were both executed in 1793.

PROVISIONAL GOVERNMENT

While elections for the convention were being held, the assembly placed the government in the hands of a provisional executive council. The Girondins, Roland and Servan, served as ministers of interior and war, respectively, posts they had held earlier under the king. The commanding figure, however, was Jacques Danton, the best known of the popular leaders. Though not the most radical, he was the darling of Paris.

Danton was gloriously ugly, careless of dress and often wine-soaked. He had the same "bad boy" appeal which had earlier been exploited by Mirabeau, whom he somewhat resembled. Danton was shorter, but he had the same bulk, pock-marked face, and mane of hair—and the same ability to adjust his language as well as his ideas, at times, to suit his audience. Danton had been an aspiring lawyer in 1789, and in 1793 was quite rich, a fact for which his courtroom labors did not altogether account. Parisians did not care; he was "one of the people." His political style resembled that of an old-fashioned American ward leader. He could mouth high-sounding ideals in the assemblies, but in the streets and bistros he talked of food and jobs and was always ready to buy a round of drinks or to take cash from his own pocket for a widow, some orphans, a wounded veteran, or an unemployed worker. He had little faith in grand schemes or in the masses. One by one, he loved the people, and they him. (Robespierre was quite different; he adored the people in the abstract, but had no rapport with them as individuals.)

At heart, Danton was a moderate who favored the use of violence only as practical political considerations demanded. His influence was destined to gradually evaporate over the next year and a half, although his popularity with the masses persisted. In August and September 1792, Paris tolerated the uninspiring and essentially Girondin provisional government because of him. Even Danton, however, could not keep Paris quiet.

THE "FIRST TERROR"

While elections for the Convention dragged on, Parisians developed an hysterical fear of enemies in their midst. It resulted from news that the Prussian army was nearing Paris, the arrest of hundreds of "enemies" by the "Watch Committee" of the Commune, and the daily spectacle of volunteers marching off for the front (mostly passing through from the provinces), which made it seem that the capital was being denuded of troops. Marat's *L'Ami du Peuple* (Friend of the People) and other newspapers warned that enemies lurked within the city —nobles, priests, and their minions, subverting the war effort and waiting for an opportunity to strike. Rumors flew that an uprising might start in the prisons, jammed with some 3000 inmates, mostly criminals, but including refractory priests and other political offenders. On 2 September news arrived that Verdun was threatened—the last fortress on the road to Paris. The Watch Committee of the Commune called the city to arms. The result was the "September Massacres." Mobs formed under self-appointed leaders and invaded the prisons, killing "priests and aristocrats" and their presumed sympathizers outright or after hearings before peoples' tribunals. Suspicious looking persons were hacked to death on the streets. In five days the people executed some 1100 "enemies." The Commune, satisfied, finally brought the violence to an end. If some innocents had perished, they congratulated themselves that only "good Republicans" now dared raise their heads.

Meanwhile the government had set up the now famous guillotine in the Place du Carrousel, before the Tuileries. The official instrument of execution (which hardly needs description) had been adopted because it was considered more merciful than other means of dispatching prisoners. It had been recommended on that basis by Dr. Joseph Guillotin, delegate to the National Assembly of 1789 (who objected to having it called after him, however, since it was the invention of Dr. Antoine Louis) and had been tested on sheep, cadavers, and finally convicted criminals. Surely its heavy blade, crashing down from a great height on the victim's neck, brought swift and sure death.[10]

INTERIM POLICY AND LEGISLATION

Danton, fully cognizant of the weakness of the French armies, made secret peace tentatives to the enemy while putting up a confident front. He may also have used bribes to damp the ardor of certain Austrian generals. At the same time, with the cooperation of the assembly and the Commune, he sent civilian commissioners to the front to supervise military decision making.

The Legislative Assembly, meanwhile, outdid itself to please Paris. It repassed legislation vetoed earlier by the king that required refractory priests to leave France within two weeks or face deportation. More classes of feudal dues (but not all) were abolished without indemnity. District governments were empowered to survey grain supplies and requisition as necessary to feed the cities. All this forecast the attitudes of the upcoming convention.

---

[10] We have no executee's testimony, but the guillotine seemed more painless than hanging or the firing squad, and eminently preferable to beheading by axe or sword (customary for nobles under the Old Regime). Executioners, though highly paid specialists, were sometimes overfortified with drink and/or had victims who flinched or dodged. If a headsman only partially severed the neck on the first blow, the prisoner might begin to thrash about, spurting blood, and the execution could turn into a gory killing as more blows were delivered. The guillotine was used by the French government until 1981, when capital punishment was abolished, though public executions had been halted in 1939. It was deemed more humane than the gas chamber or electric chair.

On 20 September 1792 the Legislative Assembly dissolved itself and the convention met for the first time. On the same day, French armies scored an astounding military victory.

VALMY

On 20 September, the French met the Prussians under the Duke of Brunswick at Valmy, and on the 21st, the enemy was in retreat. Earlier, the duke had separated two French armies, under Dumouriez and Kellerman, brushed aside Dumouriez, and moved in leisurely stages through the Argonne toward Paris. Brunswick was in no hurry. He was almost sixty (very old for a field general). He hated the French émigrés who accompanied him and who acted as if he had been sent to serve them, gave unwanted advice, and refused to keep to the rear, as he ordered. Moreover, the general suspected that Austria was pitting Prussia against France in order to best Prussia in the dispute over Polish territory. His slow movement gave Dumouriez time to join with Kellerman.

On the morning of 20 September, Brunswick found the French armies behind him on the heights of Valmy. A desultory and strange battle ensued, beginning with the fact that the Prussians fought with their backs to Paris. It was largely a long artillery duel. The French stood on the defensive all day; the Prussians charged only once, and weakly. Brunswick had not wanted to give battle at all, but simply to maintain pressure on the French by maneuvering. He had marched only because his king, more trusting of the Austrians than he, had ordered it. Moreover, the Prussian troops were wracked with dysentery, and many could hardly walk, much less fight. (They had gorged themselves on green apples in the Argonne.) The French had 50,000 men to Brunswick's 34,000. French artillery was better (designed for Louis XVI by Gribeauval, later used by Napoleon). The Prussian troops were regulars, however, and the French weakened by an infusion of volunteers and short of experienced officers.[11] Brunswick's army was superior (discounting the dysentery, which would have passed in a day or so); it seems evident that he simply did not care to fight. His losses for the day were 180; the French 500. After nightfall the Prussians reorganized, and before daybreak the next day marched around the French and retreated toward the German border.

The famous German author, Goethe, viewed the battle and drew the unfounded conclusion that inspired citizen-soldiers of the French Republic had routed the fabled Prussian army. "Here and today begins a new era in the history of the world," he pronounced. As it turned out, he was right. Surely warfare would never be the same again. Citizen armies, in ever greater mass, were the wave of the future, together with ever more complete mobilization of whole nations, civilians included, for war.

[11] See above pp. 113–114.

Fluke victory or not, Valmy was celebrated by the French as a great triumph. It had saved Paris; so much seemed beyond dispute. French morale soared at a time when a boost was badly needed. Though there were defeats ahead, the spirit of the republicans who had "routed the army of Frederick the Great" infused the entire army. As it became larger and better organized it did in fact become irresistible.

THE CONVENTION

The Convention, which on 21 September jubilantly received the news of Valmy, had 749 members, including 189 from previous assemblies. It was a middle-class body, with only two workers (both skilled artisans) and one peasant, though twenty-three nobles had been elected, including the Duke d'Orléans, who now called himself Philippe Egalité. There were only sixty-three businessmen, manufacturers, and bankers, however. The vast majority of the members were lawyers and/or officeholders with a scattering of army and navy officers, doctors, and teachers. There was one black member, J. B. Belley, a wealthy resident of France who represented Santo Domingo (Haiti). There were two foreign deputies, both honorary French citizens: Tom Paine, of American Revolutionary fame, and a German baron, long resident in France, who had adopted the name Anacharsis Clootz.[12]

The Convention met initially in the Manège, but soon moved into the Tuileries, occupying the former Salle des Machines. This was a long but narrow room with 60-foot ceilings, and seats were installed to face the rostrum in steep, semicircular tiers. The high seats to the speaker's left were taken (for no particular reason) by about 145 radicals, who, at first jokingly, began calling themselves the Montagnards (Mountaineers), or collectively the Mountain. The Girondins, some 165, ultimately the conservatives, sat on the right.[13] Those committed to neither party—the majority—took the middle seats. In the Convention the terms left, right, and center gained their present-day political connotations.[14]

In the first weeks, however, there was great unanimity. To begin with, whereas, in the previous assembly there had been officially no republicans, in this one there were no avowed monarchists. The Girondins, the "original republicans," took the lead in the Convention, and still consorted with the future Mountaineers in the Jacobin Club.

---

[12] The supposed name of a Sythian (German) friend of Solon, the Athenian reformer of the sixth century, B.C. Clootz' real name was Jean-Baptiste du Val-de-Grâce, but even that was a "translation" from the German.

[13] The term "Girondin" is used for convenience. M. J. Sydenham has clearly shown that these men were loosely associated, independent republicans, who had in common only the conviction that the Revolution was (or should be) over, since the monarchy had been overturned. There was no great class difference between them and the Montagnards.

[14] This could not have happened earlier. For one thing, the seats in the Manège encircled the speaker's platform.

THE REPUBLIC On its first full day in session, 21 September 1792, the Convention abolished the monarchy, and on 22 September decreed that all public documents henceforth be dated the "First Year of Liberty" or Year I of the Republic.[15] Finally, on 25 September, the Republic was formally proclaimed— "one and indivisible." At this point the right and left were united in their fear that France might lose its unity (one thing assured by monarchical tradition) and might fall into provincial and factional conflicts which might doom the Republic.

A committee was appointed to propose a constitution on which the Girondins had a heavy majority. The membership included Brissot, Vergniaud, Gensonné, Tom Paine, and Condorcet, along with two who later went over to the Mountain, Barère and Danton, and also Pétion, a chastened Jacobin soon denounced by the Mountain. The dominant figure was the ex-Marquis de Condorcet, the "last of the *philosophes*."

In October and November, French armies won further victories in Belgium and the Rhineland, which brought to the fore the issue of policy in conquered territories. Again, the Convention followed the Girondin lead, approving essentially the program which had been voiced in the Legislative Assembly. A short propaganda decree of 19 November 1792 set the tone for many future proclamations:

> The Convention declares, in the name of the French Nation that she will give fraternity and aid to all peoples who desire to recover their liberty.

In practice, this meant that France would encourage revolutionaries beyond her borders. It was a program of international revolution.

With the Republic proclaimed and an aggressive foreign policy enunciated, however, unanimity ended, and Girondin dominance faded. The left, some 200 strong, gradually perfected its organization, and taking advantage of its connections with the Commune of Paris, began to vie for leadership.

THE CONVENTION POLARIZES The spokesmen of the left—the Mountain—or Jacobins (since they soon drove the Girondins from that club) were those who had rallied Paris on 10 August—Robespierre, Marat, Camille Desmoulins, and (after vain attempts to mediate between the parties) Danton. They rallied to themselves the most militant of the seasoned politicians, such as Joseph Fouché and Philippe Egalité (the Duke d'Orléans) and firebrands such as the twenty-five year old Saint-Just. Their strength was in Paris. Their principal leaders were guided by Rousseau's *Social Contract* and had no doubt that they could determine the "general will" of the French, which they tended to identify with the will of Paris. They did not shrink from measures to centralize power in the capital, and even dabbled with socialism (by the definitions of the time). The Mountaineers

---

[15] The Revolutionary Calendar was not put into effect until the following year, however. It will be discussed later.

gradually learned they could gain a majority on issues by intimidating the uncommitted "Center," where sat such former legislative eminences as Sieyès and Grégoire. Initially, however, this group, derisively called the "plain," "frog pond," or "marsh," voted on most issues with the Girondins.

The Girondins depended on the same spokesmen as in the Legislative Assembly—Brissot, Vergniaud, Isnard, and Roland, in particular. They labored under the suspicion of the Paris masses (or outright hostility) because of their identification with the former government, and later with generals still in the field (Dumouriez was a hero at the beginning, but would not remain so). They were also "chronic" constitutionalists and legalists, who, to the impatient or fearful (war, another invasion, were ever-present specters) increasingly seemed habitual obstructionists. The Girondins were also vocal opponents of further popular demonstrations and opposed any measures which violated private property rights. On the control of food supplies, a vital matter to Parisians, they fought for local, decentralized authority rather than national control.

The strength of the Girondins was in the provinces and was strongest among the bourgeoisie of the cities, who feared centralization of power meant victimization by Paris. (The Girondins no more represented the peasantry than did the Mountain; both factions feared the traditionalist, royalist, religious peasantry of the remoter areas.) It was impossible to make the pressure of their constituents felt in the manner in which the Mountain could call up the Paris sections.

There was no great difference in the average wealth or social origins of the Girondins and Mountain (as was long believed). The Girondins were simply less authoritarian in outlook, less attuned to centralization and bureaucratization (one could say less modern), and more protective of property rights than the Montagnards. In the long run, their principles would guide nineteenth-century liberal constitutionalists (including the underlying assumption that the propertied classes should govern). In the short run, however, the Girondins were at a distinct disadvantage—in all things, they were too moderate.

This became apparent in the first great test of strength between the parties, which was over the fate of the king.

TRIAL OF THE KING

From the first, the problem of the disposition of Louis XVI was on everyone's mind. Yet the deputies hesitated to move precipitously against the representative of an institution over a thousand years old, an institution which many knew still had wide support among the common people (even if Louis XVI did not, and even that was doubtful). As a first step, therefore, the Convention established a committee (chaired by a Girondin, Jean-Baptiste Mailhe) to determine its legal alternatives. Under the Constitution of 1791, the king was subject to trial only if he had abdicated or led an army against the nation or condoned the attack of such an army. It was not clear that he had done any of these things.

The committee ruled that while the Legislative Assembly had been bound by the Constitution, the Convention, representing the "sovereign people," was not. Debate then went forward on what charges to bring against the king and the question of his penalty. The Girondins saw that a trial was unavoidable, but hoped to save the king's life. Some, as a last resort, favored referring the verdict and sentence to the people.

The Mountain trumpeted the feelings of the Paris street. Saint-Just, a recent law graduate and the "golden boy" of the left, summed up the case. "Louis XVI is not an accused but an enemy. One law ought to be applied to him: that which destroyed Caesar in the Senate of Rome . . . with the thrust of 22 daggers."

Most of the evidence available against Louis related to "crimes" committed long before the war—payments to nonjuring priests, subsidies to royalist newspapers, contributions to the émigré army, and the like. Much was made of Bouillé's threatening letter to the National Assembly after the flight to Varennes, which, however, only proved what everyone had known—that the king had not been kidnapped. The Convention still hesitated.

Then on 20 November, a locksmith revealed the location of a mass of documents in a secret safe which he had helped the king install in the Tuileries, and sentiment for a trial became overwhelming. Most of the material was very old and proved little more than that Louis had tried to preserve his authority. It showed that he had approved the so-called massacre of the Champ de Mars (1791), that he had planned to bribe Pétion, Santerre, and others to prevent the assault on the Tuileries of 10 August. The new evidence was not really damning, if it was voluminous (650 pages). But somehow the sensational discovery of the secret *armoire de fer* was enough in itself. The public saw its mere existence as proof of dark plotting against the nation.

Robespierre rose in the Convention to demand that Louis be condemned to death immediately without trial. This the Convention rejected, but it voted overwhelmingly to try "Louis Capet."[16] The ex-king was charged in effect with conspiracy against the nation, though his crimes were specified in great detail. It was a convenient charge, since it would not be necessary to prove that Louis had committed treason, but merely that he had planned to do so.

There was never much doubt of the verdict. Nevertheless, the trial lasted from 11 December to 15 January with the deputies often sitting seventeen hours a day. On the first day the king was brought from the Temple to hear the charges, which he vehemently denied. He was questioned for three hours about his alleged crimes, from plotting counterrevolution with Mirabeau in 1790 to the bribes offered before 10 August 1792. Though totally unprepared, he made a good showing, denying each accusation with apparent honesty, and never questioning the legality of the proceedings.

---

[16] Louis kept insisting, to no avail, that even if he were no longer king, he was not Louis Capet, either. He was descended from Hugh Capet, the tenth-century Frankish king, but his name was Louis de Bourbon.

The king's formal defense was planned by François Tronchet, an aging ex-*parlementaire* (by appointment) and the ex-minister and *philosophe*, Malesherbes, seventy-two, who felt honor bound to serve the king in bad times as he had in good. The case was presented by the young Count de Sèze, who was appointed by the Convention. Malesherbes paid for his valor with his life the next year.

The king's defense, in which he took part with great coolness, was based on his immunities under the Constitution of 1791. In addition, his counsel challenged specific counts of the conspiracy charge, which included, for example, preparing to defend the Tuileries on 10 August, which had resulted in bloodshed. The king, they argued, had done no more than oppose an illegal insurrection, and initially with the support of the municipal authorities. They made a good case, but to no avail. The king was declared guilty on 15 January by a vote of 683 to 39.

The sentence remained to be decided. The Girondins also (as they had repeatedly before) proposed a national plebiscite on the verdict and/or sentence. They had faith that the conservative peasantry would at least vote to save the king's life. The Jacobins, of course, hotly opposed a referendum, and the Convention, surrounded by the emotion-charged crowds of Paris, voted against referring any decisions to the people.

On 16–17 January the Mountain scored an additional victory—the death penalty for the king. From 8 P.M. on the 16th, all night, and into the afternoon of the 17th, deputies filed to the rostrum and voted aloud. More than expected, 288 voted for imprisonment or exile, while 46 more favored reprieve (or delay of sentence). However, 361 flatly voted for death, and 26 more for death with reprieve (delay). Thus the king was sentenced to death by a vote of 387 to 334. (The count for immediate death was 361 to 360, but it mattered little.)

On 21 January 1793, Louis XVI went to the guillotine. He died well. Paris, however, paid little tribute to his valor. Its heroes were the Jacobins and the leaders of the Mountain who had brought about the death of the "tyrant." The Girondins had discredited themselves with Paris by their defense of the king— however ineffective.[17] The factions continued to clash, though the execution of Louis XVI made the foreign war a matter of victory or death for the Republic.

WAR, CONVENTION, AND PARIS

In November 1792, Dumouriez had invaded the Austrian Netherlands, winning victory after victory. Custine, commanding the French army in the Rhineland, made major advances in the early months of 1793. Meanwhile,

---

[17] One third of them voted for death, however, in the end, for whatever reason, including Brissot and Vergniaud (though with delay or suspension of sentence, as was the case with most of the others).

Montesquiou and Anselme invaded Savoy and Nice, which were annexed to France "by popular demand," expressed in the petitions of local Jacobins. The Convention heard speeches, however, about extending France to her "natural boundaries"—the Alps, the Pyrenees and the Rhine—a goal long cherished by French kings, notably Louis XIV.

In view of the expansionist policies of the Convention, which encouraged "Jacobins" all over Europe and even in Britain, the European powers had become increasingly hostile. Britain remained neutral, however, until her commercial interests were challenged by the conquest of Belgium and the opening of the Scheldt for commerce. Spain had remained neutral because Charles IV had hoped to save his Bourbon cousin, Louis XVI.[18]

After the king's execution, Britain, Holland, and Spain withdrew their ambassadors. The Convention, its confidence bolstered by victories on all fronts, declared war on Britain and Holland in February 1793 and on Spain in March. Piedmont-Sardinia and Naples soon joined the coalition against France. The pope lent moral support, and a little later, troops as well (by subsidy). Many German states furnished troops to Austria or Prussia. Thus by mid-1793, France found herself at war with virtually all the powers of Europe except Russia.

Military reverses were almost inevitable. The French army, though now seemingly inspired, numbered only 300,000 men, distributed among armies in the Netherlands, Germany, and on the Italian and Spanish borders. Moreover, the British navy might land an invasion force from the Atlantic or Mediterranean, so that the coastal defenses had to be strengthened. The British immediately began to attack French merchantmen, interdicting essential grain shipments from the Baltic and North Africa.

In March 1793, Dumouriez was twice defeated by the Austrian general Coburg in the Netherlands. Already disheartened by the triumph of the Mountain in the Convention, Dumouriez agreed to join the Austrians in a march on Paris. When his troops refused to follow, he deserted to the enemy. In the same month, Custine sustained defeats. The desertion of Dumouriez, however, was a crowning blow to the Girondins. He was "their general."

Paris was in a black mood already because of continuous shortages of food. The Convention, though it had resisted general price controls, allowed the city to hold the price of bread at 12 sous for the four-pound loaf, and the Commune subsidized bakeries so that they could sell at that price. Flour shortages, however, produced bread shortages all the same. On uncontrolled items, prices soared. In April 1793 the price of beef was at 136 percent of the 1790 average, that of sugar 400 percent.

In the sections, Jacques Roux gained wide notoriety by demanding nationwide control of wages and prices and a full-scale assault on hoarders and profiteers, for

---

[18] He had offered to receive him as an exile and guarantee his noninterference in French affairs. His ambassador had also distributed millions in bribes—to what effect is unknown.

whom he demanded the death penalty. This ex-priest, whose followers were called the Enragés (madmen), represented the *menu peuple*, the voiceless masses, those below the status of property-owning *sans-culottes*. He had no organization, however (which proved his undoing, eventually). Nevertheless, Roux influenced opinion in Paris in the spring and early summer of 1793 and was a force to be contended with.

In April 1793 the Convention established a Committee of Public Safety as the national executive. Danton, by that time unquestionably a Montagnard, was the leading figure. Responding first to the demands of the Enragés, the committee pushed through the convention the first "Law of the Maximum." It "froze" prices on grain at the average for 1793 (through 1 May) in each department and decreed they would drop to lower maximums each month. (This assuaged the Paris masses, but not for long. The law was not vigorously enforced.)

Danton, meanwhile, urged on the armies ("Audacity and more audacity!"), but quietly undertook to negotiate peace settlements, playing especially on the antipathy between the Prussians and Austrians. To complicate his task, a domestic revolt began in the Vendée. There, the peasants rose, apparently under the leadership of nobles and clergy, some of them émigrés returned by the British navy. They formed the "Royal and Catholic Grand Army" which overran the countryside and besieged the larger towns (which were republican). National Guards had to be reinforced by the army. The movement spread into Brittany where the rebels organized into guerrilla bands, the *Chouans* (night owls). (See Map 3.2, p. 99.)

The Girondins had voted against the "Maximum," enraging the Parisians. They were blamed both for defeats in the foreign war and for the counterrevolution in the Vendée. In May the Girondins, in desperation, accused the Paris Commune of promoting disorder. The Convention approved a committee to investigate, but then repealed its resolution under pressure from the Mountain. They accused Marat of treason, and Hébert, editor of the newspaper *Père Duchesne*, which supported the Enragés, of inciting to riot. Both were tried and acquitted (Marat in absentia).

Defeated at every turn in Paris, the Girondins were, nevertheless, convinced that the majority of Frenchmen were behind them. "France will destroy Paris!" Isnard shouted to the Convention. This was on 25 May 1793. On 30 May there were anti-Girondin riots. On 2 June the Convention expelled the Girondin "enemies of the people," while 80,000 National Guardsmen, summoned by the Commune, surrounded the Tuileries and prevented interference.

Some Girondins had already fled; twenty-nine were arrested, of whom most later went to the guillotine, including Brissot and Vergniaud. Roland managed to reach safety in Belgium but Mme. Roland was made prisoner and later executed. Her husband committed suicide. Condorcet was able to hide out for a time and finished his magnificent *Progress of the Human Mind*, but he was finally captured and died in prison (probably a suicide). Perhaps the most astonished prisoner was the international revolutionary, Tom Paine, a Girondin, but arrested (technically interned) as an Englishman. It took the American minister in Paris, James Monroe, almost a year to get him freed.[19]

The Girondins, however, did in fact, have support in France at large. There were uprisings in sixty departments. And in the south and west the major cities went into revolt against the government. These included Lyons, Bordeaux, Marseilles, and Toulon. This added to the enormous pressure the government already bore and increased the fear of Parisians of assault by enemies within and without.

The situation could hardly have been worse for the Republic. Strong government was now possible, however, since the Mountain was in absolute control of the Convention and was supported by the Jacobin Club, the Commune of Paris, and the sections. The immensity of danger brought to leadership the most dedicated, forceful, and ruthless revolutionaries of the period, of whom Maximilien Robespierre (deservedly or not) was destined to become the most notorious.

[19] Even then the U.S. Government refused to allow him to return home until 1802. During the trial of Louis XVI, Paine had urged the Convention to exile the king to the United States, arguing that, whatever crimes he might have committed against the French, he had helped the Americans win independence.

The revolutionary government owes its enemies
nothing but death.
—*Robespierre*

THE TERROR
(1793–1794)

For the Republic to survive, it required a government of maximum possible decision, force, will, and imagination—one which could mobilize her resources and manpower for total war. In June 1793, France was under attack by the world's greatest powers; her major cities were in revolt against the Jacobin Convention; counterrevolutionary armies were in control of the Vendée (and most of ancient Poitou, Anjou, and Brittany); even Paris, center of Montagnard power, was surly and threatening violence. This situation produced the government of Terror, at the outset a war government granted exceptional powers.

It required a summer of fumbling, however, before the Convention resigned itself to giving power to truly audacious leaders.

LAST WHIMPERS OF MODERATION

Danton's Committee of Public Safety (the executive since April 1793), persisted in negotiating with foreign enemies and did little to strengthen France's armies. Throughout June, it temporized on the fate of the arrested Girondins. Danton involved the Convention in completing and approving the Constitution of 1793 (never promulgated)—until then a Girondin project, drafted by Condorcet—in a vain attempt to convince the provinces that the government meant well.[1] Taxes were decreased, to the advantage of the provincial bourgeoisie. The Convention also sought to quell counterrevolutionary sentiment in the countryside by abolishing (finally) feudal dues without compensation and by authorizing

---

[1] It provided for the direct election, by universal manhood suffrage, of deputies to the legislature. Local autonomy was assured, however, by provisions similar to those in the Constitution of 1791.

division of the village commons. Most peasants, however, had long since stopped paying dues, and most communes later voted *not* to parcel out the commons.

At the same time, the Paris *sans-culottes*,[2] by whose cooperation the Mountain held power, were neglected. The Law of the Maximum (passed in May), fixing grain prices, was not enforced. The Convention had authorized a "revolutionary army"—a sort of workers' militia—but declined to organize it. This denied pay to "good republicans" who were unemployed and deprived the sections of a force to arrest "suspects" and to insure the food supply. The *sans-culottes* wanted action to provide cheap food and jobs for the "deserving" workers whom they represented and among whom they lived. They got the promise, in the Constitution of 1793, of the "right to subsistence," but little more. Nevertheless, their heroes, the more radical Montagnards, Robespierre among them, went along with Danton for a time, since they were not averse to securing domestic peace without civil war.

Enemy successes, however, foreign and domestic, doomed moderation and the Danton committee. In June, French armies were defeated by the Prussians in the Rhineland and by the British-Hanovarian army in Belgium. In the west, peasant counterrevolutionary armies put republican cities, such as Nantes and Angers, under siege. The "Federal Cities" of the south and west—Lyons, Bordeaux, Marseilles, Toulon—signaled a fight to the death. Corsica revolted and got British aid. On 10 July the Convention removed Danton from the Committee of Public Safety and reduced it to nine members, seven of whom, including Couthon and Saint-Just, were militant leftists.

Paris went wild three days later (13 July), when Marat, the "Friend of the People," was murdered in his bath by Charlotte Corday, a beautiful noblewoman from Normandy. The crime had been committed almost casually, at midday, by the polite young woman who had asked for an interview with the famous journalist, working seated in his medicinal bath. Paris became paranoid; the people saw "enemies" everywhere.

In the Jacobin Club, Maximilien Robespierre called for a "Government of Terror," death to the enemies of the Republic, and a nation in arms.

THE GREAT COMMITTEE FORMS

On 27 July 1793 the Convention placed Robespierre on the Committee of Public Safety. Already established as a proponent of a strong executive, he immediately became its chief spokesman, and the Convention was sufficiently alarmed, finally, to support him. Thus, from the beginning, and increasingly over

---

[2] On the *sans-culottes*, see Chapter 1, p. 51. While older books use the term to describe all the workers—or even all those below the level of bourgeois—most scholars now use it to mean the section (ward) leaders, who were artisans, shopkeepers, and journeymen, with a few masters and others. They identified with the "respectable" workers, not the "rabble."

the next year, he was seen as the dominant figure in government—and latterly a dictator—though the policies of the committee were not always his.

The Convention expected to share power with the new committee as it had with Danton's. It was not to be. On 5 September, and again on the 6th, mobs from the sections (called up by the Paris Commune) occupied the galleries of the Convention, shouting "War on Tyrants!" "War on Aristocrats!" "War on Hoarders!" No one was harmed, but Paris made it clear that it was weary of the plodding pace of the Convention and would back direct and violent action by the committee.

If the committee could dictate to the Convention, however, it was answerable to the crowds of Paris. Jacques Roux had committed political suicide by accusing the Mountain, Jacobins, and Cordeliers of betraying the poor.[3] His Enragés program was nonetheless alive and being pushed by the followers of Jacques Hébert, editor of the newspaper *Père Duchesne*. The Hébertists demanded guaranteed jobs, food at moderate prices, death to aristocrats and the rich, aid to the sick and elderly, and free public education (all without details as to means). The movement was also violently anti-Christian (discussed further below).

Popular pressure induced Robespierre in September to admit to the Committee of Public Safety two men more radical than he—Collot d'Herbois and Billaud-Varenne, both atheists with socialist inclinations. The legislation which the committee recommended to the Convention reflected his own thinking, but priorities decidedly were influenced by these men, backed by the Commune and the street. So great was the threat to the committee, the demise of which could mean outright anarchy, that Danton was heard seconding the motions of Billaud-Varenne.

The Convention dutifully voted terror to be the "order of the day." It suspended the Constitution of 1793, approved by the electors in August. It passed a new Law of the Maximum, ordering the immediate establishment, nationwide, of maximum prices on food and other scarce items and providing for minimum wages as required. Major violation constituted treason and was punishable by death.

To complement the Committee of Public Safety, the Committee of General Security was reconstituted. (It dated from October 1792 but had been ineffectual.) Its new leaders, André Amar and Marc Vadier, were among the most zealous and merciless "guardians of the people," as befitted their mission, which was to organize a nationwide network to discover traitors. Serving this committee was the Revolutionary Tribunal, formed to render peoples' justice to those deemed dangerous to the public safety. The prosecutor was Fouquier-Tinville, a sallow middle-aged lawyer who had been a minor prosecutor under the Old Regime and

---

[3] Roux had branded the Constitution of 1793 "undemocratic." Robespierre denounced him as an enemy of public order and accused him of being in Austrian pay. He was arrested (June 1793) and condemned to death by the Revolutionary Tribunal, but after months in prison, committed suicide (1794). See p. 151, below.

who developed an overweening zeal for his new job. The tribunal was organized into four sections, of which two were in session at all times, twenty-four hours a day. There were ten to sixteen judges for each case, and some sixty jurors, but verdicts were often dictated by the gallery. There was no appeal from the tribunal. Its sentences were executed immediately (though not all were death penalties), and the property of those convicted was confiscated.

The Convention also enacted a new law of suspects in September. Under this law, anyone who by his actions, remarks, writings, or otherwise (a sour expression could be enough) revealed himself to be an "enemy of liberty" could be accused of treason. Former nobles, returned émigrés, and their relatives were automatically subject to accusation, as were those expelled from the Convention or public office or those who had been previously refused a certificate of "civism."[4] Further, reflecting Robespierre's determination to create a "Republic of Virtue," all people were suspect who could not show that they were honestly employed or performing patriotic duty. This enabled the police to clear the streets of vagabonds, beggars, prostitutes, and others. It also put in jeopardy those who lived on investments.

The committee first flaunted its strength, however, by executing those already imprisoned whose fate had been left in doubt. In October, Queen Marie Antoinette went to the guillotine, looking pitifully old and gray after a year in the Temple (she was not quite thirty-eight). Paris gave her no sympathy. "It is the greatest of all joys for Père Duchesne," wrote Hébert.[5] Following the queen in rapid succession to the "National Razor" were (among others) Philippe Égalité (the Duke d'Orléans), snatched from his seat in the Mountain; Bailly, hero of the early revolution and ex-mayor of Paris; Barnave, co-architect of most of the reforms of 1789–1791; Madame Roland, hostess and policymaker of the Girondins, and twenty-one Girondin ex-deputies. In the year of the Terror, 2600 heads were claimed by "Sainte Guillotine" in Paris alone.[6]

THE TWELVE Robespierre's committee established a government purporting to represent the common man, especially the proletariat, a task for which its membership seemed singularly unsuited. It comprised eight lawyers, one ex-Protestant minister (who had also been a ship's captain), one actor-playwright, and two army officers—both engineers. One of the lawyers, Marie-Jean Hérault de Séchelles, was an ex-noble. The other members were of comfortable middle-class origin. None had suffered privation before 1789 except Collot d'Herbois, who had run away from home as a boy to go on the stage. None had at any time worked

---

[4] These were issued by watch committees in the sections of Paris to "trustworthy citizens." It was impossible to leave Paris openly without one and very dangerous to move about.

[5] *Le Père Duchesne*, Hébert's newspaper, had taken the place of Marat's *L'Ami du Peuple* as the voice of the *sans-culottes*. The language, if anything, was more base than that of its predecessor. Hébert was known affectionately in Paris as the "Homer of Excrement."

[6] The total for France (not all by the guillotine) was perhaps 50,000, as will be discussed below. "National Razor" and "Sainte Guillotine" were Hébert's expressions.

with his hands. Hérault and Billaud-Varenne had inherited fortunes. The rest had pursued quite successful careers.

However, the opportunities of most had been limited under the Old Regime. Jeanbon Saint-André, the Protestant minister, had been without civil rights. The two army officers, Lazare Carnot and Claude-Antoine Prieur, were commoners with scant expectation of ever rising above the rank of captain. Robespierre had been a small-town lawyer with little chance of ever being admitted to the Paris bar. The same applied to Louis-Antoine Saint-Just, Georges Couthon, Robert Lindet, and Pierre-Louis Prieur.[7] All identified, however, from conviction or opportunism, with the *sans-culottes* of Paris.

Robespierre, Couthon, and Saint-Just, who set the political tone of the committee, were disciples of Rousseau and believers in government for the people by dedicated intellectuals. Collot d'Herbois and Billaud-Varenne were Rousseauists with socialist sentiments. All professed devotion to the Constitution of 1793, which they solemnly pledged to put into effect as soon as conditions allowed. If they had, France would have been the most democratic country in the world.

The justification for the committee's dictatorship and the Terror, though, was danger to the nation. The Terror, represented by the guillotine, was intended to silence any challenge to authority. This accomplished, France presumably could mobilize all her resources, human and material, to oppose the enemy within and without. The Terror was a means of discipline, therefore, a means of making every citizen contribute to the utmost to "save the nation." Presumably, with the winning of the war and restoration of domestic peace, the government of Terror would no longer be necessary.

As it turned out, the committee, usually identified with Robespierre, lasted only a year.[8] Nevertheless, its accomplishments and the plans it produced in that short time have made the Terror the most studied period of the Revolution. Thus the major members of the committee would seem to merit introductions.

Maximilien Robespierre, thirty-five, was a lawyer from Arras, who had come to Paris as a deputy to the Estates General. "The Incorruptible," as he has been justly called, was a political puritan to whom politics was a religion. Small, trim, fine-featured, and aristocratic in manner and dress, but usually severe of mien, his life was totally centered about work. He was a bachelor with no interest in money or pleasures, and who lived simply in rented rooms. Power fascinated him, but he never wavered in his conviction that he used power for the benefit of the

[7] The two Prieurs were called by their place of origin. Pierre-Louis was Prieur of the Marne; Captain Claude-Antoine was Prieur of the Côte d'Or.

[8] It is reemphasized that Robespierre did not dictate to the committee. Public opinion credited him with much more power than he had, probably because he most frequently defended the committee's policies, both in the Convention and the Jacobin Club. Barère spoke at least as often, but principally to present legislation. Robespierre also had a reputation as a proponent of radical causes dating from 1789, and was in the spotlight during the more spectacular debates and events (e.g., the "Fête of the Supreme Being," p. 155) of the Terror.

people. Robespierre inspired awe and respect, not love. He led by force of intellect and singleness of purpose. Although not a good speaker, he held audiences by his intensity and conviction. Robespierre loved the people from a distance, in the abstract, not one by one. For a time, he and "his" committee held sway over Parisians by a combination of popular acts and fear. When he lost control of the Convention, however, the people watched his destruction with indifference.

Robespierre's most loyal supporters were Saint-Just and Couthon. Louis-Antoine Saint-Just, twenty-six, was a law school graduate from Picardy. Tall, handsome, and a fire-eating orator, he was at once sublimely idealistic and bloodthirsty. A slashing political fighter, a phrasemaker, and a devout believer that men should be "forced to be free," he could shout almost in the same breath, "Human welfare is a new idea in Europe!" and "Heads! heads! and more heads!" Georges Couthon, thirty-seven, a lawyer from Auvergne, was a paralytic cripple who went about in a wheelchair and had to be lifted to the rostrum. A family man of humanitarian instincts and one of the better-read of the committeemen, he could be vitriolic in speech and ruthless in action as only a man in perpetual pain can be.

Jean-Nicolas Billaud-Varenne and Jean-Marie Collot d'Herbois were socialists in the utopian fashion of the time. Both eventually turned on Robespierre, whom they considered too conservative. Billaud-Varenne was a lawyer, writer, and sometime actor and teacher. An attractive figure, he was one of the better speakers. Collot, at forty-three, was slight, handsome, of mercurial temperament, and given to precipitous schemes, for example, blowing up the prisons to rid Paris of enemies, wholesale. Though poorly educated, he was adept at voicing borrowed ideas on the stage of the Convention.

Of the working members, the most important were Carnot and Barère. Lazare Carnot, forty, was a captain of engineers. A mathematician and expert in military construction, he was also a man of enormous organizing skill and imagination. Carnot was a Montagnard, but less interested in politics than in gearing France for war. This he did so successfully that he was dubbed the "Organizer of Victory." Bertrand Barère, thirty-eight, was a lawyer from a legal family. Had the Old Regime survived, he might still have gained eminence, but he adapted well to the new conditions. The "reluctant terrorist," Leo Gershoy called him. A master of law and of the French language, Barère eloquently delivered some of the most important policy statements of the period and drafted much of the legislation.

THE ORGANIZATION OF TERROR

The Committee of Public Safety, the executive branch, proposed legislation to the Convention, the constituted lawmaking body. Until the last days, there was little debate on issues which the committee considered vital. There was a ministry, nominally responsible to the Convention, but actually controlled in detail by the committee. Similarly, the Committee of General Security, though technically independent, was, until the very last days of the Terror, subordinate to the Committee of Public Safety.

The Committee of Public Safety exerted its power throughout France and over the armies through representatives-on-mission, appointed from its own ranks or from the Convention. These men were dispatched to supervise local governments and to dictate strategy to the generals, and in particular to take charge in rebellious areas, accompanying the armies in Vendée, Brittany, and against the "Federal Cities." The representatives had sweeping powers. They could replace army commanders, displace local officials and judges, and establish courts and order executions. They were omnipresent and in crisis situations, for short periods, omnipotent. The representatives (as discussed below in detail) were responsible for the most shocking atrocities of the Terror.

In December 1793, the government was declared "revolutionary until the peace." Thereafter the committee redesignated officials in every department, each district and municipality "National Agents," purging the untrustworthy. All were made responsible directly to Paris (or the committee's representatives-on-mission when present). The administration was centralized. Its officials were the bureaucratic predecessors of Napoleon's prefects, subprefects, and mayors.

The committee appointed and dismissed officers of the regular army and navy and had control of the National Guard. To augment these forces, it created special revolutionary armies here and there (that of Paris was most prominent), manned by the unemployed of the cities and by landless peasants. Their major function was to requisition food for the cities, but they too easily turned to pillaging and were generally disbanded in the provinces after a few weeks. (Cutting off pay usually did the trick.) That of Paris—the first and last—was abolished in March 1794.

The "party" of the Terror was made up of the scores of Jacobin Clubs (though often called by other names) in the cities and towns of France. They received bulletins from the mother club in Paris, beginning on 11 August 1792, the day after the storming of the Tuileries. These explained what was going on in Paris and later the policies and actions of the Committee of Public Safety. In September 1793 the clubs were given official status, in effect made part of the government. Their role was one of surveillance in their localities. In that connection they accused suspected traitors and recommended removal of public officials (often in favor of "good republicans" from their own ranks). The provincial clubs (like that of Paris) had earlier been dominated by liberal nobles and the richer bourgeoisie, but during 1793, in most localities, they acquired a majority of artisans, shopkeepers, and lower middle-class professionals. The leadership comprised for the most part local lawyers and sometime officials. The clubs were still dedicated to the principles of 1789, "Liberty, Equality, and Fraternity," which they interpreted in a most simplistic fashion, but the members now were enthusiastic republicans. They were also believers in the sanctity of private property, however, and were not prepared for even modest government infringement on property rights, nor sophisticated enough to appreciate any definition of equality in economic terms. They accepted wage and price controls as war measures, but when the government went further they drifted toward rebellion. These men, similarly, supported the Terror in the early months as an unpleasant necessity, but they were far from bloodthirsty, and as peace slowly returned, increasingly objected to continued executions. At the height of the Terror, however, the Jacobin clubs were a decided asset to the government.

For everyday cases the judiciary under the Terror was that prescribed by the Constitution of 1791, with predictable changes in personnel. It was the Revolutionary Tribunal of Paris, which tried treason cases, that marked the year of the Terror as a time of fear, bloodshed, and bestiality—an impression which in the popular mind is still attached to the whole Revolution. Its day-and-night sessions, particularly those in torchlight in the rock-walled cellars of the Palais de Justice, the decisions by the will of howling, often drunken people in the galleries shocked observers and have ever since inspired fiction writers.

The tribunal sent the tumbrels rolling through the streets almost daily toward the guillotine, some victims bravely maintaining their dignity, others groveling, weeping, screaming. The scenes at the Place du Carousel were equally horrifying, incredible. The mood and size of the crowd varied with the victim, but always present, seemingly, was a contingent of women who sat impassively knitting until the moment when the blade fell. When the "National Razor" was moved to the more spacious Place de la Révolution (now Concorde), a festive air was introduced into the macabre scene as hawkers went about selling food, wine, toy guillotines, pikes and liberty caps, and the like to the crowd.

The guillotine still appears to represent in the Western mind the ultimate in political repression, bloodletting, and misuse of power. Its some 2600 victims in Paris seem an insignificant number when compared to the millions executed by the Nazis during World War II or the five to ten million who died during Stalin's collectivization of farms in the Soviet Union. Yet the guillotine retains its horrible image. Perhaps this is because the Terror was the first of modern pogroms. It not only featured public executions, but carried them out with great fanfare and publicized them as necessary for the benefit of humanity. Nothing before had created such horror abroad or had so effectively intimidated a domestic population as did the Terror.

The executions in Paris are best remembered, though in fact more lives— perhaps 50,000—were taken in the provinces during the Terror by order of local tribunals or representatives-on-mission. After the capture of the Federal Cities and the defeat of the Vendéan rebels, there were so many "traitors" that the representatives considered the guillotine too slow to dispatch them (see below, p. 138).[9] At Lyons, Collot d'Herbois and Joseph Fouché had prisoners tied to

---

[9] Some books published for the 1989 Bicentenary accused the Terrorists of executing a "pogrom" against counterrevolutionaries. See footnote 4, p. 9, and, for example, Reynauld Secher, *La génocide franco-français: La Vendée-vengé* (1986).

stakes in open fields and fired upon by cannon. At Nantes, the infamous Carrier had "enemies of the people" chained in barges which were sunk in the estuary of the Loire River. At Toulon, executions, mostly by firing squads, were ordered wholesale by Augustin Robespierre (the Incorruptible's younger brother), and Barras and Saliceti (who are discussed later). It was in this way that most of the victims perished. Another long-standing misconception is that the majority of victims were nobles and priests. Donald Greer long ago demonstrated, however, that 85 percent of the victims were in neither category and that 60 percent were of the peasant or working class.[10]

THE VENDÉE

The most urgent business of the government (essential to the defeat of foreign enemies) was the suppression of internal rebellions in the Vendée and the "Federal Cities," simultaneously. For the sake of clarity, however, we shall treat the revolts separately. (See Map 3.2.)

The revolt in the Vendée had been sparked by the Convention's conscription of 300,000 men for the armies in February 1793. In the Vendée, and especially in its most medieval area, the Mauges, this seemed a final insult and oppression not to be borne. The Revolution had begun with grand promises, but to the peasants of this backward area its govermnents seemed more tyrannical and evil than those of the Old Regime. Where their old lords had been driven out, the bourgeois of the towns, who replaced them, were more hateful. The equivalent of feudal dues was still demanded (if not paid). They could afford no more land of their own, taxes were higher, inflation destroyed their meager profits, government agents "stole" their products in return for arbitrary low prices, and the rudimentary weaving industry in the villages was in depression. Worst of all, their revered priests had been impoverished and outlawed for reasons they little understood. Their field of vision hardly reached to Paris (though the execution of the king was an awful shock). To them, the Revolution had simply made them more helpless victims of the townsmen—their traditional enemies—who seemed always to find some means of robbing them of their small cash earnings. Locally, the Revolution was represented by the Jacobin clubs, merchants and officials, and middle-class National Guards of the cities and towns. The draftees of 1793 were to be selected by the local officials—that is, in the towns. It was too much.

The rebellion began feebly, in March, in the Mauges, led by refractory priests. In this trackless hedge country, as remote from France as the Bayous from Louisiana, the peasant hordes picked up recruits among the artisans and workers

---

[10] If it is considered that nobles and clergy constituted only 2 percent of the whole population, however, a greater percentage of nobles and clergy were executed than of the other classes. Greer's mistakes in statistical method are discussed by Richard Louie in *French Historical Studies*, III, No. 3 (Spring 1964), but he does not really challenge Greer's raw data.

of the villages, and even the bourgeoisie. (The real Jacobin strongholds were the larger cities, like Nantes and Angers.) Nobles and higher clerics appeared to organize the royal and Catholic army. (Some had been landed on the coast by the British.) By June 1793 the rebel army numbered some 100,000, and had taken over not only the Vendée, but most of the old provinces of Poitou, Anjou, and Brittany (except for the larger cities). The road to Paris was open to them, but their leaders chose to turn west and to besiege republican Nantes, a great port, at which they hoped the British would land supplies and reinforcements. Nantes, however, held like a rock. In July, regular republican armies belatedly took the field against the rebels, followed by representatives-on-mission, including the notorious Jean-Baptiste Carrier. He and the others "revolutionized" the towns as they were recaptured, executing rebels and their collaborators, and reconstituting city governments, National Guards, and Jacobin clubs.

The tide began to turn. It was not until the fall, however, that government troops won decisive victories, thanks to reinforcements from the Belgian and Rhine fronts (sent over loud protests). In September, Carrier entered the republican stronghold of Nantes and began to deal with royalist and Girondin sympathizers already imprisoned there and newly captured Vendéan rebels. The overflowing prisons induced him to carry out the infamous *noyades* (mass drownings) already mentioned. Hérault de Séchelles gave him the congratulations of the Committee of Public Safety: "We can be merciful when we are better assured of victory." (In February 1794, when peace was essentially restored, Carrier was recalled—to find himself no longer popular with anyone in Paris.)

Meanwhile, discipline collapsed in the French Atlantic fleet. (Already, part of the Mediterranean fleet had given itself over to the British, under Admiral Hood, at Toulon—a federal city in revolt.) Sailors took over ships in Quiberon Bay (generally without harming the officers, who threw up their hands) and sailed to Brest, where others joined the mutiny. In September, twenty-one ships-of-the-line (of fifty guns or more; half of the seaworthy battleships of the navy) and scores of lesser vessels lay at anchor at Brest while the crews vacationed.

The Committee of Public Safety, in terror that the British would seize the Atlantic ports, and/or land troops on the coast, sent two of its members, Prieur of the Marne (a lawyer) and Jeanbon Saint-André (the ex-Protestant minister) to republicanize the fleet. They arrived in mid-October, and with republican troops nearby, succeeded. Saint-André played republican evangelist aboard the ships, preaching the glories of the new order, emphasizing that every man could now be an admiral, and finishing by leading all in singing the "Marseillaise." Prieur took most of the responsibility for the harsher task of "liquidating" enemies of the people in the city. Together they restored discipline and rebuilt shore defenses.

With Brest "redeemed," Prieur was ordered to help direct the war against the royalist rebels in the Vendée. Still most fearful of British naval action, he preached a crusade against the enemy in the Jacobin clubs of the towns, often paraphrasing the Roman Senator Cato, scourge of Carthage: "London must be destroyed!

London must be destroyed!" He was soon faced, however, with the grisly task of dealing with droves of Vendéan prisoners of war, many of them ragged peasants whose leaders had fled. Ultimately he left their fate to a special military tribunal, which condemned some 3000 to death during the winter.

The relatively quick successes of the republican agents in the West were made possible by the failure of the British to exploit their opportunities. The Committee of Public Safety had overestimated the quality of British intelligence, otherwise the French navy might have been lost. As for the royalist rebellion, the government in London was both dubious of its strength and put off by the character of the Count d'Artois (brother of Louis XVI)[11] who asked permission to come to England and who demanded aid for the Vendéans (an expedition which he proposed to lead, but could not finance) and naval support. His haughty manner offended the British ministers, however, as did his dedication to a total restoration of the Old Regime (*no* constitution for him). Further, they doubted if he could raise an army, French or mercenary, even if given funds, or could command it if he did. (That he and his émigrés had been a burden to Brunswick in 1792 was well known.) Moreover, they were skeptical of Artois' reports of royalist successes in the Vendée. The count's agents in France had proved themselves incredibly inept; many had been captured, and the British feared the rest might be double agents. They gave Artois nothing (not even permission to live in England, where he already had debts of two million pounds). British aid to the Vendéans in 1793 was limited to dropping groups of émigrés on the coast, together with a few supplies. In 1795 they gave Artois what he wanted, but regretted it, as we shall see.

Without timely British aid, the valiant efforts of the poorly armed Vendéan masses were largely wasted. For example, La Carpentier, the representative-on-mission at Granville (on the Norman coast near the border of Brittany) was able to withstand a full-scale siege by the royal and Catholic army, blocking its march northward. If a British fleet had appeared in the harbor, he would have been doomed.

Once republican armies were present in force, the disorganized peasant hordes, poorly led and unsure of their objectives, were no match for them. On 23 December 1793 the battle of Savenay (west of Nantes) broke the back of the royal and the Catholic army. The remnants fled into the backwoods and swamps. Many continued to fight as guerrillas (the Chouans) for years, but the peasant rebellion was no longer a major threat after 1793.

Short as it was, the civil war in the Vendée bred much bitterness, and atrocities were committed by both sides. Unquestionably, the most frenetic bloodletters were on the government side. Carrier and Bignon (head of the special military

---

[11] The Count de Provence (Artois' elder brother) had assumed the title of regent of France in January 1793. He was in Italy for most of the year. The royalists had recognized Louis XVII, the dauphin, still imprisoned in the Temple in Paris, as king of France. He was destined to die there, however, at age ten, in 1795. The Count de Provence (later Louis XVIII), was next in line, then the Count d'Artois (later Charles X).

court) took the most lives, but almost every representative-on-mission wanted a few heads on his record, and there were dozens of ambitious representatives, if mostly short-term. Often their histrionics were more violent than their actions, as was the case with Laignelot, who replaced Saint-André at Brest. He loved to repeat the morbid epigram "Peoples will never be truly free until the last king is strangled with the bowels of the last priest!" but ordered very few executions. Nevertheless, the overall record of the Republic's missionaries was bloody indeed.

The peasants' "campaign" began as a series of marches led by priests carrying crosses. Violence was largely against property rather than persons, in the manner of the traditional food riot. As resistance stiffened, however, and marchers became soldiers, the zealots of the royal and Catholic army acquired a bloodlust akin to that of their "atheist and republican" opponents, which they exercised against prisoners and civilians as well as in battle. This produced martyrs for the terrorist government, whose sacrifices were exploited fully by republican propagandists. The most famous was Le Petit Bara, a little drummer boy captured by the Vendéans and offered his freedom (by legend) if he would shout "Vive le Roi!" He refused, and was shot, shouting "Vive La Republique!" Thousands of words were printed about him, and prints depicting his death were circulated throughout France. "Only a Republic," said Robespierre gravely, "can produce a hero of thirteen." The Incorruptible had no time to ponder the tragedy of Frenchmen killing Frenchmen. Those who resisted the "Republic of Virtue" were to him no longer citizens, and barely people.

THE FEDERAL CITIES

In June 1793 the federalist revolt, inspired by the Girondins (and in some places led by delegates who had fled the Convention), flared in sixty departments. The Montagnards' greatest fear was that the federals would make common cause with the royalists, but generally this did not occur. (The Girondin minority at Nantes, for example, balked at collaboration with the royalists and lost control to the Montagnards.) During June, Danton's conciliatory moves and the passing of the Constitution of 1793 served to neutralize the leadership, and the movements collapsed in most places with little or no bloodshed. The "Federal Cities" remained defiant, however, which kept the Convention in frantic alarm, since they included Lyons, an industrial center second in size only to Paris; Bordeaux and Marseilles, major commercial ports; and Toulon, the greatest French naval base on the Mediterranean. Moreover, it was known that the royalists still hoped to gain footholds in the cities and perhaps (depending especially on Lyons and Toulon) to reestablish the monarchy in southern France—for a start. Thus while Artois concentrated on the Vendée, the Count de Provence (regent for the boy-king, Louis XVII, in prison) moved from Germany to northern Italy— Verona, then Leghorn, where he hoped to take a ship to Toulon.

In July the Convention, spurred on by Robespierre and Saint-Just, outlawed the federalist leaders and formed armies to reduce the cities. Bordeaux, as it turned out, was no problem. Out of contact with the other cities, and finding Toulouse (blocking the route to Marseilles and Toulon) staunchly Montagnard, most of the Girondins rejected royalist overtures and made peace with the local Montagnards. When Tallien, the representative-on-mission, arrived in September, he entered the city quietly. Only about a hundred "enemies," mostly those already in prison, were executed.[12]

Marseilles witnessed a struggle between the merchant oligarchy, which favored calling in the British fleet, and the popular party, which won out. Thus, in August 1793, the republican army of General Carteaux was able to capture the city without a fight. He imprisoned a few hundred Girondins and royalists and concentrated on making Marseilles a base for the recapture of Toulon. When the representatives-on-mission, led by Barras, arrived in October, they were already preoccupied with Toulon, which the British had converted into a dangerous beachhead (see below). Fewer than 200 persons were condemned to death in Marseilles.

Lyons meanwhile had been through a municipal civil war, which ended with the Girondins wielding the guillotine against the Montagnard leaders and the flight of thousands of workers from the city. At the end of September, Lyons still held fast, flying the tricolor of the Republic (though its defenses were commanded by an émigré, the Count de Precy). It was under heavy siege, however, by regular government forces, reinforced by National Guards, contingents of the "Revolutionary Armies" (drawn largely from the unemployed), volunteers, and local conscripts.

Coordination of the attack was supplied by Couthon, who arrived on 2 October. Moving about by wheelchair and carriage, his wife helping him, he forced the five other representatives-on-mission present and a bevy of generals to agree on a plan. On 9 October the city fell.

The Convention ordered Lyons "destroyed." The homes of the rich were to be leveled to the ground. What remained—industries and homes of the workers—was to be renamed Ville Affranchie (Liberated City). Lyons would disappear from the maps. Couthon was directed to give the rebels no mercy. All this was too much for him. After tagging a few houses and setting up a tribunal, he departed, leaving the carnage to Collot d'Herbois (the actor) and Joseph Fouché (ex-cleric, professor, and future minister of police). They executed enemies wholesale, by tying them to stakes and firing on them with cannon, then resorted to the guillotine. Perhaps 2500 died—enough to appease the Convention—added to the thousands killed in battle—enough to make Lyons a major casualty of the civil war.

---

[12] He saved from the guillotine one Thérèsa Cabarrus, a beautiful divorcée, recently the wife of a nobleman. He later married her, and she became a famous hostess in Paris. It was at her salon that Napoleon was introduced to Josephine de Beauharnais.

In Toulon, royalists and Girondins cooperated in preparing the defense of the city, since the royalists, secretly organized, emerged stronger than expected, and the Girondins were made desperate by federalist defeats elsewhere. They were reinforced by émigrés and refugees from Marseilles. They raised the Lily Banner of the Bourbon dynasty and recognized Louis XVII. Thereupon Admiral Hood responded to their call and entered the harbor with units of the British Mediterranean fleet, cheered by sailors aboard French warships, whose royalist admiral had long since joined the rebels. Hood landed 12,000 British, Sardinian, and Neapolitan troops to help defend the city.

Meanwhile, in August, General Carteaux' republican army (soon taken over by Dugommier) marched from Marseilles, was reinforced to 30,000, and laid siege to Toulon. The defenders were outnumbered (the whole normal population of Toulon was perhaps 35,000), but they held the heights which ringed the city and were backed by the guns of the British fleet. They seemed impossible to dislodge, and the siege dragged on into the winter. Victory for the Republic was finally engineered, however, by an obscure young captain of artillery, Napoleon Buonaparte (Bonaparte).

NAPOLEON MOVES ON STAGE

Captain Buonaparte was available to serve at Toulon only because his family had opposed the revolt of Corsica against the French Republic and had been forced to flee to France (June 1793). (His early life will be discussed later.) Though he had been a lieutenant in the French army since 1786, he had been serving as a lieutenant-colonel in the Corsican National Guard. On his return to France, however, he was reinstated at the rank of captain. (Career officers were in short supply, and this one professed ardent Jacobinism.)

All the same, he was not assigned initially to the army at Toulon. Three "accidents" brought that about. First, one of the representatives-on-mission at Toulon was Joseph Saliceti, a Corsican and friend of the Buonaparte family. Second, the artillery commander at Toulon, General Dommartin, was wounded and relieved of duty. Third, Napoleon was nearby. Though earlier posted to Carteaux at Marseilles, he had been reassigned to the "Army of Italy" (on the frontier) but had not yet departed. Saliceti had him appointed to replace Dommartin.

In August the republican infantry began the bloody business of reducing the federal strong points on the high ground. Buonaparte pressed General Carteaux for an attack on Fort Éguillette, on a high promontory, which he considered the key to victory. From there, he calculated, his artillery could fire down on Hood's fleet, with more accuracy than the naval guns could return fire. The attack was made, but failed, and Carteaux returned to his plodding tactics, which earned him dismissal and disgrace in November. General Dugommier, who replaced him, gave Napoleon a free hand, and a month-long assault on Éguillette ensued.

Buonaparte participated with the infantry, sustaining a bayonet wound. The fort fell on 14 December, and the French began to bombard Hood's fleet the same day. On 18 December 1793, Hood evacuated Toulon, and the city fell. Six weeks later, Captain Buonaparte, twenty-four, was promoted to brigadier general. His rise to fame had begun.

The capture of Toulon marked the end of the "Federal Revolts," but this generated no magnanimity among the victors. Terror with vengeance was administered by Barras (discussed later), Saliceti, Augustin Robespierre (brother of the Incorruptible), and other representatives. Furious that many of the leaders had escaped (with Hood or otherwise), they ordered shot, by firing squads and without trial, every rebel, soldier, sailor, or official they could find—1000 or more in the first few days. Thereafter a tribunal was set up to deal with other suspects.

With domestic peace restored, the Republic could concentrate its efforts on the foreign war. Since this was the real immediate importance of the final success at Toulon, many authors have decried the emphasis generally given the role of Napoleon. Nevertheless, it was at Toulon that the government of Terror raised Buonaparte from obscurity. Saliceti, Barras, Augustin Robespierre, and the other representatives not only gave him this opportunity, but got him promoted as well. They saw to it that he was publicly praised for the victory. Napoleon was a product of the Terror. This is particularly ironic, since Maximilien Robespierre in 1792 had warned against starting a war—the same he labored to win in 1793–1794. It could end, he had said, only in the restoration of the absolute monarchy or military dictatorship. To a degree, he was right, though Napoleon would be much more than a military dictator.

ORGANIZATION FOR VICTORY

Lazare Carnot was the member of the Committee of Public Safety directly responsible for Napoleon's promotion. It was a routine action under policies that he had developed since August 1793 for restructuring the French army.

Carnot's first priority had been the implementation of the *levée en masse* (mass draft) of French manpower. The idea had originated much earlier with the Girondins, and in August 1793 had the frenetic support of Hébert and the Paris Commune. Initially, it had been conceived as a spontaneous mobilization of the nation (with a little prompting) in response to danger. The voluntary approach had not been successful, however, Carnot's contribution (with help from the minister of war, Jean Bouchotte) was to give it organization and the force of law, including penalities for "nonsubmission."

Barère, who proposed the law to the Convention (Carnot seldom spoke), prefaced the harsher requirements with an appeal in the spirit of the original concept:

> Young men will fight . . . Married men will forge arms, transport equipment . . .
> and prepare food supplies. Women, who at long last must find their true destiny in

revolution, must abandon useless occupations. [They] . . . will sew soldiers' uniforms, make tents, and serve as nurses . . . Children will make bandages . . . Old men will inflame the courage of young warriors, stir up hatred for kings, and preach the unity of the Republic.

In detail he proposed (and the Convention passed, 23 August 1793) a law requiring the registration for military service of all men over eighteen and under twenty-five. Unmarried men (only) were to be drafted as needed, but none were exempt except the physically unfit. One could not "buy" a substitute, as had been possible in the traditional militia. (This was violated in practice after 1794, however, and substitutes were legalized under the succeeding governments.) Penalties for evasion were left initially to representatives-on-mission; desertion was punishable by death. The term of service was the duration of the war.

The law created a huge pool of manpower, from which it was necessary to draft less than one in four. Resistance was, nevertheless, heavy, despite the risks—10 to 15 percent (at least) of those called in the first six months deserted and 20 percent more during 1794. Statistics on evasion are not available, but it must have been staggering by twentieth-century standards. Nonetheless, by January 1794, France had an army of 800,000 (1,200,000 on paper) the largest ever mustered by any nation.[13]

The success of conscription was aided by an enormous propaganda campaign. The *levée en masse* was touted as republican, as opposed to "recruitment" with the offer of bonus money, which was termed monarchal. Conscription, it was emphasized, would produce an army of loyal citizen-soldiers; the old system only native mercenaries. Barère warned the Convention that the aristocracy "holds in reserve gold to tempt weak or indigent citizens, deserters to dishonor the army, and royalists to corrupt its spirit." The life of the Republic depended on having incorruptible citizens in the ranks. It was not only their duty, but their privilege to defend their government. Only if they did could democracy survive.

This message was repeated in tons of posters, broadsides, and leaflets, and by speakers sent into the provinces. The names of republican heroes, such as "Le petit Bara" (see page 140 above) were made household words. Bemedaled veterans toured the country, spreading tales of glory. Citizens not privileged to bear arms

---

[13] The widespread evasion and desertion seem less startling if one considers that this was the first modern draft, that the government was quietly hated by legions of people in the areas which had revolted in 1793 (and many elsewhere), that birth and death records were spotty, and that communications and police methods were still very primitive. Thus it was fairly easy, given community sympathy, to hide out or simply ignore the law. Moreover, the law was only fully implemented in 1793–1794, and the men called then continued to serve, year after year, while younger eligibles stayed home. As the war wound down after mid-1794, desertion increased, so that by 1797, the "present for duty" army numbered scarcely 400,000. A new and more equitable system was introduced in 1798 by the Jourdan-Delbrel Law, which required the registration of those over eighteen and under twenty-five and specified that draftees in any year would come from those who turned twenty before the first day of the year. (The twenty-year-olds were called the "class" of the year.) This was a true universal conscription law, which was retained under Napoleon and by French governments until the 1870s. A similar law has remained in force ever since.

were made to feel that they had to work all the harder to make up for it. Every means was used to make *patriot* and *citizen-soldier* synonyms in the minds of the people. While real danger to the country existed, the campaign was astonishingly successful.[14]

Conscripts were sent directly to units in the field armies, named after the area of actual or proposed operation (Army of the Rhine, Army of the North, Army of Italy, etc.). There were no training camps, per se. New soldiers were simply issued arms and uniforms and assigned to units, where they were schooled by veterans. New units were formed around cadres of veterans drawn from older ones. Armies so produced lacked organization and discipline, but made up for it by numbers and an acute sense of mission.

It was repeated to recruits incessantly, until the most recalcitrant became believers, that the army would save the French Republic and would spread liberty abroad—that the Republic was the great hope of humanity and the salvation of mankind from tyranny. The army became the nation's school of patriotism. The men were fed daily on tales of glory, marched singing the "Marseillaise," "Ça Ira," and the "Carmagnole," and ordered their lives to bugles and drums and the strains of the regimental band. Always held before them was the tricolor and the flag of their regiment (their only "home"). Moreover, promotion was rapid for those who served well. Overnight, privates could become sergeants, sergeants became officers, and lieutenants and captains vaulted upward even to general—if they fought and led well. It was in Carnot's time that someone said "every private carries a marshal's baton in his knapsack." This could only build morale.

Carnot gave personal attention to purging the officer corps of the old, incompetent, or untrustworthy—mostly die-hard royalists. He displayed little prejudice against nobles, however, if they were talented and loyal to the Republic. Otherwise, Captain Buonaparte, whose father had been a count, would not have been promoted.

During 1793–1794 the whole complexion of the officer corps changed. The average age of general officers dropped drastically. Most were younger than Carnot, who was forty. All of them were battle-tested, tough, ambitious men of action. At about the same time as Carnot promoted Napoleon (twenty-four), he gave equal or higher rank to Jourdan (thirty-one), Masséna (thirty-five), Davout (twenty-three), Lefebvre (thirty-eight), Pérignon (thirty-nine), Augereau (thirty-six), Brune (thirty), and Sérurier (fifty).[15] This accounts for eight of the twenty-six

---

[14] Writes the perceptive Simon Schama: "Militarized nationalism was not, in some accidental way, the unintended consequence of the French Revolution: it was its heart and soul." *Citizens*, 858. Peter Paret holds that the *levée en masse* was instituted for domestic-political rather than military reasons in "Conscription and the End of the Old Regime in France and Prussia," in W. Treue, *Geschichte als Aufgabe* (Berlin, 1988), 169, n. 8. He holds that Robespierre and company feared losing power to the radical Hébertistes, who were pushing the draft. Gunther Rothenberg believes that, in any event, conscripts had little to do with the victories of 1793, since the first were called in September.

[15] Sérurier's rank was honorary, but he counted in the twenty-six.

men who were made marshals under the empire. In addition, there were new generals who gained eminence but never served Napoleon, such as Pichegru (thirty-two) and Hoche (twenty-five), or who served him briefly, such as Moreau (thirty).

Carnot was also involved in the mobilization of French production, including agriculture, industry, and transportation. Naturally he took a special interest in the arms industry, working to improve the former royal foundries and to create new arms works, especially in Paris. Paris factories were preferred by Robespierre's committee, which distrusted the countryside. Moreover, skilled workers and machinery could easily be assembled in Paris, and work could be provided for the unemployed. The plants also served a propaganda purpose, some of them almost purely so. For example, the shops in the gardens of the Tuileries and the Luxembourg presented a continuous spectacle of the people serving the *Patrie*. They produced mostly pikes, however, which had long been obsolete in serious warfare. Muskets, powder, and some cannon were manufactured in less conspicuous places.[16]

Carnot truly earned the sobriquet "Organizer of Victory." The success of French armies, against both foreign and domestic enemies, was spectacular.

THE WAR

In September 1793 the French scored a victory over the British under the Duke of York at Hondschoote, in the Netherlands, saving Dunkirk for France. In October 1793, General Jourdan, new commander in the Netherlands, defeated the Austrian Duke of Coburg at Maubeuge (Battle of Wattignies). In December, Hoche and Pichegru combined to defeat the Prussians at Landau in the Palatinate. In December the British were also driven from Toulon, as already noted. Toulon, was, of course, a victory over both foreign and domestic enemies. During the winter the French armies invaded Spain and held their own in the Netherlands and Germany.

In June 1794, Jourdan won a smashing victory over the Duke of Coburg at Fleurus. This forced the Austrians to evacuate Belgium, which bared the flank of the Prussians in the Rhineland. As it turned out, this was the turning point of the war. The Prussians all but stopped fighting, angry over the ineffectiveness of the Austrians and again squabbling with them (and the Russians) over Poland. In March 1795 they made peace, agreeing secretly to cede France the left (western) bank of the Rhine in return for territory in Germany. In January 1795, Pichegru took Amsterdam and, along the way (with *cavalry*), the Dutch fleet at Zeeland, which was locked in the ice. In May, he completed the conquest of Holland and

---

[16] Pikes were issued to the militia (the "revolutionary army") and they were, of course, in fashion for carrying about severed heads. This practice had begun in the early revolution, when the people searching for arms had taken whatever they could find from ancient armories and war museums.

assisted native Jacobins in converting it into the Batavian Republic.[17] In June 1795, Spain made peace. Thereafter, France had to contend with only Austria, Britain (largely at sea) and minor Italian states.

The immediate importance of the Battle of Fleurus, however, was that it relieved foreign military pressure on France. Thereafter, the acute sense of danger, which had given the Terror popular support, dissipated. From the point of view of those in power, the conduct of the war had been all too successful. Victory hastened the demise of Robespierre's committee, discussed later in this chapter.

DOMESTIC ACCOMPLISHMENTS

In our century, and especially since 1945, the Terror has been the most studied phase of the Revolution, and not without reason. The government of Terror was the "original" of modern, bureaucratic, centralized governments, which by one definition or another, are "democratic." The leaders of the Terror pushed through the Constitution of 1793 and professed to be proponents of direct representative democracy; they governed dictatorially, but (as they saw it) *for* the people, and thus, by that criterion, were democratic. Whatever kind of democrats they were, their work is now appreciated as constructive, progressive, and far-sighted, irrespective of the bloodshed they caused. They were before their time, men who grappled with ideas of social and economic equality as well as legal equality. They extended the latter by abolishing slavery in the colonies (4 February 1794), facing an issue avoided since 1789. (See p. 91.)

As already discussed, the Terror demonstrated for the first time the power of a nation totally mobilized for war. But it also set precedents in its legislation on economic matters, property, social problems, welfare, education, and much else.

The Law of the Maximum (September 1793) gave a modicum of protection to the common man by controlling prices and wages.[18] The right to subsistence,

---

[17] The French officially treated the Dutch Republic as a native creation. The Treaty of the Hague (16 May 1795) recognized the independence of the Batavian Republic and promised mutual noninterference in domestic affairs. The Dutch promised to pay an indemnity of 100,000,000 guilders (217,000,000 francs) and to make France a large loan, ceded Maastricht, Venlo, and Dutch Flanders to France, and consented to the dismantling of all frontier fortresses. The Dutch patriots, led by Pieter Paulus, also agreed, secretly and resentfully, to support 25,000 French troops until the peace. This was considered a triumph by Sieyès and Reubell, who negotiated for France.

[18] The "Maximum of May" applied only to bread and had been applied outside Paris as local authorities chose—sometimes not at all. The "General Maximum" of 29 September 1793 was nationally enforced and set prices on bread, meat, fish, wine, beer, oil, butter, salt, sugar, coal, wood, and many other items. Generally, prices were fixed at one-third above those of 1790 (local average). Wages were set at one-half greater than those of 1790. Both prices and wages were maximums. There was no minimum wage or price. Violation of the law carried the death penalty, as did hoarding, impeding the transport of grain, delaying the manufacture or sale of bread, and the like. Enforcement was supervised by representatives-on-mission.

enunciated in the Constitution of 1793, was given some substance by creating jobs in war industry. Rudimentary social security was provided by the Law of 22 Florial, Year II (11 May 1794) which granted aged, ill, or disabled countryfolk small incomes and free housing if needed.[19] Inflation was reversed by substituting republican for royal assignats. This paper was publicized as the "money of the poor," and reprisal threatened against "profiteers" who refused to accept it. Simultaneously, coin was confiscated. A compulsory loan was decreed (really a scaled income tax) that confiscated all income over 10,000 francs per year. Government bonds were converted to annuities at 5 percent, which meant that the principal was confiscated.[20]

All segments of the economy were controlled to assure the supply of the army and to insure the cities against shortages. Under penalties for violation, including death, hoarding was prohibited, farmers had to declare the amount of their harvests, and merchants' stocks were subject to inventory at any time without notice. Granaries were established in each district. A national food committee was empowered to seize food and control distribution. Another committee controlled industrial production and transportation. The Committee of Public Safety itself assumed authority over exports and imports.[21]

Feudal rights were finally abolished without any indemnity in June 1793. In the same month, a law was passed which enabled the breaking up of village commons, at the request of one-third of the members of the commune involved. The Jacobins meant thereby to provide some land for landless peasants. On this, however, they misread the desires of the brassiers. In most communes, they preferred allowing access to the commons over giving away a tiny share, and the commons were perpetuated. Some land redistribution was effected, however, by a law which confiscated the property of émigrés and required its sale in small plots on time payment.

The economic program of the Terror was capped by the famous Decrees of Ventôse, Year II (February–March 1794). They declared as forfeit the property of "recognized enemies" of the nation, and its distribution to "indigent patriots of the communes where located." The sans-culottes of Paris applauded, though most of the property involved was in rural areas, so that they had little to gain. The middle-class Convention was shocked, though, of course, it passed the laws;

[19] Incomes were surely set on the assumption that peasants would have gardens and would be helped by relatives. They were grossly insufficient for their total support. Peasants got 160 francs a year; peasant-artisans 120; widows and abandoned mothers 60 and 65 francs. Even at that, the law was never enforced.

[20] This gave the government only a short-run advantage, assuming that it really meant to pay interest in perpetuity. In fact, this legislation set the stage for repudiation of the national debt under succeeding governments.

[21] Foreign ships were outlawed from coastal traffic and a complete boycott on British goods was declared. Although British ships could not enter French harbors in wartime, British goods were coming, nevertheless, in neutral vessels, for example, those of the United States and legally or illegally over various land borders.

the majority considered them socialistic, and their hostility toward the Committee of Public Safety increased. It seems certain that Robespierre saw the laws as
an expedient to please his Paris constituency. His opponents Collot d'Herbois
and Billaud-Varenne saw them as a step toward the equalization of wealth,
however, as did Saint-Just, who usually stood with Robespierre.[22] Today, the laws
would be seen as liberal rather than socialistic since they involved only an
extension of private ownership through grant of government property.

The middle-class leaders of the time, however, felt that these laws decidedly
violated the sanctity of private property, and thereby individual liberty. While
they accepted laws controlling the economy as a wartime necessity, they recoiled
from those redistributing property without any pretense of sale and purchase.
After all, France at large was still bourgeois in mentality, so that even the
sans-culottes could not conceive of an economic system without private ownership.
Liberty, including the right to acquire and hold property, was a first principle of
the Revolution. (So much was restated in the Constitution of 1793, at the
insistence of Robespierre himself.) National financing of worthwhile projects,
however, including scientific research and education, was not considered dangerous to individual liberty.

The Terrorists were outspoken proponents of science (undifferentiated from
technology). Though they largely sponsored projects useful for war, some projects had wider potential. For example, Carnot introduced balloons for observation (these were tethered on cables near the front lines). He also established a
"telegraph" between Paris and Lille—a semaphore or "wig-wag" system that
relayed messages along a line of tall towers topped by giant arms or paddles.

The most lasting and useful innovation promoted by the Terrorists, however,
was the metric-decimal system of weights and measures, with the gram and meter
as the basic units. It was devised by Joseph-Louis Lagrange, a mathematician and
astronomer who had gained fame under the Old Regime, but who was accepted
by the Republic (and lived to receive honors from Napoleon as well). The metric
system was quickly accepted by scientists (eventually worldwide). The French
public, however, clung to its traditional livres, pieds, pounces (pounds, feet,
inches). It became fairly generally accepted only under Napoleon, who sponsored
its adoption by most other European countries.[23]

The Terrorists believed that free public education was essential to real
equality of opportunity. Public schools were also intended to produce good
republicans, and to provide schooling without religious indoctrination (or, as

---

[22] If we may judge by Saint-Just's posthumous book, *Institutions Républicains* (published in 1800).

[23] Actually, too much reverence has been given the metric system, per se. Its great advantage was the
division of units by tens, hundreds, and so on, that is, the use of the decimal system, devised about
1600 by John Napier. The meter, for example, was supposed to be one-millionth of the distance from
the equator to the North Pole on the meridian running through Paris, but it was calculated incorrectly
and is actually an arbitrary length—that of a platinum bar cut by Lagrange. Ironically, it is almost
exactly the length of the yard of the Old Regime. That—or the English yard—could just as easily
have been divided by decimal units.

some said, to substitute republicanism for Catholicism). Plans were laid down for a complete system of elementary and secondary schools, both tuition-free. Elementary education was to be compulsory for all; entry into secondary schools on the basis of merit (record in school). The top graduates of the secondary schools (five in Paris and one in each department) would go on to a university, or to one of the "Great Schools" founded by the government. At all levels, church influence was excluded.

These plans were approved by the Convention after the fall of Robespierre, but with destructive modifications. Primary schools were left dependent on local financing, and consequently few appeared. A secondary system of "central schools" (collèges) was established, but enrollment was limited and tuition was charged. The Convention at large did not share the Montagnards' enthusiasm for equality. Also, there were practical difficulties. For instance, virtually all teachers available were ex-nuns, friars, or monks, and therefore suspect. The succeeding government was forced to use these people anyway, in order to have schools at all. The primary schools drifted back under church control almost entirely.[24] In short, the public school plan failed. The Terrorists were a hundred years ahead of their time in proposing such a system.

Some institutions of higher learning *planned* under the Terror became permanent, though actually founded by the Convention after Robespierre's fall. Extant today are the École Polytechnique (Polytechnic School) and the École Normale Supérieure (High Normal School or Teachers' College), the first of the Grandes Écoles (great schools). Graduation guaranteed a position in government service or in education or was a decided advantage in seeking private employment. Others were a school of Oriental languages, a national conservatory of the arts and sciences, and a museum of natural history. To honor scholars, scientists, men of letters, and artists, the Institut de France was founded. It replaced various academies of the Old Regime and was divided into three sections: mathematics and physical sciences, moral and political sciences, and literature and fine arts.[25] In addition, the Terrorists must also be credited with the idea of establishing a National Library (Bibliothèque Nationale) and with the conversion of the old palace of the Louvre into a museum. Both of these projects, however, were really carried to completion by Napoleon.

THE MANEUVERS OF ROBESPIERRE

The domestic political history of the period has been given short shrift thus far in order to treat the highlights in one section. Hopefully, this will clarify the rise and fall of Robespierre.

---

[24] The Republic had the same problem with hospitals, orphanages, and homes for the aged, where defrocked "sisters" were quietly allowed to resume their duties.

[25] Under Napoleon, the section of moral and political sciences was divided into two sections; one of these was the reconstituted Académie Française, which dated from the time of Richelieu.

After the expulsion of the Girondins from the Convention (June 1793), the Montagnards, like other ruling factions before them, became champions of order. Thus even before becoming a member of the Committee of Public Safety, Robespierre had been denouncing Jacques Roux, leader of the Enragés, in the Convention. Roux' whole organization consisted of himself and four others, two of them women. Otherwise he simply represented the desires of the very lowest elements of society, those without property or education, and often without jobs. He demanded as a first step toward "equality" the guarantee of full stomachs for all. As noted above, the Mountain had pushed through the (first) Law of the Maximum during the spring and instituted price controls on bread in Paris. Roux was thus disarmed, and when Robespierre attacked, there was no one to defend him. Roux was arrested and left to rot in prison until 1794, when he was sentenced to die, but cheated the guillotine by committing suicide.

The destruction of Roux was also a part of the Mountain's strategy to confuse the opposition—principally the provincial followers of the Girondins, who were fomenting the "Federal Revolts." (Roux had been a *bête noir* to them.) In the same line, Robespierre, as spokesman for the Committee of Public Safety, pushed through the Constitution of 1793, giving Girondins false hopes. (The Constitution was, of course, suspended in September.) In July 1793 the committee had the first Law of the Maximum repealed, eliminating a law the Girondins had opposed tooth and nail. In September, however, it sponsored a new Maximum, with stiffer penalties for violation. Thus it appeased the Paris populace, while at the same time worked to neutralize the power of the sections.[26]

Since 10 August 1792, the section assemblies had been in "permanent session." Thus meeting halls were open day and night, and at crucial times a sufficient number of leaders were present to summon the people and put pressure on the Convention. In September 1793, Robespierre put through the Convention a law limiting meetings of the sections to two per week. Disconcertingly, he also had provided a subsidy of 40 sous to those who attended section meetings. Both measures weakened the sections, however—the first by breaking the continuity of leadership and discussion, and the second by crowding the assemblies with destitute people, usually also illiterate and politically unaware. The section leaders responded by forming societies of *sans-culottes* which charged dues. The government's next move in the sections was to form "revolutionary committees" that were authorized to apply the Law of Suspects. They were naturally responsive to the Committee of Public Safety and tended to demoralize the old section leadership.

The Commune, chosen by the sections, was gradually packed with delegates loyal to Robespierre and the committee, but cut off from the population. In the course of the winter of 1793–1794, the committee thus centralized power in Paris, as it had centralized it in France. Temporarily, this offered Robespierre a considerable advantage.

---

[26] On the provisions of the General Maximum, see footnote 18, p. 147.

At the same time, the left in Paris came under the leadership of Hébert, who spoke through his newspaper, *Père Duchesne*. He and the radicals of the Commune, such as Momoro, Vincent, and Cloots also dominated the Cordeliers, supplanting former leaders, including Danton, now more frequently seen at the Jacobins. In this power struggle, the Jacobins, while oozing sympathy for the people, backed the Committee of Public Safety and opposed disorder and excessive radicalism. Hébert, on the other hand, demanded ever more revolutionary measures, including a permanent maximum on the size of fortunes and a general redistribution of wealth. He also kept up a continual attack on unnamed monopolists, hoarders, and profiteers.[27] Hébert's proposals were always vague on specifics. A tirade in *Père Duchesne* of December 1793 was typical:

> I do not, therefore, demand the partition of the land, but what I want, damn it, is that we should make all the rich pigs who have gotten fat on the blood of the poor vomit it out, that we should make the financiers give back the money they have stolen to the Nation, and cut the fangs of all the leeches who feed on the people. . . .

Hébert was also the leader, with Pierre Chaumette, the prosecutor of the Commune, and Joseph Fouché, of the de-Christianization movement. This was something to which most members of the Convention gave lip service, since Catholicism and royalism seemed inextricably linked.[28]

On 22 September 1792, the Convention had ordered public documents dated from "Year I of the Republic." By decrees of 5 October and 24 November 1793, it approved the Revolutionary Calendar, which was distinctly an anti-Christian measure. It called for twelve months of thirty days each, with three ten-day weeks in each month. The names of the months poetically reflected the seasons of the year, which began on 22 September (23 in leap years). Sundays were eliminated, as were all church holidays. Five days left at the end of the year (six in leap years) were called *sans-culottides* and were dedicated to the celebration of revolutionary virtues.[29]

The calendar was designed to end the ordering of the lives of Frenchmen by Sundays and Saints' Days, by Easter, Christmas, and so on. This would reduce the number of public appearances by clergy and would stop the "excessive" number of "useless" processions and ceremonies. It would also limit the number of holidays and would increase the work potential of the population.

[27] He was supported by the "Femmes Révolutionaires," a small organization of women which backed all radical measures and propagandized for the equality of rights.

[28] Those who confronted the rebels in the Vendée directly, however, discovered that if the peasants were guaranteed the services of their nonjuring priests in the usual churches, their royalism tended to evaporate. (See p. 165.)

[29] Sundays were replaced by *Décadi* (tenth days). The months were Vendémiaire (harvest), Brumaire (mist), Frimaire (frost), Nivôse (snow), Pluviose (rain), Ventôse (wind), Germinal (seeding), Floréal (flowering), Prairial (meadows), Messidor (wheat harvest), Thermidor (heat), and Fructidor (ripening). The calendar was retroactive, thus 1792–1793 was the Year I, 1793–1794 the Year II, and so on.

All this was very mild, however, compared to the atheist-led de-Christianization movement, centered in Paris, and of which only a minority in the Convention approved. Hébert was the prophet; Chaumette was the pageant master; the Commune cooperated. Section leaders forced the conversion of churches into "temples of reason." Notre Dame became the scene of a gigantic "Festival of Liberty and Reason" on 10 November 1793. Staged by Chaumette, it was begun by a shapely actress in a skimpy Roman toga who placed the "torch of truth" on the "altar of reason." Chaumette then proclaimed a new religion, the worship of "gods given by nature," which required no priests. While the walls of the ancient cathedral resounded to revolutionary songs and dancing, Chaumette went to harangue the Convention, demanding that it join the worshippers. The *conventionnels* meekly followed the "Goddess of Reason" back to the cathedral. Elsewhere in France, cathedrals were converted to "temples of reason" or put up for sale. While the countryside remained stolidly Catholic in most areas, the cities imitated Paris, particularly those under the control of representatives-on-mission. In Lyons, Fouché made a ceremony of burning clerical vestments and of melting down sacred vessels. He also made a fetish of posting signs at cemeteries reading "Death Is an Eternal Sleep," as did Chaumette in Paris.

It was all too much for Robespierre, who believed, as had Rousseau, that a religion which taught a belief in a Supreme Being and an afterlife was necessary to shaping law-abiding citizens. This parading of atheism he also saw as part and parcel of Hébert's radical program, which was an affront to the "sane" revolutionary policies of the Committee of Public Safety. The Convention preferred the committee over Hébert's "mob rule and atheism."

During the winter of 1793–1794, Robespierre launched a campaign to discredit the Hébertists. In this he got the support of popular heroes who had become his opponents, notably Danton and Desmoulins. Both had been demanding moderation of the Terror and attacking the economic policies of the committee. They put that aside to assail Hébert, Chaumette, and their followers in Paris (not such as Fouché, who had operated in the provinces). Danton rallied the Convention; Desmoulins reached the people through his newspaper, the *Vieux Cordelier* (Old Cordelier).

In March 1794 the Hébertists tried to raise Paris against the Committee of Public Safety. The Parisians were sympathetic but did not move. Hébert had no specific plan to feed the people and hunger was their greatest concern. Moreover he had no organization, and Robespierre had already thoroughly disorganized the section assemblies. The threat of violence merely pushed Danton and Desmoulins into total support of the Committee of Public Safety in the interest of law and order.

In mid-March, Robespierre gave Paris telling one-two punches. On 13 March, urged on by Saint-Just, Billaud-Varenne, and Collot, he got the Laws of Ventôse passed, promising free land to the landless. While the *sans-culottes* applauded (the *menu peuple* were hungry and less impressed, but voiceless), Robespierre had Hébert and his followers arrested (15 March) and charged with conspiring with foreigners to overthrow the Republic. The Revolutionary Tribunal sent them to the guillotine on 24 March 1794. The public was puzzled and angry, but disorganized and helpless.

Robespierre now turned on his erstwhile allies, the Dantonists. The committee ruled there was no choice. Once he had destroyed the left, Robespierre had to crush the right, lest it dominate the Convention. In particular, the leftists of the Great Committee, Collot and Billaud-Varenne, who had backed him against the Hébertists were demanding Dantonist heads as the price of committee unity. On 30 March, Danton, Desmoulins, and others were arrested. They were sent before the Revolutionary Tribunal with a crowd of sometime associates imprisoned earlier. Among them was Hérault de Séchelles, dropped from the Committee of Public Safety for allegedly plotting with foreign enemies. (His aristocratic background made this believable, though the evidence against him was forged.) Others included Fabre d'Eglantine and Chabot, who were actually guilty of profiteering while arranging the dissolution of the Company of the Indies and the embezzlement of public funds. Directly or by association, each shared the accusations against the others—counterrevolutionary activity, royalism, endangering the public order, treason, and venality (profiteering). Danton was charged with everything from trying to save the queen to peculation, bribery, and bribe-taking. Probably he had greased some palms, and vice versa, but no real evidence was offered to prove this or anything else against him. It did not matter; the verdict was foredrawn. On 5 April, Danton, Desmoulins, and fifteen others went to the guillotine. (Only one of the eighteen defendants, a pregnant woman, was spared.)

Danton went jauntily, waving to the crowd from his tumbrel as if on a political campaign, and drawing laughter by shouting obscenities as he passed under Robespierre's shuttered window. On the scaffold, he rebuked the whimpering Desmoulins (who, nevertheless, struggled until his clothes were in tatters). When Danton's turn came, there was dead silence. "Show my head to the crowd," he said to the executioner, "It is a sight well worth seeing." He was joking about his ugliness, as he always had, but he also wanted to dramatize the crimes of Robespierre. Danton is murdered, the gesture said. Who will be next?[30]

THE FALL OF ROBESPIERRE

Temporarily the Committee of Public Safety was in undisputed control of Paris and France. (Though the unity of the committee itself was cracking, this was of no immediate consequence.) Robespierre, however, had cut himself off from popular support and reduced the number of his political allies. Hébert's

[30] Danton's reputation is rehabilitated in the 1989 histories, but not nearly with the effectiveness of the movie *Danton*, written by Jean-Claude Carrière and directed by Andrzej Wajda, an ex-leader of the Polish "Solidarity" movement. [Paris, 1983]

execution alienated the *menu peuple* and the rank-and-file *sans-culottes*. Danton's death both shocked the people and terrified the politicians of the Convention. Speakers avoided great issues. Even in the Jacobin Club oratorical fireworks gave way to slumber. "The Revolution is frozen," said Saint-Just.

Robespierre utilized the lull to introduce the "Cult of the Supreme Being," a new national religion which he hoped would restore public morality. Religion and terror (moderated in the countryside, but increased in Paris) were to produce the "Republic of Virtue." The cult he proposed represented a compromise among atheism, deism, pantheism, and Catholic Christianity, and, he assumed, would satisfy free thinkers and Christians alike.

The Convention dutifully established the new religion by decree. The preamble read:

> The French people recognize the existence of the Supreme Being and the immortality of the soul. They recognize that the proper worship of the Almighty celebrates the duties of man: They place first among such duties those of detesting bad faith and tyranny, of punishing tyrants and traitors and assisting the unfortunate, of defending the oppressed, of doing good unto others ... and of being unjust to none.

Festivals were ordered to celebrate the existence of the Almighty and the great days of the Revolution—14 July (fall of the Bastille), 10 August (the storming of the Tuileries), 21 January (the execution of the king), and 31 May (the fall of the Girondins). The *décadi* (tenth days of the Revolutionary Calendar) were made feast days for the worship of the Supreme Being and abstractions such as the human species, nature, the people, benefactors of humanity, martyrs of liberty, liberty and equality, true friendship, heroism, love, and the like.

On 8 June 1794 what seemed the whole of Paris trooped to the initial festival, orchestrated by the artist David in the gardens of the Tuileries. Robespierre spoke (or preached), pausing while a figure representing "Wisdom" emerged (slightly scorched) from burning effigies of "Vice," "Atheism," and "Folly." Then, cavalry led a parade to the Champ de Mars (renamed Champ de Réunion)—delegations from the Commune and sections, the whole Convention, and others, interspersed with bands. There, led by Robespierre, they placed flowers, oak branches, and other symbolic objects at the foot of an artificial mountain, representing the Republic. The officials, en masse, swore an oath to the Republic, and a hymn to the Supreme Being was sung (to the tune of the *"Marseillaise"*). At this moment Robespierre seemed unassailable. Actually, Paris had responded more out of fear than anything else. Robespierre had alienated both atheists and Christians and pleased no one. Paris was indifferent to his Supreme Being.

The term "dictator," Robespierre knew, was being used to describe him. He did not understand it, since his will did not always prevail in the committee, but he was aware that opposition was growing. Collot d'Herbois and Billaud-Varenne were now openly expressing socialist views. In the Convention there was a general fear, acute among former representatives-on-mission, that Robespierre might have them prosecuted for well-documented "crimes," committed earlier with tacit official sanction. Those most vulnerable were strong men and veteran politicians such as Fouché, Barras, Carrier, and Tallien. The Jacobin Club no longer received Robespierre warmly, and many of the provincial clubs were openly hostile.

Robespierre's response was the Law of 22 Prairial (10 June 1794), a new Law of Suspects, passed by the still docile Convention. Persons could be accused for as little as "slandering patriotism" or for spreading "discouragement." Prisoners were allowed no defense, and the sentence had to be acquittal or death. To Fouché and other vulnerable *conventionnels*, it seemed designed to destroy them. Their desperation increased and their numbers multiplied as executions accelerated. During the next seven weeks, there were 1376 executions—whereas only 1251 had been guillotined in Paris over the past fourteen months. Even the Committee of General Security, which had not been consulted on the new law, went over to the opposition.

Robespierre's enemies began to plot his overthrow. Their task was facilitated by two quite diverse factors. First, on 24 June 1794, General Jourdan won his great victory over the Austrians at Fleurus. The Republic seemed positively out of danger, and the Terror unjustified. Second, on 5 Thermidor (23 July 1794), Robespierre proposed a modification of the Law of the Maximum, which put a ceiling on wages and would have greatly reduced the salaries of many Paris workmen. This destroyed any possibility of a popular rising to save the "Incorruptible" (which was improbable anyway).

The Committee of General Security began the attack on Robespierre. Vadier and Amar charged him with association with a cult of mystics who had not renounced Catholicism, and thus were suspected royalists. Their leader, Catherine Théot, a doddering hag once imprisoned for insanity, called herself the "Mother of God," and had publicly proclaimed Robespierre to be the "True Messiah" (which was his only connection with her). It was a ridiculous charge, and Robespierre used the authority of the Committee of Public Safety to have it quashed. The Committee of General Security protested to the Convention, and there was a joint meeting of the committees, but nothing was settled. Thus Robespierre won, but in the Convention, Collot d'Herbois and Billaud-Varenne had sided with the Committee of General Security. The Committee of Public Safety was split. Fouché, Chaumette, Barras, Fréron, Tallien, and others were organizing the Convention against Robespierre, calling him a dictator who had already placed himself above the law.

The Incorruptible inadvertently helped his enemies by withdrawing to his rooms in mid-June. For almost six weeks he did not speak in the Convention, seldom visited the Jacobins, and neglected his work with the Committee of Public Safety. *Why* is a mystery. Though he was not acutely sensitive to the privations and wishes of the Parisian masses, he was not politically naïve. He may be seen either as an intellectual who had totally rationalized his behavior, and therefore felt safe, or a man oversure of his power and becoming ill and deranged.

On 8 Thermidor (26 July 1794) he emerged to take the platform in the Convention—to prolonged applause. (His opponents were organized, but unready to commit themselves. The leaders were more radical than he; their followers were conservatives from the perennially silent "plain.") For two hours he lectured, preached, and threatened. Certain "monsters" in the Mountain, he said, were calling him a dictator. Well, the Hébertists and Dantonists had made the same charge against his committee. The new faction, like those already destroyed, challenged not him, but the government, the Convention and the Republic—"Liberty" itself. "You march across volcanos!" he shouted toward the Mountain. You say "*C'est* Robespierre" who has perpetrated all the evil. But it is *you*, my accusers, who have "proliferated unjust arrests" (in the provinces), "extended the terror," cheated the government, plotted with foreigners, ruined the middle class, left the poor without food. At intervals he departed his tirade to laud the Convention for establishing the religion of the Supreme Being, which had "saved the nation" and defeated atheism and "sacerdotal tyranny" (Catholicism) at a blow. He waxed lyric over the initial festival: "Oh the divine charm of innocence and beauty!" All the while he fingered a list, presumed to be of those he would accuse. But he never read it. The nearest he got to naming enemies was during one of his flights on religion, when he intoned "No, Chaumette, no Fouché, death is not an eternal sleep . . . Death is the beginning of immortality." When he left, however, few who were present felt safe. None needed reminding that the Terror was at its height. The guillotine was delivering to "immortality" thirty to fifty persons a day. After his crazed performance, few still had confidence in Robespierre, and none could be sure his name was not on the unread list of "enemies of the people."

During the evening of the same day, Robespierre read the same speech at the Jacobins. He got the floor, however, only after a violent fight and over the bitter objections of Billaud-Varenne and Collot d'Herbois. Moreover, he might better have used the time to organize wavering politicians. As it was, he only exhausted himself further, and since he still mentioned no names, turned more neutrals into enemies.

On 9 Thermidor (27 July) Robespierre and Saint-Just, both red-eyed and numb from working through the night, appeared at the Convention to defend their government. Saint-Just rose and began a speech ("I am a member of no faction. I oppose all factions. . . . "), but he never finished it. Billaud-Varenne interrupted on a point of order. Robespierre tried to speak and was silenced with cries of "Down with the Tyrant!" "Out with the Dictator!" Tallien shouted that an "army of Cromwell" was being organized under Hanriot (commander of the Paris National Guard) to support the "tyrant Robespierre." The arrest of Hanriot and of the head of the Revolutionary Tribunal, Dumas, was voted. Vadier, the old ferret of the Committee of General Security, scenting blood, thundered accusations of dictatorship and treason against Robespierre. Pandemonium ensued, with members howling for the arrest of "the dictator." Robespierre tried to defend himself, but no one would listen. Desperate, emotionally and physically drained, he screamed, "*I demand that I be sent to death!*" When order was restored, the Convention voted the arrest of Robespierre, his brother Augustin, Saint-Just, Couthon, and others, including Hanriot and Dumas. They were taken away to various prisons.

Robespierre still controlled a majority in the Commune, however. By 10 P.M., the four principals and others had been released and were ensconced in the Hôtel de Ville. The Commune called on the sections to attack the Convention, but only sixteen (of forty-eight) responded, and the men who arrived at the City Hall were listless and uninspired.

Meanwhile the Convention went into emergency session, outlawed Robespierre (which meant he could be shot on sight by anyone), reordered the arrest of the others and the entire insurrectionary Commune. The Convention's guard of regulars and National Guardsmen from local sections seized the Hôtel de Ville at about 2:30 A.M. and broke into an upstairs room where Robespierre and company were conferring. The Incorruptible turned a pistol on himself, but the bullet only mangled his jaw.[31] Augustin jumped from a window, and Couthon went out a door in his wheelchair, only to tumble down a flight of stairs. Saint-Just, the most athletic of all, sat as if hypnotized. All were captured —Robespierre unconscious from shock and loss of blood—Couthon and Augustin stretcher cases.

There was no trial. During the night, remaining members of the two great committees went through the pretense of a hearing in the Green Room of the Committee of Public Safety in the Tuileries. Robespierre lay outside, strapped to a board, semiconscious, his jaw in a blood-soaked bandage. The others were held in the City Hall until it was over. Then all were jailed in a secret place.

On 10 Thermidor (28 July 1794), in the late afternoon, the Incorruptible and his lieutenants went to the guillotine—Couthon screaming; Saint-Just impassively; Robespierre bravely, crying out only when the bandage was ripped from his jaw. Nineteen of their followers, including Augustin, were executed at the same time. The next day, seventy-one "Robespierristes," mostly of the Commune, were beheaded.

The Terror was at an end. The authoritarian "democratic" republic was dead. Moreover, it had so alienated both Paris and France at large that the Convention was at last free to vote its will. The majority, of course, had always been conservative, though antiroyalist and anticlerical.

There followed a conservative reaction, which doomed the Constitution of 1793 and thus any hope of a representative democracy based on universal manhood suffrage. Doomed also was the more radical legislation of the terrorist government.

Ironically, this was not what had been expected by those most responsible for Robespierre's downfall. Billaud-Varenne and Collot d'Herbois of the Committee

[31] This was disputed by a soldier named Méda, who claimed to have shot him.

of Public Safety, Fouché, Tallien, and Barras of the Convention (and ex-repre-
sentatives-on-mission), and surely Amar and Vadier of the Committee of General
Security were all more radical than Robespierre. They had envisioned an even
stronger and more centralized government, and one more actively socialistic.

Astute politicans all, however, they sensed the mood of the Convention and
calculatedly tried to join the majority. Barras and Fouché were eminently successful. Some of the others (as we shall describe in detail below) were not so lucky.

SUMMARY

The greatest immediate accomplishment of the Terror government had been
the total mobilization of France for war and the saving of the Republic from its
foreign and domestic enemies. However, the Terror had also marked the high
point of revolutionary departure from the modes, practices, and institutions of
the Old Regime. It had been an experiment in authoritarian democracy and had
held out the greatest promise of more broadly based representative democracy.
It had set precedents by legislating (or proposing) a modicum of social and
economic equality and of equality of opportunity through education.

Thus the death of Robespierre marked the end of the Revolution for the more
advanced thinkers of the time. Within a year, hunger would make the Paris masses
see it that way. Especially in the twentieth century, as governments have become
more centralized, bureaucratic, and sensitive to the needs of the masses (and, in
many cases, insensitive to the shedding of blood in their name), more intellectuals
have also accepted 10 Thermidor as the end of the Revolution. They have thus
accepted that the gains (and dreams) of Robespierre and the Great Committee
were worth the bloodshed and violence wreaked on the French people.

In the decade of the 1980s, however, and especially in the Bicentennial Year
(1989), a growing number of historians (and others) decried the horrors and felt
the gains could have been wrought peacably, by evolution. They have given us
much food for thought.[32]

In any case the leftward course of the Revolution was halted. The "Thermidorian Reaction," called after the month of the Revolutionary Calendar, thus
began.

---

[32] See Introduction, p. 9, and footnote 4.

POSTSCRIPT TO TERROR

The Thermidorian Reaction
(1794–1795)

THE THERMIDORIANS

After the death of Robespierre, the Convention found itself controlling the committees, instead of the reverse. Nevertheless, the Convention comprised the same men, minus a few Montagnards. The majority was still republican and anticlerical. Thus the "Thermidorian reaction" got under way slowly, with the assembly responding cautiously to conservative public opinion, while trying to maintain a strong republican government.

The Convention had to prosecute the war, which was far from over. A revival of the Vendéan revolt had already begun. The religious problem persisted. The government was in unadmitted bankruptcy. The Terror had to be dismantled, but without precipitous action which might produce anarchy and facilitate the return to power of either Jacobins or royalists. At the same time, the Convention was determined to preserve the constructive work of the Terrorists. Finally, it had to fulfill its original purpose—to promulgate a constitution—that of 1793 or another one. The new leaders who emerged in the Convention were politicians from the Plain and deserters from the Mountain. In the first category were the Abbé Sieyès and Cambacérès, a huge, fat, but most charming gourmet and perhaps the top legal mind in France. In the second group were Fouché (temporarily), Barras, a suave, dapper, ex-viscount and ladies' man, and Jean Tallien, the former representative-on-mission at Bordeaux. They walked softly, however. It was November 1794 before the Jacobin Club was abolished and December before the Convention voted to readmit the seventy-three surviving Girondins to its ranks.

Until 1 September 1794, Barère, Collot d'Herbois, and Billaud-Varenne remained on the Committee of Public Safety, which continued to direct the government. Moreover, Barère still believed the Mountain was supreme in the

Convention and asked the deputies to strengthen the committee, describing the events of 9–10 Thermidor as "only minor disturbances which have restored the government to its full integrity." The Convention "reorganized" the committee on 31 July 1794 (13 Thermidor), three days after Robespierre's death. Actually, this involved no more than replacing those removed by the guillotine or absent on mission. The committee, nevertheless, got six new members, half its number. Of these, Tallien was the most important.

DISMANTLING THE TERROR

Gaining confidence, the Convention on 24 August 1794 removed control of the ministries and administration of justice from the Committee of Public Safety and restricted its authority essentially to matters of war and foreign policy. Other functions of government were divided among fifteen separate committees. Moreover, it decreed that one-quarter of the members of the Committee of Public Safety were to be replaced each month. Under this law, and because of resignations, there remained on the committee on 1 October 1794 only one of the original twelve—Lazare Carnot.

Meanwhile the bloodletting apparatus of the Terror had been more swiftly abolished. On 1 August (14 Thermidor), four days after Robespierre's death, the notorious Law of Prairial, defining suspects, was repealed. On 5 August, prisoners seized under this law, largely moderate bourgeoisie and *sans-culottes*, were released (five hundred in Paris alone). On 10 August the Revolutionary Tribunal was reorganized. It remained a special court for cases of treason but operated under normal rules of legal procedure. Moderates were placed on the bench, to the surprise of some Montagnards. Fouquier-Tinville, for example, the former prosecutor, asked for a judgeship. He was not only denied a post, but was arrested and ultimately guillotined. Throughout his trial he protested repeatedly "I only obeyed the law."

During the fall the new tribunal acquitted 132 prisoners who had been sent from Nantes, slowly gathering evidence about the drownings ordered by Carrier while representative-on-mission. It then tried the revolutionary committee of Nantes and finally sent Carrier to the guillotine in December. At the end of 1794, a legislative commission at last began an investigation of the past activities of Barère, Billaud-Varenne, Collot d'Herbois, and Vadier. In March 1796 the Convention ordered them sent into exile in Guiana.[1] Meanwhile, commissions were appointed to indict Terrorists in the provinces and in Paris.

---

[1] Vadier and Barère escaped. Collot died of tropical fever before the year was out, but Billaud-Varenne survived the climate and settled down contentedly with a black wife. Though granted amnesty in 1800 by Napoleon, he declined to return to France and instead moved to Haiti, where he spent his last years as a justice of the supreme court. He died in 1819.

SOCIETY In Paris, public reaction to the Terror ran well ahead of the methodical movement of the Convention. The release of the "Prairial Law" prisoners in August 1794 was celebrated by people of all classes. There were balls in the houses of the rich and influential, including some nobles, who again began appearing in public. Parties were held in the streets, warehouses, and armories for the common people. "Victims' Balls" became the rage. Those who had lost a relative to the guillotine wore red ribbons around their necks.

Freed from the Puritanistic regulations of the Terror, Paris society became increasingly licentious. The most popular salon was that of Theresa Cabarrus, who shortly became Madame Tallien, styled by a bawdy admirer "Our Lady of Thermidor." She was the daughter of François Cabarrus, a French banker with a Spanish title and fortunes in both countries, and herself the divorced wife of a French marquis. Imprisoned in 1793 at Bordeaux, she had been saved by Tallien, the representative-on-mission, who took her to Paris. There she was imprisoned again, but released after Thermidor. She in turn secured the release of Josephine de Beauharnais, widow of the Viscount de Beauharnais, a victim of the Terror, and future wife of Napoleon Bonaparte.[2]

Theresa and Josephine (called "Rose" by her friends) set the styles for Paris, where basic evening dress was the flowing "Greek" gown of diaphanous material which revealed the bust. The reigning beauty, however, was their seventeen-year-old friend, Madame Juliette Récamier, a sylph of such perfection of figure and face that painters fought to do her portrait and men of all stations were made her slaves by a glance (though she was probably the least immoral of the socialites).

The streets were taken over by the Muscadins or Incroyables (Incredibles) or "Gilded Youth"—violence-prone sons of the rich and their hangers-on. They wore their hair long, uncombed, and greasy (but perfumed), baggy coats with huge square collars, knee breeches, red-white-and-blue stockings, and boots. Fashion dictated that the clothes be rumpled and the boots muddy. Their female companions, the Merveilleuses (Wonderfuls), wore flowing dresses, boots, pounds of jewelry and "English" hats covered with stuffed birds, flowers, and the like. The angry young men flaunted their wealth, which they had been forced to hide for so long from the masses, and both insulted the people and mocked their "cowardly" fathers, who had earlier worn tattered garments and tried to make their mansions look unoccupied. They harassed *sans-culottes* and workingmen at random, but their chief targets were ex-Terrorists.

It was the Gilded Youth who set the stage for the destruction of the Jacobins. The Paris club had been closed on 10 Thermidor but reopened the next day for "honest Jacobins" (i.e., anti-Robespierrists). The Convention merely ordered the Jacobins to discontinue communicating (as a club) with clubs in the provinces. On 11 November, however, a horde of the Gilded Youth invaded the club, led by Louis Fréron (a sometime Terrorist but clever turncoat), assaulted the mem-

[2] See below, p. 185.

bers, broke up the furniture, and left the place a shambles. The next day the Convention ordered the club closed permanently.

The more radical members had already moved to the Panthéon Club (from its location near the former church where revolutionary heroes were entombed), properly called "Assembly of the Friends of the Republic." Formed by neo-Hébertists, it voiced the miseries of the masses and upheld the Constitution of 1793 as an ideal. It was destined in time to become a forum for the Communist leader, Gracchus Babeuf. (See below, p. 178.)

The Convention meanwhile ordered the remains of Marat removed from the Panthéon.[3] It, too, was invaded by the Gilded Youth, who destroyed busts and statues. There, as in Paris generally, the police watched indifferently while the Incroyables demolished monuments of the Revolution.

WHITE TERROR

Reaction was delayed in the provinces. Because of the poor communications, the destruction of the Jacobin correspondence networks and the gradualism of the Convention, the full significance of Robespierre's fall was not immediately realized. In some places, agents and representatives of the government continued to function for weeks and even months, conducting trials, ordering executions, and carrying out the de-Christianization policies.

When the reaction came, however, it struck with a vengeance. Some officials were lynched, others imprisoned. (Both Napoleon and Lucien Bonaparte were jailed for their connection with the former government, but acquitted.) In February 1795 there was a massacre of Jacobins in Lyons. In the ultra-Catholic countryside to the south, a "White Terror" was mounted against Jacobins by groups such as the Company of Jesus and the Company of the Sun. It sometimes became a pogrom against Protestants and/or Jews as well, since many of them (among city dwellers, at least) had been ardent revolutionaries. The White Terror subsided as the Thermidorian government gradually installed new local officials (some 30,000 were involved) or recognized those locally selected. The case of the Vendée, where the royalist-Catholic movement revived in force, was more difficult, and will be treated separately. (See below, p. 165.)

THE RELIGIOUS PROBLEM

Everywhere the existence of the Cult of the Supreme Being complicated matters. Although in legalizing it the Convention had reaffirmed the principle of

---

[3] The Church of Sainte Geneviève, begun by Louis XV in 1764 and finished in 1790. The National Assembly had designated it the Panthéon in 1791. Mirabeau was the first "hero" of the Revolution buried there.

freedom of religion, the cult was in fact a state religion, and those who had not accepted it had been suspect. Many churches and cathedrals had been converted into temples of the cult or had been offered for sale as National Properties. At the same time, the Civil Constitution of the Clergy had not been repealed, and the government was legally obligated to pay the salaries of juring priests (though for a year it had not).

The majority in the Convention favored maintaining the Cult of the Supreme Being and (though few said it bluntly) stamping out Catholicism. It soon became evident, however, that the cult was an intellectuals' religion which the common people scarcely understood. There was hope that the masses could be "educated" to accept it (and the Directory would later try), but, as things stood, the peasants were violently hostile to it, and even in Paris most families called in Catholic priests for last rites and burials. Civil marriage, legalized under the Terror, was practiced in Paris and the other large cities—but even there, only sophisticates considered it final. Most couples had themselves remarried by a priest. (After all, even the most rabid *sans-culotte* did not want to risk having his children called illegitimate.)

As Terrorist officials were removed, priests began to resume services. Bishop Grégoire, a member of the Convention, ordered the churches reopened in his diocese (Blois), other bishops rushed to follow his example, and a veritable Catholic revival ensued.

The Convention reaffirmed laws against nonjuring priests but took scant action to enforce them or to interfere with Catholic services. Juring priests meanwhile began demanding their salaries (reduced but not abolished under the Terror). The response of the Convention was to relieve the government of this expense by declaring the separation of church and state (September 1794).[4] The resurgence of traditional religion continued, nevertheless. The clergy got no government money (until 1801, when Napoleon concluded the Concordat with the pope), but recovered its churches and cathedrals by simply reoccupying them. Paris, as usual, was a special case. It was August 1795 before the keys to Notre Dame (officially *the* Temple of the Supreme Being) were turned over to a "Catholic Society," which reinstituted services. Even then it had to share the cathedral with the state cult and other groups.

Orators delivered dire warnings to the Convention that reviving Catholicism would mean reviving royalism. For most of the country, however, it merely meant the restoration of traditional routines of worship, which made for peace. Peasants happily began taking both Sundays and the *décadi* (tenth days) of the Revolutionary Calendar as days of rest. In the west, however, there was no peace.

---

[4] On the motion of the minister of finance, Joseph Cambon, who argued that if the state paid Catholic clergy, it would have to pay those of the Cult of the Supreme Being, or one or the other, and that the state was bankrupt and could not afford either.

AGAIN THE VENDÉE

In the Vendée and Britanny, the royalist-Catholic movement had begun to revive even before the fall of Robespierre. The bitter antipathies between country and town had persisted and been intensified by the domination of the towns by the hated "atheist" Jacobin clubs. The vicious reprisals of the terrorist government had served to drive peasants into the guerrilla bands (Chouans). In the spring of 1794 the émigré Count Joseph de Puisaye arrived in Britanny from England to coordinate the Chouans' efforts, bringing British funds and the promise of more. The French government had to reinforce its army in the west. After Thermidor, the forces of royalism increased, taking bloody vengeance on the Jacobins and putting the French army on the defensive.

In September 1794 the Convention gave command in the Vendée to General Louis Hoche, only twenty-six, but already a hero, and not a glory seeker. After battling inconclusively with the rebels, he became convinced, largely from talking with prisoners, that he could negotiate peace. What they wanted most were the restoration of their churches, the assurance that the Jacobins had fallen, and the guarantee of amnesty if they laid down their arms. The government authorized Hoche to parley on that basis. In February 1795 he signed an agreement with the major Vendéan leader François de Charette and in April and May, treaties with other leaders, including the dashing Jean Cottereau, chief commander of the Chouans. Puisaye fled to England.

Rebel priests, even ex-émigrés, were given full freedom to reopen the churches (and the requirement of the oath was ignored). Rebels not only got amnesty, but were promised compensation for damage to their property and exemption from service in the republican armies. Disarmament was carried out sloppily or not at all. The settlement was almost too good. Among the minority of militants, at least, hope was engendered that Louis XVII (the boy-king, imprisoned in Paris) would be restored to the throne. The Convention secured peace, but not for long.

QUIBERON In June 1795, Louis XVII died in the Temple (his prison) at age ten. In Verona, his uncle, the Count de Provence, was proclaimed Louis XVIII by the émigré court. He immediately issued a statement accusing the "Jacobin" government of murder and promising to return to France and wreak vengeance on the usurpers of the God-given power of his dynasty. At the same time, the British government (under Pitt) had finally granted aid to the Count d'Artois and agreed to land an émigré army on the west coast of France. Georges Cadoudal, a Chouan hero of '93, was sent ahead to rally the guerrillas in Brittany. (Refer to Map 3.2, p. 99.)

Between 27 June and 15 July the British landed some 4500 émigrés (of whom 3500 were actually impressed French prisoners of war), near Quiberon. They were reinforced by 15,000 Chouans. Meanwhile a British fleet blockaded French warships at Brest, and Charette created a diversion in the Vendée. Quiberon, however, at the end of a long, narrow peninsula, was an idiotic choice of beachhead. Hoche, warned long in advance, assembled superior forces, allowed the émigrés to land and join their allies and then drove the rebels down the peninsula and trapped them "like rats" (as he reported to the Convention). Some émigrés, including the Count de Puisaye, escaped to British vessels, but hundreds of royalists were killed and 8000 captured.

The Convention sent Tallien to supervise the trial of the prisoners. He had 748 genuine émigrés shot and freed the impressed French prisoners and Chouans. Cadoudal escaped to England. Charette, abandoned by his Vendéans, was pursued by government agents and finally captured and shot in 1796.

The Quiberon landing was part of a grand scheme hatched by the Count d'Artois to restore the monarchy in France. After the disaster, however, a British force, meant to follow up the émigré landing, turned back to England. In the Rhineland, Condé's émigré army called off a planned simultaneous invasion of France (to be facilitated by the French General Jean Pichegru, a secret royalist). Only the Count d'Artois refused to give up.

Artois was with the British invasion force, but when it was recalled, he was allowed to sail on to the island of Yeu, off the Vendéan coast. There he stayed, attempting to rally French royalists to support another invasion, until October 1795, when the British, weary of his fantasies of mass support in France, loaded him and his few troops aboard ship and returned them to England. His major contribution had been to divide émigré leadership by insisting that absolute (rather than constitutional) monarchy must be restored and by damping the ardor of the British with the same line.

Guerrilla action in the Vendée continued, but until 1798 it posed no major problem for the government. (Napoleon finally put an end to it in 1800.)

THE ECONOMIC CRISIS

The economic and financial problems of the Republic meanwhile remained acute. With the collapse of the terrorist government, the controls over production and distribution had ceased to be effective. Farmers and merchants again began hoarding grain. Supplies on the market were further decreased by natural causes; the summer of 1794 was dry, and the winter of 1794–1795 was the coldest in a hundred years. Crops were meager in both the fall and spring. In midwinter when Paris was in greatest misery, the Convention repealed the Law of the Maximum, which the sans-culottes took as evidence of the deputies' indifference. Though controls were removed to encourage the importation of grain, free-enterprise methods did not work well in wartime.

Conditions worsened as farmers, merchants, wholesalers, and bakers began refusing to accept assignats in payment for grain or bread. The paper "money of the poor" constituted the bulk of that in circulation. Under terrorist regulations (accompanied by very real punishment for violation) assignats had been very good money. Thermidorians, on laissez-faire principle, did not force businessmen to take them. Thus, while in December 1793 assignats had been worth 40 percent of face value (compared to 22 percent in July 1793), by October 1794 they were at 20 percent, by July 1795, 8 percent, and by October 1795, all but worthless. Thus the failure of the Thermidorians to enforce their use as legal tender (since hard money was in short supply) probably had more to do with the miserable plight of Parisians than the repeal of the Maximum.

The Convention did perpetuate bread price controls in Paris at 20 sous (one franc) per pound (the 1793–1794 level), but although laborers' wages had doubled since 1790 (to two francs a day), the city also established a ration of one pound per day, but four pounds a day were needed to feed a family. Moreover, the bread ration often went only to firstcomers, since there was not enough for all. The city offered rice and potatoes to supplement the ration, but since the price of fuel jumped (wood per sack was 500 francs, compared to 20 francs in 1790), workers could not afford to cook them. By April 1795 the cost of all food was eight times what it had been in 1790, and still rising.

THE UPRISINGS OF GERMINAL AND PRAIRIAL

As early as December 1794, Gracchus Babeuf, in his *Tribune du Peuple*, began a campaign to stir Parisians to action. The future Communist leader had yet to develop his program, but the misery around him excited his anger and he expressed public regret that he had earlier opposed Robespierre. He urged the *sans-culottes* to attack the Gilded Youth and to use the weight of their numbers against the Convention. There were only two parties, he said, the *sans-culotte*s and the rich. His paper was soon suppressed; most others followed the anti-Jacobin line, for example, Tallien's *L'Ami du Citoyen*.

During the winter of 1794–1795 the Commune decimated the section assemblies by indicting ex-Terrorists (200 in Paris). The people, nevertheless, found leaders. On 1 April 1795, the *sans-culottes* of the Faubourg de St.-Antoine invaded the Convention shouting "Bread and the Constitution of '93!" and held the assembly captive for hours until driven out by the National Guards of the conservative western sections. General Pichegru was authorized to place the city under martial law, and he quickly restored order.[5]

The Convention made concerted efforts to feed the City, but with scant success. Bread supplies remained insufficient even to provide the meager one-pound ration allotted workers. Hundreds died from hunger and cold. Police reports noted that people in the working-class sections all seemed palid, ill, and on the verge of collapse. Suicides increased.

---

[5] Pichegru's royalism was suspected, but Jacobinism was more feared at this time and the general was, after all, the conqueror of Belgium and Holland and a hero of the Republic. It was 1794 before he was arrested (he escaped).

The *sans-culottes* found the strength to rise again, however. On the morning of 20 May (1 Prairial) drums rolled, and the people, led by shouting women, marched from the St.-Antoine and St.-Marcel on the Tuileries. After repeated attacks, they broke into the Tuileries, killed a deputy, and waved his head on a pike before the president of the Convention. This lent force to their demands—creation of an emergency food committee, release from prison of certain "Patriots," and more. Guided by Montagnards, such as Prieur of the Marne (formerly of Robespierre's committee), the Convention "passed" legislation accordingly. Meanwhile the crowd dwindled, and at nightfall, conservative National Guardsmen cleared the Tuileries. Prieur and the other Montagnards were arrested. General Jacques Menou was called in with regular troops to insure peace.

Next morning, however, Menou was confronted before the Convention by 20,000 people, reinforced by radical National Guardsmen of the eastern sections. He accepted volunteers from the Gilded Youth and a standoff ensued; leaders of the sides parleyed; the sections agreed to submit their demands (again reduced to "Bread and the Constitution of '93") peacefully. Disorders continued in the Faubourg St.-Antoine, however. On 23 May, Menou, who had built up his army to 20,000, invaded the Quinze-Vingts and other sections, destroyed the resistance, disarmed the rebel National Guards, and arrested the leaders of the movement. The last popularly led uprising of the Revolution was over. (The crowds would move again in the fall, but, improbably, under royalist leadership.)

During the summer of 1795, economic conditions improved somewhat, the Quiberon crisis was weathered, and the Convention was finally able to complete the work before it and to prepare the way for a new government.

THE CONVENTION: CULTURAL LEGISLATION

Among other things, the Thermidorian Convention must be credited with voting into law many of the cultural and educational proposals of the Terror. The program for a complete system of tuition-free public schools, elaborated by Cordorcet (and others) before the Terror and pushed by the Great Committee was abandoned as too expensive and impractical (and because of the opposition of the resurgent Church). However, by a decree of 25 October 1795, public secondary schools were established—the "Central Schools"—one per department and five in Paris. The Museum of Natural History (founded in 1793) and the National Library (Bibliothèque Nationale, 1794) were perpetuated. The post-Thermidor Central School of Public Works (1794) became the *École Polytechnique*, a permanent school for engineers (1795). The *École Normale*, for teachers and researchers, established by the Thermidorians in October 1794, was allowed to expire in 1795 (but would be resurrected by Napoleon). The Convention, however, retained the Conservatory of Industrial Arts (Arts et Métiers) and three medical schools (at Strasbourg, Paris, and Montpelier) created in December 1794.

In its final months the Convention founded the School of Oriental Languages (March 1795), the "Bureau of Longitude" (June 1795), which included a school of astronomy, the Collège National (July 1795, formerly the Collège Royal), the Museum of the Louvre (September 1795), the Conservatory of Music, and finally (October 1795), the Institut de France. Altogether, it was an astonishing record, and as related here, ignores many worthy but unspectacular accomplishments, such as the creation of schools for the deaf, blind, and orphans of the "defenders of the Nation."

THE CONVENTION: FOREIGN POLICY

The Thermidorians also built upon earlier victories in the foreign war to conquer Belgium and the United Provinces of the Netherlands (Holland), to establish its armies firmly in the Rhineland, and to invade Spain. Prussia made peace in July 1795 (secretly promising to make over the left bank of the Rhine to France in return for territory in Germany); Spain made peace in 1795. The Thermidorian Convention annexed Belgium to France (October 1795) and oversaw the conversion of Holland into the Batavian Republic (May 1795) by the Dutch Patriot Party.

With the annexation of Belgium (the Austrian Netherlands) and the creation of the Batavian "sister" Republic, the Thermidorians had positively resumed the aggressive policy of international revolution propounded by the early Girondins. The Terrorists, oddly enough, had abandoned this policy, or seemed to have. At any rate, they had rejected overtures for aid from Dutch revolutionaries as well as Swiss, Italians, and others, on the simple ground that France was already overcommitted. For the same reason (and because Prussian-Austrian conflict over Poland benefited France), Robespierre had refused aid to General Kosciuszko, Polish hero of the American Revolution, who raised a rebellion (1794) in a last-ditch effort to save Poland as an independent nation—that is, to prevent her domination by Russia, or later her partition among Russia, Austria, and Prussia. The Polish patriots were crushed in December 1795.[6]

Carnot believed that the Thermidorians' policy was an obstacle to permanent peace, and in August 1795 he resigned from the Committee of Public Safety in protest.[7] His feeling was that whatever the monarchs of Europe agreed to in the short-run, they could not tolerate the deliberate promotion of subversion by France within their territories. Moreover, if France continued to expand her sphere of influence, the powers would eventually unite once more against her.

---

[6] Kosciuszko was imprisoned for two years in Russia, then made his way to the United States. In 1798 he returned to France where he organized a Polish legion, the first of a number to serve in the Armies of the Revolution and Napoleon.

[7] Carnot, nevertheless, became one of the first directors in the succeeding government, and later served Napoleon, but only briefly, during the peacemaking phase of the Consulate.

For the time being, however, the Thermidorians' policy was grossly offensive only to Austria. When the Convention gave way to the Directory (October 1795), only Austria and her minor allies in Germany and Italy held out on the Continent. Britain was limiting herself to war at sea.

DEMISE OF THE CONSTITUTION OF '93

After Thermidor, it had been generally assumed in the Convention that the suspended Constitution of 1793 would be put into effect—eventually. The fact that the war was still in progress was the principal argument against immediate action. Opponents of the Constitution (overt opponents at least) were in the extreme minority. After all, the Constitution had been voted by the Convention and had been heavily approved by the voters (though the turnout was light), 1,600,000 to 25,000. As the year 1794–1795 progressed, however, its strongest proponents in the Convention were gradually eliminated, and the majority came to favor radical revision or a new Constitution. The minority who still defended it strongly were true believers in democracy—ostensibly in representative democracy. Its opponents predicted that the Constitution would serve to return the Jacobins to power—if not in France at large, almost surely in Paris, where the Convention still felt uneasy. Paris herself confirmed the pessimists' fears and jolted the assembly into action on an entirely new Constitution. The insurgents of 12 Germinal (1 April 1795) had invaded the Convention shouting "Bread and the Constitution of 1793!"

Memories of the Terror were revived, and the next day a commission was appointed to consider a new Constitution. The disturbances of Prairial (20–23 May 1795) further damped the Convention's tolerance for Jacobinism. Afterward a dozen Montagnards were sent to the guillotine or committed suicide.[8] As if in penance, the Convention abolished the Revolutionary Tribunal at the end of the month. But the fear of a new Terror persisted. In addition, the Convention felt impelled to guard against a royalist revival in view of the uprisings which had culminated in the Quiberon landing, the continuing resurgence of the Catholic Church, and the concrete evidence that royalist agents were operating in Paris itself.

The Convention thus produced a Constitution designed to limit the voice of the masses, who might, out of desire for a strong government to meet their immediate needs, opt either for Jacobinism or royalism. What it produced may fairly be called a "bourgeois" Constitution, although those who wrote it felt that they were liberals rather than conservatives—liberals pushing the limits of democracy as far as possible without inviting anarchy.

---

[8] Prieur of the Marne, the most famous of those arrested, escaped, however.

CONSTITUTION OF THE YEAR III

Debate was muted and took place mostly in committee. The Convention still feared the wrath of the *sans-culottes*. Sieyès, who was the author of the passive/active citizen provisions of the Constitution of 1791, had great influence. He had always believed in equality of rights, but no more; economic inequality, he believed, was inevitable—even "assured" by equality of rights. In the end, the majority felt justified in giving power to the middle class. As Boissy d'Anglas put it:

> We ought to be governed by the best; the best are the most highly educated and those interested in the maintenance of the laws . . . you will find such men among those who, possessing property, are attached to the country in which it lies, and which has laws to protect it. . . .

In reaction against the abuse of centralized power during the Terror, the Constitution of the Year III provided for the separation of powers not only among the executive, legislative, and judicial branches, but (as will be discussed below), within the branches. In addition, democracy was revived at the local level, with the safeguard that elected officials could be suspended by the national executive in emergencies. By the summer of 1795, however, the Convention was beset with more immediate fears of royalism than of Jacobinism. Therefore the Constitution was submitted to the voters with additional decrees (passed on 22 and 30 August 1795) requiring that two-thirds of the members of the new assemblies be ex-members of the Convention. The Convention was not so much trying to perpetuate itself as to safeguard itself against a royalist coup during the transitional period to constitutional republican government, which, after all, had not been tried before. The Republic since its inception in 1792 had been governed by *ad hoc* commissions, committees and/or the Convention directly.

The Bill of Rights of the Constitution did not repeat the 1789 phrase "Men are born and remain free and equal in rights." Men were declared free and equal but duties as citizens were stressed—for example, safeguarding property and obedience to the law.[9] The "general will" was equated to law but only "as expressed by the *majority* of citizens or their representatives." The right of revolution was omitted. There was also no mention of rights to work, to public assistance, or to education.

The legislature (Corps Législatif) consisted of two houses—the Council of Elders (Anciens) and the Council of 500 (Cinq Cents). The Elders (250) had to be over forty; the deputies of the 500 over thirty. It was the right of the 500 to initiate all legislation. The Elders could only accept or reject it. One third of both

---

[9] Twenty-two rights were listed and nine duties, some in several parts.

houses were to be replaced each year, beginning in 1797, by the elections each spring.[10]

Deputies to both houses of the legislature were named by electors chosen in the cantons by the voters (male, twenty-one or over, who paid taxes). There was no property qualification for holding public office, but that for electors was very high, so that those eligible in all France numbered only about 30,000. The electors also chose five-man departmental directories and local executive committees in their municipalities and cantons. The district (arrondissement) was abolished in the new administrative system.

The national executive consisted of a Directory of five men chosen by the Council of Elders from a list supplied by the Council of 500. The directors had to be forty or over and to have served as deputies in a national legislature or ministers in the national government. After 1796, one was to retire yearly.[11] The chairmanship of the Directory was to rotate every three months—a further safeguard against tyranny. The Directory had no control over legislation or finance. The legislature, however, could not dismiss a director unless he were proven guilty of treason, embezzlement, or other high crimes. The Directory was given the power to appoint ambassadors and ministers, military officers, and members of the administration, including supervisors for elected municipal and departmental governments. However, it could declare war and make peace only with the approval of the legislature.

The judiciary was organized essentially as it had been under the Constitution of 1791. It was elective and an independent branch of the government. There were justices of the peace in the municipalities, a varying number of civil and criminal courts in the departments, and a "supreme" Court of Cassation in Paris for appeals. Government officials were tried by a special High Court.

Despite the abuse generally leveled at the bourgeois Constitution of the Year III, it was not illiberal for the time. The franchise was wider than in the United States, where voting requirements were left to the states. French voters only chose electors. However, the American Constitution also had safeguards against "popular passion." Senators were elected initially by state legislatures, which may be seen as "electors." In addition, the president of the United States was named by electors, as he technically still is.

Perhaps the major flaw in the Constitution was that there was no machinery for settling deadlocks between the legislative and executive branches. More properly there was no system for changing the Directory to suit the majority in the legislature (or naturally, vice versa). This encouraged change by coup d'état. The two-thirds decrees, already mentioned, were a sort of coup by the Convention—a violation before the fact of the Constitution. Two-thirds, or 500, of the

---

[10] For the first two years, those to retire would be chosen by lot.

[11] Those to retire were to be chosen by lot for the first four years, after which a seniority system would be applied.

750 legislators had to be former members of the Convention. Moreover, if the electoral assemblies did not return the required number, the Convention would elect them before it was dissolved.

PLEBISCITE ON THE CONSTITUTION

The Convention passed the Constitution on 22 August 1795. It was submitted to the voters (with the two-thirds decrees) on 6 September. This vote was by universal manhood suffrage—the system of 1792—since the new voting qualifications could not be applied until the Constitution was in effect. Nobles, priests, and certain Terrorists who had lost their citizenship rights were technically excluded, but universal suffrage seemed to give an advantage to Jacobins in the cities and to royalists in the countryside—an additional reason for the two-thirds laws. The moderates, however, had gained control of the press, partly through censorship, but largely through the use of subsidies granted by the Convention or private financial interests. The White Terror had all but destroyed Jacobinism in rural cities, and the Quiberon fiasco discouraged overt royalism. Neither strong Jacobin nor royalist sentiment was manifested even in Paris, but Paris was against the Constitution. There, the crowds, as usual, were influenced by hunger. The food price index was now an incredible 1000 percent over that of 1790. Bread was still scarce, the assignats were worth nothing, and unemployment was very heavy. The Constitution seemed to promise only a continuation of the Thermidorian government, and Parisians blamed the Thermidorian Convention for all their ills.

On the basis of preliminary returns, the Convention announced that the Constitution had been approved on 27 September 1795. Figures released a few days later showed the vote to have been 1,057,390 for the Constitution and 49,978 against. However, the two-thirds decrees were passed by only 205,498 to 108,794, indicating that almost 800,000 men who approved of the Constitution abstained on the decrees. In any case, the vote was light; 5,000,000 eligible men did not vote at all.

In Paris, all but one of the forty-eight sections rejected the two-thirds decrees. Eighteen sections angrily protested the adoption of the Constitution and demanded a recount of votes. The whole city reflected a sullen hostility, which the Convention pretended to ignore. After announcing elections for the new legislative councils for 12 October, it prepared to dissolve itself.

Paris, however, was unwilling to let the Convention depart in peace.

I am no longer able to obey; I have gotten a taste for command, and I would not know how to give it up.
—*Napoleon to Miot de Melito, November, 1797*

THE DIRECTORY
AND THE RISE OF
NAPOLEON BONAPARTE
(1795–1799)

THE WHIFF OF GRAPESHOT

Rumors of impending violence in Paris prompted the Convention to bring in 5000 regular troops to guard the Tuileries. Reversing its previous antiterrorist stance, it had cleared ex-*sans-culottes* to vote in the elections and had renewed laws against émigrés and nonjuring priests. Royalists, who had quietly built an organization to replace that of the suppressed Terrorists, had hoped legally to elect large contingents—perhaps majorities—in the new assemblies. The two-thirds laws meant that this would be impossible for the next two or three years, which persuaded the leaders to try to raise the sections to prevent their going into effect. The activists were constitutionalists, however, who did not parade their royalism. They did not favor restoration of the absolute monarchy, nor were they under the illusion that Paris was ready to bring back the king. Thus they kept a low profile, offering relief from the miseries of Thermidorian government to the masses and warning the bourgeoisie that the new "two-thirds" government might bring back the Terror.[1] The bourgeois leaders positively sided with the royalists when the Convention organized ex-Terrorists into battalions of "Patriots of '89" for its defense.

---

[1] The absolutist organization, formed for the Count d'Artois by the Duke d'Antraigues, refused even to communicate with the royal insurgents, whom they considered traitors because they were willing to accept a constitution.

From 27 September (5 Vendémiaire, Year IV) forward, Paris, led by the affluent Lepeletier section, signaled its intention to destroy the Convention. The deputies charged Barras, an ex-Terrorist, with the defense of the Tuileries. He called to his side Brigadier General Napoleon Buonaparte, also a one-time Jacobin, who a few weeks earlier had been struck off the army list for refusing a command in the Vendée.

Barras knew his man well. He, among others, had recommended Buonaparte's promotion at Toulon. Since the Convention had only 5000 regulars and a few hundred volunteer "Patriots" at its disposal (the National Guard was hostile or neutral, depending on the section), he needed a general who would make maximum use of available forces and would not shrink from using any and all weapons against the people. Napoleon filled the bill. He was ruthless, extremely ambitious, and a proven tactician and leader. Moreover (Barras always thought of the future), the wiry, intense, little Corsican was expendable. To many he was a foreigner, and in any case he had few connections. After he had done his work—depending on the reaction of politicians and the officer corps—he could be promoted or relegated to obscurity.

Napoleon, called to command on 4 October 1795 (12 Vendémiaire, IV), had little time to plan. He sensed immediately, however, that his infantry would never stand without heavy artillery support against the hordes of Paris. At Sablons, in the suburbs, the National Guard had the cannon he needed. At nightfall he ordered Major Joachim Murat, a tall, black-haired, arrogant Gascon, to take a troop of cavalry, seize the guns and bring them to him. Murat responded with the dash that later won him a marshal's baton and the sobriquet "first horseman of Europe," leading his men "hell for leather" through the cobblestoned streets of Paris, riding down anyone in his path. At Sablons he went through the gate at full gallop, ignoring the sentries, who watched, stunned, as his cavalry followed. At 5 A.M. on 5 October he was back at the Tuileries with forty cannon.

Napoleon now had no doubt that he could save the Convention. He concentrated on covering the approaches from the Lepeletier section, the center of the uprising, a mile to the north. To the advantage of the defenders, the streets running south all deadended into the east-west Rue St.-Honoré, one block north of the Tuileries. From there the short, wide Rue de La Convention led from the front of the Church of Saint Roch directly to the Tuileries Gardens; a few blocks to the east there was a twisting route to the Place du Carrousel, on the east side of the palace. Most of the guns were emplaced to sweep the street before Saint Roch and to guard the eastern approach; a few were trained on the single bridge over the Seine in the defender's rear (at the southern end of the Tuileries). The cannon were loaded with grapeshot, nails, links of chain, and scrap metal. On the morning of 5 October crowds began to gather on the Rue de St.-Antoine, and by noon there were 35,000 in the streets north of the Tuileries, including some 10,000 National Guards (30,000 were mobilized, but most remained in their sections). There was no immediate attack, however. The leaders palavered while the rank and file got drunk on overly ample supplies of wine furnished by sympathizers. The National Guardsmen had no artillery; the people had little but pikes, sticks, and stones. Napoleon's gunners stood by their cannon, with the infantry squared behind them.[2] As the afternoon wore on, the crowds became noisier and could be seen packing into the approach routes.

At about 4 P.M. the mass around the Church of Saint Roch suddenly surged forward toward the Tuileries Gardens along the Rue de La Convention, a roaring sea of bobbing liberty caps and pikes. The cannoneers waited, torches lit, as the people closed in. Finally, with the crowd almost upon them, the order came. FIRE! The cannon cut bloody swaths into the close-packed ranks. The people fled, leaving their dead, wounded, parts of bodies, on the bloody pavements. In the Place du Carrousel, on the other side of the palace, the scene was reenacted at almost the same time. A little later the ill-led insurgents tried to force the bridge in the defenders' rear. Again, the cannon did their work. The power of Paris was broken.

A few diehards in the Church of Saint Roch and elsewhere continued sniping into the hours of darkness, but were overcome by the infantry.[3] Wrote Napoleon to his brother Joseph at 2 A.M on 6 October: "The enemy attacked us at the Tuileries. We killed a large number of them . . . we have disarmed the sections and all is quiet. As usual I have not a scratch."

Such was Napoleon's "whiff of grapeshot."[4] By grace of General Buonaparte, the govermnent of the Directory was free to establish itself; by grace of the same general, the Directory would disappear four years later.

THE GOVERNMENT OF THE DIRECTORY: GENERAL

After reasonably peaceful elections, the National Convention dissolved itself on 26 October 1795 in favor of the new *Corps Legislatif* of 750 members (250 in the Council of Elders; 500 in the Council of 500). Technically the elections returned 507 *conventionnels* to office—more than required by the two-thirds law. However, 128 had been elected from two or more constituencies; thus the old Convention co-opted 121 more of its own to fill vacant seats before it departed. Nevertheless, the Thermidorians had not won a victory. Of the freely elected 250 members, 134 were royalists and a majority of the remainder were Jacobins. This boded ill for the future. The Directory was to experience the same assaults from the right and left that had plagued the government of Thermidor. The first

---

[2] This was normal defensive formation for close combat. The gunners fired as many times as possible to break an assault, then, if necessary, retreated into infantry squares.

[3] Saint Roch bears the marks of cannon shot and musketballs to this day.

[4] The term was coined by Thomas Carlyle in his *French Revolution* (1837) and is technically inaccurate. Napoleon was using cannister, not grapeshot, which was a naval load.

assemblies had a comfortable majority of moderate republicans and the first Directory, of which the chief members were Barras and Carnot, seemed eminently safe. Nevertheless, the Directory for the entire four years of its life was extremely unstable. It began with a "legislated violation" of the Constitution (the two-thirds law), and never ceased to reconstitute its executive and legislative branches unconstitutionally.

The Constitution of the Year III very much resembled that of the United States. An American might therefore jump to the conclusion that it should have become permanent. We should remember, however, that the French had no tradition of parliamentary government. Theirs always had been more a government of men than of laws. Thus those in power tended to refuse "bad" election results—violently if necessary. We should also remember that the French expected much more from government than did the free-wheeling Americans (whose constitution was written, initially, more to deny power to the government—prevent tyranny—than to grant or distribute it). Further, Americans were not faced with choosing between such extremes as royalism and Jacobinism, nor did they have France's religious problems. And finally, whereas France was beset by enemies on all sides, foreign powers showed little inclination to interfere with affairs in the United States (contrary to what Americans thought at the time).

Considering the conditions extant in Europe, the Constitution of the Year III gave too little power to the Executive Directory over foreign policy and war. Often it could not control its own agents—particularly generals in the field. The result was that it blundered, pell-mell, into an aggressive policy which manifested itself in the continued invasion of more territories and the creation of "sister republics." There was never an overall plan, but there seemed to be because of the repeated proclamations of the legislative branch (which became almost ritual) promising to support "free people" against tyrants, and foster liberty, equality, and fraternity throughout the world. It was this foreign policy that rendered the peacemaking of the first years temporary and led France back into full-scale war, which in turn set the stage for the collapse of the Directory.

Domestically, the government, with monotonous regularity, suffered a coup d'état after each election, beginning with the first, in 1797. Each effected changes in the Directory or legislative bodies, or both, which the voters had not authorized. In 1799 there were two coups (at least), the last of which terminated the life of the Directory and brought Napoleon to power. The object of all the coups (including the last, though it did not turn out quite as planned) was to preserve the moderate Republic by preventing either the Jacobins or royalists from gaining control.

The first Directory was elected in Year IV (1795–1796, September to September), and remained intact until the elections of the Year V (1796–1797) in the spring of 1797. The wiliest figure was Paul Barras, ex-viscount, ex-Terrorist, whom we know already. A tough, decisive, political animal, he was essentially without principles. It is significant in characterizing the government to note that he alone of the original five held office for the full four years that the Constitution of the Year III was in effect. The other directors were Carnot, the Terror's "Organizer of Victory," who continued his work with the military; Louis François Letourneur, a self-effacing expert in naval affairs dominated by Carnot; Jean François Reubell, an Alsatian firebrand determined to see France expanded to her "natural frontiers," especially the Rhine, and Louis de La Révellière-Lépaux, whose special interests were public education and destruction of the Catholic Church, but who was also the only true proponent of revolutionizing all of Europe. The presidency of the Directory rotated, but Barras and Reubell, about equally matched in willfulness, vied for leadership. To the public, Barras was "Le Roi"; in council, Reubell, while he lasted, probably dictated more decisions.

THE CONSPIRACY OF EQUALS

The first threat to the new Directory seemed to come from die-hard Jacobins who congregated in the Panthéon Club. In the fall of 1795 the outstanding figures were Robert Lindet, late of the Committee of Public Safety, and Jean Baptiste Amar, formerly of the Committee of General Security. The most vocal member, however, was François-Noel Babëuf, who called himself Gracchus Babeuf, after the leaders of a slave revolt in ancient Rome. In the club, he emphasized the return to the Constitution of 1793, which appealed to many Jacobins. To a lesser degree in the club, and more positively to a smaller circle, he advocated communism— the abolition of private property, the duty of every citizen to work, and the right of each to an equal share of the national product.

The Directory "discovered" Babeuf when his communism became the major theme of his newspaper, the *Tribune of the People*. It was ordered suppressed, and an arrest warrant was issued for him. The Panthéon Club protested the Directory's harassment of this "good republican," though few approved of his communistic schemes, or even knew much of them. The directors (February 1796) ordered the club closed (a job done by Napoleon as commander of the Army of the Interior).

Babeuf, in hiding, organized the Conspiracy of Equals, aimed at bringing down the government. Though he had Jacobin sympathizers, the core group consisted of only seven men, notably Philippe Buonarroti, an Italian revolutionary, and Augustin Darthé, a fanatic Robespierrist. They were hunted down and imprisoned in May 1796. A general pogrom against Jacobins followed, and by the time the "Equals" were brought to trial in May 1797, sixty-five persons had been indicted. (Carnot, especially, had overreacted to the Jacobin "threat.") In the end, however, only Babeuf and Darthé went to the guillotine. Buonarroti and six others were deported.

Babeuf is celebrated as the only true Communist political figure of the Revolution. At the time, however, the details of his conspiracy were vague—even to the majority of those accused of complicity. It was Buonarroti, who survived to gain a modicum of fame during the Revolution of 1830, who preserved Babeuf's schemes (unless he invented them himself) which involved the indoctrination of the people for revolution by secret agents and the infiltration and subversion of the army by Communist zealots.

At the time, the Babeuf episode served largely as an excuse for the Directory to crack down on Jacobins, nationwide. In 1796–1797, however, most Jacobins were in fact merely advocates of broader democracy, not Terrorists. Thus the conspiracy may be most important because it set the government against those with whom it might have most easily compromised and made the survival of the Republic less likely. Their suppression facilitated a royalist landslide in the elections of 1797.

THE COUPS D'ÉTAT: A SKETCH

After the elections of the Year V (in April 1797) Letourneur was replaced by royalist director, Barthélemy, with whom only Carnot sympathized. The remaining directors, with military aid (General Augereau), purged the councils of royalists (the coup d'état of 18 Fructidor, Year V), deported a number of legislators, sent Barthélemy and Carnot into exile, and replaced them with François de Neufchateau and Merlin de Douai. In 1798 the Jacobins swept to victory at the polls. The directors had François de Neufchateau replaced by Jean-Baptiste Treilhard and denied seats in the councils to 104 Jacobins (the coup of 22 Floreal, Year VI). With the onset of European war again in 1799, France sustained defeats which the councils blamed on the Directory. In May, Reubell was eliminated from office by lot. At the same time, the elections added to the opposition, allowing the legislature to turn the tables and to purge the Directory (June 1799, the coup of Prairial). Treilhard, La Révellière, and Merlin were forced out, leaving only Barras in office. Four new directors were chosen—the Abbé Sieyès, Roger-Ducos, General Moulin and Louis Gohier—the first two moderates, the latter Jacobins. Barras was an unknown quantity. The executive emerged precariously balanced and more indecisive than ever. Anything could happen. It was this situation which allowed Napoleon Bonaparte to seize power.

THE DOMESTIC RECORD

Despite the instability of the government, its domestic record was not bad. Its success was aided by successive years of good harvests and a general recovery of the economy. For Paris, the winter of 1795–1796 was perhaps the hardest of the Revolution, when bread at free-market prices was 4500 percent over the 1789 average, completely out of reach for the day laborers, who, with the unemployed, had to depend on a government dole. After the spring harvest, however, prices began to come into line, and by 1797, leveled off at about twice the 1789 average.

At the same time, wages had gradually risen by about 90 percent; thus the employed worker was in almost the same situation as in 1789. Beginning in 1797, the economy expanded steadily with resultant improvement in employment levels, and though prices rose gradually, so did wages. Overall, prosperity reigned under the Directory.

The government's economic policy was one of laissez-faire, tempered by intervention, especially to feed Paris. Firm control was established over foreign exchange and the domestic stock market. The assignats were replaced by new paper money called *mandats territoriaux* (at an exchange ratio of thirty to one), in a last effort to profit from the National Properties. When the *mandats* also depreciated in value, they were abolished as well, and the nation returned to hard currency (coin). The high tariff policy set during the Terror was maintained, to the benefit of French industry, which was also encouraged by subsidies and tax rebates. Technological research was sponsored and inventors were liberally rewarded. Under François de Neufchateau, minister of the interior (except for a year on the Directory, 1797-1798), the government began the systematic collection of agricultural and industrial statistics, reorganized poor relief, improved internal communications, and undertook comprehensive industrial planning.

There were drastic budgetary and fiscal reforms, initiated largely by Jacques Ramel de Nogaret, an unpopular but effective minister of finances. He repudiated two-thirds of the national debt by paying it in zero-interest bonds redeemable in National Properties (which meant that the bonds depreciated at the speed of assignats). The remaining one-third was placed on the Great Book of the State to be fully honored (interest bearing). This reduced state expenditures by 160,000,000 francs (out of a budget of 600,000,000) at a single blow. It also set the stage for a total repudiation of the "old" debt under Napoleon. At the same time, Ramel introduced a permanent system of direct taxes (which outlived Napoleon's regime)—on business licenses, land, personal property and servants, and doors and windows (thus the bigger the house the greater the tax). These did not meet all the government's needs, but were collectible. Additional monies were acquired by revising the system of indirect taxes (sales, excise, sumptuary, stamp taxes, etc.). Napoleon's government—and those which followed—tended to keep the direct taxes constant and to depend on indirect taxes to make up deficits. Ramel, without realizing it, established a system whereby Napoleon was able to bring the budget into balance and to hold it there until the crisis years of his regime.

Whatever favorable can be said about the Directory, however, it lacked public confidence from its inception and grew worse in this respect by the year. The executive, despite the successive coups aimed at strengthening its position, grew ever weaker. In the end, what remained of the regime could be saved only by appeal to the military. At various stages, generals whose political proclivities varied from Jacobin to royalist had exercised influence. In the end, however, only one was available and capable of rallying the army to "save" the Republic— Napoleon Bonaparte.

BONAPARTE

The man destined to be France's greatest hero was born Napoleone Buonaparte, of a proudly Italian family on Corsica, which had been French for only a
few months.

In 1768, Genoa, which had ruled Corsica for three centuries, found herself
unable to put down an independence movement led by Pasquale Paoli and sold
the island to Louis XV. French troops crushed the rebellion, and Paoli fled to
England. Most of the rebels accepted the French king's offer of amnesty, among
them Carlo (Charles) Buonaparte, who returned home to Ajaccio with his wife
Letizia Ramolino and their infant son Giuseppe (Joseph). Their second son,
christened Napoleone, was born on 15 August 1769. (He became Napoleon in
1778, when he entered school in France and changed his family name to
Bonaparte in 1796, after he became a major general.)

The Buonapartes were of Florentine nobility (Carlo entered the French
aristocracy as a count). The first Buonaparte had come to Corsica in 1567 in the
service of Genoa; the Ramolinos, Italian gentry, a little later. Neither family was
of the fierce, clannish, vendetta-prone "real" Corsican population of the wild
interior uplands. The Buonapartes had always considered themselves Italians and
educated their sons in Italy. The family had never produced a professional soldier.
Most had been lawyers, judges, officials, or churchmen—members of the largely
Italian "establishment."

Carlo Buonaparte was a lawyer trained in Pisa—slender, handsome, sandy-
haired and blue-eyed, a *bella figura*, always fashionably dressed. He was also no
man for lost causes and quickly offered his services to the French governor, the
Count de Marbeuf, to whom he made himself extremely useful. By the time of
his premature death (1785 at thirty-nine),[5] he was one of the most important men
on the island—crown judicial officer and past secretary of the Estates—and
known at the French court, where he had represented Corsica at the coronation
of Louis XVI. He easily obtained scholarships for his children from either the
crown or Church.

Letizia Ramolino, who married Carlo at fourteen, was velvet-eyed and
dark-haired, with strong classic features. "My mother," Napoleon remembered,
"was as beautiful as love." She both graced island society and delighted the clergy
(all her life she attended mass daily). And she also ran the Buonaparte farms and
mill for Carlo, a poor manager, and governed the household with an iron hand.
She gave her husband eight children—five boys and three girls—Joseph, Napoleon, Lucien, Louis, Jerome, Elisa, Pauline, and Caroline.[6] She was left a widow
at thirty-five, but managed, with Joseph's help, to care for the family until

---

[5] Of stomach cancer, which later killed Napoleon.

[6] The baptismal names of the brothers were Giuseppe, Lucciano, Luigi, and Girolamo; the girls Maria
Anna, Maria Paola, and Maria Annunziata. Four other children died in infancy.

Napoleon rose to power. Throughout her life she remained handsome and dignified, and as "Madame Mere of the Emperor," impressed the courts of Europe with her stoic serenity, which broke only after Napoleon's death at St. Helena (she outlived him by fifteen years).

Casa Buonaparte in Ajaccio was large—four floors, twenty rooms—but extremely bare. The Buonapartes' food was simple, their clothes (except Carlo's) homemade from homespun fabrics, their luxuries very few. Ajaccio was a "city" of 3000; the family lived from its farms. Napoleon's later legendary stamina surely owed much to the fact that he grew up in the country. He and Joseph roamed the hills, swam in the sea, climbed trees, rode horses, and sometimes played at working in the fields.

Joseph, the first child, was the heir, the good little boy, blessed with his father's looks, big blue eyes, and an ability to please. Napoleon, less attractive and taken for granted, fought for attention. He was belligerent, demanding, loud, and willful. He picked fights with Joseph as soon as he could stand, and while Joseph was a model student, Napoleon was a terror. He excelled only in mathematics, which he may have chosen because it was a mystery to both Joseph and his father.

From Letizia, Napoleon learned discipline, perseverance, economy (to the point of parsimony), and devotion to family. From Carlo, he got a sense of elegance, style (go hungry if necessary, but never be without a good suit), and charm, which Napoleon had in abundance, when he chose to use it. Doubtless, also, Carlo's opportunism rubbed off on him.

In December 1778, Carlo took his eldest sons to the Oratorian College of Autun where they took a "cram course" in French. Joseph remained there to train for the Church (which he later abandoned for the law). Napoleon went on to military school at Brienne on a royal scholarship. This was not because Napoleon was the favored son, however. He was bright, but had always been a disciplinary problem. Carlo had to find a career for his "little wolf." The military profession seemed suitable, though neither the army nor navy offered great opportunities. The pay was low (as a sublieutenant, Napoleon made the equivalent of about $18.50 a month). Moreover, a child of minor, "foreign" nobility could not aspire to high rank. He was likely to retire as a captain or major.

At Brienne, Napoleon was not initially the favorite of his teachers, and the students made fun of his name, appearance, and Corsican accent. He soon impressed the faculty with his ability, however, and established himself with his fists with his classmates, who were also treated with diatribes about freeing his homeland from the French oppressors. Paoli was his hero. He became a leader on the playground, but after school hours he was a lonely little boy too far from home to take advantage of weekend vacations and poor in the bargain. He buried himself in his books and made a good record. In 1784, especially because he had excelled in mathematics, he continued schooling at the École Militaire in Paris. This was the "school of future generals," which admitted largely sons of the highest nobility. As a scholarship student, however, Napoleon suffered few slights. His French had improved and the royal allowance was more generous, so that he lived in the same style as the others. He exerted himself to make friends and prudently stopped talking of Corsican independence.

He was commissioned (1785), at sixteen, after one year, but this was no extraordinary feat. Some of his classmates were younger. And he was not the top student, ranking forty-second in a class of fifty-eight.[7] He was assigned to the artillery partly because of his skill in mathematics, but more because artillerymen, though elite specialists, were expected to remain just that. Those officers destined to command armies normally were commissioned in the infantry or cavalry.

For seven years (1785–1792), Napoleon was a poverty-stricken lieutenant. He took much leave—twenty-nine months in all—most of it in Corsica (where room and board were free). What money he could save went mostly for books. He read widely—Plato, Aristotle, Thucydides, Mohammed, histories of all kinds, Fielding's *Tom Jones* (in translation), the classic French playwrights and the works of the *philosophes*. He received specialized training under the Marchal du Teil at the artillery school at Auxonne. In broader military matters, however, he educated himself, reading and making copious notes (still extant) on the campaigns of Alexander the Great, Caesar, Frederick the Great, Marlborough, Turenne, the Great Condé—and of course Charlemagne.

Of the *philosophes*, Napoleon was surely most influenced by Rousseau, who, as we noted in Chapter 2, favored government by the "general will," but defined it as what was best for the people. Napoleon later expressed similar sentiments: "Sovereignty resides in the French people, in the sense that everything without exception ought to be done in their interest, for their welfare and for their glory."

As late as 1789, Napoleon still thought vaguely of Corsican independence. He was pleased, however, when the National Assembly made the former crown colony part of France, and overjoyed when, in 1790, his hero Paoli was returned to Corsica as royal governor. Yet when Lieutenant Buonaparte met the "Babbo" (Old Papa), he was disillusioned and opined privately that Paoli knew so little of tactics that he had deserved to lose to the French. The word reached the Babbo, who judged Napoleon an egotistical "intriguer." The old man made Joseph Buonaparte one of the island's ruling directors and called Lucien to be his secretary, but would have nothing to do with "that little lieutenant."

Nevertheless, by devious means, Napoleon got himself elected lieutenant colonel in the Corsican National Guard. Paoli, at the first excuse, dispatched him to France (1792). This proved a favor, since he found that he had lost his regular commission for overstaying his leave. But France was at war and officers scarce, so that he got his commission back, with a promotion to captain. He was in Paris (unassigned) on 10 August 1792 and watched as the mobs swept into the Tuileries, slaughtering the Swiss guards, who were without orders. "If Louis XVI had mounted his horse," he wrote Joseph, "the victory would have been his." Thereafter he sided with the republicans of the Convention, and shortly was a Jacobin.

---

[7] Admittedly, he might have ranked higher if he had been at the École Militaire two years or more, as had most of his classmates.

But better a colonel than a captain. He returned to Corsica in the fall to serve with the National Guard in an expedition against Sardinia, which failed miserably. Napoleon reported at length to Paoli, blaming his commanding general; for his pains he was relieved of all duty, and he and Lucien took to organizing the Jacobins in Corsica and to establishing liaison with clubs in France.

Meanwhile, Paoli, shocked by the Terror, began negotiating secretly to put Corsica under British protection. In January 1793, when the Convention sent Louis XVI to the guillotine, the Babbo raged against the French "barbarians" to his staff. "They have killed their king, the best of men!"

Lucien, who was present, shortly sailed for France where he denounced Paoli as a traitor before the Jacobin clubs of Toulon and Marseilles. The Babbo called an assembly which declared independence and outlawed the Buonapartes and other Francophiles. The family fled to France (June 1793). Joseph settled them near Marseilles. Napoleon went back to the army as a captain, but within seven months was a general.

As we already know, it was the govermnent of Terror which snatched Napoleon from obscurity. Robespierre took over the Committee of Public Safety shortly after the Buonapartes reached France. He had an ardent supporter in Napoleon (whose "Souper de Beaucaire" has survived to prove it).[8] It was the Terrorist, Christophe Saliceti, a Corsican, who gave Napoleon his first major opportunity as a soldier—artillery commander at Toulon—where his performance gained him promotion overnight to brigadier general. (See above, p. 142)

In early 1794, General Buonaparte was assigned to the staff of the French Army of Italy, which guarded the Italian frontier, and spent much time with his family at Marseilles. Joseph soon married Julie Clary, daughter of a rich merchant, and Napoleon had a brief flirtation with Julie's younger sister Desirée.[9] The new general's future was far from assured, however, and in July 1794, when Robespierre fell from power, his career seemed to have ended. He was arrested as a Jacobin and spent a harrowing two weeks in jail. The authorities could find nothing damaging against him, however, and finally ruled that he had merely been a soldier following orders.

He returned to his duties with the Army of Italy. In March 1795 he sailed to recover Corsica with an expedition which was ignominiously turned back by the British fleet. He was then ordered to Paris and offered command of an infantry brigade in the Vendée. He saw no glory in that, and refused, whereupon he lost his commission. Barras and Saliceti managed to have his rank restored, however, and he was thus available to save the Convention in October 1795 with his "Whiff of Grapeshot." (See above, p. 174.)

---

[8] "Supper at Beaucaire" (1793), a pamphlet, recounts an imaginary conversation at a table at an inn. A "young officer" refutes the anti-Jacobin arguments of four conservative "Federalist" businessmen.

[9] Desirée later married Marshal Bernadotte, who was elected (1810) crown prince of Sweden by the Estates (with Napoleon's consent). The two eventually became king and queen of Sweden, where their descendants still reign.

Promoted to major general and shortly after made commander of the Army of the Interior, Napoleon was regarded with terror by ordinary Parisians, but not by the ladies-of-fashion, who were dying to meet the shocking master-of-cannon. He suddenly found himself a social lion.

At the salon of Madame de Tallien, he met Josephine de Beauharnais, with whom he fell in love at first sight.[10] Born in Martinique, this dark-haired, willowy beauty was the widow of the Viscount de Beauharnais, who had been a liberal in the Estates General and National Assembly, a successful general, and a Montagnard in the Convention, but, nevertheless, had been guillotined during the Terror. She had barely escaped death herself (though long separated, for alleged infidelity, from her husband). She was thirty-two, six years older than Napoleon, and the mother of two children, Eugène, fourteen, and Hortense, twelve. Very much a leader of the abandoned social life of Thermidor, she lived in luxury, but had no fortune. All Paris knew that her needs were met by "friends" in high places, including Barras. Napoleon, wise in war but naïve about women, could see in her only beauty, elegance, and sophistication. Charmed by his devotion, Josephine became Napoleon's mistress within weeks of their meeting, and, bowing to his impassioned pleas, married him in March 1796. For years, however, she took her vows very lightly, and Napoleon eventually became aware of it. Nevertheless, he never ceased to love her, defended her against his hostile family, and kept her by his side until his desire for an heir forced him to divorce her. Even then, he saw to it that she lived in imperial style.

COMMAND OF THE ARMY OF ITALY

Two days after his marriage, Napoleon was appointed commander of the Army of Italy and departed immediately (11 March 1796) for his headquarters at Nice. Enroute he began signing his name "Bonaparte"—as neatly French as Buonaparte was Italian. The name change coincided with the beginning of a rise to fame beyond even his own imagining. Even he was not talking about his "star" in 1796, however, and few would have predicted a great future for him in the military—much less the political arena.

The Directory had given him an army, but it was a motley array of ill-disciplined and ragged men who were barely able to guard the Italian border. Some said the command was Barras' reward for making Josephine an "honest woman." (Napoleon's tender letters to Josephine give this the lie, but the rumors made his task more difficult.) Another rumor had it that the directors meant to "bury" Bonaparte; the Army of Italy was not expected to play a major part in the war.

---

[10] Napoleon later gave a more "proper" version of their first meeting, which most historians have accepted. After Vendémiaire, he said, when he was disarming Paris, her son Eugène came to ask that he be allowed to keep his father's sword. Impressed with the boy's earnest manliness, he granted his request. The next day Josephine came to thank him, and they became friends.

Then, too, much about Bonaparte offended his fellow officers. Most new generals were opportunists, but his case seemed flagrant. His battle experience against foreign enemies was almost nil. He had a slight Italian accent (worse when he was angry). Most officers had some provincial accent—Gascons, Alsatians, and others—but they were French of long standing. Napoleon's size also worked against him. He was, in fact, at least 5 feet, 2 inches tall—taller than most French recruits (who had to be only 5 feet). But French officers and high officials (as in most countries in any era) were well above average height. His subordinates literally looked down on him.

Without a doubt, General Bonaparte took up his first major command with the cards stacked against him. But he saw nothing but great opportunity ahead.

THE BONAPARTE TOUCH

A high-wire walker bounces into his act not because he is "brave," but because after years of training he *knows* that he will not fall. Napoleon radiated the same sort of grim confidence when he met his officers in late March. At their head stood the formidable Generals André Masséna and Pierre Augereau—big, burly, hard-drinking ex-sergeants. As Napoleon approached, Masséna recalled, he looked like a boy riding his father's horse, but later, afoot—9 feet tall. Augereau admitted the "little bastard" somehow scared him. They had been treated to the Napoleonic presence—the eagle-sharp stare of the blue-grey eyes, the coiled-spring air of suppressed violence that demanded attention.

The officers soon also discovered that Napoleon knew more about the Army of Italy than they did. He had reviewed all available reports and plans. (In later years he would advertise himself as the unbeatable man-of-destiny; the real secret of his success was preparation and hard work.) He drove them to the wall with questions, demanded they discipline their men, round up deserters and empty the hospitals of malingerers. Thereafter he harassed them day and night. "I passed as a *homme terrible* . . . among the officers. . . . "

His approach to the men was different. He moved freely among them, tasting their food, looking over their uniforms, equipment, and arms. He learned their names and records and made promotions, out-of-hand. With the help of Joseph, consul at Genoa, a neutral port, and Saliceti, supplier to the army, he was able to get his men better food, clothing, weapons, and more prompt pay. It was not enough, but he promised in addition the wealth of Italy—there for the taking. They decided Bonaparte was a man to follow. "They had the instinct [to feel] . . . camaraderie. . . . They knew I was their patron," Napoleon said much later.

Napoleon accomplished what amounted to a miracle of leadership. In a month he marched, and what had been a disgruntled rabble proved itself a fighting force. He had breathed into it his own spirit and will to win. Carnot, now in the Directory, but still managing military affairs, saw to it that Napoleon got reinforcements and more supplies.

In all that he did in later years, Napoleon showed the same ability to influence men—in civil as well as military affairs. His presence, energy, and ferocity alternated with charm; his posing, facility with words, intelligence, and incredible memory for detail carried him through. Almost twenty years later, a prisoner aboard the British warship *Bellerophon*, he had the captain and crew at his beck and call within days.

THE FIRST ITALIAN CAMPAIGN

The Directory's objective in 1796 was to defeat Austria, the only major opponent remaining on the continent (though she had minor allies in Germany and Italy). Britain confined herself to the seas. Prussia and Spain had made peace in 1795. In 1794–1795, the Netherlands had been overrun, Belgium (the Austrian Netherlands) annexed to France, and the United Provinces converted into the Batavian Republic.

Two larger armies, under Jourdan and Moreau, were to drive on Vienna down the Danube. Napoleon's army meanwhile was to create a diversion in Italy, to tie up Austrian troops there, and to discourage Austria's allies (the principal ones Piedmont-Sardinia, the Papal States, and Naples).

General Bonaparte upset the grand strategy by turning the Italian theater into the main one. The Army of Italy marched in mid-April. In five days Napoleon had won major battles which isolated the Piedmontese; the king, Victor Amadeus, asked for a truce. Beaulieu, the Austrian commander, withdrew behind the Po River. Napoleon, however, out-flanked him by crossing in neutral territory, at Piacenza, forcing him to retreat eastward.

On 10 May, Bonaparte, in person, commanded the storming of the bridge over the Adda at Lodi and demolished the Austrian rear guard. It was not a great battle, but his valor deepened his men's belief that the "Little Corporal" was invincible. His success somehow also fired his sense of destiny. "In our time no one has done great things," he told Marmont. "It is for me to show them how." He turned aside to take Milan, where he put republicans in power. The directors ordered him to consolidate his gains, but he defied them, and they let him march.

In June he drove Beaulieu into the Tyrol and laid siege to Mantua, where an enemy garrison of 15,000 held out. (See Map 7.1.) In July, Würmser, a new Austrian commander, drove south from the Tyrol with 42,000 men to relieve Mantua, but unwisely sent 18,000 men under Quasdanovich west of Lake Garda, while he advanced on the east with 24,000 men. Napoleon, with only 30,000 disposable troops, temporarily abandoned the siege of Mantua, and on 3 August smashed Quasdanovich at Lonato, then turned to crush Würmser on 5 August at Castiglione. In September, Würmser returned with a (potentially) larger army. But Napoleon's divisions flanked him on both sides, cut him off from his reserve, and attacked his force—reduced to 19,000—from the rear at Bassano. The Austrian fought on and managed to break into Mantua with 10,000 men, but this

Map 7.1

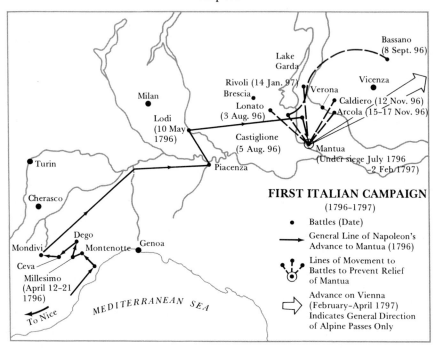

Bassano
(8 Sept. 96)

Lake
Garda

Rivoli (14 Jan. 97)
Brescia
Lonato
(3 Aug. 96)

Verona
Vicenza
Caldiero (12 Nov. 96)
Arcola (15-17 Nov. 96)

Milan

Lodi
(10 May
1796)

Castiglione
(5 Aug. 96)

Mantua
(Under siege July 1796
-2 Feb 1797)

Turin

Piacenza

Cherasco

FIRST ITALIAN CAMPAIGN
(1796-1797)

•   Battles (Date)

⟶   General Line of Napoleon's
Advance to Mantua (1796)

Lines of Movement to
Battles to Prevent Relief
of Mantua

Advance on Vienna
(February-April 1797)
Indicates General Direction
of Alpine Passes Only

Dego
Mondivi
Montenotte
Genoa
Ceva
Millesimo
(April 12-21
1796)
To Nice

MEDITERRANEAN SEA

served only to increase the trapped garrison to 25,000. In November, Alvintzy appeared to rescue Würmser, again with a superior Austrian force. Napoleon met him head-on at Caldiero and was driven back. Undismayed, he retreated through Verona, sent his army south of the Adige, recrossed the river and its tributary, the Alpone, and took Alvintzy in the flank at Arcola. French troops wavered at the Arcola bridge, but Napoleon came forward, seized a regimental standard and led the way across. Acts of personal courage of this sort—repeated often (and well publicized)—helped make him a legend. Alvintzy retreated, then returned, reinforced, in January, with 25,000 in his personal command and an equal number detached. Napoleon, with 19,000 troops, now superbly confident, defeated him at Rivoli (14 January 1797) and harried him into the Tyrol. The French lost 2200 men; the Austrians 3300 and 7000 prisoners (plus 6000 more during the retreat). On 2 February, Würmser surrendered Mantua.

Napoleon's advance divisions kept relentless pressure on the Austrians, who were now on the defensive in the passes of the Alps. Meanwhile his main army was reinforced to 40,000, and in early March he marched via the Tagliamento route on Vienna. The Austrians mustered all available troops under their best commander, the Archduke Charles, but Napoleon could not be stopped. When he reached Leoben, 100 miles from Vienna, Charles called for a truce (April 1797). The war was over. Peace was made in October 1797 at Campo Formio.

THE COUP OF FRUCTIDOR, YEAR V

Meanwhile, Napoleon had involved himself indirectly in French politics. The elections of 1797 were a royalist triumph. Almost all of the one-third new deputies were royalists, and the Elders elected a royalist director, Barthélemy, to replace Letourneur. Carnot seemed ready to cooperate with the new "moderates," but the other directors secretly called on Bonaparte to "save the Republic." He dispatched General Augereau to Paris, where the majority of the Directory, called the "Triumvirate" (Barras, La Révellière, and Reubell) appointed him commander of troops in Paris.

On 4 September 1797 (18 Fructidor, V) Augereau appeared in the Tuileries Gardens with 400 officers and demanded control of the councils' guard. It was delivered to him. The Triumvirate then directed a purge of the councils, expelling 195 members and placing under arrest the more dangerous royalists, including General Pichegru, who wounded several soldiers with a bayonet before he was taken. Pichegru, Barthélemy, and others were deported; Carnot was allowed to flee the country. François de Neufchateau and Merlin de Douai were elected to the Directory.

The Directory again presided over a middle-of-the-road government, but the coup had been accomplished with the tacit consent of the Jacobins, whose strength would be displayed in the next election. The French executive also owed its triumph to Napoleon Bonaparte, who conducted peace negotiations with Austria and her former allies as he saw fit.

KING OF MOMBELLO

After the truce of Leoben, Napoleon repaired to Mombello, the ornate palace of the Crivelli outside Milan, where he received delegates of the powers in royal style. He made no attempt to conceal his contempt for the government, "Do you think I have conquered for the benefit of the lawyers? What an idea!" He oversaw the conversion of Genoa into the Ligurian Republic and completed the formation (begun 1796) of the Cisalpine Republic, comprising former Austrian duchies , and some Papal territories,[11] and part of Venice (which he seized, despite her friendly posture). He levied indemnities at will and finally decided the terms of peace with Austria.

THE TREATY OF CAMPO FORMIO By the Treaty of Campo Formio (October 1797), Austria received Venice and her Istrian and Dalmatian possessions. However, France retained the Ionian Islands off Greece (also Venetian) as

---

[11] Milan, Modena, Mantua, Bologna, Ferrara, Romagna, and Ancona.

naval bases.[12] The Austrian emperor formally ceded Belgium to France and (as Holy Roman Emperor) the west bank of the Rhine as well. He agreed to a conference at Rastadt to provide compensation in Germany proper to princes who had lost territory on the Rhine. Finally, he gave full recognition to France's "sister republics." Napoleon had made the "Grande Nation" dominant on the Continent, encroaching on previously Austrian preserves in Germany and Italy. Austria was sure to fight back when she recovered her strength. The thought did not bother Napoleon; he helped lay plans (effected in 1798) for Roman and Swiss republics. This further extension of French power, accompanied by the imprisonment of the pope (at Valence, in France), did nothing to calm the Holy Roman Emperor.

THE CISALPINE

Napoleon's work in the Cisalpine Republic forecast his later policies and operating methods outside France. The constitution of the republic was drawn up by "sure" liberals (Melzi, Marescalchi, et al.) and not submitted to the voters. It was more democratic, however, than the current French Constitution of the Year III. Universal manhood suffrage was specified and there was to be a single-chamber legislature. The voters, however, elected delegates (who had to meet property qualifications) through a system of electors. Moreover, certification of legislators was by a *consulta* of state, initially appointed by Napoleon.[13]

The constitution, nevertheless, was radical and constructive. It abolished feudalism, including church privileges, guilds, and entail. It included a bill of rights guaranteeing equality before the law, in taxation, and of opportunity and of religious freedom. It prepared northern Italy for future Napoleonic governments, where equality, opportunity, and progress would be emphasized, but political liberty and the popular voice suppressed.

THE NEXT FIELD OF GLORY?

At the end of 1797, Napoleon returned in triumph to Paris; crowds followed his carriage everywhere. "Vive Bonaparte! Vive la Republique!" The directors, though frightened at his popularity and political potential, had no choice but to do him honor. There were parades, fireworks displays, receptions, dinners, dances, and command theater performances. The Institut elected General Bonaparte a member. "The greatest conquests," he told the intellectuals, "are those made against ignorance." He was modest, dignified, affable—but publicly criti-

---

[12] There has been much speculation about this provision. Some writers have taken it as evidence that Napoleon had a fixation on the East, and used it as part of an argument to show that his ultimate ambition was to be a "new Alexander," conqueror of an Eastern Empire. In fact, the islands proved of little use to the French navy.

[13] The Directory eliminated universal manhood suffrage in Italy in 1798; Napoleon restored it in 1800.

cized the Constitution. Privately, Napoleon told Joseph that he meant to destroy the corrupt Directory when the time was ripe. "Our dreams of a republic were illusions of youth."

Until the time was right, he determined to keep his reputation alive: that meant action. The only enemy of France still fighting was Great Britain. How could he strike at *les Anglais?* The directors offered him command of an army forming at Boulogne to invade England, but he refused it. He and Talleyrand, now foreign minister, had another plan.

Talleyrand presented it to the Institut: Seize Egypt, destroy British influence in the Ottoman Empire, cut her trade routes to India, encourage Indian rebels, perhaps invade India. Egypt, nominally a vassal state of Turkey, was ruled by the Mamelukes. Talleyrand suggested that he convince the sultan that France would restore Ottoman power in Egypt. Napoleon asked to command the expedition. The Directory agreed. Though Reubell argued that Bonaparte was treacherous and should be kept in France where they could watch him, the others were willing to gamble a small army (35,000 men) for gains that might be considerable. Britain was having economic difficulties and revolution was brewing in Ireland. Tippo Sahib, Sultan of Mysore, was giving British forces in India a serious challenge and was in contact with the French through agents in Mauritius (Île de France) in the Indian Ocean, where there was a French naval base.

If Bonaparte had even limited success, Britain might sue for peace. If he actually established a French bastion in the Middle East and could march into Asia . . . Impossible? Bonaparte had done the impossible in Italy. It was worth risking. Moreover, the directors' relations with Napoleon, whose political ambitions were fairly obvious, had been strained. If he were lost, they would not grieve.[14]

IRELAND: MISSED OPPORTUNITY?

Actually, the Directory might have been better advised to send an expedition to Ireland. The Society of United Irishmen, founded in 1792 by Wolfe Tone, a dashing Anglican lawyer, had by 1798 secretly recruited and armed 100,000 men in Ulster alone and perhaps 250,000 in all Ireland. For almost the only time in history, Protestants and Catholics stood together for Irish self-determination.[15] The British crown had been forced to concentrate 140,000 men to counter the

[14] Naturally the directors would not admit that getting Bonaparte out of Paris was a motive. La Révellière, in his memoirs, takes pains to deny it. Barras dwells at length with the difficulties Bonaparte was causing the Directory—asking to be "appointed" a director, corresponding with foreign heads of state, and so on—but says the expedition was altogether Napoleon's idea and that the Directory only gave him the means to fulfill his "dream."

[15] It is often forgotten that the Scots-Presbyterians in Ulster generally had not settled there of their own accord but had been exiled for rebellion against the English kings or for other troublemaking. Moreover, they were not part of the Anglo-Irish establishment, and were almost as much discriminated against as the native Irish Catholics. Though they had their differences with the Catholics, they exceeded them, if anything, in their hatred of the British monarchy.

threat. Wolfe Tone was in Paris and in contact with the directors—and even Napoleon—but they thought his reports were exaggerated. Moreover, French expeditions prepared in 1796 and 1797 had been thwarted by bad weather. The French did send some 900 men under General Humbert to the west coast of Ireland in 1798, but they were too few and too late. The British had forced the revolutionaries into the open before they were ready and defeated them in detail, with bloody reprisals (2000 of the luckier rebels were deported to Australia). Humbert and his men were captured. A little later, Wolfe Tone, who had been smuggled in, was betrayed to the British and committed suicide, having succeeded only in making an everlasting place for himself in Irish folklore.

Even a massive and successful French invasion of Ireland might have come to naught. On the other hand, it might have driven the British to make peace—or even freed Ireland. And it probably (and at least) would not have prompted the formation of a continental coalition against France, which was the end result of Napoleon's Egyptian adventure. Otherwise, the Egyptian adventure was notable for its glamour—partly the effect of Napoleon's showmanship on the popular mind, partly the work of his scientists and intellectuals, who, says R. R. Palmer, "virtually founded the science of Egyptology, and brought a flow of mummies and obelisks to Western Europe."

THE EGYPTIAN EXPEDITION

On 19 May 1798, Napoleon's expedition sailed from Toulon, borne by over 400 transports and escorted by thirteen ships-of-the-line and a score of lesser warships commanded by Admiral Brueys. In June, Bonaparte seized Malta, and on 1 July landed in Egypt. Only four days before his landing, Admiral Nelson, with the British Mediterranean fleet, had been lying in wait for him off Alexandria, but had left to resupply in Sicily.

On 1 August, Nelson returned to find Brueys' battleships drawn up in line in the shallows of Aboukir Bay. The French admiral hoped to force the British to attack only from one side, reducing the enemy's advantage in numbers and seamanship by firepower (his flagship alone had 120 guns). The British ships were more maneuverable than he thought, however. On Nelson's order, some slipped between Bruey's floundering vessels and the shore, and he found himself blasted from all angles. Eleven French ships-of-the-line were sunk and most of the frigates; the rest escaped under cover of darkness to Malta. Brueys was killed in action. Napoleon's army was stranded—beyond rescue—though Nelson could not prevent the conquest of Egypt.[16]

---

[16] There were less than seventy ships-of-the-line (50 guns or more) in the whole French navy. Nelson had destroyed more than a sixth in one blow—and some of the biggest and newest. This had importance beyond his immediate tactical triumph, since it took years to replace first-line ships. Even before the disaster, the French had not been able to put large fleets into the Mediterranean without baring the Atlantic and Channel coasts to attack or pulling in ships which guarded the colonies. Britain had greater commitments overseas, but had some 175 ships-of-the-line in commission.

Map 7.2

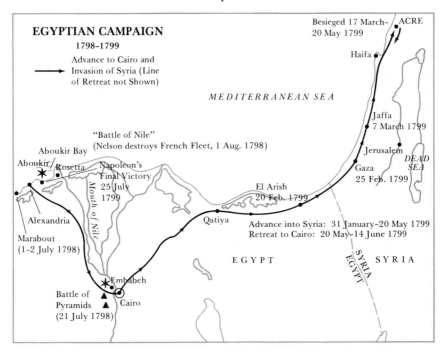

On 21 July, in a single great battle, fought before Cairo in the shadow of the Pyramids ("Forty centuries look down upon us."), Napoleon assured his mastery of the country. The Mameluke cavalry, brave to insanity, but with medieval weapons, charged again and again, only to be slaughtered by artillery and musket fire. (See Map 7.2.)

The Mameluke ruling caste had originally been the Caliph's elite guard of slave troops, taken as boys in Europe (largely the Balkans) and reared as Moslems, and still "recruited" in Europe. Napoleon admired their courage and was fascinated by their costumes—silken jackets, billowing pantaloons, turbans. He recruited some of them, who later gave an exotic touch to the Imperial Guard. The best known was his giant personal guard, Roustan, always near his master, curved scimitar at the ready.

Napoleon revolutionized (if temporarily) Egyptian institutions, establishing a rational governmental-administrative structure and a French-style system of courts. He abolished feudalism and serfdom and the dues attendant thereto and proclaimed freedom of religion and equality before the law. He gave the army's support to a contingent of scientists, *litterateurs*, and artists recruited by Gaspard Monge, the celebrated mathematician, and Claude Berthollet, an equally famed chemist. They established at Cairo the Institut d'Egypte, which propagated European culture and ideas to the East, marking the beginning of modernization in the area. Conversely, the Institut vastly expanded European knowledge of the Near East, discovering (among other things) the Rosetta stone, key to ancient hieroglyphics.[17] In February 1799, Napoleon struck into Syria (Palestine/Israel) but was stopped at Acre (Akko, near Haifa). The siege dragged on for weeks, but he was unable to take the fortress, and his troops were dying of disease, hunger, and thirst. In May he learned that the British were transporting a Turkish army to Egypt. His only choice was to retreat to Egypt in an attempt to save what he already held. (See Map 7.2.)

FRENCH AGGRESSION AND THE SECOND COALITION

After Nelson's destruction of Napoleon's fleet, the British had easily concluded an alliance with the Ottoman Empire. Before the end of 1798, they added Russia and Austria to the "Second Coalition," together with Naples and other minor Italian and German states. By March 1799, France was again at war with most of Europe.

Russia's immediate *casus belli* was the French occupation of Malta. From Rome, the Knights of Malta had appealed to Czar Paul I for aid and elected him Grand Master of the ancient order (ignoring that he was Greek Orthodox). The czar responded with alacrity because he was already deeply angered by what he interpreted as French competition for control (and ultimate partition) of the Ottoman Empire. To him, the invasion of Egypt was only a step in a process that had begun with the Treaty of Campo Formio, which transferred the Ionian Islands to France.

Austria had really been preparing since 1797 to recover from France what she considered rightfully hers—Belgium and the bulk of the Cisalpine Republic in northern Italy—and the left bank of the Rhine (not Austrian, but part of the Holy Roman Empire, for which the Austrian emperor was expected to compensate the former rulers in Germany proper).

The steady creation and manipulation of "sister republics" by France had provoked all the European monarchs, not least the Austrian emperor. The Batavian (Dutch) Republic had been established in 1795—while French troops controlled Holland[18]—with a government modeled after that of the Directory. During 1796–1797, Napoleon had put together the Cisalpine Republic, as already noted. (See above, page 190.) In 1797, Genoa had "voluntarily" become the Ligurian Republic, and in 1798 the Roman Republic had been founded after a

---

[17] The London *Times* which had surprisingly detailed information about the expedition (but not its destination) had reported (5 June 1798) that the ships had sailed carrying "An immense number of infantry, with artillery . . . *ammunition* and *men of letters*." [Italics added.]

[18] The United Provinces of the Netherlands, then as now popularly called Holland, after its major province.

French invasion from the Cisalpine. The stage had been set by a tiny minority of republicans in Rome, who fomented disturbances during which General Duphot, an aide to the French ambassador, was killed. (The French ambassador was Joseph Bonaparte.) Pope Pius VI was deported, ultimately to Valence where he died in 1799.

Meanwhile, uprisings in the Swiss cantons had been engineered by the exiles of the Club Helvetique in Paris, led by Pierre Ochs and Fédéric de LaHarpe. In January 1798 a French army moved into Switzerland and after two months of hot fighting, mostly in the rural areas, "restored order." Geneva and Mulhouse were annexed to France and the remaining cantons formed into the Helvetic Republic. Thus by mid-1798, France was ringed by puppet states, all with sizable garrisons of French troops. Before the War of the Second Coalition began, however, still another republic was established. In December 1798 the Neapolitan Bourbons, enraged by the treatment of the pope and encouraged by the Russians and Austrians, sent troops against the Roman Republic. They were thrown back by the French army of General Championnet, who seized Naples, sent the Bourbons flying to Sicily, and supported by local "patriots," proclaimed the Parthenopean Republic.

French aggression might well have provoked a Second Coalition without the ill-fated Egyptian expedition—in time. It was entrapment of that expedition, however, led by France's most feared general, which brought the powers together in 1798. And in July 1799, as he hurried the remnants of his army out of Syria and back into Egypt, the French had long since abandoned Naples and were hard pressed in northern Italy, Switzerland, Germany, and soon (August) were to be faced with a Russo-British invasion of Holland.

ABOUKIR

Barely had Napoleon regained Egypt when a fleet of 100 British, Russian, and Turkish ships were reported off the coast. On 15 July 1799 a Turkish army of 20,000 landed and went into fortified positions at Aboukir to await their cavalry, artillery, and Janissary shock troops. Napoleon mustered 7000 men and seventeen guns—all that were available—and marched to meet them before they were fully prepared. (See Map 7.2.)

On 25 July he struck with full force. His artillery shattered the enemy positions; his infantry struck frontally. Behind them came the cavalry of Murat, which veered to take the Turks on the flanks and drove them into the surf, charging, cutting, trampling until the waves frothed with blood. The awed British admiral, Sir Sidney Smith, was quick to agree to a truce and evacuated the pitiful survivors.

Napoleon had again covered himself with glory, but there was little chance he would gain more in Egypt. Since the Directory had been able to get only occasional (and useless) messages to him for six months, he held no hope of being reinforced, much less rescued. Moreover, from June issues of the London *Times* (sent him by the gentlemanly Sir Sidney Smith), he learned that France was on the defensive in Europe. Convinced that only *he* could save the country, and/or that his career was finished if he remained trapped in Egypt, he decided to give command of his army to one of his generals and return to France. The legalities (and ethics) involved could be sorted out later. It was do or die.

THE COUPS D'ÉTAT OF 1798 AND 1799

In April 1798, before Napoleon sailed for Egypt, the elections produced a flood of Jacobin deputies. However, Jacobin strength was in the provinces, not in Paris, where the police work of earlier years had been thorough. Thus the directors were able to control the existing councils, though opposed by such deputies as Generals Augereau and Jourdan (Jacobins, or more properly, dedicated republicans, but poor politicians). The Elders added the innocuous Treilhard to the Directory (replacing François de Neufchateau, who returned to the ministry of the interior). On 11 May 1798 the legislature then "legally" annulled the elections in fifty-three departments, refusing seats to 106 deputies. Half (53) were replaced by candidates suitable to the directors, the other seats were left vacant. Such was the Coup d'État of 22 Floréal, Year VI. It gave the Directory the whip hand once more, but alienated it from popular support in half the departments in the country.

In the spring of 1799 the War of the Second Coalition began. The legislative councils blamed the Directory for French reverses and the elections of April 1799 increased the number of opposition deputies. Reubell, the chief warhawk, was eliminated by lot (the prescribed yearly procedure, for a change), and retired permanently from politics. By the so-called Coup of Prairial (June 1799), the councils forced the resignation of La Révellière-Lépeaux and Merlin and voted Treilhard out. They were replaced by two moderates, the Abbé Sieyès and Roger-Ducos, and two Jacobins, General Moulin and Louis Gohier. The balance was held by Barras, whose current politics were known only to himself. The new Directory was a creature of the legislative councils, in which Jacobins emerged as the strongest leaders, and the Directory was forced to give the Jacobins key posts in the government. General Bernadotte became minister of war, Robert Lindet minister of the interior, and General Marbot commander of the Army of the Interior. The Jacobin Club revived in Paris, soon boasted 3000 members. General Jourdan proposed a new *levée en masse*, which was passed, conscripting men of twenty to twenty-five for five years' service. There was widespread fear of the revival of the Terror, bolstered in midsummer when the Council of 500 adopted a resolution to bring criminal indictments against the directors ousted in June (though no action was taken against them).

The Jacobins sought a revival of democracy—honest elections with the results respected in Paris. But they behaved under the pressures of war much like the

Jacobins of 1793–1794. Sieyès determined to exploit the fear of Jacobinism to "revise" the Constitution—only possible by a coup d'état. As matters stood, he considered that the Directory was paralyzed and wanted a provision made for a stronger executive. Sieyès was destined to get more than he bargained for—Napoleon Bonaparte.

RETURN TO FRANCE

After the victory at Aboukir, Napoleon quietly had two small ships outfitted to take him and his key subordinates to France. On 24 August, after turning his command over to General Kléber (by letter), he secretly set sail, accompanied by Murat, Alexandre Berthier (until 1814 his indispensable chief of staff), and a few others. Storms held the little vessels near the Egyptian coast for days, but they finally made headway, miraculously eluded British patrols, and after a voyage of six weeks, reached Fréjus, in southern France, on 9 October.

The news of his victory at Aboukir had just arrived. Bonaparte rode to Paris through villages full of cheering people who saw him as a savior. The Directory, which had issued orders (not received) to return *with his army* (an impossibility), bowed to his popularity and gave him a hero's welcome. His failures and abandonment of his army were ignored. Napoleon felt no guilt. He had returned to "save" France—take over the government and win the war. He would worry about the army in Egypt later. (In 1802, he did repatriate the survivors, then prisoners of the British.)[19]

THE WAR AND CONDITIONS IN FRANCE

During the spring and summer of 1799 the French had been driven out of Italy, save Genoa (under siege). The Archduke Charles threatened the Rhine frontier. Russian armies in Switzerland had put Masséna on the defensive. An Anglo-Russian army under the Duke of York had invaded the Netherlands. When Napoleon left Egypt, France seemed headed for defeat, but by the time his reception was over in Paris, things were different. Austrian armies still challenged on the Rhine and at Genoa, but the Russians had been beaten in Switzerland. More important, Czar Paul, convinced that Austria cared about nothing but recovering her own power, especially in northern Italy, ordered his troops home. The Duke of York, defeated, evacuated the Netherlands.

---

[19] Kléber was murdered and succeeded by General Menou, who in 1801 surrendered the army to a British force under Sir Ralph Abercromby, which landed at Aboukir. Another English army was being formed in India to invade via the Red Sea.

Nevertheless, French morale was low. The reinstitution of conscription in 1798 had been met with protests and widespread evasion and desertion. (Carnot's *levée en masse* had lapsed after 1794.) The elimination of paper money (both assignats and *mandats*) had resulted during 1798 and 1799 in an acute shortage of currency. Thus, though harvests were good, prices were falling. Since wages were slower to drop, some manufacturers had to cut the work force, though war-essential industries boomed (coal mining, steel production, arms production). There were pockets of heavy unemployment. Farmers were unable to sell their produce for sufficient coin to buy essentials and to pay taxes and rents, and thus turned to barter for goods. The government was forced to collect revenues in grain and other staples and to pay its civil servants (even some deputies) in kind. Ultimately, under Napoleon's government, the return to currency of intrinsic value was beneficial. The value of the franc became constant (or relatively so), and prices again rose, if slowly, while wages retained a higher purchasing power. In the short run, however, an element of chaos in the economy added to the woes of the Directory. In the fall of 1799, with war costs increasing, revenues had shrunk by half, a half-subscribed forced loan had been spent, and bankruptcy was imminent.

Generally, the people had lost faith in the government. Banditry was rife in the countryside, partly as a result of economic conditions and partly because of the laxness of local officials and the police, who were disdainful of the Directory's representatives. In the south, royalists organized a white terror against Jacobins, which evolved into outright warfare for control of Toulouse. In the chronically royalist Vendée and Brittany, guerrillas again came out in force.

During the summer of 1799, though the greatest threat to the Republic seemed to be from the right, the Abbé Sieyès, in Paris, warred against the left. The Jacobins, as noted above, had taken the lead in the councils after the spring elections. They did not have a majority, however, and lacked popular support in the capital. Nonetheless, Sieyès, possessed of an almost paranoid fear of a return of the Terror, raised the specter in the councils at every opportunity. His most dire forebodings seemed to be confirmed by the continual demands by the orators in the resurrected Jacobin Club for emergency measures and special prosecutions. The club so alarmed the councils that after repeated pleas from Sieyès, it was abolished. The Abbé then gained the reluctant support of Barras, whose vote, with that of Roger-Ducos, allowed him in August to install his friend Fouché in the ministry of police and to make General Lefebvre commander of the Army of the Interior. Sieyès' increasing power rallied to him many Jacobins (including Lucien Bonaparte) in the councils, so that when, in September, General Jourdan proposed that the legislature "declare the Nation in Danger" (which could have made way for committees with extraordinary powers, as in 1793—or meant nothing), he was roundly defeated. In the same month the directors removed Bernadotte from the war ministry, in favor of another Jacobin, but a nonentity. With the reins of the army and police in the hands of friends, Sieyès was ready to bring his new-formed political "party" into play.

THE REVISIONISITS

Since his emergence as a director in June 1799, Sieyès had been carefully organizing supporters of "constitutional revision" inside and outside the government. What he really wanted was a new Constitution—not revision—but the term salved the qualms of the timid. What he proposed was a government presided over by a "Grand Elector" (a military man with largely ceremonial duties) but controlled by two powerful civilian executives (one for domestic and one for foreign affairs). To inspire "confidence from below," elections were to be by universal manhood suffrage, but only to select "notables" eligible for local office, some of whom would be nominated for departmental offices and fewer for the national legislative bodies.

Among Sieyès' prominent collaborators were Roger-Ducos, his "echo" in the Directory; Talleyrand, the foreign minister; Cambacérès, minister of justice; and of course Fouché, minister of police. Very important to the success of the party were Napoleon's brothers, Lucien and Joseph. Both had been in the Council of 500, but Joseph had withdrawn to work for the cause outside, while Lucien was pressed upward toward the presidency of the council, which he held when Napoleon returned from Egypt. Joseph, a social lion, novelist, and *"philosophe,"* was influential among the intelligentsia—a friend of Madame de Staël, Benjamin Constant, Chateaubriand, and others. He also drew scientists, artists, politicians, and generals to his soirées at his château, Mortefontaine, near Paris. (Joseph had married a rich wife, Julie Clary, and had made a fortune himself by entering the Clary shipping business and by other enterprises, including government procurement contracts.) He won over many of his friends to the revisionists and persuaded others to remain neutral.

Though some revisionists, including Joseph, hoped for peaceful change, most knew that there was no way to change the Constitution without a coup d'état, involving at least the threat of force. For months, Sieyès had been looking for a "sword"—a general who would cooperate with him and who had stature enough to hold the loyalty of the army in the face of possible counterorders to commanders from the councils or (more likely) an uncooperative director or two, if they could not be neutralized.

General Lefebvre, commanding the Army of the Interior, would not do, though he was a friend of Sieyès. He was too much the book soldier, and rather dull-witted. Among the most celebrated generals, Moreau was suspected of having royalist sympathies; Jourdan and Bernadotte were Jacobins; and Masséna, recently covered with laurels for his victories over the Russians in Switzerland, was too brutish for other than field duty. Sieyès had settled on General Joubert, who had supported the coup of Prairial (June 1799) and sent him to win appropriate glory as commander of the Army of Italy; instead, he was killed in action. Sieyès then opted for Napoleon, though even Lucien Bonaparte warned that his brother would be difficult to control. Joseph had sent word to Napoleon to return to Paris, and though he apparently did not receive it, he turned up anyway, at just the right time.

BRUMAIRE

On arrival in Paris, Napoleon was immediately contacted by the revisionists. Inwardly enthusiastic, he played coy but pretended to be won over by Talleyrand, who served as Sieyès' intermediary. The overthrow of the Directory was planned for 18–19 Brumaire (9–10 November 1799).

On 18 Brumaire, Sieyès and Roger-Ducos resigned their directorships, as did Barras, cowed by Talleyrand (another "man of 1789," a lame, wily, ex-bishop with the inscrutable face of a tabbycat). The other directors—Gohier and Moulin—were put under house arrest. The Council of Elders was summoned and told that a major Jacobin plot was afoot—a new Terror imminent. Prompted by revisionist deputies, the Elders voted that the councils (Elders and 500) would meet the next day at the St. Cloud Palace (in the suburbs, safe from the crowd) to consider this threat. For safety they appointed General Bonaparte commander of troops in Paris, though most of the delegates knew there was no Jacobin plot.

Napoleon's assignment was opposed by Bernadotte, ex-minister of war, who could have caused trouble. "Belle-Jambe" was an ex-sergeant, popular with the rank and file. But his wife (Desirée Clary) and brother-in-law Joseph Bonaparte persuaded him not to interfere.

On 19 Brumaire the councils met amid much confusion. It was noon before the halls were ready; the palace was frigid. Troops massed in the gardens. Tempers were short. Napoleon went first before the Elders to demand revision of the Constitution. With some grumbling, the body acquiesced. In the 500 the story was different. Lucien, president of the council, could not keep order. Napoleon was greeted with anger. "Death to the traitor!" "Outlaw him!" Deputies pushed toward the front of the room. Caught in a crush, Napoleon either fainted or was knocked unconscious. He was carried from the room.

Lucien tried to restore order, and failing, rushed outside. Napoleon was trying to rally the troops but was still groggy and incoherent. Leaping on a horse, Lucien shouted that the palace was full of "assassins" and enemies of the people who must be driven out. Waving a sword, he promised to plunge it into Napoleon's heart if he betrayed the Republic. The troops cleared the halls at bayonet point. The deputies ran, tripping over their toga-like robes of office and clutching their plumed hats, through the gardens and into the woods and fields. Lucien had saved the day, but, he later said, only because, at the time, it was "do or die."

The coup had succeeded, but not as the leaders desired. Most wanted the government changed with some semblance of legality. They reconvened the chambers, insofar as possible. In the early evening a rump of the councils voted executive power to a temporary consulate—Napoleon, Sieyès and Roger-Ducos. Their responsibility was to produce a new Constitution. Moderate republican politicians were satisfied. The business community was ecstatic; prices soared on the Paris exchange.

In the face of it all, France was unmoved in its great masses. As T. S. Eliot once wrote: "Human kind cannot stand too much of reality. . . . " After ten years of revolution, unstable government, violence, and war, the people were numb. They were ready for the unreal—for the miracles Napoleon would soon promise (and in part deliver). They were ready for the strong man—the "Hero"—the man who swept petty politicians before him. They believed he could defeat their foreign enemies and restore internal order and stability—they even believed Napoleon would also "preserve the Revolution" at the same time.

In all countries force [ultimately] gives way to civil
qualification. . . . I do not govern because I am a general,
but because the nation believes I have
the proper civil qualities. . . .
—*Napoleon to the Council of State, 1802*

"THERE IS BONAPARTE"
Consulate, Empire, and Domestic Reform

CONSTITUTION OF THE YEAR VIII

France was ready for strong leadership, but Napoleon was too shrewd to say so, either to the people or the politicians (who, after all, had prepared the stage for the coup d'état of Brumaire). Thus he proceeded speedily, but quietly and cautiously, to consolidate his power. His first move was to endorse heartily the suggestion that the three provisional consuls should submit their constitution to committees of the old legislature (Elders and 500) for approval. He further allowed the legislators to presume that it would then be passed by the councils before being put to a vote of the people. This served to place the committees (commission) on the side of Napoleon, and under the leadership of the liberal theorist Pierre-Claude Danou, they produced the constitution Napoleon wanted.

Much had been made of the fact that Napoleon assumed the chair at the first meeting of the consuls without so much as a "by your leave" to Sieyès; more still of his refusal to be "Grand Elector," which office, he said, was fit for a man content to do nothing but wallow in money like a pig in his own filth. In fact, the consuls were deadlocked, and the commissions approved Danou's draft over that of Sieyès. With that, however, Napoleon showed the iron fist and insisted that the commissioners sign the constitution without reference to the old legislative bodies. They did, and it was published on 15 December 1799.

After two months of bombardment with propaganda in favor of the constitution, the people were asked to vote (February 1800). By that time, however, the government of the Consulate was already functioning.

"Constitutions," said Napoleon, "should be short and obscure." That of the Year VIII was both. The government? "There is Bonaparte," said a Parisian. Most Frenchmen did not see things that clearly, however. There was to be universal manhood suffrage; there were three "representative" bodies. The power of the electorate was in fact nullified by a complicated system of checks and balances, weighted in favor of the executive (and nominally the Senate, appointed for life). Nevertheless, the voters approved "Bonaparte"—3,011,007 to 1562—the heaviest margin ever for a constitution.[1]

The executive consisted of three consuls, named in the Constitution. Napoleon, as First Consul, had the right to promulgate laws and full executive authority—the power to appoint and dismiss members of the council of state, ministers, ambassadors, officers of the army and navy, national and local administrators, and to appoint (but not remove) most judges. His term was ten years. The second and third consuls, Cambacérès and Lebrun, had advisory functions only. Sieyès and Roger-Ducos, as ex-consuls, were relegated to the Senate but given the power, with Cambacérès and Lebrun, to appoint the majority of the Senate (thirty-one men, including themselves), which then expanded itself to sixty by co-option. From lists produced by the voters (see below for detail), the Senate appointed the members of the Tribunate (100) and Corps Législatif (300). The Tribunate could discuss legislation but not amend it, only approve or reject; the Législatif could only vote on laws reported to it by the Tribunate. All legislation was framed by the First Consul's appointive council of state.

All men over twenty-one could vote (except felons, prisoners, and the insane), but chose no representative directly. France remained divided into departments, and these into districts (abolished under the Directory), cantons (for voting only), and municipalities. In each district the voters chose one-tenth of their number as electors, who chose one-tenth of themselves for the departmental list, which then selected one-tenth for the national list. From the final list the Senate appointed deputies to the Tribunate and Corps Législatif. Only one man in 1000 had even a chance at national office.

The Constitution had no bill of rights (nor did any constitution promulgated by Napoleon). Rights were spelled out separately in the Code Napoléon (civil) and criminal law codes worked out at leisure in succeeding years. The Constitution did make clear, however, that political dissidents had no rights. The consuls (really Napoleon) had the right to order arrested any "presumed authors or accomplices in a conspiracy against the safety of the state." Technically, they could only be held ten days without charge. In practice, there was no limit.

There was no voting for electors in 1800, however. The Constitution had been proclaimed in effect on 25 December 1799. The Senate had already been formed and proceeded to fulfill its mandate to conduct "the elections entrusted to it." Lists were prepared without reference to the electorate by the Senate (in great part by Sieyès and his cronies), which selected the Tribunate and Corps Législatif therefrom. The first elections were not held until the Year IX (spring

[1] It has been alleged that the tally for this and later Napoleonic plebiscites was "rigged." No historian has been able to show, however, that Bonaparte's propositions were not overwhelmingly approved, no matter how the ballots were counted. It is true, of course, that over 50 percent of those eligible did not vote (perhaps 4,000,000), but it can only be shown that voters abstained out of opposition or despair in a few communes.

of 1801) and the required one-fifth of the legislative bodies was not replaced until the Year X.

The Senate, in the first years, could block the First Consul's projects, which was some solace to Sieyès. However, the Constitution required that it be expanded by two senators a year until it numbered eighty. The Senate elected its own, but from nominees presented by Bonaparte, the Tribunate, and the Législatif. In 1802 the Constitution was revised to allow Napoleon to appoint forty additional senators and in 1804 to give him unlimited right of appointment.

Napoleon ruled, using the *senatus consultum* (decree with the consent of the Senate) for his major pronouncements. Nevertheless, he tried to assemble a government of all talents, beginning with the selection of the second and third consuls. Cambacérès was a regicide (though he had not been a Terrorist) and a renowned legal expert. Lebrun was a former bureaucrat of the Old Regime. To heighten the contrast, Cambacérès was a huge, happy gourmet, while Lebrun was trim, austere, and all business.

TO WAR AGAIN

With his government established, Napoleon again took up the sword. Again Austria, as in 1796, was the only major enemy remaining, save Britain. He sent Moreau against the Austrians in Germany, while on the Italian front Masséna held them at bay in Genoa. In May 1800 the First Consul himself (riding a mule) led a reserve army of 40,000 from Dijon through the snow-choked passes of the Alps and captured Milan. He was behind the Austrian army of Melas. The enemy commander recovered more quickly, however, than Napoleon expected. At Marengo, on 14 June, the armies met suddenly, and what began as a skirmish grew into an all-out bloodletting. (see Map 8.1.) Napoleon, his troops dispersed, was hard pressed, but reinforcements arrived under General Charles Louis Desaix, who marched to the sound of guns. Italy was won. It was a great victory, though Desaix, the hero of the day, was killed. In December Moreau triumphed in Germany (battle of Hohenlinden) and threatened Vienna. Austria surrendered.

CONTINENTAL PEACE

The Austrian (Holy Roman) Emperor made peace at Lunéville (in Lorraine) on 9 February 1801. He confirmed French possession of Belgium and the west bank of the Rhine. A reorganization of Germany was agreed upon that would drastically reduce the number of small states, the main support of the emperor, since the minor princes (*Freiherren*, loosely "the barons" or imperial knights) could not defend themselves except in concert. Napoleon intended to expand the larger, more independent states, like Bavaria, and to make allies of them. France's

Map 8.1

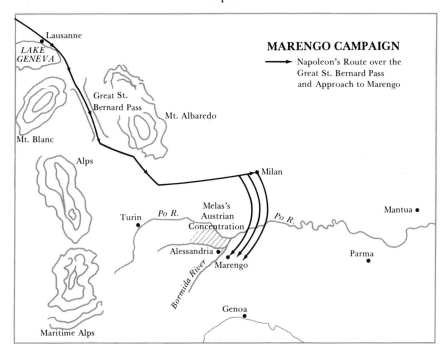

"sister republics," except those in Rome and Naples, which Napoleon chose not to restore, were recognized.

The pope was allowed his possessions in consideration of concluding a Concordat with France (see below). Naples had been reconquered by her Bourbon monarchs with heavy (if temporary) popular support. Since they agreed to admit French garrisons, reconquest seemed unnecessary—for the moment.

PEACE WITH BRITAIN

Britain, her continental allies beaten, was further shaken when Russia suspended trade. The half-mad czar, Paul I, was a great admirer of Napoleon, who impressed him by returning Russian prisoners captured in Holland without asking for a *quid pro quo*. The czar further organized the Baltic powers into a League of Neutrality, and they too closed their ports to British ships. Paul seemed ready to conclude an alliance with France. He was murdered by hostile courtiers in March 1801, however, and Alexander I, his son, assumed the throne and reversed the policy. In April a British fleet doomed the Baltic League by destroying the Danish fleet at Copenhagen. Meanwhile, however, Britain's great war minister, William Pitt, had resigned, and his successor, Addington, sued for peace with France.

The negotiators met at Amiens—Lord Cornwallis for Britain, Joseph Bonaparte for France. Cornwallis was probably the most respected public figure, save Pitt, in Britain. His defeat at Yorktown, which Americans remembered, had been the only major setback in a distinguished career which had included the Governor Generalship of India and Viceroyalty of Ireland. At sixty-seven, tall, soldierly, full of dignity, he exemplified *milord Anglais* to the French, who were honored by his coming. He refused to negotiate with "that scoundrel" Talleyrand. Joseph proved the perfect substitute; they became fast friends and completed their work in record time.

Cornwallis perhaps forgot that he was really negotiating with Napoleon. The Treaty of Amiens (signed 27 March 1802) contained no commercial agreement. There was only the promise of one, which would never be honored. The British agreed to restore all conquests except Ceylon (formerly Dutch) and Trinidad (Spanish), and to evacuate Malta and Elba. The French agreed not to garrison troops in Naples and to respect the integrity of Portugal and Holland. This meant to the British (among other things) that the ports of these countries would be open to them. They found Napoleon had another view.

THE CONCORDAT OF 1801

The Concordat of 1801 with Pope Pius VII rounded out Napoleon's peacemaking. It was an international treaty but also the key to ending the royalist-clerical rebellion in the Vendée and Brittany (intermittently in progress since 1793) and to reuniting the Catholic clergy, split since the controversy of 1791 over the oath to the government. Negotiations began after Marengo, facilitated by the restoration of the Papal States.[2] With the beginning of talks, most of the rebel leaders in France accepted the amnesty offered by Napoleon. He appointed one ex-rebel, the Abbé Bernier, chief French negotiator for the Concordat (with Joseph Bonaparte). The First Consul "encouraged" more rebels to take amnesty by hounding them mercilessly and by executing captives. The rebellion was soon dead.

The royalists hoped that since General Bonaparte was wooing the pope he might return Louis XVIII, the Bourbon pretender, to the throne. Louis wrote "his" general, asking if he would not "secure his glory" by restoring the monarchy. Impossible, Napoleon replied. "The corpses of 300,000 Frenchmen bar the way." Bonaparte knew that the Vendée rebellion had been by peasants motivated much more by religion than royalism. For the sake of his power, he made terms with the pope; he did not need the king. (The terms and implementation of the Concordat are covered below on p. 214.)

---

[2] Except those in the Cisalpine Republic.

General Bonaparte brought full peace to Europe for the first time in ten years. For good measure he ended an undeclared "corsair war" with the United States. (See below, p. 311.) Though the treaty with Britain collapsed in little more than a year, France enjoyed a respite of almost five years (1800–1805) from continental war. During this time Napoleon's government gave the nation enormous benefits and began or completed projects which are still affecting French life. (These will be treated topically below, pp. 215–227.)

CONSOLIDATION OF POWER

Reform and conciliation among all Frenchmen were the themes of the Consulate. At the same time, Napoleon quietly tightened his authority and eliminated his opposition. This was facilitated by his constitutional power to arrest "conspirators" without warrant. (See above, p. 203.)

The first minister he appointed was Joseph Fouché, minister of police, who continued in the office he had held under the Directory. Ex-cleric and teacher, polished, aristocratic in appearance, he was, nevertheless, an ex-Terrorist directly responsible for the death of hundreds. (See above, p. 141.) The First Consul knew that Fouché had to be watched, but he was a talented man, a policeman by instinct. Napoleon needed him; he used him.[3]

The restoration of law and order were much aided by the Concordat. In addition, the police were reinforced, and at times backed by the army. Highways were made safe for travel; robber bands were destroyed; city streets patrolled more efficiently and vagrants relegated to prisons or workhouses. All this was much applauded. But Napoleon's forces of order were also used for repression.

Fouché's first big case was the "infernal machine" plot—an attempt to bomb Napoleon's carriage as he drove to the Opera (Christmas Eve, 1800). A number of bystanders were killed, but not the First Consul. Within hours Fouché had identified the culprits; they were royalists. Napoleon, however, wanted to move against the "Jacobins," who were trying to strengthen the legislative bodies. He denounced them by *senatus consultum*. For the "protection of the Constitution," special tribunals sent some 120 to the Séychelles Islands (in the Indian Ocean); over 700 others were imprisoned. Three months later, Napoleon resurrected Fouché's evidence and accused the royalists. Many were imprisoned; two were shot.

In the spring of 1802 he purged the legislative bodies. One-fifth of the deputies (chosen by lot) were supposed to retire. The Senate picked their replacements from the national list, which was proper, but also chose those to retire (Napoleon's enemies), which was unconstitutional.

---

[3] Until 1810, when he caught him dealing with the British and gave his ministry to General Savary. Even so, Fouché was allowed to retain his title, Duke d'Otrante (Otranto) and was given special assignments.

Fouché had already begun the censorship of newspapers, magazines, journals, theatrical productions, and even private correspondence. Ultimately only four political papers were allowed in Paris: the *Moniteur, Journal de Paris, Journal de l'Empire, and Gazette de France*. No department could have more than one. Napoleon also "reformed" the Institut, eliminating intellectual "troublemakers." (See below, p. 213.)

In 1802, Napoleon asked the Senate to proclaim him consul for life. The Senate, in a rare moment of courage, refused; the council of state made the proclamation. A plebiscite confirmed the life consulship (3,600,000 to 8600) and amendments to the Constitution.[4] The latter authorized Napoleon to appoint forty additional senators and to call and dismiss the legislative assemblies at will. Electoral colleges, comprising only the richest citizens (though voting continued as usual) replaced departmental lists. Moreover, the Tribunate was reduced to fifty and divided into sections, each to discuss one kind of legislation only. Thus the effectiveness of the only body with a pretense to expressing the popular voice was all but destroyed. (It was dismissed permanently in 1807.) As before, the Corps Législatif voted without debating.

THE DUKE D'ENGHIEN   In 1803–1804 Napoleon and Fouché made a final end to serious Bourbon opposition. Royalists in London were hoping to assassinate or kidnap the First Consul, then return Louis XVIII to the throne backed by an army of French exiles from Germany. Fouché's agents infiltrated the group, encouraged them, and lured the leaders, Georges Cadoudal and General Pichegru, to Paris where they called on General Moreau, named to them (falsely) as a sympathizer. All three were arrested. Cadoudal was executed. Pichegru died mysteriously in prison. Moreau was exiled from France, thus eliminating a national hero and rival of Napoleon.

It remained to find the Bourbon prince supposed to lead the army from Germany. Fouché's agents fixed on the Duke d'Enghien, exiled in Baden. The duke had no army, but he was a Bourbon, the heir of the Condés, first princes of the blood, and he was nearby. Napoleon's soldiers crossed into Germany (illegally) and brought him to Vincennes (20 March 1804). He was shot at dawn the next morning. Napoleon did not apologize. It was necessary, he said, for the safety of France. He repeated this in his will.

It was an act of terror. "Bonaparte has joined the Convention," said Fouché snidely. It was a throwing down of the gauntlet to the exiled Bourbons and European monarchs in general. Napoleon meant to be emperor and defied them to interfere. In addition, he wanted to impress—dramatically, shockingly—upon the French that his life was in perpetual danger. His propaganda could then better propound that Napoleonic government, with all its benefits and the peace it had secured, depended on that life—and further, that if an hereditary monarchy were created, it could not be destroyed by removing him.

---

[4] Now termed the Constitution of the Year X.

The initial reaction of the French was adverse, even among the hardened Parisians. The Condés had produced famous soldiers for generations; the duke was young, handsome, and the last of his line. But the French soon saw Napoleon's point. A shock went through the courts of Europe, but they reacted in fear as well as horror. The weak king of Spain, Charles IV, congratulated the First Consul. (Louis XVIII sent him back his Order of the Golden Fleece.) The Austrian emperor officially ignored the incident. The czar put his court in mourning but declined to sever diplomatic relations.

THE EMPIRE

Napoleon's life-style had long since changed. In late 1802, wrote Miot: "The Tuileries and Saint-Cloud were no longer the residences of the chief magistrate of a republic, but the court of a sovereign." The same year, Napoleon founded the Legion of Honor, which conferred a decoration, rank, and pensions to its members.[5] Republicans accused him of creating a new nobility. He argued that merit was being rewarded, nothing more, but deferred awarding the medal until he was emperor.

The empire was proclaimed in May 1804 by *senatus consultum* and approved by plebiscite, 3,572,329 to 2579. By the Constitution of the Year XII, a further amended version of that of the Year VIII, Napoleon was made emperor of the French. The crown was to descend to the male heirs (if any) of Napoleon, then Joseph, then Louis. The emperor was also given the right to adopt an heir, a thing unprecedented since Roman times. He could also appoint senators without limit. The Senate instituted princely rank for Napoleon's brothers and sisters. His mother became "Madame Mère de l'Empereur." In addition, Joseph became grand elector; Cambacérès, archchancellor; Lebrun, archtreasurer; Louis Bonaparte, archconstable; and Murat, grand admiral of the empire. Eighteen generals, including Murat, Berthier, Ney, Soult, Bernadotte, and Davout, were named marshals.[6]

The coronation was staged in Notre Dame Cathedral on 2 December 1804. Pope Pius VII occupied a seat of honor, thus appearing to bless the emperor's accession, but (forewarned) he did not crown him. Napoleon crowned himself, his hand on his sword, symbolizing that he owed none of his powers to the Church but was monarch "by the unanimous will of the French people and the army." Moreover, he used the regalia and sword of Charlemagne, brought from Aix-la-Chapelle (Aachen), emphasizing that he was not the successor of the Bourbons,

[5] The medal was suspended from a blood-red ribbon (cut from revolutionary liberty caps, said English propaganda); rank was from "Grand Cross" to Chevalier (Knight). It was awarded both to military men and civilians who received from 5000 to 350 francs a year. The legion persists in France today.

[6] Four were honorary marshals—heros of the Republic; Kellerman, Lefebvre, Pérignon, and Sérurier. Others named in 1804 were Moncey, Jourdan, Masséna, Augereau, Brune, Lannes, Mortier, and Bessières.

but of the great King of the Franks. The only concrete concession to the pope was the agreement that the Revolutionary Calendar would be abolished in favor of the Christian (Gregorian) as of 1 January 1806.[7]

WAR CLOUDS   Napoleon's relations with the Vatican would worsen apace. Moreover, his assumption of the imperial dignity had been a direct affront to the Austrian Holy Roman Emperor, by tradition the successor of Charlemagne. Before that, his aggressive behavior as First Consul had alarmed not only Austria but other European powers as well. Britain had already (1803) resumed hostilities with France. In 1805 she would gain continental allies and general war would begin anew.

NAPOLEON THE GREAT?

Brute force solidified Napoleon's authority. But the real source of his power was his immense popularity with the French masses. It stemmed, in part, from the glory he brought France. The pride he excited in them, however, was mixed with trust and gratitude because he gave them perhaps the most effective government France had ever seen. In the process he reformed the nation's institutions so thoroughly that his influence is evident even today.

Napoleon was an incomparable civil executive. His domestic accomplishments certify to that; his work outside France (to be covered in later chapters) compounds the evidence. If he deserves the appellation "great," it is not merely because he was a superb soldier, but because he was also an organizer, administrator, and lawgiver.

"*Organizer* is a word of the Empire," wrote Balzac. Napoleon loved efficiency. Nothing that flawed it was allowable (within practical limits). This suited his Rousseauist philosophy. He labored to give the people what they needed but did not feel compelled to govern by their will (except as expressed in plebiscites granting very broad mandates). His approach was thus in line with the demands of the French people expressed in the *cahiers* of 1789. They had not called for destruction of the monarchy, but for more efficient government, speedier justice, equality in taxation, and elimination of privileges. He reduced liberty in France, but with the idea of introducing more equality—in the legal sense and in terms of opportunity.

SOCIETY

As First Consul one of Napoleon's earliest acts was to invite back the émigrés and exiles—royalists and republicans alike (with a few exceptions, including the royal family and its most fanatic supporters).

---

[7] The pope also remarried Napoleon and Josephine, privately, before the coronation. They had had only a civil marriage in 1796.

Why shouldn't the exiles return? Napoleon asked. "Where is the revolution-ary who would not have faith in the order of things when Fouché is minister [of police]? What gentleman, if he is French, cannot make a life where a Périgord [Talleyrand, of the high aristocracy] will have power." Careers were open to nobles, ex-Terrorists, exiles of all revolutionary governments. Carnot came back to serve briefly as minister of war, then in the Tribunate. The Marquis de Lafayette was one of the first to return.[8] He graced the salons of the Bonapartes for a few years and served them indirectly, notably in their dealings with Americans. But he was allowed no real political role—until 1815—and then it was a mistake. Most nobles employed by Napoleon were those who had not emigrated, or like Talleyrand, who had left France but briefly. Typical were the Counts de Ségur. The elder became a senator, the younger, Philippe Paul de Ségur, Napoleon's aide-de-camp and a general. The latter authored a famous account of the Russian campaign. Aristocrats were denied their ancient privileges but regained much property and used their titles socially.

The middle class (bourgeoisie), however, benefited most from Napoleon's policy of "careers open to talent" as well as his economic program (discussed below). Talent was difficult to display (except in the military, and rarely there) without education, and the bourgeoisie was educated. Moreover, there was a tacit assumption in the government that possession of wealth demonstrated talent. Thus in 1800 it was decreed that departmental and district tax collectors had to pay in advance a percentage of yearly estimated revenues. Thus the offices went to rich men. In 1802 departmental electoral assemblies were replaced by electoral colleges, which had to be selected from among the 600 richest citizens. In addition, to get the desired "tone," Napoleon directly appointed up to twenty additional members from among the thirty most heavily taxed citizens. In the cantons, candidates for municipal council had to be selected from among the hundred richest citizens, and so it went.

Members of the bourgeoisie, with fewer numbers of minor nobility and an occasional high aristocrat, populated the bureaucracy and judiciary. Outside officialdom, the middle class expanded with the growth of industry. Even in landholding, their holdings vastly outweighed those of the nobility (old and new) in 1815. Peasant holdings also increased to upward of 60 percent of all land, but a "rural bourgeoisie" of rich farmers held perhaps a third of the total.

It was the sons of the middle class who had the easiest access to the schools (see below), and thus had every opportunity to perpetuate their status. In the army, every private was given to believe that he "carried a marshal's baton in his knapsack." Joachim Murat, son of Gascon peasants, became a marshal, as did Augereau and Masséna, of equally low origins. But most of the marshals were of the middle class or minor nobility. For example, of the other "actives" appointed in 1804, Jourdan, Moncey, Bernadotte, Brune, Lannes, and Ney were sons of

---

[8] After his flight from France in 1792, he was imprisoned as a revolutionary in Austria. Though he was freed at Napoleon's request in 1797, the Directory forbade his return to Paris.

bourgeois or well-to-do artisans; Berthier, Soult, Mortier, Davout, and Bessières were nobles of the Old Regime.

Napoleon's new nobility came from the elite of government and the army. Titles derived from service and carried no privileges under the law or as to taxation. Adding a bourgeois touch, the emperor stipulated that no noble could pass his title to a son unless he bequeathed a fortune with it. Dukes had to leave incomes of 500,000 francs a year, counts 30,000, barons 15,000. Most marshals became dukes (a few princes); ministers, senators, councillors of state, and archbishops were normally made counts; barons were made from among judges, bishops, mayors of large cities, and the like. Granting titles was the privilege of the emperor, however. No one was guaranteed a title by his office. Marshal Jourdan, for example, whom Napoleon knew was always a republican at heart, was never given a dukedom.

The emperor set the social style, which could be termed royal-bourgeois. The court was magnificent, but behavior straitlaced. Napoleon had mistresses, but never paraded one in public, as had the Bourbon kings. It was understood that only wives were acceptable at the Tuileries. The emperor encouraged marshals and generals, in particular, to marry into the old nobility, and many did. "In ten years the nobility will all be one," Napoleon said. To some degree it was so. His own family, all given princely (four later royal) rank, intermarried with European royalty, and their children continued to do so after his death.[9]

Still it was the middle class and the new nobility (including nobles of the Old Regime who were promoted) who were the progressive element when the empire fell. After a short-lived triumph of the old aristocracy, the middle class and new nobility dominated the governments of the nineteenth century. While Napoleon ruled, however, there was an astonishing harmony in society.

INTELLECTUAL LIFE

Even the intellectuals, temporarily, were propitiated. Napoleon, however, soon clashed with Madame de Staël, part feminist, part aging coquette, all ego. Enamored of the First Consul, she tried to impress him at every opportunity, and was shot down repeatedly. "Who was the greatest woman of history?" she once asked. "The one who had the most children," he growled.[10] But temporarily the First Consul kept on good terms with Benjamin Constant, who was in the Institut (and briefly the Tribunate), and induced Chateaubriand to accept a diplomatic

---

[9] Lucien, who defied Napoleon's authority and married "beneath himself " in 1803, was not made a French prince, but was granted the title Prince of Canino by the pope, from whom he aquired Canino, near Rome.

[10] Anecdote attributed to General Gourgaud. Madame Germaine de Staël was famous for her novels (*Corinne; Delphine*) and literary and political tracts—and for her numerous love affairs. In her *Considerations sur la révolution française* (1818) and *Dix années d'exil* (1821), published after her death, she took revenge on Napoleon.

post. Joseph Bonaparte, co-spirit of all three, was considered by British intelligence to be the most influential man in France—until 1803.

By 1803 legal opposition to the regime had become impossible. As early as January 1800, Fouché suppressed sixty of the seventy-three newspapers in Paris. The work continued apace. Napoleon railed against the "speculative and hypothetical" in politics, blamed irresponsible intellectuals for confusing the people, creating factions, and inviting the "anarchy" common under former governments. He would not have it. "I respect public opinion . . . but it is capricious. . . . It is for the government and those who support it to enlighten it. . . . " He called for private debate but public harmony on political matters. This instruction was difficult to accept.

"Troublemakers" multiplied, particularly in the Institut. Napoleon responded by "reorganizing" the body. The sections for science and art were left intact, but that of "moral and political sciences" was dissolved, and two bodies appointed to replace it—French language/literature and history/literature. The Idéologues, including Benjamin Constant, who had dominated the old section, were not reappointed. Constant objected too vociferously and was exiled from France. Madame de Staël voluntarily followed. Chateaubriand resigned his official position and went into provincial exile.[11]

Harmony of opinion was achieved at the sacrifice of freedom of expression. In view of the benefits afforded by the new government, however, there was little objection. Some of the most vociferous came from within the Bonaparte family— from Joseph and Lucien. Few mourned the exit of the chattering Madame de Staël, and neither she nor the other exiles were hounded once they had left France. They traveled, even in French-dominated territory, and their writings were published abroad. Intellectual life did not stagnate in France either; science and the arts were nurtured and flourished. (See below, p. 225.)

It is often ignored that except for a brief period early in the Revolution, censorship had always been practiced in France and that every government since Napoleon's time has used it, including that in power today. Therefore, his system was no novelty. Admittedly, Bonaparte applied it with a severity which would have astounded the police of the Old Regime.

The clergy fell into line, devising a new catechism to teach loyalty to the regime. Napoleon was diplomatic in his management of them; privately he was cynical. "My sacred *gendarmerie*," he called them. Religion, he said, was "a mystery of the social order"—a means of controlling the populace. The Concordat had been negotiated to give him a disciplined hierarchy to inculcate proper attitudes in the people —as it had for the old kings. "One does not govern men who do not believe in God," he said, "one shoots them."

---

[11] The Idéologues were liberals who fought for active legislative bodies and freedom of the press. Benjamin Constant de Rebecque (1787–1830) had already been purged from the Tribunate for his "disruptive" oratory. A political theorist and journalist, he was much influenced by Madame de Staël. On Chateaubriand, p.225.

THE CONCORDAT/RELIGIOUS POLICY

Napoleon's Concordat with the pope (signed 15 July 1801) became law in France, along with implementing "Organic Articles" on 8 April 1802. The Concordat recognized Roman Catholicism as "the religion of the majority of Frenchmen." The French government would nominate the clergy; the pope would invest the bishops, and could reject nominees. The government agreed to pay the clergy. The pope, in effect, gave up claim to church property confiscated during the Revolution, promising that "neither he nor his successors would in any manner trouble" the new owners.

As Napoleon had expected, the Church resumed what approximated its traditional place in society.[12] This was especially important to the peasants—conservative, religious, and comprising more than 80 percent of the population. Titles to church property were guaranteed. This increased Napoleon's popularity and power also because it attached to him all those who had acquired such property. Not least important, again, were the peasants. Though their holdings were in small parcels, they owned half of the former church lands and would get more.

The Catholic Church was no longer established, thus Napoleon could proclaim religious freedom and reaffirm revolutionary laws allowing civil marriage (and divorce), which won over most anticlericals. Men could leave property to legitimate heirs not "certified" by religious marriage. Pius VII tacitly accepted all this.

The pope objected violently, however, to the Organic Articles, by which Napoleon provided "against the more serious inconveniences of a literal execution of the Concordat." Pius was particularly outraged because they were published in France with the Concordat, giving the impression that he approved them. Under the articles the Church had to perform its functions in accordance with police regulations and could do nothing presumed to disturb public tranquility. Moreover, Church doctrine was to be established by French bishops, not the pope. This was in line with Gallican tradition, as Napoleon knew, and was calculated to strengthen his hand.

Finally, regulations were provided for Protestant churches also and pay granted their ministers. Nothing was said about Jews, but by later legislation, Napoleon took them under government protection, emphasized their right to worship freely, and sponsored their integration into French society. Their money-lending activities were regulated, which inconvenienced some, but also shielded them from charges of usury. Meetings of Jewish leaders with officials were called at intervals to discuss their problems. In 1807 he staged a Grand

---

[12] Recent studies have shown, however, that a quiet rebellion was going on in the Church, in that many of the bishops increasingly favored conservative ultramontane clergy. Thus the ranks of young priests were full of men who were likely to become less docile as time went on.

Sanhedrin of Rabbis from all over Europe to inform him on Jewish practices and to advise him on regularizing his government's relations with them. The result was a decree of 1808 prescribing government of communities by consistories. The system was so successful that it is still used for religious governance in western Europe.[13] By this and other acts, he won the almost solid support of European Jewry.

Napoleon's religious policies guided later governments. The Concordat, despite the emperor's imprisonment of the pope (1809) and dismantling of the Papal States, remained the working agreement between France and the Vatican until 1905.

FISCAL AND ECONOMIC MATTERS

The most basic reforms were fiscal and economic. Faith in the government's credit had to be insured and economic growth and full employment fostered before other work could go forward.

In January 1800, Napoleon created the Bank of France, modeled after the Bank of England, with a capital of 30,000,000 francs, the stock owned partly by the government, part privately. It handled the government's money, issued its securities, and also did private business. It was shaken temporarily by the formation of the Third Coalition and the British naval victory at Trafalgar in 1805. After Napoleon's victory over the coalition it was reorganized, however, with capital of 90,000,000 and put under tighter state control. One of its functions thereafter was to lend at controlled rates when the economy required. Loans at two percent were available in 1806–1807, for example, when Napoleon's long absence on campaign caused unrest in the business community. The Bank of France is still the central financial institution of the country (though nationalized in 1945).

Fiscal administration was directed by Michel Gaudin (later a duke). A sinking fund was established—a cash reserve available to guarantee the government's debts. Part of the debt was repudiated; the rest drew regular interest. The government never failed to meet its obligations until the very last days of the regime.

For the general public, Napoleon went to a system of hard money—coin—altogether, the most stable currency.[14] He issued the *franc de Germinal* (5 grains of silver), which remained the standard in France for 123 years.[15] Direct taxes

---

[13] Napoleon flattered the Jews and gave the occasion more importance by using the term "Sanhedrin," after the Sanhedrin of Jerusalem, which, in ancient times, had ruled on Jewish civil and religious law.

[14] Bank notes, the smallest 500 francs, were used by businessmen.

[15] The ratio of value of silver to gold was set at 1 to 15.5. Silver coins of 1/4, 1/2, 1, 2, and 5 francs were minted, and gold coins of 20 and 40 francs.

were kept at a steady level; indirect taxes were adjusted upward as needed. The latter included taxes on beer, wine, liquor, liqueurs, tobacco, and salt, as well as license fees and the like. They were levied without regard to ability to pay, but caused less opposition than direct taxes on property and income since they were paid piecemeal.

The administration was purged of useless officials and was centralized; there was rigorous auditing of books at every level. "The discovery of a dishonest accountant is a victory for the administration," preached Napoleon. Collectors at departmental and district levels had to advance the government a percentage of estimated revenues each year, which limited officeholding to the rich. Nevertheless, the officials' incomes were strictly limited and they themselves were closely supervised. There was less fraud and Frenchman came closer to paying assessed taxes than at any time before, and probably since. (Tax evasion is a French national sport.) Moreover, the people complained little, though their taxes were the highest in Europe—higher even than in the satellite and puppet states created by Napoleon. The franc was the most stable currency in Europe (including Britain) during the period.

Napoleon continued the protectionist tariff policies of the Directory, which were directed primarily at Britain. The British, in turn (except in 1802–1803) ruined French overseas commerce. Napoleon ultimately countered with the Continental System (1806), an attempt to ban British goods from all of Europe. (See below, p. 243.) Tariff arrangements benefited France, however, even at the expense of her satellites. Silk manufacturing at Lyons, for example, prospered at the expense of the Cisalpine Republic (later the Kingdom of Italy). There were high import duties on Italian cloth, low duties (ultimately none) on raw silk; export duties were nil on French cloth going to Italy. French manufacturers had no competition at home, therefore, and took over part of the Italian market as well. Only Italian manufactures that the French could not produce—certain laces, velours, and gauze—found a market in France. (Despite discrimination against Italy and other countries, however, European industry expanded, and will be explained in a later chapter.)

Everything possible was done to promote industry. Loans were made to French industries at low rates, and grants were made to some, especially new industries. Tax rebates and other devices were also used. Prizes were offered to inventors.

In agriculture and commerce, public works helped. Napoleon's engineers built or repaired about 50,000 miles of roads (the figure includes some roads which ran out of France proper, however). Every village, no matter how remote, was benefited. The extinction of robber bands was also a great boon to commerce—agricultural and otherwise. Subsidies were given for new crops. Sugar beets were the most successful of these. A refining industry grew up, and by 1813 there were almost 350 factories producing a total of about 8500 tons of sugar a year. This was not enough to replace colonial cane sugar totally, but prevented a "sugar famine." Other crops included chicory, tobacco, and cotton. There was a concerted attempt to improve herds by the importation of prize breeding stock from outside the country. For example, Spanish merinos were brought in and selectively mixed with French flocks. The result was sheep producing wool of better quality than either merino or the previous variety. Expansion of the wool cloth industry was a by-product.

LABOR

Workers were required to carry the *livret* (work card-passport).[16] Their employment was recorded, but their performance was not rated. They could change jobs at will, therefore without prejudice, at least on the official record. The *livret* was issued to give protection to those gainfully employed. Those without one were assumed to be vagrants or bandits and committed to workhouses or prisons until proved otherwise. The *livret* contributed to keeping track of the work force, maintaining full employment (through the workhouses at last resort) and apprehending undesirables, criminals, and draft dodgers.

The methods of Napoleon were brutal, but the problems of beggary and banditry were very serious and required severe measures. For example, under the Directory, as a result of an investigation on theft and murder in the vicinity of Chartres, 400 "brigands" were imprisoned and perhaps 600 professional beggars interrogated and released.

Workers had the advantage of employment bureaus which transferred people from areas of low employment to places where jobs were available. Britain, where the Industrial Revolution started much earlier than in France, had nothing similar until 1909. Labor Unions were forbidden under the Chapelier Law of 1791, which remained in effect. There were, however, labor-management committees, required by the government and supervised thereby. It is true that only senior workers conferred with the managers, but at least grievances were aired.

ECONOMIC GROWTH

What were the overall results of the fiscal-economic policies? There was a growth of 25 percent in French industry; in metallurgy the percentage was higher. Much new industry was established—in metals, wool, sugar refining, tobacco processing, and even cotton, despite the blockade. Canning was invented by one Nicholas Appert who successfully preserved food in vacuum-sealed glass jars. It was produced primarily for the navy, but Napoleon's armies were the first in the world to use canned food.

---

[16] This was not entirely new. There had been worker's passes under the Old Regime, but never a uniform national system.

There was full employment except for short periods in 1806–1807 and 1810–1811. Labor was so short that an unprecedented number of women—and, unhappily, children—were hired. Several factors contributed to high employment—expanded European markets, favorable tariffs, industrial growth, demands of war, and expanding population. Finally, conscription tended to drain off surplus manpower. Its effects should not be exaggerated, however. Only 2,300,000 men were drafted during the fourteen years of Napoleon's power. Of these, 1,000,000 were called in 1813–1814. In the average department less than 3 per cent of the population was displaced (over the whole period 1800–1814).

There was expansion in agriculture as well. The growing population and the needs of war served to keep prices up. The peasantry was prosperous; more peasants acquired land than ever before. This is one reason, at least, that the farmers were Napoleonists, though their sons did most of the dying in the imperial armies.

For a long run, it may be said that the groundwork for the Industrial Revolution in France was laid during the Napoleonic Period. The same can be said of some other European countries under French control or influence for all or part of the period. The German states, for example, had a higher industrial growth rate than France—about 30 percent. Italian industry gained as well.

ADMINISTRATION AND JUDICIARY

Napoleon also reorganized the administrative-local government system. He took the basic pattern established by the National Assembly early in the Revolution, when eighty-three departments replaced the thirty-four intendencies (roughly equivalent to provinces). Departments were divided in descending order into districts (*arrondissements*), cantons, and communes (municipalities). Officials in the local governments (except under the Terror) had been elected. Napoleon appointed prefects of departments, subprefects of districts, and mayors of cities (those with over 5,000 people directly; the smaller ones through the prefects).[17] Officials were usually chosen from local electoral lists, but not always. The departmental and district councils, which advised the prefects, were also appointed from Paris. Similar arrangements applied to the officers of police. The minister of police controlled the national *gendarmerie* (previously under the army), the secret police, retained special commissioners in the larger cities and a prefect in Paris and vicinity directly answerable to him.[18] The administrative system persists today, though mayors are now elected. Police centralization is perpetuated in the Sûreté (the National Police, partly secret).

[17] The prefects were absolute governors of their departments. They were furnished detailed instructions from Paris, and ordered to follow them "literally." *Correspondence de Napoléon*, 5378 (15 February 1802).

[18] The *gendarmerie*, commanded initially by General Moncey (made a marshal in 1804), and always by a senior general, had considerable independence in practice, despite the law.

A reorganization of the judiciary was also effected. All judges were appointed. Supervising the system were the chancellor (Cambacérès after 1804) and council of state; the latter interpreted the law (a power later shared with the emperor's privy council). In the court system, the Court of Cassation stood to the top. It had civil and criminal jurisdiction but did not decide cases or interpret the laws. It merely reviewed the records of lower courts, sending cases back for retrial where there had been legal or procedural error. Beneath it were civil and criminal systems. Both terminated at the lowest level with the justice(s) of peace in the canton. Between were civil courts of first instance (one per district) and civil appeals courts (one per two or three departments) plus criminal courts (one per department). The system is essentially that of France today (though, of course, vastly expanded).

The Napoleonic administrative, judicial, and military coteries were stabilizing factors in French government in his time and have continued to be since 1815. Governments, parliaments, kings, another emperor, and presidents and their ministries have come and gone. The *fonctionnaires* have gone on "forever," each generation replacing the last.[19]

THE BUREAUCRACY

Napoleon has been credited with forming the first "police state" and alternately with establishing the first modern bureaucratic state. He controlled the law-making process through his council of state, initially about sixty men, doubled under the empire. It was divided into sections for war, marine, finance, and legislation. Councillors framed and presented his proposals to the legislative bodies and defended them (more aptly, *explained* them, especially after the Tribunate was dissolved in 1807). In 1803 the council was furnished with sixty "auditors"—young men in training. After 1804 the corps of auditors was expanded and some 120 assigned to ministers, the police, and the emperor's personal suite.

The ministers, charged with executing the law, were "political appointees." The most important was the secretary of state, initially Hughes-Bernard Maret, through whom Napoleon transmitted routine orders to the ministers of foreign affairs, police, war, administration of war, marine (including navy), interior, justice, ecclesiastical affairs, and (after 1810) the Grand Master of the Imperial University, the *de facto* minister of education. (See below.) Each minister, how-

---

[19] President Mitterand made some changes in the 80s. *Le Préfet* (so called and so ranked in the civil service) still presides over each of ninety-six departments. Officially, however, prefects are now "Commissioners of the Republic" and have less power. Laws passed during 1982–1986 transferred control of finances and some executive functions from prefects to elected departmental councils. But the prefect still controls police, is responsible to Paris for "law and order," and supervises education, health, and justice in his department.

ever, had a council of permanent career bureaucrats, comprising the heads of his departments, certain councillors of state, and accounting commissioners. Each council had a secretary who could preside in the minister's absence. Thus if Talleyrand were in Berlin or Turin, business went on as usual at the foreign office.

The councils produced administrative regulations to implement the laws. These were transmitted to the prefects of departments (and police prefects and commissioners), who also had appointed councils. Beneath them were subprefects and councils and mayors with councils, all appointed. Every detail was thus efficiently managed. Appointments were made at first (in part) from communal, departmental, and national "lists," compiled very indirectly by universal manhood suffrage. Nevertheless, at the top level, and to a lesser degree in the departments, a national civil service was created which was infinitely more powerful than the legislative branch of the government.

In short, Napoleon created the first modern bureaucracy. The cost was the obliteration of local autonomy. Whether such a system can best serve the nation (all the people) is a matter still under debate—at least in our Western democracies.

THE LAW CODES

Since 1790, revolutionary governments had labored (if sporadically) to make French law uniform throughout the nation. Napoleon gave France a common law based on the traditional, Roman, and Revolutionary laws, but laid out simply and concisely in seven codes. The first and most important was the civil code (1804), called the "Code Napoléon." It was drafted by a committee of jurists under the supervision of Cambacérès. Napoleon personally saw the final version to completion, however, presiding at fifty-seven of the 102 meetings of the commission of the council of state which approved it. The drafts bear his notes; his ideas permeate the laws.

The civil code guaranteed individual liberty, stated certain rights such as equality before the law and in taxation, freedom from arrest without due process and religious freedom as well as the right to choose one's work. It confirmed the abolition of feudalism in all its aspects, including corporate privilege such as had been held by guilds and cities. The most interesting features applied to property, marriage and divorce, and the rights of women.

There was to be equal division of property among all legitimate heirs—except that an individual might dispose of up to one-quarter by bequest. This was less radical than the revolutionary law providing for division of all without exception. Still, it made for the redistribution of property in each generation and the breaking up of great estates.

Civil marriage was required. Even if married in a church, couples had to go through a civil ceremony, thus registering the marriage with the state. Otherwise the churches (in most cases the Catholic) would still have had to certify to the legitimacy of heirs and the like. Divorce was allowed by mutual consent.[20] Other grounds were adultery, "excesses," conviction of a criminal offense of one party, or insanity. In any case the parties could not remarry for three years.

Divorce was difficult. The law was written to help keep the family together. Women were at a disadvantage in these cases. In adultery, for example, if a wife caught her husband *en flagrante delicto* and shot him (and/or his partner), she was a murderess. If the husband, under reversed circumstances, caught his wife abed with a lover and shot one or both, no charge was possible against him. Moreover, catching a wife in adultery one time was sufficient for divorce, whereas the husband had to move a mistress into the home to have the charge proved.

Women were under other disabilities as well—"less equal than men." Their property had to be managed by a husband or male relative. In law suits, they were treated as if they were minors—with the protection and disadvantages attached thereto. In civil cases the courts were sympathetic, but women's testimony was taken lightly. In criminal cases where, for example, there were lurid details, women's testimony was taken in closed court—to protect their tender sensibilities.

The French law was not amended to give women reasonable equality until the 1960s. It was 1965 before the divorce law was rewritten, and 1966 before women were allowed to own businesses and to have checking accounts.[21]

The other major code was the Criminal Code. It specified equality before the law and equality in penalties and forbade arbitrary arrest and imprisonment. Jury trial could be had in major cases at the request of the defendant. Torture by the police was allowed—under judicial restraint. This meant, in practice, that the police were rather brutal, especially to persons thought dangerous or habitual offenders. They also had the right to hold persons in custody, under warrant, for almost unlimited periods. The prosecution, in all cases, had more rights than the defense. The defense, for example, had to apprise the prosecution and judges of all witnesses and evidence it expected to bring before the court; the prosecution was not so hampered. Further, the judges could order new trials if juries ruled "illegally." For those brought up in the tradition of English and American law this seems incredible. To the French, with their inbred respect for authority of the qualified, it seemed normal—and still does. The French law did not (and does not) presume persons guilty until proven innocent. It was, however, written to protect the state, not the individual. The feeling was that it was better for some

---

[20] This would seem to have made divorce easy. One must remember, however, that in an era when marriage was the only "career" open to most women and when it was expected to produce children (literally one a year, and often did) who imposed enormous burdens on wives, women clung tenaciously to their marriages. Divorce, in practice, was a "luxury" of the upper classes. Even among the rich, however, economic considerations worked against "mutual consent."

[21] In practice, by resorting to various subterfuges, women had for decades been handling money and doing business. In cosmetics and haute couture, persons such as Coco Chanel had become millionaires despite the law.

innocents to be punished than for society to suffer. The assumption of American law (based on the English) has always been the opposite.

There was a separate penal code, which, by today's standards, was brutal. Punishments included death by guillotine, lifetime hard labor in chains, lesser terms in workhouses—for men and women—total loss of civil rights, cutting off of the right hand—and for political offenders, perpetual exile. In addition, there were codes of criminal instruction, civil procedure, and for rural and commercial cases.

For the first time all of France had the same laws; all provincial variations were nullified. The codes preserved the ideals of the Revolution while incorporating a comfortable measure of the traditional. The Code Napoléon, especially, was not a synthesis of local law, but "cut from whole cloth" by experts and imposed by authority, like the Roman Law, which Napoleon so revered.

The Napoleonic codes, expanded and amended, remain the basic law of France; they have also influenced the law of most European countries and that of many other parts of the world.

EDUCATION

In education, Napoleon's influence is often decried, but he left a lasting legacy. As to public schools, he returned the primary system to the control of the Church, favoring the teaching order of Brothers of Christian Schools, though municipal and private schools were allowed. He eliminated the secondary "central schools" of the Directory (one per department) and dismissed the Terrorists' plan for free public schools as visionary and too expensive. To replace the "central schools," he established forty-five *lycées* (roughly, high schools) and allowed municipal *collèges* and private, mostly church, schools at the same level.

The purpose of the lycées was to train future officers and civil servants. They had headmasters and administrative boards appointed by Napoleon. Inspectors general (three) visited each at least once a year. There were 6400 scholarships available, of which 2400 went to the sons of officers and civil servants, the remainder to the "best" students of lower schools. Only about 15 percent were full scholarships, however. Most students in the *lycées* paid tuition; all of them in the collèges. The curriculum included classical languages, rhetoric, morality, logic, mathematics and science. The *lycées* were under military discipline, and religious instruction was required in both *lycées* and *collèges*. Both adopted the baccalaureate examination for graduation. This exam persists in France today. Now, as then, one cannot go on to a university or one of the "Great Schools," without passing it. Every year, students still cram and work themselves into states of near hysteria over the "bacs."

Napoleon preserved the *Grandes Écoles* (Great Schools) established by the Convention. The principal ones were the École Polytechnique and the École Normale Superieure. The Polytechnic trained engineers—civil and military—

though graduates had to enter the army or navy in the latter years of the empire. The Normal School trained teachers and research men in science and the humanities. Graduation from either guaranteed a career in government service (or, generally, elsewhere, if desired).

The Great Schools still enjoy the highest prestige in France. New ones have been founded, notably the National School of Administration (1945) to train prospective *fonctionnaires*. Prior to its creation, the Polytechnique (despite its origin as an engineering school) and Normale produced most of the nation's cabinet ministers and other high officials. The two now share about equal rank. The tradition of elitism is still very much alive in theory and in practice. Any talented child of the provinces, however, has a chance to get into the Great Schools. Napoleon also must have credit for establishing the chief military academy of France, Saint-Cyr, although he had the old École Militaire, as modified by the revolutionary governments, to build on.

The Institut of France, also founded by the Convention, was preserved. It was an honorific body, but also directed to the collection of knowledge and research. Originally three sections, Napoleon organized it into four: Physical and Mathematical Sciences, French Language and Literature (the Académie Française), History and Literature, and Fine Arts. He had a political motive for reorganizing it, as mentioned earlier. But the Institut survived (though the Académie Française was suppressed temporarily in 1811). It is very much alive today.[22]

IMPERIAL UNIVERSITY

To insure control of education, Napoleon organized the Imperial University. Not a university in the ordinary sense, it was an organization of all the professors and teachers in France, who had to be members in order to teach. It was headed by a Grand Master, Louis de Fontanes, chosen by Napoleon because he was a famous essayist and poet, had political experience (president of the Corps Législatif), and was from a family of Catholics and Protestants. He was given an advisory council of thirty educators and charged with standardizing education in France from the primary to university level. The university—or rather Fontanes and his council—specified curricula, chose the texts, specified the nature of examinations and when and where they were to be held, and even the system of grading. Everyone who taught at any level in France was put under discipline—from the dons of the Sorbonne to the village schoolmasters.[23] Loyalty to the

[22] It now has five sections, the Académie Française des inscriptions et belles-lettres, des sciences, des beaux-arts, and des sciences morales et politiques.

[23] Time was required for the university to evolve. Education was first centralized under a director of education in the ministry of the interior. A uniform teaching corps was ordered formed in 1806; the university put in operation by decree of 1808. Not until 1811, however, were all teachers positively required to join. Lack of funds (within the budget, rigidly adhered to by Napoleon) for implementation of the law was one reason for delay.

emperor, the Napoleonic dynasty, and the Christian religion were mandatory. The university continued to operate in France until 1850. A centralized system, under the minister of education, has existed ever since.

WOMEN'S EDUCATION The education of women remained outside the purview of the university, and Napoleon took little interest in it. Most girls, he opined, could be educated best by their mothers. Their role was private, not public. He did authorize the opening of a finishing school (for girls of the upper classes) in the château of Écouen. He took time to dictate instructions for its operation in the midst of the 1807 campaign. Teach them good French, he wrote, a little arithmetic, geography, history, and a smattering of science. But three-quarters of their time should be spent learning sewing, "other female occupations," and good grooming. Religion and manners, though, were really all they needed to learn.

THE RECORD IN EDUCATION

Napoleon has been damned for gearing the educational system to produce soldiers and civil servants and to indoctrinate the young in loyalty to the regime. At least he made no pretense of doing otherwise. "My object in establishing a teaching corps (the university)," he told the council of state in 1806, "is to have a means of directing political and moral opinion." He also said that without "a public instruction . . . there is no equality [for the common man] except that of misery and servitude." But "public instruction" for him meant education by the state for the public good. He was determined that the Church would never regain its ancient monopoly.

Napoleon succeeded well in preserving secular control of education, though the Church has always played a major role in it. Moreover, his mark is apparent today on the French school system—at every level.

Related to education, Napoleon preserved and expanded the Bibliothèque Nationale (National Library). The Archives Nationales were given a new home in 1804—the Palace de Rohan-Soubise—where they are still located. Napoleon also must have credit for making the Louvre one of the world's great art museums—perhaps today the greatest. To accomplish this he brought art treasures from all over Europe. But they were not "stolen," as is often alleged. The Allies, after Napoleon's defeat, decided that most of them had been purchased or otherwise legally acquired, if in abnormal situations. Some were returned to their former owners, including the famous horses of St. Mark's, Venice. Most of those removed from the Louvre, however, were bought from the restored Bourbon government. The man who set the pattern was Czar Alexander I. Many of the paintings and objects which now grace the Hermitage in Leningrad (formerly St. Petersburg) were shipped from Paris in 1814–1815.

THE FATE OF THE INTELLIGENTSIA

Much has been made of the exile of Madame de Staël and Benjamin Constant. But one wonders if much of their fame was not a result of it. Surely Constant produced nothing of world-shaking value. Chateaubriand, in France, published *Le génie du Christianisme* (1802), his most famous work, and *Les Martyrs* (1809), though denied a seat in the Académie Française.[24] The verse of Jacques Delille, official poet of the empire, was praised even by Madame de Staël.

Marie-Joseph Chénier, an outstanding dramatist, was an inspector of the Imperial University. René de Pixérécourt, "father of the melodrama," set trends that lasted a century. The stage was graced by Talma, one of the greatest tragedians of all time. The Marquis de Sade, whose *Justine* has become a classic, if pornographic, was in the mental hospital at Charenton (his family approved) but wrote and produced plays to which the public was admitted. The theater and opera were very active. Napoleon patronized and regularly attended both. He loved the classics of Corneille, Racine, Molière—particularly the tragedies—and new plays on classic, especially ancient, themes. Of the new, his favorite was *Les Templiers* of Raynouard.

The emperor had a traveling library of 1000 books, which he took on campaign. It comprised 660 histories and historical memoirs, together with poetry, drama, novels, and religious works. Included (in translation) were Fielding's *Tom Jones* and Richardson's *Pamela* and classics from Homer, Lucan, and Tasso to Rousseau and Montesquieu. The works of living authors he accepted or rejected, tossing those he disliked out his carriage window. His great favorite was *The Poems of Ossian*, translated by Letourneur, which even became the basis for an opera, with music by Lesueur. We do not know what he thought of the early efforts of Stendhal. The leading novelist of the day was Ducray-Duminil, whose books are less known today than those of the "exiled" Madame de Staël, *Corinne* and *Delphine.*

In art, it is only necessary to mention the names of Jacques David, Antoine Gros, Pierre-Paul Prud'hon, Géricault, and J.-B. Wicar. In Italy, Antonio Canova was patronized by Napoleon, and in Spain, Goya.[25] The empire set a style in painting, sculpture, architecture, furniture, and dress which is distinctive; in literature the romantic period began.

Doubtless, the scientists were Napoleon's favorites. The empire boasted great names—Gaspard Monge, the father of descriptive geometry; Louis Joseph

---

[24] The Viscount François-René de Chateaubriand (1768–1848) was a royalist who returned from exile after Brumaire. The *Génie*, published after the Concordat, was dedicated "to the present government." He broke with Napoleon in 1803, however. (See above, p 213.). Author of many works, he is usually named as the founder of the romantic school in France. He wrote against Napoleon in 1814, but his *Mémoires d'outre tombe* (1849–1850) reflects a deep nostalgia for France's era of glory.

[25] Goya was court painter to King Joseph Bonaparte in Spain. His famous "Disasters of War" depicting French brutality, were probably done after Joseph's fall—at any rate he appeared with them to do court to Ferdinand VII, restored in 1814, and they saved his skin.

Lagrange, another mathematician of genius; Pierre-Simon Laplace, whose *Mécanique Céleste* pioneered in astronomy; and the zoologist, Jean Baptiste Lamarck. Napoleon fostered the work of the physicists Karl Friedrich Gauss in Germany and Alessandro Volta in Italy.

There was repression of political expression. But those who say Napoleon created an intellectual desert in France and Europe are wrong.

PUBLIC WORKS

Napoleon also left monuments and public works. The centerpiece of Paris, the Arc de Triomphe, was almost completed in 1814. The Arc du Carrousel and the column of the Place Vendôme were in place, among hundreds of other lesser monuments. The Church of the Madeleine (begun by Louis XV) was also almost completed—a shrine of the men of the Grande Armée. Some projects, mercifully, were never finished, for example, that of a huge elephant, spouting water, for the Place de la Bastille. New bridges were thrown across the Seine. Paris got a fresh water supply (via a new canal from the Ourcq River). To the chagrin of water peddlers, fountains flowed day and night in all quarters. The city sewer system was reconstructed. A number of streets were straightened and widened. The French canal system was extended by some 200 kilometers, though the major project, connecting the Rhone and the Rhine, was not finished. We have noted the roads built in France; many routes extended beyond, notably the spectacular highway across the Mt. Cenis Pass of the Alps to Italy and the Corniche, cut into the bluffs of the French and Italian Rivieras. Hardly a village is without reminders of Napoleon—practical and decorative.

CONCLUSION

"I am so much identified with our . . . monuments, or institutions, all our national acts, that one would not know how to separate me from them. . . . " said the fallen emperor in 1816. It has been true ever since: it is true today. It is patent that the Napoleonic genius still guides France through the Code Napoléon, the judiciary and administration. The Bank of France still operates. Napoleon's spirit pervades education. The Louvre museum is as much his monument as the Invalides. When the "immortals" of the Académie Française turn out, it is in the uniform Napoleon had the artist David design for them. In their insistence on constitutional government, flatly contradicted by their disdain for legislative babblers, the French maintain the emperor's own attitude. French preference for elitist leadership antedates Napoleon, as does their passion for centralized government and national planning. But he certainly brought these back into vogue with a verve Louis XIV would have approved.

Moreover, the most successful French leaders since his time have emulated him. There was an echo of his rhetoric in that of Charles de Gaulle. Said Napoleon, "My policy is to govern the people as the great number desires. That . . . is the way to recognize the sovereignty of the people." Said de Gaulle: "[My government] . . . is the system of the national majority . . . of that which emerges from the nation as a whole, expressing itself through its undivided and sovereign mass." Napoleon: "Let the legislature have the power to stop the march of government in its details—and that would result [in enfeeblement]. . . . " De Gaulle: "Under [the previous Republic] . . . the Parliament . . . [was] the exclusive source of power. . . . Such a system was not normally able to . . . accomplish all the firm and constant designs that constitute a policy, nor, all the more . . . [to lead] France in the major contemporary dramas."[26]

Never has the influence of one man been so persistent in the institutions and life of a nation as of Napoleon in France.

[26] Napoleon's words from messages to the council of state in 1800 and 1804; de Gaulle's are from a press conference of 9 November 1965. *Speeches and Press Conferences*, No. 228. (New York: Ambassade de France; Service de Presse et d'Information, 1965).

They never stop talking about my love of war. . . . Did I
ever win a single great victory without immediately
proposing peace?
—*Napoleon at St. Helena*

FORGING A
EUROPEAN EMPIRE
(1804–1812)

The Napoleonic Empire was put together by war, threat of war, and diplomacy closely connected to both. It was the creation of the *Grande Armée* and of
Napoleon's genius for war—and for taking maximum advantage of his victories.
The army was organized with great care, under the daily supervision of Bonaparte, who interested himself in the most minute details. The success of the army
Napoleon attributed "three-quarters to morale" and the rest to leadership and to
having "more forces at the point of attack than the enemy." His own genius (which
he "modestly" announced as early as 1797) he considered God-given—a "touch
for leading," a key to victory which could not be "learned from books, nor by
practice."

NAPOLEONIC WARFARE

The nucleus of the original *Grande Armée*[1] was formed at Boulogne during
1803–1804, nominally as the Army of England, that is, for a cross-channel
invasion. It was a strike force of some 200,000—half of the French army—with
a special toughness, *esprit*, and organization. The standing army from 1805 on
comprised some 600,000 men. Its officers and noncommissioned officers were
largely professionals. The ranks were filled partly by volunteers, but mostly by
conscription, which applied to men aged twenty through twenty-four. The
youngest were called first; men turning twenty in a given year were the "class" of

[1] The term *Grande Armée* was applied to the field army under Napoleon's direct command. Units left
in France, or fighting elsewhere, were not included.

that year. Married men, only sons, the physically unfit, and so on were exempt, and the "buying" of substitutes was permitted.[2] Some 1,300,000 men were drafted during 1800–1812; about 1,000,000 in 1813–1814. Through 1812, therefore, only an average of 100,000 men a year were called—less than a tenth of those eligible.

Napoleon normally took to the field with an army of 200,000 French, which was reinforced in increasing numbers from allied and satellite states as the empire evolved. He had under his personal command 300,000 in 1805, 400,000 in 1809, and 700,000 in 1812. With each campaign, however, greater numbers of French troops were fighting other than with the Grande Armée—after 1808, particularly in Spain where 250,000 to 300,000 served constantly until 1813. National Guard units were called up to reinforce the Army of the Interior in emergencies and constituted a reasonably effective reserve of 200,000 to 300,000 troops.

The basic unit below army level was the corps of 20,000 to 30,000 men, commanded by a marshal or general-in-chief.[3] The corps comprised two or more infantry divisions (10,000 to 14,000), a brigade of light cavalry (2000 to 3000 men),[4] six to eight companies of artillery, and trains. The infantry division was divided into brigades and regiments—really the only unit of standard size—ideally 3360 men (four battalions of six companies, 140 men each).[5] Total artillery support was forty-eight to sixty-four guns (six cannon and two howitzers per company), with one or two companies kept under corps control, the rest detached to divisions, brigades, and sometimes regiments. The guns were mostly fired flat out at the enemy, not used to interdict the enemy rear, or the like, since the maximum range of cannon was 900 to 1000 yards (roughly a half mile), and howitzers (six-inch mortars) about 1300 yards.

The army headquarters had its own artillery—120 to 150 guns—which brought the army average to three guns per 1000 men. The army cavalry was also

[2] The Jourdan-Delbrel law of 1798 remained in effect, modified by a 1799 amendment allowing substitutions. Napoleon limited the number of substitutes to 5 percent of draft quota in each department. The price varied with the department and the year—on the average 500 francs in 1800, 2000 in 1805, 2800 in 1809, 3500 to 5000 in 1813–1814.

[3] Officially, there were only two grades of general—"of brigade" and "of division" or brigadier general and major general. When a major general stood in for a marshal in command of a corps he was called general-in-chief, or sometimes lieutenant general. Either a marshal or general on special mission could be "Lieutenant General of the Emperor."

[4] Cavalry was termed Light (dragoons, *chasseurs à cheval*, hussars, and lancers) or Heavy (*cuirassiers*, *carabiniers à cheval*). Heavy cavalry was almost always under army command. The heavy cavalry wore armor—the *cuirass*—breast and back plates of heavy steel—and steel helmets. Both heavy and light cavalry were armed with sabres, carbines (.69 calibre) and pistols (.69).

[5] An infantry battalion had four companies of *chasseurs*, one company of *grenadiers*, and one company of *voltigeurs* (skirmishers). The grenadiers were big men used as shock troops. The *voltigeurs* were picked for small size, speed, agility, and marksmanship; they led the attack, advancing independently or in small groups. Both of the latter were elite troops. The standard infantry arm was the .69 musket; the *voltigeurs* carried carbines (.69); both weapons had bayonets. The *grenadiers* handled, if rarely, the then very dangerous grenades; *voltigeurs* could carry personal weapons, and some had hunting rifles, rare, very expensive items usually "liberated" on campaign.

separate, usually under Marshal Murat, and numbered 20,000 (1805) to 60,000 (1812). With the emperor and/or his headquarters (under Marshal Berthier) was the Imperial Guard, Napoleon's trump card.

The guard was much more than an escort force. It was a small, elite army, which numbered 8000 in 1805 and 80,000 by 1812 and had its own infantry, cavalry, artillery, military police, and train. On campaign, it was under the emperor's direct command and constituted his ultimate reserve. He delighted in deploying the artillery in battle but normally committed but few of the other *grognards* (grumblers). When he did they never failed him (until Waterloo). Their *élan* was magnificent. All men who entered the guard before 1809 (the Old Guard) had to be veterans who had distinguished themselves in at least three campaigns. The requirement was never dropped for the Old Guard. Privates ranked with sergeants of the line; sergeant-majors with lieutenants; colonels were generals of the regular army. Their pay was thus higher, their rations the best, their uniforms splendid. On campaign, Napoleon always wore the uniform of a colonel of guard cavalry *(chasseurs à cheval)*—the green coat with red facings and gold epaulets. It was part of his style to appear before the troops in the same faded green coat, by which they identified him. After 1809, when the Young Guard was formed, the Old Guard regiments were hardly ever committed in battle. Though mostly French, the guard also had regiments of Poles, Germans, Italians, and others, and a company of Mamelukes.

In general, French tactics can be described.[6] They had been developed to employ masses of half-trained troops during the wars of the Revolution. Napoleon made few changes in the overall pattern. On the defense, the two- or three-man line, or the square, was used. In the attack, the infantry carried the burden, jogging forward in battalion column—800 to 900 men with a sixty-man front. The way was prepared by the *voltigeurs* (skirmishers) who advanced, Indian fashion, taking cover as it appeared, sniping at the enemy and disrupting his formations.[7] The columns charged, shouting, bugles blowing, and delivering volleys of fire. Their object was to break through the enemy line and to open flanks. Cavalry followed up to widen the gaps and to attack the enemy rear. Artillery was used throughout to disorganize the opponent at a distance and to demolish his ranks at close quarters. These tactics worked well against continental armies, but not so well against the British, especially when commanded by Wellington. His veteran marksmen stood steady and decimated the column. If Napoleon had studied the campaigns of Wellington in Spain (where he was present for only a few months and never fought the British), he might have been better prepared for Waterloo. Instead, he disdained the "Sepoy General."

---

[6] "Tactics" will be used here as meaning patterns of battlefield action; "strategy" as the overall campaign plan (and planning) and pattern of movement to the battle area.

[7] After 1807, artillery concentrations were increasingly used ahead of or instead of *voltigeurs* to break open the enemy line.

Napoleon's personal tactics defy analysis. He never fought two battles the same way. (We shall describe several below.) His rule was "Engage and then see what develops." He normally held back a large part of his army until the pattern of enemy action became clear. Then his remarkable intuition came into play. Sensing the opponent's weak point, he would hurl overwhelming force against that point at just the right time—artillery blasting, infantry rolling forward, and cavalry moving in for the *coup de grâce*. Never, however, did he leave himself without a reserve, at least the Old Guard—until Waterloo.

"Everything is common sense," Napoleon said of war, "theory is nothing." And "All the art of war consists of a rational, extremely circumspect defense, and a daring, rapid offense." He defined the successful general as "a genius who knows that war is half science and half a gamble." But he knew the value of personal leadership as well. During the early campaigns, when a French unit wavered, Napoleon could be counted on to appear in the thick of the fighting. Later the troops came to believe the myth he carefully cultivated that "the cannonball has not been cast which will kill the Emperor" and that whenever he was on the battlefield, victory was certain. Wellington said Napoleon's presence was worth 50,000 men.

The emperor's strategy is easier to describe than his tactics. His initial movements were based on contingency plans developed long in advance by Marshal Berthier and the general staff to cover any conceivable attack by any combination of enemies. As he moved toward the enemy, the pattern was modified on the basis of intelligence, at first based on information from diplomats and others returning from the enemy side, and as he closed with the opponent, based on reports of scouts, defectors, and prisoners. (Intelligence came from spies as well, but they were the least reliable source.) It was the business of his staff to know all available routes forward, the condition of roads, bridges, and all about the terrain, especially obstacles to movement. Estimates had to be available to him on the number of troops, guns, and vehicles that could be carried by given routes—and at what speed.

Based on staff work, Napoleon moved his army along all available parallel routes so as to bring together the greatest number of men at a given place (the assumed battlefield) at a given time. His weak point was supply. Even if the roads could have borne the traffic, to keep food and materiel from distant depots constantly available would have required a second army of teamsters, wagons and horses, with a heavy guard to protect them from enemy raiders. Before a campaign, he advanced depots, supplies, food, weapons, ammunition, vehicles, and horses as far forward as possible. On his perpetual fronts—the Rhine and Elbe in Germany; the Bug in Poland; the feet of the Alpine passes in Italy—he kept fortresses heavily stocked for future action. Beyond that, however, his motto was "The war must feed the war." His troops levied off the native population. His policy was to move quickly and not to strip areas of food and horses—and to pay. (He knew well that there was no advantage in antagonizing the population more than necessary.) At times, though, his armies devastated localized areas. In this, as in other respects, they resembled the armies of the Revolution.

Napoleon used massed artillery fire better than any commander had before. His artillery, however, was inherited from the Old Regime—4-, 6-, 8-, and 12-pound guns and 6-inch howitzers, smooth bore, muzzle loading, the best in Europe. His basic offensive and defensive formations and the column attack were inherited from the Revolution. Except that he made the corps the basic unit of all arms and the division a standard fixture, his organization was a blend of the royal and revolutionary. He was not an innovator.

Bonaparte's genius was displayed in his ability to make his war machine run. He had uncanny power over men. (See above p. 186.) He could "read" a battlefield, sense an enemy's weakness, and take advantage of his mistakes. Why he was thus endowed is ultimately beyond explanation, but it was so.

It should go without saying, but somehow does not, that Napoleon did not fight for love of war or glory. He was a professional, always out to win—as decisively and quickly as possible. For one thing, there were always those in Paris anxious to take advantage of his absence. (In 1812, General Malet reported him dead in Russia and tried to seize the government.) He did not take a "sporting" attitude toward war; the greater the odds in his favor the better he liked it. He would not fight an enemy on even terms if he could assemble two or three times his numbers. Moreover, though he may have *caused* all the wars, he *started* veritably none of them until 1812. Nevertheless, Napoleon expected fruits from his victories. "To conquer is nothing," he wrote Joseph in 1808, "there must be some profit from success." The "profits" he amassed became the empire.

THE HUMAN COST

Perhaps it would be well to comment here on the cost in human lives of Napoleon's wars, since the idea persists that he destroyed a whole generation of young Frenchmen, so many that the nation was never again the same. The truth is that casualties in the Napoleonic Wars were minor compared to those of the twentieth-century wars.

As the Table below indicates, the total number of Frenchmen (from France of 1789) who died in battle or directly thereafter was 86,500 for eleven years, and adding deaths in hospital—70 percent of which were from disease, exposure, or injury—the number of deaths from all causes is 388,500. These figures do not include some 150,000 casualties from the new departments (annexed areas) and perhaps 300,000 among foreign troops serving with the Grande Armée (from satellite and allied states).

The casualties seem to have had little effect on the growth of the French population, which went from 26,000,000 in 1789 to over 30,000,000 in 1815. The average number of deaths per year in the period 1770–1784 was 837,000. The total deaths (military and civilian) in 1814 was 873,000, or only slightly more than the average for the earlier period, when the population was some 20 percent smaller.

FRENCHMEN ONLY (BY YEAR) 1803–1814

Year	Killed in Action or Died of Wounds	Died in Hospital	Prisoners and Disappeared	Hospitalized Long Absent	Totals
1803	0	1,000	500	500	2,000
1804	1,000	5,500	1,500	1,000	9,000
1805	2,000	7,000	?	5,000	14,000
1806	5,000	16,000	2,000	13,000	36,000
1807	7,500	33,000	2,000	4,000	46,500
1808	2,500	16,000	1,000	24,500	54,000
1809	19,000	32,500	14,000	12,500	78,000
1810	9,000	33,000	11,500	4,000	57,500
1811	7,500	23,500	3,500	7,000	41,500
1812*	9,000	26,500	154,000	20,500	210,000
1813	16,500	51,500	124,000	72,500	264,500
1814	7,000	52,000	53,000	66,000	178,000
Date uncertain	500	4,500	2,000	5,500	12,500
Total	86,500	302,000	369,000	236,000	1,003,500

*Russia.

Adapted from Jacques Houdaille, "Le problem des pertes de guerre," *Revue d' Histoire Moderne et Contemporaine*, XVII (1970) 418.

Napoleon was a destroyer, but not on a monstrous scale. In World War I, in four years, 1914–1918, 1,400,000 Frenchmen were killed, an average of 350,000 per year—more than were killed *and* died in hospital during the Napoleonic Wars.

As for the enemies of France: Their casualties, until 1812, were much higher, perhaps by two or three times. Between 1812 and 1814, however, the Allies went far toward restoring the balance. To hold Napoleon responsible for these deaths, though, would be to ignore the rapaciousness of other European rulers, all of whom, except for George III of England, were allied with Napoleon at one time or another.

PRELUDE TO WAR

Napoleon treated the Peace of Amiens with Britain (1802) as a truce. He kept French markets closed to the British and forced Spain[8] and the sister republics to limit theirs. He attempted to revive the French Empire in America (Louisiana and the West Indies; see below, p. 304). More alarming to George III's government, however, he extended French power on the Mediterranean shores.

In 1802, Napoleon annexed Piedmont and Elba (just evacuated by the British) to France, and took over Parma-Piacenza. Meanwhile, he was named president of the Italian (formerly Cisalpine) Republic by a Consulta elected under the supervision of troops under Murat, who was advised by francophiles such as Melzi d'Eril. His agents were at work in the Ottoman Empire, and he allowed a report on the weakness of Egyptian defenses by General Sebastiani to be published in the official *Moniteur*—hinting at a possible new invasion. He kept garrisons in Naples (until 1805). Not strangely, the British refused to give up Malta, as agreed at Amiens, but offered to negotiate. Napoleon replied by publicly insulting the British ambassador, Lord Whitworth. Britain resumed the war on the high seas in May 1803.

Napoleon immediately seized Hanover (a possession of George III), extending his power to the center of Germany. In 1803, also, Germany was reorganized under the *Reichsdeputationshauptschluss*—the decision of a deputation of the Holy Roman Empire, which went beyond what had been agreed at Lunéville. Under French influence, 112 of the smaller states disappeared, including all but one of the ecclesiastical states. Their territories went to potential allies of Napoleon, notably Bavaria, Württemberg, Saxony, and Baden. The Holy Roman Emperor, Francis II, was not pleased.

Russia's new Czar Alexander I, not so enchanted by Napoleon as his murdered father, began to see a French threat to his interests in the Baltic. He restored relations with Britain and leaned toward an alliance.

In 1804, Napoleon further shook the powers by his legalized murder of Duke d'Enghien. (See above, p. 208.) He forced Genoa to close her port to the British and the Batavian Republic (Holland) and Spain to declare war on Britain. Finally, Napoleon took the title of "Emperor," a particular blow to Francis II of Austria. (See above, p. 210.)

KINGDOM OF ITALY

In May 1805, Napoleon crowned himself "King of Italy" in the Cathedral of Milan, using the Iron Crown of the ancient kings of Lombardy. A medal struck for the occasion read "Napoleo Rex Totius Italiae" (Napoleon King of all Italy).

---

[8] Spain, defeated by France had made peace and had become an ally of France in 1795. The treaty was still in effect.

The kingdom of Italy was another incarnation of the Italian Republic. It had been ruled for President Bonaparte by its vice-president, Francesco Melzi d'Eril, who was replaced by a viceroy, Josephine's son, Eugène de Beauharnais, now a tall, handsome cavalry officer of twenty-three. Austria had consoled herself that Bonaparte's rule over a republic was temporary. However, the kingdom had to be taken more seriously. Russia felt her interests in the Balkans menaced. In addition, the "King of All Italy" style greatly alarmed the pope and the Bourbons of Naples. The success of the coronation disturbed them further. Some 30,000 people jammed the cathedral; thousands more waited outside to cheer.

Russia had allied with Britain in April 1805; Austria joined the coalition in August, by which time Napoleon had infuriated the Austrian emperor further by annexing Genoa to France. The pope lent moral support to the Allies. Naples allied with France, but Queen Marie-Caroline (sister of Marie Antoinette), was in contact with Austria and Russia, and her sympathies were not with Napoleon. "New Attila" and "Corsican Bastard" were two of her milder names for him.

INVASION OF ENGLAND?

Since 1803, Napoleon had been building an army at Boulogne, ostensibly to invade England. It is difficult to believe that in 1805 he was still serious about this. If he managed to cross the channel with an army—a chancy business—he might conquer England (British land forces were very small) but lose France to his continental enemies. In Italy he had alerted the army for Austrian attack, inspected the fortresses, and sent Masséna to assist Eugène. His correspondence indicates that his attention was more on Europe than on England. Whether or not he intended to invade, Napoleon continued to act as if he did, taking command at Boulogne on 3 August 1805.

Meanwhile, Admiral Villeneuve had begun execution of an elaborate strategy to give France naval supremacy in the Channel long enough to permit a crossing. On 30 March, with the Toulon fleet, he raced for the West Indies. Nelson, with the British Mediterranean fleet, was expected to follow him. Villeneuve was to elude Nelson, rendezvous with French fleets from Rochefort and Brest (blockaded by the British Navy), and, augmented by Spanish ships from Cadiz and Ferrol, enter the Channel at the end of August. The bulk of the French navy would thus be concentrated to protect the invasion flotilla, while British naval strength would be dispersed—long enough.

To a point, the strategy worked. Nelson was decoyed to the West Indies but discovered the ruse and sailed for Gibraltar, dispatching a fast brig to tell the admiralty that Villeneuve was bound for Europe—where, he did not know. The brig, by accident, sighted Villeneuve heading for Ferrol (northern Spain). The British were forewarned and kept the French fleet at Brest locked up. Villeneuve, meanwhile, missed his rendezvous with the Rochefort fleet, was mauled by a

British squadron off Ferrol, and made for Cadiz; where he was blockaded by Nelson's fleet (September 1805).

By this time, Napoleon had already called off the invasion of England. He nevertheless damned Villeneuve for cowardice and relieved him of his command. The admiral ignored the orders, and in October sallied forth with a combined French-Spanish fleet to meet the British. On 21 October 1805, off Cape Trafalgar, Nelson utterly destroyed Villeneuve's fleet and captured Villeneuve himself. Ironically, Nelson, the victor, was killed in the battle.[9]

Trafalgar established British supremacy on the high seas for the remainder of the Napoleonic period. At the time, however, the victory was overshadowed by the triumphs of the Grande Armée in Germany. Napoleon on 20 October had taken captive an entire Austrian army at Ulm.

CAMPAIGN OF 1805

On August 22, Napoleon had ordered Villeneuve (all too publicly): "Enter the channel, England is ours. . . . " Actually, units of the "Army of England" were already enroute to Germany. On 24 August he ordered the entire Grande Armée to march for Germany. Austrian armies, which entered Germany on 11 September, found Napoleon upon them weeks before they expected him.

At the end of September the Grande Armée was across the Rhine, 200,000 strong, including 40,000 reserve cavalry. Napoleon's generals were men who would make legend: Murat, the giant, proud Gascon horseman; Ney, the "bravest of the brave," a tall, red-haired, vain Saarlander; Bernadotte, the future king of Sweden; Soult, small, wiry, dynamic; Davout, the "bald eagle," tall, broad-shouldered, a humorless professional. The chief-of-staff was Alexandre Berthier, a severe, swarthy little gamecock.

The Austrian vanguard, 25,000 men, under General Mack, was surrounded at Ulm and captured (20 October); the other Allied forces scattered. Napoleon drove straight for Vienna, picking up 100,000 troops of German allies as he marched. He ignored the Austrian campaign in Italy. "I will lead the enemy in such a dance . . . " he wrote Eugène, "that he will have not time to bother you. . . . " This proved true. The Grande Armée, Murat's cavalry in the lead, took Vienna in November.

The Russian army had arrived late and retreated into Moravia.[10] Czar Alex-

---

[9] Villeneuve was repatriated, and on reaching France, committed suicide (April 1806). Villeneuve had fought with thirty-three ships (eighteen French, fifteen Spanish) against Nelson's twenty-seven. He lost twenty-two ships, sunk or captured. The British lost none.

[10] Chandler attributes their tardiness to a ten-day difference between the Russian calendar and the Gregorian (used by the rest of Europe). Both the Austrian and Russian staffs were so inept that this is possible. (Actually there was a twelve-day difference between the calendars, but the point is the same.)

ander I, young, full of energy, took command. Francis II of Austria joined him with a few troops. Alexander had been reared at the castle of this drillmaster father (where his mentor, a tough sergeant, had leave to beat him) and at the court of his grandmother, Catherine the Great (where he was pampered and dosed with French "philosophy"). He was alternately despot and *philosophe*. In either mood he fancied himself a soldier. He looked the part, at least—blond, tall, muscular, and superbly uniformed.

In late November, Napoleon also moved into Moravia and dispersed his corps for provisioning. This encouraged the czar to attack. His generals urged him to wait for reinforcements from Italy. The Archduke Charles (Karl) had assailed Eugène and Masséna in Italy, confidently expecting that Napoleon would again fight his major campaign there, and had scored victories. On hearing of the disaster at Ulm, however, he disengaged and marched northward at all speed. Alexander knew that Charles was on the way, but his troops were hungry and their morale was deteriorating. He believed that he had Napoleon outnumbered (he did, 87,000 to 73,000), and, not least, wanted the glory for himself. At the end of November, in the face of contrary advice from such as General Michel Kutuzov, who became famous in 1812, he chose to fight.

Alexander advanced from the vicinity of Austerlitz toward Napoleon's head-quarters at Brünn. (See Map 9.1.) To his delight, the French withdrew from the plateau of Pratzen. He decided they were retreating on Vienna. On the morning of 2 December, however, he found Napoleon's army behind the Goldbach Brook, with the south flank thinly covered by Davout's corps, and those of Soult, Bernadotte, and Lannes with Murat's cavalry behind them, on narrower fronts to the north. Alexander ordered the attack and delivered his main blow against Davout, hoping to break through and to cut the road to Vienna, Napoleon's lifeline. He might also then drive the French north, toward Prague, where the Archduke Ferdinand had a small Austrian army.

The czar, however, counted without the terrain. His troops stalled miserably in the half-frozen marshes of the Goldbach and died in hundreds under fire of Davout's infantry and artillery bombs, which shattered trees and sent lethal fragments flying. Angered that his attack was stalled, Alexander continued throughout the morning to throw reinforcements into the hellish mire of the Goldbach, until by noon, he had half his army committed there. Napoleon meanwhile nudged his northern corps forward, then in midafternoon ordered the full attack. Soult's corps crashed through the Russian center and attacked south. Lannes and Bernadotte routed the northern enemy elements; Bernadotte added strength to Soult's southward sweep. The bulk of the Russian army was driven into icy swamps and lakes. Murat's cavalry followed up, charging toward Austerlitz, cutting through the hordes fleeing northward. The "sun of Austerlitz" seemed to hang on the horizon until victory was complete. Snow fell on the retreating remnants of the Allied army, which were so scattered that Murat's horsemen could find no line of retreat to follow. Napoleon had finished the war in one blow.

Map 9.1

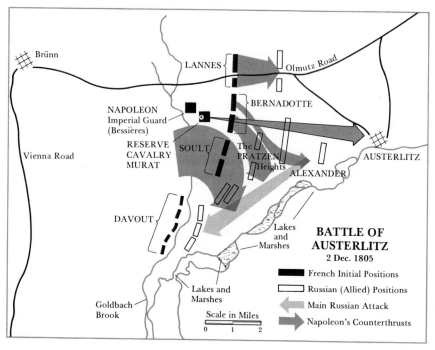

Czar Alexander escaped but made no attempt to resume hostilities—or to come to terms either. Austria made peace at Pressburg on 26 December 1805. She lost Venice and Venetian Istria and Dalmatia to the kingdom of Italy. Napoleon's allies, the Dukes of Bavaria and Württemberg were given Austrian territory (the Tyrol and Vorarlberg) and were made kings. It was a harsh settlement. Surely it made an even more implacable enemy of Austria.

NAPLES

"The dynasty of Naples has ceased to reign," Napoleon proclaimed after Austerlitz. Queen Marie Caroline had finally gone too far, and she was the real ruler; her fat easy-going husband, Ferdinand—"the Nose"—was completely under her thumb. Though allied with France, she had allowed a British-Russian force to land in Naples; it withdrew after Austerlitz. Marie pled for mercy. The "Emperor of all Europe" must know, she wrote Napoleon, that the Allies had forced themselves upon her. He thought that droll. "I will finally fix that whore," he told Talleyrand. Already Masséna was marching on Naples with 40,000 men.

In January 1806, Joseph Bonaparte was dispatched from Paris to assume the "vacant" throne. He had been recalcitrant over the creation of the empire. "Prince

Égalité," Napoleon had called him. But he accepted the crown of Naples after the emperor promised him a free hand in governing and threatened to "disinherit" him if he refused.[11]

The conquest of Naples was a walkover. The Bourbon king and queen fled to Sicily; their armies swiftly followed. Most of the nobles and the middle class remained to welcome the French, anxious that Joseph's army enter quickly and insure their property against notorious *lazzaroni* (city proletariat) of Naples. Only the fortress of Gaeta, under the bomb-shaped, hard-drinking Prince of Hesse-Philippsthal, held out (until July). The British landed 5000 men under Sir John Stuart in Calabria, where he won victories over the surprised French and badly shook their control of the south for a few months. Stuart got little support from the Neapolitan guerrillas, however, since, like it or not, he represented the Bourbons, whom they hated as much as the French. He withdrew.[12]

Meanwhile, Joseph entered his capital in mid-February 1806 through hastily erected triumphal arches. The city fathers greeted him; the clergy celebrated with a *Te Deum* at the Cathedral of Saint January, patron saint of Naples. "I compliment you on your reconciliation with Saint January," wrote Napoleon, adding snidely, "but I hope you have occupied the forts . . . and disarmed the city."

Joseph had seen to his defenses, but his mind was on other things. In early March he wrote Napoleon: "Death from starvation is common here . . . surely something can be done about it." He began widesweeping reforms which were beginning to bear fruit when he was "transferred" to Spain (1808). The new rulers, Murat and Caroline Bonaparte, continued some of them.[13]

HOLLAND

In 1806, Napoleon also converted the Batavian Republic into the kingdom of Holland under his brother Louis. The Republic's "Grand Pensionary," Rutger Jan Schimmelpennick, had governed well and also supplied money and naval units to France. But he haggled over Dutch obligations to France and argued that the Netherlands should be a vast free port, trading with all the world. France would both share the profits and would have access to anything she needed—British and colonial goods included. To Napoleon the scheme was anathema, since it would also benefit the British.

When in 1806 Schimmelpennick began to go blind, the emperor had an excuse to change the government. His first impulse was to annex Holland to

---

[11] Joseph's rights in the imperial succession were also guaranteed. This represented a new turn in Napoleon's thinking. Thereafter his rulers all had dual citizenship and would (he hoped) place France first in their allegiance.

[12] The Bourbons, with popular support, had overthrown the French-sponsored Parthenopean Republic in 1799, but they had rewarded their people with repression.

[13] Details will be given in Chapter 10 on the administration of Naples and all the other satellite and puppet states.

France. But that might alarm neutral Prussia and push King Frederick William into active alliance with the czar. And Louis, Napoleon thought, would be easy to control. Earlier a spirited soldier, and still nominally an officer, Louis had taken to dreamy intellectualism and to visiting the baths to nurse real or imagined ills.

Talleyrand informed the Dutch of Napoleon's plans for a kingdom. In April 1806, Schimmelpennick assembled a "Great Committee" (his legislature and ministry), which, after attempts to negotiate with the emperor, was told to accept a constitutional monarchy or Holland would be annexed to France. On 5 June a Dutch delegation dutifully appeared in Paris and formally petitioned the emperor to create a kingdom under Louis Bonaparte. Napoleon gracefully acceded.

On 15 June 1806, Louis departed for the Hague. Enroute he proclaimed, "I have changed my nationality." He meant it. Because he became so thoroughly Dutch, his reign was very short, but surprisingly productive.

THE USES OF HYPOCRISY Why the charade? Why the deputation, request, and the rest? Wasn't it obvious that Napoleon was forcing a new government on the Dutch? No, it wasn't, because the press was tightly controlled. The Dutch were told that their leaders had freely asked for a Bonaparte king. If rumor said otherwise, the public falsehood was easier to take. Moreover, many hoped that if liberty were lost (or reduced) by accepting Louis, Holland might be better treated because of his presence. After all, he was the emperor's brother. If he were as determined to be Dutch as he said, who could better present Dutch views? For the crowned heads of Europe, it was also convenient to accept the official fiction. Napoleon persisted in such charades, which gave an aura of legality to his actions and masked his use of force and threats.

CONFEDERATION OF THE RHINE

In July 1806, Napoleon proclaimed himself Protector of the Confederation of the Rhine *(Rheinbund)*, initially composed of sixteen German states, of which the largest were Bavaria, Württemberg, Baden, and Hesse-Darmstadt. Prussia and her allies Brunswick, Hesse-Cassel, and Saxony, did not join.[14] The Holy Roman Emperor, realizing that he had been replaced in Germany by the emperor of the French, abdicated his title and became simply the emperor of Austria.[15] For the moment, sympathy of the king of Prussia was with Francis of Austria, though the powers had long been rivals in Germany. Austria, however, was too weak to think in terms of an alliance.

Prussia had other complaints. She had been allowed to occupy Hanover in return for signing a preliminary alliance with France after Austerlitz (15 Decem-

---

[14] After 1807, only Prussia remained outside the Bund, however.

[15] Francis (Franz) II, Holy Roman Emperor, became Francis I of Austria.

ber 1805). In February 1806, Napoleon bullied King Frederick William III into signing a definitive treaty which gave him Hanover outright, but ceded more Prussian possessions to France's clients and closed Prussian ports to Britain. The British declared war on Prussia and began sweeping the sea of her commerce. Shortly thereafter, the king heard that Napoleon had offered Hanover to Britain in exchange for peace. Angry and humiliated, he still hesitated to risk war. His military advisors, however, convinced him that a preemptive strike against French forces—in Germany since 1805—would assure the aid of both Russia and Britain. He reluctantly took the role of Frederick the Great.

WAR AGAIN

Prussia allied with Russia in July 1806, mobilized in August, and without waiting for her ally sent her army southwest, toward the Thuringian Forest. The king hoped to block French forces there until the Russians reinforced him. Napoleon gave him no chance, but struck with an army of 260,000, one-fourth German. He was thirty-seven; Davout, his chief subordinate, thirty-six. The Prussians had 125,000 effectives, led by the Duke of Brunswick, seventy-one, and Prince Hohenlohe, sixty. The two hated each other, commanded an obsolete army, and coordinated nothing. On 14 October their forces were destroyed in twin battles at Jena and Auerstädt. What troops remained withdrew to East Prussia (as did Frederick William and his court). The French took Berlin and marched east.

FRIEDLAND In the winter of 1806–1807 the French pursued the Russians, who steadily refused to fight, over the vast expanses of Poland and East Prussia. It was February 1807 before a major battle was fought, at Eylau—bloody but not a Napoleonic victory, thanks to the late-day arrival of a Prussian corps. In the spring the maneuvering speeded up.

In June 1807 the enemy made a fatal error. Benningsen took the main Russian Army (60,000) across the Alle River at Friedland to crush 10,000 men under Marshal Lannes. Since there were only three bridges, it was a slow, all-night operation. Lannes got word to Napoleon at Eylau. The emperor fired off orders to scattered corps which concentrated 80,000 men at Friedland and rode there "hell for leather" to deploy them. By the time Benningsen deployed to fight (14 June), French forces could hold their own, and by afternoon, went on the attack. The Russians could not escape—driven through Friedland, which was set afire, and into the river, they were butchered, drowned, and burned alive. Victory was complete. (See Map 9.2.)

TILSIT

The czar and the king of Prussia made peace at Tilsit (7–9 July 1807). Napoleon made an ally of the czar, whom he literally met halfway—on a raft in

Map 9.2

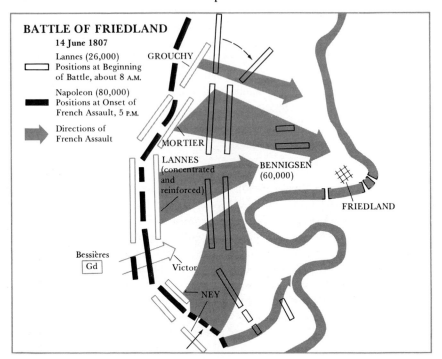

BATTLE OF FRIEDLAND
14 June 1807
Lannes (26,000)   GROUCHY
Positions at Beginning
of Battle, about 8 A.M.

Napoleon (80,000)
Positions at Onset of
French Assault, 5 P.M.

Directions of
French Assault

MORTIER

LANNES
(concentrated   BENNIGSEN
and   (60,000)
reinforced)

FRIEDLAND

Bessières
Gd

Victor

NEY

the Niemen River—and completely charmed. He gave Russia a bit of East Prussia and talked of dividing control of Europe and of partitioning the Ottoman Empire between France and Russia. Prussia was treated very roughly. She was assessed an indemnity (set in 1808 at 140,000,000 francs) and was to support French troops in her key fortresses until it was paid. Prussian Poland was taken to form the Grand Duchy of Warsaw and placed under the rule of Napoleon's ally, King Frederick Augustus of Saxony,[16] and was included, with Saxony, in the Confederation of the Rhine. Prussia also lost territory to the Grand Duchy of Berg, created for Marshal Murat in 1806, and to the new kingdom of Westphalia, to be ruled by Napoleon's brother Jerome. (See below, p. 283.) Alexander agreed to try to mediate peace between France and Britain, promising, if he failed, to ally with France, to declare war on Britain, and to close Russian ports to British commerce. Frederick William similarly agreed to close his ports and pledged Prussia to cooperate with Russia and France to force Denmark, Sweden, and Portugal to do likewise. The British, unwilling to let Denmark block the entrance to the Baltic, bombarded Copenhagen in September 1807 and sank or captured the whole Danish fleet.

---

[16] The king had been Duke of Saxony and had allied with Prussia in 1806, but switched sides after the Battle of Jena. He was king by grace of Napoleon.

Napoleon, nevertheless, controlled Europe, and was in a position to intensify economic war against Britain.

THE CONTINENTAL SYSTEM

Britain, in May 1806, had published Orders-in-Council placing the European coast from Brest to the Elbe under blockade. Napoleon struck back with the Berlin Decree of 21 November 1806, which established the Continental System (*blocus continental*). It banned British ships from all continental ports, all ships carrying British goods, and ships that had taken on cargoes at British ports, including colonial ports. It further declared a blockade of the British Isles, which he could not enforce, but hoped to.[17] British goods were made subject to confiscation.

Napoleon had multiple aims: to bankrupt the "nation of shopkeepers" by shutting off its principal markets in Europe (one-third of British exports went to Europe in 1806); to unify Europe against Britain, and, insofar as possible, to end her dependence on British trade by promoting European (particularly French) industry and by redirecting her trade to other channels; to solidify his own power by denying to Britain the advantages she had gained over the centuries by maintaining a precarious balance of power in Europe; to challenge British-inspired laws-of-the sea by upholding (or pretending to uphold) freedom of the seas and thereby to acquire the support of neutrals, such as the United States, thus gaining a modicum of world leadership. (The preamble to the Berlin Decree stressed freedom of the seas and condemned the British blockade as illegal.)

Britain responded to the *blocus* by extending her blockade to all ports controlled by France or her allies. Napoleon's *riposte* was the Milan Decrees (23 November, 17 December 1807), which made all ships forfeit that had touched a British port or had submitted to search by the Royal Navy. Neutral vessels became fair game for both the French and British. After 1807, no nation could remain aloof from the British-French struggle. The French, mostly privateers, seized vessels if they carried British goods. British vessels took them if they tried to run any other kind of goods to Europe. The United States and other neutrals were greatly affected, as well as colonial areas, notably Latin America. (This will be discussed in detail in Chapter 10.)

The Continental System did not break the British economy, but only because Europeans (never happy with the *blocus*) violated the System with gusto when Napoleon again went to war—against Spain in mid-1808, Austria in 1809, and Russia in 1812. From July 1807 until June 1808, and again from early 1810 until 1812, however, Europe was fairly well sealed to British commerce. In the first

---

[17] Napoleon refused to consider Trafalgar decisive. He was building a new navy in French, Dutch, and Italian ports. It was never strong enough to concern the British seriously, but Richard Glover estimates that it would have been if the French empire had lasted a few years longer.

case (1807–1808) Britain's exports dropped 20 percent; and her industrial production nearly 10 percent, firing off, among other disturbances, a strike of 60,000
workers in the Manchester area. In the second case (1810–1812), the System,
combined with overspeculation and overproduction during late 1808 and 1809,
caused a recession in British industry in 1810 and a depression in 1811–1812.
British exports dropped 36 percent in 1811, and industrial output 25 percent. The
Luddites, who blamed their unemployment on new technology, had been smashing machines and fomenting riots for a year when Napoleon's invasion of Russia
sparked a recovery in English industry.

The British made up for losses of legal European markets partly by smuggling,
with the help of European businessmen, dare-devil "enterprisers," and of corrupt
officials who catered to a public eager to buy. They also found new markets,
particularly in Brazil (where the Portuguese court fled on British battleships) and
in Spanish America. But it is a myth that Britain was saved by Latin American
trade. The depression of 1811–1812 was partly brought on by overextension of
credit in Central and South America. It was principally smuggling that enabled
the British to beat the Continental System. In order, at least, to share profits,
Napoleon, in 1810, began granting licenses for the importation of contraband
goods at 50 percent tariff duties. (See below, p. 261.)

For Europe, the Continental System meant lean years, but also a steady
growth of industry. (See above, p. 216 and remarks, by country, in Chapter 10.)
The closed economy, protected industry, war and the ensuing profits helped to
lay the groundwork for industrialization in the nineteenth century. Capital was
accumulated; speculators were turned into managers; labor was brought together
in factories; banking grew to accommodate the needs. The Anzin Coal Company
is a good example of an industry almost destroyed by the Revolution and revived
by Napoleon's favor and the Continental System. The Perier family, which took
control of the company in 1816, is a good example of industrial capitalists shaped
under Napoleon. In 1831–1832, Casimir Perier, who had opposed the Bourbons,
was premier of France. The family of Camillo di Cavour, future "unifier" of Italy,
made its fortune in this period. German entrepreneurs in the Ruhr laid the
foundations for the later formidable steel and arms industry.

Europe, nevertheless, hated the Continental System. It brutally subordinated
the economies of other states to that of France (as will be covered in detail in the
next chapter). Napoleon's satellite states, most directly subject to his will, were
hardest hit, including those created after Tilsit.

THE GRAND DUCHY OF WARSAW

Warsaw, placed after Tilsit under the king of Saxony, stood as a pledge to the
Poles for the resurrection of the kingdom of Poland, though Napoleon never
made specific promises to that effect. Some Poles had fought with the French
since the partitions (the last in 1795) had divided their country among Prussia,

Russia, and Austria. Dombrowski's legions had distinguished themselves. The Polish cavalry of the Imperial Guard was noted for its valor.

In 1806, Prince Joseph Poniatowski, a dashing soldier of royal blood, rallied the Poles against the Russians. In 1807 most of the high nobility cast their lot with Napoleon. He had defeated all the partitioning powers. What better hope for Poland?

Poland continued to supply troops. It was the eastern bastion of the empire until 1813, and many Poles fought with the French until Napoleon fell. The kingdom of Poland was not reconstituted, but Napoleon made a valiant attempt to give the grand duchy enlightened government.

WESTPHALIA

The kingdom of Westphalia, also created at Tilsit, comprised Prussia east of the Elbe; her late allies, Brunswick and Hesse-Cassel; part of Hanover; and some lesser states. The crown went to the youngest Bonaparte, Jerome, fifteen years Napoleon's junior. Handsome, much indulged, he was perhaps Europe's most notorious playboy. He had served in the navy, howbeit with monumental insubordination, but some valor, and as a general in the recent campaign. Napoleon admired his spirit and intelligence but did not trust him fully.

With seeming illogic, the emperor, nevertheless, expected him to make Westphalia the model state of the Rheinbund. It was to have an active parliament, French-style administration and courts, and the Code Napoléon. To a surprising degree, Jerome molded the state to Napoleon's specifications. It served France well and left an enduring legacy.

THE SPANISH ALLY

With northern Europe reorganized by the Treaties of Tilsit, Napoleon, in the latter part of 1807, turned his attention to the Iberian Peninsula. Spain and Portugal had fouled his political and economic systems.

Spain, defeated in 1794–1795 by the French Republic, had been passively allied with France since 1795. The alliance had brought her nothing but grief. The British had ruined her trade and interdicted her communications with her colonies. France had taken Santo Domingo (1795) and Louisiana (1801), lost one and sold the other. (See below, p. 304 *ff*; Chapter 11, pp. 311–314.) In 1803, Charles IV promised Napoleon a subsidy of 6,000,000 francs a year (which he never paid) in lieu of declaring war on Britain but had been forced into the war anyway in 1804. He supplied Napoleon with troops and thirty naval vessels which were shot to pieces at Trafalgar. The Spanish economy was disrupted; the port cities were wracked by labor unrest and violence. Humiliated by the French, the Spanish equally damned their own leaders.

The government was dominated by Prince Manuel Godoy, first minister, generalissimo of the army and navy, and Prince of the Peace (of 1795). He was also the lover of the queen, Maria Louisa—aging, debauched, but forceful. She scorned her husband, Charles IV, who was absorbed with horses, dogs, and hunting, and, at intervals, was insane. Ferdinand, the crown prince, intrigued constantly to seize the crown and to ruin Godoy. In his early twenties, Ferdinand was dumpy, with a low forehead and the jutting "Habsburg jaw," which, however, was the mark of highest royalty. To his subjects, he was prince charming, especially since they saw his accession to the throne as their only hope for better times. Many Spanish liberals backed him also, though in 1807, after an abortive attempt to overthrow his father (and, the queen said, to poison her), he had betrayed a number of them—including the Duke d'Infantado—to save his own skin. In 1808 he was begging Napoleon to give him a Bonaparte bride.

Not only was the dynasty degenerate, but the Spanish government was wildly ineffective, wasteful, graft-ridden, top-heavy with officials, burdened with pensioners, and unofficially bankrupt. The Church, whose hierarchy was virtually part of the government, was overstaffed and costly. Almost one man in ten was a monk or friar. The Inquisition, intent on rooting out "subversives," had imprisoned or exiled many of the king's most talented subjects.

To Napoleon, Spain had been simply a poor ally. Charles IV had given him little money, and in his judgment, untrustworthy troops and antiquated warships. He had also failed to close Portugal, as instructed, to the British, and Spain was herself violating the Continental System. To add insult to injury, Godoy had ordered Spanish forces mobilized against "the Enemy" in 1806, and then, after Jena, demobilized them, explaining to the French ambassador with incredible *sang froid* that the "Enemy" had been Portugal.

Portugal, surely, was not a friendly power. The prince regent, John (the queen was insane) professed neutrality, but worked hand in glove with the British, as had his Braganza ancestors for a hundred years.

Neither Spain nor Portugal was a military threat, but either might allow the British to land in the Peninsula. They were hurting the effectiveness of the Continental System. Moreover, Napoleon was convinced that if Portugal and Spain were properly administered, they could yield him revenues and troops. And why should the people not be grateful if he overthrew their pitiful rulers and gave them effective government?

Godoy provided a key for opening the Peninsula. Aware that his power would end with the death of Charles IV, if not before, he betrayed his country in return for the promise of a kingdom in Portugal guaranteed by Napoleon. By the Treaty of Fontainebleau (27 October 1807), Godoy agreed to allow French troops to cross Spanish territory to attack Portugal and to establish a "reserve" at Bayonne, which was actually the advance guard of an army intended to invade Spain.

A French army under General Junot seized Lisbon in November 1807. The Portuguese royal family was taken to Brazil by the British navy. More French troops gradually moved into Spain, occupied the northern fortresses, and marched on Madrid. Confused Spanish commanders reacted variously, but except at Barcelona, offered little resistance to stop the march of their French allies. By March 1808 there were 100,000 French troops in Spain. Napoleon went to Bayonne, on the Spanish border, and sent Marshal Murat to command the invasion. On 25 March, Murat entered Madrid, escorted by a part of the Imperial Guard, including Mamelukes and Polish cavalry, the band of the Guard Cavalry and 40,000 men in parade formation. The Madrileños welcomed him with applause and cheers. They thought he had come to secure the throne for Ferdinand. Murat was as jubilant as they; he thought he would be made king; his wife Caroline Bonaparte was pressing his case with the emperor. (See Map 9.3a, p. 251.)

EXIT THE BOURBONS

The Bourbons meanwhile contrived to make things easy for Napoleon. On 17 March 1808, at Aranjuez, the royal summer residence, the crown prince overthrew his father and proclaimed himself Ferdinand VII. He appealed to the French emperor for support. To Napoleon's delight, so did Charles IV and Maria Louisa. Ferdinand rode into Madrid with only two guards to greet Murat and bid for support, offering to deliver Godoy safely to Napoleon, who was at Bayonne.[18] Napoleon wanted more than Godoy, however. He had decided that the Bourbons must go. Ferdinand was a slippery character, and if the British offered him aid, he could be more dangerous than Charles IV.

The emperor ordered Murat to send both kings and all members of the royal family to Bayonne (just inside France) for "talks." Ferdinand went fearfully, but reasoned that if the emperor opposed him, he was lost. He had less courage, it proved, than his subjects. On 10 May, at Bayonne, both kings abdicated and all their possible successors renounced their rights. All were dispatched to palatial imprisonment in France. The emperor summoned Joseph Bonaparte from Naples to assume the vacant throne. Murat and Caroline would have to settle for the throne of Naples.

DOS DE MAYO

At Madrid, however, there had been trouble. On 2 May *(Dos de Mayo)*, the capital rose in insurrection. Murat was not taken by surprise, however, since Napoleon had told him to expect an uprising and even expressed hope that there

---

[18] Godoy had been captured at Aranjuez after hiding for two days rolled in a rug. His last service to Napoleon was helping persuade Charles IV to abdicate quietly. He got no reward except safe exile in France.

would be one so that the Madrileños could be treated to the "whiff of grapeshot." Murat's troops moved in from the outskirts, driving the people before them. His cannon were fired point blank into the crowds, clearing the way for infantry and cavalry.

At the Puerta de Sol, the Mamelukes, fired at from buildings, dismounted and charged inside, killing men, women, and children and rolling their heads into the streets. Spain still remembers. In popular history the Dos de Mayo is the day the demon emperor of the French set Moslems on the Christians of Madrid. There were only eighty-seven Mamelukes there, but Napoleon was from then on identified by the rebels with the Moors, ancient oppressors of the Spanish.

The rebellion was smashed. Napoleon was pleased. Surely Spanish morale was broken! Madrid, in fact, would not rise again. But Madrid was not Paris; to cow the capital was not so important as in France. The Spanish were province-oriented. The Madrileños—men, women, and children—fighting with obsolete weapons, kitchen knives, sticks and stones—heaving furniture, tiles, and chamber pots from upper floors, had set an example all Spain would follow.

JUNTA OF BAYONNE

Napoleon was further pleased—and misled—by the Spanish National Junta he called to Bayonne. In May 1808 distinguished Spaniards flooded into the little town. The Prince de Castelfranco, the Dukes del Parque and d'Infantado came, as did eminent liberals such as Francisco Cabarrus, Gonzalo O'Farrill, Pedro Cevallos, and Don Manuel Romero. Two archbishops appeared, and the heads of the Franciscan and Dominican orders. The Cardinal de Bourbon, cousin of Charles IV, sent his best wishes. Gaspar Jovellanos, Spain's most famous author, sent an encouraging letter.

The emperor wrote enthusiastically to Joseph, who was reluctant to leave Naples. Spain was a richer kingdom; the opportunities for reform were unlimited. No war of conquest would be necessary. The notables of Spain had come to greet him; they wanted a new dynasty. On 7 June, Joseph arrived at Bayonne.

Joseph was welcomed cordially by representatives of the nobility, clergy, army, and towns. The junta approved a liberal constitution. He was crowned (7 July) by the archbishop of Burgos. He easily assembled a ministry of eminent Spaniards. In high spirits, he and his cabinet left for Madrid on 9 July, escorted by Imperial and Royal (mostly French) Guards.

SPAIN IN REBELLION

Fired initially by the clergy, who saw Napoleon as the devil's servant, a grass-roots rebellion blazed up and spread. Most nobles, fearing loss of their traditional authority, happily took leadership. Those who urged moderation were often lynched. The religious peasants were easy recruits. So were the workers, already violently anti-French, especially in the ports, ruined by the Continental

System. Spanish liberals—noble and commoner—had to make a choice between the popular cause and being *afrancesados* (francophiles, with "traitor" implied). The majority sided with the rebels, including Jovellanos. But an impressive group, in numbers and talent, stuck with Joseph. (See Chapter 10, p. 279.)

Thorough provincials, the people thought of themselves as Catalans, Aragonese, Castilians. . . . They fought not for Spain but for the crown and Church. Theirs was a medieval nationalism, but, nevertheless, powerful. They identified Ferdinand VII with the "hero kings" who had freed Spain from the Moors, and because of the 700-year crusade, patriotism and church loyalty were inseparable.

In the provinces not occupied by the French, rebel juntas took over. Armies of volunteers formed around regular regiments. In the north the leaders were the aging General Cuesta, Don José Palafox, and Don Joaquin Blake, the latter two of part Irish ancestry. In the south there were Castaños, Montijo, the Irish General Felix Jones, and the French émigré Marquis de Coupigny. Later, the armies would prove extremely fragile. In the summer of 1808, however, those in the south took a toll of the overconfident and overextended French.

ENTER AND EXIT JOSEPH

Joseph proceeded easily to Madrid, the road cleared by Marshal Bessières, who set to flight disorganized rebels under Cuesta and Blake at Medina del Rio Seco. But the king was alarmed at the greeting "his people" gave him. Cities and villages fell silent on his approach; the inhabitants hid behind boarded doors and windows as he passed. He wrote Napoleon repeatedly, some days several times. The country, he said, was fused to explode. "No one has told Your Majesty the truth." Nonsense, the emperor replied. Courage. "All the better people" are for you.

Joseph found Madrid (20 July) in sinister quiet. Almost immediately, however, some of his followers began disappearing. A week after his arrival, he learned why. At Baylen, in Andalusia, General Dupont's corps of 30,000 had been captured by Castaños' rebels. Others had forced Moncey out of Valencia. French commander as well as king, Joseph had to decide whether to stand or withdraw. Rebel victories indicated there might be great hordes marching on the capital. (Actually, he had more troops than they.)

On 31 July, after eleven days in Madrid, he retreated, and in August regrouped all his forces north of the Ebro River. Napoleon was furious. "I can see . . . I must return and set the machine in motion again." Joseph was ready to call it quits. He did not want to be a king by conquest, he wrote Napoleon. "I would not live long enough to atone for all that evil." The emperor ignored his plea.

A LESSON FOR THE SPANISH   Napoleon raced to Erfurt (October 1808) to confer with the czar. Alexander renewed the alliance with France on promise of a free hand in the Ottoman Empire, with which Russia was at war. Central Europe "safe," the emperor ordered the Grande Armée from Germany to Spain.

Meanwhile, Portugal was lost. In August, Junot had pounced with careless confidence on a British invasion force at Vimiero and had been defeated by Sir Arthur Wellesley (later Duke of Wellington).[19] It was Joseph's defeat, however, which plagued Napoleon. The nation defied him in Spain. A rebel junta, governing in the name of Ferdinand VII, sat in Madrid. The Spanish victory at Baylen inspired France's enemies all over Europe. Rebel propaganda mockingly spoke of Joseph's "visit." He was now "Pepe Botellas" (Joe Bottle)—a bungling drunkard.

NAPOLEON IN SPAIN

By early November, Napoleon had 300,000 troops north of the Ebro in Spain and an elite of French commanders—Ney, Lannes, Soult, Mortier, and Lefebvre. Joseph, headquartered at Vitoria, was ordered to stand fast until the emperor arrived to take command. Departing Erfurt on 13 October, Napoleon was back in Paris on the 18th, harrying his ministers, considering reports from all parts of the empire, and bombarding Joseph for information on troops, supplies, and the situation. On 3 November at 3 A.M. he was in Bayonne, on 5 November (incognito) at Vitoria. On the morning of 6 November his presence with the army was announced by a sixty-gun salute. (See Map 9.3b.)

Intelligence revealed no more than 90,000 Spanish troops opposed him, and they were widely dispersed. He issued proclamations to the rebels, demanding that they come to their senses. "The time for illusions is over. . . . I am here with the soldiers who conquered at Austerlitz, at Jena. . . . Who can defeat them?" He lectured to Spanish delegations, including one of monks whose order was notorious for leading guerrillas. *"Monsieurs les moines* if you are determined to meddle in military affairs, I promise you I will cut off your ears." He had offered Spain the best of kings, he said repeatedly. Joseph would be restored; accept him and prosper; resist and die.

On 9 November the Grande Armée crossed the Ebro. (See Map 9.3b.) Napoleon, with Ney and the main body, drove on Madrid, while behind him Soult drove the Spanish left into the mountains of Asturias and Lannes pinned 45,000 under Palafox in Saragossa. Napoleon took Burgos and marched to the pass of the Somo Sierra in the Guadarramas, where on 30 November he was stopped by 9000 men under Benito San Juan, whose cannon raked the narrow defile. Here the Polish cavalry of the guard made legend. At the emperor's order they charged the guns head-on and routed the whole Spanish force. Half of the eighty-seven Poles were killed and the rest wounded. Napoleon glorified them in a bulletin and gave them all—living and dead—the Legion of Honor. On 4

---

[19] After the battle, by the Convention of Cintra, Junot agreed to allow his army to be returned to France by the British navy, which was done.

Map 9.3a

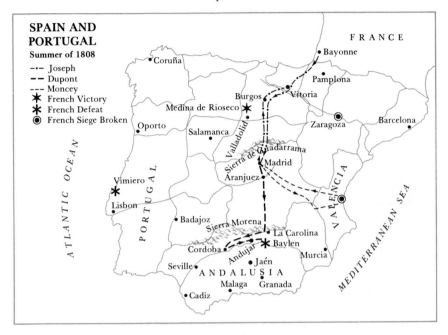

SPAIN AND PORTUGAL

Summer of 1808

—·— Joseph
— — Dupont
--- Moncey
✱ French Victory
✱ French Defeat
◉ French Siege Broken

FRANCE

• Bayonne
• Coruña
Pamplona
Burgos • — Vitoria
Medina de Rioseco ✱
• Oporto   Salamanca •   Zaragoza ◉   • Barcelona
Valladolid
Sierra de Guadarrama
• Madrid
Aranjuez •
Vimiero ✱   VALENCIA
• Lisbon
• Badajoz   Sierra Morena
La Carolina
Cordoba •   Andujar   ✱ Baylen
Seville •   • Jaén   Murcia •
ANDALUSIA
Malaga   Granada
• Cadiz

ATLANTIC OCEAN
PORTUGAL
MEDITERRANEAN SEA

Map 9.3b

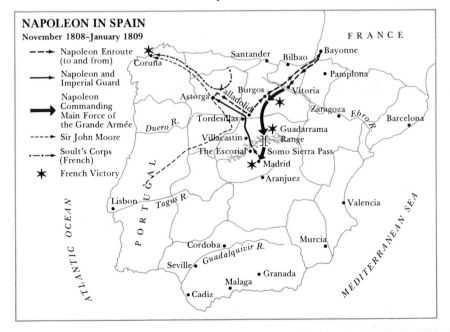

NAPOLEON IN SPAIN

November 1808–January 1809

- - ► Napoleon Enroute (to and from)
——► Napoleon and Imperial Guard
━━► Napoleon Commanding Main Force of the Grande Armée
- - - ► Sir John Moore
—·—·► Soult's Corps (French)
✱ French Victory

FRANCE

Santander   Bilbao • — Bayonne
Coruña
Pamplona •
Astorga   Burgos ✱   Vitoria
Valladolid
Zaragoza   Ebro R.   • Barcelona
Duero R.   Tordesillas •
Villacastin   Guadarrama ✱ Range
The Escorial •   Somo Sierra Pass
✱ Madrid
Aranjuez •
Lisbon •   Tagus R.   • Valencia
Cordoba •
Guadalquivir R.   Murcia •
Seville •   • Granada
Malaga •
• Cadiz

ATLANTIC OCEAN
PORTUGAL
MEDITERRANEAN SEA

December 1808, a month after he entered Spain, the Emperor entered Madrid in triumph.

Napoleon announced to the Madrileños that they had a choice between him and Joseph as king. He then offered them an oath of loyalty to Joseph, which they rushed to sign. Meanwhile, by imperial edict, he abolished the Inquisition (and seized its treasury, over 600,000 francs), suppressed most monasteries and convents, proclaimed an end to feudal privilege, and confiscated the property of rebels (dividing the proceeds between Joseph's government and his own). Then, suddenly, he was gone.

On 19 December word reached Napoleon that an English army of 30,000 under Sir John Moore was in the vicinity of Valladolid. Moore, unaware of the fate of the Spanish armies, had marched from Portugal to reinforce them, and blundered into the rear of the Grande Armée. "It is a gift of Providence. . . . " the emperor mused, hardly able to believe the reports. He would finally meet the British—on land—and with the odds ten to one against them.

Hastily restoring Joseph to his throne, Napoleon marched north with the Imperial Guard over the Guadarramas through a raging snowstorm which forced the cavalry to dismount and lead their mounts, the emperor in the vanguard. Ahead of him, Soult was in contact with Moore, Ney was moving to reinforce him, and Napoleon hoped to win a battle at Astorga. Moore, however, made for Corunna on the northwest coast. Napoleon turned back to Valladolid and gave command of the pursuit to Soult.

Messages from Paris told him that Austria was mobilizing for war, and (less serious but more infuriating) that Talleyrand, Fouché, and his sister Caroline were plotting to have Marshal Murat named his successor in case he were killed in Spain.

On 16 January 1809, Napoleon left for Paris, riding hard. He left behind orders restoring Joseph to overall command of the Army of Spain (the Grande Armée, though some units and commanders were called north in the spring). "If nothing prevents," he wrote the king, "I shall return toward the end of February."

Napoleon was destined never to return to Spain, however. If he had, the history of the empire might have been altogether different.

"THAT MISERABLE SPANISH AFFAIR"

On the day the emperor departed (16 January 1809), Soult fought Moore at Corunna. Moore died on the field, mangled by a French cannonball, but on the 17th, his troops were rescued by the Royal Navy. Still, to Napoleon, affairs in the Peninsula seemed all but settled. Spanish armies had been demolished. After Moore's defeat, Portugal seemed open to conquest. Joseph was again installed at Madrid, where the population seemed eminently docile.

Madrid was not as important as Napoleon thought, however. Moreover, the British were more stubborn than he dreamed. They returned Wellesley (Wellington) to Portugal within weeks, and the French were never able to dislodge him. Meanwhile, the Spanish armies, supplied by the British, re-formed and challenged again. For five years they lost every major battle against the French, but always reappeared.

To their aid came hordes of guerrillas. The rebel government (which retreated to Seville, then Cadiz) legalized the murder of Frenchmen. The mountainous terrain favored the bands; the people protected and supplied them. Churchmen blessed them and passed information; some monks became leaders. A widely used catechism read: "Are we at liberty to kill the French? Not only are we but it is our sacred duty to do so."

Joseph's dearest wish was to be a Spanish monarch, govern constitutionally, and bring enlightenment and prosperity to his people. But the Spanish and their British allies would give him no peace. Had Napoleon returned to Spain, the war might have been won, but he did not. The French always outnumbered the enemy, but Joseph could not coordinate their operations. Neither could Napoleon from Paris. By mid-1810, Spain, save Cadiz, was occupied. The French, however, could not drive Wellington from Portugal. He was finally recognized by the Spanish as allied commander (1812) and emerged from Portugal to take Madrid (temporarily) in 1812, and in 1813 to drive Joseph from Spain. Meanwhile the war cost the empire 300,000 men, a billion francs in specie, and untold amounts of materiel and arms. The Spanish colonies, some of which, at least, Napoleon hoped would declare for Joseph, all refused. (See Chapter 11.) "That miserable Spanish affair," Napoleon said at St. Helena, " . . . was what killed me."

Still Joseph's reign is important in Spanish history, both because of the reforms he attempted and the effect they had in promoting liberalism on the rebel side. (See Chapter 10.)

THE AUSTRIAN WAR

Arriving in Paris on 24 January 1809, Napoleon made short work of the succession plot. He drove Talleyrand into retirement, calling him "Dung in a silk stocking," accepted Fouché's "proof " of innocence (Napoleon felt he needed the policeman), and forgave Caroline.[20] He then turned to the Austrian threat.

[20] If Napoleon had been a true tyrant, he would have had Talleyrand shot. He had a peculiar loyalty, however, to those whom he owed political debts and whom he had promoted to high office. Talleyrand had displayed overweening sympathy for Austria in 1805, betrayed secrets to the czar in 1807 and 1808, and generally was in correspondence with the enemy, opining that Napoleon was stretching his power too far. The emperor knew that, but reacted only by replacing him in the foreign ministry in 1808 (J.-B. de Champagny took over, then Hughes Maret), and in 1809 only relieved him of his title of Grand Chamberlain. Talleyrand remained Prince of Benevento, a title bestowed by Napoleon, with incomes from Benevento, in Naples, and estates in France. In 1814, Talleyrand was at large, rich and available to become foreign minister of Louis XVIII. Fouché, Duke d'Otranto, was similarly keeping on good terms with certain of the enemy, especially in Britain, but was retained in the police ministry unitl 1810, then only exiled to Aix, and recalled in 1813 and in 1815. In 1815 he was instrumental in forcing Napoleon's second abdication. Caroline was not disloyal in 1809, but she and Murat put Naples in the enemy camp in 1814.

The Spanish rebellion, the withdrawal of thousands of French troops from Germany, and Napoleon's departure from Spain successively raised the hopes of the warhawks in Vienna. Lusting for revenge since 1805, they included the chancellor, Count Philip von Stadion; Maria Ludovica, the beautiful and spirited new empress (third wife of Francis I); Baron Hormayer, an Austrian nationalist born in the Tyrol, which he wanted "liberated" from Bavaria, and the Archdukes John and Ferdinand. They were encouraged by Clemens von Metternich, Austrian ambassador to Paris, who had been told by Talleyrand that the time was ripe for Austria to strike. A swarm of exiles goaded them on—Friedrich von Gentz, Baron vom Stein, August and Friedrich von Schlegel, Corsica's Pozzo di Borgo, Madame de Staël, and others. Belatedly, Archduke Charles reluctantly joined the war party.

Charles, eldest brother of the Emperor Francis, was the only general in Europe who was compared with Napoleon. (Wellington had yet to make his reputation.) Lanky, handsome, and deadly serious about his profession, he had first seen action against France in 1792, and in 1796 was promoted field marshal, at age twenty-five. It was Charles who ruined the French offensive in Germany in 1796 by driving Moreau and Jourdan back across the Rhine. Transferred to Italy, he was too late to stop Napoleon. In 1799 he distinguished himself in the Rhineland and Switzerland. After Austria's defeat in 1800, when he was too ill for active command, Charles devoted himself to reforming the army. He got only sporadic support, and in 1805 he pronounced Austria woefully unprepared and opposed resuming war against France. As a result, Quartermaster General Karl Mack got top command in Germany, and was captured at Ulm. Relegated to Italy, Charles soundly defeated Masséna and Eugène but was ordered to Moravia, where Napoleon won at Austerlitz before he arrived.

Restored to head of the *Hofkriegsrat* (War Council), Charles resumed his reforming efforts, but at the end of 1808 still considered the Austrian army unfit for action. The officer corps was overloaded with nodding veterans of past campaigns (largely unsuccessful) and young, dashing, undisciplined and untrained junior officers (all nobles, of course). The emperor would not allow conscription or commissioning of nonnoble officers, both of which policies struck him as dangerously democratic. Slavic nationalism was not yet a problem, but the largely Austro-German, Hungarian (Magyar), and foreign officers had trouble communicating with Slavic troops—and sometimes Hungarians and Rumanians as well. The Croats, under their own officers, were an exception, but were wild, like Cossacks. The training programs Charles had conceived had been ignored wherever possible; the troops were undisciplined (except for parade) and maneuvered badly. Artillery and infantry weapons were inferior to the French. Supply services were undependable. Charles had organized a National Guard *(Landwehr)* in Austria proper and in Hungary (the "Insurrection"), which he hoped would produce 400,000 troops, but time was needed. As of March 1809, Austria had 300,000 regulars and 230,000 Landwehr.

For a polyglot empire, however, Austria had developed incredible national spirit. Austrian and foreign propagandists had contributed, emulating French methods, spinning out pamphlets, placards, songs, poems, and plays often pointing to the Spanish example. German pan-nationalists, including Stein (at least at this juncture), Schlegel, and Gentz, who were in correspondence with fellow intellectuals in Prussia and the Rheinbund states, loudly predicted that Germans would rally to Austria when hostilities began. The Baron Hormayer assured the warhawks that the Tyrol would rise against Bavaria, and in fact fomented a rebellion under Andreas Hofer before the general war began. The Austrian emperor opted for war, though he could find no allies (save England).

The Archduke Charles accepted command of the armies. In March 1809 he proclaimed a war of German liberation, and on 9 April invaded Bavaria. Germans did not flock to join his forces, however. The Rheinbund states remained loyal to France, and Prussia maintained neutrality.[21]

Napoleon had begun preparations in January, calling up conscripts of the classes of 1809 and 1810. He dispatched Berthier to Germany to organize the 90,000 man Army of the Rhine and Rheinbund forces under Davout, Masséna, and Oudinot, and (recalled from Spain) Lannes, Lefebvre, and Bessières. The emperor left Paris on 13 April; on 17 April he reached his headquarters at Donauworth, in Bavaria, where he took control of an army of 170,000 men. Of these, 50,000 were Germans, however, and less than half the French troops had ever seen battle. Still in Spain were Ney, Soult, Mortier, Victor, and Junot; Murat was in Naples. The archduke's field army was slightly larger than Napoleon's, but divided north and south of the Danube River.

Napoleon struck south of the Danube, defeating Charles' forces in detail at Abensberg, Landshut, Eckmühl, and Regensburg (19–22 April). Charles withdrew his whole army north of the Danube and began regrouping in Moravia. On 13 May, Napoleon was in Vienna. The archduke had extricated the Austrian army almost intact, however, and the wide Danube lay between it and the French.

THE ITALIAN PHASE

Eugène, in Italy, commanded an army of 37,000 Italians and 15,000 French. Assailed at Sacile by superior forces under Archduke John (16 April), he was driven from Venezia and to the line of the Adige. He saved his army, but Napoleon was not pleased. "I should have sent you Masséna. . . . " he wrote. Meanwhile news from Germany reached John, and at the end of April he marched

---

[21] There was an uprising in Westphalia, led by one of Jerome's Hessian generals, but the Bonaparte king's army remained loyal to him, and the rebels were crushed within days. This crisis was followed by an invasion of the kingdom by a few hundred Prussians under Major Ferdinand von Schill (who was disowned by his king) and the young Duke of Brunswick with his "Black Legion of Vengeance." Jerome's troops drove both out. Schill was shortly trapped at Stralsund and died a hero to German nationalists. Brusnwick reached the North Sea coast near Bremen and was rescued by the British navy.

to reinforce Charles. Eugène, determined to prove himself as a general, went into pursuit.

At the crossings of the Piave and the Tagliamento, he inflicted heavy losses on the Austrians, turned aside to crush an army of Hungarians and Croats under Jelacic marching to reinforce John, and pushed the archduke into Hungary. Eugène detached 15,000 men under General Jacques Macdonald to watch John and on 27 May joined Napoleon on the Danube. The emperor was overjoyed. He reinforced Eugène to 45,000 and ordered him, at all costs, to prevent the Archduke John from reinforcing Charles. The first French attempt to cross the Danube had failed (Aspern-Essling 21–22 May); if the archdukes joined forces, the second, greater assault which Napoleon was preparing might be beaten back also.

John had moved north along the Raab River, which flows into the Danube east of Pressburg, and was within sixty miles of the main Austrian army. Macdonald had harassed him all the way, however, and his force of 50,000 was exhausted and hungry. On Eugène's approach, he took up a defensive position (15 June) near the town of Raab. Aided by the artillery of General Sorbier, later assigned to the Imperial Guard, Eugene attacked, driving his infantry forward personally and delivering the *coup de grâce* at the head of his cavalry. The archduke retreated eastward. Eugène was able to rejoin Napoleon for what proved the final engagement against the Archduke Charles.

WAGRAM

Pausing briefly at Vienna, Napoleon had moved his army rapidly down the Danube to the Island of Lobau, which divides the river. On 18 May, Masséna's corps seized Lobau, and the engineers began throwing pontoon bridges over the northern stretch of the Danube toward Aspern and Essling. On 21 May, in desperate fighting, Masséna established a bridgehead on the north bank. During the night of the 21st–22nd, Lannes came over. On the morning of 22 May, however, the Austrians cut the moorings of a floating mill upstream that swept away the French bridges. The two corps in the bridgehead were cut to pieces, Marshal Lannes was killed, and the French withdrew to Lobau under cover of darkness.

Napoleon had been defeated for the first time in a major engagement, but he would not admit it. "Only the Danube has conquered us, not the Archduke!" He refused to abandon Lobau for another crossing site, fearing it would demoralize his troops and cheer the enemy. Instead, he planned a more deliberate crossing at the same place.

The Archduke Charles made the problem of crossing easier. Leaving only 25,000 troops on the Aspern-Essling line, he withdrew his main force (115,000), to the Russbach Plateau, six miles to the north. Considering the difficulty of maneuvering the troops he commanded, Charles' moves were excellent, except

Map 9.4

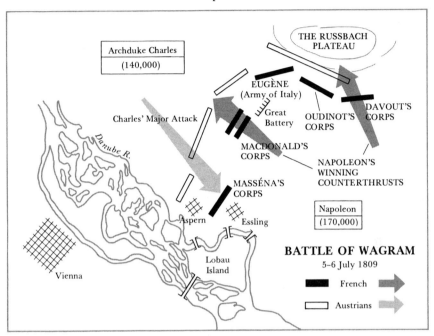

Archduke Charles
(140,000)

THE RUSSBACH
PLATEAU

EUGÈNE
(Army of Italy)

Charles' Major Attack

Great
Battery

OUDINOT'S
CORPS

DAVOUT'S
CORPS

Danube R.

MACDONALD'S
CORPS

NAPOLEON'S
WINNING
COUNTERTHRUSTS

MASSÉNA'S
CORPS

Aspern

Essling

Napoleon
(170,000)

Lobau
Island

Vienna

BATTLE OF WAGRAM
5–6 July 1809

French

Austrians

that he might have withdrawn the corps from Aspern-Essling also. His plan was based on the fair assumption that Napoleon would cross *somewhere*, but probably not precisely where he had before. Opposite Lobau alone the French could land anywhere along a five-mile stretch of riverbank. They might choose not to make their major crossing from Lobau at all, but up or downstream. On the plateau, Charles could "fix" the enemy and organize an attack at leisure. This he did—and almost beat Napoleon again.

On the stormy night of 4–5 July, Napoleon's army made the crossing flanking the Aspern-Essling line and driving the defenders westward. On the morning of 5 July, the French were arrayed before the Russbach. All day, the armies tested each other, fighting and withdrawing. At nightfall, discernible lines had formed, the French bulging northward; Charles had driven back both flanks.

On 6 July, Charles launched a major attack on the French left, driving toward Aspern, in Napoleon's rear. (See Map 9.4) By mid-morning, it appeared as if Charles would envelop the French position. But his corps commanders moved hesitantly, giving Napoleon time to shift Masséna south; he stopped them cold. Napoleon then threw Macdonald's corps into the center, augmented by reserves, Guards, and 112 cannon. Davout was already assailing the Austrian left. By midafternoon the Austrian center was giving and the left was in retreat. The

Archduke Charles, determined to save his army, broke off the engagement. The French, exhausted, did not pursue effectively.

On 10 July, Charles asked for an armistice, which Napoleon granted. The emperor's 20th Bulletin of the Grande Armée celebrated the victory and announced the promotion of Macdonald to marshal.[22] (The 19th Bulletin had glorified the victory of Eugène at Raab; Macdonald was made the hero at Wagram.)

PEACEMAKING

Napoleon had won the largest scale battle ever fought in Europe—310,000 men involved (170,000 French; 140,000 Austrians), but not by a knockout, as at Ulm and Austerlitz. He had lost 34,000 men (Charles over 40,000), but the Austrian army was still capable of fighting. It is significant that Napoleon, nevertheless, wanted peace. He repaired to the Schönbrunn Palace, in Vienna, to receive the representatives of Francis I, exiled in Budapest. The Austrian emperor delayed proceedings, however, because Charles' army was still intact, Andreas Hofer's mountaineers still held the Tyrol, and because the British, *after* Wagram, staged a long-planned amphibious assault aimed at Antwerp. Charles, however, saw no hope for victory and shortly resigned from the army—permanently. Eugène subdued the Tyrolian revolt and captured Hofer.[23] The British invasion force, slowed by French and Dutch troops, was decimated by fever on the Island of Walcheren and in September was evacuated to England.

Francis made peace at Schönbrunn on 14 October 1809. Austria ceded West Galicia to the Grand Duchy of Warsaw, part of eastern Galicia to Russia (a scrap tossed to Alexander for remaining neutral), and Balkan territory to France— Villach, Austrian Istria, Hungarian Dalmatia, and the city of Trieste. Bavaria got Salzburg, Berchtesgaden, and other small territories. Austria also sanctioned Napoleon's disposition of Tuscany and the Papal States, to be described below.

IMPERIAL PROBLEMS

Napoleon again dealt harshly with Austria. He had, nevertheless, been chastened by the experience of 1809. The Archduke Charles had challenged his

---

[22] Jacques-Etienne-Joseph-Alexandre Macdonald (1765–1840) was a descendant of Scottish supporters of England's James II who fled to France after 1688. His family had no formal title, but were treated as nobles. His father was a French army officer. He was commissioned by Louis XVI in 1787, but continued to serve in the army after 1792 under whatever government. For his service in Naples, Napoleon made him Duke of Taranto.

[23] Eugène respected the illiterate Hofer's loyalty to the Austrian emperor, his religiosity (he believed Francis I was truly God's appointed and had expected divine intervention in his behalf), and his bravery. He imprisoned him and pled with Napoleon for his life. Napoleon ordered him shot.

generalship to the limit. If the war had continued for a few more months, he thought it possible that Russia and even Prussia would have allied with Austria. The czar seemed increasingly hostile, particularly over the strictures of the Continental System and Poland, where he feared Napoleon might create an independent kingdom. The war in Spain went on. Wellesley (Wellington) had threatened Madrid in July and marched almost unscathed to safety in Portugal. There had been rumblings of discontent in France. Draft evasion and desertion were at a new high (12,000 deserters of record in 1808, 10,500 in 1809, with perhaps 7000 more among the officially "missing"). He had been forced to dismiss Bernadotte for insubordination after Wagram.[24] Lannes' death had been a terrible blow to him. He had been excommunicated by the pope, a matter he pretended to take lightly, but did not, considering its political implications. Most of all, Napoleon was concerned over the perpetuation of his dynasty. His heir, Louis' first son, had died. There was another, but the emperor felt certain that only a legitimate son of his own—by a Russian or Austrian princess—would have a chance of acceptance after his death. Dynastic marriage—a traditional solution— seemed essential. What he had won by the sword he hoped to pass on by crashing the club of hereditary monarchs.

Pending arrangements for a new marriage, he busied himself with the elaboration of his empire.

ILLYRIA AND TUSCANY

Napoleon created a state in the Balkans styled the Illyrian Provinces (after the Roman name for the area). It comprised the territory ceded at Schönbrunn by Austria, Venetian Istria and Dalmatia (given to Italy in 1805), Ragusa (seized 1808), and the Ionian Islands (captured by Russia, 1799, returned to France 1807).[25] They were declared an integral part of France and placed under the administration of Marshal Marmont, who was responsible directly to Napoleon.

Also in 1809, the emperor named his sister, Elisa Bonaparte Bacciochi, Grand Duchess of Tuscany. The kingdom of Etruria (Tuscany), a Spanish secondogeni- ture, was dissolved in 1807, and annexed to France in 1808, completing Napo- leon's control of north Italy. Tuscany remained part of France, though governed by Elisa who also ruled adjacent Parma and Piacenza.

---

[24] Napoleon, nevertheless, allowed Bernadotte to become crown prince of Sweden in 1810 after his election by the Swedish Diet. Perhaps it was because he was Joseph's brother-in-law, as noted earlier. This did not stop Bernadotte from allying Sweden with Russia in 1812, however.

[25] Italy was compensated for Istria and Dalmatia with southern Tyrol.

DEMISE OF THE PAPAL STATES

There had been a long contest of wills between Napoleon and Pius VII. The emperor claimed authority over the pope in all temporal matters. "We return to the time of Charlemagne." Pius defied him, denounced the imperial catechism (1806), stopped consecrating French bishops (1807), and refused to appoint more non-Italian cardinals. In 1808, Napoleon had Rome occupied and added the eastern Papal States to Italy.

In May 1809, Napoleon annexed to France the remaining Papal States, including Rome. Pius excommunicated him. The news reached Napoleon when he seemed to be losing the war, his army beaten back, stalled at the Danube. Short of temper, he shouted orders to arrest "that monk." His wish was conveyed to General Miollis, in Rome, who sent the pontiff off to Savona, where he was held until 1812.[26] How else, Napoleon asked, could one punish a pope "who preaches revolt and civil war?" (The reference was to Spain especially.)

The pope, though imprisoned, remained a power in Europe. Meanwhile, however, his states were subjected to vigorous rule by Napoleon's prefects.

THE AUSTRIAN MARRIAGE

If the emperor could have foreseen the future, he would have led his armies in person against Wellington and the Spanish. He was obsessed, however, with strengthening his north European system and with perpetuating his dynasty. Marriage to a Habsburg princess, he decided, might accomplish both—by making Austria a "natural" ally and by providing a wife who could give him a son.[27] In December 1809 he divorced Josephine and in March 1810 married the eighteen-year-old Archduchess Marie Louise, daughter of the Austrian emperor.

To everyone's surprise, the dynastic marriage turned into a love match. The buxom Marie Louise, at first terrified of Napoleon, gave herself to him fully. Her forty-year-old husband, the lean soldier and perpetual traveler, became a home-body. He grew fat and sedentary. His happiness influenced him to send Masséna, then Marmont, to Spain to fight *les Anglais*, when his presence there could have been decisive. After the birth of his son (March 1811), the emperor was even more tied to Paris, though preparing for war with Russia.

---

[26] In 1812 he was transferred to Fontainebleau. Forced to sign a new concordat (which he later repudiated), he was alowed to return to Rome in 1814.

[27] Napoleon had no doubt that he could father a son, since his Polish mistress, Marie Walewska, had given him one in 1809. He had another son and daughter by other mistresses, but Madame Walewska had been more of a true wife to him than Josephine, and he was certain her child was his.

CENTRALIZATION OF CONTROL

Nevertheless, Napoleon continued to centralize control of Europe. In February 1810 (before he was married), Napoleon proclaimed his prospective son "King of Rome," and Rome the second capital of the empire. Eugène, who had expected to become king of Italy, found his term as viceroy limited to twenty years, after which Italy would fall to the king of Rome (or a second son).[28] Murat rightly feared that Naples was in jeopardy as well.

Louis Bonaparte, in June 1810, found Holland occupied by French troops and French officials, enforcing the Continental System. On 1 July he abdicated and fled into exile in Austria. Holland was annexed to France. Napoleon also annexed (1810) the Hanse cities (Hamburg, Bremen and Lübeck), northern Hanover, part of Westphalia and other minor principalities, including Oldenburg, ruled by the czar's brother-in-law.

In Spain, during 1810, Joseph was relegated to Madrid, and most of the country was put under generals responsible to Paris. Napoleon took over direction of the war—from Paris. Until 1812, Joseph was king in name only.

At the end of 1810, however, the czar renounced the Continental System and the French alliance was broken. Napoleon began preparing for war and conciliated the satellite rulers.

THE GRAND EMPIRE:
STRENGTHS AND WEAKNESSES

In early 1812, Napoleon dominated Europe as had no ruler since Roman times. France was almost twice the size it had been in 1789 (130 departments and territory yet to be organized). Beyond stood the satellite kingdoms of Italy, Naples, Spain, and Westphalia. Allied with France were the States of the Confederation of the Rhine, including the Grand Duchies of Warsaw and Berg; the Swiss Confederation, Denmark-Norway, Prussia and Austria.

Despite the formidable extent of the empire and the irresistible appearance of its armies, it had weaknesses. The Spanish war had steadily sapped French strength and morale. Moreover, the rebels' stubborn resistance had awakened other European nationalities. Prussia was allied to France against her interest and will; the Austrians were not firmly attached to France by the imperial marriage. Anti-French sentiment had been increased by heavy war taxes, levies of food, equipment, and heavier conscription quotas.

In addition, the Continental System had not succeeded fully as a weapon and had been drastically modified. Napoleon had begun by allowing French grain to

[28] Eugène was compensated with the Grand Duchy of Frankfurt and promised a principality in Italy or elsewhere.

be exported to Britain in 1809—so that the peasants could pay his taxes. He shortly allowed other exports (foodstuffs and manufactures). In January 1810 he legalized the sale of prize cargoes (British goods) at 40 percent tariff. In July 1810 he authorized licenses for the importation of "contraband" on payment of 50 percent tariffs. Napoleon, nevertheless, was not displeased with the Continental System. As already noted above (p. 243), it had been partially responsible for a severe recession in Britain during 1810–1812. He intended to force Russia and her ally Sweden to rejoin the system.

By any rational criteria, Napoleon seemed destined to another triumph in 1812. The weaknesses of the empire (which are easier to see in retrospect) were more than offset by the awesome personality and seeming invincibility of the emperor of Europe. The Russians, however, responded to their czar's irrational decision to challenge him by fighting a fierce and unorthodox war, and aided by "General Winter," they beat him.

Russian success, however, was due in no small part to the fact that Napoleon had to win a quick victory. He had mobilized Europe to the maximum that his power could command but could not maintain the condition for long. His decisions (and his gambles) were based on the knowledge that if he did not win quickly and decisively, his allies probably would defect, French morale crumble, and his subject peoples rise against him.

Why might not my Code Napoléon have served as a basis for a European Code, and my Imperial University for a European University? By such means, we might have built a Europe composed of one and the same family.
—*Napoleon at St. Helena*

SATELLITES AND PUPPET STATES
Governments and Relations with France

Beyond France and the border areas annexed to her, the French Empire proper comprised states administered by rulers Napoleon appointed. Some were "independent," and others technically part of France. In the first category were the satellite kingdoms of Italy, Naples, Spain, Holland (until 1810), and Westphalia, and the grand duchies of Berg, Warsaw, and Frankfurt. In the second were the grand duchy of Tuscany, the Illyrian Provinces, and Rome.[1]

Napoleon is generally credited with "consolidating the Revolution" in France (that is, ending it and implementing its more feasible concepts). If he is to be credited with "spreading the Revolution," the evidence must come from the governmental policies he applied in non-French areas and the effectiveness of his "proconsuls" as executives.

It goes without saying that Napoleon laid down policy for the tributary states. He also expected obedience from the rulers. After designating Joseph king of Naples in 1806, he said to Miot de Melito: "I am building a family of kings . . . or rather *viceroys*." He intended to control proconsuls of lesser rank similarly. Members of his immediate family, especially, were not as subservient as he

---

[1] This list excludes such "sovereign" states as Lucca-Piombino, ruled by Elisa Bonaparte Bacciochi, and *dotations* allowed to civil and military officers to provide them incomes, for example, Benevento, in Naples (granted to Talleyrand) and Neuchâtel, annexed from Switzerland (to Marshal Berthier). Napoleon also appointed the prefects of both old French and new departments, of course, including those in Belgium and the German Rhineland, which were already integrated into France when he came to power. Only those departments are discussed herein where the prefects were responsible to an intermediate government, as in Illyria and Rome, and after 1810 in Holland.

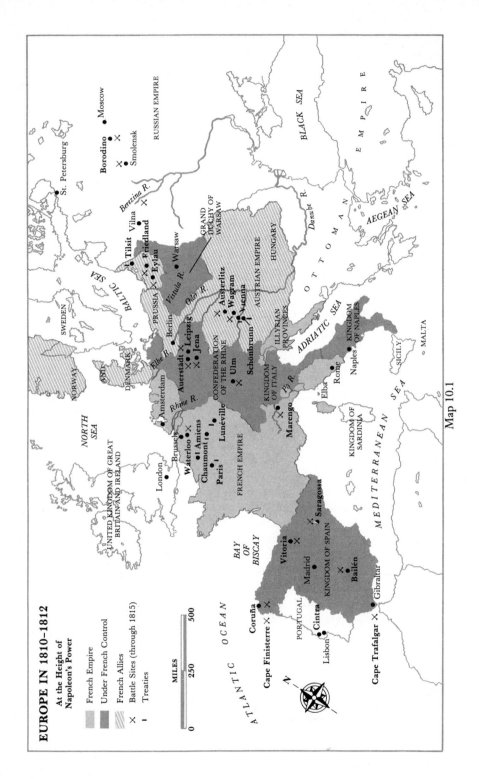

EUROPE IN 1810–1812

At the Height of Napoleon's Power

- French Empire
- Under French Control
- French Allies
- ✕ Battle Sites (through 1815)
- ┃ Treaties

MILES

0   250   500

Map 10.1

RUSSIAN EMPIRE

● Moscow
✕ Smolensk

Borodino ✕
✕ ● Smolensk

Berezina R. ✕

St. Petersburg ●

BALTIC SEA

SWEDEN

NORWAY

BLACK SEA

E M P I R E

O T T O M A N

AEGEAN SEA

GRAND DUCHY OF WARSAW

● Vilna
Tilsit ┃
✕ Friedland
✕ Eylau

PRUSSIA

● Warsaw

Vistula R.

Oder R.

Danube R.

HUNGARY

AUSTRIAN EMPIRE

Berlin ●
Elbe R.
✕ Leipzig
Auerstädt ✕✕ Jena

✕ Austerlitz
✕ Wagram
● Vienna
Schönbrunn ┃

CONFEDERATION OF THE RHINE

✕ Ulm

ILLYRIAN PROVINCES

ADRIATIC SEA

KINGDOM OF NAPLES

Po R.

● Rome
Naples ●

MALTA

SICILY

Amsterdam ●
Rhine R.

KINGDOM OF ITALY

✕ Marengo

Elba ●

KINGDOM OF SARDINIA

NORTH SEA

DENMARK

UNITED KINGDOM OF GREAT BRITAIN AND IRELAND

London ●

Brussels ●
Waterloo ✕ ● Amiens ✕
Chaumont ┃ ✕ Lunéville ┃
Paris ●

FRENCH EMPIRE

MEDITERRANEAN SEA

ATLANTIC OCEAN

BAY OF BISCAY

Coruña ● ✕
Cape Finisterre ✕

PORTUGAL

Cintra ┃
Lisbon ●

● Vitoria ✕

Madrid ●

KINGDOM OF SPAIN

Saragossa ✕

✕ Bailén

Gibraltar ●

Cape Trafalgar ✕

N

desired, but all must be credited with trying to carry out his policies. His quarrels with them resulted as much from their trying to apply the high principles he preached too literally as from their becoming "nationalists," that is, identifying with the peoples he sent them to govern.

Unquestionably, he intended to modernize governments and laws of all the states. "The peoples of Germany," he wrote Jerome, king of Westphalia, in 1807, "[like] those of France, of Italy, of Spain desire equality and want liberal ideas [applied]. . . . " Unfortunately, this was not true, notably in Spain, where the masses resisted liberalism as the work of the devil. Even where Napoleonic rulers were accepted, the price of reform was higher taxes and conscription. Thus, in the short run, the peoples did not see the benefit, for example, of the abolition of feudal dues, since it eased their financial burdens hardly at all. After 1815, his work was better appreciated. As time erased unhappy memories, his governments seemed models of efficiency and fairness compared to those of the restored *seigneurs*.

Napoleon in fact tried to offer the gains of the Revolution to all Europeans and to establish administrative and judicial systems which would better serve them. It would be idiotic to say he did so solely out of principle, of course. He hoped to win the people away from their traditional leaders, while making their states more useful to the empire. The following sections, which discuss the rulers and their states one by one, will illustrate his approach in detail.

ITALY

Eugène de Beauharnais was twenty-three when Napoleon made him viceroy of the kingdom of Italy (May 1805). Athletic, self-assured, he had his father's aristocratic features and Josephine's dark coloration. He had visited Napoleon in Italy in 1797, accompanied him to Egypt, and served as a captain of cavalry at Marengo in 1800. He was mature beyond his years, but at first was ordered to make no major decision without consulting the emperor—"Even if the moon is falling on Milan. . . ." Napoleon quickly gained confidence in Eugène's ability to govern, however, and, within a few years, his generalship. In 1805, Napoleon let Masséna command Eugène's army. In 1809, Eugène led it himself, and by his victories, helped set the stage for Napoleon's victory at Wagram.

In 1806, meanwhile, Eugène married Princess Augusta of Bavaria. A dark-haired sylph of seventeen, she was a fairy-tale princess—beautiful, good—and yet spirited enough to upbraid Napoleon for arranging marriages without regard for love. The marriage, however, was happy. She gave Eugène seven children, and the court at Milan had for some an oppressively homey atmosphere. Eugène was a model ruler, loyal to Napoleon to the end. Augusta stood by her husband, though she thought Napoleon did not reward him properly.

Eugène's constitution was that of the Italian Republic, amended to include monarchical forms. Napoleon was the executive; Eugène his deputy. The viceroy ruled with a ministry and *consulta* of prominent citizens. Laws were framed by a council of state assisted by young auditors.

The legislature, in the beginning, was a one-house body of seventy-five men elected, indirectly, by universal manhood suffrage. Had it so remained (despite property qualification for electors), the government would have been more democratic than that of France. The legislature, however, debated incessantly and accomplished little. On Napoleon's order, Eugène dismissed it after the first session (1805) and never called it again (though it was not abolished).

By amendment of the constitution, a senate was established that assumed the legislative function. The seventy-odd members were appointed by Eugène and included two deputies from each department, his ministers and grand officers of state, and a number of judges. Napoleon's purpose was to expedite reform; later, perhaps, Italy could afford a more popular government. With few exceptions, Italians, including the intelligentsia, made no objection. They found Eugène's government better than previous ones, and the viceroy himself, if not popular, was widely respected.

The constitution had a full roster of rights carried over from the Constitution of the Republic—essentially those enumerated in the French "Declaration of the Rights of Man." The constitution also declared the abolition of feudalism, guilds, and the feudal rights of the Church. The Code Napoléon, in Italian, was introduced in January 1806.

For administration, Italy was divided into twenty-four departments under prefects (*prefetto*) appointed by the viceroy; the departments were divided into districts, cantons, and municipalities. The courts were reformed, also following the French pattern, with a court of cassation at the top and justices of the peace at the bottom.

In Italy, as in France, there was a conscious effort to promote social change, principally to create an amalgam of noble and bourgeois leadership. Nobles of the Old Regime(s) were allowed to keep their titles and some were given offices, for example, Count Caprara who became grand equerry. New titles were granted for service. Francesco Melzi d'Eril, the former vice-president of Italy, was made Duke of Lodi, as well as Keeper of the Seals and senator. The middle class was represented by people like Giovanni Paradisi, Ferdinando Marescalchi, and Giuseppe Prina (who will be identified later).

Napoleon was more vitally interested in the new generation, however. "Surround yourself . . . with young men" he wrote Eugène. "The old ones are good for nothing." He saw the army, especially, as an instrument for changing society and for reducing provincialism.

"My object," he told Eugène, "is to effect a cultural revolution. . . . " The officers' schools were open to men of all provinces and classes (though few peasants or workers were educationally qualified). All lived and trained together as equals and had to use the same Italian dialect, Tuscan. It was the language of Florence (outside the kingdom) and of the Italian Renaissance, thus, to Napoleon, "pure" Italian. Elitism of talent was practiced. Those selected for the Royal Guard had special schools and developed fierce *esprit de corps* which infected the whole army.

Among the satellite armies the Italian ranked only second to the Westphalian, which was built around Hessian regiments with long military tradition. Not all the officers or men were Napoleonists, or even pro-French, but most were opposed to the return of the Old Regime. This can be said as well of Eugène's judges and bureaucrats.

For civilians, the College of Auditors, the administration, and the courts served as training grounds in efficient methods and procedures. Aristocrats generally chose the courts and the sons of the middle class chose the administration. Together, however, they formed a new breed of civil servants. Many of these men, with ex-officers of Eugène's army, became leaders in revolutions later in the nineteenth century.

Internally, laissez-faire principles ruled the economy. The government abolished internal tariffs, constructed an extensive road system in cooperation with France and latterly Illyria, and improved waterways. Napoleon affected Italy's economy drastically by gearing French tariffs to encourage Italy to produce raw materials and food for France and to purchase French manufactures. Nevertheless, domestic industry as well as agriculture prospered. Manufacturers converted to rough cloth for the domestic market and expanded the production of crepes, sheer fabrics, and other specialty items which France could not manufacture. These sold not only in France, but in Austria, Russia, and the Middle East.

In the process, Italian industry switched from the putting-out system to factory operation. In 1812 one plant at Vicenza employed 6000 people. By 1814, Bologna had 500 factories, Modena 400. The manufacturing of wool and cotton cloth had expanded. All this was done while giving Napoleon what he wanted— raw silk, some cotton, grain, meat animals, oranges, lemons, and the like. The value of silk exported in 1812 was 80,000,000 lire, 40 percent higher than in 1805.[2] The economy suffered an initial shock from the Continental System, but adjusted rapidly, taking advantage of markets lost to the British and increasing overland trade with the Middle East. It hurt less after 1810, when Napoleon's licensing system was implemented.

Italians also became master smugglers. The island of Vis, in the Adriatic, was notorious as a depot for contraband. Eugène's navy destroyed the base in 1811, but it revived. Cotton, sugar, coffee, tobacco, chocolate, and other colonial products came from Vis, the ports of the Balkans, Greece, and even the French Ionian Islands. The principal warehouses were on Malta, which became valuable to the British beyond their wildest dreams.

The minister of finances was Giuseppe Prina, who balanced the budget and kept it in balance until 1813. This he did without burdening the people greatly. His mainstay was the capitation tax on heads of families. It ran an average of 176

[2] Lire = .76 francs.

lire—about 134 francs per year. Most other regular revenues came from indirect taxes. Overall, taxes in Italy were about one-third less than in France.

Italians owed much to Prina, but hated him. He was the tax collector and not an attractive personality. Dour, businesslike, a human computer forever checking accounts, Prina was totally absorbed in his work. Efficient and incorruptible, he set high standards for his subordinates. Graft—a time-honored "sport" in Italy—was punished viciously.

Prina also managed the National Properties, largely confiscated from the monasteries, and assessed at about 500,000,000 lire (400,000,000 francs). By careful control of sales and of paper issued against the properties, the kingdom netted some 70 percent of their assessed value—much better return than any other government, including France, got from similar holdings.

Italy's ministry of waterways and roads (*Acque e Strade*) under Giovanni Paradisi greatly improved communications. Roads ran from Adriatic ports to the passes through the Alps to France or to the Po River and from its ports to the passes. Among cooperative French-Italian projects were new routes over the Mount Cenis and Simplon passes to France and between Venice and Trieste (in Illyria). Along the beautiful Riviera coast, the famous Corniche was cut into the cliffs that abut the sea. (The roadbed is still in use.) It also carried goods from the Italian departments of France, Naples, and Lucca-Piombino. All routes led to France, with the major ones from Naples bypassing Italy via Rome and the Corniche. This betrays the fact that Napoleon did not favor economic unification of the peninsula, which might promote pan-Italian nationalism. He felt that he could use and control Italian and Neapolitan nationalism, but feared a more far-reaching variety.

Paradisi, a Renaissance man—politician, poet, mathematician, and engineer—also directed public works, including the beautification of Milan. He gave a new facade to the cathedral (Duomo), second in size only to St. Peter's in Rome, and had the La Scala Opera house remodeled. Arches were built at the gates of the city, the most famous the Porta Ticinese. At Monza the palace of the Lombard kings was refurbished.

Eugène mounted public welfare and education programs which rivaled those of France. He created a National Council for Public Hygiene which enforced vaccination for smallpox, examined water and sewer systems, and supervised epidemic control. The council's advice guided the administration of hospitals, homes for orphans, the aged, and the indigent.

The viceroy placed all schools under the control of the minister of education, Giovanni Scopoli. His authority extended to the universities at Bologna, Pavia, and Padua. The work of professors and researchers was subsidized, and the faculties nominally included such literary lights as Vincenzo Monti and Ugo Foscolo. Pavia boasted Alessandro Volta, after whom the electrical unit of force is named. Higher education was expanded to include schools for engineers and veterinarians as well as military officers. Each department was given a *lycée*, and a *collège* for women was founded in Milan. The lower schools were run by the

Church under state supervision. In addition, Eugène established a Royal Academy, patronized the theaters and opera (which were put under central direction), sponsored a conservatory of music and an academy of fine arts.

Italy boasted Antonio Canova, the most renowned sculptor of his day. The handsome and willful Canova declined Napoleon's invitation to live at the imperial court, but did numerous statues and busts of the Bonapartes. His full-length nude of Pauline, called "Venus Reclining," is the most famous. Very proud of her body, she embarrassed Napoleon by repeatedly confirming that she had posed for it.[3] More representative of Canova's art, which began a classical revival, is the "Cupid and Psyche" in the Louvre and works on mythical themes held by museums in Rome, Naples, London, Munich, Berlin, and elsewhere.

Freedom was of course missing from intellectual life. Censorship was applied, though it was not severe. Vincenzo Cuoco, for example, one of the fathers of Italian unification, was able to publish a newspaper in Milan. Generally, there was little to be censored except for obscure anti-Napoleonic statements such as might be made in classical plays denouncing tyranny. The propaganda of secret nationalist societies surfaced only in 1813–1814.

The intelligentsia either supported Napoleon and Eugène (and accepted the government's largesse) or fled to Sicily or elsewhere. There is a ring of sincerity especially in the literature of the early years glorifying Napoleon and the "New Regime"—in the poetry of Vincenzo Monti and Ugo Foscolo, for example. After the loss of 20,000 Italians in Russia, there was considerable open hostility to Napoleon (not so much to Eugène). In 1813–1814, however, when intellectuals saw their choice between the return of the Old Regime and the Napoleonic system, most chose the latter, or remained silent. Ugo Foscolo, by then no longer young, insisted on joining Eugène's army to fight the Austrians.

Eugène's was a model kingdom. So solidly based was it that its army was still fighting the Austrians (and Murat, who turned his coat) when Napoleon abdicated in 1814. Had the people been allowed to vote, it is more than possible that Eugène would have retained his throne. It is not strange that northern Italy became the principal locus of revolutionary activity in the nineteenth century.

NAPLES

Napoleon seized Naples in 1806 to deny its ports to the British and to improve the French position in the Mediterranean. With Joseph in Naples, Spain his ally, and the Ottoman Empire at war with Britain and Russia, he hoped to squeeze out the British and to deliver the Levant trade to France. The scheme did not work because Spain did not cooperate, the British were able to maintain bases on Sicily (where they protected the Neapolitan Bourbons) and Malta, and

---

[3] Most shocking to Napoleon, however, was a nude of himself—for which he did not pose. It went into the cellars of the Louvre. Lord Wellington bought it in 1815, and it may be seen today in Apsley House, London.

the Turks made peace with Britain in 1809.[4] Naples retained some strategic importance, but little profit was to be gained there.

Naples was economically backward, the society feudal. Its land was held mostly by owners of gigantic *latifundia*, the crown, or the Church. Most peasants, in effect, were serfs. Poverty was extreme, starvation common, banditry rife—in Calabria, a profession, with sons following their fathers. Ignorance was incredible, and agricultural methods medieval (wooden plows, no fertilizer). Diseases such as malaria and tuberculosis were endemic. The population had a sleepy character but was prone to outbursts of inhuman brutality. The conditions of life were well reflected in the churches where the statues and paintings ran to scenes of martyrdom, with contorted figures dripping blood. It was an agricultural country with a very small middle class. Investment capital was scarce. Industry was a small factor in the economy. There was very little national or even provincial spirit, except perhaps among the *lazzaroni* of the capital, who took pride in being the slickest thieves in Christendom.

Joseph Bonaparte, styled Giuseppe Napoleone (Joseph Napoleon), was king of Naples from 1806 until mid-1808, when he went to Spain.[5] The most likable of the Bonapartes, at thirty-eight still slender and handsome, he was kingly in appearance and polished, yet democratic, in manner. As thoroughly devoted to reform as Napoleon, he was a more sincere believer in popular constitutional government. It was his plans which guided Neapolitan domestic policy until the fall of the kingdom.

Murat, styled Gioacchino Napoleone, and Caroline Bonaparte, who succeeded Joseph, were less reform-minded, but carried on most of his projects. The vain Gascon, with his shock of curly, black hair, bizarre uniforms, and jewel-studded trappings, was a king after the hearts of the *lazzaroni*. He was a creature of war, however, who, in civil affairs, depended heavily on his ministers. Caroline, fifteen years younger than her husband and quite pretty, had more political talent and a Machiavellian deviousness that even Talleyrand (one of her numerous lovers) envied. Her chief objective in life was to retain the crown for herself and her children[6] (with or without Murat). She wielded power by posing as Napoleon's defender against her increasingly nationalist husband. As the emperor's star faded, however, she became Neapolitan herself and pushed Murat, his soldier's conscience so torn that he wept, into joining the Allies (1814) to save their throne. It bought them only one troubled year.

Joseph took a positive approach to reform. He decreed feudalism abolished in August 1806. When his council of state debated too long over details of his

---

[4] Under French encouragement Turkey declared war on both in 1806. She made peace with Britain in 1809 but not with Russia until 1812.

[5] His queen, née Julie Clary, remained in France with their two daughters, though she did visit Naples briefly at the end of the reign. She never joined Joseph in Spain.

[6] Two boys and a girl. Achille, the eldest, became a prominent resident of Florida in the 1820s and is buried in Tallahassee.

decree, he lost his temper. "The people have groaned too long under . . . abuses; they shall be freed, and if obstacles appear, never doubt, I will . . . smash them." Nevertheless, his program called for gradual elimination of feudal rights, with compensation to landholders, and he delayed action on the Code Napoléon and other matters. He had plans to restructure society, the economy, the administration and courts, and much more. He elected to move slowly, though, so as not to alienate the only educated people in Naples—the nobility and the high middle class. He wanted maximum native participation in the government.

In the beginning, however, his six key ministers included three Frenchmen— Miot de Melito (interior), Pierre Louis Roederer (finance), and Christophe Saliceti[7] (police and war). The Neapolitans were Michelangelo Cianciulli (justice), Prince Pignatelli-Cerchiara (marine), and the Marquis de Gallo (foreign affairs). The reformers were Miot, Roederer, and Cianciulli. The council of state, however, which drafted laws, was overwhelmingly Neapolitan.

As a step toward greater democracy, Joseph instituted limited popular government at the local level. The existing fourteen provinces were divided into districts, "governments" (voting areas only), and municipalities. The king appointed provincial intendants, subintendants, mayors, and their councils. He made his selections, however, from lists drawn by the voters, who included all male adults who paid a minimum tax.[8] It was a modest beginning, but at least Neapolitans began developing voting experience.

The king abolished feudal and church courts (1806). Cianciulli was charged with transferring cases to existing royal courts and with planning a new judicial system. Meanwhile the judges were instructed to apply the principles of equal justice and equal penalties. French-style courts went into operation in 1808, a court of cassation at the top, justices of the peace in the "governments," with intermediate civil and criminal courts.

In the interim, the judiciary had been radically restructured to oust reactionaries and to install more liberal judges. Finesse had been applied, however; most of those retired had been given awards and shifted to ceremonial offices.

All this time the Code Napoléon and French penal code, in careful translation, were circulated by Cianciulli's ministry with interpretive tracts and other aids. Just before his departure (May 1808), Joseph ordered the penal code into effect immediately and the Code Napoléon as of 1 November 1809.

After investigating the monastic orders (one man in ten was a monk), Joseph abolished all but the Franciscans, whom he judged useful. Monastic property valued at 30,000,000 ducats together with crown lands worth 200,000,000 became the National Properties.[9] Plans called for maximum distribution to the peasants.

Joseph's program for eliminating feudalism (1806) was gradual, but effective. Proprietors lost, without compensation, all personal, juridical, and prohibitory

---

[7] The cadaverous, sinister, former patron of the Bonapartes.

[8] The amount varied with the location, but averaged about 24 ducats ($22) a year.

[9] Ducat = 4.45 francs.

rights. (The latter had allowed them to ban certain crops, building, and new methods.) Money rights (dues) were to be compensated for by the government—not the peasants. Water courses were freed, and common lands, pastures, and forests ordered divided among users. Murat continued the plan so that by 1811 legal feudalism was dead, though in Naples, law and practice were often far apart, as is the case today.

To encourage land ownership, Joseph offered low-interest loans to the peasants. The National Properties were made available for purchase by their cultivators. Nobles were not required but "encouraged" to sell by the abolition of feudalism and (later) of entail, which reduced their incomes.[10] In addition, land reclaimed from swamps and marshes and wasteland improved by new methods was offered the peasants. Here rent was low, and 95 percent of that paid in the first five years applied to the purchase price. Unfortunately, very few had enough faith in the new order and in themselves to take advantage of the opportunities offered.

Joseph also imported French experts to teach new farming techniques to the peasants, but they were slow to respond. Suspicious of foreigners, they clung to tradition. The greatest progress was made in introducing new crops, especially cotton. By 1809, Naples could supply 40 percent of the needs of the empire. Beet and cane sugar were both grown.

Products were difficult to get to market, however. Roads were lacking, partly because Neapolitans had always depended on the seaways, now under British control. Many new roads were constructed or rebuilt—from Naples to Rome, Naples to Reggio, Naples to Brindisi. The king used all available resources, including the manpower of idle French troops. The improvements helped, but commerce still moved slowly.

Roederer consolidated all banks into one, later called the "Bank of the Two Sicilies," reworked the revenue system and funded the debt. On the surface, his efforts did not seem crashingly successful. The projected deficit for 1808 (when Murat took over) was almost 8,000,000 ducats in a budget of 15,000,000. But he had paid one-half of the national debt (total 100,000,000 ducats) by use of the National Properties and was liquidating the rest. Twenty-three taxes of the Old Regime had been replaced by one tax on land and industry (though other indirect taxes remained). He had also begun the systematic repurchase of feudal rights and those of tax farmers. Murat's minister, Agar de Mosbourg, continued Roederer's policies.

Miot organized a ministry of interior (new to Naples) which supervised general administration, public works, welfare, and education. He had great success in establishing publicly financed schools, which were under secular control, though the teachers were mostly clerics or ex-clerics. Communities financed primary schools and the royal government *lycées* (high schools). Of 2520

---

[10] Entailed estates could not be sold but had to be passed down to heirs, perpetuating large holdings.

public schools planned, 1500 were operating by the end of Joseph's two-year stay. He also took steps to modernize the once famous university at Salerno.

Joseph founded a royal art museum by consolidating former monastic holdings and adding works from the royal collections. The French artist J. B. Wicar organized a School of Art and Design. Existing schools of music were consolidated and strengthened. The preservation of ruins and antiquities also became a government project. Joseph found that diggings at Pompeii, especially, were being looted for profit. He put a stop to it, and governments since have followed his lead. Otherwise, Pompeii would not be the attraction it is today.

Though a gradualist, Joseph's accomplishments were real. He had charted a course toward modernization for Naples. Decades later, Camillo de Cavour (the "unifier" of Italy) wrote in praise of his work. He regretted only that it had not been followed up after 1815.

In May 1808, just before he departed, Joseph promulgated a constitution, but Murat refused to recognize it. Instead, he promised a more liberal and truly Neapolitan one (which he never delivered). He retained the governmental organization, but replaced all the ministers but Gallo (foreign affairs).[11]

Murat's top men were Jean-Paul Daure (police), Agar de Mosbourg (finance), Giuseppe Zurlo (interior), and Francesco Ricciardi (justice)—two Frenchmen, two Neapolitans. Daure was Napoleon's spy (and as long as she needed him, Caroline's; she became his mistress). Murat came to depend on Antonio Maghella, Police Prefect of Naples (city) for information. He encouraged Murat's nationalism, as did Zurlo and Ricciardi. Agar was the king's man, even in treason (1813–1814). By 1815, Maghella had led them all into the pan-Italian independence movement. Until the latter days of the regime, however, the nationalists kept their ambitions secret—better than the king did.

Murat instituted the Code Napoléon in 1810. It was never fully enforced, however, and as to civil marriage and divorce, not at all.

Giuseppe Zurlo, meanwhile, carried forward the abolition of feudalism. With the aid of royal commissions, which settled over 8000 cases regarding compensation and the division of commons, the process was completed by late 1810. Benefits to the peasants were obscured by the assumption of some noble rights by municipalities (over waterways and mills, for example), new taxes (which, if lower, were harder to avoid), and conscription (Murat doubled Joseph's rate).

Zurlo neglected public education; the number of public schools declined. He strengthened provincial administration, however, and pushed ahead public works and economic projects. These slowly began to bear fruit. Commerce was fostered by the virtual elimination of banditry, which Murat smashed by massive use of troops and police. The king also ignored the Continental System freely and quickly bid for licenses in 1810. Olive oil, a major product unshippable in quantity except by sea, began to move to market, along with grain and other commodities

[11] Saliceti died, perhaps poisoned, in 1809; the others were given new offices.

long stockpiled. Fortunes were made, and prosperity reached even the peasantry. This added to Murat's popularity as well as his revenues.

Agar, angry over the 1808 deficit, nevertheless followed Roederer's program religiously. In 1809 his budget was almost balanced, and in 1810 and 1811 he had surpluses. By 1811 he had liquidated all but 20,000,000 ducats of the national debt. After 1811, however, Murat's increased military expenses upset the plan, forced tax increases, and brought increasing deficits.

Joseph had begun building a Neapolitan army, largely to increase national pride. "I want . . . to revive the glory of the name Italian. . . . " he wrote Napoleon. The emperor had no faith in Neapolitan troops, who excelled only in deserting, but he let him try. Joseph did reform the Royal Military Academy and founded artillery and polytechnic schools, which gave some nonnobles a chance to rise in status. He left Murat an army of fewer than 3000 men, however, disregarding French and foreign units.

Murat wanted an army to make him independent of Napoleon, and began building in 1808. After the emperor's marriage to the Archduchess Marie Louise, he worked harder, fearful that Naples would be integrated into France.[12] In 1810 he had 40,000 troops; by 1812, 80,000. His growing army made him bold. He allowed the official *Monitore* to voice nationalist sentiments, associated with the Freemasons and nascent *Carbonari* (in Naples, nationalists), and adopted a new flag to replace the French tricolor. Napoleon countered in 1811 by removing French troops (a separate army) from Murat's command—a threat to turn them against him. Murat expressed shock and swore loyalty. "Sire . . . given me your love. I will always be the first grenadier of the Emperor!" He purged his government of nationalists, and was forgiven. In 1812 he was called to the Grande Armée, and went happily.

Murat returned disillusioned, however. His army was still intact (Napoleon had taken only his guard of 7000). He recalled his old ministers and in December 1814 went over to the Allies.

TUSCANY

Tuscany had been put at Napoleon's disposal at Lunéville (1801) and converted into a Spanish *secundogeniture* (the kingdom of Etruria) in return for nearby Parma and Piacenza—and Louisiana.

The kingdom was not a success. The king died (1803) leaving a minor heir. The queen-regent, a Spanish Bourbon, was weak and unpopular. The state debt rose to 100,000,000 francs. Leghorn (Livorno) remained an unofficial *entrepôt* for

---

[12] Another possibility was that Napoleon would restore the Bourbons. Marie Louise was the granddaughter of Marie Caroline of the Two Sicilies. Murat worried more over this after the summer of 1810, when Napoleon deliberately sabotaged his attempt to invade Sicily.

British goods. Royalist and Jacobin exiles congregated at Florence. At Tilsit (1807) Napoleon decided to remove "that deformity. . . . " By the same treaty which doomed Spain (Fontainebleau, October 1807), Godoy gave up Etruria.[13] Spanish troops withdrew. A French army moved in, burned British goods at Leghorn, and occupied Florence.

In 1808, Tuscany was annexed to France and organized into four departments by Dauchy, who governed initially with a junta of Frenchmen and Italians, including General Menou, a talented eccentric who had become a Moslem in Egypt, and Cesare Balbo, *litterateur* and historian. In 1809, Napoleon pleased the natives by creating the Grand Duchy of Tuscany—technically part of France but ruled by Élisa Bonaparte Bacciochi.

Élisa, thirty-two, Napoleon's eldest sister, was handsome, regal in carriage, with strong, regular features and wide-set blue eyes which reflected rare intelligence and steady self-assurance. Educated on a royal scholarship at Saint-Cyr, under the Old Regime *the* school for young ladies, she had a polish her sisters lacked. Married in 1797 to a Corsican captain, Felice Bacciochi, she was a good wife and mother. Unlike the voluptuous Pauline, who courted scandal, her passion was for government, the arts, and literature. "We were never very close, our characters opposed," the emperor said in 1820. In truth, she was very much like him.

Élisa had proved herself as Princess of Lucca-Piombino, granted to her and Prince Bacciochi in 1805. She ruled; her husband commanded their tiny army. Napoleon had been pleased with her administration. She had abolished feudalism, applied the Code Napoléon, liquidated monastic property, and financed new schools and public works. She retained title to her principality (not annexed to France).

As Grand Duchess of Tuscany, however, she transferred her court to Florence (Firenze). Her husband again confined himself to the military. Élisa's chief subordinates were Gerando and Cesare Balbo. She had full authority over all matters—legal, administrative, and military—subject to Napoleon's approval. He seldom interfered, however, because she usually anticipated his wishes and because her grand duchy became financially independent. Moreover, by utilizing the property of the monasteries, she even paid the huge debt incurred by the preceding government.

One of Élisa's first acts was to repeal the double tax on wine—a very popular move. She then introduced equality of taxation, abolished feudalism, and instituted the Code Napoléon. At the same time, however, she introduced conscription, to which the Tuscans responded with wholesale evasion and desertion. She refused to compromise, and thus eventually had the army of 10,000 that the emperor demanded. The Tuscans, nevertheless, she wrote Napoleon, were "different from their ancestors" (doubtless thinking of the original Buonopartes).

---

[13] Whose queen, like Godoy, was promised a kingdom in Portugal.

Élisa quickly came to terms with the clergy—powerful and proud (Florence had produced many popes)—showing herself a dutiful Catholic in public, but willing to use imperial power in private. She dissolved the monastic orders, but pensioned members without prospects and provided homes for the elderly. The Church was placed under civil control, but she was careful to see that bishops had places of honor at all ceremonies. The churchmen gave her no difficulty.

Élisa's court outshone that of Italy and had a legitimate atmosphere lacking in the circles of the flamboyant Murat in Naples. She favored the French protocol of the Old Regime and presided with great dignity, which struck a respondent note among the Florentine nobility. At the same time, she patronized a swarm of artists and writers and a few scientists such as Eusebio Valli (a precursor of Pasteur).

The grand duchess took great interest in the Academy of Florence. She gave autonomy to the section for literature and language, which was actually the ancient Academy of Crusca, and backed its major project, a new Italian dictionary. The Academy's *Vocabulario*, when completed (1811), was circulated throughout the peninsula. This can be seen as Napoleon's one willful act to foster Italian unity.

She banned the works of Vittorio Alfieri, the great poet and apostle of freedom (d. 1803). She pressed and cajoled the clergy into giving him the Christian burial he had previously been denied, however, and financed a tomb, designed by Canova, in the Church of Santa Croce. There he rests with other great Florentines such as Machiavelli and Michelangelo.[14]

The Florentine theater, under state sponsorship, was very active, though weighted with French classics. For the opera, Élisa cultivated native talent and drew artists from La Scala, in Milan, and musicians from Naples. Monti, Foscolo, and other literary lights graced her court. Florence retained her time-honored place in the artistic and literary life of Italy—partly on borrowed talent, but it had always been so.

Like all Napoleon's proconsuls, Élisa left monuments to her reign. These were particularly evident along the street of Dei Calzaioli, which was straightened and widened; the facades of public buildings along the route were restored by the most skilled workmen available. Santa Croce was much beautified.

By creating a French-trained administrative and judicial corps, Élisa also made a contribution to the future of Italy. Since the eighteenth century, dukes, including Leopold, later Holy Roman Emperor, had been eminently enlightened. Nevertheless, her reign fostered later revolutions. Balbo, her minister, after 1815 in the service of Piedmont, became a leader of the *risorgimento*. Alfieri, whom she enshrined, was an inspiration to the Italian nationalists of the nineteenth century.

---

[14] She also quietly allowed Alfieri's mistress, the Duchess of Albany (the "last Stuart Queen") to live on in Florence.

ROME

Napoleon ordered the western Papal States, including Rome, annexed to France on 17 May 1809. A governing council under General Miollis began reorganizing the government. Pius VII was left in control of the Vatican, however, and granted an income of 2,000,000 francs a year. It was only when the pope responded by excommunicating the emperor that he was whisked away to Savona. (See above, p. 260.)

Miollis had already begun sweeping reforms. In June 1809, all Roman courts were dissolved, including the tribunals of the Apostolic Chamber. All feudal rights were eliminated in July 1809. At the same time, the Code Napoléon and the French commercial code were instituted. In February 1810 the territory was divided into two departments, the Trasimeno, under Antoine Roederer, and Rome, under Camille de Tournon. Overall supervision, however, remained in the hands of General Miollis, who controlled French troops in the new departments.

In February 1810 a *senatus consultum* named Rome the second city of the empire, designated the imprisoned pope chaplain of the emperor, and again offered him an income and palaces in both cities. Pius ignored the "favors," refused to take an oath to the emperor and declined even to consecrate French bishops. Napoleon ordered his life at Savona made less comfortable and for a time even his writing materials were taken away. However, the old man would not cooperate, and after a brief time the emperor, fearing for Pius' health, relented.

Meanwhile the prisoner proved able to make difficulties in Rome. He forbade the clergy to take an oath of loyalty to the emperor, and the majority obeyed. Miollis tried to compromise on the wording, but got nowhere, and had to resort to deporting nonjuring clergy, which was an embarrassment to the imperial government. When he required the oath of lawyers and booksellers many of them also refused, though they faced loss of property as well as exile. Confiscated monastic property was difficult to sell because Pius forbade purchase.

Rome was extremely difficult to govern. The French found only the nobles to be reasonably trustworthy as officials. The middle class—industrial, commercial, and professional—was geared to serve the Holy See and refused to gamble on the permanency of French rule. The common people, for the most part emotionally attached to the papacy, were appalled and angered by the regular collection of taxes and conscription. When the first draftees were called in 1810, irate mothers demonstrated in Rome, and most of the men (only 450) deserted. The Code Napoléon was never enforced, nor the courts and administration fully reformed.

The French governors had successes, nevertheless. Religious liberty was protected. Jews were granted full civil rights and the walls of the ghetto were demolished.[15] A French tax system was introduced, and monopolies held by the

---

[15] Few showed much gratitude, however. The ghetto walls had protected a thriving community which boasted many grand homes. Civil rights included the dubious privilege of being drafted for military service, which Roman Jews detested as much as other Romans.

state or nobles on items such as tobacco, liquor, and cards were abolished. Tournon did notable work in the reorganization of hospitals and prisons. Both Tournon and Roederer sponsored experimentation with new crops and were able to grow cotton successfully. By 1812 they were exporting raw fiber to France and had one cloth mill in operation. The French also began draining the Pontine marshes, a project not resumed until the 1920s, when the job was completed by Mussolini.

Almost fanatic attention was given to the preservation of Roman ruins. The various projects were supervised by Canova and Camile Denon, Director General of Imperial Museums. Work on uncovering and restoring the Colosseum went on for five years. The Arch of Titus was restored, and the Temple of Vespasian and the Column of Trajan were uncovered. Buildings (except churches) in the vicinity of the ruins were demolished to clear the view. Tons of earth and debris were removed to expose the Basilica of Constantine. Gardens to beautify the surroundings of all the ruins were planned by Berthault and 76,000 trees were ordered planted around the Forum, on the Palatine Hill, and elsewhere. Though not completed, French plans inspired work by later governments.

The Napoleonic government left physical reminders which are evident today; it also shocked the Romans with previously unknown bureaucratic efficiency. The efforts of the French were little appreciated, though Italian historians now pay them tribute. At the time the best-received innovations were champagne and the waltz.

SPAIN

Joseph entered Spain sworn to uphold the Constitution of Bayonne (1808) approved by a Spanish National Junta called by Napoleon. It provided for a single-chamber Cortes (parliament). It included nobles and clergy appointed by the king, but a majority was to be elected, indirectly by universal male suffrage, though there were property qualifications for the delegates. For Spain, however, even to have a constitution was radical, much less a single Cortes dominated by commoners.

The king had the right to appoint his ministry, council of state, and a senate. A French-style judicial system was to replace the existing tangle of royal, provincial, noble, and church courts. Certain rights were guaranteed: equality of taxation and opportunity, equality before the law, jury trial (if the Cortes approved), and freedom from arbitrary arrest. All feudal rights were abolished. Internal tariffs were to be eliminated and guilds disbanded. To conciliate the powerful clergy, the Catholic Church was declared established. After noting its part in the rebellion of 1808, however, Napoleon abolished the monastic orders and the Inquisition.

Joseph tried to govern in the spirit of the constitution, though war prevented implementing it. His continual references to it much irritated Napoleon. "Tell me," wrote the emperor in 1809, "if the Constitution prohibits the King of Spain from commanding 300,000 Frenchmen . . . if the Constitution says that at Saragossa [under siege] we may jump over the houses. . . . "

The king was able to organize his ministry and council of state as the constitution specified.[16] Throughout, the ministry was all-Spanish, even to the minister of war, Gonzolo O'Farrill. The outstanding members, François (Francisco) de Cabarrus[17] (finance) and Don Manuel Romero (interior and justice), had served the liberal Charles III (1759–1788), but had lost favor under Charles IV and had been persecuted by the Inquisition. Miot de Melito and Joseph's other French advisors were in the council of state, which, however, was overwhelmingly Spanish. Together they represented a pool of liberal talent rivaled only by the rebel Cortes at Cadiz, which sought vainly to direct the "patriot" cause. (See Chapter 11.)

Advised by Romero, Joseph planned a new administrative system (thirty-eight prefectures) with appointed prefects and elected councils, and a new judicial system. Because of the war, neither the administration nor court system was installed, except temporarily in the Madrid area, but the plans served future governments.

Beyond the requirements of the constitution, Joseph attempted to foster a free economy. Not only did he abolish feudal privileges, guilds, and internal tariffs, but he offered the royal industries for sale, including the crystal works at San Ildefonso and china works in Madrid. He abolished the royal monopolies on the manufacture and sale of tobacco, playing cards, liquor, wines, and sealing wax and on gambling. All were offered to private enterprise.

Joseph expected his liberal measures to be beneficial. In the midst of civil war, however, they only further disrupted the economy. Few investors, Spanish or foreign, were ready to risk their capital in Spain. The industries sold were on credit; some were closed. Unemployment increased, and with it sympathy for the rebels. Moreover, government revenues dropped, and to bolster them Joseph reluctantly restored the royal monopolies and reintroduced internal tariffs.

The king hoped to solve this budgeting problem and to finance progressive projects by the liquidation of the confiscated National Properties (mostly church) valued at 10,000,000,000 reals.[18] The notes issued exclusively for their purchase circulated as money, however, and rapidly depreciated. By the end of Joseph's reign they were worthless. The national (Bourbon) debt was paid in paper, and some current expenses met, but the king's deficits increased yearly. Napoleon, by 1813, had sent almost 4,000,000,000 reals in coin to Spain. Carefully planned new taxes, scaled according to ability to pay, could never be implemented. The

[16] He appointed senators as well, but the Senate never functioned.

[17] Born a Frenchman, but a Spanish count, he had founded the state Bank of Saint Charles. He was the father of the notorious Madame Tallien.

[18] Real = 0.27 francs; franc = 3.75 reals = $.20. Figures are in vellon reals (15.06 to the peso). The colonial silver peso (piece of eight) of 8 reals was the exact equivalent in weight and value of the U.S. dollar.

government lived hand-to-mouth on meager traditional revenues, loans from France, and the armies' confiscations.

Despite his financial distress, Joseph fought for progress. He established national juntas for the supervision of public welfare programs—health, hospitals, orphans homes, and homes for the aged. He decreed mass vaccination for smallpox, and had programs prepared for combating epidemics. Much of his liquid capital went into institutions of charity. He also found funds to equip Madrid with a new water system. His decorative fountains, set in public squares, are his most obvious monuments. In Spanish guide books Joseph is still "Joe Bottle," but at the same time, the "King of the Plazas" and the "King of the Fountains."

Joseph placed the universities and schools under a central junta and made plans (never operative) for a complete public school system. He did found a few *lycées*, however, and in Madrid a museum for machines and devices and a school of geometry. He had laid out the Royal Botanical Gardens, which still exist, organized a Royal Opera Company, patronized the theaters, made courtiers of the leading playwrights of the day, and retained Goya as court painter.[19] More startling, Joseph converted the Prado Palace into a museum of art. Now one of the world's greatest, its collection was begun with paintings and objects from the Royal Palace and works from confiscated monasteries. Joseph also began the restoration of the Alhambra of Granada, now one of the top tourist attractions in Spain.

In Napoleon's eyes, Joseph spent too much time on his progressive plans, not enough on war. Joseph kept trying desperately to be more than king by conquest; "I can also be king by love of the Spanish. . . . " he wrote Napoleon in 1809. The emperor was appalled and became more so as time passed. Joseph managed to repulse Wellington's attack on Madrid in 1809, and in 1810 to subdue southern Spain (assisted by Marshal Soult), where he was welcomed with astonishing warmth. Still, he continued to woo the Spanish by promising better government, dispensing gifts, awards, pensions, and titles, granting amnesty to prisoners of war and enlisting them in his Spanish army. The Spanish took his gifts and gave him nothing. Most of his enlistees deserted after receiving uniforms and arms. "El Capitan Vestuario," the rebels called him. Still the king insisted on showing faith in "his people." All the while he complained to Napoleon about French atrocities, while seeming to ignore that the guerrillas regularly tortured French prisoners (one general was boiled alive), lynched French collaborators, and massacred women and children or anyone not protected by heavy escort.

Napoleon might have tolerated Joseph's excessive charity, but the king could not balance his budget, raise a Spanish army, or contribute anything toward supporting the French army which kept him on his throne.

---

[19] See footnote 25, Chapter 8, p. 225.

By mid-1810 the emperor had had enough. He limited Joseph's authority to New Castile, Avila, and Segovia and placed most of Spain under military governors. Some were effective and just, notably Suchet in Aragon-Valencia, who destroyed guerrilla bands, organized a Spanish administration, and collected sufficient taxes to support his army. Most of the governors, however, were arbitrary, cruel, and despotic. In Joseph's opinion they embittered the Spanish, drove them into the arms of the guerrillas and made total pacification impossible. Surely he was right in part. The temper of the population was improving in 1810. When he was restored to command in 1812, it was more violent than ever. Of course in 1810 the French had been winning; Wellington held only Lisbon and the Spanish only Cadiz and a few mountain strongholds. Still, public outrage toward the French helped Wellington to easy victory in 1813.

In peaceful circumstances, Joseph might have been a progressive and well-loved monarch. The ex-rebel Count de Toreño wrote later that "he would have captivated the Spanish" if he had not represented Napoleon. If we grant that the emperor was primarily interested in conquest and profit, it still seems certain that if his government in Spain had been peacefully received, it would not simply have robbed the country and drained off its manpower. It was formed to enlighten, educate, introduce organization and efficiency, and alter society—as well as to contribute to the strength of the empire.

THE ILLYRIAN PROVINCES

Created after Wagram (1809), made part of France, the Illyrian Provinces comprised the former Balkan lands of Austria taken in 1805 and 1809. (See above, pp. 259.) The governor was Marshal Auguste-Frédéric-Louis Marmont, who had administered (1805–1809) Venetian Dalmatia (nominally for Eugène, in Italy), and added to it the republic of Ragusa (1808), after saving it from the Russians. He had devoted his time largely to the military and to roadbuilding, the latter with unusual success.

The administration of Venetian Dalmatia was organized by Dandolo, a rich Venetian Francophile who knew the area. Establishing his capital at Zara, he installed a departmental organization and a police force utilizing "pandours" furnished by the villages—a practical system among wild mountaineers.[20] At his order, the Code Napoléon (in Latin)[21] was proclaimed the law, but Dandolo did not enforce it, nor did he tamper with the feudal rights of the nobles. However, he brought the Church under secular control, abolished its tithe, confiscated

---

[20] Napoleon maintained (Austrian-organized) "Military Croatia." He kept in service six *Grenzer* (border) regiments as *Chasseurs d'Illyrie*. See Gunther E. Rothenberg, *The Military Border in Croatia, 1740–1882* (1966).

[21] Latin was the only language common to the nobles, lawyers, and clergy.

monastic property, and abolished most orders. His greatest reform was the transfer of lands in the interior, nominally state property, to the peasants, whose feudal dues were converted into a tax. With the creation of the Illyrian Provinces, Dandolo withdrew from the government.

Marmont made Liabach his capital. The whole territory was organized into four departments but ruled in essentially racial divisions (a practical measure) by six intendants through subdelegates, and Anziani (chiefs of rural districts), all appointed by the governor. Marmont was succeeded in 1811 by General Henri Bertrand, who was the last active ruler.[22] General Junot, rapidly going insane, took over briefly in 1813. Fouché saw the provinces through their final days in 1813–1814.

Bertrand extended Dandolo's reforms to the new territory, and went further. He abolished feudalism in 1811. Nobles were to be reimbursed for only one-fifth of their financial losses out of new land taxes. The peasants, however, given a taste of freedom, refused to pay and attacked their lords, many of whom fled to Austria. Bertrand was forced to use troops to restore order. The governor forged ahead, nevertheless, proclaiming the Code Napoléon in full force in 1812, and restructuring the courts. The code was never fully accepted but its influence is evident in the Yugoslav law of the present day. A French-style tax system was more effectively enforced and the consolidated debt of the provinces partially liquidated by the use of confiscated church lands.

Public works were continued. Imperial highways were completed from Liabach to Fiume and Trieste and Karlovac to Ragusa. Illyrians cooperated with Italian roadbuilders to link Trieste and Venice. Marmont and Bertrand were also able to produce a small army. Conscription never worked, but traditional local levies, most effective in Croatia, filled the ranks.

The Illyrian Provinces, however, were not a great asset to France, nor were the French well loved. The peasants were not grateful for the benefits conferred on them, and the nobles resented the loss of their privileges. The middle-class merchants hated the Continental System. Smuggling was easy along the convoluted Adriatic coastline. Trieste and other large ports suffered, however, though in 1810 licenses were granted the Illyrians (technically French) before the Italians were supplied.

Napoleon recognized his failure in the Balkans. In 1812 he promised Illyria to Austria (upon Russia's defeat) in return for the remainder of Galicia (for Poland). He again offered Illyria in return for Austrian neutrality in 1813. Nevertheless, the Napoleonic legacy to the Balkans was considerable. Feudalism could never be totally restored; memory of the Code Napoléon and the French administrative efficiency remained. The recognition of Serb and Croatian as official languages by Marmont served to promote Slavic national pride. The

---

[22] Bertrand became Napoleon's "Grand Marshal of the Palace," went into exile with him to Elba, then St. Helena, and was with the emperor when he died. He left *Mémoires*, published 1823–1825 and 1841, and *Cahiers de Sainte Hélène*, in code, which were not deciphered and published until 1949–1951.

struggles of the lower classes during the period raised hopes for greater national freedom in the future.

WESTPHALIA

King Jerome Bonaparte entered Westphalia in 1807 with a new wife—Catherine of Württemberg.[23] She was religious, well educated, fluent in French, comely, sturdy, and seemed just right to Napoleon, who wanted nephews. She in fact proved a model queen, though she could never reform Jerome, to whom *chercher la femme* was a way of life. He, nevertheless, proved an effective executive and military commander.

The emperor intended Westphalia to be a model for the other states of the Rheinbund. To insure its success, he sent a team of French experts ahead of Jerome to organize the kingdom—Joseph Siméon, Jacques Claude Beugnot, and Jean Jollivet. He appointed as minister of war General Lagrange, who had been military governor of Hesse-Cassel since 1806. When Jerome arrived, however, he took over in no uncertain way.

Napoleon and Cambacérès, advised by a hand-picked committee of Germans, had written a constitution for Westphalia. The king ruled with an appointed ministry and council of state and a 100-man *Ständeversammlung* (parliament), elected indirectly by universal manhood suffrage.

After mid-1808, Jerome governed with an all-German ministry, with two exceptions. Siméon was allowed to keep the portfolio of justice, and a succession of French generals occupied the war ministry since Napoleon would not allow a German in the office. The parliament, which even included a few peasants, functioned until 1810, when it was dismissed for opposing war taxes.

The law was the Code Napoléon in a German translation produced by Siméon with the aid of German professors and jurists. It went into effect on 1 January 1808. In the constitution and in the code, feudalism, guilds, and entail were abolished, and there was the usual roster of rights.

For administration, there were eight departments, subdivided according to the French system. The prefects were all Germans. Five were aristocrats, three from the middle class. The ratio in the ministry and council of state was also in favor of the nobles. This seemed practical for Westphalia, where the nobility was still highly respected, and Napoleon welcomed aristocrats who supported his policies, as he had in France. The king appointed prefects, subprefects, mayors, and their councils from rosters drawn up by departmental electoral colleges, which also nominated justices of the peace. The courts were organized on the French model.

---

[23] He had married Elizabeth Patterson of Baltimore in 1803 and had an American son. Though the pope refused to annul the marriage, it was done by the archbishop of Paris. The American Bonapartes were prominent at the turn of the century, when Jerome's grandson served Theodore Roosevelt as secretary of the navy and attorney general. The line is now extinct, however.

Jerome tried to pick capable men and let them do their jobs. Those who failed were replaced. He had a mind for essentials, hated detail, and was a little lazy—as some good executives are. He delegated authority freely, but never for a minute gave it up. When he worked, Jerome worked hard and thoroughly. When he was with the army, he took over. He knew his officers and his troops and cared about them, and they knew it.

The army, administration, and judiciary were all made instruments of social change. Admission to military schools and commissions were granted on merit. The officer corps remained mostly aristocratic, but the way was open for all. Prussians, Hessians, Hanoverians, Saxons, and others mingled in the military schools and in the ranks of the army. There was a "leveling" of the language. Men of all religions, similarly, marched together—Calvinists, Catholics, Lutherans, and Jews. The Westphalian army had the first Jewish officers of any German army. Social mobility was promoted, and provincialism diminished. In the judiciary and the administration there was a similar effort to keep careers open to talent. The middle class made more progress there than in the military.

The story of finances in Westphalia is a sad one. The kingdom began with a debt which got larger every year. Until 1811, however, the minister of finance, Hans von Bülow, managed to provide funds, without oppressive taxes, by selling the confiscated property of the churches (Catholic and Protestant) and by borrowing. Thus, though there were few public works and welfare projects, the kingdom served the empire well, essential institutions were maintained, and there was considerable reform.

All schools were put under a director of education, at first Johannes von Müller, an internationally known Swiss historian. In Prussian service in 1806, he had met Napoleon at Berlin and had become a disciple. Westphalia had 3100 public schools already operating, and by accident of boundaries, five universities, including Halle from Prussia[24] and Göttingen from Hanover. All the lower schools were kept open, but Müller had to close two universities (Helmstedt and Rintln) to have funds for the others—Halle, Göttingen, and Marburg—for whom students had to be imported in any case; Westphalia had only 2,200,000 people. Müller hoped that Göttingen, his alma mater, would become a center of "new European culture" in Germany. New departments were added (e.g., French literature), but the faculty wisely resisted sweeping change, particularly in science and philosophy.[25]

Jerome was no cerebral, and was given to anti-intellectual outbursts, but patronized the universities. At Göttingen, he built an observatory for Karl Friedrich Gauss (after whom the unit of magnetic flux density is named). He

---

[24] The loss of Halle prompted the founding of the University of Berlin in 1810.

[25] Göttingen became famous for physics in the nineteenth century. In the 1920s and 1930s it trained many men who were later key figures in the U.S. atomic program, including Robert Oppenheimer (an American), Edward Keller (Austrian), and Enrico Fermi (Italian). The university has revived since World War II.

named the distinguished Protestant theologian August Niemeyer rector at Marburg. He sponsored a royal society *(Societät für Wissenschaft)* as a meeting ground for French and German intellectuals. Jerome's government financed the publication of the first comprehensive German dictionary, that of Heinrich von Campe. His court librarian was Jakob Grimm, a philologist later famous for the *Fairy Tales* (with brother Wilhelm).

There was some trouble in the universities, but generally not over political matters. The first student riots occurred when Jerome suppressed the dueling societies.[26] In 1809 a few were motivated very briefly by pan-German nationalism, which, however, became important only after 1815. Students generally welcomed Jerome and, as might be expected, stood in awe of his bad reputation. Professors made snide remarks in private, but generally accepted his favors.

Jerome's public welfare programs never really got beyond the planning stage. The public debt was too heavy; the demands of Napoleon constantly increasing. However, existing hospitals and charitable institutions were kept going. The minister of the interior supervised the health program, including the enforcement of smallpox vaccination.

In terms of contribution to the empire, Westphalia ranked with Italy. Jerome supported a German army of 25,000 and varying numbers of French troops as well. He mustered 38,000 in 1812, of which 22,000 served in Russia (few returned). In addition, he sent 13,000 men to Spain and raised 20,000 to fight for Napoleon in 1813. Some of his men fought on to the end in 1814, and everywhere Westphalians distinguished themselves.

The efficiency of his government, his reforms, and the French institutions he introduced made a lasting impression. In the nineteenth century, the first revolutions in Germany were in areas once part of Westphalia.

HOLLAND

Louis Bonaparte was a man of great compassion, who in his short reign won the hearts of his subjects. Afflicted with many ills (probably mostly psychosomatic), he was flabby, balding, and looked older than Napoleon, who was nine years his senior. Married against his will to the lovely blonde Hortense de Beauharnais, he lived apart from her (even when in the same palace). They had three sons before they separated (1810), however. The last, Louis Napoleon, became Napoleon III. A half-time king, he nonetheless displayed, when well, energy, intelligence, imagination, and quiet courage—the kind that took him into plague areas to help the victims.

Louis' selection of ministers reflected his determination to be a *Dutch* king, which ultimately was his undoing. Three came from the old government, I. J. A.

---

[26] Which revived in secret. No German government has been able to suppress them totally.

Gogel (finances), Van der Goes (foreign affairs), and Admiral Verhuel (navy). The new appointees were known patriots —Roell, Mollerus, Van Hof, and Van der Heim.

The constitution of Holland provided for a legislature of thirty-eight men, comprising eighteen "High Mightinesses" of the old estates and nineteen royal appointees. Civil liberties and freedom of religion, traditional in Holland, were affirmed. The independence and territorial integrity of Holland were guaranteed, and Dutch was to remain the official language. The constitution also granted Holland favored economic treatment by France. Actually, Napoleon's policies varied with the effectiveness of Louis' enforcement of the Continental System.

Louis considered the Continental System a thing of "extreme immorality" because of the suffering it caused his nation, whose lifeblood was trade.[27] He gave appropriate orders for enforcement but seldom checked to see if Dutch officials complied with them. This was not the only thing that angered Napoleon, however. Louis consulted his legislature about everything. Even when he issued emergency decrees during epidemics and floods, he submitted them for confirmation. To the emperor's objection, Louis replied, "Do you not rule with the senate?" The king dragged his feet on the abolition of remaining feudal dues, spared the guilds, and instituted only parts of the Code Napoléon, which, said he, was un-Dutch.

Louis also rejected conscription because the Dutch had never had compulsory military service, and since few Dutch would volunteer for service, employed mercenaries, mostly German. To give the army a national character he decreed that orders be given in Dutch, but it remained a foreign legion. By 1807, however, he had the force of 20,000 that Napoleon demanded, though there was no National Guard to back it up. Still, the Dutch navy (an object of national pride) was excellent and Holland was a source of ready cash. Until 1810, Napoleon tolerated Louis' government.

The king's government lived on loans. Its borrowings averaged 104,000,000 florins a year; tax income, 53,000,000.[28] In 1809 the *interest* on the debt was 48,000,000. It was only because Louis had involved the merchant-banking oligarchy in the government that the king's credit remained good. The banks supported him, preferring to gamble on recovering their capital over raising taxes and creating public unrest.

Louis spent millions on dikes and reclaiming cultivable land from the sea and marshes. He also pressed for the implementation of a radical scheme for reducing the effects of winter floods which broke dams, inundated towns, destroyed property, took lives, and left diseases in their wake. On the advice of the Dutch hydraulic engineers Brunings and Jansz, he proposed that dikes on the Meuse, Maas, and Waal be systematically sluiced every year at flood time, allowing the water to flow overland to the sea. Structures were to be put on piles in predicted

---

[27] In his memoirs, he blamed the fall of the Napoleonic Empire on the "immoral" Continental System.
[28] Florin = 2.17 francs.

flood lanes and people and stock moved as necessary. Disasters would be avoided and alluvium left to enrich the soil. This was too extreme for the Dutch at the time, but by 1825 they had adopted the system.

Louis founded a Royal Institute of Science and Arts, composed of four royal societies for the sciences, arts, history and antiquity, and literature. Membership included the elite of the intelligentsia, such as the physicist, Van Swiden; the astronomer, Hennert; the painters, Alberti, Klein, and Teerling; and the *litterateurs*, Meerman, De Bosch, Bilderdijk, and Weyland. The king gave supervision of the schools and universities to a Director of Arts and Sciences but achieved no true centralization. The Dutch preferred and retained local control of the lower schools; the universities were adamantly self-governing. Short of funds and disinclined to buck tradition, Louis let them be.

The Dutch had veritably "invented" religious toleration. Nevertheless, in some localities, Protestants (generally in the majority) discriminated against Catholics, usually as to taxation and use of public facilities. In a few places where Catholics predominated, the reverse was true. Louis staunchly defended whichever group seemed oppressed. "When I am in Catholic territory, I am Protestant," he said, "and when in Protestant areas, I am Catholic."

The king's greatest personal crusade, however, was against disease. He organized a National Council for Public Health, planned for epidemic control, enforced smallpox vaccination, and went much further. His most grandiose scheme (never implemented) was for an international center for the collection of medical knowledge which would then be distributed worldwide. In this Louis was a century before his time. Some of his programs drew laughs—for example, a campaign for breast-feeding babies. The people, nevertheless, recognized that he was concerned about them; he proved it by such gestures as going into epidemic areas and sitting by bedsides through the night. To the consternation of professionals, he also often took control of rescue and relief in flood areas, and several times barely escaped.

Napoleon, however, was not pleased with Louis. Using nonenforcement of the Continental System as an excuse, he drove him from his throne in 1810, as already noted. Since, in fine, Louis was removed because he was too Dutch, he is well-remembered in the Netherlands.

GRAND DUCHY OF BERG

The Duchy (later Grand Duchy) of Berg was created for Murat after Austerlitz (1805) from the duchies of Cleves and Berg (respectively Prussian and Bavarian, exchanged for other territory). With the creation of the Confederation of the Rhine (1806), and again after Tilsit (1807), it was further enlarged.[29] The

---

[29] Additions were Nassau, Dillenberg, Mark, the city of Lippenstadt, Prussian Münster, Tecklenberg, and Lingen. Murat also got the postal monopoly of north Germany, held since 1615 by the house of Thurn and Taxis.

capital was Düsseldorf, and Berg included the Ruhr, already a center of mining and some metalworking.

The state was a reward to Murat for his military services. For Caroline Bonaparte, his wife, it was all too little. Unwilling to be buried in "rustic" Düsseldorf, she pursued Napoleon, constantly bidding for a kingdom until he gave her Naples in 1808. (See above, p. 247.) In 1809 the emperor gave Berg to Napoleon-Louis Bonaparte, son of Louis, age five, which the father correctly interpreted to mean that he would never inherit Holland.[30] Berg was really governed by Napoleon's administrators from the beginning. Much property, including forests and mines, was, in any case, part of the imperial domains.

The duchy was organized in 1806 by Count Agar de Mosbourg, who later served Murat in Naples. He eliminated local diets, divided the state into districts under appointed councillors (mostly German nobles), and had mayors of cities picked from lists presented by existing city councils. A common land tax was added to those of the former states and conscription was introduced. In 1809, Jacques Claude Beugnot (transferred from Westphalia) reformed the tax system, abolished guilds, and legalized marriage between nobles and commoners. He became minister of finances in 1810 when Pierre-Louis Roederer (formerly in Naples) was named chief administrator. Roederer restructured the courts and in 1812 issued a constitution, formed a council of state, and named an assembly of notables.

Meanwhile the churches were taken under civil control, the clergy was put on salary, and the monastic orders were dissolved. Roederer planned a university for Düsseldorf, but established only a few *lycées*.

Serfdom and feudalism were abolished in 1808, but peasants had to pay compensation for dues. When the Code Napoléon was introduced, belatedly, in 1811, they refused further payments, which the code made unlawful. Peasant delegations went to Paris to appeal to the emperor. Napoleon, however, unwilling to alienate the aristocracy in view of the Russian crisis, ruled against the peasants and ordered their deputies arrested on their return to Berg. It was one of Napoleon's shoddier performances. Nevertheless, the peasants benefited greatly from the decrees of 1809–1811. Property distribution was accelerated as perhaps nowhere else in the empire.

At first the industrial economy of Berg declined because of the Continental System. It shut off access to markets for its chief product, Remscheid steel, which had been exported worldwide to shipyards, barrel factories, needleworks, tool plants, and the like. The blockade also affected textiles, next in importance, since production depended on the importation of wool from Spain and England, silk from Italy, and cotton from the United States, the Spanish colonies, the Levant and elsewhere. The steel industry was able to convert to manufacturing for

---

[30] Napoleon-Louis died in 1831. It was Louis' third son, Charles-Louis Napoleon, who became Napoleon III in 1852.

imperial needs—especially for war—and was greatly expanded by 1812. Textiles declined steadily but were able to recover after 1815. Overall, however, the economy achieved a new balance, and after 1815 the Ruhr gradually became Germany's chief iron, steel, machinery, and arms-producing center.

Napoleonic rule brought difficult economic adjustments in Berg. Taxes were high. Conscription was not joyfully received and was rejected, amid rioting, after half the duchy's 5000-man army was lost in Russia. In the balance, however, the gains for Berg outweighed the losses. Industry grew, feudalism disappeared, and peasant landholding increased. Moreover, the Prussian king, after 1815, retained the French-style bureaucracy and courts and left the Code Napoléon virtually in full force.

GRAND DUCHY OF FRANKFURT

With the creation of the Rheinbund (1806), the one church state left from the Holy Roman Empire, Frankfurt, was given to the Prince Primate of Germany, Charles Theodore Dalberg, later grand duke. (After his death, it was to go to Eugène de Beauharnais. See above, p. 261.) The imposing former Archbishop-Elector of Mainz, a sincere "man of 1789," had welcomed the French invasion of the Rhineland. Lefebvre calls him a "good Catholic and a good German," but a Josephist—follower of Joseph II (d. 1790), the enlightened Austrian emperor.

The Grand Duchy of Frankfurt included the city of Frankfurt (on the Main) and environs, Aschaffenburg, Fulda, and Hanau. Dalberg's chief ministers were Albini and Beust. He promulgated a constitution and formed a council of state and an "Estates" (legislature) named by electors appointed by himself. The government modernized the administration, enforced equality of taxation and religious liberty, and declared feudalism abolished and guilds disbanded. The Code Napoléon, however, was not the law until 1810 and was enforced by traditional courts until 1813. The churches were placed under state control and the monastic orders dissolved, but religious freedom was limited by Dalberg's requirement of church marriage (Catholic or Protestant), which violated the civil code. Jews were not given full citizenship until 1812. Until then, though authorized to own land and to operate industries, they had to live in specified locations (ghettos). Until 1811 they had to pay special taxes (1813 for Fulda and Aschaffenburg). Jews were, nevertheless, appointed to high office and exerted influence. Amschel Rothschild (the *pater familias* of the international banking clan) and his fellow banker, Oppenheimer, for example, were made electors.

Nobles retained their titles and in rural areas their juridical rights. Feudal dues were nominally abolished without compensation in Fulda and Hanau (1808), but peasants were everywhere forced to buy their freedom by village, and many declined. Thus feudalism persisted in many areas despite the provisions of the Code Napoléon. Serfdom, ended by imperial decree, did not entirely disappear either.

Frankfurt was far from being a model progressive state, but for Germany, its record was not bad. The government was efficient, the administration honest, and the people reasonably satisfied. About half the peasants were freed from feudal burdens and became freeholders.

GRAND DUCHY OF WARSAW [31]

"I want a camp in Poland, not a forum. . . ." Napoleon once said in anger. He spoke the truth. What he got, however, was both. Polish troops were among his most reliable; the Polish lancers of the Imperial Guard made legend; Poniatowski became one of the twenty-six marshals of France. The chambers of the duchy's government, however, excelled in the production of words, not deeds.

Created from Prussian Poland after Tilsit (1807), the Grand Duchy of Warsaw was placed under King Frederick Augustus of Saxony. Said he, "I do my best; for the rest I trust in God and the Emperor." Old, painfully religious, sedentary and indecisive, he seldom left Dresden. His court, said the vivacious Polish Countess Potocki "resembled that of sleeping beauty."

The Baron Bignon, Napoleon's "resident," repeatedly proposed that the emperor recreate the Polish kingdom under a Bonaparte. Napoleon temporized, however, so as not to alienate Czar Alexander. Moreover, he was hesitant because, although the nobility wanted the kingdom restored, its factions violently disagreed over the form. As it was, he had the support of Prince Adam Czartoryski, head of The Family, most of its members (though young Adam served the czar), and most other great nobles. They accepted French domination as best under the circumstances. Even in 1812, Napoleon preferred to leave the Polish question open, in the hope the czar might more easily come to terms.

The grand duchy was ruled by a ministry of great nobles at Warsaw, one of whom maintained liaison with the Saxon king at Dresden. The state's constitution was published by Napoleon himself in 1807. Beneath the ministry was an appointive council-of-state, a senate of six bishops and twelve laymen, and an elected diet of 160. All were named by nobles. The diet was supposed to have a popular contingent from the cities and towns, but only "citizens" qualified for election, and the word had been translated "landholders." The diet met briefly three times and did little. The ministry, however, made some real advances.

Count Stanislas Potocki was president of the council of ministers. Elderly, tall, very thin, elegant, traveled, multilingual, he was a figurehead agreeable to all parties. An aristocrat, enormously rich, married to a Czartoryski, he was at the same time Grand Master of Freemasons in Poland (whose arms bore the Napo-

---

[31] Technically, Warsaw was a *duchy*, but then, as now, generally called Grand Duchy because it was larger than Napoleon's other grand duchies, and was power-politically more important, in that it furnished more troops and served as a buffer against Russia. See Tulard, *Dictionnaire Napoléon*.

leonic "N").[32] By instinct, he protected noble privileges, while declaiming, with utmost sincerity, on the glories of progress. This suited his ministers, who in council were called the "seven sleeping brothers" and outside did as they liked.

The most important man in the duchy to Napoleon was Prince Joseph Poniatowski, minister of war, who sent him troops and commanded a strong Polish army. "There was a Pole [out of legend]," says Mansuy, "without qualification . . . an accomplished cavalier, a prince charming." He had fought in 1794 with Kosciuszko (of American Revolutionary fame) for a free Poland, but resigned himself to the partition among Russia, Austria, and Prussia. In 1806, however, Napoleon's victory over the Prussians convinced him that backed by France, Poland might live again. He gave his allegiance to Napoleon and died fighting for him in 1813. Politically, he was not a power, but few men in Poland were more highly respected (or loved by the ladies).

The most ardent reformer was the minister of interior, Count John Paul Luszczewski. No grand seigneur, but a protégé of the French, small and fat, his life was hard and he died in office. He succeeded, nevertheless, in installing a departmental administration and populating it in part with nonnobles. The prefectures he organized lasted until 1830.

Serfdom was abolished, but the ex-serfs received no land. They had the choice of leaving the land or of remaining as rent-paying tenants, subject directly to taxes and feudal dues, which were not abolished. Those who left became day laborers, joined the proletariat of the cities (which were small and lacked in industry), or became vagabonds or bandits. In some areas the nobles took advantage of the law to expel unneeded laborers and/or troublemakers. Nevertheless, the peasantry was freed.

An embryonic middle class appeared between the nobles and the peasants. It comprised the stewarts of the nobles (some of whom did the actual work of noble prefects, subprefects, and mayors), military officers who rose from the ranks in the French or Polish armies, merchants, artisans, and some nonnoble proprietors.

There was no radical change in the character of society. However, the Continental System accelerated the impoverishment of the old aristocracy, whose fortunes depended on agriculture, by closing overseas grain markets. They sold off land to rising new men, who ultimately made it profitable again. Moreover, the system promoted industry (notably in textiles, metals, and distilling), and mining, which gave money and status to nonnoble enterprisers. Still, nobles retained control of the country, and though liberty and equality were proclaimed, Napoleonic principles were not applied.

Unlike Luszczewski, most ministers were "patriots," who meant to serve

---

[32] Freemasonry had vague origins in medieval stonemason's guilds, which supported charities. The modern lodges originated in Britain and spread to the Continent. National lodges of the eighteenth century promoted the ideals of the Enlightment. That of France, of which the Duke d'Orléans was Grand Master and Lafayette a member, was suspected of fomenting the Revolution (see Chapter 1, p. 32), but was destroyed by it. Napoleon revived the order in France. European Freemasons generally supported him.

Poland, trimming their sails as the power balance demanded. Typical was the minister of police, Count Ignatius Sobolewski, a debonaire seigneur who kept on good terms with both Poniatowski and young Adam Czartoryski (in Russia). Of like mind was the minister of justice and cults, Count Lubienski, who made a great show of installing the Code Napoléon, reforming the courts, and bringing the Church under secular control. The promulgation of the code was celebrated by a "Te Deum" in Warsaw, however, clearly forecasting that the Church would supervise its application. He restructured the courts but the judges he appointed were in vast majority noble, rich, and unsympathetic toward the Code, which was translated into Polish but not enforced.

The Church, throughout, was a bulwark of reaction. Conscious of its power over the people, Napoleon compromised. In the constitution he declared the "Christian, Apostolic and Roman" Church established, contradicting the declaration of religious freedom. Moreover, he did not replace the ultraconservative primate of Poland, Ignatius Raczynski.

Raczynski resided at Ciazno, closer to Dresden than Warsaw, and kept the pious king of Saxony subject by his towering presence and iron will. He rejected civil marriage and divorce out-of-hand. He retained the property of the Church intact, and church courts continued to function as usual. Raczynski induced the king to suspend that part of the constitution which gave the Jews full citizenship and the right to public worship. They received civil rights only upon payment and grant of patent and required special permission to buy land.

The minister of "cults," quailed before the Primate. The influence of the clergy in the council of state and senate at Warsaw was disproportionate to their numbers. There were vocal liberal nobles, among them Jan Henryk Dombrowski, who since 1795 had led a Polish legion in the French army. Liberal clergymen, however, were soon silenced by Raczynski.

In Saint Petersburg the persuasive Adam Czartoryski worked for a Polish kingdom under the czar. He had some success in 1811, after Alexander broke with Napoleon and found Russia opposed by Prussia and Austria as well. The czar offered Warsaw a Polish-Lithuanian kingdom with an outlet to the sea, a liberal constitution, and maximum autonomy. The offer was refused since Napoleon's power seemed too great to oppose. The Polish nobility, however, became even more divided, not only between Francophiles and Russophiles, but between conservatives and liberals.

In the spring of 1812, while Napoleon's armies assembled for the Russian campaign, he took steps to counter the czar's offer. At his behest, the elder Prince Adam Czartoryski presided over an extraordinary Zeym at Warsaw which founded a new Polish confederation. Simultaneously the emperor sent an ambassador (the rank appropriate to kingly courts) to Warsaw, followed by Jerome Bonaparte, who was to command the right wing of the Grande Armée. Many, including Jerome, thought he would be named king of Poland.

Napoleon, however, took no further action. Jerome marched with the army.

Apparently the emperor judged Polish opinion still too divided. Moreover, for the moment, he had what he wanted from Poland—Poniatowski and 90,000 disciplined Polish troops.

In terms of progress and enlightenment, the Grand Duchy of Warsaw cannot be rated very highly. Nevertheless, its government was superior to that it replaced, and its example undoubtedly influenced the czar to grant a constitution to the kingdom of Poland created in 1815.

The memory of the Code Napoléon, however poorly fulfilled, remained to inspire revolutionaries. Society had been shaken, inviting change. The industrial sector of the economy had gained strength. French administrative, judicial, and financial systems operated until the disastrous revolution of 1830 against Russia. Polish nationalism, reborn under Napoleon, increased in reaction to Russian tyranny after 1815, and more after 1830. The nation still honors the heroism of the Poles of the Grande Armée.

CONCLUSION

The common factors in the governance of the satellite states are obvious. All were established by force or threat of force and so held, in whole or part. Political opposition was silenced. All had constitutions, however, or came under that of France. No constitution was ever fully applied, but in every state there was some popular participation in government. In varying degree, the rights stated were enforced and reforms promised were effected. Governments, administrations, and judiciaries were remade, feudalism and serfdom were abolished, in whole or part. Equality before the law and of taxation, careers open to talent and freedom of religion become the ideal if not the rule. The Code Napoléon nominally became the law everywhere except in Spain. The churches all lost property and direct political power (except in Poland, and even there, under the law). Free domestic economies were fostered and land ownership widened (even in Spain and Poland). There was a concentrated effort to promote public welfare; improve public health; and promote education, science, the arts, and literature. Roads, bridges, canals, and harbors were built or improved. Cities got new water and sewage systems. Holland got new dikes; land was reclaimed there and elsewhere. There was also a determined attempt to sponsor social revolution. Because of the empire's short life, this worked mostly to the advantage of the rising middle class. Public education, in time, however, might have allowed more men from the lower ranks of a society to move up.

Napoleon, in short, sponsored revolution. This steeled the resolve of rulers who had lost by his remapping of Europe to strike him down when the opportunity arose. They had many aristocratic sympathizers, even among those who served Napoleonic governments across Europe. Napoleon's compromises with the old nobility, most evident in Germany and Poland, did not satisfy them and displeased the lower classes. The rising middle classes, for all the favors he did them, were frustrated by the strictures of the Continental System and by tariff arrangements which subordinated their national economies to that of France.

Especially after 1810, with the buildup for the Russian campaign, the benefits of French domination were obscured among all classes by increased taxes; higher conscription quotas; and extraordinary levies of monies, food, livestock, horses, and material. In most areas the peoples did not reach the point of open rebellion, but they were oppressed enough to welcome their old rulers when Russian-Austrian-Prussian-British power brought them back.

Europe never ceased making war on France,
on her principles, on me. . . .
The coalition was always there,
public or secret, avowed or otherwise. . . .
—*Napoleon at St. Helena*

THE WORLD AND THE FRENCH IMPERIUM

The Resistance, Allies, and the World Impact

The empire proper never submitted fully to French domination. Among the allied states of the "Greater Empire" (all Europe at the height of Napoleon's power) only those of the *Rheinbund* were reasonably subservient. Even there the response to the Napoleonic reform impulse was modest. Prussian reforms after 1807 were intended to build her military strength for the day of final reckoning. Austria, throughout the period, harbored anti-Napoleonic refugees of all nationalities, who continually incited Europeans to revolt. Europewide, latent nationalisms were awakened by the flaunting of French power, and in Germany and Italy pan-nationalism took hold among intellectuals.

Britain, of course, remained constantly at war with the French Empire. She maintained footholds in Portugal and Spain, tendered subsidies to potential European allies, financed anti-Napoleonic propaganda, and kept agents and/or spies in every capital and port. She hammered unceasingly at the Continental System and plundered French and neutral shipping on the seas. France retaliated, also punishing neutrals. (The United States, caught between two fires, "took the side of France" in the War of 1812.)

The struggle for Europe affected events in every part of the world. Napoleon embroiled Turkey and Persia with Russia. He attempted vainly to hold both the French and Dutch colonies, but ended by delivering Louisiana to the United States, Haiti to black rule, and South Africa to Britain. His invasion of Portugal drove the royal court to Brazil, which bolstered Brazilian nationalism and paved the way for independence. His conquest of Spain set the Spanish colonies adrift. Some achieved independence; others saw abortive revolutions which presaged successful ones in the nineteenth century.

In Europe, resistance to French domination paved the way for Napoleon's downfall.

REBEL SPAIN

On the fringe of the empire, the rebel *Cortes* of Cadiz stubbornly continued the pretense of governing Spain for Ferdinand VII. The Cortes was dominated by liberals whose reform objectives in 1808 had been all but identical with those of Joseph Bonaparte. Notwithstanding, the majority had supported the rebels. They were suspicious of Napoleon's motives and felt they had to respect the anti-French fury of the masses—or were intimidated by it. Melchor de Jovellanos sent warm greetings to Joseph at Bayonne, but on sensing the popular mood, broke off correspondence. Some who took oaths to the king deserted him after his retreat from Madrid (July 1808), among them Pedro de Cevallos and the Duke d'Infantado.

The liberal rebels hoped to steer their government into a progressive course. They trumpeted to Britain and Europe the news of Baylen, the exploits of the guerrillas, and the heroism of the people of Saragossa, which was besieged in 1808 and again in 1809 and taken only after it was reduced to rubble. At the same time, men such as the Count de Toreño, Jovellanos,[1] Muñoz Torrero, Arguëlles, and others, depicted the Spanish resistance as a liberal-nationalist struggle, which it was not. The resistance was led by reactionary churchmen and nobles.

A regency governing in the name of Ferdinand VII was established in 1808. The liberals got control of it in 1810, when the regency was blockaded in the port of Cadiz by Joseph's armies, where it held out by the grace of the British navy. A Cortes was assembled to write a constitution. Supposedly elected, most of the members of the Cortes were self-appointed, since the French controlled the Peninsula. It was a liberal body because only the progressives were organized and interested in reform. It was supported by the radical workers of the port, who were Francophobes and politically more sophisticated than the general peasant population.

The British happily accepted the Cortes and the regency it supported as the legitimate government of Spain. It salved the official conscience to deal with constitutionalists rather than reactionaries. It did not escape British representatives on the spot that the actual rebel leaders fighting the French paid scant attention to Cortes' orders, except when receipt of British supplies and arms were involved. It suited His Majesty's government to believe that it was helping to create a New Spain—not fighting for the return of absolute monarchy, feudalism, and the Inquisition. In any case, the defeat of Napoleon had first priority.

The Cortes' Constitution of 1812 was an exercise in one-upmanship on Joseph's Constitution of Bayonne. (See above, p. 278.) It proclaimed sovereignty

---

[1] Jovellanos died in 1811, by that time no longer trusted by the rebels because of his moderation.

of the people, equality of rights and in taxation, and inviolability of private property. It provided for an hereditary constitutional monarchy and a single-chamber Cortes elected by universal manhood suffrage, as well as for ministerial responsibility and separation of executive, legislative, and judicial powers.

The liberals had gambled that Ferdinand VII would accept the constitution when he returned. He did not. Wary on his reentry (March 1814), Ferdinand gave the reformers hope, but within weeks reasserted his absolute powers (to the plaudits of the populace). Liberals fled or were jailed and executed. A few heads were exhibited in the cities to make the king's position clear. The history of the Cadiz experiment was written by men like Toreño, who gained refuge in France.

The Cortes served its purpose in the war against Napoleon, however. It facilitated the delivery of British arms, supplies, and money to the rebel armies and guerrillas in the field. Despite its weakness, it served as a coordinating body for the war effort, ultimately appointing Wellington generalissimo of Allied forces in the Peninsula. It gave the Spanish rebellion an enormous respectability in progressive circles in Europe, Britain, and America. It allowed the Spanish intelligentsia to play a role in the national struggle. Finally, the constitution it produced was of lasting importance.

Ferdinand VII could not kill the Constitution of 1812. When revolution broke out in 1820, he was forced to accept it (if temporarily). Meanwhile, it had become a model for other revolutionaries in Europe and Latin America.

PRUSSIA

In 1807, Frederick William of Prussia gave almost dictatorial power to reform his truncated kingdom to the Baron Heinrich F. Karl vom und zum Stein, a native of Nassau (in the Rhineland). A former minister, now middle aged with a mane of greying hair and angry hooded eyes, he had earlier been too radical for conservatives and the court, and still had enemies. In 1807, Napoleon recommended him, however, as did the man he replaced as chancellor, Count (later Prince) Karl August von Hardenberg. The emperor had taken the word of Pierre Daru, his civil administrator in the conquered lands, that Stein was enlightened, and, more important, capable of reordering Prussian finances and of paying off the indemnity due France by the Treaty of Tilsit. He did not realize Stein's intense hatred of the French, which had been increased when his family's estates were lost in the reorganization of Germany.

Stein was an odd combination of progressive and romantic. He was not a Prussian but a German nationalist. His ideal Germany, however, was a federal state, which, taking into account more modern institutions, somewhat resembled the Holy Roman Empire of the twelfth century. His reforms were directed toward increasing local self-government and thus strengthening society and the state. Stein and Hardenberg, who advised him, remained a minister, and again became chancellor in 1810, agreed on the need for reform, but for different reasons.

Hardenberg, a Hanoverian educated at Göttingen, was an admirer of British institutions and a disciple of Adam Smith. Unlike Stein, he was dedicated solely to Prussian interests. Neither, however, belongs in the same category with Arndt, Fichte, Jahn, and other liberal proponents of a German nation-state.

Stein made definite beginnings in reforming a veritably medieval society. A decree of October 1807 authorized all persons to own land and to enter into any and all professions. In November 1808 taxpayers of cities were given the right to elect municipal councils, previously selected by self-appointed oligarchies. In the same month, serfdom was declared abolished as of November 1810. Stein had plans to reform the ministry, establish a parliament (*Landtag*), abolish feudal dues and the *corvée*, and limit the power of nobles in the countryside by introducing elected district councils.

Napoleon had Stein dismissed in November 1808, however, and domestic reforms ended until Hardenberg again became chancellor in 1810. The baron fled to Austria, and later Russia. (An enemy at court had sent one of Stein's anti-French letters to Napoleon. Such a letter was not difficult to come by, since he loathed the French, whom he considered irrecoverably degenerate, and had frequently damned them in writing.) Hardenberg saw to the abolition of serfdom in 1810 and in 1811 had all feudal obligations canceled (with compensation to the lords in the form of part of the peasant's land). He also carried through the abolition of compulsory membership in guilds, instituted freedom of contract, and emancipated the Jews.

More important for the immediate future, Stein encouraged military reforms, which were conceived, however, and altogether carried out, by Generals Gerhard von Scharnhorst and August von Gneisenau, aided by younger officers including the later famous Colonel Karl von Clausewitz. The *Krümpersystem* was introduced, under which men were rotated into the army for training and released to a ready reserve. By this method the standing forces were kept at 42,000, as specified by Napoleon, but the army (1812) numbered 125,000.

The existence of a Prussian army that could win victories was what enabled the king to turn on Napoleon in 1813. There was no widespread mass movement against the French. The regular army did most of the fighting, aided by some volunteers. (See page 333.) King Frederick William distrusted a "nation at arms."

Prussia had reformed herself, nevertheless, in reaction to Napoleon's challenge, and sufficiently to reassert herself in European affairs after 1813.

AUSTRIA[2]

Austria saw its only "national revival" in 1809. It was generated solely to prepare the empire for war against France, and propaganda efforts were directed

---

[2] Austria is given short-shrift in this chapter, since, as the most persistent continental enemy of Napoleonic France (and earlier Revolutionary France), it gets extensive coverage elsewhere.

largely to the German population. The Emperor Francis was deeply fearful of the consequences of stirring up popular passions even in Austria and Hungary, much less among the Slavic nationalities. He cooperated only under the influence of his beautiful new wife and the Archdukes John and Ferdinand, all under the influence of pan-German nationalists who were convinced the Germans would rally to Austria's support. Austrian writers such as Josef Hormayr and Karoline Pinchler were joined in Vienna by a swarm of German romantics such as the brothers Schlegel and Adam Muller. Francis was never a German nationalist, of course. His interest in the "German War" was only that it might make him Holy Roman Emperor again. But Germans failed to support Austria, and Francis' dream was dashed by Napoleon's victory at Wagram (July 1809).

Stadion, the chancellor, had entertained Stein-like plans for further reforms after the victory. Instead, he found himself replaced by Clemens von Metternich. The emperor returned to a policy of reactionism. Metternich guided the state on a course of cooperation with Napoleon, including a marriage between him and the Archduchess Marie Louise. In 1812 he signed an alliance which committed troops to Napoleon for the Russian campaign. Always, however, he was waiting for the moment when Austria could break free of the French yoke. It came in 1813, and he took it happily, ranging Austria with the growing Allied coalition. In terms of reform, Austria, of all the states of Europe, was least affected by Napoleon's revolutionary example.

PAN-GERMANISM

After Austria's defeat the proponents of pan-German nationalism congregated in Berlin. They were united only by a common feeling that Germans were all one people and that the French should go. The romantic poet Heinrich von Kleist made clear that he now considered Prussia the hope of Free Germany. Others, such as Adam Müller, hoped for revitalized Austrian leadership. The German Christian Roundtable, founded by Achim von Arnim, excluded "Frenchmen, Jews, and Philistines," but had no political program or even a clear program of action. Similarly, Johann Fichte, in his powerful *Addresses to the German Nation*, demanded that Germany assume "philosophical" leadership of the world. Friederich Schleiermacher was more pious but even less clear.

Friedrich Jahn founded gymnastic societies; preached fitness, readiness for leadership, racial superiority; and latterly developed a utopian scheme for the creation of a new Greater Germany, including Switzerland, with a capital to be named "Teutona" somewhere on the Elbe. Another angry man with a dream of German political unity was Ernst Moritz Arndt, whose "Lob des Eisens" damned the human lust for gold and touted the glories of "plain, black Iron." His belligerence and hatred of the French was clear enough, but he also lacked practical political vision. Patriots worked in the universities to promote the

Tugenbund, which collapsed around 1810.[3] The zealots failed to recruit the students, much less the common people.

In the last days of the Napoleonic Empire, the pan-German movement still existed largely in the minds of the intellectuals. Among the major leaders, Jahn alone could boast that he had produced fighters for the War of Liberation of 1813–1814. Many eminent intellectuals opposed the creation of a German state. Wilhelm von Humboldt, philologist and founder of the University of Berlin, would have preferred to see Germany return to its loose, federative political structure. A nation-state, he thought, would warp the outlook of German intellectuals, traditionally international, and would endanger European peace.

Others treasured the old cultural atmosphere and had looked to Napoleon to safeguard it. Schiller's son refused to fight the French in 1813. The giant of the romantics, Johann Wolfgang von Goethe, forbade his son to fight in the "War of Liberation" (though he did, briefly) and continued to wear the French Legion of Honor, even to receive an Austrian field marshal. Hegel vocally regretted Napoleon's fall—a Titan, he said, brought down by small-minded fools. We have noted the collaboration with the French of Johannes von Müller, Jakob Grimm, and others.

Nowhere, until after the Russian debacle, did cooperation with the French become disreputable. Thereafter neither the romantic nor liberal intellectuals played key roles in bringing Napoleon down. Though they surely contributed to anti-French sentiment in Germany, their thought was more important later in the nineteenth century than in 1813–1814.

CONFEDERATION OF THE RHINE

In the states allied with France, Napoleon's ambassadors were not crashingly successful in bringing about reforms. He might have applied more pressure except for the perpetual need for German troops and for supplies to maintain French garrisons. Nevertheless, there were two states which made notable progress— Württemberg and Bavaria. Baden, which we shall not discuss, ran a close third.

Duke Frederick of Württemberg (king after 1805) quarreled early with his parliament *(Landtag)*. When it refused taxes to support Napoleon's 1805 campaign, Frederick took the emperor's from-the-saddle advice—"Throw the buggers out. . . ." and never called it again. However, he and his chief minister, Ferdinand von Wintzingerode, dictated a series of useful reforms.

Administration and justice were centralized after the French fashion. Adaptations of the Napoleonic codes were instituted. Serfdom was abolished. The governmental and judicial functions of the nobles, together with their right to tax, were eliminated. Some feudal dues remained, but land ownership became the privilege of anyone, and noble-commoner marriages were legalized. The estab-

---

[3] Revived after 1815 (among students only) as the Burschenschaften.

lished Lutheran Church and other churches were deprived of feudal rights and monastic property and were put under state supervision. Religious toleration was enforced. Jews, however, did not get full citizenship, though like all others, they could hold land and enter any profession. Schools, from the University of Tübingen down, were brought under royal control.

Though the state remained despotic in form and the nobles continued to dominate society, Württemberg was much altered in its institutions and social patterns during the Napoleonic period.

In Bavaria, under the well-loved "Prince Max" (king, 1805) and his minister, Count Maximilian Joseph Montgelas, there was also change along with window-dressing. For example, the king promulgated a constitution in 1808 calling for a parliament (Landtag) elected by universal male suffrage, which he never called. Montgelas, however, organized a ministry and bureaucracy on the French model and courts that applied a modified version of the Code Napoléon and the French penal code in toto.

The churches were put under state control and monastic orders were abolished and their property confiscated. Freedom of religion was enforced and mixed marriages between Christians were legalized. Protestants were made eligible for public office, though Jews were not. Serfdom and feudalism were formally abolished, but were perpetuated, in part, in various ways. For example, former serfs were granted shares of communal lands (held by villages) but the distribution took years. Meanwhile, they continued to pay dues, and if they received land, compensation to former lords. On "mediatized" lands, formerly ruled by independent princes, the feudal system persisted undisturbed.

The crown assumed a greater role in government. The king suppressed local estates and established city governments with appointed mayors and police commissioners. He gave control of schools to a Bureau of Education, which made primary education mandatory and created new secondary schools (gymnasia), and created a National Board of Health. He enforced the adoption of the metric system of weights and measures and established a Bureau of Statistics.

What benefits resulted were offset, however, by increased taxes (partly for the Bavarian army and to support French troops on occasion, but largely to finance the expanding royal bureaucracy), conscription, and overzealousness of the state police, who ruthlessly suppressed freedom of assembly, speech, and the press (supposedly guaranteed by the constitution). As might be expected, all the unpleasant features of the regime were blamed on the French. At the extremes, the nobles blamed them for the loss of their traditional rights, and the peasants complained that their condition was unchanged or worse under the new order.

RESISTANCE IN ITALY

After mid-1809 the Italian peninsula was totally ruled by Napoleon but had not been and never was altogether submissive. The kingdom of Italy suffered minor disturbances during the suppression of the monastic orders, completed by Eugène in 1805–1806. In 1809 there were more serious outbreaks, occasioned by the imprisonment of the pope and the absence of Prince Eugène with the Grande Armée. They were local, however, and confined to rural areas, so that the disturbances were quickly brought under control.

Naples had very serious guerrilla problems in 1806–1807, but soft-hearted King Joseph had been "reinforced" by some very tough soldiers. Marshal Masséna outraged the king by executing guerrilla chiefs out-of-hand, including the Marquis de Rodio, sent from Sicily by the Bourbon queen and captured in uniform, but holding a commission to lead guerrillas. Joseph's ruthless minister of police, Saliceti, collaborated with the generals to capture Fra Diavolo, the most wily of the chieftains, and talked the king into having him shot. Saliceti also got agents into the Bourbon court at Salerno and British intelligence headquarters on Capri (headed by the boneheaded Hudson Lowe, later Napoleon's jailor at St. Helena). This enabled him to capture a number of assassins sent from Sicily to kill the king.

Murat, nevertheless, found that guerrillas were still operating, especially in Calabria. In 1809 the army, police, and provincial guards captured 33,000 (out of a population of only 5,000,000). Most were in fact bandits. Unlike the Spanish irregulars, who fought for the restoration of Ferdinand VII, most of the Neapolitans hated the Bourbons as much as the French. Their war was more one of the poor against the rich and the country against the towns. French reform efforts were poorly understood, and on the face of it, they seemed to be supporting the landholders and the bourgeois of the towns and cities.

The king opted for unusual measures and assigned General Manhès to wipe out the bands by all means. Manhès proved both merciless and shrewd. Instead of sending cavalry after the guerrillas, who camped in the roughest mountain and forest areas, he sealed off their sources of recruits and supplies. Villages were put under curfew; the death penalty was swiftly applied to anyone leaving after dark; even cows, horses, sheep, and goats had to be brought within the walls. During the severe winter of 1810–1811 most of the bands were starved out and amnestied or forced to fight and annihilated. A few "Robin Hoods" fought on, taking incredible risks to feed their bands, and made legend. Among these was Capobianco, styled "the first martyr of the Carbonari," who was captured and shot at the end of 1811.

These men did not contribute directly to the fall of Napoleon, or even of Murat. But they did account for the death of many young Frenchmen in strange and faraway places and did deplete the treasuries of both Naples and the empire.

The Italian intelligentsia can hardly take credit for that much. Opposition to the Napoleonic regimes from writers and artists was mild indeed. So little did it concern the French that the classic pan-Italian work of the period, Cuoco's *Platone in Italia*, was published by Joseph in Naples. Ugo Foscolo praised Nelson after Trafalgar, but at the same time, he was under pension and writing on patriotic themes for Eugène de Beauharnais. Perhaps the loudest protests were over the removal of Italian art works to France, made by Canova and others. Again, however, most of the artists, including Canova, were serving Napoleon and/or his rulers.

Secret patriotic societies got their start in this period. The Freemasons, first and strongest, were initially pro-Napoleonic. Notably in Naples, however, they gradually became proponents of Italian unity. There too the Carbonari, originally a kind of "poor man's Masonic Order" got its start, giving the masses equal doses of primitive Christianity (picturing Jesus, for example, as an egalitarian) and liberalism. Nascent also, in the north, were the Guelphs, Federati, Adelphi, and others. None, though, generated any widespread resistance to the Napoleonic regimes.

The great intellectual heroes of the later *risorgimento* were Alfieri, entombed with great honor at Florence by Élisa Bonaparte, and Cuoco, Joseph's and Murat's protégé, who went insane in 1815. In the "First War of Italian Independence" the secret societies supported Murat, who took advantage of Napoleon's return from Elba (1815) to try to make himself king of all Italy. (See below, p. 242.)

OTTOMAN EMPIRE

Napoleon made unconscionable use of the Turkish Empire to facilitate his schemes. He encouraged the Ottomans to make war on Britain (1806–1809) and Russia (1806–1812), the latter despite his promises to Alexander I at Tilsit and afterward. His machinations served to weaken the already "sick man of Europe" (in addition to contributing to the ultimate alienation of Russia).

The emperor sent military advisors to Selim III in 1807 to modernize his army, but they were all too vigorous. A Janissary revolt resulted (1808) that ended in the deaths of both Selim and his successor, Mustafa IV (the last of his line). The army elevated Mahmoud II, who abandoned military reforms and expelled the French.

Turkey's problems encouraged revolts among the subject Christian nationalities of the Balkans. The Greek clans rose first and appealed to the czar for aid. After Tilsit (1807), however, they turned to Napoleon, offering him, in small contingents, some 40,000 troops. He might have used them except that they volunteered only to fight the Turks.

Control of Wallachia-Moldavia (Romania), at the mouth of the Danube, was the object of greatest struggle between Russia and Turkey in the period. Russia occupied it in 1806, but finally returned it to Turkey in 1812 as part of the price of peace. However, Romanian national sentiment had been thoroughly aroused, so that the Turks found extreme difficulty in reassuming rule.

The Serbs, led by Kara George (George Petrovich) rose against the Turks in 1804 and appealed to Austria for help, which was denied, however, by the timid Francis I. Kara George turned to the czar, who was more than happy to gain an ally in the Balkans, especially after the French occupation of Dalmatia in 1806.

When in 1806 Russia invaded Wallachia and Moldavia, the Serbs were able to defeat completely their Turkish rulers and, in effect, won their independence. In 1807, Serbian forces operated with Russian armies in the south against Turkey while Alexander contended with Napoleon in the north. In December 1807, Kara George was declared hereditary chieftain of the Serbs.

Russia, however, was defeated at Friedland. A British fleet meanwhile failed to take Constantinople, where defenses were prepared by the French general, François Sebastiani. At Tilsit, Napoleon, talking of a Russian-French division of Turkey, forced the czar to terminate the Russo-British alliance while promising to mediate peace between Russia and Turkey and consenting to Russia's retention of Moldavia and Wallachia. Alexander attenuated his efforts in the Balkans and abandoned the Serbs, who were brutally crushed by the Turks and their savage Anatolian tribal allies, assisted by the Montenegrins. Kara George fled into exile.

In 1809, however, when the Russo-Turkish conflict flared anew, Alexander restored his support to the Serbian chieftain. Again the Serbs freed themselves. But again, in 1812, Alexander abandoned them to buy peace with Turkey. All his forces were needed to oppose Napoleon's invasion of "Mother Russia."

For a second time (1813) the Serbs were crushed, but their spirit was not. Under different leadership they would rise again, within two years, to win autonomy.

HAITI

Among the dreams of Napoleon while First Consul was reviving the French Empire in America.[4] He forced Spain to cede him Louisiana (1801), which he intended to be the breadbasket for the sugar producing islands of the Caribbean. The chief of these was Santo Domingo, earlier divided between the French and Spanish, but all-French since 1795. We shall refer to the French (western) half as Haiti.[5]

Haiti's history had been markedly affected by the French Revolution. Following progressively liberal pronouncements of the National Assembly, whites first battled mulattos (1790) to deny them seats in the colonial assembly, both sides using black troops. Then whites and mulattos joined to oppose the representation of free blacks (1791). A slave rebellion ensued, the huge black majority finding leaders among slaves, free blacks, and some mulattos. French forces were put on the defensive; massacres became common on both sides. Many whites and mulattos fled the country spreading tales of torture, murder, and rape. In 1793, Spain went to war with France, and Britain sent aid to the rebels. Most of the

[4] Possibly he was influenced by Josephine, born in Martinique. At least he said so on St. Helena.

[5] The French referred to the French-speaking part and/or the whole island as Saint-Domingue (a translation of Santo Domingo). Use of this term would be confusing, and French Saint-Domingue became Haiti in this period.

French-speaking black leaders took service with the Spanish of Santo Domingo against the French, among them François Dominique Toussaint Louverture (or L'Ouverture), an ex-slave who soon was a colonel in the Spanish army.

In 1794, however, inspired by the egalitarianism of the new French Republic,[6] Toussaint Louverture deserted to the French with his Haitian troops. He rescued the French governor-general, Laveaux, who was besieged near Le Cap by a black army, and was commissioned a French general and made lieutenant governor of the island. An unlikely looking leader—small, wrinkled, and awkward—he commanded respect by his intelligence, education (self-acquired), and iron will. To his aid came Christophe, a massive, imposing black, illiterate but of superb dignity, taste, and common sense; Dessalines, a raw-boned fanatic, responsible for the death of hundreds of colonists; and Pétion, a handsome French-educated mulatto.

Toussaint considered himself a Frenchman but was determined that the blacks should rule the island. In 1798 he expelled all French officials and negotiated a withdrawal of the British, who happily left the incredibly complex struggle. Toussaint then consolidated his control of Haiti and attacked Spanish Santo Domingo. In 1801 he was master of the whole island. Even so, he did not declare independence from France, but governed, unofficially, for France, and after 1799 for Napoleon. A realistic man, Toussaint restored the economy by mobilizing workers (now free men) for the planters—who in Haiti proper included as many blacks and mulattos as whites.

The arrangement displeased Napoleon, though he was not a racist. In Egypt, he had encouraged mixed marriages, emulating Alexander the Great. The massacres of the 1790s seemed to confirm the savagery of the blacks of the Indies, however, and the refugees and their allies (notably the merchants of the ports) convinced him that the colonies could be made orderly and profitable only by reestablishing the old order. By law of 10 May 1802, Napoleon restored slavery in the colonies. It was implemented promptly in Guadeloupe, Martinique, and the lesser islands, but for tactical purposes, the future status of blacks in Haiti was left unclear.[7]

Toussaint would undoubtedly have cooperated with Napoleon if left in charge of Santo Domingo, an alternative the First Consul seriously considered. In 1801 he credited General Toussaint publicly with "saving for France a great and important colony" and said he deserved to be governor. In the end, however, he decided that the "black Washington" was too independent, and determined to destroy him.

Napoleon dispatched an expedition of 23,000 men under General Leclerc, accompanied by his wife, the beautiful Pauline Bonaparte, to reassume control

---

[6] The representative of the French Legislative Assembly, Sonthonax, anticipating the action of the Convention, declared slavery abolished in 1793.

[7] The law restored the Code Noir of the Old Regime, in its entirety. Blacks were forbidden to enter France. In 1803 prefects received an administrative order forbidding them to allow the registration of mixed marriages.

of the island. In January 1802 the French fought their way ashore at Le Cap (Cap Haitien), against the resistance of the lordly Christophe, who set fire to the city as he withdrew.

Once ashore, Leclerc tried to win Toussaint over peacefully, sending him a deliberately deceptive letter from Napoleon.

> It pleases us to recognize the great services you have rendered the French people. If our flag flies over Santo Domingo, we owe it to you and your brave blacks.
>
> · · ·
>
> What is it that you want? Liberty for the blacks? You know that, in every country where we have been, we have given it to people who do not have it. Do you want [personal] consideration, honors, fortune? After the services you have rendered, you need not be in doubt about your rewards. . . .

Toussaint was not easily deceived, however, and elected to fight. It was as if he had read Leclerc's secret instructions to "promise him anything" to gain a foothold. Five months of bloody conflict ensued, with the French, supplied by sea, gaining control of the cities and steadily amassing more cannon, while the blacks occupied the backlands and increasingly suffered from lack of food, supplies, and arms. Christophe, "tired of living like a savage," defected to the French. Toussaint decided to negotiate a compromise.

The situation then became very confused, with black leaders, including Dessalines, the general the French most feared, denouncing Toussaint's "treason" and bidding for terms for themselves. Leclerc moved quickly to arrest Toussaint, who was put aboard a ship and dispatched to France. He died there within a year (April 1803) in the dank dungeon of the Fort de Joux.

During the summer of 1802, however, before Toussaint reached France, the black generals realized they had helped to make a martyr. Moreover, rumors flew that slavery was to be restored. The black armies formed again, their leaders still at odds with each other, but willing to cooperate against the enemy. Meanwhile fever began striking down the French. In September 1802, Leclerc reported that 100 to 120 men were dying daily and that 4000 had died in August. His effective army was less than 10,000, and he urgently called for reinforcements. In November 1802, Leclerc himself died of fever in the arms of his wife. Pauline was alternately hysterical and defiant, unwilling to desert other wives and the "cause," but she was finally forced to board ship for France with her husband's remains.

General Donatien Rochambeau[8] took over what remained of the French forces, but surrendered to Dessalines in 1803. Haiti was lost. Such garrisons as

---

[8] Son of the commander of French forces in the American Revolution. He was killed fighting in Napoleon's army at Leipzig in 1813.

survived retired to the former Spanish side of the island. It only remained to be decided which of the native leaders would rule.

In Spanish Santo Domingo, the French were able to hold out for a few years longer. In 1808, however, when Joseph Bonaparte was declared king of Spain, the Spanish turned against them. A colonial assembly under Juan Sanchez proclaimed loyalty to Ferdinand VII (imprisoned in France). Indifferent to the rebel government which ruled in the king's name, however, they opened trade with the British and received military aid. The French garrisons surrendered in 1809. Until 1815, Spanish Santo Domingo enjoyed peace under British protection. In time, however, black rule would come to the Spanish side of the island as well.

Napoleon, grief stricken at the death of Leclerc and horrified at the narrow escape of Pauline, renounced further ventures in America. "Damn sugar, damn coffee, damn colonies!!" He decided to sell Louisiana to the United States (1803). Without the neutrality of the British, he could not continue anyway, and war with Albion was imminent because of his moves in Europe. (See above, p. 234.) After war began (1803), other French possessions in America were taken over at leisure by the British—Guiana, Guadeloupe, Martinique, and lesser islands.

SPANISH AMERICA

In 1804, Napoleon forced Spain (once more) to join France against Britain. The British immediately cut ties between Spain and the colonies, but still found commercial opportunities limited. Briefly they considered forcing their way into Spanish American markets and in 1806 dispatched a fleet under Sir Home Riggs Popham to Buenos Aires, the capital of the Viceroyalty of La Plata (Argentina). The hostility of colonial leaders convinced them that diplomacy was the better course, however, and Popham withdrew. The colonists, however, had experienced the evident benefits of free trade. Moreover, under the leadership of Marino Moreno, the *cabildo* (city council) appointed its own viceroy.

In 1808, however, after Napoleon seized Spain, Buenos Aires refused to recognize Joseph Bonaparte (as did all the Spanish colonies) and accepted a viceroy sent by the rebel junta—Baltazar de Cisneros. His power did not rival that of Moreno. The *cabildo* at Buenos Aires, as in most capitals in Spanish America, though dominated by Creoles (American born Spaniards)[9] loudly declared its loyalty to Ferdinand VII. It paid scant attention, however, to the orders of the rebel government which ruled in his name.

In 1810, with the news of the fall of Andalusia (which made French occupation of Spain all but complete) and the flight of the regency and Cortes to the port of Cadiz, where it was totally dependent on the British navy, colonial governments

[9] The Spanish born were referred to as Peninsulars or Europeans.

became bolder. The *cabildo* of Buenos Aires deported the viceroy and set up its own junta of government; though still recognizing Ferdinand VII, Argentina moved toward independence. It grew rich on trade with Britain (and all comers, except the French) plus the retention of gold and silver previously shipped to Spain. Expeditions to annex Paraguay, Uruguay, and the mining regions of upper La Plata (Potosi, La Paz) all failed. Argentina (the United Provinces of La Plata), nevertheless, achieved lasting independence, formally declared in 1813.

In Paraguay in 1810, Dr. José Gaspar Rodriguez Francia mobilized the gauchos and Indians and routed the invading Argentinians. He then formed his own junta and with enthusiastic mass support declared Paraguay independent (1811). In answer to the proposal that Ferdinand VII be recognized, he slammed two huge pistols on the lectern: "That is my answer!" The revolution was permanent. Francia himself ruled until his death in 1846.

In Uruguay (the Banda Oriental), also attacked in 1810 by Argentina, the gauchos were rallied by one of their own, the square, tough, scar-faced José Gervasio Artigas. He too won his war hands-down, formed a junta, and declared independence. His government was destroyed, however, in 1816. Independence for Uruguay did not come until 1828.

Mexico exploded also in 1810 under the improbable leadership of a tall, gentle, superbly educated Creole priest, Father Miguel Hidalgo y Costilla. Until then, the viceroy, General Venegas, had encountered no opposition. The Inquisition handled most of the troublemakers, who included Hidalgo, a teacher too interested in Indians, blacks, and "breeds," who was exiled to the remote village of Dolores.

In September 1810, Hidalgo proclaimed a revolution, but doomed it by not soliciting the cooperation of the Creoles and by raising an army of Indians, which seemed insanely dangerous to the white minority, Creole and Peninsular. In any case, his program was more humanitarian-social than political. It proclaimed the abolition of slavery and dwelt at length on improving the standard of living of the lower classes. Supported by the white leadership, the viceroy, with an army of regulars, scattered Hidalgo's ill-equipped horde of 80,000 rebels. The priest was hunted down, stripped of his vestments, and in July 1811, shot, though he protested loyalty to his God, Church, and king to the end.

Hidalgo had one follower who would not give up, however—the Mestizo priest José Morelos, a burly, scar-faced ex-farmer and teamster. Based at Acapulco, he raised an army of peasants, proclaimed Mexico independent, outlawed slavery, and abolished most taxes. Until 1815, he held royalist forces at bay. When he was finally defeated and executed, New Spain seemed altogether her old self again. She was not. Another more successful revolution, led by Creoles, would begin in 1820.

In Venezuela in 1810, the *cabildo* of Caracas, under Vicente Emparan, charted a cautiously independent course. While professing loyalty to Ferdinand VII, it sent the young Simón de Bolívar to England to seek aid. Later one of the legendary heroes of Latin American independence, Bolívar in 1810 was merely a tall, handsome and articulate young Creole aristocrat. In London he met and was captivated by a more famous native of Caracas, Francisco de Miranda, sixty, later called "El Precursor." An ex-officer in the French army, sometime French prisoner, and exile worldwide, Miranda was a professional revolutionary. He had tried to "liberate" Venezuela in 1806, with catastrophic results, and fled to England. Miranda took over in Caracas and engineered another disaster. Disdaining the royal governor, Juan Domingo Monteverde, he called a convention which proclaimed the independence of Venezuela (July 1811). Monteverde augmented his royal army with ferocious Llaneros from the uplands and defeated the patriots under Bolívar. In 1812, Miranda, his followers scattering, was captured and sent to Spain, where he died in prison. Bolívar, however, escaped to Colombia (New Granada).

Colombia was also in revolt. In July 1810 Bogotá, the capital, had expelled the aging viceroy, Amer y Borbón, and called for a national congress. Most provinces responded, except Quito and Panama, occupied by Spanish troops. The congress, professing loyalty to Ferdinand VII, organized the United Provinces of New Granada under Camilo Torres. Bolívar joined him, helped him consolidate control of Colombia, and recruited men to recapture Caracas.

In 1813, Bolívar led an army into Venezuela through swamps and mountains, surprised Monteverde, took Caracas and again declared Venezuela independent. Monteverde returned, however, again aided by the Llaneros under José Boves, whose troops committed horrible atrocities. By early 1814 the royalists were again in control.

In 1814 the restoration of Ferdinand VII caused further defections among Bolívar's supporters, and he again fled to New Granada. Royal forces triumphed there also and Bolívar fled to Jamaica. His career had just begun, however; he was destined to become the liberator of Colombia and (with San Martín) of Peru.

Chile also formed its own government in 1810, with the usual bow to Ferdinand VII. A leader emerged in Bernardo O'Higgins, illegitimate son of the former viceroy, who united the Creole landholders and pleased the lower population with talk of democracy. Short, plump, and unheroic in appearance, he was, nevertheless, a fighter and matchless politician, and by 1814 he was *de facto* dictator of Chile. In that year, though, royalist troops returned in force and drove O'Higgins and his patriots into the mountains on the Argentine border.

O'Higgins joined forces there with José de San Martín, who was in command of an Argentine army. Tall, rugged, taciturn, San Martin had served in the rebel army of Spain, but deserted in 1811—probably because he decided an American (Creole) colonel would never get promoted. Argentina had commissioned him to acquire western territory, but he resolved to help O'Higgins liberate Chile. This he would do, beginning in 1817, and then go on (collaborating with Bolívar) to free Peru as well.

The only permanent revolutions of the period were in Argentina and Paraguay. Ecuador's (Quito's) revolution (1809) was crushed in a few months, Santo Domingo (excluding, of course, Haiti) remained loyal to Spain throughout, as did Cuba, Guatemala, and Peru. The control of the crown was restored in the remainder of Spanish America.

Spanish American independence in the end was more a product of Ferdinand's attempt at a total return to the old colonial system than to the conditions of the Napoleonic Era. Nevertheless, the process got a strong beginning while the colonies were adrift.

BRAZIL

The temporary French conquest of Portugal (November 1807) gave Portuguese America a new lease on life. The British navy ferried the royal family from Lisbon to Rio de Janeiro. The regent, Dom João (John), acting for the insane queen, Maria I, had tried to prevent French conquest by promising Napoleon that Portugal would join the Continental System. But he could not, even if he had wanted to, as Napoleon well knew, since the British could destroy Lisbon at will. (Sir Sidney Smith, who evacuated the royal family, had orders to do so if the regent actually cooperated with the French.)

The court comprised at least 10,000 persons and was joined by another 15,000 loyalists, helter-skelter. The arrival of Dom John and 25,000 Lisboans was a great shock to Rio. It was a city of 123,000, but lacked even central water and sewage systems, much less housing for princes and grandees. It had to be rebuilt, beginning with new streets. At first the court only spent, and heavily. Inevitably, however, Dom John had to levy new taxes, though he tried to make sure the affluent classes paid their share. And he reduced expenses by giving honors and titles instead of making monetary rewards, which was often more pleasing to native officials, most of whom had wealth but lacked the formal trappings of status.

Dom John worked carefully to balance officeholding between Creoles and Peninsulars, studiedly giving members of both aristocracies honor and place according to their real power over segments of the lower population. This served to attenuate vicious antagonisms that might have led to revolution, especially since most of the Brazilian Creoles were to some degree of mixed blood and had suffered discrimination because of their color.[10] (In the Spanish colonies where race was a minor factor it was, nevertheless, the Creoles who fomented revolution, both in the Napoleonic period and later.)

The British were immediately given trade rights, as were all non-belligerents. Industry and agriculture grew, land and water communications were improved, and the Bank of Rio de Janeiro was created; overall, there was unprecedented

---

[10] Brazil was the only colony where the term "Creole" applied to native-born persons who were part African or Indian. In the Spanish colonies only those who could pass for Europeans were so designated. In the French possessions, where the number of white colonists was very small, "Creole" was applied even more strictly to persons of European lineage born overseas. New Orleans, under American rule, developed a looser definition, however, so that in common parlance in the United States, "Creole" came to refer only to French-speaking persons of mixed heritage.

prosperity. Iron industries were founded. Textile production saw an immense expansion and would become Brazil's major industry in the nineteenth century.

The regent founded a royal institute, which, after 1815, recruited many Frenchmen. A royal library was established and botanical gardens created (which still thrive), in which the regent took particular interest. A naval academy and colleges of medicine and surgery were created. The first printing press in Brazil was installed at Rio.

Fortunately there was no question of war between Portuguese and Brazilian armies. The Portuguese had all along depended on local militia to control the colony. The regent created an army—but a native one—and continued to depend mostly on the militia. His regulars remained in Portugal to fight with the British and Spanish against the French.

The regent (King John VI in 1816), slight, lethargic, but a winning personality, was a great success. His advisers, the Count da Ponte and José da Lisboa, were well chosen. The latter, a disciple of Adam Smith, promoted policies perfectly geared to the needs of the time.

The king liked Brazil; Brazil liked the king. After Napoleon's fall he remained in Rio, propitiating the Congress of Vienna (which wanted legitimate monarchs back in their "proper" places) by declaring himself (1816) ruler of the United Kingdom of Portugal and Brazil.[11]

THE UNITED STATES

The United States had an alliance with France dating from the American Revolution. President Washington, however, at the onset of the wars of the French Revolution, declared the United States neutral. In 1793 he expelled the French minister Edmond Genêt for appealing directly to Americans and for trying to equip French privateers in American ports.

The French had not been too unhappy at U.S. neutrality, since she was a minor power. They had expected to get greater value from her merchant fleet and the use of her ports. France reacted violently to the Genêt affair, however, since Washington seemed to be condemning the new French Republic, which in January 1793 had sent Louis XVI to the guillotine. French ire increased when the United States settled its outstanding differences with Great Britain (the Jay Treaty, 1794).

The French began an undeclared "Corsair War" against American shipping. In the years 1797–1799 alone, privateers (and occasionally French warships) took 834 American vessels. By the time Napoleon came to power, Americans, initially pro-French, were ready to ally with Britain.

---

[11] In 1820, however, Portuguese revolutionaries demanded the king return or lose his crown. He went. In 1822, his son and regent in Rio, Dom Pedro, probably encouraged by his father, declared Brazil independent and himself emperor. The country would eventually be a republic, but not for sixty years.

President Adams decided, however, to try to deal with Bonaparte. He dispatched William Vans Murray, Oliver Ellsworth, and William Davie to bid for peace on the condition that France pay an indemnity to cover American losses and to make appropriate apologies. Napoleon, through his affable brother Joseph, asserted blandly that his government was not responsible for the conflict and opined that the "sister republics" should wipe the slate clean. He suggested that they simply cease hostilities, abrogate the alliance of 1778, and make a mutual declaration on the rights of neutrals, by this time becoming a hot issue in U.S.– British relations.

Hoping to gain a lever against Great Britain and charmed by Joseph, who brought in Lafayette and other old friends of America to reassure them, the Americans agreed. A peace convention was signed at Mortefontaine, Joseph's palatial country estate, in September 1800. The event was celebrated by days of hunts, balls, plays, and musicals. Napoleon and Josephine made a grand entrance, and the First Consul, playing the democrat, mightily impressed the Americans. William Vans Murray wrote that he hoped Bonaparte was not "too generous" to survive in French politics!

In 1801 the Americans turned to the problem of New Orleans, a vital outlet for goods carried on the Mississippi, which had been ceded to France by Spain, along with Louisiana and West Mississippi. President Jefferson (elected 1800) instructed Robert Livingston, minister to France, to try to buy it. "The Chancellor" (a former New York title), rich, refined, but big and studiedly "American," bid almost daily. Talleyrand cracked that he should get a medal for effrontery, but gave him no serious response.

Bonaparte planned to revive New Orleans, founded by Frenchmen and held by France until 1763; Louisiana was to be the breadbasket for the sugar islands of the Indies. In 1801 he appointed General (later Marshal) Claude Victor governor-general of Louisiana and organized an expedition to take over from the Spanish in New Orleans. Before Victor could sail, however, his fleet was icebound in Dutch ports (1802). Meanwhile the debacle in Haiti became known. Simultaneously, the Spanish intendant in New Orleans (probably under orders from Godoy) outraged Americans by canceling their longstanding right to free deposit of goods (October 1802) in the port, for which Napoleon was blamed. The American frontier rose in arms, demanded war on France, and Jefferson, to calm the Congress, ordered 80,000 militia called up.

In the spring of 1803, Talleyrand suddenly offered to discuss selling New Orleans with Livingston. To assist him, Napoleon sent Barbé-Marbois, the French treasurer, who had lived in Philadelphia, had an American wife, and was a friend of the chancellor. Livingston was joined by James Monroe, Jefferson's special emissary, a former minister to France with many friends in Paris. Livingston resented his coming. Monroe, enroute for London, considered himself part of a bluff being run on Napoleon. Both were startled when suddenly they were offered all of Louisiana.

Napoleon had told Marbois to sell New Orleans and everything attached to it. The price didn't matter, the more the better—cash. War with Britain was imminent. Louisiana was vulnerable to sea power and thus a liability. If the British wanted it, why not let them fight the Americans over it?

The Americans, prepared to buy only New Orleans and perhaps part of West Mississippi, wisely bargained for all offered. The price agreed upon was 60,000,000 francs in cash plus some claims, the total equivalent to about $15,000,000. The First Consul thought he had done well. "Sixty millions for an occupation that will probably last a day!" When the treaty was signed (May 1803), his tune was different. "I have just given Britain a maritime rival which in time will lay low her pride!"

France was already at war with Britain again. For a time the British tolerated American commerce with the French Indies, even accepting the "broken voyage"—Indies–United States–Europe—which "Americanized" French goods. In 1805, however, they began stopping, searching, and sometimes seizing or sinking, American merchant ships. The United States tried to negotiate for protection of legitimate neutral rights, but to no avail. In 1806, British Orders-in-Council imposed a blockade on all ports under French jurisdiction, barring American merchantmen unless they submitted to search. Napoleon replied with the Continental System (November 1806), and in 1807 declared fair prize American vessels complying with British orders.

In 1807 the French again began to seize American ships. Between 1805 and 1812, French captures probably outnumbered British (519 to an estimated 389). But the British began earlier, and the Royal Navy stopped ships and battled American vessels within sight of United States ports. Moreover, the British went in heavily for impressment of American seamen, which the French did not. By mid-1807, U.S. popular opinion was violently anti-British.

President Jefferson, however, favored economic warfare, realizing the weakness of the American navy. In December 1807 he induced the Congress to pass the Embargo Act, which closed American ports to foreign commerce. His "little Continental System" was intended to cut off American food from France and Britain, and thereby force concessions. It did not succeed, however, since both countries had bumper crops in 1807–1808. British merchants lost some £6,000,000 in sales to the United States in 1808, but Britain did not alter her policies. Napoleon applauded Jefferson's actions but confiscated American ships in French ports. In March 1809, Congress repealed the Embargo Act and replaced it with the Non-Intercourse Act, which reopened trade except with Britain and France. It was equally ineffective in winning concessions.

American commerce was the big loser, and protests from New England shippers became irresistible in Congress. The acts had also hurt American agriculture, though industrial growth had been fostered in products previously imported. In May 1810 the United States opened trade with both the British and French, with the proviso that if either lifted its blockade, America would stop trading to the other. This could only lead to economic victory over both or *de facto* alliance with one or the other.

In August 1810, Napoleon replied by decreeing the Continental System no longer applied to the United States—*if* the British revoked their Orders-in-Council. While conceding nothing, he won a propaganda victory with the American public. Moreover, the U.S. government announced nonintercourse with Britain would be resumed if the Orders-in-Council were not revoked by February 1811. In view of the industrial depression which began in 1810 and food shortages, the British were responsive, but moved very slowly. Meanwhile the United States reimposed nonintercourse, and the American temper was rasped by incidents at sea, including a British attack on the American warship *The President.*

In April 1811, Napoleon unqualifiedly revoked the Continental System for the United States. Barely had cheers died in the Congress when the British got another black mark. William H. Harrison defeated the northwest Indians at Tippecanoe and found the field littered with English weapons. The news set off the warhawks in Washington, led by the youthful Henry Clay of Kentucky. On 18 June 1812 the Congress declared war on Great Britain. The British Parliament had already decided to lift the Orders-in-Council, but it was too late. The United States was an "ally" of Napoleon.

Negotiations to end the War of 1812 began, however, before the conflict started. The British were uninterested in a fight to the death. The only real American victory was that of Andrew Jackson's collection of frontiersmen, French pirates, and local citizens arrayed behind their cotton bales at New Orleans. And it came on 8 January 1815, two weeks after the peace at Ghent.

The gains of the Napoleonic period for the United States were fabulous. Louisiana doubled the size of the country. By 1812 the American merchant fleet was nearing the size of Britain's. The American navy, though still small, had displayed valor and developed élan. American agriculture, industry, and banking had expanded. The city of Washington had been burned by the British in August 1814. But for robust, growing America this was only a ground-clearing for something bigger and better.

ASIA AND AFRICA

In 1801, Bonaparte dispatched General Charles Decaen to India as "Governor of French Establishments." His large staff was dispersed in 1803, however, when the British took Pondichéry, the last French trading station. Decaen himself remained in the Orient on various missions for Napoleon until 1811. Bonaparte never dismissed India from his mind. In addition to encouraging Persia in her war with Russia (1804–1813), he urged the Shah to attack India, offering aid. In 1807 he sent a military mission under General Claude Gardanne to reform the Persian army. British influence proved too strong, however, and Gardanne was forced to withdraw in 1808.

Meanwhile the French emperor's imagination was sparked by the rise of Mohammed Ali in Egypt. Ali had fought against Napoleon in 1798–1799, but was an admirer and much influenced by French ideas. Originally a Romanian soldier of fortune, he became chief of the Mamelukes and was named viceroy of Egypt in 1805 by the Sultan. He organized a French-style army with the aid of the renegade Joseph Sèves (Soliman Pasha), and when the Mamelukes plotted against him, massacred them (1811) and assumed absolute power. He thereafter installed the first modern government in the Middle East and oriented the economy toward the large-scale production of cotton and hemp by introducing irrigation. Napoleon hoped to make him an ally, but was too involved in Europe to do so. Mohammed Ali ruled Egypt until 1847.

On the sea route to India, Napoleon began with bases in Senegal and after the Peace of Amiens (1802), the Dutch Cape Colony (South Africa), technically the possession of the Dutch Republic. The British recaptured the cape in 1806, however, and took Senegal in 1809. Napoleon had meanwhile (1803) established a French station at Tamatave on Madagascar under Sylvan Roux. France also retained (temporarily) some of the Seychelles Islands, Mauritius, and Réunion in the Indian Ocean. The British took Tamatave also in 1810, however, and all the islands in 1811.

Napoleon's last outposts in the Far East were the Dutch East Indies, of which Java was of economic and strategic importance. Java was administered ably by the Dutch General, Daendels (who had Napoleon's blessing), for King Louis Bonaparte, and after 1810, for France. Daendels mobilized the natives, fought off desultory British attacks, and was able to get occasional cargoes of cocoa, sugar, and rubber to France or Holland. His reign was ended, however, by concerted British attack in 1811.

By that time, Napoleon's dream of Eastern conquest had evaporated in the face of the Russian challenge. Nevertheless, no part of the world, save the ancient empires of China and Japan, had escaped the impact of the Corsican's domination of Europe.

GLORY AND DISASTER
The Campaigns of Russia and Spain:
The End of the Eagles

THE RUSSIAN CHALLENGE

As mentioned at the end of Chapter 8, Czar Alexander broke with the Continental System by a Ukase of 31 December 1810. The immediate cause was Napoleon's demand that he confiscate neutral vessels in Russian ports, which were presumed to be carrying British goods. The czar's government and court, however, hated the French alliance, had opposed it in 1807, and found the attendant economic restrictions ever more insufferable. The incomes of the aristocracy, for one thing, came from the export of grain and timber, and Britain was their best customer. Moreover, Napoleon had failed to deliver on his promises of sharing power in Europe and of dividing the Ottoman Empire with Russia. Instead, he had expanded the Grand Duchy of Warsaw in 1809, married an Austrian archduchess (which seemed to indicate he would share European power with the Habsburgs, if anyone), and encouraged Turkey (*and* Persia) to heat up their wars against Russia. To add insult to injury, Napoleon in 1810 annexed to France (along with other north German territories) the Grand Duchy of Oldenburg, ruled by the czar's brother-in-law. Relatives of many Russian aristocrats already had been similarly embarrassed, since the Russian and German nobilities were heavily intermarried. Overall, the czar had reason to fear a coup d'état—perhaps assassination—if he did not stand up to the French emperor.

Alexander hardly needed to be threatened, however. In his heart he had long been ready to challenge the treacherous Napoleon. He had been tempted at Erfurt in 1808, after Talleyrand had assured him Bonaparte was headed for disaster in Spain. He was tempted again in 1809 after Napoleon committed the Grande Armée in Spain, and Austria tried to break French control of Central

Europe. But the "Crowned Jacobin" had again triumphed, and Alexander kept the peace. He was acutely aware of his nation's weaknesses. Russia's population in 1810 was no more than that of France and dispersed over thousands of square miles. Her economy was agricultural, and dependent on serfs with primitive tools; her industry was almost nil; her commerce was managed largely by foreigners and Russian Jews who had fewer rights than the foreigners. After the defeats of 1807 the czar was hesitant to commit his armies without powerful allies. Britain was ready to give limited financial aid and to send military advisers, and she could command the Baltic Sea, but this might not be enough.

Nevertheless, by the end of 1810 the czar felt he had to fight. The Continental System was wrecking his economy and he had borne all the insults he could take. In 1811 he bid for an alliance with Sweden and sued for peace with the Ottoman Empire. Napoleon facilitated his negotiations with Sweden by seizing Swedish Pomerania, in punishment for violations of the Continental System. In April 1812 the crown prince, ex-Marshal Bernadotte[1] came to terms with Alexander, promising an army of 30,000 in return for Norway, a possession of Napoleon's ally, Denmark. In May 1812, Turkey granted peace in return for Russian evacuation of Moldavia and Wallachia. The two treaties freed for service 20,000 Russian troops stationed in Finland and 60,000 on the lower Danube. With these, the czar's inept advisers promised him an army of 600,000 men by mid-1812. Actually, he had about 420,000, though less than half of them were ever massed effectively.

Napoleon, from the moment of Alexander's challenge, considered war with Russia inevitable. Throughout 1811 and into 1812, however, he blandly professed the belief that a negotiated settlement was possible and chided the Russian ambassador, who remained in Paris, over the truculence of his imperial "brother," the czar. Napoleon recalled Armond Caulaincourt, his ambassador, from St. Petersburg, but replaced him. Privately, he said that there could be no peace until England had no possible allies in Europe, which meant that the "Russian colossus" must be crushed. In February 1812, however, he wrote the czar that the "regrettable" tensions between them need not continue. "Your Majesty can make an end of it all." As late as June he was asking Alexander to come to his senses and to restore good relations.

All the while, Napoleon was carrying out a veritable mobilization of Europe, expanding the French army, the Imperial Guard, the satellite armies, and forcing even his reluctant allies Austria and Prussia to contribute troops for the coming campaign. "*Si vis pacem, para bellum,*" he said to Maret, smiling. Davout, commanding at Danzig, supervised the muster of the emperor's enormous army in

---

[1] Bernadotte was elected crown prince by the Swedish Diet in 1810 and accepted with the permission of Napoleon. Though there was bad blood between the two because of Bernadotte's blatant insubordination during the 1809 campaign, Bernadotte was a "member of the family" (married to Désirée Clary, sister of Joseph's wife Julie) and Napoleon expected him to be loyal. He was not, and by 1812 was ruling Sweden for the ailing and ineffectual Charles XIII and dealing personally with the czar.

eastern Germany and Poland, all but complete in February 1812. Hostilities began in June after the czar delivered an ultimatum promising war if the French did not evacuate Prussia and Swedish Pomerania. By that time Napoleon seemed to have unbeatable odds.

THE GRANDE ARMÉE OF 1812

In June 1812 an imperial military machine of unexampled brilliance stood poised to march into Russia from behind the Niemen in East Prussia and the Bug in Poland. The Grande Armée comprised 611,000 men, with 130,000 more service and reserve troops in depots and garrisons from Mainz on the Rhine to Königsberg on the Baltic. Of the field army about 300,000 were French (including 100,000 from new Dutch, German, and Italian departments of France), 130,000 from the German Rheinbund states, 90,000 Poles and Lithuanians, 32,000 Italians and Illyrians, and 9000 Swiss. To these, Prussia and Austria contributed token contingents of 20,000 and 30,000, respectively, after secret talks with Russia that convinced them the risk of crossing Bonaparte would be too great. Included in the totals above are troops from the satellite kingdoms—17,000 from Westphalia, 27,000 from Italy, and 5000 from Naples (the Royal Guard). Murat's army had been left behind to guard Naples against possible British invasion—and because Napoleon thought it worthless.

Spain, however, contributed no troops; Joseph, instead, retained over 200,000 French and 70,000 foreign troops to maintain himself. The few Spanish and Portuguese present were in French uniform and were mostly impressed prisoners of war. Despite the seeming invincibility of Napoleon's European army, the "Spanish ulcer" had grossly weakened the empire and continued to bleed it.

Napoleon would command the main body—the left or north wing—of 250,000 troops; Eugène the center of about 80,000; Jerome the right (south) wing, in Poland, another 80,000. Murat commanded 40,000 reserve cavalry. Guarding Napoleon's northern flank were the corps of Macdonald (30,000) and the Prussians (20,000) under Yorck von Wartenburg. To the south of Jerome's army were the Austrians under Prince von Schwarzenberg. More corps would follow.

The Imperial Guard, 47,000 strong, was an international army in itself, of which the cavalry made the most spectacular show. Each regiment had its distinctive uniform and mounts, the French in various hues of green, blue, red, and white, the Polish lancers in grey and cerise on matching grey chargers, the Italians in purple and red, the Dutch in green and yellow, Mamelukes in silks and turbans. The Imperial Guard. Master showmen. Heroes all. It alone was enough to make the enemy's blood run cold.

Closely examined, however, the guard reflected the fragility of the empire. The Old Guard remained a corps of proud veterans of at least ten years' service, but among them were only 500-odd men who had served the "little corporal" in Italy and Egypt. In the Young Guard, though its leaders were veterans, the ranks of a dozen regiments created in 1810 and 1811 were filled with new recruits and volunteer conscripts.[2]

Whatever weaknesses existed in the mighty array were not noticeable in June 1812, however. Moreover, the men were inspired by the prospect of fighting under the soldier-emperor who had never been defeated—even the Prussians, who excused their excitement by talking about a "soldier's honor" and duty to his king.

Napoleon's progress across Germany in May, escorted by cavalry of the guard, was celebrated in every village and town. Crowds jammed the streets even at night, hoping to catch a glimpse of his carriage. In the larger cities he rode on horseback, in his famous green coat, the figure of austere greatness (carefully staged) among his gaudy guard, the sinister Mameluke Roustan always behind him. He entered Dresden near midnight on 16 May, to be greeted in a blaze of torchlight by cheering throngs and at the palace of the king of Saxony by the emperor and empress of Austria and all the kings and princes of Germany (except the king of Prussia, who arrived the next day). The bells of all the churches peeled and cannon boomed a 101-gun salute. All along the route across Poland and East Prussia cannon announced his arrival and the troops massed to cheer him. On 21 June he was with the army.

Napoleon's forces outnumbered those immediately available to the czar by almost three to one (611,000 to 210,000). His strategy was simple—to close with and destroy the enemy—wherever he chose to stand—as quickly as possible.

The emperor planned to cross the Niemen near Kovno. Facing his main army (250,000) was a Russian force of 120,000 under Prince Michel Barclay de Tolly. If he could force a fight, it would all be over. If Barclay managed to join with other Russian armies, Napoleon still had overwhelming odds. Opposite Jerome, in the south, were 50,000 under Prince Piotr Bagration; farther south, beyond the almost impenetrable Prepet Marshes, another 40,000 were being organized by General Tommasov. Napoleon expected a short campaign. It would have been if the Russians had stood and fought, but they did not.

THE ROAD TO MOSCOW

On 24–25 June the vanguard of the Grande Armée crossed the Niemen, Polish cavalry scattering Cossack scouts before them. The war was on. But where was the enemy? Only vast spaces greeted the invaders.

Barclay had retreated. On 28 June, Napoleon took Vilna after brief cavalry skirmishes. In the south, Bagration also went into retrograde. Napoleon sent

---

[2] The most bizarre addition was the regiment of Pupilles, comprising orphans of veterans—French and foreign—killed in the service of the empire. To qualify, boys had to be fifteen, healthy, and at least 4 feet 11 inches tall. Most of the "Baby Guard" remained garrisoned in France in 1812 but all got their baptism of fire in 1813–1814. The whole guard numbered almost 80,000. Some regiments were in Spain, others in garrison in France and Germany. The oldest and some partly disabled veterans were permanently stationed in key fortresses.

Map 12.1

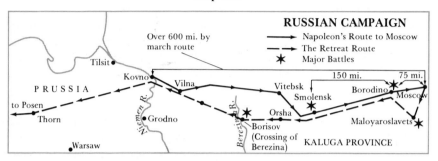

orders to Jerome to prevent the juncture of the Russian armies, and dispatched Davout with a corps of 35,000 to help. Coordination between the two was poor, however, and Bagration escaped to the east, ultimately joining Barclay in the area of Smolensk. (See Map 12.1.) Napoleon blamed Jerome and ordered him back to Westphalia, giving command of the right wing to Davout. This was unjust, but practical. Davout was a tried commander, and Jerome an unknown quantity. Nevertheless, analysis of his operation in Russia (which Napoleon did not wait to make) shows that Davout was more culpable in this instance.[3]

In any event the three wings soon became one, under Napoleon, though the strength of his main army dwindled as he drove deeper into Russia. He was forced to detach the Prussians (Yorck) and three French corps to guard him from the north and the Austrians (Schwarzenberg) and another French corps essentially to protect Poland. In addition, he garrisoned Kovno, Vilna, and six other cities as he marched, and finally Smolensk. Heat and disease also decimated his ranks, and many men, especially foreign troops, deserted. The vast spaces of Russia alone had a demoralizing effect on the Europeans, unused to endless miles of nothingness.

By his march route, dictated by Russian movements, Napoleon had penetrated almost 500 miles into Russia when he reached Smolensk on 17 August 1812. His army numbered 156,000 effectives. Bagration and Barclay had sufficient forces between them to fight, and did, but tentatively. After two days of sparring, they again retreated. Murat's cavalry led the pursuit toward Moscow, followed by the corps of Davout, Ney, Grouchy, and Eugène, flanked by Poniatowski and the cavalry of Latour-Maubourg.

Murat had led the march of the Grand Armée from the beginning, playing a role for which he seemed to have been born. Wearing a tall Polish shako, topped

---

[3] It may be that Napoleon meant Jerome's command of the army to be temporary—an excuse to send him to Warsaw—where he would be available if the emperor decided to make him king of Poland. (See Chapter 10, p. 290.) Napoleon decided against the resurrection of the kingdom, however. Jerome's Westphalians distinguished themselves during the campaign. Eighty-one were awarded the Legion of Honor, including Generals Ochs and Hammerstein. Of 22,000 (17,000 initially; 5000 replacements) only 600 returned.

with egret plumes fixed with a diamond clip, a Spanish cape, and yellow boots, astride a black charger with a leopard skin saddlecloth, the biggest of the marshals was recognizable a mile away. On the dusty plains beyond Vilna, he dashed about before his cavalry, waving his gold cane and shouting insults at the Russian scouts and rear guard. (He bragged that he never drew his sword.) The Cossacks loved him. Platoff, their commander, gave orders that "The King of Naples, with the Great Plume" was to be captured, if possible, but not killed.

Murat's fellow marshals were less enchanted. Ney complained furiously that the "Emperor's plumed cock" behaved like a madman and ignored the rest of the army. Davout said he belonged in a circus (which Napoleon had once said, referring to his uniform) and several times half drew his sword on Murat in anger. Napoleon, however, did not discourage Murat's posturing; such could be allowed the best cavalry leader in the world. On a single day, near Krasny, Murat led forty cavalry charges against Barclay's rear guard.

Beyond Smolensk, Murat doggedly attacked the Cossacks, day and night, trying to break the screen and to make the Russians stand. The rest of the army was hard pressed to keep up and the columns became much elongated (encouraging desertion) to the disgust of Davout, who was vainly trying to keep tight formations and to preserve his troops' strength. Napoleon sided with Murat, the only marshal who fully shared his optimism about the outcome of the campaign (though later he would turn morose). The heat, dirt, spaces, desertion, and perpetual marching after an elusive enemy who burned its own villages and stripped the countryside of food and forage had eroded the others' morale.

At Borodino, suddenly, the Russians turned to fight. General Kutuzov, now supreme commander of Russian forces, took command of Barclay's and Bagration's armies, which he reinforced. His forces almost matched Napoleon's—now reduced to 130,000—and he was determined to bleed the French, though he confided privately that he did not hope to defeat them. At dawn on 7 September 1812, Napoleon found the Russians in a line beyond Borodino, their positions stretching for four miles along a line of hills, anchored in the north by a "Great Redoubt"—an improvised fort—and strengthened by other hasty fortifications. (See Map 12.2.) He sent Poniatowski against the Russian south flank, backed by Murat; Eugène, commanding his corps, Grouchy's and other elements, against Borodino and the Great Redoubt; Ney and Davout, backed by Junot against the center. He turned 600 guns on the enemy, including the artillery of the guard.

Poniatowski could not turn the Russian flank, however, and the battle evolved into a bludgeoning match. Eugène, stolid and professional, captured Borodino and sent his corps against the Great Redoubt, which changed hands several times, but was finally taken. The French center also gradually gained ground, with Murat, in the frenzy which often seized him in battle, leading charges again and again against the right and then the center and dashing back to Napoleon's hilltop headquarters to give advice. As dusk fell, the Russians had been driven almost a mile from their original positions, but their lines were shorter, still intact, and

Map 12.2

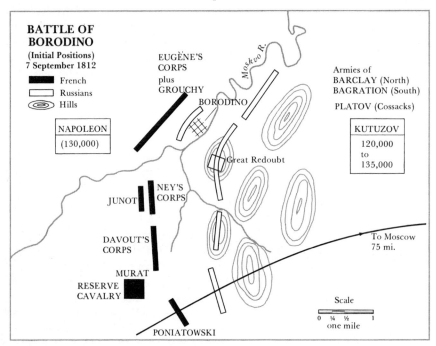

they occupied another line of hills. Napoleon called in his marshals for advice, an unusual move for him at such a juncture. The most vocal was Murat, who loudly demanded that Napoleon commit the guard. But Bessières, commanding the guard cavalry, interjected "Sire, you are 800 leagues from Paris." The emperor took his implied advice and did not gamble. He merely turned his artillery on the new Russian line in preparation for the morrow. Under cover of darkness, however, Kutuzov withdrew.

Losses on both sides had been high. French casualties were about 30,000, including ten generals killed and thirty-nine others badly wounded. The Russians had left 45,000 dead and wounded on the battlefield, but the French were impressed that they took almost no able-bodied prisoners. Napoleon claimed the victory. Ney was made the hero of the day and dubbed "Prince de Moskova." If the emperor had committed the guard he might have won. Kutuzov had committed every available man, while Napoleon had 20,000 guards and 20,000 others who had seen no action. As it was, Kutuzov could and did claim a sort of victory also. He had reduced Napoleon's forces by one-quarter. While he had plenty of reserves in the hinterland, the French had only replacements who had to be marched 700 to 1000 miles. He could supply himself easily; they could not.

Kutuzov did not care if Napoleon announced another triumph. He had made his reputation (or recovered it after Austerlitz, which Alexander chose to blame on him) against the Turks and had won repeatedly by making them come to him, stretching their supply lines, depleting their forces. On a larger scale he was doing the same with the French. The generalissimo had the confidence of the army and the people, though he was sixty-seven, tired, ill, and so fat he could not ride a horse. He overruled his generals, who wanted to fight for Moscow, arguing that the army must be saved or Russia was lost, and withdrew eastward. When the czar (at St. Petersburg) heard that the ancient capital was lost, he wept, but he left Kutuzov in command.

MOSCOW

Napoleon entered Moscow unopposed on 14 September at the head of less than 100,000 men. The city was empty except for a few hundred gaunt and bearded prisoners and madmen set loose by the mayor to make trouble for the French.[4] That night the city began to burn and blazed for five days, despite efforts of the army to stop it (the mayor had demolished all firefighting equipment). On 20 September, Napoleon wrote the czar, asking that he make peace in the name of right reason:

> The beautiful and superb city of Moscow exists no more, Rostopchin [the mayor] had it burned. Four hundred incendiaries have been arrested on that account. . . . They have been shot. The fire seems to have stopped. Three-quarters of the houses have been burned. . . . Such conduct is atrocious and without reason. Is the object to deny me resources? The supplies are in the cellars untouched by the fire. Why destroy one of the most beautiful cities in the world . . . ? I saw the same all the way to Smolensk, it has put 600,000 families in beggary.

> . . .

> If I supposed such things were done at the orders of Your Majesty, I would not be writing this letter . . . but I think that impossible of the great sovereign of a great nation. . . .
> I have made war on Your Majesty without animosity: a note from him, before or after the last great battle, would have stopped my march, and I might have been able to sacrifice the advantage of entering Moscow. . . .

Alexander did not answer. Moreover, he forbade Kutuzov to communicate with the French emperor.

---

[4] A few Russians and affluent members of the French community (merchants and others with their families) had stayed behind, but were out of sight at first. Later, they entertained the French officers. Most of them departed with the Grand Armée in October, adding to its burden.

Napoleon threw up defense lines around the city, ensconsed himself in the Kremlin, and waited. He could not believe that the Russians would not make peace. Kutuzov meanwhile reorganized his army in the Kaluga Province, to the south, where food was plentiful. He deployed only enough men to watch the city and to interdict the supply route to Smolensk and Cossacks to help volunteer peasant bands cut down French foragers who ventured too far from the walls.

Murat took over the French defense line in the southwest, opposite Russian outposts on the Nara River. For weeks, his cavalry and the Cossacks observed an unofficial armed truce. The Cossacks cheered him when he rode his line, and he had long talks with the Hetmen and Russian officers. At first cheerful (he even boasted that the Cossacks might join the French if he led them), he gradually became morose as he realized that although the Russians admired him, they considered the French doomed. His men were ever more listless from hunger and lack of action. Eugène, with Napoleon, wrote Augusta about boredom, rather than about more painful privations. They played Twenty-One, but there were no billiard tables. Maybe he would invite some artists from La Scala to entertain them later on.

All the while the situation became more desperate for the French.The blazing hot days of September gave way to freezing nights, fog, and rain in October. Food supplies ran low, even the forage for horses, who died daily— 30,000 during the month of occupation. The army was being reduced by disease and starvation, despite the occasional arrival of replacements. Russian lines around the city began to tighten; their forces, locally, grew larger than Napoleon's. On 17 October the emperor, finally convinced that the czar would not make peace, ordered preparations for withdrawal.

On 18 October the Russians broke their truce with Murat and viciously attacked across the Nara. For a time the king was surrounded, but he cut his way out with a small band of cavalry and reformed his lines. The next day (19 October) Napoleon marched from Moscow to join him, and the army marched southward toward Kaluga. The carriages of the officers and knapsacks of the men were loaded with loot, which became the first debris of the army, bound for destruction.

The "Great Retreat" had begun, but it was not planned as such. Napoleon meant to move via Kaluga and Elnya, through country not devastated by war, to Smolensk, where the army would go into winter quarters. Eugène led the way, and on 23 October occupied Maloyaroslavets (see Map 12.1) and secured the only bridge across the Luzha River. On 24 October, however, Kutuzov attacked, and a savage battle ensued during which the town changed hands ten times. The viceroy won the day by committing his Italian Royal Guard, but it was all but wiped out, and it seemed that Kutuzov meant to fight all-out to deny the Kaluga route. (The British General Wilson, with the Russians, says not; other testimony is conflicting.)

Napoleon, after the long delay in Moscow, knew that reaching winter quarters quickly was mandatory if the army were to survive. He ordered the column to take the shortest route to Smolensk, through the devastated country over which it had advanced. The rear elements were harassed from the beginning by the Cossacks, cavalry, and peasant bands. As the march progressed, attacks from Kutuzov's armies, marching parallel to the south, became bolder and more frequent. On 4 November the first snow fell, and in succeeding days more came, with temperatures dropping ever lower. The ice underfoot had slowed the pace of men and horses (for whom no spiked shoes had been ordered). Wagons and artillery became doubly hard to drag along and were gradually abandoned.

Napoleon was listless and vague. He sat for hours at a time in his carriage staring into space, breaking his stupor occasionally to issue orders. Exhausted and ill, he concentrated less on the ever more disorganized retreat than on how France and Europe would take the news, and what he must do to restore his power.

At Smolensk, the army veritably looted the supply depots, and Napoleon pronounced the city unfit for winter quarters. On 12 November the march resumed, led by the Westphalians, but the army was so disorganized that it took six days to clear the city. When Marshal Ney, with the rear guard, marched on 18 November, he found Kutuzov's main army blocking the route. To a Russian officer who rode up to offer him terms, the towering redhead shouted "A Marshal of France does not surrender!" Ney rallied his men and attacked the Russians frontally, but could not break out. That night, however, leaving his campfires burning and abandoning his wagons and artillery, he managed to get his troops across the Dneiper. The next day found him, musket in hand, on foot among his men, fighting off Platoff's Cossacks. Eugène turned back with 4000 men to help him, and Ney escaped to the main body, but with only 1000 of 6000 men who had marched with him from Smolensk.

Napoleon meanwhile learned that a Russian army under Wittgenstein threatened the northern route, and thus directed his army to march via Borisov, where he had a depot. There were three more depots between Borisov and Vilna, but the change meant that the army had to cross the Berezina River, a formidable obstacle. On the opposite bank was a Russian army of 35,000 fresh troops under Tshetshakov.

At the Berezina, however, Napoleon suddenly became the commander of old. On 26 November, while noisily focusing the Russians' attention on Borisov, he put skirmishers across the river to the north (riding behind Polish lancers), and after them infantry on rafts under the cover of artillery from the far bank. General Eblé's brave combat engineers then threw two bridges, each over 100 yards long, over the river. They broke and were repaired several times, but five decimated corps were across by noon on 28 November. By that time, Tshetshakov had caught on and attacked in force. Ney's corps held the west bank and Victor's the east, however, while thousands of stragglers poured across. During the night Victor came across. The rear guard held the bridges for more stragglers until 8:30 on the morning of the 29th, then burned them. Some 10,000 benumbed prisoners were left to the Russians; perhaps a thousand French were lost in combat or to the icy waters. Napoleon, however, had saved the bulk of his army, some 100,000 men, including detachments pulled in and the corps of Victor and Oudinot, which had not marched to Moscow. In a sense, it was one of his most inspired victories.

Napoleon considered the army still capable of fighting (had he not proved it?) and directed it to Vilna, where there were mountains of supplies. In addition to his column, Macdonald's corps of 25,000 was near Riga, as were Yorck's Prussians (20,000), their commander wavering, but not refusing orders. Poniatowski was marching for Poland, where he would reassemble 10,000. In Poland, also, there were Reynier's corps (12,000) and Schwarzenberg's Austrian army of 30,000 (which, however, had fought little, and was increasingly disinclined to do so). The emperor felt, however, that he could do little more for the army personally and was more needed in Paris. Already, General Malet had announced Napoleon dead in Russia and tried to overthrow the government. If he remained "lost" in Russia much longer, all Europe might rise against him.

MURAT AND EUGÈNE On 5 December, at Smorgoni, Napoleon gave command of the army to Murat and departed, incognito, for Paris. In the early morning hours of 19 December, he was back in the Tuileries. The 29th Bulletin of the Grande Armée admitted to the disaster that had occurred, but blamed it on the weather. It ended with "His Majesty's health had never been better," which Napoleon judged necessary to assure the French that he was far from dead.

Murat was a bad choice to command the army. Napoleon probably chose him because he was the senior officer present (a king as well as marshal) and unlikely to serve anyone else. If Murat departed, he would return to Naples, where he and Caroline might defect. Finally, considering the condition of the army, Murat's style of leadership—personal, unsophisticated bravado—was as good as any. Staff work was useless; complicated maneuvers were out of the question.

On 9 December the army reached Vilna, where it might have held out for months with the supplies available. Not under Murat. "I will not be trapped in this *pot de chambre!*" The army sacked the warehouses and marched on. On 19 December the remnants were in Königsberg, which again might have been held. But Murat led on to Posen, well inside East Prussia, where in mid-January 1813, Eugène, Berthier, Ney, and Davout began reorganizing what troops remained.

There were less than 40,000 men left of the main army, not counting perhaps 20,000 stragglers, some wounded or incapacitated by frostbite, some raving mad from the horrors they had seen. French losses had been near 400,000, plus 100,000 prisoners. Yorck, with his Prussians, had gone over to the enemy on 30 December. Schwarzenberg had assumed a neutral posture behind the Vistula. Only Macdonald, Poniatowski, and a few other lesser commanders still had viable units widely separated.

On 17 January, Murat deserted the army, leaving the command to Eugène, and galloped away for Naples. Napoleon confirmed Eugène's authority: "My son, take command. . . . It pains me that I did not give it to you before I departed." The viceroy held Posen for twelve days, then conducted a masterful retreat across

Germany. Prussia joined Russia in March, but Eugène stopped the Allies on the Elbe and held that line until Napoleon appeared with a new army in April 1813.

WHY DISASTER IN RUSSIA?

Napoleon pronounced that he had been defeated by the Russian winter. He might have added the Russian summer, which felled thousands of men and horses enroute to Moscow. This is true in that he was not beaten in open battle by the Russians. Their commanders cannot even be credited with a deliberate strategy of retreat or of "scorched earth" policy. Their withdrawal into the interior was the result of day-to-day decisions, based on their inferior strength and reluctance to match wits with Napoleon head-to-head—until Borodino. Even then Kutuzov retreated without any plan beyond saving his army to fight another day. The stubbornness of the czar and his commanders (one could say their bullheaded irrationality) gave them the ultimate victory.

Bonaparte's own bad decisions, of course, made his army the victim of the weather, inferior forces, and second-rate commanders. He advanced too far into Russia; he overstretched his supply lines; he delayed too long in Moscow.

However, what were his alternatives? He had hoped to cow the czar by massing overwhelming forces on the Vistula. When that did not work, he was committed to fight. Taking that for granted, he had to win a quick victory—within the year—or have none at all. Napoleon had the problem of supplying 600,000 men in the barren expanses of Russia. Two-thirds of his troops were foreign, and none of the rulers was willing to sacrifice indefinitely for the preservation of the Continental System. This was most true of his great-power allies, Austria and Prussia, who had contributed only token contingents in the first place. (Remember that Austria had raised 500,000 troops in 1809; she gave Napoleon *30,000* in 1812.) They were ready to turn on him at the first opportunity, and he knew it. To appease them, he had declined to reestablish the kingdom of Poland, which divided Polish leadership. The Poles sent 90,000 men in 1812, but what of the future? They did not even like fighting alongside the Austrians and Prussians, whom they knew coveted their territory—and the reverse was equally true.

In short, a long war would probably have meant the dissolution of Napoleon's army. If not that, the supply problem was sure to bankrupt the empire.

Bonaparte's decisions to pursue and pursue were based on this realization. *He had no other choice*, once committed. At Moscow, after the apparent victory at Borodino, he thought he had won. At least he had achieved maximum possible advantage. He had to delay as long as possible to exploit it—to allow the czar to "come to his senses." Otherwise a long war was in prospect. The emperor had never planned to fight for years. If that had been so, he might never have gone beyond Smolensk, which would have preserved the army, but would not have won the war. On the retreat, he might have saved more of the army if he had persisted on the Kaluga route, but he probably would have had to evacuate Russia anyway.

In broader context, Napoleon's major mistake was probably in not taking the war in Spain and Portugal seriously enough. If he had concentrated on ending that conflict, then turned on Russia, he might have won. As it was, without realizing it, he committed himself to a two-front war in 1812. While he marched into Russia, Wellington won startling victories over King Joseph Bonaparte—making quick victory over the czar even more essential.

SPAIN, 1812–1813

In April 1812, before departing for Russia, Napoleon gave King Joseph command of his armies in Spain and restored his royal authority. It seems a strange decision, especially in the critical year of 1812, and considering that since 1810 he had entrusted Joseph only with the Madrid area, directed the war from Paris, and controlled most of Spain through military governors. The probable explanation is that Napoleon expected a short campaign in Russia and felt that for a few months, Joseph, with almost 300,000 troops, could hold his own against Wellington and 30,000 *Anglais* (the Spanish and Portuguese didn't count). Further, Napoleon felt he could not trust a marshal with a kingdom. Murat had been treasonously independent in Naples in 1810–1811: Bernadotte had allied Sweden with Russia in 1812. They and others, like Soult, the best candidate for command in Spain, were *condottiere*, as he had once been himself. He knew them.

From a military standpoint, nevertheless, it was a bad decision. The situation in Spain was more dangerous than Napoleon thought, and Joseph was no general. He was eminently intelligent, and even understood military planning, but he was too softhearted to be an effective commander. Because of his lack of experience and Napoleon's violent criticism of the campaigns he had conducted, Joseph's subordinates did not take him seriously.

"Act with vigor and make yourself obeyed," Napoleon wrote Joseph. The king, instead, left the commanders of his five armies on their own until a crisis arose. They were Marshal Marmont (Army of Portugal) near Salamanca; Marshal Soult, in Andalusia; General Caffarelli, guarding the north coast and Navarre; General Dacaen, Army of Catalonia; and Marshal Suchet, in Valencia. Joseph had the Army of the Center (17,000 men) at Madrid.

Wellington meanwhile emerged from Portugal and took Badajoz and Ciudad Rodrigo on the Spanish border. (See Map 12.3.) In June with 60,000 British and Anglo-Portuguese, he marched to attack Marmont (50,000), who maneuvered to avoid contact and called for help from Joseph and Caffarelli. None came, and Marmont, on 22 July, was forced into battle alone. Wellington came off strong hill positions at Arapiles (Salamanca) and routed the French. Marmont lost an arm and was evacuated to France. Joseph, who had belatedly decided to reinforce Marmont, innocently approached on 24 July with the Army of the Center and had to flee for his life. Joseph retreated to Madrid, then Valencia. Wellington occupied Madrid, and Soult (more of necessity than in response to the king's

Map 12.3a

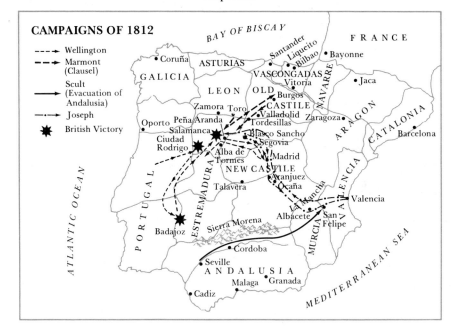

CAMPAIGNS OF 1812

- - - ► Wellington
- - ► Marmont (Clausel)
——► Scult (Evacuation of Andalusia)
—·—► Joseph
✴ British Victory

Map 12.3b

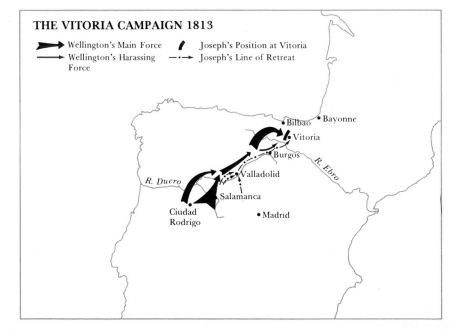

THE VITORIA CAMPAIGN 1813

►►► Wellington's Main Force
——► Wellington's Harassing Force
✦ Joseph's Position at Vitoria
—·—► Joseph's Line of Retreat

orders) evacuated Andalusia and marched to Valencia as well. Joseph's retreat was a comic opera version of Napoleon's in Russia. His army furnished escort for a column of hundreds of carriages, wagons, and carts, bearing his supporters and their families and baggage across the blistering plains of La Mancha. Guerrillas hung on the flanks, threatening and taunting, but seldom attacking, while his courtiers and their ladies carped about the inconvenience of it all.

In November 1812, Joseph and Soult retook Madrid without a fight. Wellington, faced with their advance from the east and the appearance in the north of the reorganized Army of Portugal, under Clausel, retreated to Salamanca. There Joseph combined his armies (97,000) but agonized so long over attacking that Wellington slipped away to Ciudad Rodrigo, where he prepared for action in the spring of 1813. Joseph returned in December to the comforts of Madrid.

Napoleon reached Paris from Russia at about the same time, and shortly withdrew some troops from Spain, but left Joseph with over 200,000. At the same time, he ordered the king to establish a headquarters at Valladolid, between Wellington at Ciudad Rodrigo and the main routes to France. He made clear to Joseph that his principal mission was to protect southern France. The king remained in Madrid. He was sensitive to the pleas of his courtiers and was still thinking in terms of occupying territory and preserving the semblance of a kingdom. (When he evacuated any area, his collaborators—and there were many—had to flee or be massacred by the guerrillas.) He did not march north until mid-March, after Napoleon's orders had been repeated three times. Not until mid-May did he order the last of his troops to leave Madrid. Meanwhile thousands of his courtiers and followers had converged on Valladolid, and hundreds more encumbered the march of his final elements from Madrid.

Though Napoleon was again fighting in Germany in April (see below), he took time to caution Joseph to concentrate his forces and to maintain contact with Wellington so as not to be surprised. Again, however, Joseph was slow to act. In June half of the 100,000 men under his direct command were in the vicinity of Valladolid, but the rest were scattered along the routes to Bayonne.[5]

Wellington, during the winter, had finally been made generalissimo of Allied forces in Spain, which insured Spanish cooperation lacking earlier. On 4 June he appeared northwest of Joseph with 95,000 British, Portuguese, and Spanish, and accompanied by hordes of guerrillas. He had outflanked Joseph's positions on the Duero River and threatened his communications with France. Joseph ordered his armies to concentrate on Burgos, then move north to Vitoria. Wellington detached cavalry to harass the French rear and took a parallel route north. On 15 June he was across the Ebro and marching on Vitoria. Joseph was already in Vitoria and had decided to make a stand. He had 70,000 troops, more cannon than he could use, and plenty of supplies and ammunition of all kinds. The king

---

[5] Another 100,000 men, under Dacaen and Suchet, were fighting wars of their own in Catalonia and Valencia.

allowed his generals to deploy their troops, however, and made no systematic plan for defense.

Wellington attacked at dawn on 21 June, and his advance units quickly found that all the bridges were intact over the Zadora, before Joseph's positions, and many not even covered by fire. The army poured across, and exploiting gaps between French units, caved in Joseph's center by 1 P.M. The king ordered retreat by stages, but there was no way to coordinate the maneuver. Throughout the afternoon units fought or retreated as the local situation demanded. By nightfall the retreat had turned into a rout. The French withdrew in wild disorder through Vitoria and onto the roads to the north. Joseph, abandoning his carriage and treasury, galloped away with a small party and on 28 June was in St. Jean de Luz. There on 12 July he got orders from Napoleon to retire to his estates. Marshal Soult took over the armies.

Wellington's victory at Vitoria had dire consequences for Napoleon. It not only signaled the death of the Bonaparte kingdom of Spain, it inspired Napoleon's enemies, declared and undeclared, all over Europe. In October 1813, moreover, Wellington invaded southern France.

THE WAR OF LIBERATION IN GERMANY

On 30 April 1813, Napoleon had arrived at Naumburg to take command of the reborn Grande Armée, now at 170,000. Striking across the Saale, he won victories over the Russians and Prussians at Lützen (2 May) and Bautzen (21 May). Austria meanwhile had assumed the role of mediator, renouncing her alliance with France. Metternich proposed an armistice, during which peace terms could be worked out. Czar Alexander and Frederick William of Prussia quickly accepted (4 June) and finally Napoleon, all for the same reasons—to reinforce and reorganize their armies. It was to last until 20 July, but was extended to 10 August.

The Allies were the gainers. Prussia completed her mobilization, and Prussia and Russia got British subsidies on pledge of making no separate peace with France. On 24 June, Austria agreed to join the Allies if Napoleon did not accept preliminary terms of peace, which included the dissolution of the Grand Duchy of Warsaw,[6] the return of Illyria to Austria, the return of most of Prussia's territory in Germany, and the renunciation of the German annexations of 1810. Napoleon refused in an interview with Metternich at Dresden on 26 June, offering Illyria alone to Austria in return for neutrality. They parted with an exchange of insults, Metternich in circumspect language, Napoleon damning him and expressing amazement that his father-in-law could ask him to give up "half of Europe," which, after all, would belong some day to his grandson. The same day the news of Vitoria arrived, and Francis I gained courage. Austria mobilized and on 12 August declared war on France.

---

[6] Already being organized into a kingdom under the auspices of the czar, though Poniatowski and 10,000 Poles were still with Napoleon.

The Allies gave overall command to Prince von Schwarzenberg, but he was accompanied by the rulers, and actually controlled only the main army (240,000 Austrians, Russians, and Prussians). Operating independently were Bernadotte, with 120,000 Swedes and Russians; the Prussian Field Marshal von Blücher, with 95,000 Prussians and Russians; and the Russian General Bennigsen, with 60,000 Russians and Poles. The Allied plan called for any army to retreat before Napoleon if challenged, making him extend and exhaust his forces, and to fight only when all were joined. Against Napoleon's earlier armies, such a plan would probably have netted the Allies defeat in detail and disaster. His Grande Armée of 1813, however, was composed of raw recruits, many of them mere boys, leavened with jaded veterans and led by weary and uninspired officers. Napoleon did have numbers, however. His main army stood at 250,000; Oudinot had 70,000 opposite Bernadotte in the north, the *Rheinbund* states (though wavering) had another 70,000 at his call; other corps were forming on the Rhine.

In August 1813 the fighting centered on Dresden. Napoleon defeated Schwarzenberg on 26–27 August, but the Austrian withdrew handily and the other armies gradually closed on the city. In September, Napoleon retreated to Leipzig, hoping to gain room for maneuver, but within two weeks the Allies closed in on him again, reinforced by Bavarians, who changed sides (8 October). He chose to fight, and for three days (16–18 October) the great "Battle of the Nations" raged—370,000 Allies against 220,000 French. Before dawn on 19 October, undefeated but fearing encirclement, Napoleon began an orderly withdrawal to the west. At first light, however, troops of Saxony and Baden went over to the enemy and began firing at the French. The French army's movement became increasingly frantic and confused. The Lindenau Bridge was blown up prematurely, leaving 60,000 men trapped in the city. They fought as long as they could, then some tried to escape by swimming the Elster River. Marshal Macdonald made it with some hundreds of his men; Marshal Poniatowski (given his baton just before the battle), wounded and bleeding, drowned in the attempt.

Napoleon marched for Frankfurt, then the Rhine. In Germany, his remaining allies, led by Württemberg, went over to the enemy one by one. Almost in passing, the kingdom of Westphalia was overrun. Jerome's guard of French and Westphalians conducted him safely to the Rhine, but most of the Germans then backtracked to greet their returning princes.[7] There was no popular uprising of any consequence. Jerome's officials continued to function, awaiting the pleasure of the next government; some stayed on permanently. In the popular mind, apparently, Napoleon was the villain, not Jerome. Moreover, they remained terrified of the French emperor and preferred to let the old rulers take the risk of leading opposition against him.

---

[7] The Westphalians, particulary the Hessians, took their oaths to the king very seriously. At the Rhine, they considered that they had honorably acquitted themselves of their duty since Jerome had left Germany proper. He had in fact offered to release them from duty earlier, but most of them insisted on making the final gesture of seeing him to the Rhine.

NATIONALISM IN GERMANY It is a myth that pan-German nationalism was a great factor in the "War of Liberation" against Napoleon. There was very little modern patriotism demonstrated even in the individual states. Most of the peoples behaved much as did those in Westphalia. Except in Prussia and Austria, the rulers deserted Napoleon only when they had no other choice; their people tended to be neutral or pro-French.

The proclamation "To My People" of Frederick William of Prussia is famous. He did not call for a mass national uprising, but resistance to French oppression and support for his dynasty, reminding his peoples of the glory they had won under the Great Elector and Frederick the Great. He addressed them as Prussians and Germans as well as, . . . "Brandenburgers, Prussians, Silesians, Pomeranians, Lithuanians!" He was fearful of the consequences of rousing mass enthusiasm and still doubtful about the Stein-Hardenburg reforms he had earlier authorized.

King Frederick William did not authorize conscription until 1814, and not until after 1818 did it produce a *Landwehr* and *Landsturm* (National Guard and popular militia). Those who fought with the line army were volunteers (some 28,000). However, they gave the war a certain national character in Prussia, but such nationalism as exhibited was *Prussian*, not German. The emperor of Austria put his trust solely in regular troops under aristocratic leadership. None of the shoddy business of 1809 for him!

The king of Württemberg wrote Napoleon that he was forced to join the Allies, but looked forward to the time when he could again side with France. Saxon troops, after Leipzig, mutinied when assigned to the army of Prince Blücher, an "Old Prussian" if ever there was one—at seventy in truth a holdover from the army of the Great Frederick, merciless, pipe-smoking, perpetually sipping his brandy. It was rumored he shot the Saxons in droves to restore discipline.[8] (Unlike Frederick the Great, Blücher was anti-French, almost pathologically so; a kind word about Napoleon was enough to drive him into apoplectic fury.)

The great patriotic movement of 1813 existed largely in the minds of the intelligentsia—Jahn, Arndt, Fichte, and others. All of them, in their enthusiasm for pan-Germanism, had (for the moment) abandoned liberalism, which they considered part of the baggage of the enemy. Their stirring messages, nevertheless, became part of German folklore, and contributed to the unification movement of the nineteenth century. Germans later accepted descriptions such as that of the poet Theodore Körner as real: "The people rise, the storm breaks. . . . It is a Crusade. It is a Holy War." At the time, the masses were not responsive and intellectual eminences such as Goethe, Hegel, and Jakob Grimm thought the war a tragedy.

---

[8] He admitted to ordering five shot; a Saxon commission said seven.

It was in fact a traditional war—a dynastic war—led by the old rulers to restore their traditional powers. To give them their due, they associated the Old Regime with European civilization, in all senses, and thus regarded their cause as holy.

DIPLOMATIC SPARRING/CASTLEREAGH ARRIVES

Allied success disconcerted Metternich, who became fearful that Russian hegemony would replace French in Germany. The czar was wooing Frederick William of Prussia, promising to add Saxony to his kingdom (in return for his "share" of Poland, which would become a Russian satellite). The British, though still undecided in detail on their war aims, wanted to restore a balance of power on the Continent. At this point, only Czar Alexander was determined to invade France and to destroy Bonaparte rule.

When Napoleon crossed the Rhine, therefore, Metternich, at Frankfurt, persuaded the Allies to make him a peace offer (9 November 1813). He would be allowed to retain France of the "natural frontiers"—the Alps, Pyrenees, and Rhine—which included Belgium, the Rhineland, and Savoy. The French emperor was asked only to renounce claim to Spain (already lost), Italy, and Holland, which Bülow had already invaded (and which went into revolt to restore the Prince of Orange on 15 November). With Wellington in the south of France and Allied armies poised on the Rhine, it was a very generous offer.

Bonaparte agreed to talks, and there was a short armistice, but Metternich decided the emperor was only buying time. On 1 December the Allies proclaimed they would fight until Napoleon's domination over all non-French people was ended. (They declined to threaten invasion of France, since that might strengthen Napoleon's popular support.) On 5 December, Bonaparte accepted the Frankfurt terms, but the Allies deemed it too late. Napoleon denounced them as tricksters who had hoped to make him lower his guard.

At the same time, he tried a few tricks of his own. In November 1813 he announced the restoration of Ferdinand VII to the throne of Spain—on the condition that his rebel supporters—by then in control of the country, declare neutrality. In December he told Pope Pius VII that he could return to Rome, where, he said privately, he would "lie like a bomb"—meaning that the Allies would have to decide what to do about him and his former possessions. Neither ploy worked, however. The Spanish rebel Cortes refused the condition (Ferdinand returned on his own terms in 1814). The pope's appearance in Italy (January 1814) gave Napoleon no advantage.

Meanwhile, Viscount Castlereagh, the British foreign minister, arrived on the Continent, armed with a long-sought policy statement from his government (framed on 26 December 1813). On 18 January 1814 he met with Metternich, who directed Schwarzenberg to suspend military operations until their talks were complete. Castlereagh asked that Holland (the former Dutch Republic) be combined with Belgium (the former Austrian Netherlands) under the Prince of Orange (who would become King William I of the Netherlands), that Spain and

Portugal return to their former rulers, and that Britain have a free hand in colonial settlements. (The British were bent on retaining Dutch South Africa and Malta, especially.) In return, Castlereagh was willing to support Metternich (Austria) on the reconstruction of Italy and to lend British weight in favor of a compromise settlement in central Europe. The two also agreed that for a lasting balance of power in Europe, France must remain a major power either under Napoleon or the Bourbon King Louis XVIII. The czar's candidate for the French throne, Bernadotte, was excluded, since he might become a Russian puppet. A regency under Marie Louise, ruling for the boy-emperor, Napoleon II, was also ruled out, since it might give Austria preponderance.

Under these terms, the Grand Alliance could concentrate on the task of defeating Napoleon. Britain and Austria were assured in their respective aims. Russia and Prussia could look forward to gains in central Europe—to be negotiated after the victory. Until that time, British subsidies would continue for all parties. Bernadotte meanwhile had invaded Denmark and had secured Norway for Sweden. To retain what he had gained, however, he had to fight on with the great powers. Czar Alexander remained determined that Napoleon would be dethroned, but his plans for European hegemony were thwarted.

THE CAMPAIGN IN FRANCE

On 1 January 1814, Blücher, with 110,000 men, completed his crossing of the Rhine, and Schwarzenberg entered France from Switzerland with 150,000. Behind them, in Germmany, were armies totaling another 200,000. In the south, Wellington (as already noted) had invaded France in October 1813 and was pushing methodically northward. To meet the invaders, Napoleon had 100,000 men in the north and 70,000 under Soult and Suchet in the south. His forces dwindled steadily, however, because of desertions and casualties. Eugène held out in Italy with 40,000 French and Piedmontese and 36,000 Italians.[9] The Austrians had seized Illyria, however, and were in Venetia; the British menaced the coast. Murat, in Naples, after long negotiation with the Allies, turned his coat on 11 January 1814.

Napoleon, who seemed to thrive on adversity, fought the most brilliant campaigns of his life in early 1814. He struck first in late January at Blücher along the Aube, defeating him at St. Dizier, Brienne, and La Rothière. On 1 February, however, Blücher, with reinforcements from Schwarzenberg, struck back and drove Napoleon from La Rothière toward Paris.

While the fighting went on, the Allied diplomats received France's foreign minister, Armond de Caulaincourt, and on 7 February offered Napoleon peace

---

[9] Napoleon ordered Eugène to withdraw into France *when* Murat defected (the emperor had no doubt that he would). Eugène judged that if he tried to retreat over the Alps, however, his forces would disintegrate, and thus fought on in Italy. Napoleon did not condemn him for this.

on the basis of the French boundaries of 1792—a very generous offer. The czar opposed it (unofficially); he was after Napoleon's scalp and was in touch with Talleyrand and a group of conspirators in Paris. Caulaincourt accepted the offer; Napoleon, after, a long silence, rejected it.

The emperor still thought he could win, though his effective army was now less than 50,000. In mid-February he pounced on Blücher again south of the Marne and chopped up elements of his army at Champaubert, Montmirail, Château-Thierry, and Vauchamps. He then turned on Schwarzenberg, and by 19 February had thrown him back on Troyes. Meanwhile the Allied diplomatic position hardened. On 1 March the powers pledged that none would make a separate peace and guaranteed a general peace for twenty years.

In the meantime, Napoleon had been exploiting the separation of the Allied armies. In March, they were finally joined, and he was defeated on 9–10 March at Laon, and after tearing up their rear elements and communications, at Arcis-sur-Aube on 20–21 March. Undaunted, Napoleon ordered Paris mobilized—National Guard and citizens—under Marshals Marmont and Mortier, while he continued to fight to the south. Joseph Bonaparte was "lieutenant general of the emperor" in Paris, head of the civil government, but especially charged with protecting the empress and the king of Rome. "Do not leave my son," Napoleon wrote Joseph, "and remember that I would rather have him [drowned] in the Seine than in the hands of the enemies of France."

Goaded on by the czar, Schwarzenberg directed the bulk of his combined army on Paris. With 200,000 allied troops approaching, Joseph, on 29 March, sent the empress and little king to Rambouillet and followed with members of the government the next morning. On 30 March the Allies stormed the city, driving the defenders onto the promontory of Montmartre. In the early morning hours of 31 March, Marmont went over to the enemy. Mortier had no choice but to surrender.

Napoleon gave his battered army the order to march on Paris, but his generals, even Marshals Ney and Lefebvre, refused. At Fountainebleau on 4 April 1814 he abdicated in favor of his son, but he had already been deposed by the French senate, influenced by Talleyrand and the czar. On 6 April 1814, Napoleon abdicated unconditionally. Joseph, in the interim, tried to bring the empress and king of Rome to Fountainebleau, but was turned back to Blois by enemy troops, and, on Napoleon's order, sent them to the Austrian emperor. Napoleon would never see them again.[10] In Italy, Eugène fought until 16 April, when he heard of

[10] Napoleon II (the king of Rome) was brought up at the Austrian court, bearing the title Duke von Reichstadt. He died on 22 July 1832, while on maneuvers with the Austrian army, of tuberculosis, the Habsburg curse. He had been closely watched, especially after the Napoleonic Legend took hold in France in the 1820s. The unpopular Bourbon kings feared that if he ever returned to France, he would gain mass support. After 1830, Louis Philippe was even more concerned at the prospect. The duke was mature, very intelligent and well-educated, and an extremely attractive figure, much more handsome than his father.

the abdication. He had kept most of his kingdom intact and savagely punished the Austrians (and latterly Murat's Neapolitans). He abdicated on 26 April.

By the terms of the Treaty of Fountainebleau (11 April 1814), Napoleon was made sovereign of the Island of Elba, with an income of 2,000,000 francs a year from France. The other Bonapartes were provided for with (by twentieth-century standards) incredible generosity. Marie Louise became Duchess of Parma. By the separate Treaty of Paris (3 May 1814), Louis XVIII (brother of Louis XVI) was restored to the throne of France. France retained the boundaries of 1792—larger than those of 1789 by the addition of Savoy, Avignon and the Comtat Venaissin (the papal enclave in southern France), and parts of Belgium and the Rhineland. Britain retained Malta and South Africa, but returned all other former French or Dutch colonies except Tobago, Sainte Lucia, and Mauritius. France was assessed no indemnity.

The general settlement for Europe was left to the Congress of Vienna, which met in September 1814.

EUGÈNE, MURAT, AND ITALIAN NATIONALISM

Of Napoleon's satellite states, only Naples survived, thanks to the treason of Murat and Caroline Bonaparte. Their fate was in the hands of the powers, however, and there was no consensus to maintain them on their throne. Metternich retained a free hand, since the Austrian emperor had never ratified the treaty with Murat. The British favored restoring the Neapolitan Bourbons.

Eugène, if he had chosen to betray Napoleon, would probably have had a better chance of preserving his kingdom permanently. In January 1814 the Austrian commander in Italy, Field Marshal Bellegarde, had promised the crown to him, with the guarantee of Francis I, if he would join the Allies. He was supported by his father-in-law, the king of Bavaria (who urged him to defect), and greatly respected by the Austrians and British. Eugène, however, could not be won over. Nevertheless, after Napoleon's abdication, there still seemed a chance for him. His military position was such that the Austrians happily settled for an armistice (16 April) and left him in control of his Italian army and major fortresses (though the French contingents were evacuated). There had been no uprising against him. On 17 April the Italian senate reaffirmed support of Eugène's government and dispatched delegates to the Allies in Paris. There were disorders in Milan, however, fomented by Eugène's enemies, the Austrian Marshal Bellegarde occupied the city, and the politicians deserted the viceroy en masse. The people, generally, took a detached attitude and seemed to desire nothing more than peace. Eugène was left with his small army, but even if it remained totally loyal, which was doubtful, he could hardly hope to survive among the great powers on military might alone. He abdicated and went into exile in Bavaria, where the king treated him well.

Murat had agonized long before betraying Napoleon. For almost a full year, while negotiating with the Austrians and British, he had continued to protest his loyalty to the emperor, and even went north to fight for him at Dresden and Leipzig. Only a week before he signed a treaty with Austria (11 January 1814), he wrote Napoleon to expect hostile acts, but to trust him. He could not admit his treason even to himself; he was too simple and honest a man for the business. Napoleon recognized the real villain: "His wife made him defect, Caroline, my sister, has betrayed me!"

The Gascon had also been propelled into action, however, by his ministers, Antonio Maghella and Giuseppe Zurlo, both high in the Carbonari and Masonic Order, and a number of similarly connected generals and officials. They encouraged him to believe that the people of the whole peninsula would rise to his support in the name of Italian unity —that he could be king of Italy, not merely Naples. Murat entered Rome with his Neapolitans on 24 January 1814, proclaiming himself the "Liberator of Italy," and was cheered, which was misleading. The Romans saw him as a protector against the return of the French. At Bologna, just liberated from Eugène by the Austrians, he drew only a small crowd, which stared blankly at a claque hired to shout *"Viva Il Re d'Italia."* Maghella and his cohorts had been wrong. The people were interested only in staying out of the way of the armies and protecting their property. They were war weary, and, in any event, not politically aware.

In 1814, Italian pan-nationalism was even less vital than pan-Germanism. Murat turned to the business of war, but less than half-heartedly. He managed to avoid attacking Eugène until 14 April—two days before the armistice. So strange were his maneuvers that the Austrian generals and British observers in Italy were ready to accuse him of betraying them as well as Napoleon. His emotional attachment to the emperor had in fact almost ruined Caroline's plan to save their kingdom. After the abdication, he wrote Napoleon: "Never doubt my heart, it is worth more than my head!" He should have followed one or the other. As it was, his crown remained in jeopardy.

He was destined to blunder again in 1815 and to lose his kingdom and his life.

EMPEROR OF ELBA

Napoleon never thought to blame his fall on himself. The traitors were responsible. Traitors! Marmont. Ney. Lefebvre. His own family. Even Roustan was gone! Talleyrand—he should have been shot in 1809. All those he had raised so high had brought him low. He became despondent, and on the night of 12–13 April took a vial of poison he had carried on the retreat from Russia, but he did not die.

On 20 April he was himself again, and departed in his inimitable theatrical style. He reviewed the Old Guard in the court of the Château of Fountainebleau and addressed them:

For twenty years, I have found you constantly on the road of honor and glory. . . .
Adieu, Mes Enfants! Would that I could press you all to my heart; at least I embrace
your banner!

General Petit came forward with the Eagle and Napoleon kissed it. Amid the
sobs of the guardsmen he got into his carriage and was driven away.

On 3 May he landed on Elba. His empire had been reduced to eighty-six
square miles—sixteen miles across at the widest point. It had 12,000 Italian-speak-
ing inhabitants whom he had kept under military government since 1802, and
who did not love him. He set to work with his usual zest, however, creating a
court, a government, an army of 1600, including 600 of his Old Guard, and a
"navy" of one brig and four other little ships. He decorated a palace in
Portoferraio and four other residences.

He poured money into improving mining, agriculture, and fishing. The
population prospered—but largely from officeholding and the spending of rich
visitors. At the end of 1814, Napoleon had spent 1,000,000 francs and netted only
200,000 from taxes. His stipend from France had not arrived (and never would),
so he had to make up the deficit from his own funds. This was only one of his
discontents, however.

More than anything else, he wanted Marie Louise and his son with him. But
the Allies were deaf to his pleas. Napoleon fumed that Francis I was holding the
boy hostage in the manner of ancient barbarian rulers and blackened with anger
at reports (ultimately true) that the ex-empress had become the mistress of her
"guardian," Count von Neipperg. He was consoled somewhat by his mother, who
came to stay with him. And his sister Pauline commuted continually from Italy,
arranging balls and other entertainments. Madame Walewska visited him
briefly.[11] He received a stream of curious travelers. Island society, however, was
deadly dull.

Moreover, Napoleon lost interest in governing. He had organized everything
he could, and it appeared he would soon be bankrupt. In that context, news of
dissension among the Allies at Vienna and the troubles of Louis XVIII in France
encouraged him to try to recover his throne.

THE CONGRESS OF VIENNA/
LOUIS XVIII AND THE FRENCH

In September 1814 the Congress of Vienna had met, amid extravagant
celebrations, to settle the fate of Europe. The czar and emperor of Austria were
there, along with most of the kings and princes of Europe, all with their foreign
ministers and platoons of advisers. With Napoleon banished, however, the Allies
lacked an enemy to unite them. Talleyrand, the master survivor, representing

[11] His Polish mistress, by whom he had a son. (See Chapter 9, p. 260, footnote 27.) She came to stay,
but he felt her presence might give the Allies another excuse to keep his wife and son from him.

Louis XVIII, was smugly aware that conflicts were inevitable. "Allies?" he said to Metternich. "What Allies? Against whom? . . . Surely not against the king of France: He is the guarantee . . . of the peace." He expected France to have a great-power role, and got it for her. The czar held out for all of Poland—an "independent" kingdom under the Russian crown; the king of Prussia supported him on promise of receiving Saxony, occupied by Russian troops. Metternich of Austria and Castelreagh of Britain opposed, fearing Russian domination of central Europe. Talleyrand broke the deadlock by ranging France on the side of Austria and Britain. (In January 1815, the three signed a secret military alliance.) Saxony was preserved; the czar got only the core of Poland.

Talleyrand had supported the Saxon king in the name of "legitimacy"—restoration of the traditional rulers. On the same basis he demanded that Murat be removed from Naples in favor of the Bourbon king, Ferdinand (of the Two Sicilies). Metternich supported Murat formally because of his treaty with Austria, but actually only to maintain quiet in Italy until the affairs of northern Europe were settled. Castlereagh backed him because he had promised Austria a free hand in Italy in return for a free hand in colonial matters. However, the British leaders detested Murat as a turncoat. The czar, a liberal-moralist of sorts, preferred Murat to the "butcher king" Ferdinand, but cared really only about northern Europe, as was the case with Frederick William of Prussia. At the beginning of 1815, only Metternich stood between Murat and oblivion, and he tentatively—on the basis of an unratified treaty. Murat was not long in discovering his vulnerable position.

Napoleon took pleasure in the troubles of the Allies, and even more in those of Louis XVIII. The Bourbon king returned with the unqualified support of only a small number of Frenchmen—those who had followed him in exile and royalists who had somehow survived at home. The *émigrés*, especially, expected power, influence, and restoration of their property. The king could not deliver. In order to rule, he had to employ ex-revolutionaries and Bonapartists in the government and administration, and to control the army he had to leave Napoleon's marshals virtually in charge. He returned property still in the hands of the state to his nobles, but that did not satisfy them and alarmed other citizens who had purchased National Properties.

Louis XVIII tried to please the people with a "Constitutional Charter," which provided for a British-style monarchy with a two-house legislature and guaranteed civil rights and religious freedom. But the people still equated his return with the restoration of the Old Regime. Moreover, the charter declared the Roman Catholic Church reestablished and this fact was overemphasized by the clergy, who in some areas even refused absolution to owners of National Properties. In the eyes of most Frenchmen, the fact that the Bourbon flag had replaced the tricolor was more significant than the constitutional professions of the king. Moreover, he increased rather than reduced taxes.

The army was as unhappy as the people. The draftees, of course, had happily returned home. The marshals and senior generals (not without qualms of conscience) swore loyalty to Louis in return for office and income. But the great mass of professional officers and NCOs (noncommissioned officers)—the product of Napoleon's wars—remained loyal to the emperor. Moreover, the army was drastically reduced in size by requirement of the Allies, which meant the dismissal of thousands of officers and NCOs. To ease their lot, Louis put them on half pay, but they were not grateful. Instead, they became even more violent Bonapartists.

The intelligentsia was pleased at the outset by the proclamation of freedom of the press and of speech. For a while it worked largely to the advantage of royalist propagandists, but gradually republicans and Bonapartists took advantage of it. The crown reimposed censorship, over the loud protests of former anti-Napoleonic writers such as Madame de Staël and Benjamin Constant.

Napoleon decided that France was ready to take him back and that the Allies—considering their differences, and if he promised to keep the peace—would not unite to reimpose Louis XVIII on the French. On the night of 26 February 1815 he blithely sailed for France with his staff and Old Guards aboard the Brig *Inconstant*.

FLIGHT OF THE EAGLE

On 1 March 1815, Napoleon landed on the Gulf Juan, between Cannes and Antibes, and marched north along the flanks of the Alps, avoiding the royalist Rhone valley. He was cheered in every village and town. On 7 March, however, near Grenoble, his guard confronted troops deployed by General Marchand to capture him. He recognized the standard of the 5th regiment of the line. He pushed past his men and displaying the courage, dramatic flair, and gambler's instinct that had made him great, opened his coat and walked forward. "There he is, Fire!" shouted a young captain. There was dead silence.

"Soldiers of the 5th," Napoleon shouted, "I am your Emperor. . . . If there is a man among you who would kill his Emperor, here I am!" There was none. Cheering *"Vive l'Empereur! Vive l'Empereur!"* the troops rushed to join his little army. More regiments followed their example.

The "thunderer of the scene" (Lord Byron's words) began a triumphal procession to Paris, his forces growing as he went. At Grenoble, crowds greeted him, and since Marchand had fled with the keys to the city, tore down the gates and presented them to the emperor. Lyons welcomed him frenetically. At Auxerre, Marshal Ney, who had vowed to bring Napoleon to King Louis in an iron cage, fell into his arms. On 20 March 1815 the emperor entered Paris, from which the rotund and puffing Louis XVIII had fled, and was carried on the shoulders of a riotously happy crowd into the Tuileries. He was destined to rule France again, however, for only a "hundred days," (20 March–22 June 1815).

THE HUNDRED DAYS

Napoleon promised the French more democratic government, backing his words by issuing an "Additional Act" to the Imperial Constitution. The document was framed by Benjamin Constant, exiled for his liberalism in 1803, and provided for a freely elected Chamber of Deputies. It was approved overwhelmingly by plebiscite, though the vote was light, and elections were promptly held. He assembled a ministry of all talents, including Joseph Fouché, Caulaincourt, and Lazare Carnot, the old "Organizer of Victory." His brothers Joseph, Jerome, and (to his surprise) Lucien rallied to him.[12] He recalled his veterans on half-pay service to active duty and began rebuilding the army.

To the Allies, Napoleon promised peace—over and over—emphasizing that he was now content to rule France within her existing borders. His constitution, which gave the power to declare war to the legislature, was designed as much to impress the powers as the French. The Congress of Vienna, however, had declared him an outlaw (13 March) before he even reached Paris and branded him "an Enemy and Disturber of the Tranquility of the World." On 25 March, Austria, Prussia, Russia, and Britain pledged to keep 150,000 troops each in the field until he was totally defeated. The emperor kept Caulaincourt busy protesting his pacific intentions, nevertheless, and tried to divide the Allies by sending Czar Alexander a copy of Talleyrand's secret military alliance with Austria and Britain. It was to no avail.

MURAT IN ITALY

Murat, meanwhile, confirmed the Allies' worst suspicions of Napoleon by proclaiming himself the emperor's ally and attacking the Austrians (19 March) in northern Italy. It pleased the Gascon to imagine that he was recovering his honor by rallying to the emperor, but in fact he was fighting to save and enlarge his kingdom. He had been strengthening his armies so as to maintain himself by force, and Napoleon's return seemed a godsend. While the Allies were mesmerized by the threat from France, Murat hoped to demolish the weak Austrian garrisons in Eugène's former kingdom and to unite Italy. Whether Napoleon won or not, he, Murat, would have to be dealt with as king of all Italy.

Caroline thought their only chance was to remain loyal to the Allies and feared Napoleon. "I know him. He will kill us!" Murat, however, listened to the Carbonari leaders, who assured him that the societies would raise the whole nation for him. He marched north with 40,000 men and at Rimini proclaimed the independence of Italy. Italians, however, generally ignored him, as in 1814. The Austrians, at first wary (they thought he had 100,000 men, which he did, on

---

[12] Lucien had gone into voluntary exile in Rome after Napoleon disapproved of his marriage to Madame Jouberthon in 1803, and in 1810 had sailed for America with his family, only to be captured by the British. He had lived comfortably in the country in England (though technically a prisoner of war) until 1814, then returned to Rome. He had guilt feelings about his desertion of his brother, especially since British propaganda had pictured him as a refugee from Napoleon's tyranny, and the only brother with the courage to oppose the emperor, which was not quite true.

paper), soon realized he was a paper tiger, and on 3 May at Tolentino, totally destroyed his army. He fled to France, where he offered his services to Napoleon. The emperor ignored him. Caroline gave over Naples to the Austrians and British and went into exile in Vienna. Italian historians later portrayed Murat as a pioneer of Italian unification, and often refer to his campaign as "the First War of Italian Independence." At the time, however, he was not mourned even by the nationalist intelligentsia; their valiant fool had failed them.[13]

WATERLOO

Whether Napoleon meant to keep the peace is unknown, and, in any case, is an academic question. He was forced to begin preparing for war from the moment he entered Paris. When the Allies proved totally unresponsive to his diplomacy, he determined to attack them as soon as possible. They had the potential of raising 700,000 troops, already had 400,000, if in scattered garrisons, and were backed by the Bank of England. He would be lucky to have half their numbers by the summer. His government was living on credit. Moreover, the French were in no mood for a long war, despite the tumultuous reception they had given him. Royalists were making trouble in the countryside; the new legislative chambers were demonstrating alarming independence. For the most part, the "little people" supported him, but the noble and middle-class politicians took a barely disguised wait-and-see attitude. He had little faith that a "jacquerie," without the leadership element could keep him on the throne. As so often in his career, he needed a quick victory over his foreign enemies to survive.

By June 1815 he had raised almost 300,000 men—an incredible[14] achieve-ment—of which 125,000 could constitute a strike force. He badly missed Marshal Berthier, his perennial chief-of-staff, who had gone into exile, as had Macdonald, Marmont, and others. The "names" he could call on were few, but he made do, if some of his judgments seem strange. He appointed Marshal Davout, probably his best commander ever, minister of war, and made Marshal Soult chief-of-staff. The reverse might have been a better arrangement; the explanation probably is that he feared leaving Soult in Paris. He made the impetuous Ney, in effect, his deputy field commander. The Marquis de Grouchy, the one general he promoted to marshal, would fail him badly in the coming campaign. His corps commanders were brave and competent soldiers, but lacked the aura of legend. Napoleon could have used Murat, though it is understandable that he refused to employ him. The emperor's brother Jerome, who fought heroically as a division commander, probably should have been allowed a corps.

[13] In October 1815, Murat, vowing to recover his kingdom or "die like a king," returned to Naples with a small band of freebooters, mostly Corsicans. He was captured at Pizzo and shot.

[14] He also had mobilized 170,000 National Guards, but did not count on them heavily.

Napoleon's plan was to strike at the nearest Allied armies in Belgium. Wellington, with an Anglo-Dutch force of about 80,000, was at Brussels; Blücher was east of Liège with 90,000 Prussians and Saxons. Schwarzenberg was assembling a mass of 250,000 in Germany. The Allied plan was for all three armies to close on Paris, with the czar following with a huge reserve. Napoleon planned to march on Brussels, crush Wellington, and then turn on Blücher. However, the seventy-year-old Prussian was lashing his troops toward the French border.

On 15 June 1815, Napoleon crossed the Sambre at Charleroi and put Ney on the route to Brussels via Quatre Bras with 45,000 men. Early on the 16th, however, the emperor encountered Blücher's advance elements, and directed his remaining 80,000 men on Ligny. Wellington meanwhile had ordered his army to shift southward, but did not hear of Napoleon's advance until midnight on the 15th while at a ball given by the Duchess of Richmond in Brussels (only thirty miles from Charleroi). Scribbling orders for his army to concentrate on Quatre Bras, Wellington continued to dance until 2 A.M.; at dawn on the 16th he was galloping south. Meanwhile on the same morning (16 June), his advance elements, under the Prince of Orange, engaged Ney at Quatre Bras. Seven miles to the east, Napoleon attacked Blücher at Ligny and forced him to retreat, exacting 5000 casualties. Ney, fighting against ever-increasing forces, late in the day commanded by Wellington, was stalemated. On the morning of the 17th, Wellington heard of Blücher's defeat and ordered a retreat to Mont St. Jean, signaling Blücher that he would fight Napoleon there "if I am supported by even a single Prussian corps." Blücher retreated parallel to Wellington and within easy reach.

Napoleon dispatched Grouchy with 33,000 men to pursue Blücher and to prevent his junction with Wellington. The emperor marched for Quatre Bras, linked up with Ney, and on the 17th, in driving rain, pursued Wellington northward. Grouchy meanwhile lost Blücher and quartered for the night. Only in the late morning of 18 June did he discover that Blücher had regrouped at Wavre and was marching to reinforce Wellington, at Waterloo (Mont St. Jean) only nine miles away. Even then Grouchy made no move to threaten Blücher's advance—or later to "march to the guns." Napoleon was thus deprived of almost one-third of his army at Waterloo—almost doomed before the battle began.

On the morning of 18 June the Anglo-Dutch army was arrayed south of Waterloo, straddling the highway to Brussels before Mont St. Jean. (See Map 12.4.) Most of Wellington's army was on the reverse slope of rolling hills, with advance posts in the Chateau of Hougomont west of the highway and in the farm of La Haye Sainte, on the highway. Napoleon's army flanked the highway a mile south at La Belle Alliance, on the same undulating plateau. Ney was in command of the forward corps, under Reille and d'Erlon; behind them the corps of Lobau backed by cavalry corps under Kellermann and Milhaud; and behind them, massed on either side of the road, was the Imperial Guard. The day was bright and sunny, but both armies were soaked and exhausted from the previous day's march, and the ground was muddy.

Map 12.4

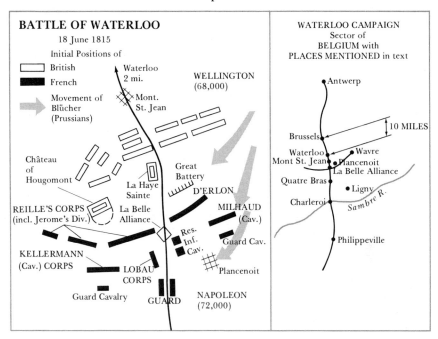

Napoleon and Wellington had one thing in common: they liked to let the enemy attack first, then to develop a decisive counterattack. Wellington was a man of maddening patience. In Spain he had beaten the French again and again (but never Napoleon; they had never met) by standing stonily in carefully chosen defensive positions until his more impetuous opponents exhausted themselves in the attack, then crushing them (or casually withdrawing to a better position). He veritably never went on the offensive unless he was certain the enemy was staggering (as at Vitoria). At Waterloo, he had several reasons for standing fast: Napoleon had him slightly outnumbered (71,000 to 68,000). With any luck, Blücher would reinforce him before the day was out. He had fewer guns than the French (156 to 246), and those he had could be used to better effect in defense.

Napoleon, on the other hand, had to carry the battle to Wellington. If he delayed he would be outnumbered. Grouchy, if he handled himself well (which he didn't), might hold Blücher at bay for a day, perhaps longer. Eventually, however, the "Old Wolf" would come at him with two- or three-to-one odds. Napoleon had to defeat Wellington quickly, then make junction with Grouchy and go after Blücher if the campaign was to be won. The emperor judged that he had not even time for a flanking movement (which might only drive Wellington into retreat anyway). He had to attack frontally, and he did, though he waited until almost midday to let the ground firm up.

At about 11:15, Reille's corps moved against Wellington's right. It was a feint for the main attack on the left and center by D'Erlon, which began shortly afterward. Reille became heavily engaged, however, and had to bypass Hougomont, where Jerome's division fought all day, with enormous losses. D'Erlon's attack stalled at about 2 P.M. before the defenses hinged on the Farm of La Haye Sainte.

At about the same time, Napoleon's scouts reported—and he could soon see—Prussian masses advancing from the east. He dispatched Lobau's corps to cover his right and returned to the main battle. He had committed his last infantry (combined) corps, however, and now had to win with the artillery, the cavalry of Kellermann and Milhaud, and the guard infantry and cavalry. Napoleon concentrated his artillery on Wellington's center. D'Erlon renewed the attack on the center, followed by Milhaud's cavalry. La Haye Sainte held, but the Anglo-Dutch line withdrew behind crests. About 4 P.M., Ney, assuming they were in retreat, led the cavalry in a general charge, which beyond the crests met murderous fire from the English, Scottish, and Dutch squares, backed by artillery which fired and was withdrawn into the squares. Ney retreated. At about 6 P.M., Ney led another attack, with the same results, except that La Haye Sainte fell, and the Allied line showed signs of crumbling in the center.

Napoleon meanwhile saw the Prussians drive Lobau into Plancenoit, on his right, and reinforced him with units of the guard. The French held. Napoleon returned to the main battle, in the center. He gave Ney nine of the remaining eleven battalions of the guard to prepare for a final assault, then rushed off to observe action on the right. When he returned, Ney had committed the guard infantry, accompanied by all the cavalry he could find, and was charging again against the center. His third horse had been shot from under him, and he was on foot, waving a broken sword, leading the guard forward. As the guard topped the crest of the enemy position, seemingly numberless infantry suddenly appeared before them. (They had been lying in the tall wheat and were ordered to stand up.) For the first time in its history, the guard faltered, then broke and retreated. With the repulse of the Old Guard about 8 P.M., the French army began falling to pieces, assailed frontally by Wellington's cavalry and from the east by Bulow's Prussians (30,000), with more under Blücher close behind. Four battalions of the Old Guard formed squares south of La Haye Sainte, but the army swirled past them, and most of them perished. "The Guard dies; It does not surrender!" Two other battalions of guards, squared near La Belle Alliance, with the emperor in the center, made a final attempt to rally the army, then escorted Napoleon southward.

TO ST. HELENA

The Emperor reached Paris on 21 June to find the government in the hands of a committee dominated by Fouché. It demanded that he give up the throne, seconded by the Chambers, led by the Marquis de Lafayette. On 22 June, he abdicated in favor of his son, Napoleon II (the king of Rome). The Chambers tentatively resolved to accept Napoleon II, but Fouché and Lafayette secured the support of the Allies for the restoration of Louis XVIII.[15] Napoleon meanwhile retired to Malmaison, where he received supporters and said farewells, the last to his mother. On 29 June he fled, fearing capture by Blücher's cavalry. It was well known that the Prussian marshal wanted Napoleon shot. On 3 July he was at Rochefort, where Joseph had a ship ready to sail for America and offered to impersonate him while he made good his escape. Napoleon declined.

On 15 July, he surrendered himself to Captain Maitland of the *Bellerophon*, handing him a letter for the prince regent of England asking for asylum. "I have finished my political career, and I come, like Themistocles, to sit at the hearth of the British people. I put myself under the protection of . . . Your Royal Highness, as the most powerful, constant and generous of my enemies." By the time the warship reached Plymouth, however, the powers at Paris had ruled that Napoleon was a prisoner of war (2 August 1815), and he was not allowed even to land. Britain was charged with selecting a place of confinement from which another return would be impossible. The place chosen was the island of St. Helena, in the south Atlantic near the 15th parallel, 1300 miles from Africa, 2400 from Brazil. It was a volcanic rock, twenty-eight miles across, with valleys of lush vegetation and fierce winds and tides. A more remote location could hardly have been found. It took three months for the *Northumberland*, which carried the ex-emperor to his island prison, to reach St. Helena.

CONGRESS OF VIENNA

Meanwhile the Congress of Vienna completed its remapping of Europe and issued its final act (8 June 1815). The "Principle of Legitimacy"—restoration of traditional rulers—was generally applied for the major powers, but otherwise loosely indeed. It had been enunciated by Talleyrand, initially, to strengthen the position of France, but he came not to need it. (see Map 12.5)

A kingdom of Poland was created, with the czar of Russia as king (but with its own constitution). It comprised the former Grand Duchy of Warsaw—less Galicia (to Austria), Thorn and Posen (to Prussia), and Cracow, which became a free state. Austria was restored to her boundaries, and also received Salzburg and the Tyrol (from Bavaria), Lombardy and Venetia, and the Illyrian Provinces. In addition, Habsburg princes took the thrones of Modena and Tuscany, and Parma went to former Empress Marie Louise (also a Habsburg). Prussia was essentially restored, and in addition to Posen and Thorn, received Danzig, Swedish

---

[15] Louis XVIII reentered Paris on 7 July 1815. By the second Treaty of Paris (20 November 1815), France was reduced to the boundaries of 1789 and assessed an indemnity of 700,000,000 francs.

EUROPE IN 1815

After the Congress of Vienna

☐ German Confederation

MILES

0   250   500

Map 12.5

ATLANTIC OCEAN

PORTUGAL

Lisbon

KINGDOM OF SPAIN

Madrid

KINGDOM OF FRANCE

Loire R.

Seine R.

Paris

London

UNITED KINGDOM OF GREAT BRITAIN AND IRELAND

NORTH SEA

Amsterdam

UNITED NETHERLANDS

Brussels

(PR.)

Rhine R.

HANOVER

Frankfurt

Copenhagen

DENMARK

Elbe R.

Berlin

KINGDOM OF PRUSSIA

Oder R.

KINGDOM OF SWEDEN (INCLUDES NORWAY)

Stockholm

BALTIC SEA

FINLAND

St. Petersburg

RUSSIAN EMPIRE

Moscow

Warsaw

Vistula R.

Dniester R.

Vienna

AUSTRIAN EMPIRE

SWITZERLAND

LOMBARDY

VENETIA

Po R.

Rhône R.

KINGDOM OF SARDINIA-PIEDMONT

CORSICA (FR.)

PAPAL STATES

Rome

Naples

KINGDOM OF THE TWO SICILIES

ADRIATIC SEA

Danube R.

MONTENEGRO

OTTOMAN EMPIRE

BLACK SEA

Constantinople

AEGEAN SEA

MEDITERRANEAN SEA

N

Pomerania, almost half of Saxony (the former ruler kept the rest), and territories in the Rhineland including Cologne and Mainz.

Belgium and the former Dutch Republic were united to form the kingdom of the Netherlands, under King William I of Orange. Belgium was the price Britain paid for retention of the Dutch colonies of Cape Town (South Africa) and Ceylon. Britain also kept the French islands of Tobago, Sainte Lucia, and Mauritius—and Malta. Spain and Portugal were restored to their Bourbon and Braganza rulers. Naples (with Murat and Caroline swept away) went back to the Bourbons, along with Sicily. Sardinia reannexed Piedmont and added Genoa as well. The pope reassumed rule of his states in central Italy.

The German states, their number reduced to thirty-nine, were loosely united in a confederation. Austria was given membership, however, and moreover the permanent presidency of the Diet. Thus a shadow of the Holy Roman Empire returned.

The French settlement was left for the Second Treaty of Paris, signed 20 November 1815. Louis XVIII was re-restored to the throne, but France was reduced to the boundaries of 1789 (instead of 1792). This meant ceding Savoy to Sardinia-Piedmont, the Saarland to Prussia, and small territories to the Swiss Confederation and the Netherlands. To safeguard Europe against any future French aggression, the Quadruple Alliance was concluded (20 November 1815), among Britain, Russia, Austria, and Prussia.

NAPOLEON'S DEATH AND ENSHRINEMENT

Napoleon died on St. Helena on 5 May 1821 of stomach cancer, and was buried on the island. He had asked in his will, however, that he be laid to rest "on the banks of the Seine, among the French people whom I have loved so much." In December 1840, his wish was granted. At the behest of King Louis Philippe, seconded by a somewhat guilt-ridden British government, his remains were brought to Paris and interred with great ceremony under the dome of the Invalides, where he now lies.

"AND THE REST IS LEGEND . . . "

Napoleon spent much of his time during the final years dictating his inter-pretation of the history of his era—formally to Emmanuel de Las Cases, in conversation to Generals Bertrand, Montholon, Gourgaud, the Irish surgeon Barry O'Meara, and scores of others. He did not attempt to add lustre to his military reputation (which he surely knew was unshakable); indeed, he said that Waterloo would "eclipse the memory" of his other battles. Instead, he fiercely challenged those who called him a tyrant and destroyer and elaborated on an image of himself as a man who had tried to govern in the interests of all the French and the other peoples of Europe. He asserted that his ultimate goal was to create a European "federation of free peoples" and to bring the benefits of the French Revolution to all. "The Imperial Guard always marched to the 'Marseillaise.'"

On his deathbed, he dictated advice to his son, whom he believed would one day be emperor:

> Regenerate [Europe] through laws; establish above all institutions which destroy all traces of feudalism, which assure the dignity of man [and] develop the germs of prosperity which have lain dormant for centuries; see that the masses share in that which is today the province of the few. . . .

In addition, he presented himself dramatically as a martyr to the cause of human liberty, struck down by the evil forces of the Old Regime, and bound to the God-forsaken "rock" of St. Helena to die. The British, he said, had deliberately put him in a climate and environment which would kill him speedily. Of that he convinced few, but he won the sympathy of almost everyone—not just including, but especially, the British. He charmed everyone who got to know him, from little children to admirals and diplomats—everyone except his dour "jailer," Sir Hudson Lowe. In the end, in the eyes of the world, he did become a martyr. And, as he had predicted, this image, verging on apotheosis, guaranteed that he would never be forgotten.

Thus Napoleon's principles, aims, and character continue to mystify and fascinate—and always will. Not only do arguments about him rage on among historians and other specialists, but some of the most talented writers of every generation have chosen to present their own interpretations of him in fiction.[16] In our own century, he has been portrayed also in films and television dramas. In all these forms, whether he is presented in a favorable light or not—and he often is not—he is remembered. He looms larger than life. The legend begun by Napoleon's propagandists—writers and painters—and by himself through his bulletins, proclamations, and writings, has been perpetuated. It is difficult to separate the legend from real history.

Napoleon *is* a legend as well as a historical figure. The historian must try to separate the true from the fictional about him. This inevitably involves crossing pens with Napoleon himself, and dealing with the fact that a good part of his interpretation of his career was accurate. His genius is evident in the brief he presented for himself on St. Helena. Napoleon did not try to perpetrate falsehoods (with a few exceptions, which *can* be blamed on Las Cases or other writers); he merely emphasized the constructive parts of his work.

---

[16] Among these are: Heinrich Heine, Stendhal, Victor Hugo, Balzac, Alexandre Dumas (père et fils), Rudyard Kipling, Tolstoy, Nietzsche, Thomas Hardy, Edmond Rostand, Arthur Conan Doyle, George Bernard Shaw, Anatole France, Louis Aragon, Jean Anouilh, and, in the 1970s, Anthony Burgess. None, of course, devoted his time exclusively to Napoleon.

Without question he deliberately spread revolutionary concepts throughout Europe. He came closer to creating a European Empire than any ruler since Roman times. If it little resembled a federation of free peoples, one can choose to believe that it might have, in time, if his government had survived—or even that he would have founded a centralized European state. The impact of his laws and institutions is still markedly evident in France and, in varying degrees, throughout Europe and the world.

Even discounting the magnificent drama of his passing, it is difficult to believe that history would have been the same without Napoleon Bonaparte. As Hegel recognized in his own time, he was a true "World Historical Individual." He shook the world. As he predicted it would, his reputation "echoes down the generations." Even in China and Japan, his effigy is instantly recognized today by people whose ancestors were unaware of his existence.

AFTERWORD

The introduction drew many conclusions, which might better have been put here, at the end of the book. Perhaps the reader can now return to them with profit. It depicted the Revolutionary Napoleonic Era as an "overture to modern times." It remains to be emphasized, however, that, without Napoleon, it might have been a very muted "overture."

In France, the Revolution left as permanent legacies the principles of "Liberty, Equality, and Fraternity," popular constitutional government, and guaranteed rights. It originated modern nationalism, mass armies, and total war. Under the Terror, it produced a recognizable model for contemporary bureaucratic governments, with their twin penchants for tyranny and promoting welfare.

Without Napoleon, however, the Revolution might have been largely a French affair. Its great energy might have been dissipated in the floundering of a nineteenth-century "bourgeois" republic—an extension of the Directory. Because of Napoleon, however, the Revolution spread in Europe—it blazed, it shocked, it was fixed forever by trauma in the European mentality. In part deliberately, in part despite himself, Napoleon made the Revolution a crucial event in European and world history.

BIBLIOGRAPHY

What follows is essentially a list of selected books (syntheses, monographs, etc.) on the French Revolutionary-Napoleonic Era and its eighteenth century background, arranged by period or category. It is intended to represent all possible opinions and to supply the nonspecialist with an extended reading list. For the research-minded, there is a section (at the end) on Bibliographies of the Revolutionary-Napoleonic Era. Primary sources (documents of the period) are not listed here; the bibliographies list the printed ones as well as guides to major archives with unpublished materials. The *historiography* of the Era is discussed at the end of the Introduction.

Ahead of our book list, it seems appropriate to pay tribute to the authors of textbooks, surveys, and other works that have introduced most twentieth century American scholars, save only the emerging generation, to French Revolutionary-Napoleonic studies, *viz.*: Louis R. Gottschalk, *The Era of the French Revolution* (1929); Leo Gershoy, *The French Revolution and Napoleon* (1933, 1964); and John Hall Stewart, *Documentary Survey of the French Revolution* (1951). And in the *Rise of Modern Europe* series, edited by William L. Langer: Leo Gershoy, *From Despotism to Revolution* (1944, 1963); Crane Brinton, *A Decade of Revolution, 1789–1799* (1934, 1963); and Geoffrey Bruun, *Europe and the French Imperium* (1938, 1963). Finally, Georges Lefebvre's long-lived *La Révolution française*, 4th ed. (1951) and *Napoléon*, 4th ed. (1953) *Peuples et civilisations*, vols. 13 and 14, edited by Louis Halphen and Philippe Sagnac. *The French Revolution*, 2 vols. [Vol. 1 translated by Elizabeth Moss Evanson (1962); Vol. 2 translated by John Hall Stewart and James Friguglietti [1961–1962]; and *Napoléon*, 2 vols. translated by Henry Stockhold (1969). A fifth edition of *La Révolution française* (1963) was prepared by Albert Soboul.

FRENCH REVOLUTION: GENERAL

Bosher, J. F. *The French Revolution.* New York, 1988.

Carlyle, Thomas. *The French Revolution.* Edited by K. J. Fielding and David Sorensen. 1989. 1st ed., 1837.

Doyle William. *Oxford History of the French Revolution.* 1989.

Ford, Franklin. *Europe, 1780–1830.* 2d ed., 1978.

Furet, François, and Denis Richet. *La Révolution française*. 1965 and 1973. Translated as *The French Revolution* by Stephen Hardman. 1970.

Gaxotte, Pierre. *La Révolution française*. 1928. New ed., 1975.

Godechot, Jacques. *France and the Atlantic Revolution of the 18th Century*. Translated by Herbert H. Rowen. 1965.

———. *La Grande Nation: L'Expansion révolutionnaire de la France dans le monde*. 2 vols. 1956. 2d ed., 1983.

———. *La Révolution française: chronologie commentée 1787–1799*. 1988.

Goehring, Martin. *Geschichte der Grossen Revolution*. 2 vols. 1950–1951.

Hampson, Norman. *Social History of the French Revolution*. 1963.

Hobsbawm, Eric. *The Age of Revolution, 1789–1822*. 1962.

Kafker, Frank A., and James M. Laux. *The French Revolution: Conflicting Interpretations*. 4th ed. 1989.

Kennedy, Emmet. *Cultural History of the French Revolution*. 1989.

Mathiez, Albert. *La Révolution française*. 2 vols. 1927.

———. *The French Revolution*. Translated by C. A. Phillips. 1928.

Palmer, R. R. *The World of the French Revolution*. 1971.

———. *The Age of Democratic Revolution, 1770–1799*. 2 vols. 1959–1964.

Reinhard, Marcel. *Paris pendant la Révolution (Cours de Sorbonne)*. 2 vols. 1966.

Rudé, George. *Revolutionary Europe, 1783–1815*. New York, 1964.

Schama, Simon. *Citizens: A Chronicle of the French Revolution*. 1989.

Soboul, Albert. *A Short History of the French Revolution*. Translated by Geoffrey Symcox. 1977.

———. *Précis d'histoire de la Révolution française*. 1962.

———. *The French Revolution, 1787–1799: Storming of the Bastille to Napoleon*. Translated by Alan Forrest and Colin Jones. 1975.

Sutherland, Donald M. G. *France, 1789–1815: Revolution and Counter-revolution*. 1986.

Thompson, J. M. *The French Revolution*. 2d ed. London, 1951.

Tulard, Jean. *Révolutions de 1789 à 1851*. Vol. 4 of *Histoire de France*. 1985.

Vovelle, Michel. *1789–1799: La Révolution française: images et récits*. 5 vols. 1986.

FRENCH REVOLUTION: EXTENDED MONOGRAPHS AND SPECIAL STUDIES

Ackerknecht, E. *Medicine in the Paris Hospital, 1794–1848*. 1966.

Agulhon, Maurice, *Republic in the Village: The People of the Var from The French Revolution to the Second Republic*. Translated 1982.

Applewhite, Harriet B., and Darlene G. Levy, eds. *Women and Politics in the Age of the Democratic Revolution*. 1989.

Aulard, Alphonse. *Le Christianisme et la Révolution française*. 1924. (*Christianity and the French Revolution*.) Translated by Lady Frazer, 1967.

Baker, Keith, and Colin Lucas. *The French Revolution and the Creation of Modern Political Culture.* Vol. 1 of *The Political Culture of the Old Regime.* 1987.

Baker, Keith. *Inventing the French Revolution: Essays on French Political Culture in the Eighteenth Century.* 1990.

Bernard, H. C. *Education and the French Revolution.* 1969.

Blumenkranz, Bernhard. *Histoire des Juifs en France.* 1972.

———. *Juifs et la Révolution Française.* 1976.

Bringemeier, Martha. *Ein Modejournalist erlebt die Franzosische Revolution.* 1981. Bryson, N. *Tradition and Desire: From David to Delacroix.* 1984.

Carlson, Marvin. *The Theater of the French Revolution.* 1966.

Chadwick, Owen. *The Popes and European Revolution.* 1981.

Clère, Jean-Jacques. *Les paysans de la Haute-Marne et la Révolution française: recherches sur les structures foncières de la communaute villageoise (1780–1825).* 1988.

Cobb, Richard. *The Police and the People: French Popular Protest, 1789–1820.* 1970.

Darnton, Robert, and Daniel Roche, eds. *Revolution in Print: The Press in France, 1775–1800.* 1989.

David, Marcel. *Fraternité et Révolution française: 1789–99.* 1987.

Fayet, Joseph. *La Révolution et la science.* 1959.

Forrest, Alan I. *French Revolution and the Poor.* 1981.

Genty, Maurice. *Paris, 1789–1795: l'apprentissage de la citoyenneté.* 1987.

Godechot, Jacques. *Pensée révolutionnaire en France et en Europe, 1780–1799.* 1964.

———. *La Révolution française dans le Midi toulousain.* 1986.

Gough, Hugh. *The Newspaper Press in the French Revolution.* 1988.

Gullickson, Gay L. *Spinners and Weavers of Auffay: Rural Industry and Sexual Division of Labor in a French Village, 1750–1850.* 1986.

Hales, E.E.Y. *Revolution and Papacy, 1769–1846.* 1960.

Hemmings, F.W.J. *Culture and society in France, 1789–1848.* 1987.

Huard, Pierre. *Sciences, Medicine, Pharmacie de la Revolution et l'Empire.* 1970.

Hunt, Lynn Avery. *Politics, Culture, and Class in the French Revolution.* 1984.

Jones, Colin. *Charity and Bienfaisance: The Treatment of the Poor in the Montpellier Region, 1740–1815.* 1982.

Jones, Peter. *The Peasantry in the French Revolution.* 1988.

Kennedy, Michael L. *The Jacobin Clubs in the French Revolution.* Vol. 1: *The First Years,* 1982. Vol. 2: *The Middle Years,* 1988.

Leveque, Jean-Jacques. *L'art et la Révolution française: 1789–1804.* 1987.

Landes, Joan B. *Women and the Public Sphere in the Age of the French Revolution.* 1988.

Lateille, André. *L'Eglise catholique et la révolution française.* 2 vols. 1946–1950.

Leith, James A. *The Idea of Art as Propaganda in France, 1750–1799: A Study in the History of Ideas.* 1972.

Léon, A. *La Révolution française et l'education technique.* 1968.

Lewis, Gwynne, and Colin Lucas, eds. *Beyond the Terror: Essays in French regional and social history, 1794–1815.* 1983.

Mahler, Raphael. *A History of Modern Jewry, 1780–1815.* 1971.

Mansel, Philip. *The Court of France, 1789–1830.* 1988.

Margadant, T. W. *Urban Rivalries in the French Revolution.* 1990.

Marion, Marcel. *La vente des biens nationaux pendant la Révolution.* 1908. Reprint, 1975.

Martin, M. *Les origines de la presse militaire en France.* 1975.

Mathiez, Albert. *La Révolution et l'Eglise.* 1910.

McKeown, Thomas, *The Modern Rise of Population.* 1976.

Nationalism in the Age of the French Revolution. Edited by Otto Dann and John Dinwiddy. 1988.

Ozouf, Mona. *Fête révolutionnaire, 1789–1799.* 1976. Translated as *Festivals and the French Revolution* by Alan Sheridan. 1988.

Palmer, R. R. *The Improvement of Humanity: Education and the French Revolution.* 1985.

———., ed. *The School of the French Revolution: A Documentary History of the College of Louis-le-Grand . . . 1762–1814.* 1975.

Parker, Harold T. *The Cult of Antiquity and the French Revolutionaries.* 1937 and 1965.

Plongeron, Bernard. *Les reguliers de Paris devant le serment constitutionnel . . . 1789–1801.* 1964.

Poland, Burdette C. *French Protestantism and the French Revolution . . . 1685–1815.* 1957.

Popkin, Jeremy D. *News and Politics in the Age of Revolution: Jean Luzac's "Gazette de Leyde."* 1988.

Ramsey, Matthew. *Professional and Popular Medicine in France, 1770–1830.* Cambridge History of Medicine Series. 1988.

Robert, Daniel. *Eglises Reformées en France, 1790–1830.* 1961.

Roche, Daniel. *The People of Paris.* 2 vols. Translated by Marie Evans and Gwynne Lewis. 1987.

Sédillot, René. *Le Coût de la Révolution française.* 1988.

Sewell, William H., Jr. *Work and Revolution in France: The Language of Labor from the Old Regime to 1848.* 1980.

Shulim, Joseph I. *Liberty, Equality, and Fraternity: Studies in the Era of the French Revolution and Napoleon.* 1989.

Soboul, Albert. *Problèmes paysans de la Révolution.* 1976.

Soprani, Anne. *La Révolution et les femmes: 1789–1796.* 1988.

Vess, David. *Medical Revolution in France, 1789–1796.* 1975.

Wills, Antoinette. *Crime and Punishment in Revolutionary Paris.* 1981.

18th CENTURY BACKGROUND: GENERAL

Aliverti, Maria Ines. *Il ritratto d'attore nel settecento francese e inglese.* 1986.

Behrens, C.B.A. *The Ancien Régime.* In *History of European Civilizaton Library.* Edited by Geoffrey Barraclough. 1967.

De Vries, Jan. *European Urbanization, 1500–1800.* 1984.

Dévèze, M. *Europe et le monde à la fin du XVIIIe siècle.* 1971.

Frey, Linda, and Marsha Frey. *Societies in Upheaval: Insurrections in France, Hungary, and Spain in the Early Eighteenth Century.* 1987.

Hall, Thadd E. *France and the Eighteenth Century Corsican Question.* 1971.

Labrousse, Ernest, Pierre Léon, Pierre Goubert. *Des derniers temps de l'âge seigneurial aux préludes de l'âge industriel.* 2 vols. 1970.

Mousnier, Roland, Ernest Labrousse, and Marc Bouloiseau. *Le XVIIIe siècle: Révolution intellectuelle, technique, et politique, 1715–1815.* Vol. 5 of *Histoire générale des civilisations.* Edited by Maurice Crouzet. 1953.

Post, John D. *Food Shortage, Climatic Variability, and Epidemic Disease in Preindustrial Europe: The Mortality Peak in the Early 1740s.* 1985.

Reese, Armin. *Europaische Hegemonie und France d'outre mer: koloniale Fragen in der franzosischen Aussenpolitik 1700–1763.* 1988.

Riley, James C. *Population Thought in the Age of Demographic Revolution.* 1985.

———. *The Eighteenth-Century Campaign to Avoid Disease.* 1987.

Zeeden, Ernst Walter. *Europa im Zeitalter des Absolutismus und der Aufklarung.* 1981.

18th CENTURY FRANCE: SOCIAL, CULTURAL INSTITUTIONAL

Barber, Elinor G. *Bourgeoisie in 18th Century France.* 1955.

Benabou, Erica-Marie. *La prostitution et la police des moeurs au XVIIIe siècle.* 1987.

Bergeal, Catherine. *Protestantisme et tolerance en France au XVIIIe siècle: La Révocation a la révolution: (1685–1789).* 1988.

Bluche, François. *Les magistrats du Parlement de Paris au XVIIIe siècle.* New ed., 1986.

Braham, Allan. *Architecture of the French Enlightenment.* 1987.

Brennan, Thomas Edward. *Public Drinking and Popular Culture in Eighteenth-Century Paris.* 1988.

Bryson, Norman. *French Painting of the Ancien Régime.* 1983.

Censer, Jack and Jeremy Popkin, eds. *Press and Politics in Pre-Revolutionary France.* 1987.

Charlton, D. G. *New Images of the Natural in France: A Study in European Cultural History, 1750–1800.* 1984.

Fairchilds, Cissie C. *Domestic Enemies: Servants & their Masters in Old Regime France.* 1984.

———. *Poverty and Charity in Aix-en-Provence, 1640–1789.* 1976.

Ford, Franklin L. *Robe and Sword.* 1953.

Forster, Robert. *The Nobility of Toulouse.* 1960. Reprint, 1977.

———. *The House of Saulx-Tavanes . . . Versailles and Burgundy, 1790–1890.* 1971.

Forster, Robert, and Orest Ranum, eds. *Medicine and Society in France.* Translated by Elborg Forster and Patricia M. Ranum. 1980.

French Women and the Age of Enlightenment. Edited by Samia I. Spencer. 1984.

Gand, Michel. *Le Loiret dans la tourmente révolutionnaire: emeutes et mouvéments populaires, 1789–1795.* 1982.

Garrioch, David. *Neighbourhood and Community in Paris, 1740–1790.* 1986.

Gelbart, Nina Rattner. *Feminine and Opposition Journalism in Old Regime France: Le Journal des Dames.* 1986.

Gelfand, Toby. *Professionalizing Modern Medicine: Paris Surgeons and Medical Science and Institutions in the 18th Century.* 1980.

Goubert, Pierre. *L'Ancien régime.* 2 vols. 1969–1973.

Grand, Serge. *Ces bonnes femmes du XVIIIe: flaneries à travers les salons litteraires.* 1985.

Gruder, Vivian. *The Royal Provincial Intendants.* 1969.

Hill, Peter P. *French Perceptions of the Early American Republic, 1783–1793.* 1988.

Hufton, Olwen. *Poor of 18th Century France, 1740–1789.* 1974.

Isherwood, Robert M. *Farce and Fantasy: Popular Entertainment in Eighteenth-Century Paris.* 1986.

Kaplan, Steven L. *Le complot de famine: histoire d'une rumeur au XVIIIe siècle.* Traduit de l'americain, 1982.

Kaplow, Jeffry. *The Names of Kings: The Parisian Laboring Poor in the Eighteenth Century.* 1972.

Labrosse, Claude, and Pierre Retat. *L'instrument périodique: la fonction de la presse au XVIIIe siècle.* 1985.

Le Roy Ladurie, Emmanuel. *Les paysans de Languedoc.* 2 vols. 1966. Translated as *The Peasants of Languedoc* by John Day, 1974.

Lebrun, Francois. *Se soigner autrefois: medecins, saints et sorciers aux 17e et 18e siècles.* 1983.

Lough, John. *An Introduction to Eighteenth Century France.* 1968.

Mackrell, J.Q.C., *The Attack on Feudalism in Eighteenth Century France.* 1973.

Maza, Sarah. *Servants and Masters in Eighteenth Century France: The Uses of Loyalty.* 1983.

McManners, John. *Abbés and Actresses: The Church and the Theatrical Profession in Eighteenth-Century France.* 1986.

———. *Death and the Enlightenment: Changing Attitudes to Death among Christians and Unbelievers in Eighteenth-Century France.* 1981.

———. *French Ecclesiastical Society . . . Ancien Regime.* 1961.

Meyer, Jean. *Le noblesse Bretonne au XVIIIe siécle.* 1966.

Noone, John. *The Man Behind the Iron Mask.* 1988.

Palmer, R. R. *Catholics and Unbelievers in 18th Century France.* 1939.

Phillips, Roderick. *Family Breakdown in Late Eighteenth-Century France: Divorces in Rouen, 1792–1803.* 1980.

Pluchon, Pierre. *Negres et juifs au XVIIIe siècle: le racisme au siècle des Lumières.* 1984.

Richard, Guy. *Noblesse d'affairs au XVIIIe siècle.* 1974.

Roche, Daniel. *The People of Paris: An Essay in Popular Culture in the 18th Century.* Translated by Marie Evans and Gwynne Lewis. 1987.

Root-Bernstein, Michele. *Boulevard Theater and Revolution in Eighteenth-Century Paris.* 1984.

Schwartz, Robert M. *Policing the Poor in Eighteenth Century France.* 1988.

Sheppard, Thomas F. *Lourmarin in the Eighteenth Century: A French Village.* 1971.

Sonnet, Martine. *Education des filles au temps des lumières.* 1987.

Steinbrugge, Lieselotte. *Das moralische Geschlecht: Theorien und literarische Entwurfe uber die Natur der Frau in der Franzosischen Aufklarung.* 1987.

Tarczylo, Theo. *Sexe et liberté au siècle des lumières.* 1983.

Vernus, Michel. *Le presbytére et la chaumière: curés et villageois dans l'ancienne France, XVIIe et XVIIIe siècles.* 1986.

Vovelle, Michel. *Piété baroque et déchristianisation en Provence au XVIIIe siècle.* 1973.

Walter, Gérard. *Histoire des paysans de France.* 1963.

Welch, Cheryl B. *Liberty and Utility: The French Ideologues and the Transformation of Liberalism.* 1984.

18th CENTURY EUROPE: SOCIAL, CULTURAL, INSTITUTIONAL

Donakowski, Conrad L. *A Muse for the Masses: Ritual and Music in an Age of Democratic Revolution, 1770–1870.* 1977.

Ebeling, Dietrich. *Burgertum und Pöbel: Wirtschaft und Gesellschaft Kölns im 18. Jahrhundert.* 1987.

Erbe, Michael. *Deutsche Geschichte, 1713–1790: Dualismus und Äufgeklarter Absolutismus.* 1985.

Hertz, Deborah Sadie. *Jewish High Society in Old Regime Berlin.* 1988.

Herzig, Arno. *Unterschichtenprotest in Deutschland 1790–1870.* 1988.

La Vopa, Anthony J. *Grace, Talent, and Merit: Poor Students, Clerical Careers, and Professional Ideology in Eighteenth-Century Germany.* 1988.

Melton, James Van Horn. *Absolutism and the Eighteenth-Century Origins of Compulsory Schooling in Prussia and Austria.* 1988.

Nenon, Monika. *Autorschaft und Frauenbildung: das Beispiel Sophie von la Roche.* 1988.

Pallach, Ulrich-Christian. *Materielle Kultur und Mentalitaten im 18. Jahrhundert: wirtschaftliche Entwicklung und politischsozialer Funktionswandel des Luxus in Frankreich und im Alten Reich am Ende des Ancien Regime.* 1987.

Schieth, Lydia. *Die Entwicklung des deutschen Frauenromans im ausgehenden 18. Jahrhundert.* 1987.

Schleuning, P. *Das 18. Jahrhundert: der Burger erhebt sich.* 1984.

Lis, Catharina. *Social Change and the Labouring Poor: Antwerp 1770–1860.* 1986.

Seidler, Eduard. *Lebensplan und Gesundheitsführung: Franz Anton Mai und die medizinische Aufklärung in Mannheim.* 2. Aufl. 1979.

Sherwood, Joan. *Poverty in Eighteenth-Century Spain: The Women and Children of the Inclusa.* 1988.

Ziessow, Karl H. *Landliche Lesekultur im 18.-19. Jahrhundert: das Kirchspiel Menslage und seine Lesegesellschaften 1790–1840.* 1988.

18th CENTURY ECONOMIC AND FINANCIAL: FRANCE AND EUROPE

Antonetti, Guy. *Une maison de banque à Paris au XVIIIe siècle: Greffulhe Montz et Cie.* 1963.

Bamford, Paul W. *Privilege and Profit: A Business Family in Eighteenth-Century France.* 1988.

Bosher, J. F. *French Finances, 1770–1795: From Business to Bureaucracy.* 1970.

Bruguière, Michel. *Gestionnaires et profiteurs de la Révolution: l'administration des finances françaises de Louis XVI à Bonaparte.* 1986.

Carrière, Charles. *Négociants Marseillais au XVIIIe siècle.* 1973.

Chaussinand-Nogaret, Guy. *Gens de finance au XVIIIe siècle.* 1972.

Crouzet, F. *Capital Formation in the Industrial Revolution.* 1972.

Durand, Yves. *Les fermiers généraux au dix-huitième siècle.* 1971.

Hofer, Peter. *Deutsch-französosische Handelsbeziehungen im 18. Jahrbundert: die Firma Breton frères in Nantes (1736–1766).* 1982.

Kaplan, Steven. *Bread, Politics and Political Economy during the Reign of Louis XV.* 1976.

Kaplan, Steven L. *Provisioning Paris: Merchants and Millers in the Grain and Flour Trade during the Eighteenth Century.* 1984.

Komlos, John. *Nutrition and Economic Development in the Eighteenth-Century Habsburg Monarchy.* 1989.

Labrousse, Ernest. *Esquisse du mouvément des prix et des revenus en France au XVIIe siècle.* 2 vols. 1933.

Luthy, Herbert. *La Banque Protestante en France: De la révocation de l'édit de Nantes à la Révolution.* 2 vols. 1959–1960.

Markovitch, Tihomir. *Histoire des industries françaises: Les industries lainières de Colbert à la Révolution.* 1976.

Matthews, George T. *The Royal General Farms in the Eighteenth Century.* 1958.

Morineau, Michel. *Faux-semblants d'un démarrage économique: Agriculture et demographie en France au XVIIe siècle.* 1971.

Mousnier, Roland. *Progrès scientifique et technique au VIIIe siècle.* 1958.

Parker, Harold T. *The Bureau of Commerce in 1781 and Its Policies with Respect to French Industry.* 1979.

Riley, James C. *International Government Finance and the Amsterdam Capital Market, 1740–1815.* 1980.

———. *The Seven Years War & the Old Regime in France: The Economic and Financial Toll.* 1986.

Sonenscher, Michael. *The Hatters of Eighteenth-Century France.* 1987.

———. *Work and Wages: Natural Law, Politics and the Eighteenth Century French Trades.* 1989.

Stein, Robert Louis. *The French Sugar Business in the Eighteenth Century.* 1988.

Steur, J. J. *Herstel of ondergang: de voorstellen tot redres van de Verenigde Oost-Indische Compagnie, 1740–1795.* 1984.

Ulbricht, Otto. *Englische Landwirtschaft in Kurhannover in der zweiten Halfte des 18, Jahrbunderts: Ansatze zu historischer Diffusionsforschung.* 1980.

THE ENLIGHTENMENT, SCIENCE AND RELATED

Albury, W. R. *The Logic of Condillac and the Structure of French Chemical and Biological Theory, 1780–1801.* 1972.

Aldridge, A. Owen. *Voltaire and the Century of Light.* 1975.

Baker, Keith M. *Condorcet: From Natural Philosophy to Social Mathematics.* 1975.

Bazzoli, Maurizio. *Il pensiero politico dell'assolutismo illuminato.* 1986.

Bien, David D. *The Calas Affair: Persecution, Tolerance, and Heresy in Eighteenth Century Toulouse.* 1960.

Blum, Carol. *Diderot, the Virtue of a Philosopher.* 1974.

——. *Rousseau and the Republic of Virtue: The Language of Politics in the French Revolution.* 1988.

Bollème, Geneviève. *Les Almanachs populaires aux 17e et 18e siècles.* 1969.

——. *La bibliotheque bleue.* 1971.

——, ed. *Contes bleus.* 1983.

Carpanetto, Dino. *L'Italia del Settecento: illuminismo e movimento riformatore.* 1981.

Cassirer, Ernst. *The Question of Jean-Jacques Rousseau.* Translated by Peter Gay. 1988.

Chisick, Harvey. *The Limits of Reform in the Enlightenment: Attitudes to the Education of the Lower Classes in France, 1762–1789.* 1981.

Cobban, Alfred, ed. *The Eighteenth Century: Europe in the Age of the Enlightenment.* 1969.

Cranston, Maurice W. *Philosophers and Pamphleteers: Political Theorists of the Enlightenment.* 1986.

Darnton, Robert. *Mesmerism and the End of the Enlightenment in France.* 1968.

Domergue, Lucienne. *Censure et lumières dans l'Espagne de Charles III.* 1982.

——. *Le Livre en Espagne au temps de la Révolution française.* 1984.

Du Pont de Nemours, Pierre Samuel. *The Autobiography of Du Pont de Nemours.* Translated and edited by Elizabeth Fox-Genovese. 1984.

Eisenstein, Elizabeth. *Print Culture and Enlightenment Thought.* 1986.

Ellenburg, Stephen. *Rousseau's Political Philosophy.* 1976.

Fox-Genovese, Elizabeth. *The Origins of Physiocracy: Economic Revolution and Social Order in Eighteenth Century France.* 1976.

Frijhoff, Willem, and Dominique Julia. *Education et Société dans la France de l'ancien régime.* 1975.

Garrett, Clarke. *Respectable Folly: Millenarians and the French Revolution in France and England.* 1975.

Gay, Peter. *The Enlightenment: An Interpretation.* 2 vols. 1966–1969.

Gillmor, G. Stewart. *Coulomb and the Evolution of Physics and Engineering in Eighteenth Century France.* 1971.

Godechot, Jacques. *La pensée révolutionnaire, 1770–1789.* 1969.

Goodman, Dena. *Criticism in Action: Enlightenment Experiments in Political Writing.* 1988.

Halevi, Ran. *Les loges maçonniques dans la France d'Ancien Régime aux origines de la sociabilité démocratique.* 1984.

Harari, Josue V. *Scenarios of the Imaginary: Theorizing the French Enlightenment.* 1987.

Herr, Richard. *The Eighteenth Century Revolution in Spain.* 1958.

Hertzberg, Arthur. *The French Enlightenment and the Jews.* 1968.

Jacob, Margaret C. *The Radical Enlightenment: Pantheists, Freemasons, and Republicans.* 1981.

Kors, Alan C. *D'Holbach's Coterie: Enlightenment in Paris.* 1976.

Korshin, Paul J., ed. *The Widening Circle: Essays on the Circulation of Literature in 18th Century Europe.* 1976.

Lough, John. *The Encyclopédie of Diderot and d'Alembert.* 1968.

Mandrou, Robert. *Culture populaire aux 17e et 18e siècles.* 1964.

May, Henry. *The Enlightenment in America.* 1976.

McDonald, Joan. *Rousseau and the French Revolution.* 1965.

Meek, R. L. *The Economics of Physiocracy.* 1963.

Miller, James. *Rousseau: Dreamer of Democracy.* 1984.

Mornet, Daniel. *Origines intellectuelles de la Révolution française.* 1933. 4th ed., 1947. Translated as *The Intellectual Origins of the French Revolution,* 1954.

Nixon, Edna. *Voltaire and the Calas Case.* 1961.

Pangle, Thomas L. *Montesquieu's Philosophy of Liberalism.* 1973.

Payne, Harry C. *The Philosophes and the People.* 1976.

Perkins, Jean. *Concept of Self in the French Enlightenment.* 1969.

Picon, Antoine. *Architectes et ingenieurs au siècles des lumières.* 1988.

Placanica, Augusto. *Il filosofo e la catastrofe: un terrmoto del Settecento.* 1985.

Proust, Jacques. *Encyclopédisme dans le Bas-Languedoc au XVIIIe siècle.* 1968.

Razzell, P. E., *The Conquest of Smallpox.* 1977.

Richter, Melvin. *The Political Theory of Montesquieu.* 1977.

Rousseau, G. S., and Roy Porter, eds. *Sexual Underworlds of the Enlightenment.* 1988.

Shackleton, Robert. *Montesquieu.* 1961.

Sozzi, Lionello. *Jean-Jacques Rousseau.* 1985.

Starobinski, Jean. *Jean-Jacques Rousseau: Transparency and Obstruction.* Translated by Arthur Goldhammer. 1988.

Staum, Martin S. *Cabanis: Enlightenment and Medical Philosophy in the French Revolution.* 1980.

Tortarolo, Edoardo. *Illuminismo e Rivoluzioni: Biografia politica di Filippo Mazzei.* 1986.

Vaggi, Gianni. *The Economics of François Quesnay.* 1987.

Van Kley, Dale K. *The Jansenists and the Expulsion of the Jesuits from France, 1757–1765.* 1975.

Venturi, Franco. *Settecento riformatore.* 1969. Translated as *The First Crisis* by R. Burr Litchfield, 1989.

Wade, Ira O. *The Intellectual Development of Voltaire.* 1969.

———. *Intellectual Origins of the French Enlightenment.* 1971.

Zmijewska, Helena. *La critique des salons en France du temps de Diderot (1759–1789).* 1980.

INTERNATIONAL/ENLIGHTENED MONARCHS

Asprey, R. B. *Frederick the Great: The Magnificent Enigma.* 1986.

Bellatalla, Luciana. *Pietro Leopoldo di Toscana granducaeducatore: teoria e pratica di un despota illuminato.* 1984.

Bernard, Paul. *Joseph II and Bavaria.* 1965.

———. *Jesuits and Jacobins: Enlightenment and Enlightened Despotism in Austria.* 1971.

Blanning, T.C.W. *Joseph II and Enlightened Despotism.* 1970.

Bruun, Geoffrey. *The Enlightened Despots.* 1929.

Caizzi, Bruno. *Industria, commercio e banca in Lombardia nel XVIII secolo.* 1968.

Carter, Alice C. *Dutch Republic in the Seven Years War.* 1971.

Castries, René de la Croix, Duc de. *La France at l'independance Americaine.* 1975.

Cone, Carl. *The English Jacobins.* 1968.

Davis, David Brion. *The Problem of Slavery in the Age of Revolution.* 1974.

Dollinger, Hans. *Friedrich II, von Preussen: sein Bild im Wandel von zwei Jahrhunderten.* 1986.

Duffy, Christopher. *Military Life of Frederick the Great.* 1986.

Fontana, José, ed. *Carlos III, Madrid, y la Ilustracion: contradicciones de un proyecto reformista.* 1988.

Frostin, Charles. *Les révoltes blanches à Saint-Domingue aux XVIe et XVIIe siècles: Haiti avant 1789.* 1975.

Gagliardo, John G. *Enlightened Despotism.* 1967.

Gooch, G. P. *Frederick the Great.* 1947.

Grey, Ian. *Catherine the Great.* 1962.

Hamilton, Earl J. *War and Prices in Spain, 1651–1890.* 1947.

Henderson, W. O. *Economic Policy of Frederick the Great.* 1963.

Hubatsch, Walther. *Frederick the Great of Prussia: Absolutism and Administration.* Translated by Patrick Doran. 1975.

———. *Friedrich der Grosse und die preussische Verwaltung.* 1982.

Knopp, Werner. *Erinnerung an einen Konig.* Translated as *In remembrance of a king: Frederick II of Prussia, 1712–1786.* 1986.

Langford, Paul. *The Eighteenth Century, 1688–1815.* In *Modern British Foreign Policy* Series. London, 1976.

Leeb, I. Leonard. *Ideological Origins of the Batavian Republic: History and Politics in the Dutch Republic, 1741–1800.* 1973.

Magnan, André. *Dossier Voltaire en Prusse: 1750–1753.* 1986.

Melton, James Van Horn. *Absolutism and the Eighteenth-Century Origins of Compulsory Schooling in Prussia and Austria.* 1988.

Mervaud, Christiane. *Voltaire et Frederic II: une dramaturgie des lumières, 1736–1778.* 1985.

Padover, S.K. *Revolutionary Emperor: Joseph II.* 1967.

Reinalter, Helmut. *Aufgeklarter Absolutismus und Revolution: zur Geschichte des Jakobinertums und der frühdemokratischen Bestrebungen in der Habsburgermonarchie.* 1980.

Ritter, Gerhard. *Friedrich Der Grosse.* 3d ed. 1954.

Schama, Simon. *Patriots and Liberators: Revolution in the Netherlands, 1780–1813.* 1977.

Schieder, Theodor. *Friedrich der Grosse: ein Konigtum der Widerspruche.* 1983.

Soliday, Gerald L. *A Community in Conflict: Frankfurt Society in the 17th and Early 18th Century.* 1974.

Stroup, John. *The Struggle for Identity in the Clerical Estate: Northwest German Protestant Opposition to Absolutist Policy in the Eighteenth Century.* 1984.

Treue, Wilhelm, ed. *Preussens grosser Konig: Leben und Werk Friedrichs des Grossen.* 1986.

Ullmann, Hans-Peter. *Staatsschulden und Reformpolitik: die Entstehung moderner offentlicher Schulden in Bayern und Baden 1780–1820.* 1986.

Venohr, Wolfgang. *Fridericus Rex: Friedrich der Grosse, Portrat einer Doppelnatur.* 1985.

de Wit, C.H.E. *De Nederlandse revolutie van de achttiende eeuw, 1780–1787. Oligarchie en proletariat.* 1974.

Zavala, Iris M. *Masones, Comuneros y Carbonarios.* 1971.

PREREVOLUTION/ONSET OF REVOLUTION

Berlanstein, Leonard R. *The Barristers of Toulouse in the 18th Century, 1740–1793.* 1975.

Bosher, J. F. *French Finances, 1770–1795: From Business to Bureaucracy.* 1970.

Doyle, William. *The Parlement of Bordeaux and the End of the Old Regime, 1771–1790.* 1974.

———. *Origins of the French Revolution.* 2d ed. 1988.

Egret, Jean. *Louis XV et l'opposition parlementaire, 1715–1774.* 1970.

———. *Necker: Ministre de Louis XVI, 1770–1790.* 1975.

———. *La Prerévolution française.* 1962. Translated as *The French Prerevolution, 1787–1788,* 1977.

Emmanuelli, Francois-Xavier. *Pouvoir royal et vie regionale en Provence au déclin de la monarchie . . . 1795–1790.* 1974.

Faure, Edgar. *La disgrâce de Turgot.* 1961.

Gooch, G. P. *Louis XV: The Monarchy in Decline.* 1956.

Grange, Henri. *Les idées de Necker.* 1974.

Harris, R. O. *Necker: Reform Statesman of the Old Regime.* 1979.

Hyslop, Beatrice F. *Guide to the General Cahiers.* 1936.

———. *French Nationalism in 1789 according to the General Cahiers.* 1934. Reprint, 1968.

Labousse, Ernest. *La crise de l'economie française à la fin de l'Ancien Régime et au début de la Révolution.* 1944.

Lefebvre, Georges. *The Coming of the French Revolution.* Translated by R. R. Palmer, 1947, from *Quatre-Vingt-Neuf,* 1939. Reprint, 1970.

Vovelle, Michel. *La Chute de la monarchie, 1787–1792.* 1972. English translation, 1984.

REVOLUTION (1789–1792)

Acomb, Frances. *Mallet du Pan (1749–1890): A Career in Political Journalism.* 1973.

Barton, H. A. *Count Axel von Fersen.* 1975.

Bastid, Pierre. *Sieyès.* 1939.

Bernardin, Edith. *Strasbourg et l'institution de l'état civil laic au début de la Révolution française.* 1986.

Bernier, Olivier. *Secrets of Marie Antoinette.* 1985.

Brinton, Crane. *The Lives of Talleyrand.* 1936.

Brucker, Gene A. *Jean-Sylvain Bailly, Revolutionary Mayor of Paris.* 1984.

Castelot, André. *Marie Antoinette.* 1961.

Censer, Jack R. *Prelude to Power: The Parisian Radical Press, 1789–1791.* 1976.

Chevallier, J. J. *Mirabeau.* 1947.

Cubells, Monique. *Les horizons de la liberté: naissance de la révolution en Provence (1787–1789).* Aix-en-Provence, 1987.

Dawson, Philip. *Provincial Magistrates and Revolutionary Politics in France, 1789–1795.* 1972.

Destremau, Noëlle. *Soeur de Louis XVI, Madame Elisabeth.* 1983.

Doyle, William. *Origins of the French Revolution.* 1980.

Dumont, Franz. *Die Mainzer Republik von 1792/93: Studien zur Revolutionierung in Rheinhessen und der Pfalz.* 1982.

Dupuy, Roger. *La Garde nationale et les débuts de la Révolution en Ille-et-Vilaine, 1789–1793.* 1972.

Garrett, M. B. *The Estates General of 1789.* 1935.

Gerson, Noel B. *Statue in Search of a Pedestal: A Biography of the Marquis de Lafayette.* 1976.

Godechot, Jacques. *La prise de la Bastille.* 1965. Translated as *The Taking of the Bastille* by Jean Stewart, 1970.

Gottschalk, Louis. *Lafayette.* 6 vols. 1935–1973. Vol. 6: Louis Gottschalk with Margaret Maddox, *Lafayette in the French Revolution: From the October Days through the Federation,* 1973.

———. *Marat.* 1927.

Greenbaum, Louis. *Talleyrand: Statesman-Priest.* 1970.

Harris, Robert D. *Necker and the Revolution of 1789.* 1986.

Harris, S. E. *The Assignats.* 1930.

Haslip, Joan. *Marie Antoinette.* 1988.

Higonnet, Patrice L. R. *Sister Republics: The Origins of French and American Republicanism.* 1988.

Hunt, Lynn. *Revolution and Urban Politics in Provincial France: Troyes and Reims, 1786–1790.* 1978.

Johnson, Hubert C. *The Midi in Revolution: A Study of Regional Political Diversity, 1789–1793.* 1986.

Jordan, David P. *The King's Trial: The French Revolution vs. Louis XVI.* 1979.

Kates, Gary. *The Cercle Social, The Girondins, and the French Revolution.* 1985.

Kermina, Françoise. *Hans-Axel de Fersen.* 1985.

Kessel, Patrick. *La nuit du 4 Aout 1789.* 1969.

Lafebvre, Georges. *La Grande Peur de 1789.* 1932. New ed., 1970. Translated as *The Great Fear of 1789* by Joan White, 1972.

————. *Les paysans du Nord pendant la Révolution française.* 1924. New ed., 1972.

Lever, Everlyne. *Louis XVI.* 1985.

Luc, Jean-Noël. *Paysans et droits féodaux en Charente-Inférieure pendant la Révolution française.* 1984.

Murray, William James. *The Right-Wing Press in the French Revolution, 1789–92.* 1986.

Necheles, Ruth F. *L'Abbé Grégoire (1787–1831): The Odyssey of an Egalitarian.* 1971.

Neely, Sylvia. *Lafayette and the Liberal Ideal.* 1990.

Orieux, Jean. *Talleyrand, the Art of Survival.* 1974.

Picq, A. *Législation militaire a l'époque révolutionnaire.* 1931.

Rose, R. B. *The Enragés: Socialists of the Revolution?* 1965.

Roudinesco, Elizabeth. *Théroigne de Méricourt: Une femme mélancolique sous la Révolution.* 1989.

Slavin, Morris. *The Making of an Insurrection: Parisian Sections and the Gironde.* 1986.

Smith, Edwin B. *Jean-Sylvain Bailly.* 1964.

Tackett, Timothy. *Religion, Revolution, and Regional Culture in Eighteenth-Century France: The Ecclesiastical Oath of 1791.* 1986.

Vovelle, Michel. *The Fall of the French Monarchy, 1787–1792.* Translated by Susan Burke, 1984.

CONVENTION AND TERROR

Bernardine Melchior-Bonnet. *Charlotte Corday.* 1972

Bianchi, Serge. *La révolution culturelle de l'an II: elites et peuple (1789–1799).* 1982.

Blanc, Olivier. *Olympe de Gouges.* 1981.

Bonnet, Jean-Claude. *La mort de Marat.* 1986.

Bouloiseau, Marc. *The Jacobin Republic, 1792–1794.* Translated by Jonathan Mandelbaum, 1984.

Bouloiseau, Marc. *Le Comité de salut public, 1793–1795.* 1968.

————. *République Jacobine.* 1972.

Bregeon, Jean-Joel. *Carrier el la Terreur nantaise.* 1987.

Balossier, Jacques. *La Commission extraordinaire de douze (18 mai 1793–31 mai 1793): l'ultime sursaut de la Gironde contre la prise du pouvoir par les Montagnards.* 1986.

Brinton, Crane. *The Jacobins.* 1930.

Broilliard, Jean-Louis. *Aubusson sous la Terreur: 1793–1794.* 1981.

Blanc, Olivier. *Last Letters: Prisons and Prisoners of the French Revolution, 1793–1794.* Translated by Alan Sheridan. 1987.

Castelnau, Jacques de. *Histoire de la Terreur.* 1970.

Cobb, Richard. *Terreur et subsistances, 1793–1795.* 1965.

————. *Paris and its Provinces, 1792–1892.* 1975.

————. *Armées révolutionnaires.* 1960–1961. Translated as The People's Armies: The Armées Révolutionnaires, Instrument of the Terror in the Departments . . . by Marianne Elliot, 1987.

Conté, Arthur. *Sire, Ils ont voté la mort: La Condamnation de Louis XVI.* 1966.

Dauxois, Jacqueline. *Charlotte Corday.* 1988.

Duras, Louise-H.-C.-P. de Noailles de Durfort, duchesse de. *Journal des prisons de mon père de ma mère et des miennes.* 2d ed. 1889. Reprint, 1989.

Gallo, Max. *Robespierre the Incorruptible: A Psychobiography.* 1971. Translated from *Histoire d'une solitude.* 1971.

Gershoy, Leo. *Bertrand Barère: A Reluctant Terrorist.* 1962.

Godfrey, James L. *Revolutionary Justice.* 1951.

Gouges, Marie-Olympe de. *Politische Schriften in Auswahl.* Hrsg. Margarete Wolters and Clara Sutor. 1979.

Greer, Donald M. *The Incidence of Terror During the French Revolution.* 1935.

Guilaine, J. *Billaud-Varenne: L'Ascète de la Révolution.* 1969.

Guilhaumou, Jacques. *La mort de Marat.* 1989.

Hampson, N. *Life and Opinions of Maximilien Robespierre.* 1974.

Jordan, David P. *The Revolutionary Career of Maximilien Robespierre.* 1988.

Kennedy, Michael. *Jacobin Club of Marseilles, 1790–1794.* 1973.

Kerr, Wilfred B. *The Reign of Terror.* 1927.

Krivanec, Ernest. *Jean-Paul Marat: Fremd unter Fremden.* 1986.

Lenotre, G. *Le tribunal Révolutionnaire, 1793–1795.* 1959.

Levy, Barbara. *Legacy of Death: A History of the Sanson Family, Official Executioners of the Kings of France.* 1976.

Lucas, Colin. *The Structure of the Terror: The Example of Javogues and the Loire.* 1973.

Markov, Walter. *Exkurse zu Jacques Roux.* 1970.

Martin, Gaston. *Les Jacobins.* 1963.

Mathiez, Albert. *Vie chère et le mouvement social sous la terreur.* 1927.

———. *Etudes sur Robespierre.* 1973.

Matrat, Jean. *Robespierre, or the Tyranny of the Majority.* 1975.

Mazauric, Claude. *Babeuf.* 1988.

Olivier, Albert. *Saint-Just et la force des choses.* 1954.

Palmer, R. R. *Twelve Who Ruled: The Year of the Terror in the French Revolution.* 1941. Reprint, 1970.

Patrick, Alison. *Men of the First French Revolution: Political Alignments in the National Convention of 1792.* 1972.

Rudé, George. *Robespierre Revolutionary Democrat.* 1975.

Scott, Otto J. *Robespierre: The Voice of Virtue.* 1974.

Scott, William. *Terror and Repression in Revolutionary Marseilles.* 1973.

Soboul, Albert. *Les sans-culottes parisiens de l'an II: Mouvement populaire et gouvernement revolutionnaire, 2 juin 1793–9 Thermidor an II.* 1958.

———. *Les soldats de l'an II.* 1959.

———. *Paysans, Sans-Colottes, et Jacobins.* 1966.

———. *La Première République: 1792–1804.* Paris, 1968.

——. *Mouvement populaire et gouvernement revolutionnaire.* 1968. Translated as *The Sans-Culottes* by Remy Inglis Hall, 1972.

Sydenham, M. J. *The Girondins.* 1961.

——. *The First French Republic, 1792–1804.* 1974.

Traeger, Jorg. *Der Tod des Marat.* 1986.

Vignery, Robert J. *The French Revolution and the Schools: Educational Policies of the Mountain, 1792–94, 1965.*

Vovelle, Michel. *Religion et Révolution: La déchristianisation de l'an II.* 1976.

Walzer, Michael, ed. and trans. *Regicide and Revolution: Speeches at the Trial of Louis XVI.* 1974.

EMIGRATION AND COUNTERREVOLUTION

Baldensperger, Fernand. *Mouvement des idées dans l'emigration française, 1789–1815.* 2 vols. 1924.

Beik, Paul H. *The French Revolution Seen from the Right.* 1956. Reprint, 1970.

Billaud, A.-M. Vaillant. *La guerre de Vendée.* 1972.

Bordonove, Georges. *La vie quotidienne en la Vendée pendant la Révolution.* 1974.

Boutier, Jean. *Campagnes en emoi: révoltes et révolution en Bas-Limousin, 1789–1800.* 1987.

Chardon, Henri. *Les Vendéens dans la Sarthe.* 3 vols. 1976.

Cobbard, Alfred. *The British Secret Service.* 1954.

Diesbach, Ghislain de. *Histoire de l'immigration, 1789–1814.* 1984.

Du Rostu, Loic. *Histoire extérieure et maritime des guerres de Vendée.* 1987.

Gallet, Jean. *Les paysans en guerre.* 1988.

Godechot, Jacques. *Counter-Revolution: Doctrine and Action.* 1971. Translated from *La Contre-revolution.* 1961.

——. *Le comte d'Atraigues: Un espion dans l'Europe des émigrés.* 1985.

Greer, Donald M. *The Incidence of Emigration during the French Revolution.* 1951.

Mackesy, Piers. *The Strategy of Overthrow, 1798–1799.* 1974.

Mitchell, Harvey. *The Underground War Against Revolutionary France: The Missions of William Wickham, 1794–1899.* 1965.

Montagnon, André. *Guerres de Vendée, 1793–1832.* 1974.

Paret, Peter. *Internal War and Pacification: The Vendée 1789–1796.* 1961.

Picheloup, René. *Les ecclesiastiques français emigrés ou deportés dans l'Etat pontifical, 1792–1800.* 1972.

Portes, René Bittard des. *Histoire de l'armée de Condé pendant la Révolution française, 1791–1798.* 1891. Reprint, 1975.

Racineux, Alain. *Les brigands du roi: episodes de la chouannerie en Haute-Bretagne.* 1985.

Tilly, Charles. *The Vendée.* 1964 and 1976.

Weiner, Margery. *The French Exiles, 1789–1815.* 1950.

THERMIDOR AND DIRECTORY (1794–1799)

Beale, Georgia R. *Révellière-Lépeaux: Citizen Director.* 1938.

Buonarroti, Philippe M. *History of Babeuf's Conspiracy for Equality.* 1966. Translation of *Conspiration pour l'égalité.* 1828.

Cole, Hubert. *Fouché, the Unprincipled Patriot.* 1971.

Eisenstein, Elizabeth L. *The First Professional Revolutionist: Filipo Michel Buonarroti.* 1959.

Garnier, Jean-Paul. *Barras, le roi du Directoire.* 1970.

Godechot, Jacques. *La vie quotidienne en France sous le Directoire.* 1977.

Homan, Gerlof D. *Jean-Francois Reubell: French Revolutionary Patriot.* 1971.

Howard, Martha W. *That Roland Woman.* 1984.

Lafebvre, Georges. *The Directory.* 1966. Translation of *Le Directoire,* 3d ed., 1958.

Lyons, Martyn. *France under the Directory.* 1975.

Madelin, Louis. *Fouché.* 1955.

Mathiez, Albert. *The Thermidorian Reaction.* 1931.

———. *Le Directoire.* 1934.

———. *Le Théophilanthropie et le culte décadaire.* 1928. Reprint, 1975.

Mazauric, C. *Babeuf et la conspiration pour l'égalité.* 1962.

Popkin, Jeremy. The Right-Wing Press in France, *1792–1800.* 1980.

Reinhard, Marcel. *La France du Directoire.* 2 vols. 1956.

Rose, R. B. *Babeuf: The First Revolutionary Communist?* 1977.

Soboul, Albert. *Le Directoire et le Consulat.* 1967.

Thompson, David. *The Babeuf Plot: The Making of a Republican Legend.* 1975.

Tonnesson, Kare D. *La défaite des sans-culottes: Mouvement populaire et réaction bourgeoise en l'an III.* 1959.

Vess, David M. *Medical Revolution in France, 1789–1796.* 1975.

Woloch, Isser. *Jacobin Legacy: The Democratic Movement under the Directory.* 1970.

Woronoff, Denis. *La République bourgeoise.* 1972.

———. *The Thermidorian Regime and the Directory, 1794–1799.* Translated by Julian Jackson. 1984.

FRENCH REVOLUTION: INTERNATIONAL IMPACT

Artola, Miguel. *Los origines de la España contemporanea.* 2 vols. 1958.

Bemis, Samuel Flagg. *Diplomatic History of the United States.* Rev. ed. 1950.

Biro, Sidney. *The German Policy of Revolutionary France.* 1957.

Blanning, T.C.W. *Reform and Revolution in Mainz, 1743–1893.* 1974.

Cone, Carl. *The English Jacobins.* 1968.

DeConde, Alexander. *The Quasi-War: The Politics and Diplomacy of the Undeclared War with France, 1791–1811.* 1966.

Devleeshouwer, Robert. *Arrondissement du Brabant sous l'occupation francaise, 1794–1795.* 1965.

Dozier, Robert R. *For King, Constitution, and Country: The English Loyalists and the French Revolution.* 1983.

Droz, Jacques. *L'Allemagne et la Révolution française.* 1949.

Ergang, Robert R. *Herder and the Foundations of German Nationalism.* 1931.

Gerth, Hans H. *Burgerliche Intelligenz um 1890: Zur Soziologie des deutschen Frühliberalismus.* 1935, Reprint, 1977.

Gooch, G. P. *Germany and the French Revolution.* 1920.

Hayes, Richard. *Ireland and Irishmen in the French Revolution.* 1932.

Hokkanen, Kari. *Krieg und Frieden in der politischen Tagesliteratur Deutschlands zwischen Baseler und Luneviller Frieden, 1795–1891.* 1975.

Kaplan, L. S. *Jefferson and France.* 1967.

Kocoj, Henryk. *Wielka Rewolucja a Polska.* 1987.

Kohn, Hans. *Prelude to the Nation States: The French and German Experience, 1789–1815.* 1967.

Krieger, Leonard. *The German Idea of Freedom: History of a Political Tradition.* 1957.

Kuhn, Axel. *Jacobiner im Rheinland: Der Kölner Konstitutionelle Zirkel von 1798.* 1976.

Leeb, L. *Ideological Origins of the Batavian Revolution.* 1973.

Lyon, E. Wilson. *Louisiana in French Diplomacy, 1759–1894.* 1934.

Meikle, A. W. *Scotland and the French Revolution.* 1912.

Noether, Emiliana. *Seeds of Italian Nationalism, 1700–1815.* 1951.

O'Gorman, F. *The Whig Party and the French Revolution.* 1967.

Perotin-Dumon, Anne. *Etre jacobin sous les tropiques* [Guadeloupe]. 1985.

Polasky, Janet. *Revolution in Brussels, 1787–1793.* 1987.

Ritter, Joachim. *Hegel und de franzosische Revolution.* 1957.

Roider, Karl A., Jr. *Baron Thugut and Austria's Response to the French Revolution.* 1987.

Romano, Ruggiero. *Prezzi, Salari e Servizi a Napoli nel secolo XVIII, 1734–1806.* 1965.

Ross, Steven T. *European Diplomatic History, 1789–1815: France against Europe.* 1969.

Rufer, Alfred. *Suisse et la Révolution.* 1973.

Schama, Simon. *Patriots and Liberators: Revolution in the Netherlands, 1780–1813.* 1977.

Sherwig, John M. *Guineas and Gunpowder: British Foreign Policy in the Wars with France, 1793–1815.* 1969.

Sorel, Albert. *L'Europe et la Révolution française.* 8 vols. 1885–1904.

Strange, M. N. *Société russe et la Révolution française.* 1961.

Streisand, Joachim. *Deutschland, 1789–1815.* 1959.

Tervooren, Klaus. *Die Mainzer Republik 1792/93: Bedingungen, Leistungen und Grenzen eines burgerlichrevolutionaren Experiments in Deutschland.* Frankfurt am Main, 1982.

Wangermann, Ernst. *From Joseph II to the Jacobin Trials: Government Policy and Public Opinion in the Habsbourg Dominion in the Period of the French Revolution.* 1959.

Ward, A. W., and G. P. Gooch. *Cambridge History of British Foreign Policy.* Vol. 1: 1783–1815. 1922.

Watson, J. Steven. *The Reign of George III.* Vol. 12 of the *Oxford History of England.* 1960.

Weis, Eberhard. *Montgelas: 1759–1799: Zwischen Revolution und Reform.* 1971.

Zaghi, Carlo. *Potere, chiesa e societa: studi e ricerche sull'Italia giacobina e napoleonica.* 1984.

NAPOLEON: BIOGRAPHIES AND LIFE AND TIMES

Bainville, Jacques. *Napoléon.* 1962.

Cambridge Modern History. Vol. 9: *Napoleon.* 1906.

Collaveri, François. *Napoleon, empereur franc-maçon.* 1986.

Cronin, Vincent. *Napoleon.* 1971.

Driault, Edouard. *La vraie figure de Napoléon.* 3 vols. 1928–1930.

Frayling, Christopher. *Napoleon Wrote Fiction.* 1972.

Herold, J. Christopher. *Horizon Book of Napoleon.* 1963.

Herold, J. C. *The Mind of Napoleon.* 1955.

Kircheisen, F. M. *Napoleon I: Sein Leben und seine Zeit.* 9 vols. 1911–1934.

Latreille, André. *L'Ere Napoléonienne.* 1974.

Lefebvre, Georges. *Napoléon.* 5th ed. 1965. English translation in 2 vols. by Henry Stockhold, 1969.

Lysiak, Waldemar. *Empirowy pasjans.* Wyd. 2. 1984.

Madelin, Louis. *Consulate and the Empire.* 2 vols. Translated by E. F. Buckley. 1934–36.

Manfred, Albert Zakharovich. *Napoleon Bonaparte.* 1972. [Available in Russian and French.]

Markham, Felix. *Napoleon.* 1963.

Markov, Walter M. *Die Napoleon-Zeit: Geschichte und Kultur des Grand Empire.* 1985.

Ravignant, Patrick. *Napoléon* 1985.

Sieberg, Heinz Otto, ed. *Napoleon und Europa.* 1971.

Soboul, Albert. *Le premier Empire.* 1973.

Tarle, E. V. *Bonaparte.* Translated from the Russian. 1937.

Thompson, J. M. *Napoleon Self-Revealed: . . . Selected Letters.* 1934.

——. *Napoleon Bonaparte; His Rise and Fall.* 1952.

Tulard, Jean. *Napoléon: Ou le mythe du Sauveur.* 1977. Translated as *Napoleon: The Myth of the Savior* by Theresa Waugh, 1984.

——, ed. *Oeuvres litteraires et écrits militaires de Napoléon.* 3 vols. 1968.

NAPOLEON AND FRANCE

Albert, Phyllis C. *The Modernization of French Jewry: The Consistory and Community in the Nineteenth Century.* 1978.

Anchel, R. *Napoléon et les Juifs.* 1928.

Arnold, Eric A. *Fouché, Napoleon and the General Police.* 1979.

Baelen, Jean. *Benjamin Constant et Napoléon.* 1965.

Bellenfant, Michel. *Le departement du Var sous le Consulat et l'Empire: aspects economiques et sociaux*. 1981.

Bergeron, Louis. *Négociants et manufacturiers parisiens: Du Directoire a l'Empire*. 1975.

———. *L'Episode Napoleonien: Aspects intérieurs*. 1972. Translated as *France under Napoléon* by R. R. Palmer, 1981.

Bertaud, Jean Paul. *La France de Napoleon, 1799–1815*. 1987.

Burton, June K. *Napoleon and Clio: Historical Writing, Teaching, and Thinking during the First Empire*. 1979.

Cabanis, André. *La presse sous le Consulat et l'Empire*. 1975.

Chatelain, J. *Dominique V. Denon et le Louvre de Napoléon*. 1973.

Durand, Charles. *Auditeurs au conseil d'état de 1803 à 1814*. Reprint, 1973.

Erlanning, E. *La resistance bretonne à Napoléon. 1799–1815*. 1986.

Festy, O. *L'Agriculture française sous le Consulat*. 1952.

Fohlen, Claude. *Naissance d'une civilisation industrielle*. 1961.

Geiger, Reed G. *The Anzin Coal Company, 1800–1883: Big Business in the Early Stages of the French Industrial Revolution*. 1974.

Guerrini, M. *Napoléon et Paris*. 1975.

Guillemin, H. *Mme. de Staël, Benjamin Constant, et Napoléon*. 1959.

Herold, J.C. *Mistress to an Age: . . . Madame de Staël*. 1955.

Holtman, Robert B. *Napoleonic Propaganda*. 1950

———. *The Napoleonic Revolution*. 1967.

Horricks, Raymond. *In Flight with the Eagle: A Guide to Napoleon's Elite*. 1988.

Katz, Jacob. *Out of the Ghetto: The Social Background of Jewish Emancipation, 1770–1870*. 1973.

Kobler, Franz. *Napoleon and the Jews*. 1976.

Latreille, André. *L'Eglise catholique et la Révolution française*. Vol. 2: *L'ère Napoléonienne*. 1950.

Lentz, Thierry, and Denis Imhoff. *La Moselle et Napoleon: Etude d'un departement sous le Consulat et l'Empire*. 1988.

Lombard, Paul. *Par le sang d'un prince: le duc d'Enghien*. 1986.

Poisson, G. *Napoléon et Paris*. 1964.

Poniatowski, Michel. *Talleyrand et le Consulat*. 1986.

Reddy, William M. *The Rise of Market Culture: The Textile Trade and French Society, 1750–1900*. 1984.

Robert, Daniel. *Les églises reformées de France, 1800–1830*. 1961.

Schwarzfuchs, S. *Napoleon, the Jews, and the Sanhedrin*. 1979.

Soboul, Albert. *Problèmes paysans . . . 1789–1848*. 1976.

Tulard, Jean. *Consulat et l'Empire*. 1970.

Villefosse, L. de, ed. *L'Opposition de Napoléon*. 1969.

Vinnet, Odette. *Napoléon et l'industrie française: la crise de 1810–1811*. 1947.

Vion, A. *Vie Calaisienne sous le Consulat et l'Empire*. 1972.

Walter, Gérard. *Histoire des paysans de France*. 1963.

Woronoff, Denis. *L'industrie siderurgique en France pendant la Révolution et l'Empire*. 1984.

DIPLOMACY (NAPOLEONIC PERIOD)

Bertier de Sauvigny, G. de. *Metternich*. 1959. New ed., 1986.

Bourgeois, Emile. *Manuel historique de politique étrangère*. 6th ed. Vol. II: *Les Révolutions, 1789–1830*. 1920.

Butterfield, H. *The Peace Tactics of Napoleon, 1800–1808*. 1929.

Deutsch, H.C. *Genesis of Napoleonic Imperialism*. 1938.

Fisher, H.A.L. *Napoleonic Statesmanship: Germany*. 1903.

Fugier, André. *La révolution française et l'empire napoléonienne*. Vol. IV: *Histoire des relations internationales*. Edited by Pierre Renouvin. 1954.

Grimstead, Patricia. *The Foreign Ministers of Alexander I*. 1969.

Hales, E.E.Y. *Napoleon and the Pope*. 1961.

Horne, Alistair. *Napoleon, Master of Europe, 1805–1807*. 1979.

Kissinger, Henry. *A World Restored: Metternich, Castlereagh and the Problems of the Peace, 1812–1822*. 1957.

Kraehe, Enno E. *Metternich's Germany Policy*. Vol. 1: *Contest with Napoleon, 1799–1814*, 1963. Vol. 2: *The Congress of Vienna*, 1983.

Lefebvre, Armand. *Histoire des cabinets de l'Europe pendant le consulat et l'empire*. 3 vols. 1845–1847.

Manique, Antonio Pedro. *Portugal e as potencias europeias, 1807–1847: relaçoes externas e ingerencias estrangeiras em Portugal na primeira metade do seculo XIX*. 1988.

Mowat, R. B. *The Diplomacy of Napoleon*. 1926.

Nicolson, Harold G. *The Congress of Vienna: A Study in Allied Unity, 1812–1822*. 1946 and 1960.

Palmer, Alan Warwick. *The chancelleries of Europe*. 1983.

Ragsdale, Hugh. *Detente in the Napoleonic Era: Bonaparte and the Russians*. 1980.

Ross, Stephen T. *European Diplomatic History, 1789–1815: France Against Europe*. 1969 and 1981.

Rössler, Hellmuth. *Oesterreichs Kampf um Deutschlands Befreiung: Die deutsche Politik der nationalen Führer Oesterreichs, 1805–1815*. 2 vols. 1945.

Saul, Norman E. *Russia and the Mediterranean, 1798–1897*. 1970.

Sorel, Albert. *L'Europe et la révolution française*. 8 vols. 1885–1904.

Srbik, Heinrich. *Metternich: Der Staatsmann und der Mensch*. 3 vols. 1925.

Vandal, Albert. *Napoléon et Alexandre Ier*. 3 vols. 1891–1896.

Ward, A. W., and G. P. Gooch. *Cambridge History of British Foreign Policy*. Vol. 1: *1783–1815*. 1922.

Webster, C. K. *The Congress of Vienna*. 2d ed. 1934.

Whitcomb, Edward A. *Napoleon's Diplomatic Service*. 1979.

NAPOLEON AND EUROPE; NAPOLEON AND THE WORLD

**GENERAL

Andreas, Willy. *Das Zeitalters Napoleons und die Erhebung der Völker.* 1955.

Aziz, Philippe. *L'Europe sous la botte française.* 1983.

Collaveri, François. *La franc-maçonnerie des Bonaparte.* 1982.

Connelly, Owen. *Napoleon's Satellite Kingdoms.* 1965, 1969, 1990.

Driault, Edouard. *Napoléon et l'Europe.* 5 vols. 1910–1927.

Göhring, Martin. *Napoléon: Vom alten zum neuen Europa.* 1959.

Lovie, Jacques, and André Palluel. *L'Episode Napoléonien: Aspects extérieurs.* 1972.

Markham, Felix. *Napoleon and the Awakening of Europe.* 1954.

O'Dwyer, Margaret M. *The Papacy in the Age of Napoleon and the Restoration: Pius VII, 1800–1823.* 1985.

Mistler, Jean, ed. *Napoléon et l'empire.* 2 vols. 1969.

New Cambridge Modern History. Vol. 9: *War and Peace in an Age of Upheaval, 1793–1840.* 1965.

Tulard, Jean. *Le Grand Empire, 1804–1815.* 1982.

Zaghi, Carlo. *Napoleone e L'Europa.* 1969.

**GREAT BRITAIN

Dickinson, H.T., ed. *Britain and the French Revolution, 1789–1815.* 1989.

Elliott, Marianne. *Partners in Revolution: The United Irishmen and France.* 1982.

Hueckel, Glenn R. *The Napoleonic Wars and Their Impact on Factor Returns and Output in England, 1793–1815.* 1985.

Mackesy, Piers. *War without Victory: The Downfall of Pitt, 1799–1802.* 1984.

Watson, J. Stephen. *The Reign of George III.* Vol. 12: *Oxford History of England.* 1973.

Severn, John. *The Wellesley Affair: Richard Marquess Wellesley and the Conduct of Anglo-Spanish Diplomacy.* 1981.

**SPAIN AND PORTUGAL

Artola, Miguel, *Los Afrancesados.* 1953.

———. *Los origines de la España contemporanea.* 2 vols. 1959.

———. *La Hacienda del siglo XIX: Progresistas y Moderatos.* 1986.

Aymes, Jean-René. *La deportation sous le Premier Empire: Les Espagnols en France (1808–1814).* 1983.

Chastenet, J. *Godoy, Master of Spain, 1792–1808.* 1953.

Fernandez de Castro, Ignacio. *Las Cortes de Cadiz al plan de desarrollo.* 1968.

Fugier, André. *Napoléon et l'Espagne, 1799–1808.* 2 vols. 1930.

Grandmaison, Geoffroy de. *L'Espagne et Napoleon, 1804–1814.* 3 vols. 3d ed. 1908–1933.

Lovett, Gabriel H. *Napoleon and the Birth of Modern Spain.* 2 vols. 1965.

Marti Gilabert, Francisco. *Motin de Aranjuez*. 1972.

Martinez de Velasco, Angel. *Formaçion de la Junta Central*. 1972.

Mercader Riba, Juan. *La organizaçion administrativa françesa en España*. 1959.

―――. *José Bonaparte Rey de España (1808–1813): Estructura del estado español bonapartista*. 1983.

Solis, Ramon. *El Cadiz de las Cortes*. 1958 and 1969.

**NORTHERN AND CENTRAL EUROPE

Anderson, E. N. *Nationalism and Cultural Crisis in Prussia*. 1939.

Berding, Helmut. *Napoleonische Herrschafts und Gesellschaftspolitik im Königsreichs Westfalen, 1807–1813*. 1973.

―――. *Privat Kapital, Staatfinanzen und Reformpolitik im Deutschlander Napoleonische Zeit*. 1981.

Droz, Jacques. *Le romantisme allemagne et l'état: Resistance et collaboration dans l'Allemagne napoléonienne*. 1966.

Dunan, Marcel. *Napoléon et l'Allemagne: Le système continental et les débuts du royaume de Bavière, 1806–1810*. 1942.

Ellis, Geoffrey. *Napoleon's Continental Blockade: The Case of Alsace*. 1981.

Ford, G. S. *Stein and the Era of Reform in Prussia*. 1922.

Hau, Michel. *L'Industrialisation d'Alsace (1803–1939)*. 1987.

Holtzle, E. *Das alte Recht und die Revolution: Ein politische Geschichte Württembergs in der Revolutionszeit, 1789–1815*. 1931.

―――. *Württemberg im Zeitalter Napoleons*. 1937.

Junkelmann, Marcus. *Napoleon und Bayern: von den Anfangen des Königreiches*. 1985.

Kisch, Herbert. *From Domestic Manufacture to Industrial Revolution: The Case of the Rhineland Textile Districts*. 1989.

Kleinschmidt, A. *Geschichte des Königreichs Westfalen*. 1893.

Kohn, Hans. *Prelude to the Nation States: The French and German Experience*. 1967.

Koppen, Wilhelm. *Deutsche gegen Deutschland: Geschichte des Rheinbundes*. 1936.

Langsam, W. C. *Napoleonic Wars and Nationalism in Austria*. 1930.

Lésage, C. *Napoléon I, Creancier de la Prusse, 1801–1814*. 1924.

Meinecke, Friedrich. *Das Zeitalter der deutschen Erhebung*. 6th ed. 1957. Translated as *The Age of German Liberation* by Peter Paret, 1977.

Paret, Peter. *Yorck and the Era of Prussian Reform, 1808–1815*. 1966.

―――. *Clausewitz and the State*. 1976 and 1985.

Raack, R. C. *The Fall of Stein*. 1965.

Rambaud, Alfred. *L'Allemagne sous Napoleon Ier, 1804–1811*. 1874.

Rossler, Helmuth. *Oesterreichs Kampf um Deutschlands befreiung*. 2 vols. 1945.

Schmidt, C. *Le Grand-Duché de Berg, 1800–1813*. 1904.

Shanahan, William O. *Prussian Military Reforms, 1780–1813*. 1954.

Simon, Walter M. *The Failure of the Prussian Reform Movement, 1801–1819*. 1955.

Streisand, Joachim. *Deutschland, 1789–1815*. 1959.

White, Charles E. *Enlightened Soldier: Scharnhorst and the Militärische Gesellschaft in Berlin, 1801–1805.* 1989.

Woeste, Dietrich. *Der Osemund: Ein Beitrag zur Wirtschaftsgeschichte des Markischen Sauerlandes und zur Geschichte des Eisens.* 1985.

Wohlfiel, R. *Spanien und die deutsche Erhebung, 1808–1814.* 1965.

**THE NETHERLANDS

Caumont La Force, Marquis de. *L'architrésorier Lebrun, gouverneur de la Hollande, 1810–1813.* 1907.

Colenbrander, H. T. *Konig Lodewijk 1806–1810.* 2 parts. 1909–1910. Vol. 5 of *Gedenkstukken der Algemeene Geschiedenis van Nederland 1795–1840.* 10 vols. 1905–1922.

———. *Schimmelpenninck en Konig Lodewijk.* 1911.

Geyl, Pietr. *Geschiedenis van de Nederlandse stam.* vols. 6 and 7. 1948–1958. New Ed., 1965.

Kikkert, J. G. *Koning van Holland, Louis Bonaparte.* 1981.

Shama, Simon. *Patriots and Liberators: Revolution in the Netherlands, 1780–1813.* 1977.

Van Houtte, J. A., ed. *Algemene geschiedenis der Nederlanden.* 12 vols 1949–1956.

**POLAND

Askenazy, Szymon. *Napoléon et la Pologne.* 1925. Translated from the Polish, 1925.

Kallas, Marian. *Konstytucja Ksiestwa Warszawskiego.* 1970.

Kukiel, Marjan. *Czartoryski and European Unity, 1770–1861.* 1965.

Mansuy, Abel. *Jérôme Napoléon en la Pologne en 1812.* 1931.

Tranie, J. *Les Polonaise de Napoléon.* 1982.

Senkowska-Gluck, Monika. *Donacji napoleonskie w Ksiestwie Warszawskim.* 1968.

Sobocinski. W. *Historia Ustroju i prawa Ksiesta Warszawskiego.* 1964.

**ITALY

Bressan, Edoardo. *Poverta e assistenza in Lombardia nell'eta napoleonica.* 1985.

Bucci, Sante. *La Scuola Italiana Nell'Età Napoleonica: Il Sistema Educativo e Scolastico Francese nel Regno d'Italia.* 1976.

Butera, Maria Maddalena. *Campagne italiane nell'eta napoleonica: la prima inchiesta agraria del Italia moderna.* 1981.

Caldora Umberto. *Calabria Napoleonica, 1800–1815.* 1960.

Capra, Carlo. *L'età rivoluzionaria e napoleonica in Italia, 1796–1815.* 1978.

Driault, Edouard. *Napoléon en Italie, 1800–1812.* 1906.

Dupont, M. *Murat, Cavalier, Maréchal . . . prince et roi.* 1980.

Fugier, André. *Napoléon et L'Italie.* 1947.

Guagnini, E. *L'età dell'illuminismo e l'età napoleonica.* 1979.

Johnston, R. M. *The Napoleonic Empire in Southern Italy and the Rise of the Secret Societies.* 2 vols. 1904. Reprint, 1973.

La Volpe, G. *Gioacchino Murat: Administrazione e reforme economiche.* 1931.

Lazzareschi, Eugenio. *Elisa Buonaparte Baciocchi nella vita e nel costume del suo tempo.* A cura del s. o. Italo Pizzi. 1983.

Madelin, Louis. *La Rome de Napoléon.* 1906.

McClellan, G. B. *Venice and Bonaparte.* 1931.

Morachiello, Paolo, and G. Teyssot. *Nascita delle citta di Stato: ingegneri e architetti sotto il Consolato e l'Impero.* 1983.

Naselli, Carmelo Amedeo. *la soppressione napoleonica delle corporazioni religiose: contributo alla storia religiosa del primo Ottocento italiano, 1808–1814.* 1986.

Natali, Giovanni. *L'Italia durante il regime Napoleonico.* 1950.

Rath, R. John. *Fall of the Napoleonic Kingdom of Italy.* 1941.

———. *The Provisional Austrian Regime in Lombardy-Venetia, 1814–1815.* 1969.

Pingaud, Albert. *La domination française dans l'Italie du nord, 1790–1805.* 2 vols. 1914.

Rambaud, Jacques. *Naples sous Joseph Bonaparte, 1800–1808.* 1911.

Rodocanacchi, E. *Elisa Bacciochi en Italie.* 1900.

Rossi, Pietro. *L'Alba dell'Italia moderna: Republica Romana, 1796/1799.* 1978.

Spinosa, Antonio. *Murat: da stalliere a re di Napoli.* 1984.

Tavera, Nedo. *Elisa Bonaparte Baciocchi: principessa de Piombino.* 1982.

Tulard, Jean. *Murat, ou, L'Eveil des nations.* 1983.

Valente, Angela. *Gioacchino Murat e l'Italia meridionale.* 1965.

Villani, Pasquale. *La vendita dei beni dello stato nel Regno di Napoli, 1806–1815.* 1964.

———. *Italia napoleonica.* 1978.

Woolf, Stuart Joseph. *A History of Italy, 1700–1860: The Social Constraints of Political Change.* 1979.

Zaghi, Carlo. *Napoleone e l'Italia.* 1966.

**BALKANS AND MIDDLE EAST

Bjelovucic, Harriet. *The Ragusan Republic: Victim of Napoleon and Its Own Conservatism.* 1970.

Bundy, Frank J. *The Administration of the Illyrian Provinces of the French Empire, 1809–1813.* 1987.

Ciragan, E. O. *La politique ottomañe pendant les guerres de Napoléon.* 1954.

Driault, E. *La politique oriental de Napoleon, 1806–1808.* 1904.

Georges, Spillmann. *Napoléon et l'Islam.* 1969.

Ghorbal, Shafik. *The Beginnings of the Egyptian Question and the Rise of Mehemet Ali.* 1929.

Pisani, P. *La Dalmatie de 1797 à 1815.* 1893.

Pivec-Stele, M. *La vie économique des Provinces Illyriennes, 1890–1913.* 1931.

Puryear, Vernon. *Napoleon and the Dardanelles.* 1951.

Shaw, Stanford J. *Between Old and New: The Ottoman Empire under Sultan Selim III, 1789–1807.* 1971.

**UNITED STATES, LATIN AMERICA, AND THE WORLD

Alperovich, M. S. *Historia de la independencia de Mexico, 1810–1924.* 1964. Translated from the Russian, 1967.

Bonnel, Ulane. *La France, Les Etats-Unis et la guerre de course, 1797–1815*. 1961.

Cole, Herbert. *Christophe, King of Haiti*. 1967.

Collier, Simon. *Ideas and Politics of Chilean Independence, 1808–1833*. 1967.

Dangerfield, G. *Chancellor Robert R. Livingstone*. 1960.

DeConde, Alexander. *Entangling Alliance: Politics and Diplomacy under George Washington*. 1958.

———. *The Quasi-War: The Politics and Diplomacy of the Undeclared War With France, 1792–1801*. 1966.

Fagg, J. E. *Latin America: A General History*. 2d ed. 1969.

Egan, Clifford. *Neither War Nor Peace: Franco-American Relations, 1803–1812*. 1983.

Hamill, Hugh M., Jr. *The Hidalgo Revolt: Prelude to Mexican Independence*. 1966.

Hill, Peter P. *William Vans Murray, Federal Diplomat: The Shaping of the Peace with France*. 1968.

Horsman, Reginald. *The War of 1812*. 1969.

———. *Diplomacy of the New Republic [U.S.], 1776–1815*. 1985.

Humphreys, R. A. *Liberation in South America, 1800–1817*. 1952.

Humphreys, R. A., and J. Lynch, eds. *The Origins of Latin American Revolutions*. 1967.

James, C.L.R. *The Black Jacobins: Toussaint L'Ouverture and the San Domingo Revolution*. 1938.

Korngold, Ralph. *Citizen Toussaint*. 1969.

Lynch, John. *Spanish American Revolutions, 1808–1826*. 1973.

Lyon, E. Wilson. *Louisiana in French Diplomacy, 1759–1804*. 1934.

Malone, Dumas. *Jefferson the President, 1801–1805*. 1970.

Murat, Ines. *Napoléon et le rêve americain*. 1975. Translated as *Napoleon and the American Dream* by Frances Frenaye. 1981.

Pluchon, Pierre. *Histoire des Antilles et de la Guyane*. 1982.

Prado, C. *Formação do Brasil contemporaneo*. Vol 1. 1945.

Robertson, James A. *Louisiana under the Rule of Spain, France and the United States*. 1911.

Robertson, William S. *France and Latin American Independence*. 1939.

———. *Rise of the Spanish American Republics*. 1918 and 1965.

Saintoyant, J. *La colonisation française pendant la période Napoléonienne*. 1931.

Scharon, Faine. *Toussaint Louverture et la révolution de Saint-Domingue*. 1957.

Shulim, Joseph I. *The Old Dominion and Napoleon Bonaparte: A Study in American Opinion*. 1952.

Smelser, Marshall. *The Democratic Republic, 1801–1815*. New American Nation Series. 1968.

Tallant, Robert. *The Louisiana Purchase*. 1952.

Tyson, George F., ed. *Toussaint L'Ouverture*. 1973.

Verna, Paul. *Pétion et Bolivar: Cuarenta anos 1790–1830 de relaçiones haitiano-venezolanas*. 1969.

THE BONAPARTES
(See also under Napoleon and Europe)

Adelbert von Bayern, Prince. *Eugen Beauharnais: Der Stiefsohn Napoleons.* 1940.

Amelunxen, Clemens. *König und Senator: Jerome und Lucien, zwei Bruder Napoleons.* 1980.

Aronson, Theo. *The Golden Bees.* 1964.

Aubrey, Octave. *The King of Rome.* 1930. Translated from French, 1932.

Bernardy, Françoise de. *Eugene de Beauharnais, 1781–1824.* 1973.

Castelot, André. *King of Rome.* Translated from French, 1960.

Castries, René de La Croix, Duc de. *La reine Hortense: fille d'impératrice et mère d'empereur.* 1984.

Chastenet, Geneviève. *Marie-Louise: l'impératrice oubliée.* 1983.

Cole, Herbert. *The Betrayers: Joachim and Caroline Murat.* 1972.

Connelly, Owen. *The Gentle Bonaparte: A Biography of Joseph, Napoleon's Elder Brother.* 1968.

F.M. Kircheisen. *Jovial King* [Jerome]. Translated from the German, 1932.

Geer, Walter. *Napoleon and His Family.* 3 vols. 1927–1929.

Girod de l'Ain, G. *Joseph Bonaparte.* 1970.

Garnier, Jean-Paul. *Murat: Roi de Naples.* 1959.

Kikkert, J.G. *Köning van Holland, Louis Bonaparte 1778–1846. 1981.*

Knapton, E. J. *Empress Josephine.* 1963.

Labarre de Raillicourt, D. *Louis Bonaparte: Roi de la Hollande.* 1963.

Martineau, Gilbert. *Le roi de Rome.* 1982.

Masson, Frédéric. *Napoléon et sa famille.* 13 vols. 1900–1919.

Melchior-Bonnet, Bernardine. *Jérome Bonaparte: ou, L'envers de l'epopée.* 1979.

Mercader Riba, Juan. *José Bonaparte, rey de España, 1808–1813.* 1972.

Nabonne, Bernard. *Pauline Bonaparte: La Venue impériale.* 1963.

Oman, Carola (Lady Lenanton). *Napoleon's Viceroy: Eugene de Beauharnais.* 1966.

Prieur, Jean. *Murat et Caroline.* 1985.

Seward, Desmond. *Napoleon's family.* London, 1986.

Stirling, Monica. *Madame Letizia.* 1961.

Stoeckl, Agnes. *Four Years an Empress: Marie-Louise.* 1962.

Sutherland, Christine. *Marie Walewska: Napoleon's Great Love.* 1979.

Tessadri, Elena S. *Il vicere Eugenio di Beauharnais.* 1982.

Weiner, Margery. *Parvenu Princesses: Napoleon's Sisters.* 1964.

Wright, Constance. *Daughter to Napoleon* [Hortense de Beauharnais]. 1961.

OTHER BIOGRAPHIES

Adelbert, Prince von Bayern. *Eugen Beauharnais, der Stiefsohn Napoleons.* 1940.

Almedingen, Martha E. *The Emperor Alexander I.* 1964.

Brinton, Crane. *The Lives of Talleyrand.* 1936 and 1960.

Cardigny, Louis. *Les marchaux de Napoleon.* 1977.

Colomba, Hélène. *Madame Walewska . . . belle histoire d'amour.* 1964.

Criste, O. *Erzherzog Carl von Osterreich,* 3 vols. 1912.

Delderfield, R. F. *The March of the Twenty-Six: The Story of Napoleon's Marshals.* 1962.

Dupré, Huntley. *Lazare Carnot.* 1940. Reprint, 1975.

Durova, Nadezhda Andreevna. *The Cavalry Maiden: Journals of a Russian Officer in the Napoleonic Wars.* Translation and notes by Mary Fleming Zirin. 1988.

Foster, J. T. *Napoleon's Marshal: The Life of Michel Ney.* 1968.

Gallaher, John G. *The Iron Marshal: Louis N. Davout.* 1976.

Garros, Louis. *Ney: Le brave des braves.* 1964.

Glover, Michael. *Wellington as Military Commander.* 1968.

Herold, J. C. *Mistress to an Age: Madame de Staël.* 1955.

Holland, Vyvyan. *Goya: A Pictorial Biography.* 1961.

Hourtoulle, H.F.G.L. *Davout le terrible.* 1975.

Kammacher, Léon. *Joseph Fouché: Du révolutionnaire au ministre de la police.* 1962.

Longford, Elizabeth. *Wellington: The Years of the Sword.* 1969.

Madelin, Louis. *Fouché.* 1955.

Marshall-Cornwall, J. H. *Massena* [sic]. 1965.

Melchior-Bonnet, Bernardine. *Un policier dans l'ombre de Napoleon: Savary, duc de Rovigo.* 1962.

Morton, J. B. *Marshal Ney.* 1958.

Nabonne, Bernard. *Bernadotte.* 1946.

Oman, Carola. *Sir John Moore.* 1953.

———. *Nelson.* 1954.

Palinson, Roger. *The Fox of the North: . . . Kutuzov.* 1977.

Papillard, François. *Cambacérès.* 1961.

Reinhard, Marcel. *Le grand Carnot.* 2 vols. 1950–1952.

Thrasher, Peter A. *Pasquale Paoli: An Enlightened Hero.* 1970.

Wast, T. du Nicole. *Laure Junot, duchesse d'Abrantès.* 1985.

Watson, S. J. *By Command of the Emperor: A Life of Marshal Berthier.* 1957.

Willette, L. *Maréchal Lannes: d'Artagnon sous l'empire.* 1979.

Young, Peter. *Napoleon's Marshals.* 1974.

Zweig, Stefan. *Fouché.* 1930.

WAR: INTERPRETIVE AND THEORETICAL

Anderson, M. S. *War and Society in Europe of the Old Regime, 1618–1789.* 1988.

Barker, Thomas Mack. *Army, Aristocracy, Monarchy: Essays on War, Society, and Government in Austria, 1618–1780.* 1982.

Best, G. *War and Society in Revolutionary Europe.* 1982.

Childs, J.C.R. *Armies and Warfare in Europe, 1648–1789.* 1982.

Duffy, Christopher. *Military Experience . . . Age of Reason.* 1987.

Elting, John R. *The Superstrategists.* New York, 1982.

Gat, Azar. *The origins of Military Thought from the Enlightenment to Clausewitz.* 1989.

Griffith, Paddy, ed. *Wellington [as] Commander.* 1985.

Ingrao, Charles W. *The Hessian Mercenary State: Ideas, Institutions, and Reform under Frederick II, 1760–1785.* 1987.

Kemp, A. *Weapons and Equipment of the Marlborough Wars.* 1980.

Kennett, Lee. *The French Army in the Seven Years War.* 1967.

Kessel, Eberhard. *Militargeschichte und Kriegstheorie in neuerer Zeit.* Ausgewahlte Aufsatze. Herausgegeben und eingeleitet von Johannes Kunisch. 1987.

Marines de guerre européennes, XVII–XVIIIe siècles. Edité par Martine Acerra, Jose Merino, et Jean Meyer. 1985.

Marshall-Cornwall, James. *Napoleon as Military Commander.* 1968.

Oman, C.W.C. *Studies in the Napoleonic Wars.* 1930.

Paret, Peter, ed., with Gordon Craig and Felix Gilbert. *Makers of Modern Strategy.* 1968.

Parker, Geoffrey. *The Military Revolution: Military Innovation and the Rise of the West, 1500–1800.* 1988.

Yorck von Wartenburg, M. *Napoleon as a General.* 2 vols. 1902.

WARS OF THE FRENCH REVOLUTION

Blanning, T.C.W. *Origins of the French Revolutionary Wars.* 1986.

Bertaud, Jean-Paul. *La Révolution Armée: Les soldats-citoyens et la Révolution française.* Paris, 1979. Translated as *The Army of the French Revolution: From Citizen Soldiers to Instrument of Power* by R. R. Palmer, 1988.

Chuquet, Arthur-Maxime. *Les Guerres de la Révolution.* 11 vols. 1914.

Lynn, John A. *The Bayonets of the Republic: Motivation and Tactics of the Army of Revolutionary France, 1791–94.* 1984.

Paret, Peter. ""Conscription and the End of the Old Regime in France and Prussia." In W. Treue, *Geschichte als Aufgabe.* Berlin, 1988.

Phipps, Ramsey W. *The Armies of the First Republic and the Rise of Napoleon's Marshals.* 5 vols. London, 1926–29. Reprint, 1985.

Quimby, Robert S. *The Background of Napoleonic Warfare.* 1957.

Rodger, A. B. *The War of the Second Coalition, 1798–1801: A Strategic Commentary.* 1964.

Ross, Steven T. *Quest for Victory: French Military Strategy, 1792–1799.* 1973.

———. *From Flintlock to Rifle Infantry: Tactics, 1740–1866.* 1979.

Scott, Samuel F. *The Response of the Royal Army to the French Revolution.* 1978.

Wetzler, Peter. *War and Subsistence: The Sambre and Muese Army in 1794.* 1985.

Woloch, Isser. *The French Veteran from the Revolution to the Restoration.* 1979.

ARMIES: OLD REGIME, REVOLUTION, NAPOLEON and OPPONENTS

Blond, Georges. *La Grande Armée, 1804–1815*. Paris, 1979.

Choury, Maurice. *Les Grognards de Napoléon*. Paris, 1968.

Davies, G. *Wellington and His Army*. London, 1954.

Elting, John R. *Swords Around a Throne: Napoleon's Grande Armée*. 1987.

Esdaile, Charles J. *Spanish Army in the Peninsular War*. 1988.

Forrest, Alan. *Conscripts and Deserters: The Army and French Society during the Revolution and Empire*. 1989.

Johnson, David. *Napoleon's Cavalry and Its Leaders*. 1978.

Lachouque, Henry. *Napoléon et la garde impériale*. 1957. Translated as *The Anatomy of Glory: Napoleon and His Guard* by Anne S. K. Brown. 1961.

Paret, Peter. *Yorck and the Era of Prussian Reform, 1807–1814*. 1966.

———. *Clausewitz and the State*. 1976 and 1985.

Pivka, Otto von. *Napoleon's German Allies*. London, 1978.

Rogers, Hugh C. B. *Napoleon's Army*. London, 1974.

———. *Wellington's Army*. London, 1979.

Rothenberg, Gunther E. *The Military Border in Croatia, 1740–1882*. 1966.

———. *The Art of Warfare in the Age of Napoleon*. 1978.

———. *Napoleon's Great Adversaries: The Archduke Charles and the Austrian Army, 1792–1814*. 1982.

Shanahan, W. O. *Prussian Military Reforms, 1786–1813*. 1954.

Ward, S.G.P. *Wellington's Headquarters, 1809–1814*. London, 1957.

NAPOLEON: CAMPAIGNS, GENERAL

Chandler, David G. *The Campaigns of Napoleon: The Mind and Method of History's Greatest Soldier*. 1966.

Connelly, Owen *Blundering to Glory: Napoleon's Military Campaigns*. 1987.

Dodge, Theodore A. *Napoleon: A History of the Art of War*. 4 vols. 1904–1907.

Dupont, M. *Napoléon en campagne*. 3 vols. 1950–1955.

Esposito, Vincent J., and J. R. Elting. *A Military History and Atlas of the Napoleonic Wars*. 1964.

Lachouque, Henry. *Napoléon et la garde impériale*. 1957. Adapted as *The Anatomy of Glory: Napoleon and His Guard* by Anne S. K. Brown. 1961.

———. *Napoléon: 20 ans de campagnes*. 1964. Translated as *Napoleon's Battles: A History of His Campaigns* by Ray Monkcom. 1967.

Parker, H. T. *Three Napoleonic Battles*. 1944 and 1983.

NAVAL WARFARE

Aman, Jacques. *Les officiers bleus dans la marine française au XVIIIe siècle*. 1976.

Farrère, Claude. *Histoire de la Marine française*. 1962.

Keegan, John. *The Price of Admiralty*. 1988.

Longridge, C. N. *The Anatomy of Nelson's Ships*. Drawings and Plans by E. Bowness and G. F. Campbell. 1955–1974. Revised by E. Bowness, 1977 and 1985.

Mackesy, Piers. *The War in the Mediterranean*. 1957.

Mahan, A. T. *The Influence of Seapower Upon the French Revolution and Empire, 1793–1815*. 2 vols. 14th ed. 1919.

Maine, Ren. *Trafalgar*. 1960.

Marcus, G. J. *Royal Navy in the Age of Nelson, 1793–1815. 1971*.

Merino Navaro, J. P. *Armada Española en el siglo XVIII*. 1981.

Palmer, Michael. *Naval Operations during the Quasi-War with France, 1798–1801*. 1988.

Pritchard, James Stewart. *Louis XV's Navy, 1748–1762: A Study of Organization and Administration*. 1987.

THE CAMPAIGNS

Alexander, Don. *Rod of Iron: French Counterinsurgency Policy in Aragon during the Peninsular War*. 1985.

Aymes, J. R. *La guerre d'independance espagnole*. 1973.

Barthorp, Michael. *Napoleon's Egyptian Campaigns*. 1978.

Belis, Roger. *La campagne de Russie, 1812*. 1966.

Benoist-Mechin, J.G.P.M. *Bonaparte en Egypte*. 1966.

Bond, Gordon C. *The Grand Expedition: The British Invasion of Holland in 1809*. 1979.

Cate, Curtis. *The War of the Two Emperors: The Duel Between Napoleon and Alexander: Russia 1812*. 1985.

Davies, D. W. *Sir John Moore's Peninsular Campaign*. 1974.

Duffy, C. J. *Austerlitz, 1805*. 1977.

———. *Borodino*. 1972.

Dupont, M. *Napoléon et la trahison des marchaux, 1814*. 1970.

Ellis, Geoffrey. *Napoleon's Continental Blockade*. 1981.

Epstein, Robert M. *Eugene at War, 1809*. 1984.

Eyck, F. Gunther. *Loyal Rebels: Andreas Hofer and the Tyrolian Uprising of 1809*. 1986.

Fleishmann, Theo. *Expedition anglaise . . . en 1809: Conquete de l'Ile de Walcheren et menace sur Anvers*. Brussels, 1973.

Foucart, Paul J. *Bautzen . . . 20–21 mai 1813*. 1897.

Friedrich, R. *Die Befreiungskreig 1813–1815. 4 vols. 1911–13*.

Gates, David. *Spanish Ulcer: . . . the Peninsular War*. 1986.

Glover, Richard. *Britain at Bay . . . 1803–1814*. 1973.

Herold, J. Christopher. *Napoleon in Egypt*. 1961.

Horward, Donald D. *Napoleon and Iberia: The Twin Sieges of Ciudad Rodrigo and Almeida, 1810*. 1984.

Jackson, Wm. *Attack in the West: Napoleon's First Campaign*. 1953.

Josselson, Michael, and Diana Josselson. *The Commander: Barclay de Tolly*. 1980.

Lachouque, H. *Napoléon en 1814*. 1959.

Lachouque, Henry. *Napoléon Austerlitz*. *1960*.

———. *Jena*. 1961.

Lachouque, H., J. Trainie, and J. C. Carmigniani. *Napoleon's War in Spain*. Translated by Janet Mallender and J. R. Clements. 1982.

Lapouge, Gilles. *La bataille de Wagram*. 1986. Translated as *The Battle of Wagram* by John Brownjohn. 1988.

Lawford, J. P. *Napoleon: The Last Campaigns, 1813–1815*. 1977.

Lloyd, Christopher. *The Nile Campaign*. 1973.

Maude, F. N. *The Jena Campaign, 1806*. London & NY, 1909.

———. *The Ulm Campaign, 1805*. NY & London, 1912.

Melchior-Bonnet, B. *La conspiration de . . . Malet*. 1963.

Myatt, Frederick. *British Sieges of the Peninsular War*. 1987.

Napier, Sir William F. P. *History of the War in the Peninsula and in the South of France, 1807 to 1814*. 6 vols. 1886.

Nicolson, Nigel. *Napoleon 1812*. 1985.

Olivier, Daria. *The Burning of Moscow, 1812*. 1966.

Oman, C.W.C. *History of the Peninsular War*. 7 vols. 1902–1930.

Palmer, Alan W. *Napoleon in Russia*. 1967.

Parker, H. T. *Three Napoleonic Battles*. 1944. New ed., Durham, NC, 1983.

Parkinson, Roger. *Fox of the North: The Life of Kutuzov*. 1976.

Pelet, J. J. *The French Campaign in Portugal, 1810–1811*. Translated and edited by Donald D. Horward. 1973.

Petre, F. L. *Napoleon at War*. Edited by A. A. Nofi. 1984.

Read, Jan. *The War in the Peninsula, 1807–1814*. 1977.

Riehn, Richard K. *1812: Napoleon's Russian Campaign*. 1990.

Rodger, A. B. *War of the Second Coalition, 1798 to 1801*. 1961.

Ross, Steven T. *Quest for Victory: French Military Strategy, 1792–1799*. 1973.

Roux, Georges. *Napoléon et le guepier espagnol*. 1970.

Schreiber, Hermann. *Das Volk steht auf: Europas Befreiungskampf gegen Napoleon*. 1982.

Thiry, Jean. *Bonaparte en Egypte*. Paris, 1973.

———. *Bonaparte en Italie*. 1974.

Tranie, J., and J. C. Carmigniani. *Napoléon: 1813, la campagne d'Allemagne*. 1987.

Tranie, J., and J. C. Carmigniani. *Napoléon et Austriche . . . 1809*. 1984.

Tranie, Jean, and Jean-Carlos Carmigniani, eds. *Napoléon et la Russie . . . 1805–1807*. 1984.

———. *Napoleon et l'Allemagne: La Prusse, 1806*. Edited 1984, 1989.

Troyat, Henri. *Alexander of Russia, Napoleon's Conqueror*. Translated by Joan Pinkham. 1983.

Warner, Oliver. *The Battle of the Nile*. 1960.

Young, Peter, and J. P. Lawford. *Wellington's Masterpiece: The Battle and Campaign of Salamanca*. 1973.

THE LAST DAYS

Artom, Guido. *Napoleon Is Dead in Russia: The Extraordinary Story of One of History's Strangest Conspiracies*. 1970.

Blond, Georges. *Les Cent-Jours*. 1983.

Bluche, Frédéric. *Le plébiscite des cent-jours*. 1974.

Chalfont, Lord, ed. *Waterloo: The Battle of Three Armies*. 1980.

Chandler, David. *Waterloo: The Hundred Days*. 1980.

Christophe, Robert. *Napoleon on Elba*. 1959. Translated from the French. 1964.

Cubberly, Ray E. *Role of Fouché During the Hundred Days*. 1969.

Duhamel, Jean. *The Fifty Days: Napoleon in England*. 1969. Translated by R. A. Hall. 1970.

Godlewski, G. *Trois-cents jours d'exil: Napoléon à Elbe*. 1961.

Hillemand, Pierre. *Pathologie de Napoléon*. 1970.

Houssaye, Henri. *1814*. 1888.

———. *1815*. 3 vols. 1889–1902.

Howarth, David. *Waterloo: Day of Battle*. 1968.

Hubert, Emanuelle. *Les cent jours*. 1966.

Kemble, James. *Napoleon Immortal: The Medical History and Private Life of Napoleon Bonaparte*. 1959.

Korngold, Ralph. *The Last Years of Napoleon*. 1959.

Lachouque, Henry. *Last Days of Napoleon's Empire: From Waterloo to Saint Helena*. 1965. Translated by L. F. Edwards. 1966.

———. *Waterloo, 1815*. 1972. Translated from the French. 1975.

Longford, Elizabeth. *Wellington: The Years of the Sword*. 1969.

MacKenzie, Norman. *The Escape from Elba: The Fall and Flight of Napoleon, 1814–1815*. 1985.

Martineau, Guilbert. *Napoleon's Saint Helena*. 1969.

Melchior-Bonnet, B. *La conspiration du général Malet*. 1963.

Primrose, A. P., Lord Rosebery. *Napoleon: The Last Phase*. 1900.

Richardson, James. *Napoleon's Death: An Inquest*. 1974.

Saunders, Edith. *The Hundred Days*. 1963.

Thornton, Michael J. *Napoleon after Waterloo: England and the Saint Helena Decision*. 1968.

Weider, Ben and David Hapgood. *The Murder of Napoleon*. 1982. Based on Sten Forshufvud, *Who Murdered Napoleon?* 1961.

REFERENCES

Braesch, Fritz. *Finances et monnaies révolutionnaires*. 1937.

Chandler, David G. *Dictionary of the Napoleonic Wars*. 1979.

Connelly, Owen, ed., with P. W. Becker, H. T. Parker, June Burton and Janice Berbin. *Historical Dictionary of Napoleonic France*. 1985.

Coppa, Frank J., ed. *Dictionary of Modern Italian History*. 1985.

Dainville, F. de, and Jean Tulard. *Atlas administratif de l'Empire*. 1973.

Furet, François, and Mona Ozouf. *Dictionnaire critique de la Révolution française, 1988*. Translated as *Critical Dictionary of the French Revolution* by Arthur Goldhammer, 1989.

Godechot, Jacques. *Les institutions de la France sous la Révolution et l'Empire*. 2d ed. 1968.

———. *Les constitutions de la France*. 1970.

Jourquin, Jacques. *Dictionnaire des maréchaux du Premier Empire: Dictionnaire analytique statistique et compare des vingt-six maréchaux*. Nouv. ed., 1986.

Marion, Marcel. *Dictionnaire des institutions de la France aux XVIIe et XVIIIe siècles*. 1923.

McKeown, Thomas. *The Rise in Modern Population*. 1977.

Mousnier, Roland. *Les institutions de la France sous la monarchie absolue*. 2 vols. 1974–1976. Vol. 1: *Society and the State*, translated by Brian Pearce, 1985. Vol 2: *The Origins of State and Society*, translated by Arthur Goldhammer, 1985.

Reinhard, M. *Etude de la population pendant la Révolution et l'Empire*. 1963.

Reinhard, Marcel, and A. Armengaud. *Histoire générale de la population mondiale*. 3d ed. 1968.

Ross, Steven T. *European Diplomatic History, 1789–1815: France Against Europe*. 1969.

Scott, Samuel F., and Barry Rothaus, eds. *Historial Dictionary of the French Revolution, 1789–1799*. 1985.

Shepherd, William R. *Historical Atlas*. 8th ed. 1956.

Soboul, Albert. *Dictionnaire historique de la Révolution française*. Edited by Jean-René Suratteau and François Gendron. 1989.

Tulard, Jean, ed. *Bibliographie critique des mémoires sur le Consulat et l'Empire*. 1971.

———. *Dictionnaire Napoléon*. 1987.

JOURNALS

Annales Historiques de la Révolution française, published 1924–present, with a break 1941–1946, by the Société des Etudes Robespierristes. (Called *Annales révolutionnaires* from 1908 to 1923).

Bulletin de la Société Belge d'Etudes Napoléoniennes (Belgium).

French Historical Studies (1959ff.) (United States.)

Revue des Etudes Napoléoniennes (1912–1940, with some breaks), succeeded by a *Bulletin* (1947), and (since 1954) by the *Revue de l'Institute Napoléon*.

Rivista Italiano di Studi Napoleonici (Italy).

The *American Historial Review* and *Journal of Modern History* both carry articles and reviews of books on Revolutionary/Napoleonic period. The same is true for the *Canadian Historical*

Review, the *Bulletin des Recherches Historiques* (Quebec Archives), the *English Historical Review*, the *Historische Zeitschrift* (Germany), the *Revue Historique* (France), *Voprosy Istorii* (USSR), and many others.

BIBLIOGRAPHIES

American Historical Association's Guide to Historical Literature. Edited by George F. Howe. 1961.

Bestermann, Theodore. *A World Bibliography of Bibliographies*. 4th ed. 5 vols. 1965–1966.

Bibliographie annuelle de l'histoire de France. 1955ff.

Blumenkranz, Bernhard. *Bibliographie des Juifs en France*. 1974.

Caldwell, Ronald J. *The Era of the French Revolution: A Bibliography of the History of Western Civilization, 1789–1799*. 1985.

Caron, Pierre. *Manuel pratique de l'étude de la Révolution française*. 1912. New ed., 1947.

Cioranescu, Alexandre. *Bibliographie de la littérature française du 18e siècle*. 2 vols. 1969.

Godechot, J. *L'Europe et l'Amerique a l'époque Napoléonienne*. *Nouvelle Clio*, No. 37 1967.

———. *Les Révolutions, 1770–1799*. *Nouvelle Clio*, No. 36. 4th ed. (1986).

Guide to Historical Literature. Edited by G. M. Ducher, 1931, Reprint, 1949.

Horward, D. D. *Napoleonic Military History: A Bibliography*. 1986.

Kircheisen, Friedrich M. *Bibliographie des Napoleonischen Zeitalters*. Berlin, 1902. French edition: *Bibliographie Napoléonienne*. 2 vols. Paris, 1908–1912. [Incomplete.]

Mandrou, Robert. *La France aux XVIIe et XVIIIe siécles*. *Nouvelle Clio*, No. 33. 1967.

Martin, André, and Gérard Walter. *Le catalogue de l'histoire de la Révolution française: Ecrits de la période révolutionnaire, 1789–1799*. 5 vols. 1936–1943.

Mauro, Frédéric. *L'Expansion Européenne, 1600–1870*. *Nouvelle Clio*, No. 27. 1964.

Meyer, Jack A. *A Bibliography of the Napoleonic Era: Recent Publications, 1945–1985*. 1987.

Monglond, André. *Annales de bibliographie méthodique et descriptive.* . . . 10 vols. 1930–1965.

Ross, Steven T. *French Military History, 1661–1799: A Guide to the Literature*. 1984.

Tourneux, Maurice. *Bibliographie de l'histoire de Paris pendant la Révolution française*. 5 vols. 1890–1913.

Tuetey, André. *Répertoire général des sources manuscrites de l'histoire de Paris pendant la Révolution française*. 11 vols. 1890–1914. [Incomplete.]

Tulard, Jean. *Bibliographie critique des mémoires sur la Consulat et l'Empire écrits ou traduits en Français*. 1971.

Villat, Louis. *La Révolution et l'Empire*, *Clio*, 2 vols., 3d ed. 1947.

Walter, Gérard. *Répertoire de l'histoire de la Révolution française: Travaux publiés de 1890 à 1940*. 2 vols. 1941–1951.

INDEX

Académie Française, 26, 39, 75, 150 fn, 223, 225, 226
Acre (Akko), 194
Adams, John, 32
Additional Act (to French Constitution, 1815), 341–342
Administration in France: under the Consulate and Empire, 207–210, 218–219, 226; under the convention, 121–123, 129–134, 141–142, 149–150, 152, 155, 161, 166–169, 171–174; under the Directory, 4, 172, 176–178, 189, 196–197, 207; under the National Assembly, 90–91, 98, 100,218
Administration in the satellites and lesser states. See Berg, Grand Duchy of; Frankfurt, Grand Duchy of; Holland; Illyrian Provinces; Italy, Kingdom of; Naples, Kingdom of; Rhine, Confederation of the; Rome; Spain; Tuscany, Grand Duchy of; Warsaw, Grand Duchy of; Westphalia, Kingdom of
Africa, 6, 15, 314–315, 347
Agar de Mosbourg, Count, 272–274, 288
Aiguillon, Duke d', 40, 46, 48, 63, 83, 105, 117
Alembert, Jean d', 25, 27
Aboukir, 192, 195–196, 197 fn
Absolutism, French, 2, 15, 23, 26, 27, 35–37, 37 fn, 38–43, 62, 98, 101, 166, 174, 174 fn; strengths and weaknesses of, 38
Alexander I, Czar of Russia, 205, 224, 234, 236–238, 240–242, 249, 253 fn, 259, 261, 262, 290, 303, 304, 316–318, 322–324, 327, 328, 331, 331 fn, 334–336, 339, 340, 342, 344, 347
Alvintzy, 188
Amar, André, 131, 156, 159
American Revolution, 15, 18, 169: and France, 3, 13, 32–35, 58, 61, 83, 98, 104, 110, 113, 121, 290, 311
Amiens, Treaty of (1802), 206, 234, 315
Amis de la Vérité (Friends of Truth), 89, 96
Amis des Noris, Société des (Friends of the Blacks), 91, 109
Annexation: under the Consulate and Empire, 259–261, 275, 277, 281, 316, 331; under the Convention, 126, 169, 187; under the Directory, 195, 235
Architecture, 75, 255
Argentina, 307–309

Armée revolutionnaire (armées revolutionnaires, 1793–1794). See Revolutionary Armies
Army, French: under the Consulate, 204–206, 228; under the Convention, 122, 125–128, 138, 139, 141–147, 160, 161, 165, 166, 183, 185; under the Directory, 178, 179, 194, 196, 198, 199; under the Empire, 228–232, 274, 280, 291, 318–319, 322–326, 343–346; under the Legislative Assembly, 112, 113, 113 fn, 114, 119, 120; under Louis XVIII, 340–341; under the Old Regime, 47, 181. See also Grande Armée; National Guard
Army of Italy, 142, 184–187, 199
Arndt, Ernst Moritz, 298, 299, 333
Art (including painting and sculpture), 96, 150, 168, 193, 199, 213, 223, 225, 269, 273, 275, 276, 280, 286, 293, 303
Artois, Count d', (later Charles X), 82, 108, 110, 139, 139 fn, 140, 166, 174 fn
Asia, 8, 15, 16, 20, 191, 314, 315
Assemblies, Revolutionary. See Constitutions of France; Estates General; Assembly, Legislative; Assembly, National
Assembly, Legislative (1791–1792), 100, 106, 106 fn, 108–111, 111 fn, 112, 114–117, 119, 120, 122–124
Assembly, National, 69–72, 74, 77, 81–92, 94–96, 96 fn, 100–105, 107, 108, 110, 115, 119, 124, 163 fn, 183, 185, 307
Assembly of Notables, 62, 65, 104
Assignats, 92–93, 115, 148, 166–167, 173, 180, 198
Atlantic Revolutions and enlightened monarchies, 15, 34–35
Augereau, Pierre, General, 145, 179, 187, 189, 196, 209 fn, 211
August, Day of 10 August, 115–118, 122, 124, 151, 155
August, Night of 4 August, 83–84, 105
Austerlitz (1805), 237, 238, 240, 250, 258, 322
Austria, 4, 7, 57, 96, 112–114, 117, 119, 120, 126, 127, 146, 147, 156, 169, 170, 187–190, 194, 195, 197, 204, 209, 210, 211 fn, 235, 236, 236 fn, 237–238, 240, 243, 245, 252, 252 fn, 253–258, 258 fn, 259–261, 267, 269, 281, 282, 289, 290, 292, 294, 295, 298, 298 fn, 299, 300, 303, 316–320, 327, 331–333, 335, 336 fn, 337–340, 342, 343, 347, 349; in the